ENCYCLOPAEDIA OF
BRITISH
POTTERY AND PORCELAIN
MARKS

ENCYCLOPAEDIA OF BRITISH POTTERY AND PORCELAIN MARKS

By

GEOFFREY A. GODDEN

F.R.S.A.

Schiffer Publishing Ltd

Box E, Exton, Pennsylvania 19341

Contents

Preface

The material incorporated in this book has been built up over many years and is arranged in alphabetical order, with numerous cross-references. The reader does not have to know the manufacturer or the place of production before tracing the mark.

After much practical experience in operating a "Mark Research and Dating Service", the writer is confident that this book will enable the reader to find with ease the information he requires. In the case of the more important "collectable" factories the reader is referred to specialised books where he may obtain detailed information on a factory's history and illustrations of typical specimens.

Emphasis has been placed on the correct *dating* of each mark and, apart from the writer's personal observations and correspondence with present-day manufacturers, local libraries and museum curators, information has been collected from the following authoritative sources:

The Board of Trade Files of Dissolved Companies.
The Board of Trade Registers of Designs etc. 1839 onwards.
The Companies Registration Office.
The Patent Office—Registers of Trade Marks.
Local Directories.
The Public Record Office, London.
Rate Records of the Staffordshire Potteries.
The Trade Marks Journal.

The yearly *Pottery Gazette Diary* published by Scott, Greenwood & Son Ltd. from 1882 to the present day has been a most valuable source of information on changing marks and manufacturers. The late Alfred Meigh's comprehensive records* on the Staffordshire potters has also been of the greatest assistance and the writer is greatly indebted to him for his mass of stable information gathered together over more than 25 years of painstaking study.

This book contains over 4,000 British china marks and these range in date from 1650 to the present day. Each mark is numbered for easy reference. In many cases the firm's predecessors and successors are given so that the whole history of the firm can be followed. Modern marks have been included as these appear on examples that may well prove to be collector's specimens of the future; the Studio Potters already have their followers, a trend that must spread with time. The marks of over three hundred post-war Studio Potters are recorded, the majority for the first time.

The writer would welcome information on any mark not included in this book or any corrections or observations on material incorporated in it, so that subsequent editions may be presented in a form as complete and perfect as possible. Information from manufacturers on new marks would also be very welcome.

Geoffrey A. Godden,
14, Sompting Ave.,
WORTHING, SX.

*The Meigh records are now in the writer's possession and are covered by copyright.

Acknowledgements

I wish to record my gratitude to the late Alfred Meigh for his painstaking work in taking extracts from the Staffordshire rate records before they were destroyed during the last war. Without this material, now in my possession, the accurate dating of the working periods of many of the smaller firms and the correcting of other dates which have previously been accepted and copied by one authority after another, would have been impossible.

The preparation of this book would have been far more difficult had it not been for the ready assistance I have received from present-day manufacturers, Studio Potters (many of whom I have visited) and local Librarians, all of whom have answered my enquiries in a most courteous and detailed manner. My particular thanks are also due to A. H. Hall, Esq., the Librarian at the Guildhall Library.

I would also like to acknowledge the very kind co-operation received from Messrs. Scott, Greenwood & Son Ltd., the publishers of the monthly trade magazine *Pottery Gazette* and of the yearly *Pottery Gazette Diary*. I have had their permission to use and reproduce information contained in these publications and, in particular, their lists of marks in current use. I must also acknowledge the source of much interesting information gleaned from reference books written by Reginald G. Haggar.

I am also grateful to the many collectors, dealers and museum officials who have sent me details of hitherto unrecorded marks. The staff at the Craftsmen Potters Shop in Lowndes Court, London W.1, and the Information Officer at the Rural Industries Bureau have also been most helpful and have enabled me to trace many modern potters.

Several ornate printed marks on specimens in my own reference collection could not be reproduced in photographic form in this book; in many cases the marks have been accurately drawn for me by Mr. Donald F. Abbott, F.R.S.A. Other photographs of clear marks have been taken by Mr. D. Gardiner, A.I.B.P.

My final remarks must be to express my thanks to my publishers and their printers for their helpful advice in preparing my manuscript for publication in its present form.

Introduction and General Notes

The principal function of a trade-mark is to permit the identification of the manufacturer of a product; but the fact that even slight changes in the standard trade-mark will assist in the *dating* of an object is of still greater importance to the collector. An example of this that springs readily to mind is the changes in colour and form of the standard anchor mark of the Chelsea factory which have resulted in the porcelain produced there being divided into four main periods: the raised anchor period (c. 1749–53), the red anchor period (c. 1753–8), the gold anchor period (c. 1758–70) and the Chelsea-Derby period (c. 1770–84), the last with its distinguishing anchor and D mark. The products of many other ceramic factories, especially those of the 19th century, may be similarly dated by means of variations in their standard marks, all of which will be found in this book.

The adoption of certain general rules would save many errors in the dating of English trade-marks. The fact that "England" was added to marks from 1891 (to comply with the American McKinley Tariff Act) is given in previous mark books, but it should be remembered that "Made in England" signifies a 20th century dating. The use of "Limited" in various abbreviations: Ld., Ltd., etc. after a pottery firm's title indicates a date after 1860 and was not generally used in ceramic marks before the 1880's. The Old Hall Earthenware Company of Hanley was the first Staffordshire pottery firm to become a Limited Liability Company, in March 1861. The very fact that the words "Trade-Mark" occur in certain marks signifies a date subsequent to the Trade-Mark Act of 1862 and the words normally denote a date after 1875. The occurrence of "Rd. No." followed by a number signifies a date after 1884; if the number is above 360,000 the date is subsequent to 1900 (see page 527).

Examination of over 3,500 English china marks in the writer's records suggests the following further *general* rules of dating:

A. Any printed mark incorporating the Royal Arms (or versions of the Arms) are 19th century or later.
B. Any printed mark incorporating the name of the pattern may be regarded as being subsequent to 1810.
C. Use of the word "Royal" in the manufacturer's title or trade-name suggests a date after the middle of the 19th century; obvious examples of this include "Royal Cauldon", "Royal Grafton", "Royal Worcester".
D. The words "Bone China," "English Bone China", etc. denote a 20th century date.

Many 19th century printed marks are based on stock designs—variations of the Royal Arms, a garter-shaped mark (crowned or uncrowned) or the Staffordshire knot (see page 13). These may be found with the initials or names of the relevant manufacturers. The Royal Arms marks were employed from the early part of the 19th century but clear impressions which show the quartered Arms *without* a central inescutcheon are subsequent to 1837 (see page 552). The garter-shaped mark was extensively used from the 1840's onwards and the Staffordshire knot may occur from about 1845; it was much used in the 1870's and 1880's and continues in some instances to the present day. As the name implies, this form of mark points to a Staffordshire manufacturer. Any object bearing the diamond shaped registration mark was produced after 1843, see page 526.

Several English manufacturers employed private methods of dating their wares. Messrs. Minton introduced their impressed cyphers from 1842 (see page 440 for key chart). Messrs. Josiah Wedgwood's impressed three-letter system (used from 1860) is given on page 658. The Kerr & Binns Company at Worcester incorporated the last two digits of the year in their shield-shaped mark (reserved for the finest quality pieces) from 1856 to 1862. The "Royal Worcester" Company, from 1862, also employed a system of yearly dating, as did the Royal Crown Derby Company later in the century.

Some late 19th century manufacturers dated their ware in full, a notable example being Messrs. Doulton of Lambeth. Many other manufacturers impressed their ware with numbers denoting the month and last two figures of the year, e.g. $\frac{1}{75}$ for January 1875. By this means the manufacturers could ensure that stocks of white undecorated ware were used in chronological order and so not spoiled by being kept in the factory store for an unreasonable period. Dates incorporated in printed marks generally relate to the claimed date of the factory's establishment, *not* the date of production.

Many English marks consist of the firm's initials; these often appear in triangular form; $\frac{F\&R}{B}$ or $\frac{H\&G}{B}$. In these cases the bottom letter denotes in which town in the Staffordshire Potteries the factory was situated. The first example given here is Ford & Riley of Newcastle Street, Burslem, the second Heath & Greatbatch, Union Pottery, Burslem. Serious confusion may arise when the town's initial letter was placed directly after the firm's initials, as in the case of Edwards & Brown of Longton who used the initials E. & B.L. The main towns and initials are Burslem (B), Cobridge (C), Fenton (F), Hanley (H), Longton (L)* and Tunstall (T).

Many impressed marks are indistinct but can often be deciphered if held up to a strong light with the marks outermost. A pencil may accentuate other faint marks; ink should not be used as it may stain the body.

The major London retailing establishments used a variety of printed marks on their merchandise. Marks with the names of Daniell, Goode or Mortlock, which often occur, relate not to the manufacturer but to the retailer, and the same is true of several marks that give the names of smaller shops with addresses in St. Paul's Churchyard. Many retailers' marks are listed with the date of use.

Several of the marks used on the more collectable wares have been reproduced on forgeries; in these cases the reader is warned of this fact. The marks of manufacturers from about 1830 onwards have not been reproduced and they form a reliable guide to the source and date of the example.

Many present-day manufacturers claim dates of establishment that do not agree with information contained in this work. This is due to the fact that the firms claim the earliest date of their *predecessors*. An example of this is Messrs. W. T. Copeland & Sons Ltd. "Estd. 1770". The Copeland firm came into being in 1847 and the date 1770 claimed relates to the original Spode firm which was succeeded in 1833 by Copeland & Garrett and then by W. T. Copeland. As each firm used different marks they are treated separately in this book.

Working periods left open, e.g. "1890– ", indicate that the firm is still operating. Open dates after a mark indicate that the mark is in current use. Many dates will be found to differ from those

---

* Some French firms at Limoges used as a mark their initials over the letter L. These French specimens are of a hard, glassy porcelain and unlike the Longton bone china or earthenware.

given in previous books but the dates here given have been checked with available contemporary records.

Irish marks have been incorporated in the general alphabetical list of British marks.

The V. & A. prints referred to are a collection of pulls from potters' copper plates housed in the Print Room at the Victoria and Albert Museum. Many of these printed designs bear the marks of the manufacturers for whom the prints were engraved. These cover a period of about fifty years from the 1820's.

It should be noted that the marks are not necessarily reproduced to scale in this book. The size of the mark does not affect the date of attribution. Several marks, in fact, occur in different sizes on specimens from the same service. The mark on a large article—e.g. a tureen—will usually be larger than the same mark on a small object such as a cup or saucer.

The Appendix contains marks that cannot be identified or dated with certainty and which have therefore been omitted from the main section. The Appendix will also be found to contain information on doubtful marks or on foreign marks that can be mistaken for British marks. All entries in the Appendix are indexed in the main section. Terms used in the main section are listed in the glossary, and reference books in the bibliography.

For the purpose of the alphabetical arrangement of this book the abbreviated "and" sign "&" has been disregarded; the alphabetical arrangement is by surname, then Christian name or initial, so that "Thomas Godwin" should be regarded as Godwin, Thomas, and as such follows Godwin, Rowley & Co.

All English porcelains are "soft paste" or bone china unless otherwise stated.

The manner in which each mark appears is given i.e. "Printed". The addition of "Etc." indicates that the mark is *normally* printed but not invariably so.

The initial J may appear as I on 18th and 19th century marks.

English earthenwares prior to c. 1770 are usually unmarked. English delft-type earthenwares with a coating of white tin glaze are also unmarked as are also salt glazed wares. *Porcelain* was not made in England before the 1740's. Porcelains are normally translucent, earthenwares are opaque.

Many 19th century printed marks are based on the Staffordshire knot, the garter, crowned or uncrowned, or variations of the Royal Arms, see below.

Staffordshire Knot mark, often with the manufacturer's initials or name in the segments.

Royal Arms mark, of which many variations occur. These marks have the manufacturer's name etc. under the arms. See also page 552.

Garter mark, with or without crown over. Many variations occur in the 19th century. The firm's initials or name may occur in the centre or in the border.

Recently introduced or discovered potters' marks have been added up to the time of going to press and after the consecutive numbering of the main section was completed. This necessitated some amendments to the numbering and to the subdivision of some mark numbers by the addition of letters.

Several marked examples mentioned as being in the Godden Collection are on public display at the Art Gallery & Museum, Worthing, Sussex.

KEY TO GENERAL PLAN FOR EACH ENTRY

Number
column

SHORT NAME   FULL TITLE. Subsequent additions (Ltd) etc. given in
                                         brackets. Address. Duration of firm's operation. N.B.
                                         Dates left open show that the firm is still in operation. *Type of
                                         ware(s) produced.* Predecessor, and subsequent firm, where
                                         relevant.

1   MARKS   Notes on each mark (printed, impressed etc.) with period of
Mark   or initials* used, *given*   use, general observations, etc.
Number   *in date order.*

                                         Title of reference book(s) giving full information on the
                                         factory's history and illustrations of typical products.

The reader should in all cases locate the mark in the main section by means of any initials, name
or device.   This will lead directly, or by cross reference, to the correct factory and further details of the
period of the mark, etc.

Lists of complicated monograms or signs will be found listed between pages 746 and 765.

In tracing the correct potter or firm, the *surname* will be found listed in alphabetical order.

---

* It should be remembered that in most cases the basic, key, initials of a firm can only be given.   These initials
occur in countless different marks, some of which are pictorial and relate to individual patterns.   Most printed marks
also include the trade name of the pattern.

Map showing the Location of the Principal Pottery Centres

PUBLISHER'S NOTE

Numerous references will be found in these pages to typical or documentary specimens illustrated in *British Pottery and Porcelain: an illustrated Encyclopaedia of Marked Specimens.* . . . This book is planned as a companion volume to the present work and illustrates a wide range of marked English wares of the period prior to 1900.

TYPES OF CERAMIC MARKS

On this page, and on the seven pages that follow, are reproduced some typical examples of different types of ceramic marks. The numbers printed below the marks refer to the entries in the main section of this book.

INCISED MARKS

605

Incised Marks are scratched into the body before the first firing process and before decoration. Signature and initial marks particularly lend themselves to this form of marking. The edges often show a ploughed-up effect which does not occur with impressed marks

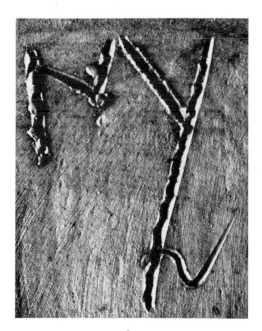

2840

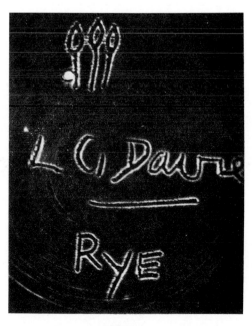

1199

IMPRESSED MARKS

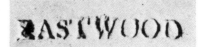

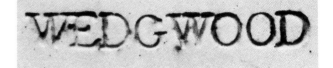

3701   4075

Impressed marks are made by applying a metal die to the ware before the first firing and before decoration. The process is most commonly used with simple name-marks, of which the standard WEDGWOOD mark is a good example

SEAL-TYPE MARKS

3238   3069   3573   3566

Much 20th-century studio pottery bears an impressed seal-type mark made up of initials, monogram or other device. These marks normally have the circular or ·shaped outline, common to all seal devices

PRINTED MARKS

1871

1095

Printed marks first came into general use in about 1800, though they were in use on porcelains decorated with underglaze blue patterns as early as 1760.

In course of manufacture the pattern or mark is transferred to the pottery from engraved copper plates by means of special paper which picks up ink from the plate and deposits it on the surface of the china. This process may take place either before or after glazing. As a general rule pottery having a printed pattern also has a printed mark.

Some 20th-century potters apply their printed marks by means of a rubber stamp or stencil

1739

2529

2760

PRINTED MARKS

2301

2574

3889

4348A

3868

1172

74

PRINTED MARKS

2694

1919

3258a

1101

2761

1938

3358

2633

PRINTED MARKS

3988

910

2542

3345

1099

PAINTED MARKS

Spode
2004

3648b

SPODE
3095

3648b

N2 M3

2873/4

3947

3645

Painted marks are applied over the glaze during or after decoration. Typical examples are the red or gold anchor marks of Chelsea, and the painted "Spode" mark. Some early porcelains decorated in underglaze blue have factory or workman's marks painted in blue under the glaze. The "crescent" and "square" marks of Worcester are painted in this manner, giving rise to the description "painted in underglaze blue"

APPLIED MOULDED MARKS

2690

2616

2701

2621

3988

Applied marks are rare. They should really be classed with impressed marks as, in the majority of cases, they are impressed marks on a raised pad. The potter forms them quite separately from the pieces he is making, placing them in position before firing. An early example is the raised anchor mark of Chelsea. Some 19th-century marks appear to be applied but are not so. They were cast in position at the same time that the pottery was formed in the mould

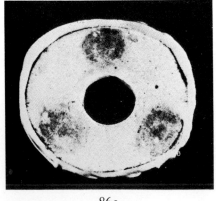

863

PAD MARK

Photograph of the base of a Derby porcelain figure, c. 1775, showing three "pad" marks of dark tone where the figure was supported during the firing process. Many 18th-century Chelsea-Derby and Derby figures and groups show these marks on the base

A

—	A	*See* Appendix
125		*See* Peter G. Arnold.
169–70		*See* Avoncroft Pottery.
997a		*See* Angela Colegate.
—		*See* Group letters.
138	A. BROS.	*See* G. L. Ashworth Bros. (Ltd.).
130	A. & CO.	*See* Edward Asbury & Co.
603	A. B.	*See* Briglin Pottery Ltd.
649	AB	*See* Alan Brough.
745	(monogram)	*See* Alan Caiger-Smith.
11a	A. B. SHELTON	*See* Adams & Bromley.
11	A. & B.	*See* Adams & Bromley.
94	A. B. & Co.	*See* Allman, Broughton & Co.
704a		*See* A. Bullock & Co.

ABBEY

RICHARD ABBEY, Liverpool. 1773–80*. *Engraver and Printer.*

Abbey was apprenticed to, and worked for, the famous Liverpool printer John Sadler, but his early work was rarely signed.

It is most unlikely that Abbey himself manufactured the wares he printed. He left Liverpool about 1780 and then worked in Scotland and in France. He returned to Liverpool in the early 1790's and founded a pottery, later to become the

Herculaneum Pottery. A printed and signed teapot will be found illustrated in *British Pottery and Porcelain: an illustrated Encyclopaedia of Marked Specimens.*

1 **ABBEY LIVERPOOL**

The name Abbey occurs on several prints engraved by Richard Abbey. 1773–80.*

* By December 1773 Abbey was working on his own account and advertised:

" . . . begs leave to inform his friends and the public; That he has open'd his shop at No 11 in Cleveland Square. Where he manufactures and sells all sorts of Queen's Ware Printed in the neatest manner and in Variety of Colours . . . ."

ABBEYDALE

2

ABBEYDALE NEW BONE CHINA CO. LTD., Duffield, Derbyshire. 1962– . *Porcelain.*

Printed mark, 1962– .

ABBOTT

ANDREW ABBOTT, Lane End. Staffordshire Potteries. 1781–3. Subsequently Turner & Abbott, q.v. *Earthenwares.*

Andrew Abbott is listed in London directories of 1804 and 1808 as at 82 Fleet Street, London. This relates to a retail shop.

3 ABBOTT POTTER   Impressed mark, 1781–3.

ABBOTT

ABBOTT & MIST, Lane End. Staffordshire Potteries. 1787–1810. *Earthenwares.* Subsequently J. Mist, q.v.

London directories of 1794 and 1799 list a partnership between Abbott and Newbury but marks in this form are not recorded.

4 ABBOTT & MIST   Impressed or painted mark, 1787–1810.

3 ABBOTT POTTER   *See* Andrew Abbott.

2198 A. B. J.   *See* A. B. Jones & Sons (Ltd.).

2190 A. B. J. & S.   *See* A. B. Jones & Sons (Ltd.).

2191 A. B. J. & Sons   *See* A. B. Jones & Sons (Ltd.).

133 A. B. R.   *See* Ashby Potter's Guild.

ABSOLON

WILLIAM ABSOLON, The Ovens, and 25 Market Row, Yarmouth, Norfolk. 1784–1815. *Decorator of Earthenwares and Glass.*

For further information on William Absolon and his work see the *Transactions of the English Ceramic Circle*, vol. 5, part 1. Typical examples will be found illustrated in *British Pottery and Porcelain: an illustrated Encyclopaedia of Marked Specimens.*

5   Painted Yarmouth mark, 1784–1815.

6   *Absolon yarm*   Painted name-mark, 1784–1815.

7   Absolon Yarm·N°25   Painted mark, 1790–1815. "N 25" refers to the address 25 Market Row and dates from 1790.

997   A. C. C.   *See* A. Colegate.

ACTON

LEONARD ACTON, Bramber, Sussex. 1945– . *Individual hand-made Pottery, Animals, etc.*

8   L. A   Incised initials, 1945– .

9   Incised outline of a bridge, sometimes accompanied by the initials L. A., 1945– .

116   AD   *See* Dorothy Annan.
4375   (monogram)   *See* Wye Pottery.

18, 25   ADAMS   *See* William Adams & Sons Ltd.

ADAMS

BENJAMIN ADAMS, Greengates, Tunstall. Staffordshire Potteries. c. 1800–20. *Earthenwares and Jasper-type wares.*

A selection of Benjamin Adams wares will be found illustrated in *British Pottery and Porcelain: an illustrated Encyclopaedia of Marked Specimens.*

10   B. ADAMS   Impressed mark, c. 1800–20.

ADAMS		**ADAMS & BROMLEY**, Victoria Works, Hanley. Staffordshire Potteries. 1873–86. *Earthenwares, Jasper wares, Parian, Majolica, etc.* Formerly John Adams & Co.

For further information see L. Jewitt's *The Ceramic Art of Great Britain* (1878 and 1883).

11	A & B	Marks 11, 11a and 12 impressed or printed. Used from 1873 to
11a	A. B.	1886.
	SHELTON	
12	ADAMS & BROMLEY	

15a	Adams & Co.	*See* John Adams & Co.
17		*See* William Adams & Sons Ltd.

ADAMS		**ADAMS & COOPER**, Carlisle Works, Longton. Staffordshire Potteries. 1850–77. *Porcelain.* Subsequently Edward Adams.
13	A. & C.	Initial mark occurring on blue printed porcelain tea cups and saucers in the Willett Collection, Brighton Museum. These examples are of the 1862 period.

ADAMS		**HARVEY ADAMS & CO.**, High Street and Sutherland Road, Longton. Staffordshire Potteries. 1870–85. *China and Earthenwares.* Formerly Adams & Scrivener. Subsequently Hammersley & Co.
	H. A & Co.	
14		Printed mark, 1870–85.

ADAMS		**JOHN ADAMS & CO.**, Victoria Works, Hanley. Staffordshire Potteries. 1864–73. *Earthenwares, Jasper wares, Parian, Majolica, etc.* Subsequently Adams & Bromley, q.v.
15	J. ADAMS & CO.	Impressed mark, 1864–73.
15a	ADAMS & CO.	Impressed mark, 1864–73.

ADAMS		**ADAMS & PRINCE**, Lane Delph. Staffordshire Potteries. Late 18th or early 19th century. *Earthenwares.*
16	ADAMS & PRINCE	Impressed mark (rare). Late 18th or early 19th century.

ADAMS		WILLIAM ADAMS & SONS (POTTERS) LTD. (and earlier titles: W. Adams, W. Adams & Co., W. Adams & Son), Greengates etc. Tunstall and Stoke. Staffordshire Potteries. 1769– . *Earthenwares, Basaltes, Jaspers, Parian, etc.*

For further information on the Adams family the reader is referred to:
William Adams, an old English Potter, W. Turner (1904).
The Adams Family, P. W. L. Adams (1914).
British Potters and Pottery Today, C. G. E. Bunt (1956).
A Pride of Potters, D. Peel (1959).

An interesting article on Adams ware is contained in the *Apollo* magazine, April 1953.

17	ADAMS & CO.	Impressed mark, 1769–1800.
18	ADAMS	Impressed mark, 1787–1805 on Jasper wares. 1800–64 on general earthenwares.
19		Printed mark on blue printed earthenwares, 1804–40.
20		Impressed mark on earthenwares, 1810–25.
21	W. ADAMS & CO.	Rare impressed mark, c. 1815.
22 23	W. ADAMS & SONS W. A. & S.	Distinguishing details of several printed marks of differing design: name of the individual pattern is often included, as mark no. 24, 1819–64.
24		Mark no. 24 is an example of the initials W. A. & S. occurring as part of an ornate printed mark, with the name of the pattern, 1819–64.
25	ADAMS	Impressed mark found on parian figures and groups, 1845–64.
26	W. ADAMS	Distinguishing detail of several printed marks of differing design: name of the individual pattern is often included, mid-19th century.

27   W. A. & CO.   Distinguishing initials found on several printed marks of differing design: name of the individual pattern is often included, 1893–1917.

28–32

A selection of printed marks used from c. 1879 into the 20th century. Variations occur in marks 28 and 29, a crown in place of the eagle, etc. The word "ENGLAND" occurs on marks after 1891.

34      Printed mark introduced in 1879. "England" added from 1891.

35   Printed mark on Ironstone type wares, 1890–1914. The word "TUNSTALL" occurs on Adams marks from 1896.

36–7   ADAMS   Printed marks from 1896 and continued into the 20th century.
                       ESTBD 1657   The names of different bodies—"Imperial Stone Ware", etc.—
                       TUNSTALL,   were sometimes added to mark no. 36. Mark no. 37 was used
                       ENGLAND   on Jasper wares from 1896.

38   Printed mark, 1914–40.

39	CALYX WARE	20th century trade-name found impressed or incorporated in printed marks.

40–2

W. Adams & Sons
England

1950+   1950+   1962—

Nos. 40–2. The basic post-war printed marks.

42a	MICRATEX	Trade-name for new, extra strong body, introduced commercially in 1963. This name will be incorporated in some marks from 1963 onwards.

ADAMS

43

PATTERN.
W & T ADAMS.
TUNSTALL.

WILLIAM & THOMAS ADAMS, Greenfields, Tunstall. Staffordshire Potteries. 1866–92. *Earthenwares.*

Printed mark, 1866–92. Emblems other than the Royal Arms were also used with the name in full.

Adderley
Adderley & Co.

See Adderleys Ltd.

ADDERLEY

ADDERLEY FLORAL CHINA, Sutherland Road, Longton. Staffordshire Potteries. 1945– . *Bone China Figures and Ornaments.*

   This is a branch of Ridgway Potteries Ltd. that continues to operate under original title.

44

Printed mark. 1945– .

ADDERLEY

J. FELLOWS ADDERLEY, Jubilee Works, Longton. Staffordshire Potteries. 1901–5. *Porcelain.*

| 45 | J. F. A. | Distinguishing detail of several printed marks of differing design: name of the individual pattern is often included, 1901–5. |

| 46 | | Printed trade-mark, 1901–5. |

ADDERLEY — **WILLIAM ALSAGER ADDERLEY (& Co.)**, Daisy Bank Pottery, Longton. Staffordshire Potteries. 1876–1905. *China and Earthenwares.* Subsequently Adderleys Ltd., q.v.

| 47 | W. A. A. | Distinguishing detail of several printed marks of differing design: name of the individual pattern is often included, 1876–85. |

| 48 | W. A. A. & Co. | "& Co." added to mark 47 from January 1886 to 1905. |

| 49 | | Printed trade-mark, 1876–1905. Also occurs with initials W. A. A. below (1876–85) and with W. A. A. & Co.(1886–1905). This mark was later used by Adderleys Ltd. |

ADDERLEYS — **ADDERLEYS LTD.**, Daisy Bank Pottery (renamed Gainsborough Works), Longton. Staffordshire Potteries. 1906– . *China and Earthenwares.* Formerly William Alsager Adderley & Co.

| 50 | | Printed mark, 1906–26. Also used from 1876 by predecessors, see mark 49. |

| 51–5 | | |

1912–26   1912–26   1926+   1926+   1929–47

Printed marks together spanning the years 1912–47.

56–8

1947–50

1950–62

1962–

Messrs. Adderleys Ltd. were taken over in 1947 by Ridgway Potteries Ltd. but the Adderleys title has been retained. Marks from 1947 include nos. 56–8.

742   AE   *See* Alan Caiger-Smith.
          (monogram)

502   AF   *See* Bow China Works.
          (monogram)

1536   A. F. & S.   *See* Alfred Fenton & Son.

2207   A. G. H. J.   *See* A. G. Harley *Jones*.

3242   A. G. R.   *See* Albert G. Richardson.

3243   A. G. R. & CO. LTD. *See* A. G. Richardson & Co. Ltd.

1875–6   AH   *See* Anna Hagen.
2101   (monogram)   *See* Agnette Hoy.

AINSLIE   **PETER AINSLIE**, Leicester (1948–56). Chester (1956–). 1948– .* *Studio-type Pottery, Stonewares.*

59–60   Impressed seal-type marks, 1948– *.

* Peter Ainslie produced no stonewares after moving to Chester in 1956, nor very much pottery. He hopes soon to be able to start potting seriously again. (*G.G. 1964.*)

AINSWORTH

W. H. & J. H. AINSWORTH, Stockton Pottery, Stockton-on-Tees, Co. Durham. 1865–1901. *Earthenwares.*

61

Impressed mark, 1865–1901.

2795   A. J.
           M.

See Arthur J. Mountford.

72

See Alcock, Lindley & Bloore Ltd.

ALBERT

ALBERT POTTERIES LTD., Albert Street, Burslem. Staffordshire Potteries. 1946–54. *Earthenwares.*

62

Printed or impressed, 1946–54.

63

Printed or impressed, 1946–54.

1292   **ALBION CHINA**
            or
1294   **ALBION WORKS**

See J. Dimmock & Co.

486   **ALBION POTTERY**

See Bourne & Leigh Ltd.

ALCOCK

HENRY ALCOCK & CO. (LTD.), Elder Pottery, Cobridge. Staffordshire Potteries. 1861–1910. *Earthenwares.* Formerly John Alcock. Subsequently The Henry Alcock Pottery, see next entry.

| 64 | H. A. & Co. | Distinguishing detail of several printed marks of differing design: name of the individual pattern is often included, 1861–80. |

| 65 | | Printed mark, 1880–1910. "England" added from 1891. "Ltd." added from 1900. |

ALCOCK THE HENRY ALCOCK POTTERY, Clarence Works, Stoke. Staffordshire Potteries. 1910–35. *Earthenwares*. Formerly Henry Alcock & Co. (Ltd.), q.v.

| 66 | | Printed mark, 1910–35. |

ALCOCK JOHN ALCOCK, Cobridge. Staffordshire Potteries. 1853–61. *Earthenwares*. Subsequently Henry Alcock & Co., q.v.

| 67 | JOHN ALCOCK COBRIDGE | Distinguishing detail of several printed marks of differing design, 1853–61. |

A typical marked jug will be found illustrated in *British Pottery and Porcelain: an illustrated Encyclopaedia of Marked Specimens*.

ALCOCK JOHN & GEORGE ALCOCK, Cobridge. Staffordshire Potteries. 1839–46. *Earthenwares*.

| 68 | J. & G. ALCOCK COBRIDGE | Impressed mark, 1839–46. |

| 69 | ORIENTAL STONE J. & G. ALCOCK | Impressed mark, 1839–46. "Oriental Stone" refers to the name of the body. |

| 69a | J. & G. A. | Distinguishing detail of several printed or impressed marks of differing design: name of the individual pattern is often included, 1839–46. |

| 70 | ALCOCKS INDIAN IRONSTONE | Impressed mark on Ironstone wares, believed to relate to this firm. |

ALCOCK

JOHN & SAMUEL ALCOCK, JUNIOR, Cobridge. Stafford-shire Potteries. c. 1848–50. *Earthenwares.*

This partnership probably succeeded that of John & George Alcock, q.v.

71   J. & S. ALCOCK JR.   Printed or impressed name-mark, c. 1848–50.

ALCOCK

ALCOCK, LINDLEY & BLOORE (LTD.), Vulcan Pottery, Hanley. Staffordshire Potteries. 1919– . *Earthenwares, mainly teapots.* Formerly Smith & Co.

72

Printed or impressed mark, 1919– .

ALCOCK

SAMUEL ALCOCK & CO., Cobridge c. 1828–53. Hill Pottery, Burslem, c. 1830–59. Staffordshire Potteries. c. 1828–59. *China, Earthenwares, Parian, etc.* Subsequently Sir J. *Duke* & Nephews, q.v.

For further information see *British Pottery and Porcelain, 1780–1850.* Typical specimens will be found illustrated in *British Pottery and Porcelain: an illustrated Encyclopaedia of Marked Specimens.*

73   SAM^L ALCOCK & CO.   Printed or impressed name-mark with "Cobridge" address,
         COBRIDGE   c. 1828–53.

74   SAM^L ALCOCK & CO.   Printed, impressed or moulded marks with "Burslem" address,
         BURSLEM   c. 1830–59. The date of publication of many models is incor-porated in many marks. See Plate 4.

75   S. A. & CO.   Many different printed, painted or impressed marks were used
76   S. ALCOCK & CO.   by this firm and incorporate either the initials or name. Several
77   SAM^L ALCOCK & CO.   of these marks include the Royal Arms, or a bee-hive device. On some specimens only the initials S. A. & Co. or the name was added, without any pictorial device, c. 1830–59.

78   This version of the Royal Arms mark occurs on Alcock wares, with or without the initials, S. A. & Co., or the name below it.

70	ALCOCKS INDIAN IRONSTONE	*See* John & George Alcock.
125a	ALDERNEY	*See* Peter G. Arnold.

ALDRIDGE

ALDRIDGE & CO., Normacot Works, Longton. Staffordshire Potteries. 1919–49. *Earthenwares.* Subsequently Aldridge Pottery Co. (Longton) Ltd.

80	ALDRIDGE & CO LONGTON	Impressed mark, 1919–49.

350 588	ALDWYCH CHINA	*See* Beswick & Son. *See* Bridgett & Bates.

3272	ALE (monogram)	*See* A. Lewis-Evans.

ALLANDER

ALLANDER POTTERY (Hugh Allan), Milngavie, Nr. Glasgow, Scotland. 1904–8. Studio-type Pottery (glaze effects).

81	ALLANDER H. A. 1905	Incised or painted mark, in writing letters or italics, with year of production added. 1904–8.

ALLASON

JOHN ALLASON, Seaham Pottery, Seaham Harbour, Nr. Sunderland, Durham. 1838–41. *Earthenwares.*

82	JOHN ALLASON SEAHAM POTTERY	Rare printed mark, 1838–41.

ALLER

ALLER VALE ART POTTERIES, Newton Abbott, Devon. 1887–1901. *Earthenwares.* Formerly J. Phillips & Co. Subsequently Royal Aller Vale & Watcombe Pottery Co., q.v.

83	ALLER VALE	Impressed mark, 1887–1901.

ALLERTON

CHARLES ALLERTON & SONS, Park Works, Longton. Staffordshire Potteries. 1859–1942. *China, Earthenwares, Lustre decoration, etc.* Formerly Allerton, Brough & Green. Taken over in 1912 by Cauldon Potteries Ltd., from which date they operated under the name of Allerton's Ltd.

Early wares were unmarked.

84 CHAS ALLERTON & SONS ENGLAND — Distinguishing details of several printed or impressed marks of differing design: name of the individual pattern is often included, c. 1890–1942.

85 C. A. & SONS

86–8

c. 1890+ c. 1890+ c. 1903–12

Printed marks 1890–1912.

89–93

c. 1912+ c. 1915+ c. 1915–29 c. 1929–42

Printed marks together spanning the years 1912–42 used by Allertons Ltd.

ALLERTONS LTD. *See* Charles Allerton & Sons, previous entry.

ALLMAN

ALLMAN, BROUGHTON & CO., Overhouse Works, Burslem. Staffordshire Potteries. 1861–8. *Earthenwares.* Formerly Morgan Wood & Co. Subsequently Robinson Kirkham & Co.

94 A. B. & CO.
95 A. B. & CO. WEDGWOOD PLACE BURSLEM — Distinguishing details of several printed or impressed marks of differing design: name of the individual pattern is often included, 1861–8.

ALLSUP

JOHN ALLSUP, 16, St. Paul's Churchyard, London.   1832–58.   *Retailer.*

96   JOHN (or J) ALLSUP
ST. PAUL'S CHURCH-
YARD, LONDON

Printed mark on Grainger Worcester and other wares, 1832–57. Specimens bearing the address, 22 Ludgate Street, are believed to date to 1858.

ALPHA

ALPHA POTTERIES, Sidcup, Kent.   1954–8.   *Individually designed Studio Pottery.*

97   *Alpha*   Written mark, 1954–8.

98   ∝   Incised mark, 1954–8.

99   ∝   Impressed seal-mark, 1954–8.

1025   ALMA WARE   *See* Thomas Cone Ltd.

3073   ALP
(monogram)

See Alfred L. Pocock.

2130a   ALPHA WARE   *See* William Hulme.

ALSOP

JAMES ALSOP (SENR.), 9 Water Lane and Temple Street, Bristol.   1770+.   *Stonewares and Earthenwares.*

100   ALSOP   Impressed mark, 1770+.   It is presumed that this mark relates to James Alsop, senior, but other potters of this name worked in Bristol early in the 19th century.

ALTON

ALTON CHINA CO. LTD., Kingcross Street, Longton. Staffordshire Potteries.   1950–7. *Bone China Figures, Birds, Animals, etc.*

101   ALTON
BONE CHINA

Printed mark, 1950–7.

102   BONE CHINA
ALTON ENGLAND

Printed mark, 1950–7.

ALTON   **ALTON TOWERS HANDCRAFT POTTERY (STAFFS) LTD.**, Alton Towers, Stoke. Staffordshire Potteries. 1953– . *Earthenwares.*

103   ALTON TOWERS   Marks 103, 104 and 105, printed or impressed, often in cir-
         HANDCRAFT   cular outline, as mark no. 105, 1953– .
           STAFFS
          ENGLAND

104   TOWERS CRAFT WARE

105

3824

                              See Tenby Pottery.

2826   AM   *See* Andrew Mackee.
          L

3560   AMBASSADOR WARE   *See* Simpsons (Potters) Ltd.

1035   AMBLESIDE   *See* G. Frederick Cook.

AMISON   **CHARLES AMISON (& CO. LTD.)**, Stanley China Works, Wedgwood St. (renamed Amison St., 1953), Longton. Stafford-shire Potteries. 1889–1962. *Porcelains.* Formerly Amison & Lawson, c. 1878.
                                   Charles Amison 1889–1916. Charles Amison & Co. 1916+. Charles Amison & Co., Ltd. 1930+.

106   C A   Impressed initials, 1889+. The L stands for the place name
          L   Longton.

107

                              Printed mark, 1906–30.

108

                              Printed mark, 1930–41. Factory closed 1941–45. A similar mark with "Made in England" used 1946–49.

| 109 | | Printed mark, 1949–53. |

| 110 | | Printed mark, 1951–62. Used on floral china only. (The moulds for floral wares were purchased by Longton New Art Pottery Co. Ltd. in 1962; production of these wares is continued by the later Company.) |

| 111 | | Printed mark, 1953–62. |

| — | A. M. S. | *See* Appendix, page 708. |

ANCHOR

ANCHOR PORCELAIN CO. LTD., Anchor Pottery, Anchor Road, Longton. Staffordshire Potteries. 1901–18. *China.* Formerly T. Morris.

| 112 | A. P. CO. | Impressed initial marks, 1901–18. |

| 113 | A. P. CO. L. | |

| 114 | | Impressed or printed mark, 1901–15. |

| 114a | | Printed mark, 1915–18. |

ANGLESEA

ANGLESEA POTTERY, Miss B. Carpenter, Llanfaethlu, North Wales. 1954– .* *Studio-type Pottery.*

| 115 | ANGLESEA crest POTTERY | Impressed or incised name-mark with crest of the Carpenter family (a lion arising from a crown), 1954– .* |

* Since 1959 little pottery has been produced.

ANNAN   DOROTHY ANNAN, London N.W.3. 1949– . *Studio-type Pottery ; also Murals and Mosaics.*

116   Incised or painted mark, 1949– .

—   ANNFIELD POTTERY *See* J. Thomson.

162   AP   *See* Ault Potteries Ltd.
161   (monogram)   *See* William Ault.
173, 175   *See* Aylesford Priory Pottery.
743   *See* Alan Caiger-Smith.
2974   *See* Judith Partridge.
3128   *See* Alfred & L. Powell.

112   A. P. CO.   *See* Anchor Porcelain Co.

113   A. P. CO. L.   *See* Anchor Porcelain Co.

ARBEID   DAN ARBEID, Abbey Art Centre, New Barnet, Hertford-shire. 1956– . *Studio-type Pottery, Stonewares.*

117   D. A.   Painted or impressed initial and name-marks, 1956– .

118   ARBEID   The name occurs on large vases etc., the initials on small specimens.

121   ARCADIAN   *See* Arkinstall & Son (Ltd.).
             or
       ARCADIAN CHINA

803b   ARDEN   *See* Barbara Cass.

1693   ARF   *See* Annette Fuchs.
         (monogram)

ARISTOCRAT   ARISTOCRAT FLORALS & FANCIES, Heathcote Works, Longton. Staffordshire Potteries. 1958– . *Bone China Floral Fancies, Jewellery, etc.*

119	ENGLISH *Aristocrat Florals* BONE CHINA	Printed mark, 1958– .

ARKINSTALL

ARKINSTALL & SONS (LTD.), Trent Bridge Pottery, (subsequently Arcadian Works), Stoke-on-Trent. Staffordshire Potteries. 1904–24. *China.* This firm was taken over by Robinson & Leadbeater, 1908. Subsequently by A. J Robinson & Sons and later by Cauldon Ltd., 1925.

120   A & S   Distinguishing initials found on several printed marks of differing design: name of the individual pattern is often included, 1904–12.

121   ARCADIAN
or
ARCADIAN CHINA   Trade-name incorporated in marks, 1904–24.

122   Printed mark, 1904–24.

ARMSTRONG

LADY HESTER ARMSTRONG, London, N.W.1. 1959– . *Studio-type Ceramic Sculpture.*

123   H. A.   Initials, impressed or painted, on small pieces, 1959.

124   H. ARMSTRONG   Signature in full on large pieces, 1959 .

ARNOLD

PETER G. ARNOLD, Leatherhead, Surrey (1958–62). Alderney Pottery, Channel Islands (1962–). 1958– . *Studio-type Pottery.*

125   Painted mark, 1958– .

125a   ALDERNEY   Painted or incised place name-mark on wares made after 1962 and sold in Alderney.

125b   Impressed AY monogram mark, 1962– .

—	ARROW DEVICES	*See* Appendix.
499		*See* Bow China Works.
3050–1		*See* Pinxton Works.

ART

ART POTTERY CO., Anchor Works, Hanley. Staffordshire Potteries. *1900–11. Earthenwares.* Formerly Physick & Cooper. Subsequently Cooper's Art Pottery Co., q.v.

126

Printed mark, 1900–11. Mark continued by successors.

ARTONE

ARTONE POTTERY, Burslem. Staffordshire Potteries. *1946– . Studio-style Pottery, Figures and Fancies.*

127

ARTONE
ENGLAND
HAND PAINTED
BONE CHINA

Printed mark, within an outline of an artist's palette, 1946–

—	AS	*See* A. Singer (Appendix).
3456	(monogram)	*See* Audrey Samuel.
3681	A. S.	*See* A. Stanyer.
	B.	
3682	A S	*See* A. Stanyer.
	ENG	
	B	
—	A. S. & CO.	*See* Appendix, page 709.
3575		*See* Ambrose Smith & Co.
120	A & S	*See* Arkinstall & Son (Ltd.).

ASBURY

EDWARD ASBURY & CO., Prince of Wales' Works, Longton. Staffordshire Potteries. *1875–1925. China and Earthenwares.* Formerly Hammerley & Asbury, q.v.

For further information see L. Jewitt's *The Ceramic Art of Great Britain.*

128		Printed mark, 1875–1925.
129	ASBURY LONGTON	Mark no. 128 also occurs with the name ASBURY and the place name LONGTON added above the crest.
130	A & CO.	Distinguishing initials found on several printed marks of differing design: name of the individual pattern is often included, 1875–1925.

ASHBY

ASHBY POTTERS' GUILD, Woodville, Nr. Burton-on-Trent, Derbyshire. 1909–22. *Earthenwares*. Subsequently Ault & Tunnicliffe Ltd., q.v.

131 — Impressed mark, 1909–22.

132–4 — These initial marks are to be found on individual examples from c. 1909 and relate to the artist or potter.

ASHTEAD

ASHTEAD POTTERS LTD., Victoria Works, Ashtead, Surrey. 1926–36. *Earthenwares*.

135 — Printed mark, 1926–36.

136   W. GREEN   This signature mark occurs on some Ashtead wares painted or designed by this artist.

ASHWORTH   **G. L. ASHWORTH & BROS. (LTD.)**, Broad Street, Hanley. Staffordshire Potteries. 1862– . *Earthenwares, Ironstone, etc.* Succeeded Francis Morley, q.v.

For further information on Ashworth wares see L. Jewitt's *Ceramic Art of Great Britain* (1883), C. G. E. Bunt's *British Potters and Pottery Today* (1956).

137   ASHWORTH   Impressed mark, 1862–80.

138   A. BROS.
139   G. L. A. & BROS.   Distinguishing details of several printed marks of differing design: name of the individual pattern is often included, 1862–c. 90. Typical examples are reproduced as nos. 140–2.

140–2

As manufacturers of Mason's "Patent Ironstone" Messrs. Ashworths first adopted the printed mark originally used by Masons (Mark 143). They later added their own name (Mark 144) and in 1891 added the word "England" (Mark 145). They also used similar marks in which the word "Real" was used in place of "Patent", so that the wording "Real Ironstone China" occurs.

143–5

Former Mason   Name Ashworth   "England" added
mark continued   added 1862+   below standard
                                                    mark 1891+

146   The printed Royal Arms mark occurs on Ashworth earthenwares from 1862. The impressed name ASHWORTH is also normally present.

147      Printed mark c. 1880 onwards. Slight variations occur with the wording "A Bros" or "Ashworths".

148		20th century version of printed mark. "England" or "Made in England" frequently occur below.
149	LUSTROSA	Trade-name on some earthenwares having special glaze effect, c. 1900.
150		Printed mark, 1932 onwards. Several similar marks occur with the names of special patterns or styles, as in this case the name Masons also occurs.
151–2		Printed ironstone marks used from 1957 onwards.
—	JOHN ASQUITH	*See* Nottingham Stonewares.

ASTBURY

ASTBURY, Shelton. Staffordshire Potteries. Mid-18th century. *Earthenwares.*

153   ASTBURY   Incised or impressed mark on red earthenwares. Mid-18th century.

Copies of Chinese seal-type marks also occur impressed on Astbury unglazed red earthenwares. See two interesting Papers by Robin Price in the *Transactions of the English Ceramic Circle*, vol. 4, part 5 and vol. 5, part 3.

An "Astbury" covered jug will be found illustrated in *British Pottery and Porcelain: an illustrated Encyclopaedia of Marked Specimens.*

N.B. Several potters of this name were working in Staffordshire from c. 1720 onwards. Most of their wares are unmarked.

ASTBURY

RICHARD MEIR ASTBURY, Foley Pottery, Lane End, Shelton. Staffordshire Potteries. 1790. *Earthenwares.*

154   R. M. A.   Impressed mark, late 18th century.

155	ASTBURY	Impressed mark, late 18th century. A moulded "Fair Hebe" jug sold at Sotheby's in 1962 had the impressed mark R. M. A. on the edge and ASTBURY on the base. This jug was modelled by Voyez in 1788. See *British Pottery and Porcelain: an illustrated Encyclopaedia of Marked Specimens*.
3427	A. S. W.	*See* Rye Pottery.
744	AT	*See* Alan Caiger-Smith.
3830	(monogram)	*See* Anne H. Thalmessinger.

ATKINSON   **ATKINSON & CO.**, Southwick Pottery, Sunderland, Co. Durham. 1788–99. *Earthenwares.* Succeeded by Anthony Scott & Co., see Southwick Pottery.

156	ATKINSON & CO.	Impressed or printed, 1788–99.

ATLAS   **ATLAS CHINA CO. LTD.**, Atlas Works, Wolfe Street, Stoke. Staffordshire Potteries. 1906–10. *China.* Formerly Chapman & Sons Ltd. Taken over by Grimwades Ltd., and name revived. 1930–6.

157		Printed mark, 1906–10. Variation of former Chapman mark. A similar Atlas mark was used on tiles by the Atlas Tile Works, Vine St., Hanley, 1907–20.
1834	ATLAS	*See* Grimwades Ltd.
1312	AT R	*See* Don Pottery.

AULD   **IAN AULD**, Wimbish, Saffron Walden, Essex. 1959 . *Studio-type Pottery, Stonewares.*

158	IA.	Impressed seal-type mark, 1959– .
159		Painted mark, 1959– . Other initials occur on Ian Auld's wares. These relate to the glaze, etc., used.

AULT

WILLIAM AULT, Swadlincote, Nr. Burton-on-Trent, Staffordshire. 1887–1923. *Earthenwares.* Subsequently Ault & Tunnicliffe, q.v.

160

Printed mark, 1887–1923.

The signature mark of Chr. Dresser occurs on Ault wares designed by him, see mark no. 1400. Typical examples will be found illustrated in *British Pottery and Porcelain: an illustrated Encyclopaedia of Marked Specimens.*

161

Printed or impressed monogram, 1887+. Also used by Ault Potteries Ltd., 1937+.

AULT

AULT POTTERIES LTD., Swadlincote, Nr. Burton-on-Trent, Staffordshire. 1937–present day. *Earthenwares.* Formerly Ault & Tunnicliffe.

162

Impressed or printed mark, 1937– .

AULT

AULT & TUNNICLIFFE LTD., Swadlincote, Nr. Burton-on-Trent, Staffordshire. 1923–37. *Earthenwares.* Formerly Ault, Wm. and Ashby Potters' Guild, q.v. Subsequently Ault Potteries Ltd., q.v.

163–5

Printed or impressed marks, 1923–37.

AVON

AVON ART POTTERY LTD., Jubilee Works to 1961 (continued at Edensor Rd.), Longton. Staffordshire Potteries. 1930– . *Earthenwares.*

166

Printed or impressed mark, 1930–39.

167      Printed mark, 1939–47.

168      Printed mark, 1947– . Slight variations occur.

AVONCROFT   AVONCROFT POTTERY (Geoffrey Whiting), Hampton Lovett, Nr. Droitwich, Worcestershire. 1952– . *Studio-type Stonewares* (rarely Porcelain).

169–70      Standard Avoncroft impressed seal-marks within circular outline, 1952– .

171   Personal impressed seal-mark of Geoffrey Whiting, 1952– .

166–8	AVON WARE	*See* Avon Art Pottery Ltd.
3996	AW	*See* Alan Wallwork.
4378–9	(monogram)	*See* Arthur & Aileen Wyllie.
4233	A. W. L.	*See* Arthur Wood.
892	A. W. R. (or monogram)	*See* Kenneth Clark Pottery.

AXE   AXE VALE POTTERY (DEVON) LTD., Seaton, Devon. 1959– . *Hand painted Earthenwares.*

172   Printed mark, 1959– .

125b   AY   *See* Peter G. Arnold.
            (joined)

AYLESFORD   **AYLESFORD PRIORY POTTERY**, Aylesford, Nr. Maidstone, Kent. 1955– . *Stonewares.*

173-4   Impressed seal-marks, 1955– .

175   Impressed mark, 1955– .

176-7   Nos. 176 and 177 are personal marks of Colin Pearson at Aylesford Priory up to mid-1962.

188   AYNSLEY   *See* John Aynsley & Sons (Ltd.).

AYNSLEY   **H. AYNSLEY & CO. (LTD.)**, Commerce Works, Longton. Staffordshire Potteries. 1873– . *Earthenwares.*

178   H. AYNSLEY & CO.   Distinguishing details of several printed marks of differing
          LONGTON   design: name of the individual pattern is often included,
179   H. A. & CO.   1873–1932. "England" sometimes added from 1891 onwards.
          L.   "Ltd" added to most marks from 1932.

180

181-3   VOGUE MODERNE

           1946-54   1951+   1955

Printed or impressed marks, 1946 onwards.
   Variations of mark no. 183, with "Vogue Moderne" replaced by the name of some other style or pattern, also occur.

AYNSLEY		JOHN AYNSLEY (or ANSLEY), Lane End. Staffordshire Potteries. 1780–1809. *Printed Earthenwares.*

184	AYNSLEY LANE END	Several different printed name-marks occur incorporated in the printed design. Nos. 184–7 are the basic forms of signature found, 1780–1809.
185	I. AYNSLEY	
186	J. AYNSLEY LANE END	See *British Pottery and Porcelain : an illustrated Encyclopaedia of Marked Specimens.*
187	JOHN AYNSLEY LANE END	

AYNSLEY

JOHN AYNSLEY & SONS (LTD.), Portland Works, Longton. Staffordshire Potteries. 1864– . *Porcelains.*
The early wares were unmarked.

| 188 | AYNSLEY | Impressed mark, 1875+. |

| 189 | | Printed mark, 1875–90. |

| 190–4 | |

Printed marks from 1891, after which the name "ENGLAND" was added.

B

—	B	*See* Appendix.
196		*See* John & Edward Baddeley.
267		*See* Thomas Barlow.
268		*See* T. W. Barlow & Son Ltd.
284		*See* Paul Barron.
285		*See* Basing Farm Pottery.
404		*See* Blair & Co.
503		*See* Bow China Works.
614		*See* Bristol Porcelain.
1507		*See* Eos Pottery.
—		*See* Group letters.
2511		*See* Ray Marshall.
3357		*See* Rockingham Works.
4334		*See* Worcester, Barr period.
577	B (in triangle)	*See* Noel Brannan.
—	B & CO	*See* Appendix.
376–7		*See* L. A. Birks & Co.
419		*See* Bodley & Co.
467		*See* Boulton & Co.
272–3	B. Ltd.	*See* Barlows (Longton) Ltd.
427	B & Son	*See* Bodley & Son.
526	B. A. & B.	*See* Bradbury, Anderson & Bettany.
1974	baba	*See* Barbara Hauber.

BABBACOMBE		**BABBACOMBE POTTERY LTD.**, Torquay, Devon. 1952– . *Earthenwares.*
195	BABBACOMBE POTTERY LTD. MADE IN TORQUAY, DEVON	Printed mark, in circular form, 1952– .
199	BADDELEY	*See* Ralph & John Baddeley.

BADDELEY		**JOHN & EDWARD BADDELEY**, Shelton. Staffordshire Potteries. 1784–1806. *Earthenwares.* Subsequently Hicks & Meigh, q.v.
196	B	Impressed initial marks, 1784–1806.
197	I.E.B.	A marked dessert service (illustrated in *British Pottery and*
198	I.E.B. W.	*Porcelain: an illustrated Encyclopaedia of Marked Specimens*) has most of the main pieces impressed with the initials I.E.B., some with W. below. The plates have only the initial B impressed.

BADDELEY		**RALPH & JOHN BADDELEY**, Shelton. Staffordshire Potteries. 1750–95. *Earthenwares.*
199	BADDELEY	Impressed marks, 1775–95.
200	R & J BADDELEY	

BADDELEY		**THOMAS BADDELEY.** Various addresses. Hanley. Staffordshire Potteries. 1800–34. *Engraver.*
201	T. BADDELEY HANLEY	Signature marks on prints engraved by Thomas Baddeley, 1800–34.
201a	THOS BADDELEY PRINTER & ENAMELLER HANLEY	An interesting signed and dated (1804) earthenware jug with spinning machine subject print will be found illustrated in *British Pottery and Porcelain: an illustrated Encyclopaedia of Marked Specimens*. A similar example, dated 1822, was sold at Sotheby's in 1963.

BADDELEY		**WILLIAM BADDELEY,*** Eastwood, Hanley. Staffordshire Potteries. 1802–22. *Earthenwares, of Wedgwood types.*
202	EASTWOOD	Impressed mark, 1802–22. See Plate 2.

N.B. "EAST" is sometimes indistinct, so that the mark might pass as Wedgwood. The mark is sometimes placed in unusual places, at the front lower edge of a teapot, etc. A fine bulb pot will be found illustrated in the companion illustrated encyclopaedia of marked specimens.

* A potter of this name was working at Longton, c. 1864–75, see next entry.

BADDELEY

WILLIAM BADDELEY,* Drury Court Works, Longton. Staffordshire Potteries. 1864–75. *Terra-cotta wares, etc.*

203   W. BADDELEY

Impressed mark, 1864–75.

* A potter of this name was working at Hanley, c. 1802–22, see previous entry.

BAGGALEY

E. BAGGALEY LTD., Branksome China Works, Bournemouth, Hants. 1957– . *Earthenwares.* Formerly Branksome Ceramics Ltd., q.v.

204

Printed mark, used by Branksome Ceramics Ltd. and the present Company from 1947.

205

A similar mark with the addition of the words "Super-Fine" has been used on some wares since 1957, as has been this variation with the words "Hand Painted".

BAGGALEY

JACOB BAGGALEY, Hill Works, Liverpool Road, Burslem. Staffordshire Potteries. 1880–6. *Earthenwares.* Formerly Wood & Baggaley.

206   J B

Impressed initials, 1880–6.

BAGGERLEY

BAGGERLEY & BALL, St. James' Place, Longton. Staffordshire Potteries. 1822–36. *Earthenwares.*

207

Printed mark, in underglaze blue, 1822–36.

N.B. This basic *form* of mark occurs with the initials of other manufacturers.

This mark occurs on a dated jug (1823) illustrated in my *British Pottery and Porcelain 1780–1850*. The name Baggerley is spelt in various ways in contemporary records. This mark has in the past been attributed, incorrectly, to other manufacturers.

BAGSHAW

BAGSHAW & MEIR (or **MAIER**), Burslem. Staffordshire Potteries. 1802–8. *Earthenwares.*

208   B & M

Impressed or printed initial marks, 1802–8.

BAGULEY

ALFRED (and **ISAAC**) **BAGULEY**, Rockingham Works (c. 1842–65) and Mexborough (c. 1865–91). Yorkshire. 1842–91. *Porcelains, etc., in Rockingham styles.* Isaac Baguley 1842–55. Alfred Baguley 1855–91.

Alfred Baguley decorated porcelain purchased in the white, he was not a manufacturer.

209

Printed mark, 1842–65. A variation has the words "Royal Rockingham Works, Baguley".

N.B. This mark was also used from 1842 to 1855 by Isaac Baguley and by his son Alfred from 1855 to 1865.

210   BAGULEY
         ROCKINGHAM
         WORKS

The above griffin mark may have been used on examples made for the Fitzwilliam family, other examples bear only the painted name and address, 1842–65.

211 ROCKINGHAM WORKS
         BAGULEY
         MEXBRO.

Printed or painted mark, 1865–91. Note the word Mexborough or Mexbro used after 1865. Very rarely found.

BAGULEY

C. BAGULEY, Hanley. Staffordshire Potteries. Early 19th century.

212   PUB^d BY
       C. BAGULEY
       HANLEY
    STAFFORDSHIRE
    20 JULY 1810

Relief mark on group (of parian type body) of two children and a rabbit.

N.B. The year is indistinct.

This name-mark probably refers to the modeller of this group as I cannot trace a potter of this name.

—   ISAAC BAGULEY   *See* Alfred (and Isaac) Baguley.

BAILEY   **C. J. C. BAILEY** (or **BAILEY & CO.**), Fulham Pottery, London S.W.6. 1864–89. *Stonewares, Terra-Cotta, etc., Porcelain* (c. 1873). Subsequently Fulham Pottery & Cheavin Filter Co. Ltd., q.v.

For further information see Jewitt's *Ceramic Art of Great Britain* (1883). A vase will be found illustrated in *British Pottery and Porcelain: an illustrated Encyclopaedia of Marked Specimens.*

213   BAILEY   Distinguishing details of several incised or impressed marks of differing design, 1864–89. The year of production is sometimes added.
           FULHAM
214   C. J. C. BAILEY
           FULHAM POTTERY
           LONDON

215   Incised monogram mark, of the initials C. J. C. B. often with wording FULHAM POTTERY, etc., and the date, 1864–89.

BAILEY   **BAILEY & BATKIN**, Lane End, Longton. Staffordshire Potteries. 1814–27.* *Earthenwares (lustre decorated).*

216   BAILEY & BATKIN   Impressed or moulded marks, 1814–27.*
217   BAILEY & BATKIN   The reference to "Sole Patentees" refers to the article (not
           SOLE PATENTEES   the lustre decoration). The object a "Perdifume" was patented (c. 1824) by "William Bailey, the younger, of Lane End, Staffordshire Potteries. Manufacturer and ornamenter of lustreware". The earthenware "Perdifume" (generally decorated with silver lustre) was an improved fume consumer for consuming the smoke arising from gas burners and lamps. See *British Pottery and Porcelain: an illustrated Encyclopaedia of Marked Specimens.* Also *Old English Lustre Pottery* by John and Baker.

The order books of a small china seller in Boston, America, have recently been discovered. In 1816 Bailey & Batkin supplied 50 tea services "Lustre edged female figures, ten sets" spotted lustre tea sets, also gold lustre landscape pattern services, also jugs, teapots, sugars, creamers and coffee pots in silver and gold lustre.

217a   B & B   Lustre wares with these initials were probably made by this firm, c. 1814–27.

* The date that this partnership ceased is open to some doubt. Bailey & Co. is listed in 1829. William Bailey was potting at Lane End to 1832.

BAILEY		BAILEY & HARVEY., Longton. Staffordshire Potteries. 1834–5. *Earthenwares (lustre decorated).*
218	BAILEY & HARVEY	Impressed mark, 1834–5.

BAILEY

WILLIAM BAILEY & SONS, Gordon Pottery, Longton. Staffordshire Potteries. 1912–14. *Earthenwares.*

219 Printed mark, 1912–14.

BAILEY

W. & J. A. BAILEY, Alloa Pottery, Alloa, Scotland. 1855–1908. *Earthenwares.* Formerly Anderson & Gardner.

220 BAILEY Rare printed marks occur with the name of the pattern and "BAILEY".

220a W. & J. A. BAILEY ALLOA Impressed marks on leaf pattern majolica type plate in the Godden Collection, c. 1855–90.

221 Late printed mark, 1890–1908.

BAILEY

BAILEY POTTERIES LTD., Fenton. Staffordshire Potteries. 1935–40. *Earthenwares.*

222 BEWLEY POTTERY MADE IN ENGLAND Distinguishing detail of several printed marks of differing design: name of the individual pattern is often included, 1935–40. Mark no. 223 is a typical example.

223

BAIRSTOW

P. E. BAIRSTOW & CO., Mount Pleasant (and Trent Walk Pottery from 1938), Shelton, Stoke-on-Trent. 1954– . *Bone China Fancies.* Formerly Fancies Fayre Pottery, q.v.

224 Former mark of Fancies Fayre Pottery continued by Bairstow, 1946– .

225   Printed Bairstow mark, 1954– . Slight variations occur.

2192–3   B. A. J. & SONS   *See* A. B. Jones & Sons (Ltd.).
and
2197

BAKER   **BAKER, BEVANS & IRWIN,** Glamorgan Pottery, Swansea,
                   Wales. 1813–38. *Earthenwares.*

226   B. B. & I.   Distinguishing details of several printed or impressed marks of
227   BAKER BEVANS   differing design: name of the individual pattern is often included,
        & IRWIN   1813–38.
                            Examples will be found illustrated in the companion encyclo-
                        paedia of marked specimens.

228   B. B. & CO.   Marks may occur with the initials B. B. & Co. or G. P. Co.—for
229   G. P. CO.   Glamorgan Pottery Co., 1813–38.

BAKER   **(W.) BAKER & CO. (LTD.),** Fenton. Staffordshire Potteries.
                   1839–1932. *Earthenwares.*

230   W. BAKER & CO.   Distinguishing detail of several printed or impressed marks of
231   BAKER & CO.   differing design: name of the individual pattern is often in-
                        cluded, from about 1860.   Ltd. was added to the firm's style
                        in 1893.

232–5

          c. 1893–1928   c. 1928–30   c. 1930–2   c. 1930–2

                   Printed marks, c. 1893 onwards.

BAKEWELL   **BAKEWELL BROS. LTD.,** Britannic Works, Hanley.
                   Staffordshire Potteries. 1927–43. *Earthenwares and Stonewares.*

236	BAKEWELL BROS. LTD.	Distinguishing detail of several printed marks of differing design: the name of the body "Royal Vitreous", etc., is often added, 1927–43.

                  N.B. The addition of "Stoke-on-Trent" in marks indicates a date after 1931.

BALAAM

W. BALAAM, Rope Lane Pottery, Ipswich, Suffolk. 1870–81. *Slip decorated Earthenwares.* Pottery formerly worked by the Schulens.

237	W. BALAAM ROPE LANE POTTERY IPSWICH	Impressed mark, 1870–81.

238	ROPE LANE POTTERY IPSWICH	Impressed mark used by Schulen or Balaam, 1840+. A slip ware oval dish with combed decoration and bearing this rare mark will be found illustrated in *British Pottery and Porcelain: an illustrated Encyclopaedia of Marked Specimens.*

BALFOUR

BALFOUR CHINA CO. LTD., Royal Crown Pottery, Longton. Staffordshire Potteries. 1947 to January 1952. *Bone China.* Subsequently Trentham Bone China Ltd.

239	BALFOUR ROYAL CROWN POTTERY BEST BONE CHINA ENGLAND	Circular printed mark with crown above, 1947–52.

BALL

BALL BROTHERS, Deptford Pottery, Sunderland, Durham. 1884–1918. *Earthenwares.* Established 1857 as William Ball. "Bros." added from 1884.

240	COPYRIGHT BALL BROS. SUNDERLAND	Printed on design of one teapot pattern* of about 1890. Most pieces are unmarked.

        See *The Potteries of Sunderland and District* (1961).

    * This teapot will be found illustrated in *British Pottery and Porcelain: an illustrated Encyclopaedia of Marked Specimens.*

BALL

IZAAC BALL, Burslem. Staffordshire Potteries. Late 17th century to early 18th century. *Slip decorated Earthenwares.*

241	I. B.	These initials occur on several examples of Staffordshire type, slip-decorated earthenwares. These examples have been tentatively attributed to Izaac Ball, a potter who is included in Wedgwood's list of Burslem potters, c. 1710–15.

1056 BALMORAL *See* Co-op Wholesale Society.

3343 BALTIMORE CHINA *See* W. H. Robinson.

BANCROFT   **BANCROFT & BENNETT,** Newcastle St., Burslem. Staffordshire Potteries. 1946–50. *Earthenwares.*

242 Printed mark, 1946–50.

BARBER   **BARBER, ERIC,** Newcastle upon Tyne and Sunderland, Co. Durham. 1951– . *Non-commercial studio-type Earthenwares.*

243 Incised or painted initial mark, with year of production, 1951– .

BARINA   **BARINA POTTERIES LTD.,** Luton, Bedfordshire. 1949–55.* *Earthenwares.*

244 BARINA The name Barina was registered as a trade-mark in 1949.
244a BARINA
    STUDIOS

245 ST. ALBAN The name "St. Alban ware" is also recorded.
    WARE

       * The date of closure is open to doubt.

BARKER   **BARKER** (three brothers, John, Richard and William), Lane End. Staffordshire Potteries. c. 1800. *Earthenwares, Basalt, etc.*

246 BARKER Impressed name-mark, late 18th century, early 19th century.
      The Victoria and Albert Museum contains a moulded basalt creamer and a moulded earthenware teapot (of Pratt type) both marked "Barker". See *British Pottery and Porcelain: an illustrated Encyclopaedia of Marked Specimens.*

BARKER   **BARKER BROS. LTD.,** Meir Works, Barker St. Longton. Staffordshire Potteries. 1876– . *China and Earthenwares.*

247	B.B.	Impressed mark c. 1876–c. 1900. "LTD" occurs on most marks from 1901.
248		Printed mark, c. 1880+.
249–51		Printed marks, 1912–30.
252–3		1930–7.
254–5a		1937– ; slight variations occur, in which different pattern or style names are added.

BARKER

BARKER & SON, Hill Works, Burslem. Staffordshire Potteries. c. 1850–60. *Earthenwares.*

256	B. & S.	This initial mark occurs on a printed pattern registered by this firm in June 1850. The initials were presumably also used on other wares made by Barker & Son, c. 1850–60.
256a	BARKER & SON	Printed or impressed name-mark, c. 1850–60.
—	E. BARKER	*See* Appendix.

BARKER

BARKER POTTERY CO., New Brampton, Chesterfield, Derbyshire. 1887–1957. *Stonewares.*

257		Printed or impressed mark, 1928–57.

BARKER

BARKER, SUTTON & TILL, Sytch Pottery, Burslem. Staffordshire Potteries. 1834–43. *Earthenwares.* Subsequently Barker & Till (see Appendix—B & T.).

258 B. S. & T.
259 B. S. & T.
      BURSLEM

Distinguishing details of several printed or impressed marks of differing design: name of the individual pattern is often included, 1834–43.

An impressed marked pottery bust will be found illustrated in *British Pottery and Porcelain: an illustrated Encyclopaedia of Marked Specimens.*

BARKER

SAMUEL BARKER & SON, Don Pottery, Swinton, Nr. Rotherham, Yorkshire. 1834–93. *Earthenwares.* See also "Don Pottery".

260 BARKER
    DON POTTERY

Impressed mark, c. 1834+.

261

Printed or impressed mark. c. 1834– . "B" may occur above the crest in place of "Barker".

262

Rare mark used, . 1850.

263

Printed mark c. 1851–93 with or without "Don Pottery". N.B. "& SON" or "& S" occurs from 1851 on all marks.

257 BARKER WARE

See Barker Pottery Co.

BARKERS

BARKERS & KENT LTD., Foley Pottery, Fenton. Staffordshire Potteries. 1889–1941. *Earthenwares.*

264	B. & K.	Distinguishing details of several printed or impressed marks of differing design: name of the individual pattern is often included, 1889–1941. "L" or "Ltd." was added from 1898. Mark no. 266 is a typical example.
265	B. & K. L.	

266 — Standard printed mark, 1898–1941.

—   C. BARLOW   *See* Appendix, page 710.

BARLOW

THOMAS BARLOW, Market Street Works, Longton. Staffordshire Potteries. 1849–82. *Earthenwares and Porcelain.*

267   B.   Impressed initial mark, 1849–82. Some lustre wares marked with an impressed B have been attributed to this potter but the initial could also relate to other potters.

BARLOW

T. W. BARLOW & SON LTD., Coronation Works, Commerce St., Longton. Staffordshire Potteries. 1882–1940. *Earthenwares.*

268	B	Wares from 1882 largely unmarked. An impressed B or B & S may rarely occur.
269	B & S	

270 — Printed or impressed mark, 1928–36.

271 — Printed mark, 1936–40.

BARLOWS

BARLOWS (LONGTON) LTD., Melbourne Works, Longton. Staffordshire Potteries. Barlows Ltd. 1920–22. Barlows (Longton) Ltd. 1923–52. *Earthenwares.*

272   B. LTD   Impressed mark, 1920+.

273   Printed mark, 1920–36.

274   MELBAR WARE
       LB
       'VITRIC'
       SEMI PORCELAIN
       ENGLAND   Printed mark, 1936–52.

737   BARMOUTH   *See* Bwthyn Pottery.

BARNES   **WILLIAM BARNES**, Swinton, Manchester. Pre-war and 1945– . *Studio-type Pottery.*

275   *WB*   Incised or painted initial mark 1945– .

275a   From 1948 to 1957 William Barnes worked at the Royal Lancastrian Pottery (Pilkingtons). Such wares bear the P mark.

BARNHOUSE   **BARNHOUSE POTTERY**, Margaret Leach & L. A. Groves (1946–7), Brockweir, Monmouth, Wales. 1946–October 1951. *Studio-type pottery.*

276   W\/   Impressed seal mark or written monogram of the initials W.V. (Wye Valley). Margaret Leach continued potting at Aylburton, Gloucestershire, but a new mark was then used, see Margaret Leach, mark no. 2353.

BARON   **W. L. BARON**, Rolle Quay Pottery, Barnstaple, Devon. 1899–1939. *Earthenwares.*
       W. L. Baron was formerly employed at C. H. Brannam's, Litchdon Pottery, Barnstaple, see page 98.

277   BARON. BARNSTAPLE   Incised mark written 1899–1939.

4339–
4342

BARR
and
BARR, FLIGHT & BARR

See Worcester Porcelains, page 695.

BARRATT'S

BARRATT'S OF STAFFORDSHIRE LTD., Royal Over-house Pottery, Burslem. Staffordshire Potteries. 1943– .
Earthenwares. Formerly known as Gater Hall & Co., q.v. (and King & Barratt).

278–9

Former Gater Hall & Co.'s (pre-war) marks continued, 1943+.

280–80a

Printed marks, 1945+.

281

DELPHATIC

"Delphatic" body and special marks date from 1957.

282–82a

Printed marks, 1961– .

BARRETT

DORA BARRETT, Harpenden, Herts. 1938– . *Terra-cotta and Stoneware Models of Animals, etc.*

283

Incised initial mark, 1938– .

BARRON

PAUL BARRON, Bentley, Nr. Farnham, Surrey. 1948– .
Studio-type Pottery.

284

B

Impressed seal mark B in square, 1948– .
   A fine stoneware jar by Paul Barron is illustrated in *Artist Potters in England*, M. Rose (1955).

569 576	BARUM	*See* C. H. Brannam Ltd.

BASING — **BASING FARM POTTERY** (John N. S. Green), Ashington, Sussex. 1962– . *Studio-type Pottery.*

285 — Impressed Basing Farm Pottery seal mark, 1962– .

286 — Seal type mark of three incised lines within an impressed outline, 1962– .

BATES — **BATES & BENNETT**, Lincoln Pottery, Cobridge. Staffordshire Potteries. 1868–95. *Earthenwares.*

287   B & B   Distinguishing detail of several printed or impressed marks of differing design: name of the individual pattern is often included, 1868–95.

BATES — **BATES, BROWN-WESTHEAD & MOORE**, Cauldon Place, Shelton, Hanley. Staffordshire Potteries. 1859–61. *Porcelain and Earthenwares.* Formerly J. Ridgway, Bates & Co., q.v. Subsequently Brown-Westhead, Moore & Co., q.v.

288   B. B. W. & M.   Distinguishing initials found on several printed or impressed marks of differing design: name of the individual pattern is often included, 1859–61.

Some decorative vases with classical figure motifs were produced.

BATES — **BATES ELLIOTT & CO.**, Dale Hall Works, Burslem. Staffordshire Potteries. 1870–5. *Earthenwares, Porcelain, etc.* Subsequently Bates Walker & Co., q.v.

289   B. E. & Co.   Distinguishing initials found on several printed marks of differing design, 1870–5.

290 — Staple trade-mark incorporated in many marks and continued by successors.

291	TURNER JASPER WARE	Impressed mark on Jasper wares made in Turner's old moulds, 1870–5.

BATES   **BATES, GILDEA & WALKER**, Dale Hall Works, Burslem. Staffordshire Potteries. 1878–81. *Earthenwares and China.* Formerly Bates Walker & Co., q.v. Subsequently Gildea & Walker, q.v.

292	B. G. & W.	Distinguishing initials found on several printed marks of differing design: name of the individual pattern is often included, 1878–81.

BATES   **BATES WALKER & CO.**, Dale Hall Works, Burslem. Staffordshire Potteries. Late 1875–8. *Earthenwares, Jaspers and China.* Formerly Bates Elliot & Co., q.v. Subsequently Bates, Gildea & Walker, q.v.

293	B. W. & Co.	Distinguishing details of several printed marks of differing design: name of the individual pattern is often included, 1875–8. The boy crest, mark no 290, is often included.
293a	BATES WALKER & CO.	

1632	BATH POTTERY	*See* Richard Freeman.
3514		*See* John Shelly.

BATHWELL   **BATHWELL & GOODFELLOW**, Upper House Works, Burslem (and at Tunstall, 1820–2). Staffordshire Potteries. 1818–23. *Earthenwares.* Formerly T. & E. Bathwell.
    This firm is listed in most books as *B*othwell & Goodfellow, an early error that has been repeated, without checking.

294	BATHWELL & GOODFELLOW	Impressed name-mark, 1818–23.

BATKIN   **BATKIN, WALKER & BROADHURST**, Church Street, Lane End. Staffordshire Potteries. *Earthenwares, Stone-china, etc.* 1840–5.

295	B. W. & B.	Distinguishing initials found on several printed marks of differing design: name of the individual pattern is often included, 1840–5. A marked plate is illustrated in H. Wakefield's *Victorian Pottery* (1962), Plate 3, and in *British Pottery and Porcelain: an illustrated Encyclopaedia of Marked Specimens.*

BATTAM

296   B ⫶ S.

BATTAM & SON, Gough Sq., London. c. 1830–70's. *Decorators.*

Painted mark on ceramics decorated at Battam & Sons, London decorating establishment. Such examples often bear the initials of the Ceramic and Crystal Palace Art-Union which was formed by Thomas Battam in 1858, see page 713. Thomas Battam, one time art-director at Copelands, died in 1864 but his son continued the London decorating establishment. His paintings in the manner of Limoges enamels were included in several international exhibitions, noticeably that of 1862 and 1871. Three marked examples will be found included in the companion illustrated encyclopaedia.

BATTEN

297   IAN BATTEN
Chard,
Hand Made.

IAN BATTEN, Chard Pottery Studio, Chard, Somerset. December 1961– . *Studio-type Pottery.*

Impressed or printed mark, the name Ian Batten is written in script. December 1961– .

BATTERHAM

298   R. B.

RICHARD BATTERHAM, Durweston, Blandford Forum, Dorset. 1959– . *Studio-type Pottery.*

Impressed seal mark, initials R.B. in oval, with or without "ENGLAND" under, 1959– .

BATTLE

299   BATTLE POTTERY

BATTLE POTTERY, Bernard J. Cotes, Battle, Sussex. 1961– . *Studio-type Pottery.*
  B.J. Cotes was formerly at the Orchard and Hastings Potteries, q.v.

Painted or incised mark in writing letters, 1961– .

299a
BATTLE

Personal mark of Bernard Cotes, incised or painted, "Battle" added from November 1962. Basic mark formerly used at Hastings Pottery, and continued at Battle. With or without the word "BATTLE".

BAXTER

JOHN DENTON BAXTER, High Street, Hanley. Staffordshire Potteries. 1823–7. *Earthenwares.*

300	I.D.B.	An attractive blue printed dish in the Godden Collection bears a printed mark incorporating the name of the pattern, the Staffordshire knot and the initials I.D.B. Illustrated in *British Pottery and Porcelain: an illustrated Encyclopaedia of Marked Specimens*.
301	J.D.B.	Similar marks have been recorded with the initials J.D.B. No other potter of the period had these initials, c. 1823–7.
301a	Prince of Wales's feather crest CELTIC CHINA STAFFORDSHIRE KNOT DEVICE	A mark comprising the Prince of Wales feather crest, with the initials J. D. B. below, together with a Staffordshire knot containing the words "Celtic China" has been seen on an earthenware plate. The plate also bears an impressed Staffordshire knot, c. 1823–7.

BAXTER

BAXTER, ROWLEY & TAMS, Park Place Works, Longton. Staffordshire Potteries. 1882–5. *China*. Subsequently Rowley & Tams.

302	B. R. & T.	Impressed initial mark, 1882–5.

BAYER

RICHARD, FRANZ BAYER, Shipley, Yorkshire. 1939–   .
Studio-type Pottery.
  Mr. Bayer has produced very little pottery in recent years.

303	*rfb*	Impressed or painted initial mark, 1939– .

BAYLEY

BAYLEY MURRAY & CO., Saracen Pottery, Possil Park, Glasgow, Scotland. 1875–84. *Earthenwares*. Subsequently Saracen Pottery Co.

304	B. M. & Co. SARACEN POTTERY	Distinguishing detail of several printed or impressed marks of differing design, 1875–84.
—	BAYLON	*See* Appendix, page 710.
—	B B	*See* Appendix.
242		*See* Bancroft & Bennett.
247 & 250		*See* Barker Bros. (Ltd.).
2705		*See* Mintons.

456	B. B. B.	*See* Booths (Ltd.).
586	B. B. B.	*See* Bridgett, Bates & Beech.
—	B & B	*See* Appendix.
207		*See* Baggerley & Ball.
217a		*See* Bailey & Bennett.
287		*See* Bates & Bennett.
398		*See* Blackhurst & Bourne.
587		*See* Bridgett & Bates.
3507	B. B. C.	*See* John Shaw & Sons (Longton) Ltd.
228	B. B. & CO.	*See* Baker, Bevans & Irwin.
	and	
226	B. B. & I.	
252	B. B. Ltd.	*See* Barker Bros. Ltd.
288	B. B. W. & M.	*See* Bates, Brown-Westhead & Moore.
803	B. C.	*See* Barbara Cass.
590	B. & C.	*See* Bridgwood & Clarke.
616 & 618	B. C. CO.	*See* Britannic China Co.
1724	B. C. G.	*See* B. C. Godwin.
3825	B D	*See* Terrington Pottery.

BEALE		**EVELYN BEALE, MISS**, Glasgow, Scotland. c. 1920–35. *Earthenware.*
305	Evelyn Beale	Signature mark, painted or incised, c. 1920–35.

BEARDMORE		**BEARDMORE & EDWARDS**, Union Square, Longton. Staffordshire Potteries. 1856–8. *Earthenwares.*
306	B. & E.	Distinguishing detail of rare printed marks of differing design, c. 1856–8.

BEARDMORE

FRANK BEARDMORE & CO., Sutherland Pottery, High St., Fenton. Staffordshire Potteries. 1903–14. *Earthenwares.* Formerly Christie & Beardmore, q.v.

307   F. B. & CO.   Distinguishing initials found on several printed or impressed
             F.   marks of differing design, with or without F. under, 1903–14.

307a   Printed mark, 1903–14.

289   B. E. & Co.   *See* Bates Elliot & Co.

BECKLEY

D. BECKLEY, Seaview Pottery, Isle of Wight, Hampshire. October 1958– . *Hand-made Pottery.* Formerly "Island Pottery Studio", q.v.

308   SEAVIEW POTTERY ISLE OF WIGHT   Printed or impressed mark, 1958–9.

308a   Printed or impressed mark, 1959– .

BEDDGELERT

BEDDGELERT POTTERY (Mrs. A. Davey and Mrs. P. Hancock), Beddgelert, North Wales. June 1962– . *Studio-type Earthenwares.*

309   Painted mark, 1962– . The name Beddgelert may also occur.

3119   BEDFORD   *See* Ridgways (Bedford Works) Ltd.

BEDNALL

BEDNALL & HEATH, Wellington Pottery, Hanley. Staffordshire Potteries. 1879–99. *Earthenwares.* Subsequently Wellington Pottery Co., q.v.

| 310 | B. & H. | Distinguishing initials found on several printed marks of differing design: name of the individual pattern is often included, 1879–1900. "England" should occur added from 1891 to 1899. |

| — | Beehive marks | *See* Index, Hive marks, page 760. |
| — | BEECH | *See* Appendix, page 710. |

BEECH

BEECH, HANCOCK & CO., Swan Bank Pottery, Burslem. Staffordshire Potteries. 1851–5. *Earthenwares.*

In some directories this firm is listed as Beech & Hancock, a form of title normally used after 1857.

| 311 | B. H. & CO. | Distinguishing initials found on several printed marks of differing design: name of the individual pattern is often included, 1851–5. |

BEECH

BEECH & HANCOCK, Church Bank Works (c. 1857–61), Swan Bank Pottery (c. 1862–76), Tunstall. Staffordshire Potteries. 1857–76. *Earthenwares.* Formerly R. Beswick. Subsequently James Beech, see next entry.

N.B. A firm with a similar title was working at Burslem c. 1851–5, but "& Co." should occur after their title or initials, see previous entry.

| 312 | BEECH & HANCOCK | Distinguishing details of several printed marks of differing design: name of the individual pattern is often included, |
| 313 | B & H | 1857–76. A swan device may occur on some printed marks of the 1862–76 period. |

BEECH

JAMES BEECH, Swan Bank Works, Tunstall and Burslem. Staffordshire Potteries. 1877–89. *Earthenwares.* Formerly Beech & Hancock, q.v. Subsequently Boulton, Machin & Tennant, q.v.

N.B. This firm should not be confused with James Beech & Son of Longton.

| 314 | SWAN J. B. | Printed mark of a Swan over the initials J. B., often with name of pattern added, 1877–89. |

BEECH

JAMES BEECH & SON, Albert & Sutherland Works, Longton. Staffordshire Potteries. 1860–98. *China.* Subsequently D. Chapman & Sons, q.v.

315	J. B. & S.	Distinguishing details of several printed marks of differing design: name of the individual pattern is often included, 1860–98. A crowned Staffordshire knot with these initials and ENGLAND occurs, 1891–8.
315a	J. B. & SON	

BELFIELD

BELFIELD & CO., Prestonpans Pottery, Prestonpans, Scotland. c. 1836–1941. *Earthenwares.*

316 BELFIELD & CO., PRESTONPANS Various impressed or printed name and address marks occur. Most of these marks are on wares made after c. 1870.

399 BELGRAVE *See* Blackhurst & Hulme.

3525–6 BELL CHINA *See* Shore & Coggins.

319–20 BELL mark *See* J. & M. P. Bell & Co.
321 & 323 *See* Belle Vue Pottery.

2701 JOHN BELL *See* Mintons.

BELL

J. & M. P. BELL & CO. (LTD.), Glasgow Pottery, Dobbies Loan, Glasgow, Scotland. 1842–1928. *Earthenwares, Parian, etc.*

See also Jewitt's *Ceramic Art of Great Britain* (1878 and 1883) and J. A. Fleming's *Scottish Pottery* (1923).

317 J. B. Distinguishing initials found on several printed or impressed marks of differing design: name of the individual pattern is often included, c. 1842–60.

318 J & M. P. B. & CO. Distinguishing initials found on several printed marks of differing design: name of the individual pattern is often included, c. 1850–70. A bell or an eagle often occur in these marks.

319   Bell mark impressed or printed with or without initials "B" or "J. B."
N.B. LTD or L^D occurs from 1881.

320   Printed mark from c. 1881 to 1928.   Several variations occur.

BELLE   **BELLE VUE POTTERY,** Hull, Yorkshire.   Various owners from c. 1802.   *Earthenwares.*

321   Distinguishing detail of two bells, found on several printed or impressed marks of differing design, c. 1826–41.

322   BELLE VUE   The name Belle Vue occurs in some printed marks without the bell device, c. 1826–41.

323   TWO BELLS DEVICE   Two bells as no. 321 occur impressed on some wares without the above title, c. 1826–41.

The above marks have previously been attributed to an earlier period but they were probably introduced by William Bell in 1826.

BELLEEK   **BELLEEK POTTERY** (David McBirney & Co., etc.), Belleek, Co. Fermanagh, Ireland.   1863– .   *Parian, Porcelain, etc.*

324   BELLEEK   Impressed or relief name-mark, 1863–90.
        CO. FERMANAGH

324a   FERMANAGH   Rare impressed mark, recorded on lithophanes, 1863–90.
         POTTERY

325   Impressed or printed crowned harp mark, rarely used, 1863–80.

326   Printed or impressed standard trade-mark (first version), 1863–91.

327  Second version of standard printed trade-mark (slight variations occur). Note the addition of "Co. Fermanagh" and "Ireland" added from c. 1891 and continued to the present day. The engraving on later marks is less detailed than that on 19th century marks.

Typical examples will be found illustrated in *British Pottery and Porcelain: an illustrated Encyclopaedia of Marked Specimens*. See also Jewitt's *Ceramic Art of Great Britain* (1883).

BELPER

BELPER POTTERY, Nr. Derby, Derbyshire. 1809–34. *Stonewares.*

Works closed 1834 and transferred to Denby. See page 89. See Jewitt's *Ceramic Art of Great Britain* (1878 and 1883).

328   BELPER   Impressed marks, 1809–34.
329   BELPER & DENBY
       BOURNES
       POTTERIES
       DERBYSHIRE

BEMBRIDGE

BEMBRIDGE POTTERY (T. R. Parsons and Sybil Finnemore, formerly of Yellowsands Pottery), Bembridge, Isle of Wight. 1949–61. *Studio-type Pottery.*

330 Seal or painted mark, 1949–61.

331–2 T R P   1960   Painted personal marks of T. R. Parsons, with year, 1949–61.*

333 &   FINNEMORE   Personal marks used by Sybil Finnemore (Mrs. Parsons). 1949–53.*
333a

* These personal marks were also used at the Yellowsands Pottery, c. 1927–39.

BENHAM

TONY BENHAM, Kensington Church Street, London W.8. 1958– . *Studio-type Pottery.*

334   TONY BENHAM   Incised or painted written signature marks, often with year added, 1958– .

—   BENTLEY   *See* Josiah Wedgwood (& Sons Ltd.).

BENNETT   **GEORGE BENNETT & CO.**, Victoria Works, Stoke. Staffordshire Potteries. 1894–1902. *Earthenwares.*

335   G. B. & Co.   Impressed or printed initials, with or without the word "STOKE", 1894–1902.

BENNETT   **J. BENNETT & CO.**, Hanley. Staffordshire Potteries. 1896–1900. *Earthenwares.* Subsequently Bennett & Shenton.

336   J. B. & Co.   Distinguishing initials found on several printed or impressed marks of differing design: name of the individual pattern is often included, 1896–1900.

BENNETT   **WILLIAM BENNETT (HANLEY) LTD.**, Cleveland Works, Hanley. Staffordshire Potteries. 1882–1937. *Earthenwares.* Firm retitled "William Bennett (Hanley) Ltd." from c. 1922.

337   W. B.   Distinguishing details of several printed or impressed marks of
           H.   differing design: name of the individual pattern is often
338   WILLIAM BENNETT   included, 1882–1930.
         HANLEY

339   Printed mark, 1930–7.

BENSON   **AGNES BENSON**, Kings College Road, Ruislip, Middlesex. 1951– . *Studio-type Pottery.*

340   "Gigs" mark painted or incised, 1951– .

341   G. M. initials or monogram, 1959– .

BENTLEY		**G. L. BENTLEY & CO. (LTD.), Old Cyples Pottery,*** Longton. Staffordshire Potteries. 1898–1912. *China.*
342	G. L. B. & Co. LONGTON	Distinguishing initials found on several printed marks of differing design. With or without "Longton" under, 1898–1912. "Ltd" may occur from 1904.

* Messrs. J. T. Fell & Co. worked this pottery from c. 1923 and used this name as a mark, see page 245.

BENTLEY		**BENTLEY, WEAR & BOURNE,** Vine Street, Shelton. Staffordshire Potteries. 1815–23. *Printers and Enamellers.* Subsequently Bentley & Wear, 1823–33.
343	BENTLEY, WEAR & BOURNE ENGRAVERS & PRINTERS SHELTON, STAFFORDSHIRE	The name-mark of this firm of engravers occurs on some printed wares of the period 1815–23. The name is usually on the printed design, not on the base. Several designs were engraved for the American market.

BERRY		**JOHN BERRY,** London S.E.26. 1954– . *Studio-type Pottery.*
344	J. B.	Initials in circular seal mark used 1951–4 while employed at the Seviers and Sun Potteries, London.
345	JOHN BERRY	Name in full, incised or painted, 1954– .
4025	BERYL	*See* Warrington Pottery Co. Ltd.

BESWICK		**JOHN BESWICK (LTD.),** Gold Street, Longton. Staffordshire Potteries. 1936– . *Earthenwares.* Formerly J. W. Beswick. Early wares not marked.
346	*Beswick Ware.* MADE IN ENGLAND	Printed mark, 1936– .
347–8	BESWICK · ENGLAND (circular) BESWICK ENGLAND	Post-war marks include the words "Beswick, England". This simple form of mark may also be found on earlier wares, "Staffordshire Dogs" etc., from the 1920's.

BESWICK

BESWICK & SON, Warwick Works, Longton. Staffordshire Potteries. 1916–30. *China.* Formerly Bridgett & Bates, q.v.

349   B & S
Distinguishing initials found on several printed or impressed marks of differing design, 1916–30.

350   ALDWYCH CHINA
Trade-name, formerly used by Messrs. Bridgett & Bates (from c. 1912) and continued by Beswick & Son to 1930.

346   BESWICK WARE
See John Beswick (Ltd.).

1274   BETWS-Y-COED
See Derlwyn Pottery.

BEVINGTON

BEVINGTON & CO., Swansea, Wales. 1817–21. *Cream-wares and Porcelain.* Subsequently T. & J. Bevington. See also Swansea, page 605.

351   BEVINGTON & CO.
SWANSEA
Impressed mark, rarely used, 1817–21. Mainly found on earthenwares.

BEVINGTON

JOHN BEVINGTON, Kensington Works, Hanley. Staffordshire Potteries. 1872–92. *Porcelains.*

352
Painted mark in underglaze blue, 1872–92.

353   BY ROYAL LETTERS
PATENT
JOHN BEVINGTON
KENSINGTON WORKS
HANLEY, STAFFS
Printed mark, with Royal Arms above, 1872–92.
    John Bevington advertised reproductions of old Dresden, Derby, Chelsea and Worcester patterns in figures, vases, candelabra, baskets, etc. These Bevington pieces are often called Coalbrookdale or Derby in error.
    Two examples will be found illustrated in *British Pottery and Porcelain: an illustrated Encyclopaedia of Marked Specimens.*

BEVINGTON

JOHN BEVINGTON & CO., Elm St., York St. and Clarence St., Hanley. Staffordshire Potteries. 1869–71. *Earthenwares.* Formerly Bevington & Bradley.

354	J. B. & Co. H.	Distinguishing initial found on several printed marks of differing design: name of the individual pattern is often included, 1869–71.

BEVINGTON		**JAMES & THOMAS BEVINGTON**, Burton Place Works (and other addresses), Hanley. Staffordshire Potteries. 1865–78. *China, Parian, etc.* Formerly S. Bevington & Son. Subsequently T. Bevington.
355	J. & T. B.	Impressed initial mark, 1865–78.

BEVINGTON		**THOMAS BEVINGTON**, Burton Place Works (Mayer St. Works c. 1890–1), Hanley. Staffordshire Potteries. 1877–91. *China, Parian and Earthenwares.* Formerly J. & T. Bevington, q.v. Subsequently Hanley Porcelain Co., q.v.
356	T. B.	Distinguishing initials found on several printed marks of differing design, 1877–91. Mark no. 357 is a typical example.
357		

223	BEWLEY POTTERY	*See* Bailey Potteries Ltd.
1579	B. F.	*See* Benjamin Floyd.
728–9	BF (monogram)	*See* Burmantofts.
4339	B. F. B.	*See* Worcester-Barr Flight & Barr period.
722–3	B. G.	*See* Benjamin E. Godwin.
667	B. G. P. CO.	*See* Brownfield's Guild Pottery Society Ltd.
292	B. G. & W.	*See* Bates, Gildea & Walker.
— 311	B. H. & CO.	*See* Appendix, page 711. *See* Beech, Hancock & Co.
310 311	B. & H.	*See* Bednall & Heath. *See* Beech & Hancock.

319	B. & H.	*See* Blackhurst & Hulme.
431		*See* Bodley & Harrold.
400	B. & H. L.	*See* Blackhurst & Hulme.

BIGGS   JOAN A. BIGGS, MISS., Princedale Pottery (April 1958 to September 1961), London S.W.16. (September 1961–) 1958– . *Studio-type Pottery.*

358   *PP*   Painted or incised Princedale Pottery mark, April 1958 to September 1961.

359   JB   Painted or incised initial mark of Joan Biggs, September 1961– .

BILLINGE   THOMAS BILLINGE, Liverpool. c. 1760–80. *Engraver.*

360   BILLINGE SCULP LIVERPOOL   Rare signature marks on engraved patterns, by Billinge at Liverpool, c. 1760–80.

BILLINGSLEY   WILLIAM BILLINGSLEY, Mansfield, Nottingham. c. 1799–1802. *Porcelain.*

     William Billingsley was a famous ceramic painter employed at Derby, Pinxton, Nantgarw, Swansea and Worcester, c. 1790–1828. The late Mr. C. L. Exley's researches indicate that Billingsley was only at Mansfield from mid-1799 to about June 1802. See also Mansfield.

361   BILLINGSLEY MANSFIELD   Written signature on porcelain decorated at Mansfield. Very rare, c. 1799–1802. Several slight variations occur in the form of signature.

     Marked specimens will be found illustrated in *British Pottery and Porcelain: an illustrated Encyclopaedia of Marked Specimens.*

BILLINGTON   DORA, MAY, BILLINGTON, various addresses. Artist and potter. 1912+.* *Studio-type Pottery.*

362   Painted mark on Bernard Moore wares, 1912–15.

363   Incised or painted mark on studio-type pottery, 1920+.

* At the time of writing (1964) Dora Billington was not actively engaged in potting.

BILTONS

BILTONS (1912) LTD. (Biltons Ltd. from c. 1900 to 1912), London Road, Stoke. Staffordshire Potteries. 1900– . *Earthenwares.*

364   BILTON   Impressed marks, 1900+.
365   BILTONS

366   Printed mark, 1912+.

367   Standard post-war mark. Variations occur with different style titles, "Elegance by Biltons" etc., 1947+.

BINGHAM

EDWARD BINGHAM, Hedingham Art Pottery, Castle Hedingham, Essex. 1864–1901. *Early styled Earthenwares, Relief Motifs, etc.* Subsequently Essex Art Pottery.

368   Applied pad mark in relief, 1864–1901. This mark is given in several books as being "c. 1848"; this is an error. Typical examples will be found illustrated in the companion encyclopaedia of marked specimens.

369   E. BINGHAM   Incised signature mark, 1864–1901.
    CASTLE HEDINGHAM
    ESSEX

369a	ROYAL ESSEX ART POTTERY WORKS	Incised mark on some specimens made by E. Bingham within a few years of 1901. An example dated 1904 bears this mark with Bingham's signature and mark no. 368.

BINGLEY

THOMAS BINGLEY (& CO.), Swinton, Yorkshire. 1778–87. *Earthenwares.* Subsequently Greens, Bingley & Co.

370   BINGLEY   Impressed mark, 1778–87.

BIRCH

EDMUND JOHN BIRCH, Albion St., Shelton. Staffordshire Potteries. 1796–1814. *Wedgwood-type wares, Basaltes, etc.* Formerly Birch & Whitehead, see below.

371   BIRCH

372   E. I. B.

Impressed name or initial marks, 1796–1814.

Typical examples of Birch-marked basalt will be found illustrated in *British Pottery and Porcelain: an illustrated Encyclopaedia of Marked Specimens.*

BIRCH

BIRCH & WHITEHEAD, Albion Street (?), Shelton, Hanley. Staffordshire Potteries. c. 1796. *Basaltes and Creamware.* Subsequently E. J. Birch, see previous entry.

373   B. & W.

Rare impressed mark on basalt teapot formerly in Captain Grant's collection and illustrated in his *The Makers of Black Basaltes* (1910), Plate II. c. 1796.

Attribution of this mark is open to some doubt as the initials also fit Breeze & Wilson of Hanley. c. 1809–17. An open-work creamware basket in the Godden Collection also bears the impressed initials B. & W.

BIRKS

BIRKS BROTHERS & SEDDON, Cobridge Works, Cobridge. Staffordshire Potteries. 1877–86. *Ironstone wares.* Formerly Cockson & Seddon.

374

IMPERIAL IRONSTONE
CHINA
BIRKS BROS. & SEDDON

Royal Arms printed mark with type of ware and title in full below, 1877–86.

BIRKS		**L. A. BIRKS & CO.**, Vine Pottery, Stoke. Staffordshire Potteries. 1896–1900. *China and Earthenwares.* Subsequently Birks, Rawlins & Co.
375	BIRKS	Impressed mark, 1896+.

376–7  B & CO. Initial marks in various printed forms, 1896–1900.

BIRKS

BIRKS, RAWLINS & CO. (LTD.), Vine Pottery, Stoke. Staffordshire Potteries. 1900–33. *China.* Formerly L. A. Birks & Co., see previous entry.

378–9 Several printed marks occur incorporating the initials B. R. & Co. or the title in full, 1900+.

380–1 Printed marks, c. 1917+.

382–3	SAVOY CHINA CARLTON CHINA	Trade-names and marks used, c. 1930.
389–91	BISHOP	*See* below.

BISHOP

BISHOP & STONIER (LTD.), various addresses, Hanley. Staffordshire Potteries. 1891–1939. *China and Earthenwares.* Formerly Powell, Bishop & Stonier, q.v.

384   B & S   Distinguishing initials found on several printed or impressed marks of differing design: name of the individual pattern is often included, 1891–1910.

385–6  Printed marks of predecessors continued with or without "Bisto" under, 1891–1936.

387–8  Printed marks, 1899–1936.

389–91   Printed or impressed marks, 1936–9.

BISHOPS		**BISHOPS WALTHAM POTTERY**, Bishops Waltham, Hampshire. 1866–7. *Terra-cotta.* See also Chaffers' *Marks and Monograms . . .*, 15th Edition.
392	BISHOPS WALTHAM	Printed mark, within double lined oval, 1866–7.

A group of typical examples will be found illustrated in *British Pottery and Porcelain: an illustrated Encyclopaedia of Marked Specimens.* The Bishops Waltham Clay Company Ltd. exhibited pottery, terra-cotta and ornamental bricks at the 1867 Paris Exhibition.

BISSELL		**HOWARD BISSELL**, Swincraft Productions,* Oldswinford, Worcestershire. 1960– . *Studio-type Pottery.*
393	H. B.	Impressed seal type initial mark, used prior to 1962.
394	H. B.	Incised initials in flowing writing letters, 1962– .

     * Howard Bissell was formerly at the "Oldswinford Pottery", q.v.

385–6	BISTO	*See* Bishop & Stonier (Ltd.).
3067–8	BK (monogram)	*See* Katharine Pleydell-Bouverie.
264	B. & K.	*See* Barkers & Kent Ltd.
265	B. & K. L.	
266	B. & K. LTD.	

713–14	BL	*See* Burgess & Leigh (Ltd.)
2346–7a	(also monogram)	*See* Bernard Leach.
482, 487	B. & L.	*See* Appendix, page 711.
712, 715,		*See* Bourne & Leigh (Ltd.).
722		*See* Burgess & Leigh (Ltd.).
719	B. & L. Ltd.	*See* Burgess & Leigh (Ltd.).
1220	BLACK WORKS	*See* Thomas Dean (& Sons) (Ltd.).

BLACKHURST   JABEZ BLACKHURST, Boston Works, Sandyford, Tunstall. Staffordshire Potteries. 1872–83. *Earthenwares.* Formerly. Knapper & Blackhurst.

395   JABEZ BLACKHURST   Distinguishing detail of several printed marks of differing design: name of the individual pattern is often included, 1872–83. Mark no. 396 is a typical example.

396

BLACKHURST   JOHN BLACKHURST & CO. LTD., Prospect Works, Cobridge. Staffordshire Potteries. 1951–9. *Earthenwares.*

397   Printed mark, 1951–9.

397a   J. BLACKHURST ENGLAND   Name-mark in written form, 1951–9.

BLACKHURST   BLACKHURST & BOURNE, Hadderidge Pottery, Burslem. Staffordshire Potteries. 1880–92. *Earthenwares.* Formerly Heath & Tunnicliffe, q.v.

398   B. & B.   Distinguishing initials found on several printed marks of differing design: name of the individual pattern is often included, 1880–92.

BLACKHURST

BLACKHURST & HULME, Belgrave Works, Longton. Staffordshire Potteries. 1890–1932. *China.*

399   B. & H.   Distinguishing initial found on several printed marks of differing design: name of the individual pattern is often included, 1890–1914.

400   THE BELGRAVE CHINA B & H L ENGLAND   Printed mark, c. 1914+.

BLACKHURST

BLACKHURST & TUNNICLIFFE, Hadderidge Pottery, Burslem. Staffordshire Potteries. c. 1879. *Earthenwares.* Formerly Heath & Blackhurst. Subsequently Blackhurst & Bourne, q.v.

401   B & T   Distinguishing initials found on several printed marks of differing design: name of the individual pattern is often included, c. 1879.

BLACKMAN

MRS. AUDREY BLACKMAN, West Wood House, Oxford. 1949– . *Individual Figures and Groups.*

402   A. BLACKMAN   Signature mark. 1949– .

BLADES

JOHN BLADES, Ludgate Hill, London. c. 1800–30. *Retailer.*

403   BLADES LONDON   Written mark on wares *sold by* Blades, c. 1800–30.

BLAIR

BLAIR & CO., c. 1880–1911, **BLAIRS LTD.**, c. 1912–23, **BLAIRS (LONGTON) LTD.**, 1923–30, Beaconsfield Pottery, Longton. Staffordshire Potteries. 1880–1930. *China.*

404   B   B within diamond impressed or printed mark, 1880–1900.

405   BLAIRS CHINA ENGLAND   Impressed or printed mark, 1900+.

406   BLAIRS CHINA   Printed mark, 1900+.

407   Printed mark, 1914–30.

BLASHFIELD   JOHN MARRIOTT BLASHFIELD, Southwark Bridge Road
                          and Mill Wall, London. c. 1840–75. *Terra-cotta, Architec-
                          tural wares and Tiles.* See also Jewitt's *Ceramic Art of Great
                          Britain* (1878).

408   BLASHFIELD   Impressed marks, 1840–58.
409   J. M. BLASHFIELD

409a   BLASHFIELD,   Impressed mark, 1858–75.
            STAMFORD   N.B. "Stamford" from 1858.

BLENSDORF   E. M. BLENSDORF, Bruton, Somerset. c. 1950– .*
                          Studio-type Pottery.

410   Incised or painted monogram mark, c. 1950– .

                            * Of late years Professor Blensdorf has concentrated on sculpture rather
                          than pottery.

BLIK   BETH BLIK, Victoria Studios, Tollesbury, Essex.   May
                          1963– . *Functional Pottery.*
411   BLIK.   Painted or incised signature mark on wares made by Beth Blik,
                          1963– .

411a   Circular mark on wares made by potters working under Beth
                          Blik.

1259–60   BLOOR   *See* Derby Porcelain Works.

2417   BLUE BELL   *See* Longton Pottery Co. Ltd.

BLUE JOHN   BLUE JOHN POTTERY LTD., Union St., Hanley. Staf-
                          fordshire Potteries. 1939– . *Earthenwares.*

| 412 | | Printed mark, 1939+. |

| 412a | | Printed mark, 1947–9. |

| 413 | | Printed mark, 1949– . |

| 459 | BLUE MIST | *See* Booths & Colcloughs Ltd. |

| 4221 | BLUESTONE WARE | *See* Winterton Pottery (Longton) Ltd. |

| 497 | BLUE WATERS POTTERY | *See* Bovey Pottery Co. Ltd. |

BLYTH

BLYTH PORCELAIN CO. LTD., Blyth Works, High St., Longton. Staffordshire Potteries. c. 1905–35. *China.* Formerly Dresden Porcelain Co., q.v. Taken over by A. T. Finney in 1935.

| 414 | B. P. CO. LTD | Distinguishing initials found on several printed marks of differing design: name of the individual pattern is often included, 1905–35. |

| 415 | | Printed mark, c. 1905+. |

| 416 | | Printed mark, c. 1913+. |

417 Printed or impressed mark, c. 1925–35.

| 2736 | BM | *See* Bernard Moore. |
| 2752 | | *See* Moray, Barbara, The Countess of. |

| 304 | B. M. & CO. | *See* Bayley Murray & Co. |
| 3462 | | *See* Saracen Pottery. |

| — | B. & M. | *See* Appendix, page 711. |
| 208 | | *See* Bagshaw & Meir. |

| 469 | B. M. & T. | *See* Boulton, Machin & Tennant. |

| 489a | B N & CO. | *See* Bourne Nixon & Co. |

BOARDMAN

BOARDMAN (BENSLEY & BOARDMAN?), Liverpool, Lancashire. Late 18th century. *Earthenwares*.

418 BOARDMAN — Impressed mark, reported as occurring on earthenwares. Very rare.

BODLEY

BODLEY & CO., Scotia Pottery, Burslem. Staffordshire Potteries. 1865. *Earthenwares*.

419 Printed mark, 1865.

BODLEY

EDWARD F. BODLEY & CO., Scotia Pottery, Burslem. Staffordshire Potteries. Est. 1862. *Earthenwares*.

N.B. There is confusion over this firm in local records and directories. It would seem that Bodley & Co., Bodley & Harrold and E. F. Bodley & Co. overlapped during the 1863–5 period.

Subsequently E. F. Bodley *& Son*, q.v.

420	E. F. B. & CO.	Distinguishing initials found on several printed marks of
421	E. F. B.	differing design: name of the individual pattern is often in-
		cluded, 1862–81.

422	SCOTIA POTTERY	Printed mark, Staffordshire knot with "Scotia Pottery" within, 1862–81.
423	BODLEY	Impressed mark. 1870+ but this could be the mark of other firms of this name.

BODLEY

EDWARD F. BODLEY & SON, New Bridge Pottery, c. 1883+(formerly Scotia Pottery, Burslem), Longport. Staffordshire Potteries. 1881–98. *Earthenwares.* Formerly E. F. Bodley & Co., see previous entry.

424	E. F. B. & SON	Distinguishing initials found on several printed or impressed marks of differing design: name of the individual pattern is often included, 1881–98.
425	E. F. B. & S.	

426		Printed mark, 1883–98.

BODLEY

BODLEY & SON, Hill Pottery, Burslem. Staffordshire Potteries. 1874–5. *China.* Formerly Bodley & Diggory. Subsequently E. J. D. Bodley, q.v.

    N.B. This firm should *not* be confused with E. F. Bodley & Son of Longport.

427	B. & SON	Printed mark within Staffordshire knot, 1874–5.

BODLEY

E. J. D. BODLEY, Hill Pottery (and Crown Works from 1882), Burslem. Staffordshire Potteries. 1875–92. *China and Earthenwares.* Formerly Bodley & Son, see previous entry.

428	E. J. D. BODLEY	Impressed name-mark on porcelains, 1875+.

429	E. J. D. B.	Distinguishing initials found on several printed or impressed marks of differing design: name of the individual pattern is often included, 1875–92. The initials J and B are often joined, as in mark no. 430.
430		

BODLEY

BODLEY & HARROLD, Scotia Pottery, Burslem. Staffordshire Potteries. 1863–5. *Earthenwares.*

431	B & H	Distinguishing details of several printed marks of differing design: name of the individual pattern is often included, 1863–5.
432	BODLEY & HARROLD	

433   SCOTIA POTTERY   Printed within Staffordshire knot—a mark also used by E. F. Bodley & Co.

BONASSERA   LEO BONASSERA, Church Street, Kensington, London W.8. 1961– . *Studio-type Pottery*.

434      Painted or incised initials, 1961– .

BONE   CHARLES BONE, A.R.C.A., Brighton College of Art, Brighton, Sussex. 1952– . *Studio-type Pottery, Stonewares*.

435   Incised or painted initial mark, 1952–.   A similar mark is used by Graham Burr, see page 119.

—   IOSEPH BOON   *See* Appendix.

BOOTE   T. & R. BOOTE LTD. (Etc.), Waterloo Pottery (and other addresses), Burslem.   Staffordshire Potteries.   1842– . *Earthenwares*, *Parian wares*, *Tiles*, *etc*.
                                  See Jewitt's *Ceramic Art of Great Britain* (1878).

436   T. & R. B.   Distinguishing details of several printed or impressed marks of
437   T. & R. BOOTE   differing design: name of the individual pattern is often in-
438   T. B. & S.   cluded, 1842 onwards.   The Royal Arms were often included in Boote's Victorian marks.

439–41

Printed marks 1890–1906.
        N.B. Waterloo Pottery was closed in 1906 and the firm has subsequently concentrated in the manufacture of tiles.

—	ENOCH BOOTH	*See* Appendix, page 712.

BOOTH		**EPHRAIM BOOTH & SON,** Cliff Bank, Stoke. Staffordshire Potteries. c. 1795. *Earthenwares.* Formerly Ephraim Booth.
442	E. B. & S.	Impressed initials attributed to E. Booth & Son, c. 1795.

BOOTH		**FREDERICK BOOTH,** Broad St., Bradford, Yorkshire. c. 1881. *Earthenwares.*
443	F. B.	Ornate mark of quartered shield with a potter at the wheel, and the initials F and B were registered by Frederick Booth in 1881.

BOOTH		**G. R. BOOTH (& CO.),** Waterloo Works, Canal Side, Hanley. Staffordshire Potteries. 1829–44. *Earthenwares.*
444	PUBLISHED BY G. R. BOOTH & CO. HANLEY STAFFORDSHIRE	Impressed marks of this form occur with various dates, 1829–44. N.B. "& Co" added from c. 1839.

BOOTH		**HUGH BOOTH,** Cliff Bank, Stoke. Staffordshire Potteries. 1784–9. *Earthenwares.* Subsequently Ephraim Booth.
445	H. BOOTH	Impressed on creamwares, etc., 1784–9.

BOOTH		**BOOTH & SONS,** Church St., Lane End. Staffordshire Potteries. 1830–5. *Earthenwares.*
446	BOOTH & SONS	Impressed mark, 1830–5. Also listed in Rate Books as Richard and Abel Booth.

BOOTH		**THOMAS BOOTH & CO.,** Knowles Works, Burslem (c. 1868) and Church (Bank) Works, Tunstall. Staffordshire Potteries. 1868–72. *Earthenwares.* Subsequently Thomas Booth *& Son,* q.v.
447	T B & CO.	Distinguishing detail of several printed marks of differing design: name of the individual pattern is often included, 1868–72.

BOOTH

THOMAS BOOTH & SON, Church Bank Pottery, Tunstall. Staffordshire Potteries. 1872–6. *Earthenwares*. Formerly T. Booth & Co., q.v.   Subsequently T. G. Booth, q.v.

448   T. B. & S.

Distinguishing initials found on several printed marks of differing design: name of the individual pattern is often included, 1872–6.
    N.B. These initials were also used by T. & R. Booth, q.v.

BOOTH

THOMAS G. BOOTH, Church Bank Pottery, Tunstall. Staffordshire Potteries. 1876–83. *Earthenwares*. Formerly T. Booth & Son, q.v. Subsequently T. G. & F. Booth, q.v.

449

Printed mark, 1876–83.

BOOTH

T. G. & F. BOOTH, Church Bank Pottery, Tunstall. Staffordshire Potteries. 1883–91. *Earthenwares*. Formerly T. G. Booth, q.v.   Subsequently Booths (Ltd.), see next entry.

450   T G & F B

Distinguishing initials found on several printed marks of differing design: name of the individual pattern is often included, 1883–91.

BOOTHS

BOOTHS (LIMITED), Church Bank Pottery (and Swan and Soho Potteries from c. 1912), Tunstall. Staffordshire Potteries. 1891–1948. *Earthenwares*. Formerly T. G. & F. Booth, see previous entry.   Subsequently Booths & Colclough Ltd., see next entry.

451

Printed mark, 1891–1906.

452

Painted or printed mark on reproductions of antique Worcester porcelains.   The Worcester square seal mark (no. 4315) also occurs.   It should be noted that these Booth reproductions are in opaque earthenware, not porcelain as are the originals. Variations of this mark occur, 1905+.

453　　　Printed mark c. 1906+ with or without "England".

454　　　Printed mark 1912+ with or without "England" or "Made in England" under or with 1750 divided each side of mark.

455-6　 　1930+ marks or BOOTHS LIMITED ENGLAND with variations to 1948.

BOOTHS

BOOTHS & COLCLOUGHS LTD., Hanley. Staffordshire Potteries. 1948–54. *Bone China and Earthenwares.* Formerly Booths Ltd. and Colclough China Ltd., q.v.

Continued as Ridgway, Adderley, Booths & Colcloughs Ltd. from January 1st 1955 and retitled Ridgway Potteries Ltd. from February 28th, 1955. See page 536.

457-9　

　　　　　　1948–54　　　　　1948–54　　　　　1950+

460-2　

　　　　　　1950–54　　　　　1950–54　　　　　1954–50

Printed marks.

Marks nos. 457 and 458 were formerly (c. 1945–8) used by Messrs. Colclough China Ltd.

BOSCEAN		BOSCEAN POTTERY (Scott Marshall and Richard Jenkins), St. Just-in-Penwith, Cornwall. February 1962– . *Studio-type Stonewares.* Both Scott Marshall and Richard Jenkins formerly worked at the Leach Pottery.
463	B	Impressed seal mark, February 1962– .
BOSSONS		W. H. BOSSONS (SALES) LTD., Brook Mills, Congleton, Cheshire. 1956– . *Earthenware Figures, etc.*
464	BOSSONS	Printed or impressed name-mark, 1956– .
—	BOTHWELL & GOODFELLOW	*See* Appendix.
BOTT		BOTT & CO., Lane End. Staffordshire Potteries. c. 1810. *Earthenwares, sometimes with silver lustre decoration.* Local records show two firms of this style: John Bott & Co., Lane End., c. 1810. Thomas Bott & Co., Lane End, c. 1811.
465	BOTT & CO.	Impressed mark. Early 19th century. A typical marked bulb pot is illustrated in *British Pottery and Porcelain: an illustrated Encyclopaedia of Marked Specimens.*
BOUGH		BOUGH POTTERY (Mrs. E. Amour-Watson), Edinburgh, Scotland. 1925–42. *Earthenwares.*
466	E. A. BOUGH	Impressed or incised signature mark, used on earthenwares, 1925–42.
4401	BOULTON	*See* Postscript, page 745.
BOULTON		BOULTON & CO., Mill Street Works, Longton. Staffordshire Potteries. 1892–1902. *China.* Succeeded by John Chew.
467	B. & Co.	Distinguishing initials found on several printed marks of differing design: name of the individual pattern is often included, 1892–1902.

468   Printed or impressed shield mark, 1900–2.

BOULTON   BOULTON, MACHIN & TENNANT, Swan Bank Pottery,
                            Tunstall. Staffordshire Potteries. 1889–99. *Earthenwares*.
                            Formerly James Beech, q.v.

469      Printed or impressed mark, 1889–99.

BOURNE   CHARLES BOURNE, Grosvenor Works, Fenton. Stafford-
                            shire Potteries. 1817–30. *Porcelain*.
                            This potter is mainly known for his teawares but some very
                            fine vases in the Spode tradition were also made. See *British
                            Pottery and Porcelain: an illustrated Encyclopaedia of Marked
                            Specimens*.

470   CB   Painted marks, initials CB over the pattern number, which
           No. 7   naturally varies with different designs, c. 1818–30.

471   CHARLES BOURNE   Painted mark, the name in full on rare specimens, c. 1817–30.

BOURNE   EDWARD BOURNE, Longport. Staffordshire Potteries.
                            1790–1811. *Earthenwares*.

472   E. BOURNE   Impressed mark, 1790–1811.
                            A fine pair of jardinière vases with relief motifs and "Pratt"
                            type colouring will be found illustrated in *British Pottery and
                            Porcelain: an illustrated Encyclopaedia of Marked Specimens*.

BOURNE   JOSEPH BOURNE & SON LTD., Bourne's Pottery,
                            Denby, Derbyshire. Est. c. 1809:
                                 Mr. Jager, c. 1809–12.
                                 William Bourne, 1812–33.
                                 Joseph Bourne, 1833–60.
                            Stonewares.

473   BOURNES   Various 19th century impressed marks. Marks with the
           WARRANTED   addition of "Codnor Park" relate to the period 1833–61.

474   J. BOURNE & SON   "& Son" was added to the style from about 1850.
         PATENTEES
       DENBY POTTERY
        NEAR DERBY

475   BOURNES POTTERIES
     DENBY & CODNOR
         PARK
       DERBYSHIRE

476   Impressed or printed mark, in circle from c. 1895, in square form from c. 1910.

477–80   BOURNE, DENBY, ENGLAND.   **Є**PIC   *Danesby Ware*

Impressed and printed marks, c. 1930+.

481   Impressed or printed basic mark, c. 1948– . Other marks occur with the name of the pattern and the trade-name "Denby"
             N.B. Many Bourne wares are unmarked.

BOURNE

BOURNE & LEIGH (LTD.), Albion & Leighton Potteries, Burslem. Staffordshire Potteries. 1892–1941. *Earthenwares.* Formerly Blackhurst & Bourne, q.v.

482   B. & L.   Distinguishing details of several printed marks of differing
483   E. B. & J. E. L.   design: name of the individual pattern is often included,
484   E. B. J. E. L.   1892–1939. The firm's name also occurs printed in full.
485   E. B. & J. E. L.
          B.

486   Printed mark, c. 1912+.

487–8   Printed marks of the 1930's. Note the addition of "Leighton Pottery".

BOURNE		BOURNE NIXON & CO., Tunstall. Staffordshire Potteries. 1828–30. *Earthenwares.*
489	BOURNE NIXON & CO.	Impressed mark, 1828–30.
489a	B N & Co.	Distinguishing detail of printed marks of differing design, 1828–30.

BOURNE		SAMUEL BOURNE, Shelton, Hanley. Staffordshire Potteries. Early 18th century. *Earthenware Figures, Animals, etc.*
490	S. BOURNE	Rare impressed mark on figure of a hind in the Hanley Museum, c. 1803–13.

BOURNEMOUTH		**BOURNEMOUTH POTTERY CO.**, Sylvan Pottery, Hanley. Staffordshire Potteries. Est. at Bournemouth in 1945. *Earthenwares.* At Hanley from 1952.
491	BOURNEMOUTH POTTERY ENGLAND	Printed or impressed mark, 1945–51.
492		Printed or impressed mark, 1952–7. Note the word "Hanley". An initial may occur in the centre of this mark.
473	BOURNES	*See* J. Bourne & Sons (Ltd.).

BOVEY		**BOVEY POTTERY CO. LTD.**, Bovey Tracey, Devon. 1894–1957. *Earthenwares.* Formerly Bovey Tracey Pottery Co., see next entry. Early wares usually unmarked.
493		Printed or impressed mark, c. 1937–49.

494   Printed or impressed mark, 1949–56.

495   E II R BOVEY POTTERY CO. LTD. 1952   Printed mark, 1952.

496–7      Printed marks, c. 1954–7.

BOVEY

BOVEY TRACEY POTTERY COMPANY, Bovey Tracey, Devon. 1842–94. *Earthenwares.* Subsequently Bovey Pottery Co. Ltd., see previous entry.

498   B. T. P. Co.

Distinguishing initials found on several printed or impressed marks of differing design: name of the individual pattern is often included, 1842–94.

Two typical examples will be found in the companion illustrated encyclopaedia of marked specimens.

BOW

BOW CHINA WORKS, Stratford, West Ham, London. c. 1747–c. 1776. *Porcelain.*

For further information on Bow Porcelain see:
Chaffers' *Marks and Monograms...*, revised 15th edition. H. Tait's British Museum Catalogue of the Bow Porcelain Exhibition of 1959, and a paper by Mr. Tait in the *Transactions of The English Ceramic Circle*, vol. 5, part 4.

B. Watney's *English Blue and White Porcelain of the 18th Century* (1963).

499–500

Early incised marks c. 1750. An incised anchor mark has also been recorded but is very rare.

501–3   R A̶ B

Rough incised workmen's marks occur, c. 1750–60.

Various small numbers and letters occur painted in under-glaze blue, on examples painted in this colour. Also various mock Chinese characters.

504	MADE AT NEW CANTON	This inscription occurs on rare circular inkwells. Dated examples include 1750 and 1751. See companion illustrated encyclopaedia of marked specimens.

505   The painted anchor and dagger mark was the standard Bow mark from c. 1760 to 1776. As this mark was painted by hand many slight variations occur. On some rare examples only the dagger was painted.

506   The crescent mark in underglaze blue occurs on some specimens, also on figures. This should not be confused with the Worcester crescent mark.

507–8   T T°   The impressed marks of the repairer Tebo occur on Bow figures, etc., see page 612.
       N.B. Most Bow porcelain is unmarked.

BOWERS

GEORGE FREDERICK BOWERS (& CO.), Brownhills Works, Tunstall. Staffordshire Potteries. 1842–68. *Porcelain and Earthenwares.* Subsequently F. T. Bowers.

509   G. F. B.
510   G. F. B. B. T.
511

Distinguishing initials found on several printed marks of differing design: name of the individual pattern is often included, 1842–68. The initials often occur inside a Staffordshire knot device, as mark no. 511.

512   G. F. BOWERS
        OR
512a   G. F. BOWERS & CO.

513   IRONSTONE CHINA
       G. F. BOWERS

514   G. F. BOWERS TUNSTALL POTTERIES

Printed or impressed marks, 1842–68.

BOWKER

ARTHUR BOWKER, King Street, Fenton. Staffordshire Potteries. 1948–58. *Porcelain Figures, etc.*

515   STAFFORDSHIRE FINE BONE CHINA OF ARTHUR BOWKER MADE IN ENGLAND

Printed mark, 1950–8. Slight variations occur.

BOYD		DAVID & HERMIA BOYD, Chelsea, London S.W.3. 1950–
		5* and 1962– . *Studio-type Pottery.*
516	BOYD	Incised or painted name-marks, in writing letters, 1951–5.
517	DAVID BOYD	
518	BOYD ENGLAND	
519	D & H BOYD	Incised or painted name-marks, in writing letters, often with
	ENGLAND 1963	year added, 1962– .
520	DAVID & HERMIA	
	BOYD ENGLAND 1963	

* David Boyd started potting in Australia. He came to England in 1950 and worked here until 1955 (except in 1952 when the Boyds were potting in France). From 1955 to the end of 1961 they were in Australia and were then in Italy until returning to England in August 1962.

BOYLE		ZACHARIAH BOYLE (& SONS), Hanley (1823–30), Stoke
		(c. 1828–50). Staffordshire Potteries. 1823–50. *Earthenwares*
		and Porcelain.
521	BOYLE	Impressed mark, 1823–50.
522	Z. B.	Distinguishing initials found on several printed marks of
523	Z. B. & S.	differing design: name of the individual pattern is often
		included, 1823–8 and with "& S" added from 1828 to 1850.
463	BP	*See* Boscean Pottery.
	(monogram)	
330	B. P.	*See* Bembridge Pottery.
3018		*See* Baajie Pickard.
414	B. P. CO.	*See* Blyth Porcelain Co. Ltd.
585		*See* Bridge Products Ltd.
671–2		*See* Brownhills Pottery Co.
415–16	B. P. CO. LTD.	*See* Blyth Porcelain Co. Ltd.
620		*See* Britannia Pottery Co. Ltd.
636	B. P. LTD.	*See* British Pottery Ltd.
378 &	B. R. & CO.	*See* Birks Rawlins & Co.
381		

BRACKLEY		THOMAS BRACKLEY, Buckland, Nr. Aylesbury, Bucking-
		hamshire. Mid-18th century. *Earthenwares.*

524   THOMAS BRACKLEY   This incised inscription occurs on an earthenware jug, dated
           POTTER AT   1759.   There was a pottery at Buckland during most of the
BUCKLAND COMMON   18th century but the normal products are unmarked.

BRADBURY

G. ERIC BRADBURY, London S.W.4., and Ringmer, Sussex. c. 1910–54. *Earthenware Figures.*

G. E. Bradbury's father, Frederick George Bradbury, also made pottery figures.

525   ERIC BRADBURY   Incised mark on individual figures and groups in pottery mainly,
           LONDON 1928   c. 1920–30.
       MADE IN ENGLAND

BRADBURY

BRADBURY ANDERSON & BETTANY, Crown Works, Longton. Staffordshire Potteries. 1844–52. *Earthenwares, Parian, etc.*

526   B A & B   Distinguishing initials found on several printed marks of differing design: name of the individual pattern is often included, 1844–52.   The Royal Arms occur in several marks.

BRADEN

NORAH BRADEN, Miss, Leach Pottery, St. Ives (c. 1924–28) and Coleshill, Wilts. (c. 1928–36). 1924–36. *Studio-type Pottery.*

527-9

Impressed seal mark and incised monograms, 1924–36.

For illustrations of Miss Braden's work see *Artist Potters in England,* M. Rose (1955).

BRADLEY

BRADLEY & CO., Coalport,* Shropshire. Early 19th century.

530   BRADLEY & CO.   Impressed mark on an oval basalt teapot in the Victoria and
           COALPORT   Albert Museum (number c. 204–1926).   See *British Pottery and Porcelain: an illustrated Encyclopaedia of Marked Specimens.*

* Local directories do not list a firm of this name.   A firm of decorators and retailers, J. Bradley & Co., was listed in London directories, c. 1813–20, see J. Bradley & Co.   In directories of 1813 and 1814 the entries are "J. Bradley, Colebrook-dale China Manufact. 54 Pall-Mall".   It is possible that this firm were the London agents for the Coalport (Colebrooke-dale) factory.

BRADLEY

F. D. BRADLEY, various addresses, Longton. Staffordshire Potteries. 1876–96. *Porcelain*.

531   BRADLEY

Impressed mark on decorative porcelains in the style of Messrs. Moore Bros, 1876–96.

In 1889 this firm advertised "Table decorations, time pieces, candelabras, lamps, tazzas, fruit and flower bowls, centres, &c. &c.". The Bradley wares are often similar to Moore Bros. pieces.

See *British Pottery and Porcelain: an illustrated Encyclopaedia of Marked Specimens*.

BRADLEY

J. BRADLEY & CO., Pall Mall, London. c. 1813–20. *Decorators and Retailers*.

The brothers J. and T. Bradley were talented ceramic artists. Swansea porcelains are known to have been sold by this firm.

532   J. BRADLEY & CO.
533   J. BRADLEY & CO.
         47 PALL MALL
         LONDON

Printed or painted name-marks on porcelain or pottery decorated by this firm, c. 1813–20. The address 54 Pall Mall also occurs. Part of a marked piece of a dessert service is illustrated in *British Pottery and Porcelain: an illustrated Encyclopaedia of Marked Specimens*.

BRADLEYS

BRADLEYS (LONGTON) LTD., Crown Clarence Works, Longton. Staffordshire Potteries. 1922–41. *China*.

534

Printed mark, 1922–8.
A similar mark with the word "Bradleys" was also used by Salisbury (Crown) China Co., q.v.

535

Printed mark, c. 1928–41.

BRAIN

E. BRAIN & CO. LTD., Foley China Works, Fenton. Staffordshire Potteries. 1903– . *Porcelain*. Formerly Robinson & Son, q.v.

536	HARJIAN ENGLAND	Trade-mark used from 1903.
537	E. B. & CO. F.	Impressed mark, early 20th century.
538		Printed mark, 1903+.

| 539-43 | | |

Printed marks, 1905+   1913+. Later "Made in England" replaces "England"   1930+   1936+   1936+

| 544 | | Printed mark, 1948–63.*

   * Messrs. E. Brain & Co. Ltd. took over the business of Coalport China Ltd. in 1958. At the time of writing (early 1963) it is planned to cease production of "Foley" china on July 21st 1963 and to then concentrate on production at the Coalport Works. Mark no. 544 will then cease to be used. |
| 3351
3355 | BRAMELD
or
BRAMELD & CO. | *See* Rockingham Works. |

BRAMELD   **JOHN WAGER BRAMELD** (Brameld & Co.), Piccadilly, London W.1. c. 1830–50. *Retailer.*

    John Wager Brameld was one of the partners in the Rockingham concern. He was a fine artist but his time was mainly devoted to travelling for the firm and to the management of the London shop. He died in 1851.

| 565 | I. W. BRAMELD
PICCADILLY
LONDON | Very rare printed mark on porcelain jug in the Godden Collection, c. 1830–4. Directories of 1832–4 list Brameld & Co. at 174 Piccadilly and to 1850 at 3 Titchborne St. |
| 2992 | BRAMFIELD | *See* James Pearson Ltd. |

3494	BRAMPTON	*See* William Sharpe & Co.

BRANKSOME

BRANKSOME CERAMICS LTD., Surrey Road, Bournemouth, Hants. 1945–56. *Earthenwares, Stonewares, etc.* Subsequently E. Baggaley Ltd., q.v.

566–8

Printed marks. Slight variations in the wording occur, c. 1945–56.

BRANNAM

C. H. BRANNAM LTD., Litchdon Pottery, Barnstaple, Devon. 1879– . *Earthenwares.*
   Charles Brannam's father, Thomas, potted at Barnstaple for many years and exhibited at the 1851 Exhibition.

569   C. H. BRANNAM
          BARUM

Incised signature in writing letters, often with date added 1879+.

570   C. H. BRANNAM

Impressed mark, 1879–1913.

571   C. H. BRANNAM LTD.
          BARNSTAPLE

Impressed mark, 1913+. Note addition of "Ltd.".

572

Printed or impressed mark, 1929+.

573   CASTLE WARE
     ROYAL BARUM WARE

Trade-names used in the 20th century.

575   C. H. BRANNAM
          LTD.
       BARNSTAPLE

Impressed marks, 1930's– . Often with "Made in England" added.

576   C. H. BRANNAM
       BARUM DEVON

BRANNAN

NOEL BRANNAN, Burbage, Leicestershire. 1947–
Studio-type Pottery.

577

Incised or painted mark, 1947– . The name Noel may replace the initial "N" in some marks.

BRAUNTON

BRAUNTON POTTERY CO. LTD., various owners. Station Road, Braunton, N. Devon, Est. 1910– . *Earthenwares.*
     Early wares unmarked.

578

Printed or impressed mark, c. 1947– .

BREEZE

JOHN BREEZE & SON, Greenfield, Tunstall. Staffordshire Potteries. 1805–12, see note below. *Earthenwares and Porcelain*

579   BREEZE

Incised or painted mark in writing letters, late 18th, early 19th century. This mark could relate to several potters of this name:
     John Breeze of Burslem in the 1790's.
     John Breeze & Son of Tunstall, c. 1805–12.
     William Breeze of Shelton, c. 1812–20 or
     Jesse Breeze (son of John) of Tunstall, c. 1812–26.
     An unusual pair of marked sauce-tureens from a porcelain dessert service are illustrated in *British Pottery and Porcelain : an illustrated Encyclopaedia of Marked Specimens.*

2097   BRENTLEIGH WARE   *See* Howard Pottery Co.

3870   BRETBY   *See* Tooth & Co. (Ltd.).

BRETBY

BRETBY BRICK & STONEWARE CO. LTD., Newhall, Nr. Burton-on-Trent. *Ornamental Wares* from c. 1957. *Stonewares.*

580–80a, b

B
BURTON
R

Printed or impressed marks, 1957 to present day.

BRICKHURST

BRICKHURST POTTERY, Keith & Fiona Richardson, Laughton, Nr. Lewes, Sussex. August 1952– . *Earthenwares.*

581	BRICKHURST POTTERY SUSSEX
581a	BRICKHURST POTTERY ENGLAND
581b	BRICKHURST ENGLAND

Impressed marks, no. 581, a and b, 1952– .

582   F R

Painted initials of Mrs. Fiona Richardson on rare examples of tin glazed Delft-type earthenware made and decorated by Mrs. Richardson.

Mr. Richardson at one time worked at the near-by Dicker Pottery, and now employs the last of the Dicker potters (Mr. Robb). The Brickhurst wares carry on the Dicker tradition, the lustrous black glaze is noteworthy.

BRIDDON

SAMUEL & HENRY BRIDDON, Brampton, Derbyshire. Mid-19th century. *Stonewares.*

Many members of the Briddon family were potting at or near Brampton in the 19th century. A Henry Briddon was still working in the 1880's. The most important Briddon pottery was the Walton Pottery built by the first William Briddon in 1790 and which was continued by two further generations of the same name.

583   S & H BRIDDON

Impressed mark, c. 1848–c. 1860.

BRIDGE

BRIDGE POTTERY (Dorothy Watson), Rolvenden, Kent. Est. 1921 to present day. *Earthenwares.*

584

Impressed or printed mark, 1921– .

BRIDGE

BRIDGE PRODUCTS CO. (H. C. Swann), Bridge House, Winscombe, Somerset. 1954–63. *Earthenwares.*

585

Printed or impressed mark, 1954–63.

BRIDGETT

BRIDGETT, BATES & BEECH, King Street, Longton. Staffordshire Potteries. 1875–82. *China.* Subsequently Bridgett & Bates, q.v.

586

Printed or impressed mark, 1875–82.

BRIDGETT

BRIDGETT & BATES, King Street, Longton. Staffordshire Potteries. 1882–1915. *China.* Formerly Bridgett, Bates & Beech, see previous entry.

587   B & B

Impressed initials, or used with printed marks, 1882–1915.

588

Printed mark, c. 1912+, also used by successors, Messrs. Beswick & Son, q.v.

BRIDGWOOD

BRIDGWOOD & CLARKE, Churchyard Works, Burslem (also Tunstall, c. 1864). Staffordshire Potteries. 1857–64. *Earthenwares.* Subsequently Edward Clarke (& Co.), q.v.

589   BRIDGWOOD &
          CLARKE

Impressed mark, 1857–64.

590   B & C
590a   B & C
          BURSLEM

Distinguishing details of several printed marks of differing design: name of the individual pattern is often included, 1857–64. The name of the body is often added—"Opaque China", etc.

BRIDGWOOD

SAMPSON BRIDGWOOD & SON (LTD.), Anchor Pottery, Longton. Staffordshire Pottery. Est. c. 1805. *Earthenwares (Porcelain prior to 1887).*

591   BRIDGWOOD & SON
592   S. BRIDGWOOD &
          SON

Impressed name-marks mid-19th century.

593

Printed mark c. 1853+. A variation of this crest mark occurs from 1884; the device is enclosed in a shield with "Bridgwoods China" above.

594–7

1885+
"England" added
from 1891

1885

"Parisian Granite"
wares. 1870+

1910+

598–600

1912+
"Ltd" added from c. 1933

1950+

1961– .

Printed marks, 1885 onwards.

BRIGHT

JOHN BRIGHT, Temple Street, Bristol, Gloucestershire. c. 1820–45.* *Stonewares.* Formerly Hope & Bright.

601 J. BRIGHT

Rare impressed mark on a stoneware goblet, c. 1820–43, illustrated in *British Pottery and Porcelain: an illustrated Encyclopaedia of Marked Specimens.*

* J. Bright is listed in local directories of 1824, 1831 and 1841. In 1850 and 1854 the style is J. & A. Bright and in 1853 Bright & Co. The name does not occur after 1854.

BRIGLIN

BRIGLIN POTTERY LTD., Crawford Street, London W.1. Est. 1947 to present day. *Earthenwares.*

602 BRIGLIN

Impressed mark, 1947– . Circular, "Hand made BRIGLIN in England" mark used from 1957.

603 A. B.

Painted initial mark on wares decorated by Anthony Barson.

BRINDLEY

DONALD BRINDLEY POTTERY LTD., Chelson Street, Longton. Staffordshire Potteries. Est. 1961 to present day. *Earthenware Figures, etc.*

604

Printed or impressed mark, 1961– .

BRINK

MRS. HELEN BRINK, Canonbury Square, London N.1. 1960–1. *Studio-type Pottery.*

Mrs. Brink is a Canadian potter; her work in England was confined to the period 1960–1. She started potting in Toronto in 1957.

605	BRINK	Incised mark, c. 1960–1. See Plate I.

606	BRISTOL	*See* below, also.
3108		*See* Pountney & Co. (Ltd.).
3131 & a		*See* William Powell.

BRISTOL

BRISTOL PORCELAIN, Bristol, Gloucestershire. c. 1750–52 and 1770–81. *Porcelain (hard paste during 1778–81 period).*

For detailed information on Bristol Porcelain the reader is referred to:
Bristol Porcelain, F. Hurlbutt (1928). *Champions Bristol Porcelain,* F. Severne Mackenna (1947).
Chaffers' *Marks and Monograms* . . . revised 15th edition and the Catalogue of the Alfred Trapnell collection of Bristol and Plymouth Porcelain, published by Messrs. Albert Amor in 1912.

Typical examples are illustrated in *British Pottery and Porcelain: an illustrated Encyclopaedia of Marked Specimens.*

606	BRISTOL	Moulded relief marks on early wares, sauce-boats, etc.,
607	BRISTOLL	c. 1750–2. Very rare, only one marked enamelled example has been noted and a few decorated in underglaze blue. A blue example will be found illustrated in the companion illustrated encyclopaedia of marked specimens.

Painted marks, c. 1770–81:

608–14	

Many variations of these painted marks occur, different workmen's numbers of signs with the cross mark or with the crossed swords (in imitation of the Dresden mark). The sword marks are usually painted in underglaze blue. Reproductions (in soft porcelain) were made by S. J. Kepple early in the 20th century and these examples often bear the cross mark with a date, as mark no. 610.

508

T°

Impressed or moulded mark found on figures, baskets and other ornate articles.   This personal mark also occurs on Bow and Worcester porcelains.

BRISTOL

BRISTOL POTTERY, Water Lane, Bristol, Gloucestershire. c. 1785–1825. *Earthenwares.*
   For further information see "Old Bristol Potteries", W. J. Pountney, 1920.

615   BRISTOL POTTERY

Impressed or painted mark, c. 1785+. Early in the 19th century this wording occurs in an oval outline.

   For other Bristol *Pottery* marks and manufacturers see:
      J. Bright, page 102.
      Pountney & Co. (Ltd.), page 506.
      Pountney & Allies, page 507.
      Pountney & Goldney, page 507.
      Powell W. (& Sons), page 509.
      Ring & Co., page 540.

619   BRITANNIA, MARK
620
970
1412–13

See Britannia Designs Ltd.
See Britannia Pottery Co. Ltd.
See Cochran & Fleming.
See Dudson, Wilcox & Till Ltd.

BRITANNIA

BRITANNIA CHINA COMPANY, Edensor Road, Longton. Staffordshire Potteries. 1895–1906. *China.*

616   B. C. Co.

Impressed mark, 1895–1906.

617

Printed mark, 1900–4.

618

Printed or impressed mark, 1904–6.

BRITANNIA

BRITANNIA DESIGNS LTD., Townstal Pottery, Dartmouth, Devon. 1961– . *Decorators.*

619

Printed mark, 1961– .

BRITANNIA

BRITANNIA POTTERY CO. LTD., St. Rollox, Glasgow, Scotland. 1920–35. *Earthenwares.* Formerly Cochran & Fleming, q.v.

620

Printed trade-mark. 1920–35. A similar mark occurs with the initials "B.P. Co. Ltd." and "Made in Scotland".

621   HIAWATHA

Trade-name used on wares. c. 1925+.

—   BRITANNICUS
        DRESDEN CHINA

See Appendix, page 712.

BRITISH

BRITISH ANCHOR POTTERY CO. LTD., Anchor Road, Longton. Staffordshire Potteries. 1884. *Earthenwares.*

Printed or impressed marks:

622–4

1884–1913
"England" added from 1891

BRITISH ANCHOR
POTTERY
ENGLAND

1910 onwards

1913–40
Works closed 1940–5

625–7

1945+

BRITISH ANCHOR
ENGLAND

1945+
The name on various patterns or styles occurs with this mark

1950+
Initial "B" etc. in centre

628-30

Regency
BRITISH ANCHOR
ENGLAND
EST.1884

1952+

BRITISH ANCHOR
ENGLAND
EST.1884

1954+

MONTMARTRE
WARE
BRITISH ANCHOR
MADE IN ENGLAND

1954+

631-3

RICHMOND
BRITISH ANCHOR
ENGLAND
EST. 1884

1958+

Hostess
Table Ware
British Anchor
EST.1884
Staffordshire
England.
4-61

1961+

TRIANON
WARE
BRITISH ANCHOR
ENGLAND
EST.1884

1961+

BRITISH	**BRITISH ART POTTERY CO. (FENTON) LTD.**, Rialto Works, Fenton. Staffordshire Potteries. 1920–6. *China.*
634	Printed or impressed mark, 1920–6.
BRITISH CROWN WARE	*See* Lancaster & Sons (Ltd.). *See* Lancaster & Sandland Ltd.
BRITISH	**BRITISH POTTERY LTD.**, High Street, Tunstall. Staffordshire Potteries. 1920–6. *Earthenwares.*
635	Printed mark, 1920–6.
BRITISH 636 B. P. LTD.	**BRITISH POTTERY LTD.**, Melbourne Works, Longton. Staffordshire Potteries. c. 1930– . *Manufacturers' Agents.* These initials incorporated in printed mark of potter's kiln sometimes occur on wares made by firms for whom the above company act as agents, from about 1930 onwards.
BRITTON	**RICHARD BRITTON & SON**, Leeds Pottery, Leeds, Yorks. 1872–8. *Earthenwares.* Formerly Richard Britton, Subsequently Taylor Bros.

637	R. B. & S.	Distinguishing initials found on several printed marks of differing design: name of the individual pattern is often included 1872–8.

638   Impressed mark, date uncertain, c. 1853–78.

BROADHURST

JAMES BROADHURST & SONS LTD., Portland Pottery, Fenton. Staffordshire Potteries. c. 1862 at Longton, to 1870. 1870 to present day at Fenton. *Earthenwares.* Formerly Broadhurst & Sons of Longton.

639   J. B.   Distinguishing initials found on several printed marks of differing design: name of the individual pattern is often included, 1862–70.

640   J. B. & S.   Distinguishing initials found on several printed marks of differing design: name of the individual pattern is often included, 1870–1922.

641   J. B. & S. Ltd.   "Ltd." added to marks from 1922.

642   Printed mark from 1957.

642a   Printed mark from 1961. Other post-war marks occur with the name "Broadhurst" in full.

1134   BROADWAY   *See* G. M. Creyke & Sons.

BROADWAY

BROADWAY POTTERY (A. E. Wheeler), Broadway, Worcestershire. 1959– . *Studio-type Pottery.*

643   BROADWAY POTTERY   Impressed mark, in writing letters, 1959– . Wares bearing this mark and the name "Tudor Jones" were made before 1963, see "Campden Pottery".

BRONTE

BRONTE POTTERY (Mrs. M. Jackson), Harpenden, Herts. 1956 to present day. *Earthenwares.*

644   BRONTE POTTERY   Incised or painted mark in writing letters, 1956– .

BROOKER   **CLIVE BROOKER**, Stanmore and Enfield, Middlesex.
                                         1956 to present day. *Studio-type Pottery.*

645   CLIVE BROOKER   Incised or impressed signature mark, 1956–60.

646   C B   Impressed seal mark, 1960– .

—   A. BROOM   *See* Appendix, page 712.

BROUGH   **ALAN BROUGH**, London (1946–56), Brixham, Devon
                                         (1956–). 1946– . *Studio-type Pottery.*

647   AB   Painted initial mark, 1946– .

BROUGH   **BROUGH & BLACKHURST**, Waterloo Pottery, Longton.
                                         Staffordshire Potteries. 1872–95. *Earthenwares.*

648   BROUGH &   Distinguishing detail of several printed or impressed marks of
         BLACKHURST   differing design: name of the individual pattern is often in-
                                     cluded, 1872–95. "England" may be added after 1891.

BROUGHAM   **BROUGHAM & MAYER**, Newfield, Tunstall. Staffordshire
                                         Potteries. 1853–5. *Earthenwares.*

649   BROUGHAM &   Distinguishing detail of several printed marks of differing
         MAYER   design: name of the individual pattern is often included,
                                     1853–5.

BROWN   **PERCY BROWN**, Twickenham, Middlesex.   1938– .
                                         Studio-type Pottery.

650   P B   Initial or simple monogram mark, 1938–47.

651   PB   Monogram mark, 1947– .

652   BROWN PAISLEY   *See* Robert Brown & Co., below.

BROWN   **ROBERT BROWN & CO.,** Ferguslie Fire-Clay Works, Paisley, Scotland. 1876–1933. *Earthenwares.*

652   BROWN PAISLEY   Printed or impressed mark, 1876–1933.

BROWN   **BROWN & STEVENTON LTD.,** Royal Pottery, Burslem. Staffordshire Potteries. 1900–23. *Earthenwares.* Subsequently J. Steventon & Son, q.v.

653   B. & S.   Distinguishing initials found on several printed marks of differing design: name of the individual pattern is often included, 1900–23.

654   Printed mark, 1920–3.

BROWN   **T. BROWN & SONS LTD.,** Ferrybridge Pottery, Ferrybridge, Yorks. 1919– . *Earthenwares.* Formerly Sefton & Brown, q.v.

655   T. B. & S.
F. B.   Impressed mark, only on wares made for export. Other wares unmarked.

BROWN   **MRS. YVETTE (AND PAUL) BROWN,** Low Hole Bottom, Harrogate, Yorks. 1956 to present day. *Studio-type Pottery.*

656–7   Impressed seal marks of Mrs. Y. Brown, 1956– .

658   p
b   Impressed initials of Mr. Paul Brown. Most pieces are unmarked, 1956– .

BROWNE   **IRENE M. BROWNE,** Miss, London S.W.6. c. 1920's–30's. *Earthenware Figures.*

659   I. M. BROWNE   Incised signature mark, c. 1920's–30's. A signed example in the Hanley Museum was purchased in 1925.

BROWNFIELD

WILLIAM BROWNFIELD (& SON(s)), Cobridge. Staffordshire Potteries. 1850–91. *Earthenwares, Porcelain from 1871.* Formerly Wood & Brownfield, q.v. Subsequently Brownfields Guild Pottery Society Ltd., see next entry.

For further information see Jewitt's *Ceramic Art of Great Britain* (1878 and 1883), and Rhead's *Staffordshire Pots and Potters* (1906)

660	W. B.	Distinguishing initials found on several printed impressed or moulded marks of differing design, 1850–71. Many moulded parian jugs bear these initial marks, see companion illustrated encyclopaedia.
661		

662	BROWNFIELD	Impressed marks 1860 onwards. The printed name also occurs
663	BROWNFIELDS	with a crown above.

664	W. B. & S.	Printed initial marks with addition of "& S" or "& Son" are
665	W. B. & SON	subsequent to 1871.

665a	& SONS	After 1876 the earlier "Son" became "Sons" but this is not shown on marks engraved before 1876.

666 Printed mark 1871–91. A variation occurs with the words "Trade Mark", on a bar across the centre of this mark.

BROWNFIELDS

BROWNFIELDS GUILD POTTERY SOCIETY LTD. (and Brownfields Pottery Ltd. c. 1898–1900), Cobridge. Staffordshire Potteries. 1891–1900. *China and Earthenwares.* Formerly William Brownfield & Sons, see previous entry.

See Rhead's *Staffordshire Pots and Potters* (1906).

667	B. G. P. CO.	Impressed mark, 1891–1900.

668–9 Printed marks, 1891–8.

670 Printed mark, 1891–1900, used by the Guild and also by the subsequent Brownfields Pottery Ltd.

BROWNHILLS

BROWNHILLS POTTERY CO., Tunstall. Staffordshire Potteries. 1872–96. *Earthenwares.* Subsequently Salt Bros., q.v.

671   B. P. CO.

Distinguishing initials found on several printed or impressed marks of differing design, 1872–96. Mark no. 672 is a typical example.

672

Printed mark. 1872–96. "England" added from 1891.

673-4

Printed marks, c. 1880–96.

BROWN-WESTHEAD

BROWN-WESTHEAD, MOORE & CO., Cauldon Place, Hanley. Staffordshire Potteries. 1862–1904. *Earthenwares and Porcelains.* Formerly Bates, Brown-Westhead & Moore, q.v. Subsequently Cauldon Ltd., q.v.

 For further information see Jewitt's *Ceramic Art of Great Britain* (1878 and 1883).

675   B. W. M.
676   B. W. M. & CO.

Distinguishing initials found on several printed or impressed marks of differing design: name of the individual pattern is often included, 1862–1904.

677 T. C. BROWN-
   WESTHEAD MOORE
    & CO.

Impressed marks, 1862+.

678 BROWN-WESTHEAD
    MOORE

679

Printed mark, 1862+.

680 Printed or impressed mark, 1884+.

681 Printed or impressed mark, 1891+.

CAULDON WARE
BROWN-WESTHEAD, MOORE & CO.

682 Printed mark. 1890+. Slight variations of wording occur.

POTTERS TO HER MAJESTY

683–4a

BROWN WESTHEAD, MOORE & CO.

CAULDON   WARE

ENGLAND

Printed marks used, c. 1895–1904.

302 B. R. & T. *See* Baxter, Rowley & Tams.

BRUCKNER **LASZLO BRUCKNER**, London N.19. 1949*– . *Pottery Animals, etc., also Ceramic Jewellery.*

685 *B̶R* Impressed initial mark with the words "Made in England" arranged around this device, 1952– .

685a L. B. On small items the initials L. B. are impressed with a wavy line below, 1950– . The initials L. B. have also been used as an *incised* mark from 1949.

* Laszlo Bruckner first produced animal figures in Vienna in 1936. These bore an initial mark similar to the Bernard Leach mark no 2347. His London studio was established in 1949.

BRUNT		**JOHN (& THOMAS) BRUNT**, Rawdon Pottery, Nr. Burton-on-Trent, Derbyshire. c. 1830–61. *Earthenwares*. Formerly John Hall. Subsequently Smith, Dooley & Co.
686	BRUNT	This name-mark has been recorded on useful earthenwares. Thomas succeeded his father, John Brunt, and continued to c. 1861.

BRUNTON		**JOHN BRUNTON**, Wear Pottery, Southwick, Sunderland, Durham. 1796–1803. *Earthenwares*. Subsequently Samuel Moore & Co., q.v.
687	J. BRUNTON	Printed mark, 1796–1803.

BRYN		**BRYN RHODIAN POTTERY**, The Baroness Bonner of Main, Bryn-y-Gwalia Hall, Llangedwyn, Wales. c. 1957– . *Studio-type Pottery*.
688	BRYN	Written mark on small articles, c. 1957– .
688a	BRYN-Y-GWALIA	Written mark on large articles, c. 1957– .

296	B •:• S	*See* Battam & Son.
— 256 269 349 384 653	B. & S.	*See* Appendix, page 712. *See* Barker & Son. *See* T. W. Barlow & Son Ltd. *See* Beswick & Son. *See* Bishop & Stonier (Ltd.) *See* Brown & Stevenson Ltd.
733	B. S. A.	*See* Burslem School of Art.
1922	B. S. & H.	*See* B. & S. Hancock.
258	B. S. & T.	*See* Barker Sutton & Till.
— 401	B. & T.	*See* Appendix, page 712. *See* Blackhurst & Tunnicliffe.
498	B. T. P. CO.	*See* Bovey Tracey Pottery Co.
—	B. T. & S.	*See* Appendix, page 713.

BUCHAN		**A. W. BUCHAN & CO. (LTD.),** Portobello Pottery, Portobello, Nr. Edinburgh, Scotland. 1867– . *Stonewares.*
689	STAR DEVICE	Impressed or printed star mark, 1867 onwards.
690 690a 691	PORTOVASE CENOLITH SENOLITH	Trade-names used in the 1920's and 1930's.

692   Printed trade-mark, 1949– . "Finest Stoneware" sometimes added below this mark.

BUCKFAST

BUCKFAST ABBEY POTTERY (Miss M. Gibson-Horrocks), Buckfast, Devon. 1952– . *Studio-type Pottery.*

693   BUCKFAST ABBEY CRAFTS CERAMICS   Printed or impressed mark of running deer, surrounded by this wording, 1952– .

694-5 $\begin{smallmatrix}M\\H\\G\end{smallmatrix}$ M   g   H   Incised or impressed personal marks used by Miss Gibson-Horrocks, 1952– .

BUCKLE

J. T. BUCKLE & CO., Low Ousegate, York, Yorks. c. 1840. *Retailers.*

696   J. T. BUCKLE & CO. YORKS   Printed marks in various forms occuring on wares sold by this firm in the 1840's.

3672   FRANK A. BUCKLEY   *See* Staffs. Teaset Co. Ltd.

BUCKLEY

BUCKLEY HEATH & CO., Union Pottery, Burslem. Staffordshire Potteries. 1885–90. *Earthenwares.*

697   Printed or impressed mark, 1885–90.

BUCKLEY

BUCKLEY WOOD & CO., High Street Pottery, Burslem. Staffordshire Potteries. 1875–85. *Earthenwares.* Formerly Whittingham Ford & Co.

698	B. W. & CO.	Distinguishing initials found on several printed or impressed marks of differing design: name of the individual pattern is often included, 1875–85.

604	BULL mark	*See* Donald Brindley Pottery Ltd.

BUHLER

KIRSTI BUHLER, Hale, Cheshire. 1957– . *Studio-type Pottery.*

699	K. B.	Painted or impressed initial marks, 1957– . "F" was added
700	K. B. F.	below the initials K. B. in 1959.

BULLERS

BULLERS LTD., Milton, Nr. Hanley. Staffordshire Potteries. *Decorative wares* c. 1937–48.

This firm produced mainly industrial wares, but decorative pottery and figures were produced from 1937–55.

701	BY BULLERS	Painted marks, c. 1937–48.
702	BULLERS MADE IN ENGLAND	
703	MADE IN ENGLAND BY BULLERS	The signature mark of Anne Potts occurs on figures. The initials J. R. occur on examples decorated by James Rushton. AH monograms occur on specimens modelled or decorated by Agnete Hoy.

BULLOCK

A. BULLOCK & CO., Waterloo Pottery. c. 1895–1902. Kensington Pottery. c. 1903–15. 1895–1915. *Earthenwares, Majolica.*

N.B. A firm of this style was also in operation c. 1881–6.

704	A. B. & CO. H.	Distinguishing initials found on several printed or impressed
704a	A. B. & Co.	marks of differing design: name of the individual pattern is often included, 1895–1915.

—	W. BULLOCK	*See* Appendix, page 713.

BULMER

M. E. BULMER, MISS, Burrill, Yorkshire. 1956–60. *Studio-type Pottery; also Figures and Animal models.*

705		Incised or painted monogram mark, 1956–60.

BURCH		**PHILIP BURCH**, Barnstaple, Devon. 18th century. *Earthenwares*.
706	PHILIP BURCH MAKER 1788	A red earthenware harvest jug with white slip and incised decoration is in the Glaister Collection at the Fitzwilliam Museum, Cambridge; it bears this signature mark with an inscription. See *British Pottery and Porcelain: an illustrated Encyclopaedia of Marked Specimens*.
BURCHARD		**RUTH BURCHARD**, Mrs., London N.W.11. 1955– . *Studio-type Pottery*.
707	R. B.	Incised mark of initials, 1955– .
709	BURCRAFT	*See* Burgess Bros.
BURGESS		**BURGESS BROS.**, Carlisle Works, Longton. Staffordshire Potteries. 1922–39. *Earthenwares*.

708–9   Printed marks, a more ornate version occurs with the name "Burgess Bros." in full, 1922–39.

BURGESS		**HENRY BURGESS**, Kiln Croft Works, Burslem. Staffordshire Potteries. 1864–92. *Earthenwares*. Formerly T. & R. Boote.

710   H B   Printed or impressed Royal Arms with initials or name below, 1864–92.

711   HENRY BURGESS

BURGESS		**BURGESS & LEIGH (LTD.)**, Hill Pottery, c. 1867–89, Middleport Pottery, c. 1889+, Burslem. Staffordshire Potteries. 1862– . *Earthenwares*.

712   B. & L.   Distinguishing initials found on several printed or impressed marks of differing design: name of the individual pattern is often included, 1862– . The place name Burslem may be added to these initials.

713–14 Monogram mark, impressed or printed, 1862+.

715  Printed mark, 1862+. Many variations occur.
     N.B. The basic beehive mark was used by other earlier manufacturers: e.g. S. Alcock & Co.

716 Printed mark, 1880–1912.

717 Printed mark, 1906–12.

718 Printed mark, c. 1912+.
     N.B. "Ltd." added to style in 1919.

719  Printed mark, c. 1919. Note addition of Ltd. to B & L initials.

720–3

Printed marks of the 1930's.

724

Printed mark, c. 1940– .

725

Printed mark on Ironstone wares, c. 1960– .

BURGESS

THOMAS BURGESS, Mount Pleasant Works, Hanley. Staffordshire Potteries. 1903–17. *Earthenwares.* Formerly Harrop & Burgess, q.v.

726

Printed or impressed mark formerly used by Harrop & Burgess continued to 1917.

708   BURGESS WARE   *See* Burgess Bros.

720–5   BURLEIGH   *See* Burgess & Leigh (Ltd.).

3505–7   "BURLINGTON"   *See* John Shaw & Sons (Longton) Ltd.

BURMANTOFTS

BURMANTOFTS (Messrs. Wilcox & Co. (Ltd.)), Leeds, Yorks. 1882–1904.* *Art Pottery (glaze effects, etc.).*

  * Art Pottery was discontinued in August 1904, later Terra-cotta wares produced by the Leeds Fire-Clay Co. Ltd.

727   BURMANFOFTS FAIENCE   Impressed mark, with or without monogram mark, 1882–1904.

728–9

Impressed monogram mark. The shape number also occurs under these marks, 1882–1904.

BURN		HILDA BURN, Miss, Edinburgh, Scotland. c. 1920's–30's. *Earthenwares.*

730

Incised or painted mark of the 1920–30 period.

BURR

GRAHAM BURR, London S.E.5. 1952– . *Studio-type Pottery.*

731

Painted or incised initial (G. B.) mark, 1952.
    A similar initial mark was used by Charles Bone, see page 84.

4267   BURSLEY WARE   *See* H. J. Wood (Ltd.).

580–2   BURTON (WARE)   *See* Bretby Brick & Stoneware Co. Ltd.

BURSLEM

BURSLEM POTTERY CO. LTD., Scotia Works, Burslem. Staffordshire Pottery. 1894–1933. *Earthenwares.*

732

Printed mark, 1894–1933.

BURSLEM

BURSLEM SCHOOL OF ART, Burslem. Staffordshire Potteries. 1935–41. *Pottery Figures, etc.*

733

Impressed mark on pottery figures, groups, etc., 1935–41. Some specimens with this mark also bear the name of the instructor—William Ruscoe—or of the pupils, and a date.

580   B
       BURTON   *See* Bretby Brick & Stoneware Co. Ltd.
       R

BURTON

SAMUEL & JOHN BURTON, New Street, Hanley. Staffordshire Potteries. 1832–45. *Earthenwares.* Formerly James Keeling.

734	S. & J. B.	Impressed initials on raised pad, with model number, c. 1832–45. This rare mark occurs on a moulded jug in the Godden Collection. John Ward mentions this firm in 1843. N.B. The initials also fit Samuel and James Boyle of Church Street, Stoke. c. 1842–3.
581	BURTON WARE	*See* Bretby Brick & Stoneware Co. Ltd.

BURTON   WILLIAM BURTON, Codnor Park, Derbyshire. c. 1821–32. *Stonewares.*

Works subsequently taken by Joseph Bourne of the Denby Pottery.

735	W. BURTON CODNOR PARK	Impressed name-marks, 1821–32.
735a	WM. BURTON	
3003	BUSHEY HEATH	*See* Ida S. Perrin.
373	B. & W.	*See* Birch & Whitehead.
295	B. W. & B.	*See* Batkin Walker & Broadhurst.
293 698	B. W. & CO.	*See* Bates Walker & Co. *See* Buckley Wood & Co.
675 & 680 676 & 679	B. W. M. or B. W. M. & CO.	*See* Brown-Westhead, Moore (& Co.).

BUTTERFIELD   WILLIAM & JAMES BUTTERFIELD, Globe Pottery, Tunstall. Staffordshire Potteries. 1854–61. *Earthenwares.* Subsequently W. & C. Butterfield.

736	W. & J. B.	Distinguishing initials found on several printed marks of differing design: name of the individual pattern is often included, 1854–61.
3622	I. BUTTON	*See* Soil Hill Pottery.
803a	B. W.	*See* Barbara Cass.

BWTHYN

BWTHYN POTTERY, Barmouth, Wales. 1956– . *Studiotype Pottery.*

737

Impressed or printed mark, 1956– .

—

B. Y.

See Group Letters, page 295.

C

—	C	*See* Appendix, page 713.
811–12		*See* Caughley Works.
—		*See* Group Letters, page 295.
1953		*See* Jeremy Harper.
748	C & CO.	*See* Calland & Co.
924		*See* Clokie & Co. (Ltd.).
983		*See* Colclough & Co.
1064		*See* J. H. Cope & Co. (Ltd.).
3676		*See* Stanley Pottery Ltd.
106	C. A. L.	*See* Charles Amison (& Co. Ltd.).
829	C. A. & CO. LTD.	*See* Ceramic Art Co. Ltd.
85	C. A. & SONS	*See* Charles Allerton & Sons.
—		*See* Appendix, page 713.

CADBOROUGH

CADBOROUGH POTTERY, Nr. Rye, Sussex. Established c. 1807 by James Smith. *Earthenwares.*

Taken over c. 1840 by William Mitchell. William Mitchell & Sons 1859–69. Frederick & Henry Mitchell until 1871.

Cadborough pottery is seldom marked but these marks occur and should not be confused with those of the Rye Pottery.

738	OLD SUSSEX WARE RYE	Incised marks mid-19th century to 1871. The marks should not be confused with Rye Pottery marks, see page 558.
738a	RYE POTTERY	
739	MITCHELL	Various incised signature marks also occur on 19th century wares; on some specimens the initial M only was incised.
740	M	

CAIGER   ALAN CAIGER-SMITH, Aldermaston, Berks. 1955– . *Studio-type Pottery.*

741   Incised or painted personal mark of Alan Caiger-Smith, 1955– .

742–5

Other monogram marks of potters working with Alan Caiger-Smith at Aldermaston as Messrs. Eastop, Tipler, Partridge and Blakiston. These are sometimes written quickly and may not always appear exactly as here printed.

CALLAND   JOHN F. CALLAND & CO., Landore Pottery (or Swansea Vale Pottery), Swansea, Wales. 1852–6. *Earthenwares.*

746	CALLAND SWANSEA	Distinguishing detail of several printed or impressed marks of
747	CALLAND & CO. LANDORE, SWANSEA	differing design, 1852–6.
748	C & CO.	The "C & CO" mark with the words "Improved Willow"
749	J. F. CALLAND & CO. LANDORE POTTERY	occurs on a copper plate in the Godden Collection and its attribution to this firm is only tentative.

39   CALYX WARE   *See* William Adams & Sons (Potters) Ltd.

3758–60   CAMBRIA   *See* Swansea Pottery.
     CAMBRIAN   *See* Swansea Pottery.
     CAMBRIAN POTTERY   *See* Swansea Pottery.

CAMBRIAN   CAMBRIAN POTTERY CO. LTD., Llandudno, Wales. 1958– . *Studio-type Pottery.*

750–1   CAMBRIAN STUDIO WARE MADE IN WALES   CAMBRIAN STUDIO WARE LLANDUDNO   Impressed or printed marks, 1958– .

| 750–1 | CAMBRIAN STUDIO WARE | *See* Cambrian Pottery Co. Ltd., above. |

CAMM

CAMM BROTHERS, Smethwick, Staffordshire. 1870–80. *Mainly Tiles and Plaques* (decorated *by this firm*). Formerly T. W. Camm.

| 752 | CAMM BROTHERS SMETHWICK | Impressed or printed mark, 1870–80. |

CAMPAVIAS

ESTELLA CAMPAVIAS, Miss, Burgh Street, London N.1. 1954– . *Studio-type Earthenwares* (c. 1954–6); *Stonewares with glaze effects*, c. 1957– .

Most examples of Miss Campavias individual pottery are unmarked.

| 753 | E\|C | Incised or painted mark on earthenwares, 1954–6. |

| 753a | E | Incised, impressed or painted mark on stonewares, 1957– . |

CAMPDEN

CAMPDEN POTTERY, Muriel Tudor-Jones (Miss), Chipping Campden, Gloucestershire. April 1963*– . *Studio-type Pottery.*

* Muriel Tudor-Jones has worked at several well-known potteries since 1947. From 1959 to 1962 she worked the Broadway Pottery with two partners.

| 754 | CAMPDEN POTTERY | Impressed mark, April 1963– . |

| 754a | Muriel (or M) Tudor-Jones | Signature mark in incised or painted writing letters. This may occur from 1959 with the "Broadway Pottery" mark, or after April 1963 with the "Campden Pottery" mark. |

CAMPBELL

CAMPBELL TILE CO. (LTD.), Stoke. Staffordshire Potteries. 1882– . *Tiles.* Formerly Campbell Brick & Tile Co.

755		Impressed or moulded mark, 1882– .
756		New version of trade-mark, 1962– .

CAMPBELLFIELD

CAMPBELLFIELD POTTERY CO. (LTD.), Springburn, Glasgow, Scotland. 1850–1905. *Earthenwares.*
　　See J. A. Fleming's *Scottish Pottery.*

757 758 759	CAMPBELLFIELD C. P. CO. 	Distinguishing detail of several printed or impressed marks of differing design, 1850–84.
760	C. P. CO. LTD.	"Ltd" added to style, c. 1884.
761		Printed mark, c. 1884–c. 1905.

CANDY

CANDY & CO. LTD., Great Western Potteries, Newton Abbot, Devon. 1882– . *Earthenwares.*

762	C N A	Distinguishing detail of several printed or impressed marks of differing design on 20th century wares.
763		Printed or impressed mark, c. 1916+.
764	CANDY WARE	Trade-name 20th century.

CANNING

CANNING POTTERY CO., Fenton. Staffordshire Potteries. 1907–35. *Earthenwares.*

| 765 | DECORO | Printed or impressed mark comprising the name Decoro on a bar, across the outline of a vase, with "Made in England", 1923-35. |

| — 3230 | CANONBURY STUDIO | *See* Sally Dawson. *See* Christa Reichel. |

CAPEL

CAPEL CERAMICS (Anthony and Elizabeth Lane), London S.W.1.* 1962– . *Studio-type Pottery, Jewellery, Dishes, etc.*

766

Impressed seal or painted initial mark of Capel Ceramics, 1962– .

  * Mr. and Mrs. Lane hope to establish a pottery at St. Ives, Cornwall, during 1963.

CAPPER

CAPPER & WOOD, Bradwell Works, Longton. Staffordshire Potteries. 1895–1904. *Earthenwares.* Subsequently Arthur Wood, q.v.

767   C & W

Distinguishing initials found on several printed or impressed marks of differing design: name of the individual pattern is often included, 1895–1904.

CARA

CARA CHINA CO., Uttoxeter Road, Longton. Staffordshire Potteries. 1945– . *China Figures and Floral Ornaments.*

768   CARA CHINA

Distinguishing name found on several printed marks of differing design, c. 1945– .

CARDEW

MICHAEL AMBROSE CARDEW, Winchcombe, c. 1926–39. Wenford Bridge, c. 1939–42.* Cornwall. 1926–42. *Studio-type Pottery.*

  Michael Cardew was a very early pupil of Bernard Leach, he started in August 1923. For further information see G. Wingfield Digby's *The Work of the Modern Potter in England* and Muriel Rose's *Artist Potters in England.*

769

Impressed seal mark, c. 1926+.
  See also Wenford Bridge and Winchcombe.

  * Michael Cardew moved to the Gold Coast in 1942 and established the Vume Pottery in 1945.

CARDIGAN

CARDIGAN POTTERIES (Woodward & Co.), Wales. c. 1875–90. *Earthenwares.*

770   CARDIGAN
        POTTERIES

771 WOODWARD & CO.
      CARDIGAN

Distinguishing detail of several printed marks of differing design, c. 1875—about 1890.

CAREY

THOMAS & JOHN CAREY, Anchor Works (etc.), Lane End. Staffordshire Potteries. c. 1823*–42. *Earthenwares.*

772   CAREYS

Impressed or printed marks with the name Careys and an anchor, c. 1823–42. Many printed marks occur with the name Careys, the name of the pattern, type of body—"Saxon Stone", etc.

* The first reference to the partnership seems to date from 1823 but "Carey Bros" and John occurs before this date. The partnership was dissolved in January 1842.

CARISBROOKE

CARISBROOKE POTTERY WORKS, Newport, Isle of Wight. 1929–32. *Earthenwares.* Formerly Isle of Wight Pottery Co.

773

Impressed mark, 1930–2. See also S. E. Saunders.

383 CARLTON CHINA

See Birks, Rawlins & Co. (Ltd.).

CARLTON

CARLTON WARE LTD., Carlton Works, Stoke. Staffordshire Potteries. January 1958– . *Earthenwares.* Formerly Wiltshaw & Robinson Ltd.

774–6

Former printed marks used by Messrs. Wiltshaw & Robinson Ltd. continued by new company from 1958.
See also Wiltshaw & Robinson Ltd.

CAROLINE

CAROLINE POTTERY LTD., Caroline Street, Longton. Staffordshire Potteries. 1946–53.* *Earthenwares.*

777   CAROLINE WARE
MADE IN ENGLAND

Printed mark, including word "Caroline," c. 1946–53.

* This firm has subsequently acted as retailers only.

CARR

JOHN CARR (& CO.) (& SON), Low Lights Pottery, North Shields, Northumberland. c. 1845–1900. *Earthenwares.* Formerly Carr & Patton.

778   J. CARR & CO.

A printed plate, with moulded floral edge, in the Godden Collection bears this rare mark, c. 1850. "& Co." occurs in a directory of 1850 but in 1845 the style was J. Carr only. In 1854 the style was changed to "& Son" and "& Sons" from 1861 onwards.

779   STAG'S HEAD

Jewitt writing of the firm of John Carr & Sons in 1878 noted "The mark, which, however, has been seldom used, is a stag's head".

780   CARRIG WARE

See Carrigaline Pottery Ltd., below.

CARRIGALINE

CARRIGALINE POTTERY LTD., Carrigaline, Co. Cork, Ireland. Est. 1928 to present day. *Earthenwares.*

780   CARRIG WARE
781   CARRIGALINE
POTTERY

Printed marks with name CARRIG or CARRIGALINE, or the style in full, c. 1928– .

781a

CARRUTHERS

HILARY CARRUTHERS, Miss, Malvern, Worcestershire. 1960– . *Studio-type Pottery.*

782

Incised or painted initial mark, 1960– .

CARTER		**CARTER & CO. (LTD.)**, Poole, Dorset. 1873–1921. *Earthenwares, Art Pottery and Tiles.* Subsequently Carter, Stabler & Adams, see next entry.
783 784	CARTER & CO. CARTER POOLE	Distinguishing details of several printed, impressed or incised marks of differing design, 1873–1921.
785		
CARTER		**CARTER, STABLER & ADAMS (LTD.)***, Poole Pottery, Poole, Dorset. 1921 to present day.* *Earthenwares.* Formerly Carter & Co., see previous entry.
786		Impressed monogram mark of initials, C. S. A. This mark rarely occurs with that given below, c. 1921+.
787		Impressed or printed c. 1921+, with or without border lines.
788		Impressed or printed mark, c. 1921+. N.B. A pre-1925 version omits "Ltd." after the style.
789		Dolphin mark introduced in 1950–1 (not 1919 as has been recorded in other books, in error).
790		Redrawn version of above printed mark, used from 1956 onwards.
791		Incised or painted mark on individual pieces by the designer, R. B. Jefferson, c. 1959– .

792 Version of standard mark used on oven tableware introduced c. 1961.

792a Special printed marks on individual "Studio" wares, first exhibited in October 1963.

* In February 1963 the firm's title was changed to Poole Pottery Ltd.

CARTLEDGE

JOHN CARTLEDGE, Cobridge.   Staffordshire Potteries. c. 1800. *Earthenware Figures.*

793   JOHN CARTLEDGE AT THE LODGE IN THE PLANTATION, COWBRIDGE 1800

This inscription is recorded on a very rare pair of earthenware figures, see *British Pottery and Porcelain: an illustrated encyclopaedia of Marked Specimens.*

CARTLIDGE

F. CARTLIDGE & CO., Normacott Road, Longton. Staffordshire Potteries.   1889–1904. *China.*

794   F. C.
795   F. C. & CO.

Distinguishing initials found on several printed or impressed marks of differing design: name of the individual pattern is often included, 1889–1904. "& Co." may occur after 1892.

CARTWRIGHT

CARTWRIGHT & EDWARDS (LTD.), Borough Pottery, 1869+.   Victoria Works, 1912+.   Longton and Heron Cross Pottery 1916+. Fenton.   Staffordshire Potteries.   c. 1857–. *Earthenware and China.*

Messrs. Cartwright & Edwards Ltd. have been a branch of Alfred Clough Ltd. from 1955.

796   C & E

Distinguishing initials found on several printed or impressed marks of differing design: name of the individual pattern is often included, c. 1880 onwards.

797

Initials in diamond, impressed or printed, used from c. 1900+.

798

Printed mark used on wares made at Victoria Works, c. 1912+.

799	C & E. Lᵀᴰ "BORONIAN" WARE	Printed and impressed mark, c. 1926+. Note addition of "Ltd." to initials.

800–2	BORONIAN WARE MADE IN ENGLAND C&E Lᵀᴰ c. 1929+	*Norville* WARE C & E LIMITED ENGLAND c. 1936+	VICTORIA C & E BONE CHINA ENGLAND	Printed marks, c. 1929+.

CASS

BARBARA CASS, York (1952–61), Arden Pottery (1962–), Henley-in-Arden, Warwickshire. 1952– . *Studio-type Pottery.*

803	B C YORK	Painted or incised initial mark with name "York", April 1952–September 1960.
803a	B W YORK	Painted or incised initial mark, September 1960–August 1961. The initials B W relate to Miss Cass's married name, Mrs. B. Wolstencroft.
803b	B C ARDEN	Painted or incised initial mark with place name "Arden". 1962– .

CASSON

MICHAEL (& SHEILA) CASSON, Prestwood, Bucks. 1953.* *Earthenwares and Stonewares.*

For further information on Michael Casson and illustrations of his work, see *Apollo* magazine, December 1961.

804	Cᴍ	Impressed seal or painted mark, 1953–5.
805	M̶	Impressed seal mark, 1955– .
805a	W S	Impressed seal or written initial mark used by Mrs. Sheila Casson from c. 1951 to 1959.

805b		Impressed seal mark used by Mrs. Sheila Casson, 1959– .

          * Michael Casson started potting at Russell Square, London, in 1963. Prestwood Studio dates from 1959.

573	CASTLE WARE	*See* C. H. Brannam Ltd.

CASTLE   **CASTLE ESPIE POTTERY**, Comber, Co. Down, Ireland. 1870–88. *Earthenwares.*

806	CASTLE ESPIE WORKS, COMBER	Impressed mark, 1870–88.

CASTLE   **CASTLE WYND POTTERIES**, Gifford, East Lothian, Scotland. Established c. 1950 at Castle Wynd, Edinburgh. Moved to Gifford late in 1953. *Earthenwares.*

807		Printed or impressed marks, late 1953– .

—	CASTLECLIFFE WARE	*See* Westminster Pottery Ltd.
1417–18	CASTLEFORD	*See* David Dunderdale & Co.

CAUGHLEY   **CAUGHLEY (OR SALOPIAN) WORKS** (of Thomas Turner), Nr. Broseley, Shropshire. 1775–99. *Porcelain.* Subsequently J. Rose & Co., see *Coalport.*

808	TURNER	Impressed name-marks (rare), c. 1775–80. The word "Salo-
809	TURNER GALLIMORE	pian" normally occurs in lower-case letters and very rarely in
	or	upper-case letters.
	GALLIMORE TURNER	N.B. The impressed mark "Turner" also occurs on *earthen-*
810	SALOPIAN	*wares* of other manufacture.

811–12		Crescent or "C" marks in underglaze blue. The filled in or shaded crescent occurs on blue printed pieces. Variations occur—initials, etc., within the crescent or C. Similar to Worcester marks. c. 1775–90.

813–17 *S S× S× S₀ S* Printed marks in underglaze blue, c. 1775–90.

818–20

Printed mock Chinese signs with English numerals. Printed in underglaze blue, c. 1775–90.

N.B. Most examples of Caughley porcelain decorated with enamelled decoration are unmarked. Blue painted (or printed) pieces bear marks nos. 811–20.

820a H. An incised H occurs on some specimens. The Worcester hunting horn marks may also have been used on Caughley porcelain.

The reader is referred to F. A. Barrett's *Caughley and Coalport Porcelain* (1951). Typical examples will be found illustrated in *British Pottery and Porcelain: an illustrated encyclopaedia of Marked Specimens*, and in B. Watney's *English Blue and White Porcelain of the 18th century* (1963).

681–4a CAULDON *See* Brown-Westhead, Moore & Co.
See Cauldon Ltd., below.

CAULDON **CAULDON LTD.**, Cauldon Place, Shelton, Hanley. Staffordshire Potteries. 1905–20. *China and Earthenwares.* Formerly Brown-Westhead, Moore & Co., q.v. Subsequently Cauldon Potteries Ltd.

821 CAULDON ENGLAND Distinguishing name "Cauldon" on several printed marks of differing design: name of the individual pattern is often included, 1905–20. Mark nos. 822–3 are typical examples. On some marks "Ltd." or "Limited" is added to Cauldon.

822–3

Some former Ridgway and Brown-Westhead, Moore & Co. marks used with addition of "Cauldon" or "Cauldon Ltd." and "England", 1905–20.

CAULDON **CAULDON POTTERIES LTD.**, Stoke. Staffordshire Potteries. 1920–62. *China and Earthenwares.* Formerly Cauldon Ltd., see previous entry.

Cauldon Potteries Ltd. was acquired by Pountney & Co. Ltd. of Bristol during the later part of 1962.

Some former Cauldon Ltd. marks were continued after 1920.

824

MADE IN ENGLAND
Royal Cauldon
England
Est 1774

Printed mark, 1930–50. Slight variations occur.

825

Royal Cauldon
Bone China
17 74
Made in England

Standard printed mark, 1950–62.

CAZIN

CHARLES CAZIN (d. 1901), Fulham, London. 1871–4. *Stonewares*.

Cazin returned to France c. 1874. Examples of his work on English pottery are rare.

See Jewitt's *The Ceramic Art of Great Britain* (1878 and 1883).

**826 &
826a**

C Cazin Cazin. 1872

Incised signatures on rare examples of stoneware designed by Cazin at C. J. C. Bailey's Fulham works, c. 1871–4.

470	C. B.	*See* Charles Bourne.
646		*See* Olive Brooker.
1008		*See* Collingwood Bros.
884		*See* Christie & Beardmore.
435	CB	*See* Charles Bone.
452	(joined)	*See* Booths (Ltd.)
731		*See* Graham Burr.
857		*See* Bernard H. Charles.
885–6	C. B. F.	*See* Christie & Beardmore.
1005	C. B. L.	*See* Collingwood Bros.
886	C. & B.	*See* Christie & Beardmore.
1116		*See* Cotton & Barlow.
3070	C. B. P.	*See* Thomas Plowman.

—	C. C.	*See* Appendix, page 713.
766		*See* Capel Ceramics.
976	C. C. & CO.	*See* Cockson & Chetwynd.
—	C. & C. P. (Art Union)	*See* Appendix.
942 1108 1206	C. D.	*See* Coalport Porcelain Works. *See* Daphne Corke. *See* Clare Dawkins.
1040	C. & D.	*See* Cooper & Dethick.
941	C. DALE	*See* Coalport Porcelain Works.
1103	CDK (monogram)	*See* Daphne Corke.
4018	C. D. W.	*See* Christopher D. Warham.
796–8 & 801–2 1097–8	C. & E.	*See* Cartwright & Edwards (Ltd.). *See* Cork & Edge.
799–800	C. & E. Ltd.	*See* Cartwright & Edwards (Ltd.).
2227	CECILE	*See* Cecile Joynson.
301a	CELTIC CHINA	*See* John Denton Baxter.
1101–2	C. E. & M.	*See* Cork, Edge & Malkin.
CEMAES		**CEMAES POTTERY** (W. L. Rees), Parc-y-Gilwen, Pembroke-shire, Wales. 1957– . *Studio-type Earthenwares and Stone-wares.*
827	CEMAES	Incised mark, 1957– .
690a	CENOLITH	*See* A. W. Buchan & Co. (Ltd.).
1554	CERAMART	*See* Fine Arts Porcelain Ltd.
CERAMIC		**CERAMIC ART CO. LTD.**, Stoke Road, Hanley. Stafford-shire Potteries. 1892–1903. *Decorators.*

828	THE CERAMIC ART CO. LTD. HANLEY STAFFORDSHIRE ENGLAND	An ornate printed mark with outline of vase and this wording occurs on wares made for, or decorated by, this firm, 1892–1903. N.B. The addition of Hanley differentiates between this firm and the following entry.

CERAMIC   **CERAMIC ART CO. (1905) LTD.**, Crown Pottery, Stoke. Staffordshire Potteries. 1905–19. *Earthenwares.*

829	C. A. & CO. LTD.	Distinguishing initials found on several printed or impressed marks of differing design: name of the individual pattern is often included, 1905–19.
830	CERAMIC ART CO. LTD. CROWN POTTERY STOKE-ON-TRENT, MANUF: OF FAIENCE	Printed mark with title in full arranged around central crown, 1905–19.

2489	CETEM	*See* C. T. Maling & Sons (Ltd.).
1593–4	C. F.	*See* Charles Ford.
968 or 969	C & F C & F. G.	*See* Cockran & Fleming.
1012 1088	C & G.	*See* Collingwood & Greatbatch. *See* Copeland & Garrett.
—	C. G. W.	*See* Robert Wilson.
1884 2039	C. H.	*See* Christine Hall. *See* Charles Hobson.
1939	C. H. CO.	*See* Hanley China Co.
977 982 1158	C. & H.	*See* Cockson & Harding. *See* Coggins & Hill. *See* Cumberlidge & Humphreys.
—	CHAFFERS	*See* Appendix, page 713.

CHAILEY

CHAILEY POTTERY, Sussex. Late 18th century into 19th century. *Earthenwares.*

831   CHAILEY SOUTH COMMON POTTERY SUSSEX. 1792

Impressed (inlaid) mark on dated presentation bowl* in the Sussex Archaeological Society's Museum, Lewes, Sussex.

832   MADE BY ROBT BUSTOW, CHAILEY SOUTH COMMON, 1791

A similar large bowl is recorded with this inscription.

833   SOUTH CHAILEY POTTERY

Impressed (inlaid) mark on flask dated 1800, in the Fitzwilliam Museum, Cambridge.

* This bowl also bears the name of the Sussex potter, Thomas Alcorn. His son, John of South Common, Chailey, was described as a brickmaker in 1841. See *British Pottery and Porcelain: an illustrated Encyclopaedia of Marked Specimens.*

CHALLINOR

C. CHALLINOR & CO., High Street, Fenton. Staffordshire Potteries. 1892–6. *Earthenwares.* Formerly E. & C. Challinor, q.v.

834   C. CHALLINOR & CO. ENGLAND

Distinguishing detail of several printed marks of differing design: name of the individual pattern is often included, 1892–6.

CHALLINOR

EDWARD CHALLINOR, Pinnocks Works (Unicorn Pottery, c. 1862–7), Tunstall. Staffordshire Potteries. 1842–67. *Earthenwares.*

835   E. C.
835a   E. CHALLINOR

Distinguishing detail of several printed marks of differing design: name of the individual pattern is often included, 1842–67.

CHALLINOR

E. CHALLINOR & CO., Fenton Potteries*, Fenton.* Staffordshire Potteries. 1853–62. *Earthenwares.* Subsequently E. & C. Challinor, see next entry.

836   E. CHALLINOR & CO.

Distinguishing detail of several printed marks of differing design, 1853–60.

* A firm of this title is also recorded at Tunstall in 1851 and 1853–4.

CHALLINOR

E. & C. CHALLINOR, Fenton Pottery, Fenton. Staffordshire Potteries. 1862–91. *Earthenwares, Ironstones, etc.* Formerly E. Challinor & Co., q.v. Subsequently C. Challinor & Co., q.v.

837	E & C. C.	Distinguishing initials found on several printed marks of differing design: name of the individual pattern is often included, 1862–91.
838	E. & C. CHALLINOR FENTON	Other marks incorporate the title in full. The printed marks include the Royal Arms, and the Staffordshire knot, with name or initials, 1862–91.

CHAMBERLAIN

CHAMBERLAIN(S) (& CO.), Worcester. c. 1786–1852. *Porcelains.* Subsequently Kerr & Binns, q.v.

839	Chamberlains	Early written marks, including the name and often the pattern number, c. 1786–1810. Many wares of this period were unmarked. These early written marks were often painted inside the cover of a teapot, or other article.
840	Chamberlains Worcester, No. 70	
840a	Chamberlains Worcester Warranted	

841	T	An incised initial T occurs on some pre-1800 dishes and plates.

842	Chamberlain's Worcester, & 155, New Bond Street, London. Royal Porcelain Manufactory.	Written or printed mark, c. 1811–40. Note the addition of a crown and the word "Royal".

843	H. Chamberlain & Sons	Rare form of mark sometimes found incised, c. 1811–27.

844	Chamberlain's Worcester, & 63, Piccadilly, London.	Written or printed mark, c. 1814–16. Note the Piccadilly address.

845	Chamberlain's Regent China, Worcester, & 155, New Bond Street, London.	Printed mark used on "Regent" body, c. 1811–20. This mark is mainly found on services made from this special and expensive body. Several variations of the above basic marks may be found. The addresses are an important guide to dating. Some marks incorporate the words "Porcelain Manufacturers to H.R.H. the Prince Regent".

846	CHAMBERLAINS ROYAL PORCELAIN WORCESTER	Rare incised mark, c. 1815–25. Some examples made c. 1840 may bear both Flight, Barr & Barr and Chamberlain marks.

847

CHAMBERLAIN & CO.
WORCESTER
155 NEW BOND ST.
& No. 1
COVENTRY ST.
LONDON.

Printed mark, c. 1840–5. Note addition of "& Co." (and Coventry St. address). The first three lines of this mark were also used at this period mainly on small examples.

848   CHAMBERLAIN & CO. Written or printed mark in various forms c. 1846–50 with or
             WORCESTER   without crown above.

849   CHAMBERLAINS   Impressed or printed mark, with or without "Worcester" below, c. 1847–50.

850

Printed mark, c. 1850–2.

    See *Worcester Pottery and Porcelain, 1751–1851*, R. W. Binns, "A century of Potting in the city of Worcester 1865 and 1877", Chapter XX. Many typical examples are illustrated in *British Pottery and Porcelain: an illustrated Encyclopaedia of Marked Specimens.*

3626–7   CHAMBERS   *See* South Wales Pottery.

1914   CHAMELEON WARE   *See* George Clews & Co. (Ltd.).

2173–4 CHANNEL ISLANDS   *See* Jersey Potteries Ltd.

3617   CHANTICLEER WARE   *See* Soho Pottery (Ltd.).

CHAPMAN

DAVID CHAPMAN & SONS, Atlas Works, Longton. Staffordshire Potteries. 1889–1906. *China.* Firm renamed "Chapman & Sons (Stoke-on-Trent) Ltd." from 1904. Address: Atlas Works, Stoke. Former mark continued but without "Longton" under. Subsequently Atlas China Co. Ltd., q.v.

851   Printed mark, with or without "Longton" under, 1889–1906.

CHAPMANS

CHAPMANS LONGTON LTD., Albert Works, Longton. Staffordshire Potteries. 1916– . *China.*

852			Printed mark, 1916–30.

853–6

| c. 1930–49 | 1930–49 | 1938–41 | 1949– |

Printed marks from 1930.

| 297 | CHARD | *See* Ian Batten. |

CHARLES   **BERNARD H. CHARLES,** Parkstone, Poole, Dorset. 1955– . *Studio-type Pottery (Stonewares) and Architectural Ceramics.*

857   Incised initial mark, 1955– .

| 2794 | CHARNWOOD CISTERCIAN | *See* Mount St. Bernard Abbey. |

| 890 | CHEAM POTTERY | *See* Henry Clark. |

CHEESMAN   **VERA CHEESMAN,** Mrs., Marlow, Bucks. 1947– . *Studio-type Pottery Figures in Terra-cotta, etc.*

858   Vera Cheesman   Signature mark, incised or painted, 1947– .

859   19 ⩔ 62   Monogram mark, with year of production.
     N.B. A similar form of mark was used by Charles Vyse but this potter was not producing figures at the period that Mrs. Cheesman uses this mark.

| 2965 | CHEF WARE | *See* Paramount Pottery Co. Ltd. |

865	CHELSEA	*See* Chelsea Porcelain Works.
2858–61		*See* New Chelsea Porcelain Co. (Ltd.).
2968		*See* Gwendolen Parnell.
3945		*See* Charles Vyse.
4112–13		*See* Reginald F. Wells.
2070	CHELSEA ART POTTERY	*See* Hollinshead & Griffiths.
2969	CHELSEA, CHEYNE	*See* Gwendolen Parnell.
3950		*See* Charles Vyse.
4113	CHELSEA COLDRUM	*See* Reginald F. Wells.

CHELSEA-DERBY

CHELSEA-DERBY. *Porcelain.*

In 1769 William Duesbury of the Derby Porcelain Works purchased the Chelsea factory. Porcelains were decorated* at Chelsea until c. 1784 and this period of the Chelsea and Derby factories history is known as the "Chelsea-Derby" period. Marks include

860–2

all normally painted in gold. The gold anchor mark was previously used at Chelsea c. 1756 69. The Chelsea Derby examples are more restrained in taste. A bowl in the Victoria and Albert Museum is dated 1779 and has a gold anchor mark. The so-called Chelsea-Derby figures and groups were probably made at Derby, rather than at the old Chelsea works. These figures are seldom marked but show three unglazed darker patches (or "pad marks") under the base; these marks were caused by the manner in which the pieces were rested during the firing process. The base of a figure with these darker pad marks is reproduced in Plate 8, mark 863. Derby figures also show this feature.

863   See photographic reproduction, Plate 8

Representative examples of "Chelsea-Derby" porcelains will be found illustrated in *British Pottery and Porcelain: an illustrated Encyclopaedia of Marked Specimens.*

---

* It would appear from original accounts quoted by L. Jewitt that porcelain continued to be made and fired—as well as decorated at the Chelsea Works—after they were purchased by Duesbury. In some instances the models were made of clay sent from Derby—"48 compotiers, all made with the Derby clay".

CHELSEA

CHELSEA PORCELAIN WORKS, London. c. 1745–69.
Porcelain (soft paste).

864–5   Incised triangle mark sometimes with addition of "Chelsea" and year (1745), c. 1745–50. Two examples have been recorded with the triangle painted in blue.

866 Rare early mark painted in underglaze blue, c. 1748–50.

867 Anchor mark on small oval raised pad, c. 1749–52. Sometimes the anchor is picked out in red (c. 1751–2). This mark, no. 867, is known as the "Raised anchor" mark.

868 Anchor painted in red (of small size *). Numerals sometimes painted with this mark. Other colours and slight variations occur. "Red anchor" period, c. 1752–6. On very rare underglaze blue examples the anchor is painted in blue.

869 Anchor mark in gold.* This mark occurs on *many* reproductions. "Gold Anchor" period, c. 1756–69.
   N.B. The anchor in gold sometimes occurs on Derby porcelains decorated at Chelsea, c. 1769–75.

870 R Impressed R mark on "gold anchor" period figures, vases, etc.

860 Chelsea-Derby mark in gold or enamel, c. 1769–84. See also Chelsea-Derby.

For further information on Chelsea porcelains see:
Chaffers' *Marks and Monograms* . . . revised 15th edition;
Blunt's *The Cheyne Book of Chelsea China and Pottery* (1924);
F. S. Mackenna's *Chelsea Porcelain, The Triangle and Raised Anchor Wares* (1948);
F. S. Mackenna's *Chelsea Porcelain, The Red Anchor Wares* (1951);
F. S. Mackenna's *Chelsea Porcelain, The Gold Anchor Period* (1952); and
A. Lane's *English Porcelain Figures of the 18th century* (1961); also
British Pottery and Porcelain: an illustrated Encyclopaedia of Marked Specimens.

   * All Chelsea anchor marks were painted very small; any anchor mark over a quarter of an inch in height should be treated with suspicion.

CHELSEA

CHELSEA POTTERY (Rawnsley Academy Ltd.), Radnor Walk, Chelsea, London S.W.3. 1952– . *Earthenwares.*

871   CHELSEA POTTERY   Incised mark with or without circular seal mark, 1952– .

872

Impressed or incised Chelsea Pottery mark, 1952– . The wording "Chelsea Pottery. Hand made in England" may occur arranged round this mark.

   The name or initials of many individual potters working at the Chelsea Pottery Studio occur on their wares, e.g. "Jem" used by Joyce Morgan.

2857   CHELSEA CHINA   *See* New Chelsea Porcelain Co.

CHERNIAVSKY

PEGGY CHERNIAVSKY, Mrs., London S.W.3. 1951– . *Pottery Figures, etc.*

873

Impressed or painted mark, 1951–4.

873a   Peggy Cherniavsky   Incised or painted signature mark, 1951– .

CHESWORTH

CHESWORTH & ROBINSON, Lane End. Staffordshire Potteries. 1825–40. *Earthenwares.* Formerly Chesworth & Wood.

874   C & R   A printed mark occurs of the Staffordshire knot with the initials C & R but this mark could also be that of Chetham & Robinson, 1822–37.

CHETHAM

CHETHAM (& SON), Longton. 1810–34. *Earthenwares.* Formerly Chetham & Woolley, q.v. Subsequently Chetham & Robinson, q.v.

   Rate records from May 1810 list "Widow Chetham". This was Ann Chetham.

875   CHETHAM   Impressed mark, 1810–18.

876   CHETHAM & SON   Impressed mark, 1818–34.

CHETHAM		**JONATHAN LOWE CHETHAM**, Commerce Street, Longton. Staffordshire Potteries. 1841–62. *Earthenwares*.
877	J. L. C.	A printed mark occurs with the initials J. L. C. in writing letters, under the Royal Arms, 1841–62.

CHETHAM		**J. R. & F. CHETHAM**, Commerce Street, Longton. Staffordshire Potteries. 1846–69. *Earthenwares*.
878	J. R. & F. C.	Distinguishing initials found on several printed marks of differing design: name of the individual pattern is often included, 1846–69.

CHETHAM		**CHETHAM & ROBINSON**, Commerce Street, Longton. Staffordshire Potteries. 1822–37. *Earthenwares*. Formerly Chetham & Son, q.v.
879	C & R	Distinguishing initials found on several printed marks of differing design: name of the individual pattern is often included, 1822–37.
		Similar marks were used by Messrs. Chesworth & Robinson (1825–40).
		A typical blue printed earthenware plate is illustrated in the companion illustrated encyclopaedia of marked specimens.

CHETHAM		**CHETHAM & WOOLLEY**, Commerce Street, Lane End, Longton. Staffordshire Potteries. 1796–1810. *Earthenwares*.
		Continued by Ann Chetham, Richard Woolley set up his own factory and became bankrupt in 1814, see page 692.
880	CHETHAM & WOOLLEY LANE END	Incised mark, 1796–1810.
881	PEARL WARE	Impressed mark on "Pearl" body earthenwares, 1796–1810. This mark was also used by other manufacturers.

CHEW		**JOHN CHEW**, Mill Street Works, Longton. Staffordshire Potteries. 1903–4. *China*. Formerly Boulton & Co.
882	J. C. L.	Impressed mark of initials inside a diamond, 1903–4.

| 2968 | CHEYNE | *See* Gwendolen Parnell. |
| 3950 | | *See* Charles Vyse. |

| — | CHIEFTAIN WARE | *See* Govancroft Potteries Ltd. |

CHILD

SMITH CHILD (*CHILD* is the surname), Newfield, Tunstall. Staffordshire Potteries. 1763–90. *Earthenwares.*

| 883 | CHILD | Impressed mark, 1780–90. |

| 1428 | CHILDREN'S VILLAGE | *See* Duxhurst. |

| 3801 | CHININE | *See* John Tams (& Son) (Ltd.). |

| 3229–30 | CHRIS | *See* Christa Reichel. |

| — | CHRISTIAN | *See* Appendix, page 714. |

CHRISTIE

CHRISTIE & BEARDMORE, Sutherland Pottery, Fenton. Staffordshire Potteries. 1902–3. *Earthenwares.* Formerly Hulme & Christie, q.v. Subsequently F. Beardmore & Co., q.v.

884	C. B.	Distinguishing initials found on several printed marks of
885	C. B.	differing design: name of the individual pattern is often in-
	F.	cluded, 1902–3. Mark no. 886 is a typical example.

886

| 2153 | CHRISTOPHER PAUL | *See* Christopher P. Jackson. |

| 2040 | C. H. & S. | *See* C. Hobson (& Son). |

| 1797–1801 | CHURCH MARK | *See* T. G. Green & Co. (Ltd.). |

| 2853 | CIENNE | *See* C. Newbold. |

1708	CIMS	*See* Glebe Pottery.

CINQUE   **CINQUE PORTS POTTERY (LTD.),** The Mint, Rye, Sussex. 1957– . *Earthenwares.*

887   Printed or impressed mark, 1957– .

CIRCLE   **CIRCLE POTTERY CO.,** Crown Pottery, Stoke. Staffordshire Potteries. 1936–8. *Earthenwares.*

888   Printed mark, 1936–8.

1031	CJ (joined)	*See* Joanne Connell.
2531–3	C. J. M. & CO.	*See* Charles James Mason.
4158	C. J. W.	*See* James & Charles Wileman.
2240	C. K.	*See* Charles Keeling.
—	CK (monogram)	*See* Appendix.
1036	C··K	*See* G. Frederick Cook.
4119	C. K. A.	*See* Wenford Bridge Pottery.
3872	CLANTA	*See* Tooth & Co. (Ltd.).
2225	CLAPHAM	*See* J. F. Jordan.

CLARE   **CLARE CHINA CO. LTD.,** Ruby Works, Longton. Staffordshire Potteries. 1951– . *Decorators of Bone China useful wares.*

889   BONE CHINA CLARE MADE IN ENGLAND   Printed mark, with addition of crown, on porcelains decorated by this firm, 1951– .

| 1061–2 | CLARENCE | *See* Co-op Wholesale Society Ltd. |

| 2878 4172–3 | CLARICE CLIFF | *See* Newport Pottery Co. Ltd. *See* Arthur J. Wilkinson (Ltd.). |

CLARK　　　　　　　　　　　**HENRY CLARK**, Cheam Pottery, Cheam, Surrey. 1869–1880. *Red-bodied Earthenwares.*

890　　HENRY CLARK CHEAM POTTERY　　Impressed or incised mark, 1869–80.

CLARK　　　　　　　　　　　**KENNETH CLARK POTTERY**, London W.1. 1952– . *Studio-type Pottery, Tiles, etc.*

891　　KENNETH CLARK POTTERY　　Impressed or printed mark, 1952– .

891a　　*KC 61.*　　Painted initial mark of Kenneth Clark with last two numerals of year, 1952– .

892　　*AWR*　　Painted mark of Ann Wynn Reeves (Mrs. K. Clark) on individual pieces.

CLARKE　　　　　　　　　　　**EDWARD CLARKE (& CO.)**, Phoenix Works, Tunstall, c. 1865–77. Churchyard Works, Burslem, c. 1878–87. 1865–87. *Earthenwares.* Formerly Bridgwood & Clarke, q.v. Subsequently A. J. Wilkinson, q.v.

893　　EDWARD CLARKE (TOWN)

894　　EDWARD CLARKE & CO. (TOWN)

Distinguishing name found on several printed marks of differing design: the address of the firm is often added and is a guide to dating.
　　Tunstall address used, c. 1865–77.
　　Longport address used, c. 1878–80.
　　Burslem from 1880 to 1887.

895　　　　Printed mark, with Burslem address, c. 1880–7.

896	ROYAL SEMI-PORCELAIN	Impressed or printed term used from c. 1877.

CLARKE   JOAN CLARKE, MISS, Brundall, Ludham, Norfolk. 1950– . *Studio-type Pottery.*

897	JOAN CLARKE BRUNDALL	Signature mark with place name, Brundall, 1950–8.
898	JOAN CLARKE LUDHAM	Signature mark with place name, Ludham, 1958– .

CLARKSON   DEREK CLARKSON, Bacup, Lancs. 1961– . *Studio-type Pottery.*
       Derek Clarkson has held various teaching posts from 1950.

899		Impressed seal type mark used from January 1961– .

CLAVERDON   A. BOURNE CLAVERDON (Alice Buxton Winnicott, b. 1891). London N.W.3. c. 1947–50. *Studio-type Pottery.*

900		Impressed on printed mark, also the name "CLAVERDON" alone. 1947 to about 1950.

CLAVERING   CLAVERING POTTERY (Mrs. E. Barnett), Clavering, Essex. 1956– . *Studio-type Pottery and Figures.*

900a	CLAVERING	Incised, stamped or written mark, 1956– .
900b	LISA	Christian name added to the basic mark, on some individual specimens, 1956– .

CLAYBURN   CLAYBURN STUDIO POTTERY LTD., Milner Street, Hanley. Staffordshire Potteries. 1953–7. *Earthenwares.*

901	CLAYBURN STUDIO POTTERY	Distinguishing detail of several marks of differing design, 1953–7.

CLAYPITS

CLAYPITS POTTERY (Thomas Jenkins & Sons), Ewenny, Bridgend, Glamorgan, Wales. Pottery established c. 1700. *Earthenwares.*

902   CLAY PITS   Incised mark in writing letters. 20th century.
           EWENNY

CLAYTON

CLAYTON BONE CHINA (LTD.), St. Georges Works, Longton. Staffordshire Potteries. 1958–62. *Bone China Animals, Floral Ornaments, etc.*

903,   CLAYTON   Printed marks, 1958–62.
903a   MADE IN ENGLAND
        BONE CHINA
        HAND MADE

          —

    HAND PAINTED
      BONE CHINA
   MADE IN ENGLAND
     BY CLAYTON

CLEE

CLEE POTTERY, Anthony Clee, Kent (1958–9) then Eton, Windsor, Berkshire. August 1958– . *Studio-type Pottery.*

904   CLEE   Impressed mark used at Fawkham Green, Kent, August 1958 to May 1959.

904a   CLEE ETON   Impressed mark used at Eton, May 1959 to August 1960.

904b   HAND MADE AT   Impressed mark, August 1960 to December 1962.
      THE CLEE POTTERY
      ETON, WINDSOR

904c   CLEE POTTERY   Impressed mark, December 1962– .

CLEMENTSON

CLEMENTSON BROS. (LTD.), Phoenix Works and Bell Works, Hanley. Staffordshire Potteries. 1865–1916. Formerly J. Clementson, q.v.

905      Distinguishing detail of several printed marks of differing design, 1867–80.

CLEMENTSON BROS.

906–7

Printed marks, c. 1870+. Note addition of "Limited" on mark no. 907; this is subsequent to the year 1910.

908

Printed mark, 1901–13.

909

Printed mark, 1913–16.

CLEMENTSON

JOSEPH CLEMENTSON, Phoenix Works, Shelton, Hanley. Staffordshire Potteries. c. 1839–64. *Earthenwares*. Subsequently Clementson Bros. (Ltd.), see previous entry.

910   J. C.
910a   J. CLEMENTSON

Distinguishing detail of several printed marks of differing design: name of the individual pattern is often included, 1839–64. See Plate 6. The attribution of some of these J. C. marks is proved by Patent Office records. A mark of the 1840 s onwards has the Phoenix bird with the name J. CLEMENTSON under.

910b   MANUFACTURED BY
            J. CLEMENTSON
            BROAD STREET
            SHELTON
            STAFFORDSHIRE

A printed earthenware plate in the Godden Collection has the name and address in full. The subject is dated November 1839.

CLEMENTSON

CLEMENTSON & YOUNG, Broad Street, Shelton, Hanley. Staffordshire Potteries. 1845–7. *Earthenwares*. Formerly Clementson, Young & Jameson, q.v.

911   CLEMENTSON &
            YOUNG

Distinguishing detail of impressed or printed marks of differing design: name of the individual pattern is often included, 1845–7. Some printed wares were made for the American market.

CLEMENTSON

CLEMENTSON, YOUNG & JAMESON, Broad Street, Shelton, Hanley. Staffordshire Potteries. 1844. *Earthenwares.* Subsequently Clementson & Young, see previous entry.

912   C Y & J

A printed mark occurs in the Patent Office records (October 1844) in the name of the above firm. This mark comprises the name of the printed pattern, the body (Ironstone) and the initials C Y & J.

339   CLEVE WARE

See William Bennett (Hanley) Ltd.

CLEWS

GEORGE CLEWS & CO. (LTD.), Brownhills Pottery, Tunstall. Staffordshire Potteries. 1906–61. *Earthenwares.*

913

Printed globe mark with name of pattern or title of firm on central band, 1906+.

914   CHAMELEON WARE

Trade-name impressed or incorporated in marks, 1906+.

915–17

1935+   1935+   1947–61

Printed marks from 1935.

CLEWS

JAMES & RALPH CLEWS, Cobridge Works, Cobridge. Staffordshire Potteries. 1818–34. *Earthenwares (China, c. 1821–5*).*

The works were rented from William Adams in September 1817, but were not then in good repair. The firm became bankrupt in 1834 or 1835.

918   CLEWS WARRANTED
            STAFFORDSHIRE

Impressed mark, with crown above. The initials G. R. sometimes occur each side of the crown and this indicated an early (Georgian) date.

918a   CLEWS
            DRESDEN
         OPAQUE CHINA

The wording no. 918a occurs as part of a large pre-Victorian Royal Arms mark on a decorative plate in the Godden Collection. This specimen also bears the impressed mark, no. 918.

919

Impressed mark often found on good quality blue printed earthenwares. The wording reads: "Clews, Warranted Staffordshire". See companion illustrated encyclopaedia. Many printed marks also occur and these incorporate the name "Clews", c. 1818–34, see note below.

On bill-heads these potters are described as "Potters to Her Imperial Majesty, the Empress of all the Russians".

N.B. Reproductions have been made of Clews blue printed earthenwares; these have a faked mark similar to mark no. 919. The faked marks are very clearly stamped, not blurred as are most of the marks on original specimens.

* The china wares produced c. 1821–5 do not seem to be marked but some examples bear the same floral moulded borders as occur on *marked* earthenwares.

| 1291 | CLIFF | *See* J. Dimmock & Co. |

CLIVE

JOHN HENRY CLIVE, Newfield, Tunstall. Staffordshire Potteries. 1802–11. *Earthenwares.* Subsequently Child & Clive.

920 CLIVE Impressed name-mark, 1802–11.

CLIVE

STEPHEN CLIVE, Well Street Pottery, Tunstall. Staffordshire Potteries. 1875–80. *Earthenwares.*

921 S. C.
922 S. C. & CO.

Distinguishing detail of several printed marks of differing design: name of the individual pattern is often included, 1875–80. From 1876 "& Co." may be added to the initials S. C.

CLOKIE

CLOKIE & CO. (LTD.), Castleford, Yorkshire. 1888–1961. *Earthenwares.* Formerly Clokie & Masterman, see below.

923–5 CLOKIE & CO.

Printed marks with title or initials of firm occur, c. 1888–1961. N.B. "Ltd." added from c. 1940.

CLOKIE		**CLOKIE & MASTERMAN**, Castleford, Yorkshire. 1872–87. *Earthenwares.* Formerly Thomas Nicholson & Co. Subsequently Clokie & Co. Ltd., above.
926	C. & M.	Distinguishing details of several printed or impressed marks of
927	CLOKIE & MASTERMAN	differing design, 1872–87.

CLOSE		**CLOSE & CO.**, Church Street, Stoke. Staffordshire Potteries. 1855–64. *Earthenwares.*
928	CLOSE & CO. LATE W. ADAMS & SONS STOKE-UPON-TRENT	Distinguishing detail of several printed or impressed marks of differing design, 1855–64.

CLOUGH

ALFRED CLOUGH (LTD.), St. Louis Works, Longton. Staffordshire Potteries.
     Alfred Clough, c. 1913–56.
     Alfred Clough Ltd., c. 1956–61.*
    Parent company to Barker Bros., Cartwright & Edwards, W. H. Grindley, Royal Art Pottery, Sampson Smith.

    * Continued as Clough's Royal Art Pottery, see next entry.

CLOUGH'S

CLOUGH'S ROYAL ART POTTERY, Barford Street, Longton. Staffordshire Potteries. 1961– . *Earthenwares.* Formerly Alfred Clough Ltd. (Royal Art Pottery).

929   Printed mark, c. 1961– . Formerly used by "Royal Art Pottery" (Alfred Clough Ltd.), 1951–61.

CLOWES		**WILLIAM CLOWES**, Longport, Burslem. Staffordshire Potteries. c. 1783–96. *Earthenwares, Basaltes, etc.*
930	W. CLOWES	Impressed mark, 1783–96.

CLULOW		**CLULOW & CO.**, Fenton. Staffordshire Potteries. c. 1802. *Earthenwares.*
931	CLULOW & CO. FENTON	This "mark" occurs in the design of a moulded Castleford type teapot, in the Newark Museum, U.S.A. c. 1802. See the companion illustrated encyclopaedia of marked specimens.
		N.B. Meigh's list includes Robert Clewlow (or Clulow) & Co. c. 1802.

CLYDE		**CLYDE POTTERY CO. (LTD.)**, various managements,* Greenock, Scotland. Est. c. 1815–1903. *Earthenwares.*

For further information see J. Arnold Fleming's *Scottish Pottery.*

932	CLYDE	Distinguishing details of several printed or impressed marks of
933	GREENOCK	differing design.
934	G. C. P. CO.	N.B. "Ltd." used in marks c. 1857–63.
935	C. P CO.	Most early wares are unmarked, marked pieces probably date
936	G. P. CO.	from c. 1850–1903.
	G.	

* From c. 1840 to c. 1857 Thomas Shirley & Co. used their initials T. S. & Coy, see page 574.

769	CM	*See* Michael Ambrose Cardew.
804	(also joined)	*See* Michael Casson.
2479		*See* Christopher Magarshack.
2503		*See* Carlo Manzoni.
2614a		*See* Charles Meigh.
769		*See* Wenford Bridge Pottery.
769		*See* Winchcombe Pottery.
926	C. & M.	*See* Clokie & Masterman.
1158		*See* Cumberlidge & Humphreys.
2620	C. M. & S.	*See* Charles Meigh & Son.
2624	C. M. S. & P.	*See* Charles Meigh, Son & Parkhurst.
2852	C. N.	*See* C. Newbold.
762	C N. A.	*See* Candy & Co. Ltd.

COALBROOK		**COALBROOK POTTERIES**, Cleveland Works, Shelton. Staffordshire Potteries. 1937– . *Floral wares.*
937		Printed mark, c. 1948– . Other marks occur with the name "Coalbrook".

938–9   COALBROOKDALE   *See* Coalport Porcelain Works, below.

COALPORT

COALPORT PORCELAIN WORKS (John Rose & Co.), Coalport, Shropshire. c. 1795– (at Stoke-on-Trent from c. 1926). *Porcelain.*

The early Coalport porcelains are mostly unmarked. The two painted marks below are very rare and occur on two plates in the Godden Collection and on one in the Victoria and Albert Museum, see *British Pottery and Porcelain: an illustrated Encyclopaedia of Marked Specimens*. The period is c. 1805–15.

938–9

Other early Coalport porcelains of the 1810–25 period will be found bearing the following marks painted in underglaze blue. Many examples with these marks are of the colourful, floral encrusted type. Typical examples are illustrated in the companion illustrated volume mentioned above. The crossed swords also occurs on porcelains made at other factories and is a copy of the Dresden factory mark.

940–3

944

This impressed mark will be found on many examples of Coalport plates, dishes, etc., of the 1815–25 period, other numbers 1 or 6 rarely occur. See companion illustrated encyclopaedia.

The printed marks reproduced below were used for a few years from June 1820. Several slight variations were used, the first two are very rarely seen. It is probable that version number 948, with the addition of the word "improved", was used slightly later than mark number 947.

945–8

The marks are reproduced from specimens illustrated in *British Pottery and Porcelain: an illustrated encyclopaedia of Marked Specimens*.

| 949 | JOHN ROSE & CO. COALBROOKDALE SHROPSHIRE | Many written and printed marks occur during the period 1830–50; all give the title, often with the address, as these two samples, nos. 949 and 950. |

| 950 | | |

| 951 | JOHN ROSE COLEBROOK DALE 1850 | Mark no. 951 occurs painted on plates presented to the Victoria and Albert Museum by John Rose in 1850. One is illustrated in the companion illustrated encyclopaedia. |

| 951a | MADE AT COALBROOK DALE | This rare moulded mark occurs on a parian figure of Wellington in the Godden Collection. This example is of the 1850 period. |

| 952 | J. R. & CO. or I R & CO. | Several printed marks incorporate the initials J. R. & Co. (or I R & Co.) during the 1850–70 period. Similar initial marks were also used by J. Ridgway & Co., see page 534. The Coalport marks sometimes include the words "English Porcelain". |

| 953 | | This anchor mark with a "C" above occurs painted in blue on a Coalport copy of a Chelsea porcelain vase in the Victoria and Albert Museum. See *British Pottery and Porcelain: an illustrated Encyclopaedia of Marked Specimens*. Other Coalport copies of Chelsea have a gold anchor, larger in size than that found on the originals, c. 1845–55. |

| 954 | | Painted mark in colours or in gold, c. 1851–61. |

| 955 | | Painted mock Sevres mark on ornate specimens, c. 1845–55. The gold anchor mark of Chelsea was also copied. |

| 956 | | Painted or gilt "ampersand" mark, c. 1861–75. |

956a Printed mark, c. 1870–80. A saucer with this mark in the Godden Collection has the impressed date 1877.

957 COALPORT AD 1750 Printed or painted mark, c. 1875–81.

958–9   Printed crown marks, c. 1881–1939+.
N.B. "England" added c. 1891. "Made in England" occurs from c. 1920.

960–1   Printed marks of post-war period. Variations occur, as no. 961, which give details of the pattern or style.

962 Revised standard mark, 1960+.

963 COALBROOKDALE BY COALPORT MADE IN ENGLAND Painted mark, in writing letters on the reintroduced, floral encrusted "Coalbrookdale" wares, c. 1960+.
For information on 19th century Coalport porcelain and artists see *Victorian Porcelain* (1961).

COBHAM **COBHAM (SURREY) POTTERY LTD.** (D. Zadek), Cobham, Surrey. 1947–56. *Earthenwares*. Subsequently D. Zadek, q.v.

964 D Z COBHAM Written or incised mark, 1947–56.

COCHRAN **R. COCHRAN & CO.**, Verreville Pottery (also Britannia Pottery to 1896), Glasgow, Scotland. 1846–1918. *Earthenwares, Stonewares and China (China ceased c. 1856)*.

965 R. C. & CO. Impressed initials, 1846+.

R, COCHRAN & CO.

966

GLASGOW

Distinguishing name found on several printed or impressed marks of differing design, 1846–1918.

967   COCHRAN,
       GLASGOW

Printed mark of the seated figure of Britannia and "Cochran, Glasgow" occurs on a design registered in September 1875.

COCHRAN

COCHRAN & FLEMING, Britannia Pottery, St. Rollox, Glasgow, Scotland. 1896–1920. *Earthenwares*. Formerly R. Cochran & Co., q.v. Subsequently Britannia Pottery Co. Ltd., q.v.

For further information see J. Arnold Fleming's *Scottish Pottery* (the author was the partner in the above firm).

968   C & F
969   C & F
       G

Distinguishing initials found on several printed or impressed marks of differing design from 1896.

970

ROYAL
IRONSTONE CHINA

The seated figure of Britannia appears on many printed marks with the style "Cochran & Fleming", 1896–1920.

971

COCHRAN & FLEMING
GLASGOW.   BRITAIN

Printed mark, 1900–20.

972   FLEMING
973   PORCELAIN OPAQUE
       GLASGOW. BRITAIN
       FLEMING

The impressed mark FLEMING also occurs, as do several printed marks based on this wording, with the addition of a crown, 1900–20.

COCKER

GEORGE COCKER, Derby, etc. c. 1808–40. *Modeller*.

George Cocker was a figure modeller trained at the Derby works. He subsequently modelled for various firms or on his own account. Figures and groups in unglazed porcelain or parian occur with his incised signature. G. Cocker died in 1868.

974 G. COCKER
DERBY

Incised written signature:

Derby periods   1808–c. 17 and 1821–40.
Coalport period   1817–19.
Worcester period   1819–21.
London period   c. 1840–50.
and at Mintons   c. 1850–60.

The signature mark D. Cocker has been noted on a white bust and this probably relates to one of George Cocker's sons.

COCKSON

COCKSON & CHETWYND (or Cockson Chetwynd & Co.), Globe Works, Cobridge. Staffordshire Potteries. 1867–75. *Earthenwares*. Subsequently Cockson & Seddon, q.v.

975 COCKSON &
CHETWYND
976 C. C. & Co.

Distinguishing details of several printed marks of differing design: name of the individual pattern is often included, 1867–75. The initials also fit other firms.

COCKSON

COCKSON & HARDING, New Hall Works, Shelton. Staffordshire Potteries. 1856–62. *Earthenwares*. Formerly Hackwood, q.v. Subsequently W. & J. Harding, q.v.

977 C & H
978 C & H
LATE HACKWOOD

Distinguishing details of several printed or impressed marks of differing design: name of the individual pattern is often included, 1856–62. Mark no. 979 is a typical example.

979

COCKSON

COCKSON & SEDDON, Globe Works, Cobridge. Staffordshire Potteries. 1875–7. *Earthenwares*. Formerly Cockson & Chetwynd, q.v. Subsequently Birks Bros. & Seddon, q.v.

980

IMPERIAL IRONSTONE
CHINA
COCKSON & SEDDON

Printed mark, 1875–7.

COFFEE		**WILLIAM COFFEE,** Derby. c. 1805–16. *Figure modeller.*
		See F. Brayshaw Gilhespy's *Crown Derby Porcelain* (1951).
981	W. COFFEE DERBY	Incised signature (in writing letters) on rare figures, c. 1805–16.
COGGINS		**COGGINS & HILL,** High Street, Longton. Staffordshire Potteries. 1892–8. *Porcelain.*
982	C & H	Distinguishing initials found on several printed or impressed marks of differing design: name of the individual pattern is often included, 1892–8. The word "England" may also occur.
1401	H Co. D &	*See* Henry Dreydel & Co.
457–8 & 460 990 991–3 3286, 3290	COLCLOUGH	*See* Booths & Colclough. *See* H. J. Colclough. *See* Colclough China Ltd. *See* Ridgway Potteries Ltd.
COLCLOUGH		**COLCLOUGH & CO.,** Stanley Pottery (and other addresses), Longton. Staffordshire Potteries. 1887–1928. *China and Earthenwares.* Subsequently Stanley Pottery Ltd., q.v.
		Early wares unmarked.
983		Printed mark, 1903–19.
984		Printed mark, 1919–28.

COLCLOUGH

H. J. COLCLOUGH, Vale Works, Goddard Street, Longton. Staffordshire Potteries. 1897–1937. *China and Earthenwares.* Subsequently Colclough China Ltd., q.v.

985   H. J. C.   L.

Distinguishing initials found on several printed marks of differing design, 1897 onwards.

986–7

Printed marks, 1908–28.

988–9

Printed marks, 1928–37.

990

Printed mark, 1935–7.

COLCLOUGH

COLCLOUGH CHINA LTD., Longton. Staffordshire Potteries. 1937–48. *China.* Formerly H. J. Colclough, q.v. Subsequently Booths & Colcloughs Ltd., q.v. (who continued to use mark nos. 991–3).

From 1937 to 1939 the former marks (nos. 989–90) of H. J. Colclough were used by this new company.

991

Printed mark, 1939+.

992–4

Post-war printed marks., c. 1945–8.

COLDRUM

COLDRUM POTTERY, Reginald F. Wells, West Malling, Kent. c. 1904–9. *Earthenwares.*
  Reginald F. Wells, a noted 20th century potter subsequently worked at Chelsea. See under R. F. Wells.

995   COL'RUM   Impressed mark, c. 1904–9.

COLDSTONE

COLDSTONE KILN, Chris Harries, Ascott-under-Wychwood, Oxford. 1953– . *Slip decorated Earthenwares.*

996   COLDSTONE   Impressed or incised name-mark, 1953– .

996a   Impressed CK (Coldstone Kiln) seal mark, 1953– .

COLEGATE

ANGELA COLEGATE, MISS, Malvern, Worcestershire. 1960– . *Studio-type Pottery.*

997   A. C. C.   Incised or painted initial mark, 1960–2.

997a   Impressed seal type mark, 1962– .

COLLARD

C. COLLARD, Honiton Art Potteries, Ltd., Honiton, Devon. 1918–47. *Earthenwares.* Formerly Foster & Hunt. Subsequently Norman Hull, q.v.

998   COLLARD HONITON   Impressed mark, 1918–47.
           ENGLAND

COLLEY

ALFRED COLLEY & CO. LTD., Gordon Pottery, Tunstall. Staffordshire Potteries. 1909–14. *Earthenwares.*

999   Printed or impressed mark, 1909–14.

COLLIER

S. & E. COLLIER (LTD.), Grovelands Potteries, Reading, Berks. Est. c. 1848–1957. *Terra-cotta wares.*
Early wares unmarked.

1000   Impressed mark, c. 1870–1905.

1001      Impressed or printed standard mark, c. 1905–57.

1002   THUMB PRINT   A mark of a thumb print was registered in 1906.

1003   SILCHESTER WARE   This trade-name occurs impressed, in a pointed oval, c. 1907+.

COLLINGWOOD

COLLINGWOOD BROS. (LTD.), Crown Works (St. George's Works from 1919), Longton. Staffordshire Potteries. 1887–1957.* *China.* Formerly Collingwood & Greatbatch, q.v.

1004   COLLINGWOOD   Impressed mark, 1887–1900.

1005   C B
     L   Printed mark of initials with crown above, c. 1887–1900.

1006   Printed mark, 1900–12.

1007   Printed mark, 1912–24.

1008–9   Printed mark, 1924–30.

1010   Printed mark, 1930–40.

1011

Printed mark, 1937–57.*

* From March 1948 to 1957 this firm was "Collinwood China Ltd." but the former marks were continued. The works were then taken by Messrs. Clayton Bone China Co., q.v.

COLLINGWOOD

COLLINGWOOD & GREATBATCH, Crown Works, Longton. Staffordshire Potteries. 1870–87. *China.* Subsequently Collingwood Bros., see previous entry.

1012

Printed or impressed crown mark, with or without initials C & G, 1870–87.

COLLINSON

CHARLES COLLINSON & CO., Burslem. Staffordshire Potteries. 1851–73. *Earthenwares.*

1013   C. COLLINSON & CO. Distinguishing name found on several printed marks of differing design: name of the individual pattern is often included, 1851–73. Mark no. 1014 is a typical example.

1014

COLLYER

ERNEST COLLYER & MRS. COLLYER (PAMELA NASH), Stanmore, Middlesex. 1950– . *Studio-type Pottery, Tiles and Panels.*

1015   E. C./1963

Incised or painted initial mark of Ernest Collyer, with year, 1950– .

1016   P. N.

Incised or painted initial mark used by Mrs. Collyer (Pamela Nash), 1950– .

1017   COLLYER-NASH

Name-mark on ceramic panels decorated by Mr. and Mrs. Collyer, 1950– .

1017   COLLYER-NASH

See Ernest Collyer, above.

4215   COLONIAL POTTERY *See* F. Winkle & Co. (Ltd.).

995   COL'RUM   *See* Coldrum Pottery.

4111–13   COL'RUM   *See* Reginald F. Wells.

COMMONDALE   **COMMONDALE POTTERY**, Nr. Stokesley, Yorkshire.
                              Various firms from c. 1861. *Earthenwares.*

1018   COMMONDALE   Impressed mark, in circular form. Late 19th century.
        POTTERY

1019   CROSSLEY   Impressed mark, c. 1872–90.*
        COMMONDALE

                                      * The production of *decorative* and *domestic* earthenwares ceased about
                              1884.

COMPTON   **COMPTON POTTERY**, Nr. Guildford, Surrey. Est. c. 1902
                              by Mrs. G. F. Watts. *Earthenwares.* The Potters Art Guild
                              Ltd. continued from 1936 to 1956.

1020   COMPTON   Impressed mark, c. 1902+.
        POTTERY

1021   COMPTON   Printed or impressed mark, the wording enclosed by outline of a
     GUILDFORD SURREY   bowl, c. 1945–56.

CONE   **THOMAS CONE LTD.**, Alma Works, Longton. Stafford-
                              shire Potteries. 1892– . *Earthenwares.*

1022   T. C.   Distinguishing details of several printed or impressed marks of
            L.   differing design: name of the individual pattern is often in-
1023   T. C.   cluded, 1892–1912.
        LONGTON

1024   Printed mark, 1912–35.

1025   Printed mark, 1935+.

1026–7		Printed marks, 1946+ and (no. 1027) 1950+.

CONEY   JOHN CONEY, Hutton, Nr. Weston-super-Mare, Somerset; Glastonbury, Somerset; and Bedhampton, Havant, Hampshire. 1927– . *Studio-type Pottery*.

1028	Mendip	Incised or painted mark in writing letters, 1927–30.
1029	Glaston	Incised or painted mark, often with year, 1933–5.
1030	*J Coney 1962*	Incised or painted signature mark, with year, 1927– .

CONNELL   JOANNA CONNELL, MISS. (Mrs. F. Constantinidis), Great Baddow, Chelmsford, Essex. 1950– . *Studio-type Porcelain and Stonewares*.

1031		Impressed seal mark, in circle, 1950– . Some wares are unmarked.

CONWAY   CONWAY POTTERY CO. LTD., Fenton. Staffordshire Potteries. 1930– . *Earthenwares*.

1032–4	CONWAY POTTERY ENGLAND 1945+	CONWAY Lavender Blue ENGLAND 1945	"Rose Pink" CONWAY ENGLAND 1960+

Post-war printed marks.

COOK   G. FREDERICK COOK, The Potter's Wheel Studio, Ambleside, Westmorland. 1948– . *Studio-type Pottery and Stonewares*.

1035	AMBLESIDE	Incised or painted place name-mark, 1948– .

1036   **C..K.**   Impressed personal mark on individual specimens, 1948– .

COOKE   **COOKE & HULSE**, Stafford Street, Longton. Staffordshire Potteries. 1835–55. *Porcelains*.

1037   COOKE & HULSE   Rare printed name-marks, incorporating the name of the pattern, "Alma Japan", etc., 1835–55.

COOKSON   **DELAN COOKSON**, West Bridgford, Nottinghamshire. 1958– . *Studio-type Pottery*.

1038   **D**
        C   Impressed seal mark, 1961– . Earlier wares are rarely marked.

COOMBES   **COOMBES**, Queen Street, Bristol. 1775–1805. *China Repairer*.

1039   COOMBES
        QUEEN ST.
        BRISTOL   Signature in writing letters on 18th century porcelains repaired and refired by this person. Some examples have the date and price added. The early date 1776 has been noted.
        An interesting article by G. Wills in *Country Life*, December 4, 1958, illustrates some Coombes repaired articles with signature marks.

—   COOPER & CO.   *See* Appendix, page 714.

COOPER   **COOPER & DETHICK**, Viaduct Works, Longton. Staffordshire Potteries. 1876–88. *Earthenwares*.

1040   C. & D.   Distinguishing initials found on several printed marks of differing design: name of the individual pattern is often included, 1876–88.

COOPER   **FRANCIS GLANVILLE COOPER**, Sheffield, Yorkshire. 1945– . *Studio-type Pottery*.

1041   Incised initials or impressed seal type mark, also painted, 1945– .

1042

COOPER

J. COOPER & CO., Ducal Works, Burslem. Staffordshire Potteries. 1922–5. *Earthenwares.*

1043

Printed or impressed mark, 1922–5.

COOPER

MAUREEN COOPER, MRS., Roehampton Village, London S.W.15. 1955– . *Studio-type Pottery and Panels.*

1044   MAUREEN HARRINGTON COOPER

Incised signature in flowing writing, 1955– .

1045

Incised or painted monogram of initials M. H. C., 1955– .

COOPER

RONALD G. COOPER, Hornsey College of Art, London. Also lecturer at other Schools of Art. 1946– . *Studio-type Pottery.*

1046

Painted or incised initial mark, c. 1946– , often with year of production.

COOPER

SUSIE COOPER CHINA LTD., Longton, c. 1950–9. Burslem, c. 1959+. Staffordshire Potteries. 1950–61. *Bone China.* Subsequently "Susie Cooper Ltd.", same mark used.

1047

Susie Cooper
BONE CHINA
ENGLAND

Printed mark, 1950– .

COOPER

SUSIE COOPER POTTERY (LTD.), Burslem. Staffordshire Potteries. c. 1930– . *Earthenwares and China.*
Miss Cooper (Mrs. C. F. Barker) was formerly employed decorating wares for A. E. Gray & Co., c. 1925–30.
Renamed "Susie Cooper Ltd." c. 1961.

1048–9

Printed marks, also signature alone, c. 1930– . The name "Crown Works" does not occur before 1932.

COOPER

WAISTEL COOPER, Porlock (c. 1952–7), Culbone (c. 1957–), Somerset. 1952– . *Studio-type individual Stonewares.*

1050   WAISTEL

Brush written mark in writing letters, 1952– .

COOPERS

COOPERS ART POTTERY CO. (and subsequent titles), Anchor Works, Hanley. Staffordshire Potteries. c. 1912–58 (with changes in style). *Earthenwares.* Formerly Art Pottery Co., q.v.

1051

Printed mark, formerly used by the "Art Pottery Co.", q.v., continued by succeeding firms:
Cooper & Co. (c. 1930–6).
Coopers (Anchor Pottery) Ltd. c. 1936–41 and c. 1947–58.

1052   COOPER ENGLAND

Printed marks occur with the words "COOPER" "ENGLAND" in conjunction with an anchor, c. 1936–58.

CO-OPERATIVE

CO-OPERATIVE WHOLESALE SOCIETY LTD., Crown Clarence Pottery, Longton. Staffordshire Potteries. 1946– . *Earthenwares.*

1053–7

1946+   1946+   1950+   1962+   1962+

Post-war printed marks on earthenware. See next entry for china.

CO-OPERATIVE

CO-OPERATIVE WHOLESALE SOCIETY LTD., Windsor Pottery, Longton. Staffordshire Potteries. 1922– . *China.*

1058

Printed mark, c. 1946+.

1059–62

Printed marks of the 1950's and early 1960's.

COOTE

AUBREY R. COOTE, Wanstead, London E.11. 1955– *Studio-type Pottery.*

1063

Impressed or incised mark on red bodied earthenwares, 1955–

COPE

J. H. COPE & CO. (LTD.), Wellington Works, Longton. Staffordshire Potteries. 1887–1947. *China.*

1064   C. & CO.   Impressed or printed initial mark, 1887+.

1065   J. H. C. & CO.   Distinguishing initials found on several printed marks of differing design: name of the individual pattern is often included, c. 1900 onwards.

1066

Printed mark, c. 1906+.

1067

Printed mark, c. 1924–c. 47.

COPELAND		**W. T. COPELAND (& SONS LTD.),** Spode Works, Stoke. Staffordshire Potteries. 1847 to present day. *Porcelain, Parian and Earthenwares.* Formerly Copeland & Garrett, q.v.
1068	COPELAND, LATE SPODE	Impressed or printed name alone or with other devices, c. 1847–67.
1069	COPELAND	
1070	COPELAND'S PORCELAIN STATUARY	Rare printed mark on early parian figures, etc., c. 1847–55.

1071	COPELAND	Printed mark, c. 1847–51, but see later variation mark no. 1073.
1072		Printed mark, 1850–67. An *impressed* mark of a crown and the word "Copeland" occurs on earthenwares. Sometimes the word "Copeland" was impressed in curved form without the crown. These marks were used into the 20th century.
1072a	COPELAND	
1073	COPELAND	Printed mark, 1851–85. An earlier, simpler version is mark no. 1071.
1074		Printed mark, 1875–90.
1075		Printed mark on earthenwares, 1867–90.
	Y 88	Impressed date marks showing the month letter and last two numerals of the year—July 1888. This system was continued into the 20th century, 08 = 1908, etc.

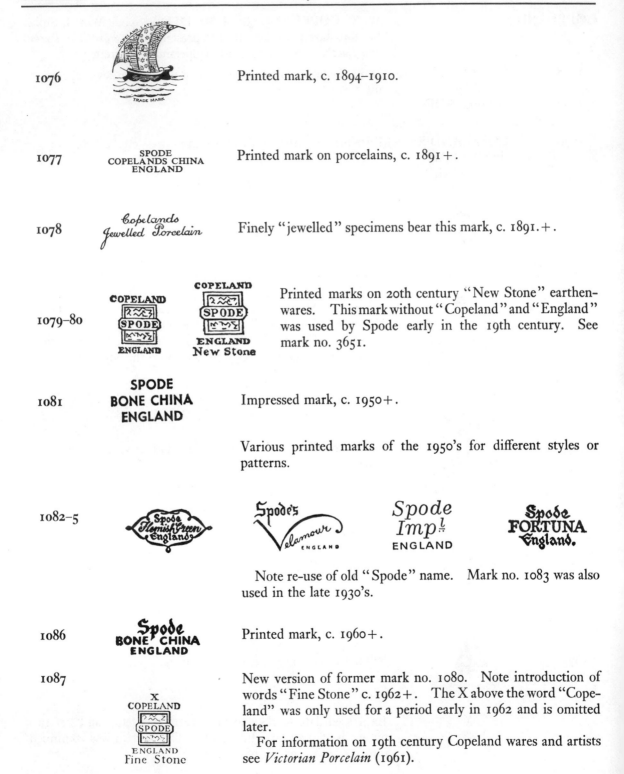

1076   Printed mark, c. 1894–1910.

1077   SPODE
        COPELANDS CHINA   Printed mark on porcelains, c. 1891+.
        ENGLAND

1078   *Copelands*   Finely "jewelled" specimens bear this mark, c. 1891.+.
        Jewelled Porcelain

1079–80   COPELAND   COPELAND   Printed marks on 20th century "New Stone" earthen-
                                    wares. This mark without "Copeland" and "England"
           SPODE   SPODE   was used by Spode early in the 19th century. See
                    ENGLAND   mark no. 3651.
           ENGLAND   New Stone

1081   SPODE
        BONE CHINA   Impressed mark, c. 1950+.
        ENGLAND

        Various printed marks of the 1950's for different styles or
        patterns.

1082–5   Spode   Spode's   Spode   Spode
          Flemish Green   Velamour   Impl   FORTUNA
          England   ENGLAND   ENGLAND   England.

        Note re-use of old "Spode" name. Mark no. 1083 was also
        used in the late 1930's.

1086   Spode   Printed mark, c. 1960+.
        BONE CHINA
        ENGLAND

1087   New version of former mark no. 1080. Note introduction of
        words "Fine Stone" c. 1962+. The X above the word "Cope-
        X   land" was only used for a period early in 1962 and is omitted
        COPELAND   later.
        SPODE   For information on 19th century Copeland wares and artists
        ENGLAND   see *Victorian Porcelain* (1961).
        Fine Stone

COPELAND		**COPELAND & GARRETT**, Spode Works, Stoke. Staffordshire Potteries. March 1833–47. *Porcelain, Earthenwares and Parian*, *etc.* Formerly Spode, q.v. Subsequently W. T. Copeland, see previous entry. Typical specimens will be found illustrated in *British Pottery and Porcelain : an illustrated Encyclopaedia of Marked Specimens.*
1088	C. & G.	Initials used in several printed marks, and rarely painted with the pattern number, c. 1833–47.
1089	N. S.	Impressed initials in Spode's "New Stone" body, c. 1820–40.
1090	COPELAND & GARRETT	Several printed marks, incorporating the name of the firm, the pattern or the type of body occur. The marks printed below are typical, c. 1833–47.

1091–3	

A mark similar to no. 1091 has been reported with the date 1846 in the centre and "Stone China" below.

1094		Printed mark used on "New Japan Stone" china body, c. 1833–47.
1095		Rare printed mark, in gold on a porcelain plate in the Godden Collection, 1833–47.
COPER		**HANS COPER**, Digswell House, Welwyn Garden City, Herts. (Formerly Albion Mews, London.) 1947– . *Studiotype Pottery, Stonewares.* Typical examples of Hans Coper's pots are illustrated in Muriel Rose's *Artist Potters in England.*
1096	**HC**	Impressed or incised initials in seal form, 1947– .

CORK | CORK & EDGE, Newport Pottery, Burslem. Staffordshire Potteries. 1846–60. *Earthenwares.* Subsequently Cork, Edge & Malkin, see next entry.

1097   C & E   Distinguishing initials found on several printed marks of differing design, 1846–60. The name in full occurs on other marks, see below.

1098–1100

The mark incorporating the American Eagle occurs on a moulded pattern jug, "Babes in the Wood", in the Godden Collection. See *British Pottery and Porcelain: an illustrated Encyclopaedia of Marked Specimens.*

CORK | CORK, EDGE & MALKIN, Newport Pottery, Burslem. Staffordshire Potteries. 1860–71. *Earthenwares.* Formerly Cork & Edge, see above. Subsequently Edge & Malkin, q.v.

1101
1102   C E & M   Distinguishing initials found on several printed marks of differing design: name of the individual pattern is often included, 1860–71. Mark no. 1102 is a typical example.

CORKE | DAPHNE CORKE, Lexden, Colchester, Essex. 1951– . *Studio-type Pottery.*
From 1951 to 1956 Miss Corke worked at the Chelsea Pottery.

1103   Incised or painted monogram mark, 1951– .

1104   DAPHNE CORKE   Various name or initial marks used from 1959– .
1105   D. CORKE
1106   CORKE
1107   D. C.

1108

CORN

W. & E. CORN, Top Bridge Works, Longport. Staffordshire Potteries. (At Burslem, c. 1864–91.) 1864–1904. *Earthenwares.*

1109   W. & E. C.
1110   W. E. C.

Distinguishing initials found on several printed marks of differing design: name of the individual pattern is often included, c. 1864–1900. Most pre-1900 wares are unmarked.

1111–13

Printed marks, c. 1900–4.

279   CORONA
1673

See Barretts of Staffordshire Ltd.
See Gater Hall & Co.

270–1 CORONATION (WARE)
1935

See T. W. Barlow & Son Ltd.
See S. Hancock.

CORONATION

CORONATION POTTERY CO. (LTD.), Lonsdale Street, Stoke. Staffordshire Potteries. 1903–54. *Earthenwares.*
    Early wares unmarked.

1114

Printed or impressed post-war mark, c. 1947–54. "Ltd." added to style from 1947.

COTTIER

COTTIER & CO., various addresses in London, with branches in other cities. c. 1867–1902. *Decorators and Designers.*

1115   COTTIER & CO.
      LONDON

Rare painted mark on earthenware decorated by this firm, c. 1867+. A marked Minton dish with this mark in the Godden Collection is dated 1882.

COTTON

COTTON & BARLOW, Commerce Street, Longton. Staffordshire Potteries. 1850–5. *Earthenwares.*

1116   C & B

Distinguishing initials found on several printed marks of differing design: name of the individual pattern is often included, 1850–5.

COTTON   **ELIJAH COTTON (LTD.)**, Nelson Pottery (from 1889), Hanley. Staffordshire Potteries. 1880– . *Earthenwares.* Early wares unmarked.

1117–18   Printed marks, c. 1913+.

1119   Printed mark, 1956– .

2433 & 2435   COURT CHINA   *See* William Lowe.

1265   COURTNEY   *See* Derby Porcelain Works.

COUTTS   **DIANE COUTTS, MISS**, Ovingdean, Brighton, Sussex. 1956– . *Studio-type Pottery.*

1120   Impressed seal type mark, 1956– .

2370c   COWES   *See* Jo Lester.
2500a   *See* J. H. Manning.

COWLISHAW   **WILLIAM HARRISON COWLISHAW**, Letchworth, Hertfordshire. 1908–14. *Earthenwares.*
1121   ICENI WARE   Impressed mark, within a circle, 1908–14.

1145   *See* Crowan Pottery.

176	C. P.	*See* Aylesford Priory Pottery.
2338	CP (joined)	*See* Langton Pottery Ltd.
761	C. P. C. LTD.	*See* Campbellfield Pottery Co. (Ltd.).
758 935	C. P. CO.	*See* Campbellfield Pottery Co. (Ltd.). *See* Clyde Pottery (Co. Ltd.).
935	C. P. Co. G.	*See* Clyde Pottery (Co. Ltd.).
760	C. P. Co. Ltd.	*See* Campbellfield Pottery Co. (Ltd.).
1155	C. P. P. CO.	*See* Crystal Porcelain Pottery Co. Ltd.
874 879	C & R	*See* Chesworth & Robinson. *See* Chetham & Robinson.
1143a	CRAB MARK	*See* Cromer Pottery.

CRANE

WALTER CRANE, R. W. S., worked for Wedgwoods, Mintons, and Pilkingtons, and as an *Independent Designer*.

1122

Personal mark on wares or patterns designed by this artist, c. 1865–1915.

A Maw & Co. vase (c. 1889) decorated with a pattern designed by Walter Crane will be found illustrated in *British Pottery and Porcelain: an illustrated Encyclopaedia of Marked Specimens.*

CRAVEN

CRAVEN DUNNILL & CO. LTD., Jackfield, Shropshire. 1872–1951. *Decorative tiles, etc.* Formerly Hargreaves & Craven.

1123	CRAVEN & CO.	Several impressed marks were used by the above firm from
1124	CRAVEN DUNNILL & CO. JACKFIELD SALOP	about 1872; most include the name in full, but sometimes only the place name "JACKFIELD" was used, 1872–1951.
1125	JACKFIELD	

CRAWFORD

JOAN CRAWFORD (Mrs. J. Faithfull), Isle of Mull and Dalkeith, Nr. Edinburgh, Scotland. 1951– . *Studio-type Pottery.*

1126		Painted initial marks, 1951–8. The initials were sometimes incised on early wares. The name "Mull" occurs on specimens made in the Isle of Mull. Wares made at Dalkeith have only the initials "JC".
1127		Painted initial marks used from 1958.

CREIGIAU

CREIGIAU POTTERY (R. G. Southcliffe & Co. Ltd.), Creigiau, Nr. Cardiff, Wales. 1948– .

1128–31

CREIGIAU POTTERY WALES	SOUTHCLIFFE POTTERY CREIGIAU	SOUTHCLIFFE CREIGIAU WALES	CREIGIAU CARDIFF WALES

Several variations of the above name and place marks have been used impressed or printed since 1948.

2218–19 CRESCENT *See* George Jones (& Sons, Ltd.).

506 CRESCENT SHAPED *See* Bow China Works.
811–12 MARKS *See* Caughley Works.
2447–8 *See* Lowestoft Porcelain Factory.
4313–14a *See* Worcester Porcelains.

CRESSWELL

J. & W. CRESSWELL, London S.E.18. 1962– . *Studio-type Earthenwares and Stonewares.*

1132   Impressed seal mark, 1962– .

CREYKE

G. M. CREYKE & SONS, Bell Works, Hanley. Staffordshire Potteries. 1920–48. *Earthenwares.*

1133 G M C Distinguishing initials found on several printed or impressed marks, 1920–48.
1133a

1134	Made in *Broadway* ENGLAND	Printed marks, 1935+.

1135	*G.M.B.* HANLEY ENGLAND	Printed marks, 1930–48.

CRICKLADE

CRICKLADE POTTERY, Ivan and Kay Martin, Cricklade, Wiltshire. 1950– . *Studio-type Pottery.*

1136 CRICKLADE — Impressed pottery mark, 1950– .

1137 K M — Impressed initial seal type mark of Mrs. Kay Martin.

1138 — Impressed seal mark of Ivan Martin, on special pieces, 1950– .

2182 CRISTAL — *See* H. & R Johnson (Ltd.).

CROCKER

W. H. CROCKER, Bideford, Devon. Est. in 18th century. Works rebuilt in 1870. *Earthenwares.*

1139 W. H. CROCKER BIDEFORD — Incised or impressed marks, 1870–c. 1900.

CROFTS

STELLA REBECCA CROFTS, Norsey Wood, Billericay, Essex. 1925– . Individual *Animal and Bird studies in Earthenwares.*

1140 *STELLA. R. CROFTS* — Incised or painted signature, in writing letters, 1925– .

CROME

CROME POTTERY (Ethel M. Fitt), Church Road, Lowestoft, Suffolk. 1921–7. *Earthenwares.*

1141 CROME POTTERY — A circular trade-mark was registered in 1921; this comprises the end view of a sailing ship with the words "CROME POT-TERY" above, 1921–7.

CROMER

1142
1143
1143a

CROMER POTTERY
R.M.

CROMER POTTERY (Rosemary Middleton), Aylmerton, Nr. Norwich, Norfolk. 1952– . *Earthenwares.*
The incised mark "Cromer Pottery" or the painted initials "RM" (joined) occur on wares from 1952. Also the impressed crab mark.

CROSSKEYS

1144

CROSSKEYS POTTERY, Jan and Zoe Ellison, Cambridge. 1951–60.* *Studio-type Stonewares.*

Impressed seal mark used at Crosskeys Pottery, 1951–60 and subsequently as the personal mark of Mrs. Ellison on her individual stonewares made at Swaffham Bulbeck, Cambridge, from 1960.

> * Mr. Jan Ellison helped to start the first Canadian Art Pottery in the Rockies in 1919; he subsequently concentrated on sculpture in Paris and London. After the war Mr. and Mrs. Ellison turned to pottery and studied under the leading English potters before starting their own Crosskeys Pottery at Cambridge.

1019   CROSSLEY

See Commondale Pottery.

CROWAN

1145

CROWAN POTTERY (Harry and May Davis), Praze, Cornwall. 1946 to July 1962. *Studio-type Pottery.*
Mr. and Mrs. Davis emigrated to New Zealand in July 1962 and there continued potting.

Impressed seal mark, 1946 to July 1962.

1012   CROWN MARK
1322
1743a
2023
3055
3086
3258a
3376

See Collingwood & Greatbatch.
See Doric China Co.
See Goodwins & Harris.
See Hicks, Meigh & Johnson.
See Enoch Plant.
See Thomas Poole.
See John Ridgway (Co.).
See Roper & Meredith.

2846		*See* James Neale (& Co.).
4198		*See* Robert Wilson.

2781–2	CROWN CHELSEA CHINA	*See* Thomas Morris.

1904a		*See* Hammersley & Co.

CROWN   **CROWN CHINA CRAFTS LTD.**, Crown Works, Stoke. Staffordshire Potteries. 1946–58. *China and Earthenware Floral Wares.*

1146		Printed marks, 1946–58.

1053–7	CROWN CLARENCE	*See* Co-op Wholesale Society.
278	CROWN CORONA	*See* Barratts of Staffordshire Ltd.
1673a		*See* Gater Hall & Co.
1547 & 1550	CROWN DEVON	*See* S. Fielding & Co. (Ltd.).
2323	CROWN DRESDEN WARE	*See* Lancaster & Sons (Ltd.). *See* Lancaster & Sandland Ltd.
3243	CROWN DUCAL	*See* A. G. Richardson & Co. Ltd.
1590–2	CROWN FORD or CROWNFORD	*See* Ford & Sons (Ltd.).
1753	CROWN GOVAN	*See* Govancroft Potteries Ltd.
2771	CROWN MANOR	*See* Morley Fox & Co. Ltd.
3793 & 3795	CROWN POTTERY	*See* John Tams (& Sons) (Ltd.).

CROWN

CROWN STAFFORDSHIRE PORCELAIN CO. LTD.,
Minerva Works, Fenton. Staffordshire Potteries. 1889– .
China. Formerly T. A. & S. Green, q.v.
Firm restyled Crown Staffordshire *China* Co. Ltd. in 1948.

1147

Printed mark, 1889–1912.

1148–50

Printed marks, 1906+. "England" or "AD 1801" sometimes added. These marks occur on copies of antique porcelains.

1151

Printed mark, 1930+. Other examples were used for special patterns, the name "CROWN STAFFORDSHIRE" is incorporated in these marks.

1152

Standard printed trade-marks from the 1930's onwards. Various slight changes have been made over the years.

1153–4

Printed marks on specially designed tablewares, c. 1956–   and c. 1962– .

—

C R & S
or
C R & Son

See Appendix, page 715.

—

CRYSTAL PALACE
ART UNION

See Appendix, page 713.

CRYSTAL

CRYSTAL PORCELAIN POTTERY CO. LTD., Elder Road, Cobridge. Staffordshire Potteries. 1882–6. *Porcelain (and Pottery) Tiles and Plaques.*

1155 1156	C P P Co.	Distinguishing initials found on several printed or impressed marks of differing design. The dove mark, no. 1156, often occurs with these initials, 1882–6. N.B. Firms with similar title and initials are recorded.
—	CRYSTAL WARE	This painted mark occurs on an earthenware plate (in the Victoria and Albert Museum) of c. 1820–30, painted with fruit, within a gilt border. It is not a true factory mark.
3683–5	C S Co.	*See* Star China Co.
2486b & 2487	C T M	*See* C. T. Maling.
2488	C T M & SONS	*See* C. T. Maling & Sons (Ltd.).

CUBE

CUBE TEAPOTS LTD., Campbell Yard, Leicester. 1917–51. *Teapots.*

1157	CUBE	Printed or impressed marks, comprising or incorporating the name "CUBE", 1917–51.

—	CULLUM & SHARPUS	*See* Sharpus.
2471	CUMBERLAND POTTERY	*See* A. Schofield.

CUMBERLIDGE

CUMBERLIDGE & HUMPHREYS, Gordon Pottery, Tunstall. Staffordshire Potteries. 1886–9 and 1893–5.* *Earthenwares.*

1158 1158a	C & M C & M TUNSTALL	Distinguishing detail of several printed or impressed marks of differing design: name of the individual pattern is often included, 1886–9 and 1893–5.

* From 1889 to 1892 Messrs. Cumberlidge Humphreys & Hele were working the Gordon Pottery (this firm may have used a mark similar to the above but with the initials "C H & H"). In 1893 the style returned to that of Cumberlidge & Humphreys.

CURTIS		**G. R. CURTIS**, Littlethorpe Potteries, Nr. Ripon, Yorkshire. *Earthenwares.*
		The Littlethorpe Potteries (established in 1839) produce mainly unmarked horticultural pottery. Rare post-war individual pottery by Mr. Curtis is sometimes marked as nos. 1158b and c.
1158b	G. R. C.	Incised initial mark, in writing letters.
1158c	LITTLETHORPE CURTIS RIPON	Impressed mark, in circular form.
CUTTS		**JAMES CUTTS**, Shelton. Staffordshire Potteries. c. 1834–70.
1159	J. CUTTS	This signature (in writing letters) occurs on rare printed patterns, designed or engraved by this talented artist, c. 1834–70.
859 3944–5 & 3947	C V	*See* Vera Cheesman. *See* Charles Vyse.
3950	C V P	*See* Charles Vyse.
1122	C V V	*See* Walter Crane.
3974–6	C W or C W LTD.	*See* Charles Waine (& Co.) (Ltd.).
767 4163	C & W	*See* Capper & Wood. *See* James & Charles Wileman.
1968	C & W K H	*See* C. & W. H. Harvey.
—	C. Y.	*See* Group letters.
912	C Y & J	*See* Clementson, Young & Jameson.
3771	CYMRO STONE WARE	*See* Swansea (Pottery).

CYPLES

CYPLES: JOSEPH   c. 1784–95.
        MARY   c. 1795–1812.
        JESSE   c. 1805–11.
        LYDIA   c. 1812–34.
        R & W
        CYPLES   c. 1834–40.
Market St., Lane End. Staffordshire Potteries. c. 1784–1840.
Earthenwares. Subsequently Cyples, Barlow & Cyples.

| 1160 | CYPLES | Impressed name-marks occur, normally without initials to |
| 1160a | I CYPLES | show which potter of this name was responsible for the specimen. Dating by mark alone is therefore difficult. |

CYPLES

CYPLES & BARKER, Market Street, Longton. Staffordshire Potteries. 1846–7. *Earthenwares.*

| 1162 | CYPLES & BARKER | Impressed mark, 1846–7. |

| 1529 | CYPLES OLD POTTERY | *See* J. T. Fell & Co. |
| — | C. Z. | *See* Group letters. |

D

860, 1243 1250, 1253, 1261 1297–8 2349 3770	D	*See* Derby Porcelain Works. *See* Thomas Dimmock & Co. *See* David Leach. *See* Swansea Pottery.
3760	D. & CO.	*See* Swansea Pottery.
117	D. A.	*See* Dan Arbeid.
505	DAGGER DEVICE	*See* Bow China Works.

DAKIN

THOMAS DAKIN, Shelton. Staffordshire Potteries. Early 18th century. *Earthenwares.*

1163   THOMAS DAKIN MADE THIS CUP 1710   This name occurs on a slip decorated earthenware Posset pot in the Victoria and Albert Museum.

2349a   D. A. L.   *See* David Leach.

DALE

JOHN DALE, Burslem. Staffordshire Potteries. Early 19th century. *Earthenware Figures.*

     N.B. The only written reference to this potter is a record of his marriage in 1825.

1164	J. DALE BURSLEM	Impressed mark on two figures (of the Elements) in the Victoria and Albert Museum. A marked bust of Wesley is also known. Early 19th century.
1165	I. DALE BURSLEM	

The marked figures noted above are illustrated in *British Pottery and Porcelain: an illustrated Encyclopaedia of Marked Specimens.*

2830–1	DALMENY	*See* Charles W. McNay & Sons.

DALTON

WILLIAM B. DALTON, London.* 1900– .* *Studio-type Stoneware and Porcelain.*

1166 — Incised or painted monogram mark, 1900– .

* William Dalton emigrated to the United States of America in 1941. He is the author of several books on pottery.

DAN

JOHN DAN, Wivenhoe Pottery, Wivenhoe, Essex. 1953– . *Studio-type Pottery.*

1167   J. D.   Impressed seal mark of the initials J.D., 1953– .

1168   —   Incised mark of the Wivenhoe Pottery, 1953 .

480	DANESBY WARE	*See* Joseph Bourne & Son (Ltd.)

DANIEL

DANIEL & CORK, Navigation Road, Burslem. Staffordshire Potteries. 1867–9. *Earthenwares.*

1169   DANIEL & CORK   Printed mark with name of pattern, Nankin, 1867–9 on mug in Godden Collection. See *British Pottery and Porcelain: an illustrated Encyclopaedia of Marked Specimens.*

DANIEL

HENRY & RICHARD DANIEL, London Road, Stoke (also Shelton). Staffordshire Potteries. 1820–41. *Fine quality Porcelains and Pottery.*

Henry Daniel died in 1841. The Stoke works were continued by Richard Daniel.

| 1170 | H. & R. Daniel | Written mark, 1820–41. |

| 1171 | H. Daniel & Sons | Written mark, 1829–41. |

1172   Ornate printed mark on examples made for the Earl of Shrewsbury in 1827.* See also photographic reproduction on Plate 4.

* See Godden's *British Pottery and Porcelain, 1780–1850.* Chaffers' *Marks and Monograms . . .*, 15th edition, and *British Pottery and Porcelain: an illustrated Encyclopaedia of Marked Specimens.*

| 1171 | H. Daniel & Sons | *See* Henry & Richard Daniel, above. |

DANIEL

JOHN DANIEL, Cobridge. Staffordshire Potteries. c. 1770–86. *Earthenwares.*

The working period of this potter is open to some doubt. A John Daniel signed the agreement dated February 1770 not to undersell their wares. A creamware covered basket and stand is in the British Museum and is inscribed "John Daniel 1775". John Daniel is included in Tunnicliff's survey of 1786 as a manufacturer of "cream-colour and red earthenware". He may have worked later than 1786.

| 1173 | JOHN DANIEL | Incised signature mark, 1770–86. |

DANIEL

S. DANIEL, Stoke. Staffordshire Potteries. c. 1810. *Earthenwares.*

| 1174 | S. DANIEL STOKE | Printed name "mark" on earthenware mug in the Victoria and Albert Museum, c. 1810. It is probable that this "mark" relates to the engraver of the printed design, not the manufacturer. |

DANIEL

THOMAS DANIEL, Burslem. Staffordshire Potteries. 18th century.* *Earthenwares.*

| 1175 | THOMAS DANIEL | Impressed mark, in circular form, found on a fragment of an earthenware butter dish excavated at Burslem. See *Transactions of the English Ceramic Circle,* no. 1: "Excavations in North Staffordshire", by H. W. Maxwell. |

* A Thomas Daniel is recorded working at Burslem in 1785. A Cobridge potter of this name was working from at least 1750.

DANIELL

1176

A. B. & R. P. DANIELL (and other styles), New Bond St. and Wigmore Street, London W.1. c. 1825–1917. *Retailers.* Printed mark on Coalport and other wares made for this firm of retailers. Such marks would not occur before 1860 and are prior to the closure of this firm in 1917. Several other printed marks occur with Daniell's name.

DARTMOUTH

1177   DARTMOUTH HAND MADE IN ENGLAND POTTERY

1178

DARTMOUTH POTTERY LTD., Dartmouth, Devon. 1947– . *Earthenwares.* Printed or impressed mark, 1947– .

Printed mark, 1947– .

DAVENPORT

1179   Davenport
1179a   DAVENPORT

DAVENPORT (various styles: W. Davenport & Co., Davenports Ltd., etc.), Longport. Staffordshire Potteries. c. 1793–1887. *Earthenwares, Creamwares, Porcelains, Ironstone, etc.*

For further information see Jewitt's *Ceramic Art of Great Britain* (1878 and 1883).

Impressed marks with the name Davenport alone, or with an anchor. The lower-case marks (as no. 1179) are of the 1793–1810 period. Upper-case marks are subsequent to 1805.

A selection of early marks is given below, others occur.

1180–3

c. 1805–20

c. 1795+ *
Longport may occur in place of Davenport.

c. 1805–20
on "Stone china".

c. 1805–20
on "Stone china".

1181a

* A later variation of mark no. 1181 was used up to about 1860, in several instances the last two numerals of the year were placed each side of the anchor, as no 1181a. See companion illustrated encyclopaedia of marked specimens.

1184

The anchor alone occurs impressed on porcelains and earthenwares, including fine services of the 1820 period.   See *British
Pottery and Porcelain: an illustrated Encyclopaedia of Marked
Specimens*.   On a fine creamware service of 1820, some
pieces bear the impressed mark 1181, some the anchor alone.

Many different printed marks occur on earthenwares of the
1820–60 period.   A selection is reproduced but others occur
with names of different patterns and the name "Davenport".

1185–7

1188   DAVENPORT   Printed mark on porcelains, c. 1815+.   A later version is given
            LONGPORT   as mark no. 1194.

1189   DAVENPORT   Impressed mark, with or without anchor.   Note the numbers
            LONGPORT   9.80, being month and year numerals in this case for September
            9.80   1880.   Sometimes these are placed each side of an anchor;
                               these date marks only seem to occur on mid-19th century
                               earthenwares, not on Davenport porcelains.

1190

Rare mark on porcelains, c. 1830–40.
   Shaw, writing in 1837, lists William Davenport & Co. as
"Manufacturers of China to His Majesty and the Royal
Family".

            DAVENPORT   Impressed mark on porcelain plaques, often sold in the white
            PATENT   and decorated by non-Davenport artists, c. 1850–70.

1191

Printed mark in underglaze blue on porcelains, c. 1850–70.
But rarely used on pre-1830 wares.   On pre-1830 pieces the
mark is in black or colours other than blue.

1192  Printed mark on wares of registered form or pattern. For key to date of registration see page 527, c. 1842–83.

1193  Printed mark on wares sold by the firm's Liverpool shop, c. 1860–87.

1194 Printed mark on porcelains, c. 1870–86. An earlier version is given, as mark no. 1188.

1195   DAVENPORTS LTD.

1195a   DAVENPORTS LIMITED

Printed marks on earthenwares, c. 1881–7. Note use of Ltd. or Limited.

DAVENPORT

1196   D. B. & CO.

DAVENPORT BANKS & CO., Castlefield Pottery, Hanley. Staffordshire Potteries. 1860–73. *Earthenwares, Majolica, etc.* Subsequently Davenport Beck & Co., see below.
Distinguishing initials found on several printed marks of differing design; name of the individual pattern is often included, 1860–73. These initials were also used by Davenport Beck & Co., see no. 1197.

1196a   DAVENPORT BANKS & CO. ETRURIA

The name in full occurs, impressed or printed on some specimens, 1860–73.

DAVENPORT

1197   D. B. & CO.

DAVENPORT BECK & CO., Castlefield Pottery, Hanley. Staffordshire Potteries. 1873–80. *Earthenwares, Majolica, Jet, etc.* Formerly Davenport, Banks & Co. see above.
A printed mark was used, comprising a castle, the initials D. B. & Co. and "Etruria" within an oval garter, 1873–80.

DAVIE

1198 L. G. D.

LESLIE G. DAVIE, The Needles Studio, Rye, Sussex. 1954–62. *Studio-type Pottery.*
Incised initials, 1954–62.

1199

RYE

Needles mark with RYE under or L. G. DAVIE, RYE. The major pieces are signed and dated, 1954–62. See Plate I.

DAVIES

1200 H. DAVIES
PILL POTTERY

H. DAVIES, Pill, Nr. Bristol. Early 19th century. *Earthenwares.*
Unique incised mark in writing letters on red earthenware figure of a recumbent lion in the Glaisher Collection (Fitzwilliam Museum, Cambridge). See companion illustrated encyclopaedia of marked specimens.

Rhead, *British Pottery Marks*, lists this potter as DOVIES. This would appear to be incorrect although there is no record of a potter of either name at Pill.

DAVIES

1201 DAVIES & CO.

DAVIES & CO., Tyne Main Pottery, Sheriff Hill, Newcastle upon Tyne, Northumberland. 1833–51. *Earthenwares.*
Rare impressed mark on small plate, dated 1847, in the Godden Collection. Jewitt noted that this firm produced "white, printed, and lustre ware, chiefly for the Norwegian market". The above-mentioned plate is decorated with a formal floral motif in enamel and silver lustre. See *British Pottery and Porcelain: an illustrated Encyclopaedia of Marked Specimens.*

DAVIS

1202

C. DAVIS, MISS, Gwern-y-Steeple, Glamorganshire, Wales. c. 1958– . *Ceramic Jewellery, Figures and Plaques.*

Painted or incised mark, c. 1958– .

DAVIS

1203 DAVIS

DEREK M. DAVIS, Duff House, Arundel, Sussex. 1953– . *Studio-type Earthenwares.*
Painted or incised mark, 1953–9. Stonewares and tiles, c. 1959–62, are unmarked.

1203a		Painted or incised mark introduced early in 1963.

DAVIS

JOHN HEATH DAVIS, Trent Pottery, Eastwood, Hanley. Staffordshire Potteries. 1881–91. *Earthenwares.* Formerly J. H. & J. Davis.

1204	J. H. DAVIS HANLEY	Printed mark, with name of pattern. 1881–91.
1204a		Printed mark, c. 1881–91.

DAVISON

DAVISON & SON (LTD.), Bleak Hill Works, Burslem. Staffordshire Potteries. c. 1898–1952. *Earthenwares.*
    No early marks are recorded.

1205		Printed trade-mark registered in 1948, c. 1948–52.

DAWKINS

CLARE DAWKINS, MRS., Snaresbrook, London E.11. 1951– . *Studio-type Pottery.*

1206	C. D. WANSTEAD	Incised or painted mark in writing letters, 1951– .

DAWSON

DAWSON (John Dawson & Co., etc.), South Hylton and Ford Potteries, Sunderland, Durham. c. 1799–1864. *Earthenwares (printed and lustred wares, etc.)*

    For further information see *The Potteries of Sunderland and District* (1961) (Sunderland Libraries publication). Some examples will be found illustrated in the companion illustrated encyclopaedia to this mark book.

1207	DAWSON	Distinguishing details of several printed or impressed marks of
1207a	I. DAWSON	differing design, c. 1799–1848. In 1837 the firm's style was
1208	DAWSON & CO.	"Thomas Dawson & Co".

1209	DAWSON & CO. LOW FORD	Many printed marks occur, some as part of the printed design. All include the name "DAWSON", "FORD" or "SOUTH HYLTON", 1800–64.
1210	J. DAWSON & CO. LOW FORD	
1211	FORD POTTERY	
1212	J. DAWSON SOUTH HYLTON	

1208–9	DAWSON & CO.	*See* Dawson, above.
1207a	I. DAWSON	
1212	J. DAWSON	

DAWSON

SALLY DAWSON, MISS, Canonbury Studio, London N.1. September 1962*– . *Studio-type Pottery.*

| 1213 | DAWSON | Incised or painted name-mark, 1962– . |

| 1214 | | Impressed seal type mark, 1963– . The name "Canonbury Studio" may occur with these name or initial marks. |

* Miss Dawson formerly potted in Canada.

DAY

GEORGE DAY, Albion Works, Longton. Staffordshire Potteries. 1882–9. *Earthenwares.* Formerly G. & T. Day.

| 1215 | | Printed mark, 1882–9. |

| — | JOSEPH DAY | *See* Appendix, page 715. |

DAY

DAY & PRATT, Mount Pleasant Works, Longton. Staffordshire Potteries. 1887–8. *China.* Formerly J. Day & Co.

| 1216 | DAY & PRATT | Printed or impressed name-mark, 1887–8. |

| 283 | DB | *See* Dora Barrett. |
| 363 | (joined) | *See* Dora May Billington. |

| — | D. & B. | *See* Appendix, page 715. |

1196	D. B. & CO.	*See* Davenport, Banks & Co.
1197		*See* Davenport, Beck & Co.
1421		*See* Dunn, Bennett & Co. (Ltd.)

899	DC	*See* Derek Clarkson.
1038	(also joined)	*See* Delan Cookson.
1108		*See* Daphne Corke.
1120		*See* Diane Coutts.
1306		*See* R. F. Dixon & Co.

| 1280 | D & C
L | *See* Dewes & Copestake. |

| 1416–18 | D. D. & CO. | *See* David Dunderdale & Co. |

| 1459 | DE | *See* David Eeles. |
| 1487 | (also joined) | *See* Derek Emms. |

DEACON

DEACON POTTERY, London W.C.1. 1952–8. *Studio-type Pottery.*

1217

Impressed circular seal mark, 1952–8.

647   A_B

Individual examples made by Alan Brough bear his initials and indicate a date prior to 1956.

DEAKIN

DEAKIN & SON, Waterloo Works, Lane End. Staffordshire Potteries. 1833–41. *Earthenwares.*

At later dates the style was James Deakin & Co. and/or James Deakin & Son.

1218

Printed mark, 1833–41. An earthenware plate, from a dinner service, with this mark is illustrated in *British Pottery and Porcelain: an illustrated Encyclopaedia of Marked Specimens.*

DEAN

S. W. DEAN, Newport Pottery, Burslem. Staffordshire Potteries. 1904–10. *Earthenwares.* Formerly Edge, Malkin & Co., q.v. Subsequently Deans (1910) Ltd., q.v.

1219  Printed mark, 1904–10.   Other marks occur with the firm's title in full.

DEAN   THOMAS DEAN (& SONS) (LTD). Black Works, Tunstall. Staffordshire Potteries. 1789–1947.* *Earthenwares.*

1220 Printed mark, 1896–1947.

1221   Printed mark, 1937–47.
      * From 1947 to 1952 this firm operated from Adderley Teapot Works, Tunstall.

DEANS   DEANS (1910) LTD., Newport Pottery, Burslem.   Staffordshire Potteries. 1910–19. *Earthenwares.* Formerly S. W. Dean, q.v.

1222   DEANS (1910) LTD.   Printed mark with the title in full occur, 1910–19.
         BURSLEM
         ENGLAND

765   DECORO   *See* Canning Pottery Co.

DECORO   DECORO POTTERY CO. (R. H. & S. L. Plant Ltd.), Tuscan Works, Longton.   Staffordshire Potteries. 1933–49. *Earthenwares.*

1223–5

Printed marks, 1933–49.

DELAMAIN   HENRY DELAMAIN, "Irish Delft Ware Manufactory", Dublin, Ireland. c. 1752–7.* *Tin Glazed Delft-type Earthenwares.*

1226

Most of Delamain's delft wares were unmarked but some *rare* specimens have painted in underglaze blue; the initials may be read as H.D. for Henry Delamain, with Dublin added.

Henry Delamain introduced, c. 1753, the firing of delft wares by coal instead of wood as hitherto. A rare bowl dated 1753 and with an inscription relating to coal firing is in the British Museum. This and a "H.D." plate will be found illustrated in *British Pottery and Porcelain: an illustrated Encyclopaedia of Marked Specimens.*

Interesting information on Delamain is contained in Jewitt's *Ceramic Art of Great Britain* (1878).

* After the death of Delamain in January 1757 the works were continued by his widow, and then by executors until about 1770. The "H.D." examples can probably be dated 1752–7.

DE LELIVA

TRENTHAM DE LELIVA, London University. 1962– . *Studio-type Pottery, Stonewares.*

1227

Painted monogram mark, 1962– .

2257a   DELAWARE

See Henry Kennedy & Sons (Ltd).

DELLA-ROBBIA

DELLA ROBBIA COMPANY LTD. (Harold Rathbone), Birkenhead, Cheshire. 1894–1901. *Earthenwares, Tiles, Plaques, etc.*

For an early account of Harold Rathbone's Della Robbia Pottery, see *The Magazine of Art* (1896). Two examples are illustrated in II. Wakefield's *Victorian Pottery* (1962). An interesting 1896 photograph of typical wares is reproduced in the companion illustrated encyclopaedia.

1228   DELLA ROBBIA

Impressed or incised mark, c. 1894–1901.

1228a

Incised mark, c. 1894–1901. The initials above vary and relate to the decorator. These initials include C. (Charles Collis), C. A. W. (C. A. Walker), C. M. (Carlo Manzoni), L. W. (Liza Wilkins), R. B. (Ruth Bare).

| 281–2a | DELPHATIC | *See* Barratts of Staffordshire Ltd. |

| 2110a | DELPHINE | *See* Hudson & Middleton. |
| 2660–2 | | and J. H. Middleton & Co. |

| 3003 | D. E.
M. | *See* Ida S. Perrin. |

DE MORGAN

WILLIAM DE MORGAN, Chelsea, Fulham, etc., London. c. 1872–1907.* *Earthenwares, Fine glaze effects, Tiles, Vases, etc.*
   Early wares unmarked and mainly decorated blanks made by other potters.

1229   Early impressed mark, c. 1880–2.

1230   Name-mark, c. 1882+. Many name-marks occur in various forms:
   De Morgan,
   W. De Morgan,
   Wm. De Morgan,
   or D.M.
   N.B. "& Co." added to most marks after 1888.

   *William De Morgan retired from potting in 1907 but his former partners and artists continued decorating wares to about 1911.

1231   Merton Abbey address mark, other marks incorporate this name, all relate to the period 1882–8.

1232   Impressed or painted mark, 1882+.

1233   Sands End address mark. Others were used, all may be dated from 1888 onwards.

1234		Impressed initial mark, with the last two numerals of the year.
1235	D.I.P.	Several marks incorporate these initials which relate to the partners, W. De Morgan, Frank Iles, Charles and Frederick Passenger. c. 1898–1907.*
1236	F. P.	Initial marks used by the individual decorators: Frederick
1237	J. J.	Passenger (see also mark 1240), Joe Juster, Charles Passenger,
1238	C. P.	J. Hersey. These initials usually occur on 20th century speci-
1239	J. H.	mens only.
1240	F. P.	The initials F.P. also denote Fulham Pottery and were used on examples made after 1907.

    See the Victoria and Albert Museum's *Catalogue of Works by William De Morgan* (1921), H. Wakefield's *Victorian Pottery* (1962) and the companion illustrated encyclopaedia of marked specimens. *Old English Lustre Pottery* by W. John and W. Baker includes a chapter on De Morgan ware.

    *William De Morgan retired from potting in 1907 but his former partners and artists continued decorating wares to about 1911.

4017	DENABY POTTERY	*See* John Wardle & Co.
476–8 & 481	DENBY	*See* Joseph Bourne & Son (Ltd.)
DENNIS		WALTER PEN DENNIS, Ruabon, Wales. c. 1891–1901. *Tiles, etc.*
1241		Printed or impressed mark, c. 1891–1901.
DENTON		DENTON CHINA (LONGTON) LTD., Longton. Staffordshire Potteries. 1945– . *China Figures and Jewellery.*

1242   BEST BONE *Denton China* ENGLAND   Printed mark, 1945– .

1243   DERBY   *See* Derby Porcelain Works.
1247   *See* Derby Pot Works.
1263   *See* Richard Lunn.
1269
1272
2455

DERBY   **DERBY PORCELAIN WORKS** (W. Duesbury, Bloor, Royal
                     Crown Porcelain Co.), Derby. c. 1750–1848 and c. 1878– .
                     Porcelain.
                         For further information on Derby Porcelain see:
                     The Old Derby China Factory . . . , J. Haslem (1876).
                     William Chaffers' *Marks and Monograms* . . . , 15th edition.
                     Crown Derby Porcelain, F. Brayshaw Gillespy (1954).
                     Derby Porcelain, F. Brayshaw Gillespy (1961).
                     Victorian Porcelain, G. A. Godden (1961).
                         Typical specimens will be found illustrated in *British Pottery
                     and Porcelain : an illustrated Encyclopaedia of Marked Specimens.*

1243–5   *D Derby*   W D.Co   New D

          Early incised marks, all rare, c. 1750–5.   Most Derby porce-
          lains of the 1750–80 period are unmarked.

863   See photographic   Figures and groups often have unglazed bases with three darker
       reproduction,   patches or "pad" marks, showing the method by which the
       Plate 8   figure was stood during the firing process. A typical base
                           showing these patches is reproduced in Plate 8.

1246   A small painted anchor, in red, brown or gold sometimes occurs
          ⚓   on Derby porcelains of the 1760–80 period.
                               N.B. This is normally a Chelsea mark.   See also Chelsea-
                           Derby, page 141.

1247		Rare mark, incorporated in the printed design on wares printed by Richard Holdship, c. 1764–9.
1248		Painted mark, on Chinese-type patterns, variations occur, c. 1765–80.
1249		Incised mark, found on dishes, etc., and rarely on figures, c. 1770–80.

From c. 1769 to 1775 William Duesbury was working the Chelsea factory in London and then at Derby. This period is known as the Chelsea-Derby period; the following three marks were used, usually painted in gold.

860–2

Typical examples of Derby porcelains will be found illustrated in *British Pottery and Porcelain: an illustrated Encyclopaedia of Marked Specimens*.

1250		Painted Derby porcelain mark, c. 1770–82.
1251		Several copies of foreign marks have been recorded on Derby porcelains. These marks include the C.T. monogram of the Frankenthal factory. These rare marks were probably placed on replacements made at the Derby works.
1252	No. 173	Many Derby figures and groups have only the model number incised under the base, c. 1775 into Bloor period.
1253		Standard painted mark. c. 1782–1825. Painted in various colours: puce, blue and black, c. 1782–1800; red, c. 1800–25. As this mark was hand painted by different artists, many slight variations occur.

1254		Very rare painted mark, c. 1795.
1255		Mock Dresden mark painted in blue, c. 1785–1825.

1256–8

The above three marks were recorded by William Chaffers but they are *very* rare variations of the normal marks, c. 1800.

BLOOR PERIOD

1259		Printed (transferred by the thumb) mark, the earliest Bloor mark, c. 1820–40.
1260	BLOOR DERBY	Printed or painted marks occur with the words Bloor Derby surmounted by a crown or in an oval, c. 1830–40.
1261		Printed mark in red, c. 1825–40.
1262		Painted mock Sèvres mark, c. 1825–48.
1263		Printed mark in red, c. 1830–48.

The old works were closed in 1848. Some of the former artists and workmen opened a small factory in King Street,

Derby, and continued the tradition of Derby Porcelain; their marks were:

1264-6

       c. 1849-59   c. 1849-63   c. 1859-61

1267

Painted mark (or thumb transferred) used from 1861 to 1935, when the King Street factory was taken over by the Royal Crown Derby Company Ltd. See Stevenson & Hancock, page 597.

DERBY CROWN PORCELAIN COMPANY LTD. Est. 1876.

1268

Printed mark, c. 1878–90. Year cyphers occur below this mark, see table, page 204.

1269

Impressed mark on "Crown" earthenware. Potting dates may occur under this mark, i.e. 3.99 for March 1899. The word "Derby" occurs alone on porcelains, c. 1878–1900.

ROYAL CROWN DERBY PORCELAIN CO. LTD.

1270

Printed mark, c. 1890– . "Made in England" replaced the word "England", c. 1921. "Bone China" occurs on post-war marks. Year cyphers occur with this mark, see table, page 204.

DERBY YEAR CYPHERS WHICH APPEAR BELOW MARKS 1268 AND 1270.

1271

1882	1883	1884	1885	1886	1887	1888
1889	1890	1891	1892	1893	1894	1895
1896	1897	1898	1899	1900	1901	1902
1903	1904	1905	1906	1907	1908	1909
1910	1911	1912	1913	1914	1915	1916
1917	1918	1919	1920	1921	1922	1923
1924	1925	1926	1927	1928	1929	1930
1931	1932	1933	1934	1935	1936	1937
1938 I	1939 II	1940 III	1941 IV	1942 V	1943 VI	1944 VII
1945 VIII	1946 IX	1947 X	1948 XI	1949 XII	1950 XIII	1951 XIV
1952 XV	1953 XVI	1954 XVII	1955 XVIII	1956 XIX	1957 XX	1958 XXI ETC.

DERBY

1272

1273   T. RADFORD SC.
                DERBY

1273a   RADFORD fecit
          DERBY POT WORKS

DERBY POT WORKS, Cockpit Hill, Derby.   c. 1751–80. *Earthenwares (Creamware).* See *Transactions of the English Ceramic Circle*, vol. 3, part 4.

Signature or rebus marks on wares bearing printed designs by Thomas Radford or Richard Holdship, c. 1760–71. Other wares are not marked.

DERLWYN

DERLWYN POTTERY (Misses Campion & Pritchard), Betws-y-Coed, Wales. 1959– . *Studio-type Pottery.*

1274

BETWS-Y-COED

Incised or painted swallow mark, with place name and often with the initial of the potter, 1959– .

3396   DEVON MOTTO WARE

See Royal Aller Vale.

1549   DEVON WARE

See S. Fielding & Co.

DEVONMOOR

DEVONMOOR ART POTTERY (LTD.), Liverton, Newton Abbot, Devon. Est. 1913, closed c. 1914; re-opened c. 1922– . *Earthenwares.*

1275   DEVONMOOR
1276   DEVONMOOR MADE IN ENGLAND

Impressed or printed name-marks, c. 1922– .

DEVONSHIRE

DEVONSHIRE POTTERIES LTD., Bovey Tracey, Devon. 1947– . *Earthenwares.*

1277

Printed mark, 1947– .

1278

Printed or impressed mark 1956– .

1279

Printed mark or seal, 1959– .

DEWES		**DEWES & COPESTAKE,** Viaduct Works, Longton. Staffordshire Potteries. 1894–1915. *Earthenwares.*
1280	D & C L	Distinguishing detail of several printed marks of differing design: name of the individual pattern is often included, 1894–1915.
1785	D. G.	*See* David Green.
1215	DG (joined)	*See* George Day.
2035	D. H.	*See* David Hilton.
2006	DH (joined)	*See* Daphne Henson.
2137a	d i or DI (joined)	*See* D. Illingworth.
—	DIAMOND SHAPED DEVICE	*See* Registration marks, page 527.
415–17	DIAMOND CHINA	*See* Blyth Porcelain Co.
DIAMOND		**DIAMOND POTTERY CO. (LTD.),** Diamond Pottery, Hanley. Staffordshire Potteries. 1908–35. *Earthenwares.* Formerly Pearl Pottery Co.
1281 1281a	D. P. CO. D. P. CO. LTD.	Distinguishing initials found on several printed marks of differing design: name of the individual pattern is often included, 1908–35.
DIANE		**DIANE POTTERY CO.,** Heathcote Works, Longton. Staffordshire Potteries. 1960– . *China, Floral Ornaments, etc.*
1282	DIANE POTTERY LONGTON STAFFORDSHIRE	Distinguishing detail of several printed marks of differing designs, 1960– .

DICKER

DICKER POTTERY, Uriah Clark & Nephews (Ltd.), Dicker Potteries Ltd. from 1946, Lower Dicker, Sussex. 1843–1959. *Earthenwares.*

1283   DICKER   Early incised mark.   Most early wares are unmarked.

1284   DICKER, SUSSEX   Impressed marks on two specimens, c. 1911, in the Fitzwilliam
1285   U. C. & N.   Museum, Cambridge.   It should be noted that these two speci-
            THE DICKER   mens bear very early dates—1782 and 1801—and are mislead-
            SUSSEX   ing.   Similar examples are in the Godden Collection and are copies of Sussex traditional pottery with inlaid inscriptions, dates, etc.

1286   DICKER WARE   Trade-name registered in 1933.

1286a   DICKER WARE   Impressed mark in circular form, c. 1933–59.
            MADE IN ENGLAND

DICKINSON

N. DICKINSON, Worthing, Sussex.   1948– .   *Studio-type Pottery.*

1287   [N]   Initial mark, 1948– .

DILLON

FRANCIS DILLON, Cobridge. Staffordshire Potteries. 1834–43. *Earthenwares.*

1288   DILLON   Impressed name-mark, 1834–43.

1288a   F. D.   Distinguishing detail of several printed marks of differing design: name of the individual pattern is often included, c. 1834–43.

3768   DILLWYN   *See* Swansea (Porcelain **or** Pottery).
3754   DILLWYN & CO.
3764

3772   DILLWYN'S   *See* Swansea (Pottery).
            ETRUSCAN
            WARE

DIMMOCK

J. DIMMOCK & CO., Albion Works, Hanley.   Staffordshire Potteries.   1862–1904.   *Earthenwares.*   Formerly Thomas Dimmock & Co., q.v.

1289   J. D. & CO.

1290

Distinguishing initials or monogram found on printed marks of differing design: name of the individual pattern is often included, 1862–78.

From c. 1878 this firm was under the proprietorship of W. D. Cliff and his name occurs in most marks.

1291–2   CLIFF
         ALBION CHINA

Impressed marks, c. 1878–90.

1293–6

Printed marks, c. 1878–1904.

DIMMOCK

THOMAS DIMMOCK (Junr) **& CO.**, Albion St. (c. 1828–59), Tontine St. (c. 1830–50), Shelton (also at Hanley).   Staffordshire Potteries.   1828–59.   *Earthenwares.*

1297   D.

Distinguishing initial found on several printed marks of differing design: name of the individual pattern is often included, 1828–59.   Mark no. 1299 is a typical example.

1298

Although this initial fits other firms of the period (Davenports, etc.) the mark reproduced occurs on a design registered by this firm in 1844.

1299

Many such marks occur and may be dated, c. 1828–59.

1300

This monogram mark occurs impressed or in conjunction with printed marks as no. 1301, 1828–59.

1301  N.B. There were many potters named Dimmock working in the Staffordshire Potteries during the 19th century.

DIMMOCK

1302   D. & S.   **DIMMOCK & SMITH,** Tontine Street, Hanley. Staffordshire Potteries. 1826–33 and 1842–59. *Earthenwares.* Distinguishing initial of several printed marks of differing design: name of the individual pattern is often included. By the general style of the wares these marks would seem to relate to the second period of this firm—1842–59.

DINKY

    DINKY ART POTTERY CO. LTD., Ruby Works, Longton. Staffordshire Potteries. 1931–47. *Earthenwares.*

1303      Printed mark, 1931–47.

1235   D. I. P.   *See* William De Morgan.

2907   DISLEY   *See* C. D. Nowell.

3743   DIXON & CO.   *See* Sunderland.
3744   DIXON AUSTIN
3746   (& CO.)
3745   DIXON AUSTIN, PHILLIPS & CO.

DIXON

    JAMES DIXON & SON(S), Cornish Street, Sheffield 1. 1822–33 and "& Sons" from 1833– . *Manufacturers of Sheffield Plate, Britannia Metal and Silver Wares.*

1304   PUBLISHED BY JAS DIXON & SONS SHEFFIELD MARCH 1st 1842   Attractive earthenware jugs (with metal covers) in the Godden Collection bear these marks. The second mark appears on a jug which was the first ceramic object registered under the 1842–83 Design Registration Act. See *British Pottery and Porcelain: an illustrated Encyclopaedia of Marked Specimens.*

1305   Messrs. James Dixon & Sons did not manufacture earthenwares; the designs were registered in their name and the objects were mounted by them.

3747 DIXON PHILLIPS *See* Sunderland.
      & CO.

DIXON R. F. DIXON & CO.,* Ruby Porcelain Works, Longton. Staffordshire Potteries. 1916–1929. *China and Earthenwares.*

1306   Printed mark, 1916–29.

    * Messrs. Dixon & Co. were London retailers and importers. At the period listed they employed this mark on wares made for them at the Ruby Porcelain Works, Longton.

2254–5 DK   *See* Dorothy Kemp.
        (joined)
—   D. & K. R. *See* Appendix, page 715.
1444   *See* Edge Malkin & Co.

2940   D. K. W.   *See* Oxshott Pottery.

2869   DL   *See* Newlyn Harbour Pottery.
        (joined)

2403   D. L. & CO. *See* David Lockhart & Co.

2404   D. L. & S. *See* David Lockhart & Sons.
2405   or
        D. L. & SONS.

1232   D. M.   *See* William De Morgan.
1234   *See* Donald Mills.
2678

2523   DMB   *See* Dorothy B. Martin.
        (joined)

2651   D. M. & S. *See* David Methven & Sons.

1287	ⅅ	*See* N. Dickinson.

1948	D. N. H.	*See* D. N. Harding.

DODD

R. DODD, Dykes Studio, Henfield, Sussex. 1961– . *Studio-type Pottery.*

1307	Ⲙ𝖯	Impressed seal type mark, 1961– .

DOE

DOE & ROGERS, High St., Worcester. c. 1820–40.
Doe & Rogers were *decorators* of porcelain at Worcester. Each was formerly employed at the Chamberlain Works; their wares are normally marked in writing letters:

1308, 1308a

Doe & Rogers, Worcester, or rarely Doe & Rogers, 17 High St., Worcester.
Typical examples are illustrated in *British Pottery and Porcelain: an illustrated Encyclopaedia of Marked Specimens.*

1313 261 263	DON	*See* below and Samuel Barker & Son.

DON

DON POTTERY, Swinton, Yorkshire. 1790–1893 (various proprietorships). *Earthenwares.*

1309	DON POTTERY	Impressed or painted mark, c. 1790–1830.
1310	DON POTTERY GREEN	Distinguishing detail of several impressed or printed marks of differing design, 1800–34.
1311	GREEN DON POTTERY	
1312	A T R	These initials have formerly been ascribed to the Don Pottery. It would not seem to have been a regular mark and may not relate to this pottery.
1313	DON	A relief pad mark occurs on some specimens, with the one word "Don", 1810–30.

1314   Impressed or printed crest mark, 1820–34. A variation has the words "Green Don Pottery".

1315 BARKER DON POTTERY The above mark occurs from 1834 with the name "Barker", see page 55 where other late Don Pottery marks are recorded under Samuel Barker & Son. c. 1834–93.

DONOVAN JAMES DONOVAN, George's Quay, Dublin, Ireland. c. 1770–1829.

James Donovan (& Son) *decorated* English porcelain and earthenwares. The last entry in local directories is for the year 1829. Some examples are signed as marks nos. 1316–18. Painted name-marks, c. 1790–1829.

1316 DONOVAN
1317 DONOVAN DUBLIN

1318 DONOVAN'S IRISH MANUFACTORY The name rarely occurs *impressed* on wares made to the order of James Donovan. The last mark occurs on a mug in the Godden Collection painted over the Derby factory mark of c. 1790.

DONYATT DONYATT (PIT POTTERY), Somerset.

From the 17th century into the 20th century there were small country potteries in and around Donyatt. Most of their earthenwares are unmarked.

Examples made at the Pit Pottery, Donyatt, in 1910 for Dr. J. W. L. Glaisher bear incised marks:

1319, 1320 DONYATT   DONYATT POTTERY
See also James Rogers.

DORIC DORIC CHINA CO., China St., Fenton. (c. 1924–6), High St., Longton. Staffordshire Potteries. 1924–35.* *China.*

1321 DORIC Impressed or printed Doric marks, 1924–35.

1322–3 Printed marks, 1926–35.*

1324 Printed mark, 1934–5.

* Firm taken over by Royal Albion China Co., q.v., who used similar "Doric" marks.

DORINCOURT

DORINCOURT POTTERS, Leatherhead Court, Surrey. 1952. *Decorated Tiles, etc.*

1325 DORINCOURT POTTERS

Impressed or printed marks, 1952– .

1326

1587 DOROTHY DALE *See* Ford & Sons (Ltd).

DOULTON

DOULTON & CO. (LTD.),* Nile St., *Burslem.* Staffordshire Potteries. c. 1882– . *Earthenwares and Porcelains.*

* Formerly Pinder Bourne & Co., q.v. Retitled Doulton Fine China Ltd. from October 1955.

1327 DOULTON Impressed mark, 1882+.

1328–32 DOULTON & SLATERS PATENT

Early printed or impressed, c. 1882–1902. "England" added in 1891. The production of china was added to that of earthenware in 1884.

1333–4  Standard printed mark, no. 1333, c. 1902– . "Made in England" added from c. 1930 onwards. Variations occur with names of different effects under "Flambe", "Titanian", etc.

1335-6	ROYAL DOULTON FLAMBÉ ROYAL DOULTON KALON	Special marks for individual styles of decoration, c. 1900+.
1337		Variation of mark no. 1333, used c. 1922-7.
1338	ENGLISH TRANSLUCENT CHINA	Wording added below standard mark no. 1334 from January 1960 to denote new type of body.

DOULTON

DOULTON & CO. (LTD.), *Lambeth*, London S.E.   c. 1858–1956. *Earthenwares and Stonewares.* Formerly Doulton & Watts, q.v.

* Production ceased at Lambeth in March 1956, the Burslem works continued.

1339	DOULTON LAMBETH	Impressed mark, c. 1858+. N.B. Decorative wares date from c. 1870 onwards.
1340		Impressed mark, c. 1869–77. The year of production appears in the centre of this mark from 1872. A circular variation of this mark was rarely used.
1341		Impressed mark, c. 1877–80. The year of production is normally incised in the clay.
1342		Impressed or printed mark on earthenware (not stoneware), c. 1872+.
1343		Impressed mark on stonewares, c. 1880–1902. "England" added from 1891. N.B. From 1872 to 1888 the year of production was impressed or incised on each piece, with the mark of the artist, see pages 216–19.
1344	DOULTON LAMBETH ENGLAND	Impressed mark on stonewares of small size, c. 1891–1956.

1345   Impressed mark on Impasto wares, c. 1879–1900.

1346   Impressed mark on special wares, c. 1886–1914.

1347   Impressed or printed mark on special wares, c. 1887–1900.

1348   Impressed mark on Silicon wares, c. 1881–1912. "England" added from 1891.

1349   Impressed mark on earthenwares, c. 1881–1910.

1350   Impressed mark on Carrara wares, c. 1888–98.

1351   Standard impressed mark, c. 1902–22 and c. 1927–36.

From 1902 to 1914 an impressed shield occurs with lower-case letters. These denote the year of potting. c = 1902, d = 1903 and so on to o for 1914.

1352   Impressed mark on wares produced by the slip cast method, c. 1912–56.

1353		Rare monogram mark on hard paste white figures, c. 1918–32.
1354–5		Variations of mark no. 1351 but without crown under lion, c. 1922+.
1356		Printed or impressed mark on Persian styled wares, c. 1920–8.

MONOGRAMS USED BY SOME DOULTON ARTISTS
(Compiled from information kindly supplied by the former Doulton employee and historian, Mr. W. T. Fairhall.)

1357		Arthur B. Barlow, c. 1872–9.
1358		Florence E. Barlow, c. 1873–1909.
1359		Hannah B. Barlow, c. 1872–1906.
1360		John Broad, c. 1873–d. 1919.
1361		Frank A. Butler, c. 1873–1911.
1362		Mary Butterton, c. 1875–c. 1890.
1363		Mary Capes, c. 1876–83.

1364	Ⓜ	Miss F. M. Collins, c. 1875–80.
1365	ℚℳ	Minna L. Crawley, c. 1876–83.
1366	𝔇	Louisa J. Davis, c. 1873–90.
1367	W𝔈	William E. Dunn, c. 1883–95.
1368	³L𝓔	Louisa E. Edwards, c. 1873–90.
1369	J𝔈	John Eyre, c. 1884–90.
1370	**AH**	Miss Agnete Hoy, c. 1952–7, or signature in full.
1371	F ℰL	Francis E. Lee, c. 1875–90.
1372	ℱ	Florence Lewis, c. 1875–97.
1373	ℱL	Florence M. Linnell, c. 1880–5.
1374	ℰDL	Edith D. Lupton, c. 1876–89.
1375	JHM	John H. McLennan or signature in full, c. 1880–1910.
1376	M·V·M	Mark V. Marshall, 1876–1912.

1377	Mary Mitchell, 1876–87.
1378	Arthur E. Pearce, 1873–1930.
1379	Frank C. Pope, 1880–1923.
1380	Florence C. Roberts, c. 1879–1930.
1381	Kate Rogers, c. 1880–92.
1382	William Rowe, 1883–1939.
1383	Henry Simeon, 1894–1936.
1384	Eliza Simmance, c. 1873–1928.
1385	Katie Sturgeon, c. 1880–3.
1386	George Hugo Tabor, c. 1878–90.
1387	Margaret E. Thompson, c. 1900.
1388	George Tinworth, 1867–1913.

1389	**Watt**	Linnie Watt, c. 1880–6.

N.B. These artist's monograms are not indexed. For further information on Doulton wares and artists, see:
The A.B.C. of XIX Century English Ceramic Art, J. F. Blacker (ND).
Marks and Monograms ..., W. Chaffers' new 15th edition (1964).
Victorian Pottery, H. Wakefield, 1962.
Typical examples will also be found illustrated in *British Pottery and Porcelain: an illustrated Encyclopaedia of Marked Specimens*.

—   Doulton Fine China Ltd.   *See* Doulton & Co. (Ltd.), *Burslem*.

1346   DOULTON & SLATER'S PATENT   *See* Doulton & Co. Ltd., Burslem and Lambeth.

DOULTON

DOULTON & WATTS, Lambeth, London S.E. c. 1815–58. *Stonewares and Terra-cotta*. Subsequently Doulton & Co., *Lambeth*.
For further information and illustrations of typical specimens see Blacker's *The A.B.C. of English Salt Glaze Stoneware* (1922).

1390   DOULTON & WATTS   Distinguishing detail of several impressed, moulded or incised
1391   DOULTON & WATTS   marks of differing design, c. 1815–58.
    LAMBETH POTTERY
    LONDON
1392   LAMBETH POTTERY
    DOULTON & WATTS
    I HIGH STREET
    LAMBETH

Items printed on a Doulton & Watts bill-head of 1847 include: "Chemical apparatus of every description . . . made to the size of 3co gallons, Royal Patent Water Filters, Bottles & Jars, Ale & Porter Bottles, covered jars, &c. &c. Terra Cotta vases, Statues, Fountains and all kinds of Architectural Work". Unusual items on this 1847 bill include "1 Gross Whistles, 1 Gross Toy Faces, 3 dozen Bacchus creams".

307	DOVE AND BRANCH	*See* Frank Beardmore & Co.
886	MARK	*See* Christie & Beardmore.
1156		*See* Crystal Porcelain Pottery Co. Ltd.
2127		*See* Hulme & Christie.

DOVE   DOVE POTTERY (Audrey Martyn), Hammersmith, London W.6. 1959– . *Earthenwares.*

1393	THE DOVE POTTERY	Painted mark, 1959– .

—	H. DOVIES	*See* H. Davies.
1217	ℙ	*See* Deacon Pottery.
1281	D. P. CO.	*See* Diamond Pottery Co. (Ltd.).
1396	or	*See* Dresden Porcelain Co.
1397–9	D. P. CO. L	
1281a	D. P. CO. LTD.	*See* Diamond Pottery Co. (Ltd.).
3141	D/PW	*See* Powell & Wells Studio Pottery.
3246	D. R.	*See* Donald Richards.
1228a	D. R. (& Ship)	*See* Della Robbia Company Ltd.
—	DRAB PORCELAIN	*See* Appendix, page 715.

DRESDEN   DRESDEN FLORAL PORCELAIN CO. LTD., Longton. Staffordshire Potteries. 1945–56. *China Figures and Floral Wares.*

1395		Printed mark, 1945–56.

DRESDEN   DRESDEN PORCELAIN CO., Blythe Works, Longton. Staffordshire Potteries. 1896–1904. *Porcelains.* Formerly T. Forrester & Son, q.v. Subsequently Blyth Porcelain Co. Ltd., q.v.

| 1396 | D. P. CO. | Distinguishing initials found on several printed or impressed |
| 1397 | D. P. CO. L. | marks of differing design: name of the individual pattern is often included, 1896–1904. |

1398   Printed mark, 1896–1903.

1399   Printed mark, 1903–4.

DRESSER
1400   CHR. DRESSER   **CHRISTOPHER DRESSER** (1834–1904). *Designer*.
This signature, in writing letters, occurs on Ault (1891–6) and Linthorpe pottery (c. 1879–82) designed by Dresser who also designed for Mintons and Wedgwoods.

DREYDEL   **HENRY DREYDEL & CO.**, London. Late 19th century. *Retailers and Importers*.

1401   This mark usually occurs on foreign china imported and sold by this firm but some examples bearing this mark are of English manufacture. Late 19th century.

1214	D. S.	*See* Sally Dawson.
—	D. & S.	*See* Appendix, page 715.
1302		*See* Dimmock & Smith.
3882		*See* Marianne de *Trey*.
1226	DUBLIN	*See* Henry Delamain.
1934	DUCHESS	*See* A. T. Finney & Sons (Ltd.).
1458	DUCHESS CHINA	*See* Edwards & Brown.
1934		*See* S. Hancock & Sons.

DUCKWORTH RUTH DUCKWORTH, Kew, Surrey. 1956– . *Studio-type Pottery and Sculpture.*

1402   Painted or incised mark, 1956– .

DUCROZ DUCROZ & MILLIDGE, Lane End, Staffordshire Potteries. Mid-19th century. *Earthenwares.*

1403 DUCROZ & MILLIDGE This potter is listed by Chaffers and other authorities, but the present writer has not traced this firm in the Staffordshire rate records nor does it occur in the lists compiled by Alfred Meigh.

The above name occurs with the Royal Arms and the words "Royal Terra Cotta Porcelain" on a sauce tureen stand in the Victoria and Albert Museum (c. 2600 –1901)

1404   DUDSON *See* Dudson Bros. (Ltd.) below.
1407–9 *See* James Dudson.

DUDSON DUDSON BROS. (LTD.), Hope Street, Hanley. Staffordshire Potteries. 1898– . *Earthenwares, Jaspers, etc.* Formerly J. T. Dudson, q.v.

1404 DUDSON ENGLAND Impressed or printed marks, 1898+. "Hanley" may be
1405 DUDSON BROTHERS ENGLAND incorporated in these marks.

1406   Printed mark, 1936–45.

1407   Printed mark, 1945– .

1408	DUDSON HANLEY ENGLAND VITRIFIED STONEWARE	Impressed or printed mark, 1945– . Year numbers occur under this mark.

DUDSON

JAMES DUDSON, Hope & Hanover Streets, Hanley. Staffordshire Potteries. 1838–88. *Earthenwares, Figures, etc.* Subsequently J. T. Dudson, see next entry.

1409   DUDSON   Impressed mark, found on mid-19th century moulded jugs. Most Dudson wares were unmarked but an advertisement of 1886, reproduced in the companion illustrated encyclopaedia of marked specimens, shows typical Dudson type Jasper wares in the Wedgwood style.

DUDSON

J. T. DUDSON, Hope Street, Hanley. Staffordshire Potteries. 1888–98. *Earthenwares, Jaspers, etc.* Formerly James Dudson, previous entry. Subsequently Dudson Bros., q.v.

1410   J. DUDSON   Impressed marks, 1888–98.
1411   J. DUDSON
        ENGLAND

DUDSON

DUDSON, WILCOX & TILL LTD., Britannic Works, Hanley. Staffordshire Potteries. 1902–26. *Earthenwares.*

1412–13   Printed or impressed marks, 1902–26.

DUKE

SIR JAMES DUKE & NEPHEWS, Hill Pottery, Burslem. Staffordshire Potteries. c. 1860–3. *Porcelains, Parians, etc.* Formerly S. Alcock & Co. Subsequently Hill Pottery Co. Ltd.

    See Jewitt's *The Ceramic Art of Great Britain* and *British Pottery and Porcelain: an illustrated Encyclopaedia of Marked Specimens.*

1414  Impressed hand mark, c. 1860–3.

DUNCOMBE E. DUNCOMBE, MISS, Wimbledon, London S.W.19. 1953– . *Studio-type Pottery.*

1415 Incised or painted mark, 1953– . Stonewares have been produced from 1962.

DUNDERDALE DAVID DUNDERDALE & CO., Castleford Pottery, Castleford, Yorkshire. c. 1790–1820. *Earthenwares, Creamwares, Jasper-type Stonewares.*

Pottery subsequently worked by many different firms, see T. Nicholson & Co.

See Jewitt's *The Ceramic Art of Great Britain.* Marked examples will be found illustrated in *British Pottery and Porcelain: an illustrated Encyclopaedia of Marked Specimens.*

1416	D. D. & CO.	Distinguishing detail of several impressed marks, c. 1790–1820.
1417	D. D. & CO. CASTLEFORD	The typical so-called Castleford Jasper-type stoneware teapots, etc., are seldom marked. Some bear only a number, usually
1418	D. D. & CO. CASTLEFORD POTTERY	"22".

DUNMORE DUNMORE POTTERY (CO.), (Peter Gardner), Airth, Stirlingshire, Scotland. c. 1860–1903. c. 1903–11. *Earthenwares.*

See J. Arnold Fleming's *Scottish Pottery* (1923) and *British Pottery and Porcelain: an illustrated Encyclopaedia of Marked Specimens.*

1419	PETER GARDNER DUNMORE POTTERY	An impressed mark occurs comprising the name Peter Gardner in the border of a circle with the name "Dunmore Pottery" in
1420	DUNMORE	the centre of the circle. The impressed mark Dunmore also occurs, c. 1860–1903. From 1903–c. 1911 the style was the "Dunmore Pottery Co."

DUNN		**DUNN BENNETT & CO. (LTD.)**, Royal Victoria Works, Burslem. Staffordshire Potteries. Established at Hanley, 1875– . *Earthenwares.*
1421	D. B. & CO.	Distinguishing initials found on several printed marks of differing design, c. 1875–1907. The basic mark shows a beehive, as no. 1422. "Ltd." may occur from 1907 onwards.

1422 —

1423 — Printed mark, 1937– .

1424 — Printed mark on wares made of Ironstone body, 1955– .

DUNN CONSTANCE DUNN, MRS. (Miss Wade), various addresses. 1924– . *Studio-type Pottery.*
   See G. Wingfield Digby's *The Work of the Modern Potter in England* (1952).

1425 — Incised mark, 1924– .

2058	DUNSTER	*See* George F. Holland.
3176		*See* Protean Pottery.

DURA DURA PORCELAIN CO. LTD., Empress Pottery, Hanley. Staffordshire Potteries. 1919–21. *Porcelain.*

1426 — Printed mark, 1919–21.

DURHAM DURHAM CHINA CO. LTD., Earlsway Team Valley, Gateshead, Co. Durham. 1947–57. *China and Earthenwares.*

1427   Printed or impressed marks based on this device occur. The style in full and "Made in England" also occurs, 1947–57.

DUXHURST   **DUXHURST,** Children's Village Potters (Lady Henry Somerset), Homes of the Holy Redeemer, Duxhurst, Surrey. 1919–23. *Earthenwares.*

1428   CHILDREN'S VILLAGE POTTERS DUXHURST   A circular mark, comprising a small boy on a duck, surrounded by the words "Children's Village Potters, Duxhurst" was registered in 1919.

A company styled Duxhurst Pottery Ltd. was probably a continuation of this venture, see next entry.

DUXHURST   **DUXHURST POTTERY LTD.,** Duxhurst, Reigate, Surrey. c. 1923–4. *Earthenwares.*

1429   DUXHURST   Impressed or printed mark, c. 1923–4.

—   D. W.   *See* Appendix, page 715.
1624   DW (joined)   *See* Robert & Sheila Fournier.

1757   D. W. G.   *See* Dorothy W. Gow.

964   D. Z.   *See* Cobham Pottery Ltd.
4398   *See* Douglas Zadek.

E

| | E. | *See* Appendix, page 716. |
| 753a | | *See* Estella Campavias. |

| 1853 | EAGLE mark | *See* F. Grosvenor (& Son). |

| 262 | EAGLE & CORONET | *See* Samuel Barker & Son. |

EARDLEY

EARDLEY & HAMMERSLEY, Church Bank Works, Tunstall. Staffordshire Potteries. 1862–6. *Earthenwares.* Formerly Beech & Hancock, q.v. Subsequently Ralph Hammersley, q.v.

| 1430 | E. & H. | Distinguishing initials found on several printed marks of differing design: name of the individual pattern is often included, 1862–6. |

EARDLEY

EARDLEY, SPEAR & CO., Well Street Pottery, Tunstall. Staffordshire Potteries. 1873. *Earthenwares.*

| 1431 | E. S. & CO. | A printed mark comprising these initials and the name of the pattern was used c. 1873. |

EARTH

EARTH POTTERIES (John Cole), London S.E.3. c. 1937. *Studio-type Pottery.*

| 1432 | EARTH | Impressed marks on specimens in Victoria and Albert Museum, |
| 1433 | EARTH POTTERIES | purchased in 1937. |

EASTGATE		**EASTGATE POTTERIES LTD.,** Withernsea, E. Yorkshire. 1955– . *Earthenwares.*

1434

A printed mark depicting a gate on which is added the word Eastgate, with England under, 1955– .

1435   WOODLAND   Trade-name on animal models.

202   EASTWOOD   *See* William Baddeley.

—   E. B.   *See* Appendix, E. Booth.
243   *See* Eric Barber.
544   *See* E. Brain & Co. Ltd.

1437   E. B. & B.   *See* Edge, Barker & Barker.

540–1   E. B. & CO.   *See* E. Brain & Co. Ltd.
1438   *See* Edge Barker & Co.

537–8   E. B. & CO. F.   *See* E. Brain & Co. Ltd.

1513   E. & B.   *See* Evans & Booth.

429   E. B. J. D.   *See* E. J. D. Bodley.

483   E. B. & J. E. L. or E. B. J. E. L.   *See* Bourne & Leigh Ltd.

1458   E. & B. L. or   *See* Edwards & Brown.
1457   E. & B. L.

2521a   E. B. M.   *See* Martin Bros.

442   E. B. & S.   *See* Ephraim Booth & Son.

835   E. C.   *See* Edward Challinor.
1015   *See* Ernest Collyer.

753	E ⊥ C	*See* Estella Campavias.
837	E. & C. C.	*See* E. & C. Challinor.
—	E. C. & C.	*See* Appendix.
1415	E. D.	*See* E. Duncombe.

EDGE

WILLIAM & SAMUEL EDGE, Market Street, Lane Delph. Staffordshire Potteries. 1841–8. *Earthenwares.*

1436   W. & S. E.   Distinguishing initials found on several printed marks of differing design: name of the individual pattern is often included, 1841–8.

EDGE

EDGE, BARKER & BARKER, Fenton. Staffordshire Potteries. 1836–40. *Earthenwares.* Formerly Edge Barker & Co., see next entry.

1437   E. B. & B.   Distinguishing initials found on several printed marks of differing design, 1836–40. One example occurs on a jug depicting William IV (1830–7).

EDGE

EDGE BARKER & CO., Fenton and Lane End. Staffordshire Potteries. 1835–6. *Earthenwares.* Subsequently Edge, Barker & Barker, see previous entry.

1438   E. B. & CO.   Distinguishing initials found on several printed marks of differing design: name of the individual pattern is often included, 1835–6.

EDGE

EDGE & GROCOTT, Tunstall. Staffordshire Potteries. *Earthenware Figures.*

This partnership is not mentioned in the Staffordshire directories or rate records. Daniel Edge worked at Waterloo Road, Burslem, c. 1834–42 and Samuel Grocott at Liverpool Road, Tunstall, 1828–30. The above partnership would appear to be of short duration, c. 1830.

1439	EDGE & GROCOTT	This mark occurs on rare Staffordshire figures (of Walton type), c. 1830.

EDGE

EDGE MALKIN & CO. (LTD.), Newport and Middleport Potteries, Burslem. Staffordshire Potteries. 1871–1903. *Earthenwares.* Formerly Cork, Edge & Malkin, q.v. Subsequently S. W. Dean, q.v.

1440	EDGE, MALKIN & CO.	Impressed mark, c. 1871–1903.
1441 1442	E. M. & CO. E. M. & CO. B.	Distinguishing initials found on several printed marks of differing design: name of the individual pattern is often included, 1871–1903. "Ltd." may be added from 1899.
1443		A typical printed mark, c. 1871–80.
1444	D. & K. R.	A printed mark of the Royal Arms above these initials occurs on a design registered at the Patent Office in 1873 in the name of Edge, Malkin & Co. The initials probably relate to the firm for whom the pattern was made.
1445		Standard printed mark registered in 1873. Slight variations occur—the name of the pattern in place of the words "trade mark", c. 1873–1903.
1456	EDWARDS	*See* James & Thomas Edwards.
1448	EDWARDS D. H.	*See* James Edwards & Son.

EDWARDS

JAMES EDWARDS & SON, Dale Hall, Burslem. Staffordshire Potteries. 1851–82. *Earthenwares, Ironstone, etc.* Formerly James Edwards, c. 1842–51. Subsequently Knapper & Blackhurst, q.v.

1446	J. E. & S.	Distinguishing detail of several printed or impressed marks of
1447	STONE CHINA JAMES EDWARDS & SON. DALE HALL	differing design. DALE HALL or D. H. occurs on most marks of this firm, c. 1851–82.
1448	EDWARDS D. H.	

EDWARDS

JOHN EDWARDS (& CO.), King St., Fenton. Staffordshire Potteries. 1847–1900. *China and Earthenwares.*

John Edwards commenced potting at Longton, c. 1847; he moved to Fenton, c. 1853.

1449	J. E.	Distinguishing initials found on several impressed or printed
1450	J. E. & Co.	marks of differing design, 1847–73. "& Co." added to style for period c. 1873–9.

1451–2		Printed marks, c. 1880–1900.

EDWARDS

J. C. EDWARDS (J. C. Edwards (Ruabon) Ltd.), Trefynant Works, Ruabon, N. Wales. 19th century to 1958. *Terra-cotta and Earthenware Tiles, etc.*

1453	J. C. E.	Impressed mark, c. 1880–1958.

EDWARDS

JAMES & THOMAS EDWARDS, Kilncroft Works, c. 1839, Sylvester Street, c. 1841, Burslem. Staffordshire Potteries. 1839–41. *Earthenwares.*

1454	J. & T. E.	Distinguishing detail of several impressed or printed marks of
1455	J. & T. EDWARDS B.	differing design: name of the individual pattern is often included, 1839–41.
1456	EDWARDS	A printed pattern was registered in September 1841 and this has a mark comprising a sailing vessel, with the words "Boston Mail" above, and "Edwards" below, see companion illustrated encyclopaedia.

EDWARDS		**EDWARDS & BROWN**, Victoria Works, Longton. Staffordshire Potteries. 1882–1933. *China.*
1457	E. & B. L.	Distinguishing initials found on several impressed or printed marks of differing design: name of the individual pattern is often included, 1882–1910.
1458		Printed mark, 1910–33.

EELES		**DAVID EELES**, Shepherd's Well Pottery, London N.W.3. 1955–1962. Mosterton, Dorset (from July 1962–). *Studio-type Pottery, Tiles, etc.*
1459	D. E.	Incised, impressed or painted initials on wares made by David Eeles, 1955– .
1460		Impressed mark of the Shepherd's Well Pottery, c. 1955– .
4264	E. & E. W.	*See* Enoch Wood & Sons.
421	E. F. B. or	*See* Edward F. Bodley & Co.
420	E. F. B. & CO.	
425	E. F. B. & S. or	*See* Edward F. Bodley & Son.
424	E. F. B. & SON	
1561	E. F. K. L.	*See* John Thomas Firth.
—	E. G.	*See* Appendix, page 716.
1519b	E. G. & C.	*See* Everard, Glover & Colclough.
3008a	E. & G. P.	*See* Edward & George Phillips.
—	E. H.	*See* Appendix.
2004	EH	*See* E. Henderson.
3836	(monogram)	*See* Theda Pottery.

1430	E. & H.	*See* Eardley & Hammersley.

EHLERS A. W. G. EHLERS, Lowerdown Cross, Bovey Tracey, Devon. 1946–55. *Studio-type Pottery.*

1461   Incised or painted mark, 1946–55.

372	E. I. B.	*See* Edmund John Birch.
2214	E. J.	*See* Elijah Jones.
429	E. J. D. B. or	*See* E. J. D. Bodley.

430

1464	E. K. B.	*See* Elkin Knight & Bridgwood.
1466	E. K. & CO.	*See* Elkin Knight & Co.
2256	E. K. N. N.	*See* Kenn Pottery.
2371	E. L.	*See* Eileen Lewenstein.

ELEKTRA ELEKTRA PORCELAIN CO. LTD., Edensor Works, Longton. Staffordshire Potteries. 1924– . *Earthenwares.*

1462   Printed mark, 1924– .

1463   Printed mark, c. 1940– .

3798 ELEPHANT BRAND *See* John Tams (& Sons) (Ltd.).
      or mark

ELKIN		**ELKIN, KNIGHT & BRIDGWOOD,*** The Foley Potteries, Fenton. Staffordshire Potteries. c. 1827–40. *China and Earthenwares.* Formerly Elkin Knight & Co. and Elkin Knight & Elkin. Subsequently Knight & Elkin or Knight Elkin & Co.
1464	E. K. B.	Distinguishing initials found on several printed marks of differing design: name of the individual pattern is often included, 1827–40.

     * The records of this firm and the various partnerships are very complicated. The rate records change almost yearly, sometimes this firm is listed as "Knight, Elkin & Bridgwood" and marks occur with the initials K. E. & B. See page 376.

ELKIN		**ELKIN KNIGHT & CO.,** Foley Potteries, Fenton. Staffordshire Potteries. 1822–6. *Earthenwares.* Subsequently Elkin, Knight & Bridgwood, q.v.
1465	E. K. & CO.	Distinguishing detail of several impressed or printed marks of
1466	ELKIN KNIGHT & CO.	differing design: name of the individual pattern is often included, 1822–6.

ELKIN		**ELKIN & NEWBON,** Stafford Street, Longton. Staffordshire Potteries. c. 1844–5. *Earthenwares.*
1467	E. & N.	Distinguishing initials found on several printed marks of differing design, 1844–5.

ELKIN		**SAMUEL ELKIN,** Stafford St. (1856–9), Mill St. (c. 1860–4), Longton. Staffordshire Potteries. 1856–64. *Earthenwares.*
1468	S. E.	Distinguishing initials found on several printed marks of differing design: name of the individual pattern is often included, 1856–64.
1468a	ELKINS & CO.	*See page 242.*

ELLGREAVE		**ELLGREAVE POTTERY CO. LTD.,** Ellgreave St., Burslem. Staffordshire Potteries. 1921– . *Earthenwares.* Early wares are unmarked.
1469–71		

Printed marks, c. 1947.

ELLIOT		**LIDDLE, ELLIOT & SON,** Dale Hall Pottery, Longport. Staffordshire Potteries. 1862–71. *China and Earthenwares.* Formerly Mayer & Elliot.
1472	L. E. & S.	Distinguishing initials found on several impressed or printed marks of differing design: name of the individual pattern is often included, 1862–71.

ELLIS		**JOHN ELLIS,** Bristol and/or Bovey Tracey. Late 18th century, early 19th century. *Earthenwares.*
1473	J. ELLIS	Impressed marks. Late 18th century, early 19th century.
1474	JOHN ELLIS	

—	J. ELLIS & CO.	*See* Appendix.

ELLIS		**ELLIS, UNWIN & MOUNTFORD,** High Street, Hanley. Staffordshire Potteries. 1860–1. *Earthenwares.* Subsequently Ellis, Unwin, Mountford & Taylor.
1475	E. U. & M.	Printed mark with initials and name of pattern, 1860–1.

2731	E L M	*See* Esmé Moody.

ELSMORE

ELSMORE & FORSTER, Clayhills Pottery, Tunstall. Staffordshire Potteries. 1853–71. *Earthenwares, Parian, etc.* Subsequently Elsmore & Son, see below.

1476 ELSMORE & FORSTER Distinguishing name found on several printed marks of differing design, 1853–71.

1477 Slight variations of the Royal Arms mark occur, with the name on a ribbon below. A jug with mark no. 1477 in the Godden Collection is dated 1859.

ELSMORE

ELSMORE (THOMAS) & SON, Clayhills Pottery, Tunstall. Staffordshire Potteries. 1872–87. *Earthenwares.* Formerly Elsmore & Forster, see above.

| 1478 | ELSMORE & SON ENGLAND | Impressed mark, on printed earthenware plate in Godden Collection, 1872–87.   Note early, pre-1891, use of "England". |

ELTON

SIR EDMUND ELTON, Sunflower Pottery, Clevedon, Somerset. 1879–1930. *Earthenwares.*

See J. F. Blacker's *The A.B.C. of XIX century English Ceramic Art.*

| 1479 | *Elton* | Painted or incised mark, 1879–1920.   The date may occur on some specimens. |
| 1480 | *Elton*⁺ | Painted mark 1920–30. Note the cross added after Sir Edmund's death in 1920.   An Elton vase is illustrated in H. Wakefield's *Victorian Pottery* (1962). |

ELTON

J. F. ELTON & CO. LTD., Belle Works, Burslem.   Staffordshire Potteries. 1901–10. *Earthenwares.*

| 1481 | J. F. E. CO. LTD. BURSLEM | Distinguishing initials or monogram found on printed or impressed marks of differing design, 1901–10. |
| 1481a | | |

| 2567 | ELTON POTTERY | *See* Thomas Mayer (Elton Pottery) Ltd. |

ELWOOD

PATTY ELWOOD, Mrs., Newlyn, Cornwall and West Meon, Hampshire. 1953– . *Studio-type Pottery, mainly Tablewares.*

| 1482 | | Impressed seal mark, 1953– . Mrs. Elwood moved to the Meon Pottery at West Meon in 1962. |

| 2731a | E. M. | *See* Esmé Moody. |

EMBERTON

THOMAS, ISAAC & JAMES EMBERTON, Highgate Pottery, Brownhills, Tunstall. Staffordshire Potteries. 1869–82. *Earthenwares.* Formerly William Emberton, q.v. Subsequently James Emberton.

1483   Printed garter shaped mark with the initials T I & J E, 1869–82.

1484   T. I. & J. EMBERTON The name in full was also used and occurs on a mug in the Godden Collection.

EMBERTON

WILLIAM EMBERTON, Highgate Pottery, Brownhills, Tunstall. Staffordshire Potteries. 1851–69. *Earthenwares.* Formerly W. Emberton & Co. Subsequently T. I. & J. Emberton, q.v.

1485   W. E. Distinguishing initials found on several printed marks of differing design: name of the individual pattern is often included, 1851–69. Several garter shaped marks were used.

1528   EMBOSA WARE *See* J. T. Fell & Co.

1441   E. M. & CO. *See* Edge, Malkin & Co. Ltd.
         or
1442   E. M. & CO.
           B.

EMERY

FRANCIS J. EMERY, Bleak Hill Works (and other addresses), Burslem. Staffordshire Potteries. c. 1878–93. *Earthenwares.*

1485a   F. J. EMERY. Printed marks incorporating these initials and name, often with the name of the pattern, c. 1878–93. "England" may be added, c. 1891–3.

EMERY

JAMES EMERY, Mexborough, Yorkshire. 1837–61. *Earthenwares.*

1486   J. EMERY Incised mark, in writing letters, 1837–61.
             MEXBRO

EMMS		**DEREK EMMS**, Longton. Staffordshire Potteries. 1955– . *Studio-type Pottery.*
1487		Impressed seal type mark, 1955– . Some wares are unmarked.
EMPIRE		**EMPIRE PORCELAIN CO.** (Ltd.), Empire Works, Stoke. Staffordshire Potteries. 1896– . *Earthenwares.*
1488		Printed mark, 1896–1912.
1489		Printed mark, 1912–28.
1490		Printed mark, 1928–39. Note month and year potting numbers incorporated in this and later marks.

1491–4

1495–8

The marks reproduced above are a selection of those used during the 1930's.

1499–
1502

**EMPIRE
ENGLAND**

Printed or impressed marks of the late 1940's and 1950's.
Month and year numbers normally occur with these marks and
show the date of manufacture.

1503–5

Printed marks of the 1960's. "Ltd." may be added to the title
on marks from mid-1963.

1488–97
& 1499

EMPIRE WARE
or WORKS

See Empire Porcelain Co.

2725   EMUNDU   *See* Mogridge & Underhay.

2619   ENAMEL PORCELAIN   *See* Charles Meigh.

ENGLAND   Occurs on most English marks after about 1891.

3975   ENGLISH CHINA   *See* Charles Waine (& Co.) (Ltd.) (also used by other manufacturers).

EOS

EOS POTTERY (Bryan Newman and Reg Mussett), Dulwich,
London S.E.22.   December 1961– . *Studio-type Pottery.*

1506   EOS   Incised, impressed or printed mark, December 1961– .

1507   B   The initial B often appears on wares made by Bryan Newman.

1488–90   E. P. CO.   *See* Empire Porcelain Co.

479   EPIC   *See* Joseph Bourne & Son Ltd.

3142   E/PW   *See* Powell & Wells Studio Pottery.

3421	ER (monogram)	*See* Evadne Russell.
ERA		**ERA ART POTTERY CO.**, Sutherland Street, Stoke. Staffordshire Potteries. 1930–47. *Earthenwares.*
1508–9		Printed marks, 1930+.
1510–11		Printed marks, 1936+.
1512		Printed mark, 1939–40 and 1946–7. *N.B.—The trade-name "Ranleigh Ware" was reintroduced early in 1964, on pottery marketed by BAIFIELD PRODUCTIONS LTD., a subsidiary of S. Fielding & Co., Ltd.*
1508–9, 1511	ERA WARE	*See* Era Art Pottery Co.
1986–7	ERICA	*See* J. E. Heath Ltd.
2695	E. S.	*See* Eileen Stevens.
1431	E. S. & CO.	*See* Eardley Spear & Co.
3915	ET (monogram)	*See* Eleanor Tydeman.
—	ETRUSCAN MAJOLICA	*See* Appendix (G.S.H.), page 719.
1475	E. U. & M.	*See* Ellis, Unwin & Mountford.
—	EVANS (on printed patterns)	*See* Samuel Gilbody.
EVANS		**EVANS & BOOTH**, Knowles Works, Burslem. Staffordshire Potteries. 1856–69. *Earthenwares.* Subsequently Evans & Tomkinson.

| 1513 | E. & B. | Distinguishing initials found on several printed marks of differing design: name of the individual pattern is often included, 1856–69. |

| | EVANS & CO. | *See* D. J. Evans & Co., below. |

EVANS

D. J. EVANS & CO., Cambrian Pottery, Swansea, Wales. 1862–70. *Earthenwares.* Formerly Evans & Glasson, q.v.

1514	D. J. EVANS & CO. SWANSEA	Distinguishing detail of several printed marks of differing design: name of the individual pattern is often included, 1862–70. Mark nos. 1517–18 are typical examples.
1515	EVANS & CO.	
1516	D. I. EVANS & CO.	N.B. Some marks may give D. I. Evans & Co.

1517–18

| 1516 | D. I. EVANS & CO. | *See* D. J. Evans, above. |

EVANS

EVANS & GLASSON, Cambrian Pottery, Swansea, Wales. 1850–62. *Earthenwares.* Formerly Dillwyn & Co., q.v. Subsequently D. J. Evans & Co., q.v.

| 1519 | EVANS & GLASSON | Distinguishing detail of several impressed or printed marks of differing design, 1850–62. |
| 1519a | EVANS & GLASSON SWANSEA | |

EVERARD

EVERARD, GLOVER & COLCLOUGH, Lane End. Staffordshire Potteries. c. 1847. *China & Earthenwares.* Formerly Everard Colclough & Townsend (c. 1837–45), Everard & Glover, c. 1846.

| 1519b | E. G. & C. | Distinguishing detail of several printed marks of differing design: name of the individual pattern is often included, c. 1847. |

EVERETT

RAYMOND R. EVERETT, Raymond Everett Pottery, Rye, Sussex. March 1963– . *Studio-type Earthenwares.*

1520   Painted initial mark on special wares, 1963– .

1520a   Printed or impressed mark, 1963– . The place name RYE may replace the initial R on some marks.

3994	E. W.	*See* E. Wallis.
4249		*See* Enoch Wood.
4126	E. W. B.	*See* Elizabeth Whitehouse.
4260	E. W. & S.	*See* Enoch Wood & Son.
4399	EZ (monogram)	*See* Elsa Zerkowitz.

POSTSCRIPT

ELKINS

ELKINS & CO. (Elkin, Knight & Elkin), Lane End Staffordshire Potteries. c. 1822–30. *Earthenwares.*

1468a   ELKIN & CO.   Distinguishing detail of printed mark, just reported, with pre-Victorian Royal Arms. This mark probably relates to Elkin, Knight & Elkin, c. 1822–30.

F

3726	F	*See* Harry H. Stringer.
1533	F. & CO.	*See* Thomas Fell (& Co.).
1585	F. & SONS or	*See* Ford & Sons.
1584	F. & SONS LTD.	
—	W. FAIRBAIRNS	*See* Appendix, page 716.
2342–4 4045–6	FALCON WARE	*See* Thomas Laurence (Longton) Ltd. *See* J. H. Weatherby & Sons (Ltd.), page 653.

FANCIES   **FANCIES FAYRE POTTERY**, Britannia Works, Hanley, c. 1946–51. Mount Pleasant, Shelton, c. 1951– . Staffordshire Potteries. 1946– . *Earthenwares, Figures and "Fancies".*

1521	FANCIES FAYRE ENGLAND	Printed or impressed mark, 1946+.*
1522	KNICK KNACKS ENGLAND	Printed or impressed mark, 1949+.*
1523	STAFFORDSHIRE F. F. ENGLAND	Printed or impressed mark, 1950+.*

1524		Printed or impressed mark, c. 1953+, continued in use by P. E. Bairstow & Co. after 1954.*

                                                * Continued as P. E. Bairstow & Co., q.v.

FARNHAM

FARNHAM SGRAFFITO POTTERY (Ada K. Hazell), Farnham, Surrey. c. 1897–8. *Earthenwares.*

1525	F. S. P.	A circular mark, comprising these initials and three hazel nuts, was registered in 1897.
443	F. B.	*See* Frederick Booth.
4343	F. B. B.	*See* Worcester, Flight Barr & Barr, page 696.
306	F. B. & CO.	*See* Frank Beardmore & Co.
	or	
307	F. B. & CO. F.	
4335	F. & B.	*See* Worcester, Flight & Barr, page 695.
794	F. C.	*See* F. Cartlidge & Co.
1041–2		*See* Francis G. Cooper.
795	F. C. & CO.	*See* F. Cartlidge.
1595		*See* Ford, Challinor & Co.
1595a	F. & C.	*See* Ford, Challinor & Co.
1572	FCP (monogram)	*See* Walter J. Fletcher.
1288a	F D	*See* Francis Dillon.

FEATHERSTONE

FEATHERSTONE POTTERIES, Falcon Works, Stoke. Staffordshire Potteries. 1949–50. *Earthenwares.*

| 1526 | F. P. | Distinguishing initials found on impressed or printed marks of |
| 1527 | F. N. P. | differing design, 1949–50. |

FELL   **J. T. FELL & CO.**, Cyples Old Pottery, Longton. Staffordshire Potteries. 1923–57. *Earthenwares.*

1528   EMBOSA WARE   Printed or impressed marks, 1923–57.

1529   MADE BY CYPLES   The date 1793 is the claimed date of establishment of the
         OLD POTTERY   original Cyples pottery, and does not relate to the age of the
             1793   ware.

FELL   **THOMAS FELL (& CO.) (Ltd.)**, St. Peter's Pottery, Newcastle upon Tyne, Northumberland. 1817–90. *Earthenwares, Creamwares, etc.*

1530   FELL   Impressed marks, 1817–30.

1531–2

1533   F. & CO.   Distinguishing detail of several impressed or printed marks of
1534   T. F. & CO.   differing design. Note addition of "& Co.". c. 1830–90.
1535   T. FELL & CO.   Marked specimens will be found illustrated in *British Pottery and Porcelain : an illustrated Encyclopaedia of Marked Specimens.*

—   FEN   *See* Appendix, page 716.

FENTON   **ALFRED FENTON & SONS**, Brook St., Hanley. Staffordshire Potteries. 1887–1901. *China and Earthenwares.*

1536   A. F. & S.   Distinguishing initials found on several impressed or printed
1537   marks of differing design: name of the individual pattern is often included, 1887–1901. Mark no. 1537 is an example.

2541   FENTON   *See* G. M. & C. J. Mason.
      STONE WORKS

324a   FERMANAGH   *See* Belleek Pottery.
       POTTERY

FERRYBRIDGE		**FERRYBRIDGE POTTERY** (called Knottingley Pottery, prior to 1804) (various partnerships), Nr. Pontefract, Yorkshire. 1792 to present day. From 1792 to 1804 the works were known as the Knottingley Pottery. *Earthenwares.*
		See O. Grabham's *Yorkshire Potteries, Pots and Potters* (1916).
1538	TOMLINSON & CO.	Impressed or printed marks, 1792–6 and 1801–34.
1539	WEDGWOOD & CO.	Impressed, c. 1796–1801.
1540	FERRYBRIDGE	Impressed mark, c. 1804+.
1541	FERRYBRIᴄGE	N.B. "D" sometimes reversed.
	R & T	Subsequent owners were Tomlinson Plowes & Co. (1834+); Wigglesworth & Ingham; Reed Taylor & Kelsall, Reed & Taylor (c. 1843–56). This firm also worked the Rock Pottery and used the initials "R & T" as a mark. See also Reed & Taylor, page 525.
	L. W.	The Royal Arms mark was used by Lewis Woolf & Sons from 1856 to 1883. The words "OPAQUE GRANITE CHINA" occur in the central shield. "Ferrybridge and Australian Potteries" may occur with this mark from 1857. The initials "L. W." found on many printed marks probably relate to Lewis Woolf, c. 1856–70. See Appendix, page 726.
	P. B. P. BROS. POULSON BROTHERS	These initials, etc., occur with the Royal Arms mark, or in other forms, from c. 1884–97.
	S. B. F. B. T. B. & S. F. B.	Several marks incorporating the initials "S. B." were used by Messrs. Sefton & Brown 1897–1919 when they were succeeded by T. Brown & Sons, who use the initials "T. B. & S.".
1523	F. F.	*See* Fancies Fayre Pottery.
511	F. G. B.	*See* George Frederick Bowers (& Co.).
1898 2063	F. H.	*See* Frank Hamer. *See* W. Fishley Holland.
1634	FH (monogram)	*See* H. M. French.

1611	F. & H.	*See* Forester & Hulme.

FIELDING

S. FIELDING & CO. (LTD.), Railway Pottery, Devon Pottery (from 1911 onwards), Stoke. Staffordshire Potteries. 1879– . *Earthenwares, Majolica, etc.*

1542	FIELDING	Impressed mark, c. 1879– .
1543	S. F. & CO.	Distinguishing initials found on several printed marks of differing design: name of the individual pattern is often included, 1880–1917.
1544	GAME COCK MARK	L. Jewitt, in the revised (1883) edition of his *Ceramic Art of Great Britain*, states "The mark of the firm is a game cock". The present writer has not seen this mark.
1545–6		Standard printed marks, c. 1891–1913.
1547		Printed mark, c. 1913+.
1548–50		

Printed marks, c. 1917–30.

1551		Printed trade-mark, c. 1930– . Slight variations occur.
1542a	FIELDING 12 A 52	Impressed mark, showing the date of manufacture, April 12th, 1952.

—   FIFE POTTERY   *See* Appendix, page 717.

FIFIELD

1552	W. FIFIELD	
1553	W. F.	
1553a	W F B	

WILLIAM FIFIELD, b. 1777, d. 1857, Ceramic Painter, Bristol. c. 1810–55. *Decorator*.

The painted signature or initials of this artist occur on Bristol creamwares, etc., c. 1810–55. Some examples are dated. Both father and son painted on earthenwares at this period. The initial B may be added after the initials W F.

    Examples decorated by this artist are illustrated in *British Pottery and Porcelain: an illustrated Encyclopaedia of Marked Specimens*.

FINE

FINE ARTS PORCELAIN LTD., Charlton, London S.E.7. 1948–52. *Earthenwares*.

1554   Printed mark, 1948–52.

333a	FINNEMORE
4389	

See Bembridge Pottery.
See Yellowsands Pottery.

FINNEY

A. T. FINNEY & SONS (LTD.), Duchess China Works, Longton. Staffordshire Potteries. 1947– . *Porcelain*. Formerly Blythe Porcelain Co. Ltd., which was taken over by A. T. Finney in 1935.

1555   DUCHESS   Trade-name incorporated in many marks, c. 1947+.

1556   Printed mark, c. 1947–60.

1557   Printed mark, 1961– . Slight variations occur, names of patterns or styles added.

1558		Printed mark, 1962– .

FIRTH

JOHN THOMAS FIRTH, Mill Brow, Kirkby Lonsdale, Westmorland. Late 19th century to early 20th century. *Pottery, glaze and sgraffito effects.*

See A. Lomax's *Royal Lancastrian Pottery, 1900–38* (1957). John Thomas Firth's name appears in local directories of 1894 and 1897 but not in that of 1910.

1559	J. T. F. K. L.	Incised initials of J. T. Firth, c. 1890–1910.
1560	S. F. K. L.	Incised initials of Sydney Firth.
1561	E. F. K. L.	Incised initials of Ellen Firth.

FISHER

JOHN FISHER, with Denis Rock, Rowlands Gill, Co. Durham. 1950– . *Studio-type Pottery.*

1562		Painted or incised mark, 1950–9.
1563		Incised or painted monogram of John Fisher, 1950– .
1564		Personal rebus of John Fisher, 1950– .

FISHLEY

EDWIN BEER FISHLEY (b. 1832, d. 1912), Fremington, Devonshire. 1861–1906. *Earthenwares.* Formerly Edmund Fishley.

1565	E. B. FISHLEY FREMINGTON N. DEVON

Incised mark, 1861–1906.

Bernard Leach has described E. B. Fishley as the last of the English peasant potters, his utilitarian pitchers and baking

dishes were pointed out to Leach's students as representing the
true English tradition in pottery.

Other members of the Fishley family have potted in the West
Country:

George. Late 18th–early 19th century.
Edmund. c. 1839–61.
Edwin. c. 1861–1906.
W. Fishley Holland. c. 1900–   , see pages 330–1.
George Fishley Holland. c. 1955–   , see page 330.

FISHLEY

1566   F. FISHLEY
FREMINGTON
DEVON

GEORGE FISHLEY, Fremington, Devonshire. Late 18th to
early 19th century. *Earthenwares.*
This impressed mark has been recorded. Various signature
type marks also occur. Subsequent members of this important
family of potters are listed above. George Fishley was succeeded by Edmund in about 1839.

FIVE

1567   FIVE TOWNS CHINA
CO. LTD.
ENGLAND

FIVE TOWNS CHINA CO. LTD., Park Works, Middleport.
Staffordshire Potteries. 1957–   . *Floral Porcelains.*
Distinguishing name found on several printed marks of differing
design: a potter's kiln is depicted in several marks, 1957–   .

2299   FK
(monogram)

See Frank Kneller.

—   F
R   L
R

See Appendix (F. Raymond).

FLACKET

1569   F. T. & R.

FLACKET, TOFT & ROBINSON, Church Street, Longton.
Staffordshire Potteries. 1857–8. *Earthenwares.* Formerly
Flacket & Toft.
Distinguishing initials found on several printed marks of differ-
ing design: name of the individual pattern is often included,
1857–8.

3961	FLAXMAN	*See* Wade, Heath & Co. (Ltd.).
	or	
3960	FLAXMAN WARE	

972	FLEMING	*See* Cochran & Fleming.

FLETCHER

THOMAS FLETCHER, Shelton, Hanley. Staffordshire Potteries. c. 1786–1810.

1570	T. FLETCHER SHELTON	These "marks" are recorded but Thomas Fletcher was a printer and decorator, not a manufacturer, c. 1786–1810.
1571	T. FLETCHER & CO.	(These dates are only approximate.)

A signed example will be found illustrated in *British Pottery and Porcelain : an illustrated Encyclopaedia of Marked Specimens.*

FLETCHER

WALTER J. FLETCHER, Cleeve Prior, Evesham, Worc. 1960– . *Studio-type Pottery.*

1572 3

Impressed seal marks 1960. The initials stand for "Frogland Cottage Pottery" & "Frogland Pottery".

—	FLIGHT	*See* Worcester, pages 694–6.
—	FLIGHT & BARR	
—	FLIGHT, BARR & BARR	

110	FLORAL	*See* Charles Amison & Co. Ltd.

FLORAL

FLORAL CHINA CO. LTD., Sutherland Road, Longton. Staffordshire Potteries. 1940–51. *China floral wares.*

1574-5

Printed marks, c. 1946–51. Slight variations occur.

FLORAL

FLORAL PRODUCTIONS, Liverpool Road, Newcastle. Staffordshire Potteries. 1952–62. *China Fancies and Jewellery.*

1576	FLORAL PRODUCTIONS BONE CHINA ENGLAND	Printed or impressed mark, 1952–62.
2560	FLOREAT	*See* Maw & Co. Ltd.

FLOWERS

		JOSEPH FLOWERS, Redcliff Backs, Bristol, Gloucestershire. c. 1740–85. *Tin glazed (delft type) Earthenwares.*
1577	JOSEPH FLOWER SCULP 1741	Signature or initial marks occur on very rare examples of 18th century Bristol delft. Most examples are unmarked.
1578	J. F. 1751	

FLOYD

BENJAMIN FLOYD, Anchor Lane, Lane End. Staffordshire Potteries. c. 1843. *Earthenwares.*

1579	B F	Distinguishing initials found on several printed marks of differing design: name of the individual pattern is often included, c. 1843.

N.B. Some English looking marks incorporating the initials B. F. were made by Boch Freres of Belgium, c. 1850–60. This point is proved by initial and name-marked plate in the Godden Collection.

FLOYD

R. FLOYD & SONS, Lovatt and Hall Street Works, Stoke. Staffordshire Potteries. 1907–30. *Earthenwares.* Formerly R. Floyd & Co.

1580	R.F.&S.	Printed or impressed mark, 1907–30.
2759	F. M.	*See* Francis Morley (& Co.).
2760	or F. M. & CO.	
1527	F. N. P.	*See* Featherstone Potteries.

FOLCH

STEPHEN FOLCH, Church St., Stoke. Staffordshire Potteries. 1820–30. *Earthenwares, Ironstone, etc.*

1581 | FOLCH'S GENUINE STONE CHINA | Rare impressed mark on transfer printed Ironstone wares, 1820–30.

538 | FOLEY | *See* E. Brain & Co. Ltd.
539 | (FOLEY ART CHINA, | *See* James & Charles Wileman.
540–4 | FOLEY CHINA)
4163

1599 | FORD | *See* Ford Pottery.

FORD

FORD & SONS (LTD.), Newcastle St., Burslem. Staffordshire Potteries. c. 1893–1938, then Ford & Sons (Crownford) Ltd. *Earthenwares.* Formerly Ford & Riley, q.v. Subsequently Ford & Sons (Crownford) Ltd., see below.

1582 | F & S | Distinguishing detail of several printed marks of differing
1583 | F & S / B | design: name of the individual pattern is often included, 1893–1938. "& SONS" occurs in full, in place of "& S"
1584 | F & SONS LTD. | on some marks, as nos. 1585–6.

1585–6 | "Ltd." may occur from 1908

Printed marks of the 1930's include:

1587–90

1591 | Standard mark from the 1930's and continued by *Ford & Sons (Crownford) Ltd.* from c. 1938.

1592 | Printed mark, c. 1961– , used by Ford & Sons (Crownford) Ltd.

FORD		CHARLES FORD, Cannon St., Hanley. Staffordshire Potteries. 1874–1904. *China*. Formerly T. & C. Ford, q.v. Works sold to J. A. Robinson & Sons Ltd. in 1904.
1593		Impressed or printed monogram mark, 1874–1904.
1594		Swan mark, impressed or printed, c. 1900–4.

FORD   FORD, CHALLINOR & CO., also listed in records as **FORD & CHALLINOR**, Lion Works, Sandyford, Tunstall. Staffordshire Potteries. 1865–80. *Earthenwares*.

1595 & 1595a		Printed marks incorporating the initials F. C. & Co. or F. & C. occur 1865–80.

FORD   JOHN FORD & CO., 39 Princes St., Edinburgh, Scotland. 1891–1926. *Retailers*.

1596	JOHN FORD & CO. EDINBURGH	Distinguishing name found on several printed marks of differing design, 1891–1926.

FORD   FORD & PATTERSON, Sheriff Hill Pottery, Newcastle upon Tyne, Northumberland. c. 1820–30.* *Earthenwares*. Formerly Patterson & Co., q.v.

1597	FORD & PATTERSON Sheriff Hill Pottery	Impressed mark, rarely found on lustre decorated earthenwares. c. 1820–30. Two marked plates are in the Laing Art Gallery and Museum, Newcastle.

      * The working period of this partnership is open to doubt. Marked examples appear to be of this date and a directory of 1837 lists Patterson & Co. rather than Ford & Patterson. Several other potters named Patterson were working in the district.

FORD   FORD & POINTON LTD., Norfolk Works, Hanley. Staffordshire Potteries. 1917–36.* *China*. Formerly Pointon & Co. Ltd.

1598   Printed mark, c. 1920–36.

* This firm was amalgamated with the Cauldon group c. 1921.

FORD

1599
1600

FORD
FORD POTTERY
SOUTH HYLTON

FORD POTTERY, South Hylton, Sunderland, Durham. 1799–1864. *Earthenwares, Creamwares, Lustrewares.* Distinguishing detail of several impressed or printed marks of differing design, 1799–1864. See also "Dawson", page 193.

FORD

1601
1602–3

F & R

FORD & RILEY, Newcastle St., Burslem. Staffordshire Potteries. 1882–93. *Earthenwares.* Formerly Whittingham, Ford & Riley, q.v. Subsequently Ford & Sons, q.v. Distinguishing initials found on several printed marks of differing design: name of the individual pattern is often included, 1882–93. Mark nos. 1602–3 are examples.

FORD

SAMUEL FORD & CO., Lincoln Pottery, Crown Pottery (from c. 1913), Burslem. Staffordshire Potteries. 1898–1939. *Earthenwares.* Formerly Smith & Ford, q.v.

1604      Printed mark (previously used by Smith & Ford). The initials F. & Co. may occur in place of S. & F., 1898–1936.

1605   Printed mark, c. 1936–9.

FORD

THOMAS FORD, Cannon St., Hanley. Staffordshire Potteries. 1871–4. *China.* Formerly C. & T. Ford. Subsequently Charles Ford, q.v.

1606	T. F.	Distinguishing initials found on several impressed or printed marks of differing design, 1871–4. Mark nos. 1607–8 are examples which are based on the registration device, see page 527. The month and year of manufacture are impressed on many pieces— $\frac{12}{73}$ stands for December 1873, and so on.
1607		
1608		

FORD

T. & C. FORD, Cannon Street, Hanley. Staffordshire Potteries. 1854–71. *China*. Subsequently Thomas Ford, q.v.

1609	T. & C. F.	Distinguishing initials found on several impressed or printed marks of differing design, 1854–71. Mark no. 1610 is a typical example and is normally impressed.
1610		

FORESTER

FORESTER & HULME, Sutherland Pottery, Fenton. Staffordshire Potteries. 1887–93. *Earthenwares*. Subsequently Hulme & Christie, q.v.

1611		Printed mark, 1887–93. "England" added below from c. 1891.

FORESTER

THOMAS FORESTER & CO., Melbourne Works, Longton. Staffordshire Potteries. c. 1888. *Earthenwares*. Formerly Meigh & Forester.

1612		Printed mark, c. 1888.

FORESTER

THOMAS FORESTER SON & CO., Sutherland Pottery, Fenton. Staffordshire Potteries. 1884–8. *China and Earthenwares*. Subsequently Forester & Hulme, q.v.

1613 Printed mark, 1884–8.

1613   FORESTER'S   *See* Thomas Forester Son & Co., above.

FORESTER

1614   T. F. & S.

THOMAS FORESTER & SONS (LTD.), Phoenix Works, Longton. Staffordshire Potteries. 1883–1959. *China and Earthenwares.* **Formerly Thomas Forester.**
Distinguishing initials found on several marks of differing design, 1883–91. An advertisement of 1890, showing typical vase forms and patterns, will be found in the companion illustrated encyclopaedia.

1615 Printed mark, 1891–1912. Note addition of "LD" or "LTD".

1616 Printed mark, 1912–59.

1617   PHOENIX CHINA
1617a   PHOENIX WARE

Distinguishing names found on several marks of differing design, 1910–59.

FORSE

AUDREY H. FORSE, MISS, Lasallos Street, Polperro, Cornwall. 1959– . *Studio-type Pottery.*

1618   **ⅩF** Pbb.   Incised or painted mark, 1959. With or without "P66".

FORSTER

JOHN FORSTER, Hanley. Staffordshire Potteries. c. 1820 *Earthenwares.*

1619	JOHN FORSTER MADE THIS HANLEY AGUST THE 29.1820	It is possible that John Forster was a workman, rather than a manufacturer. A John For*e*ster is however listed in rate records for Lane End between 1807 and 1830. Incised mark on base of figure inkstand in the Fitzwilliam Museum, Cambridge.

FORSYTH

MOIRA FORSYTH, MISS, St. Oswald's Studios, London S.W.6. c. 1930– .* *Earthenware figures and groups.*

Miss Moira Forsyth is the daughter of the celebrated ceramic artist-designer, Gordon M. Forsyth (1879–1953).

1620 1621	MOIRA FORSYTH M. F.	Signature or initial marks, painted or incised, c. 1930– .*

* Few figures have been produced in recent years as Miss Forsyth's main concern is with glass work, windows, etc.

—	FOSTERS STUDIO POTTERY CO.	*See* Appendix.
3520	FOSTON	*See* Ralph Shirley.

FOURNIER

ROBERT & SHEILA FOURNIER, Ducketts Wood, Ware, Herts. c. 1946–61. Greenwich Studios, London S.E.10. c. 1962– . 1946– . *Studio-type Pottery.*

1622–3		Personal impressed seal marks of Sheila and of R. Fournier, 1946– .
1624		Incised or painted Ducketts Wood mark, 1946–61. The numbers denote the year, e.g. 57 = 1957.

FOWLER

FOWLER THOMPSON & CO., Watson's Pottery, Prestonpans, Scotland. c. 1820–40. *Earthenwares.* Pottery established by Watson, c. 1750.
See J. Arnold Fleming's *Scottish Pottery.*

1625	FOWLER THOMPSON & CO.	Printed or impressed mark, c. 1820–40.

FOWNHOPE		**FOWNHOPE POTTERY** (Dennis Lacey), Fownhope, Hereford. 1956– . *Studio-type Pottery.*
1626	HEREFORDSHIRE	Impressed mark, 1956–8.

1627 *Fownhope.* Painted mark, 1958– .

FOX-

SYLVIA FOX-STRANGWAYS, MISS, Dartington Hall Estates, Totnes, S. Devon. 1921–30. *Studio-type Pottery.*

1628 Painted or incised mark, 1920's–30's.

FOY

PEGGIE E. FOY LTD., West Wickham, Kent. 1945– *Earthenwares.*

1629 Impressed or printed mark, 1945– .

1236	F. P.	*See* William De Morgan.
1526		*See* Featherstone Potteries.
3004a		*See* Ida S. Perrin.
1573	FP (monogram)	*See* Walter J. Fletcher.
1598	F. & P.	*See* Ford & Pointon.
3241	FR (monogram)	*See* Frances E. Richards.
1601	F. & R. or	*See* Ford & Bailey.
1603	F. & R. B	
—	T. FRADLEY	*See* Appendix, page 717.

FRANCEYS

FRANCEYS & SPENCE, Pleasant Street, Liverpool. c. 1820–1830.

1630	PUBD. MARCH 1820 T. FRANCEYS & SPENCE LIVERPOOL W. SPENCE FECIT. PUBD. BY W. SPENCE 1829	These copyright marks (see page 516) occur on portrait plaques and busts modelled in a black or a white jasper-type body, c. 1820–30.
1631		

3672	FRANK BUCKLEY	*See* Staffordshire Teaset Co. Ltd.
—	FREELING & CO.	*See* Appendix, page 717.

FREEMAN

RICHARD FREEMAN, Bath Pottery, Bath, Somerset. 1956– . *Studio-type Pottery.*

1632

Impressed seal mark, 1956– .

1633   BATH POTTERY

Impressed mark, 1956– . This mark was also used by John Shelly from c. 1949.

2619 (note)	FRENCH CHINA	*See* Charles Meigh & Son.

FRENCH

H. M. FRENCH, MISS, Peckham, London S.E.13.   1945*– . *Studio-type Pottery.*

1634

Incised initial mark, 1945*–55 or similar impressed seal mark, 1955– .

   * Miss French was assistant to Charles Vyse at his Chelsea pottery before the war, and examples produced in the 1930's may bear the F. H. monogram.

2370a	FRESHWATER	*See* Jo Lester.
	THE FRIARS	*See* Aylesford Priory Pottery.

3143	F. & R. P.	*See* F. & R. Pratt Co. (Ltd.).
	or	
3144	F. & R. P CO.	

FRY

ROGER FRY, Omega Workshops,* 33 Fitzroy Square, London. c. 1913–19. *Tin-glazed Earthenwares.*

Impressed or incised mark, often of large size, c. 1913–19.

1635

* The Omega Workshops sold Roger Fry's pottery which was made at Camberwell, London, and at the Poole pottery of Carter, Stabler & Adams.

FRYER

J. FRYER & SON (LTD.), Roundwell St., Tunstall. Staffordshire Potteries. 1945– . *Earthenwares.*

1636–7   *J. Fryer & Son, Tunstall, England*   Printed marks, c. 1945– .

1638   Printed marks, 1954– .

333		*See* Bembridge Pottery.
4388		*See* Yellowsands Pottery.

3739	FS	*See* Felix Summerly.
	(monogram)	

1582	F & S	*See* Ford & Son (Ltd.).
	or	
1583	F & S	
	B	

—	F S C	*See* Appendix, page 717.

1960	F S H	*See* Frederick Harrop.

1525	F S P	*See* Farnham Sgraffito Pottery.
1569	F T & R	*See* Flacket, Toft & Robinson.

FUCHS   ANNETTE FUCHS, MISS, London W.9. 1961– . *Studio-type Pottery.*

1639   **ARF**   Painted mark, 1961– .

FUCHS   TESSA FUCHS, MISS, London W.9. 1961– . *Studio-type Pottery.*

1640–1   *Tessa Fuchs*   Painted marks, 1961– .

213	FULHAM	*See* C. J. C. Bailey, and entry below.
1642		

FULHAM   **FULHAM POTTERY & CHEAVIN FILTER CO. LTD.,** Fulham Pottery, London S.W.6. 1889– . *Vases and Utilitarian store wares.* Formerly C. J. C. Bailey, q.v.

1642	FULHAM	Early incised marks, rarely used, c. 1889–1920.
1642a	FULHAM POTTERY LONDON	Impressed mark, in oval, on vases, c. 1948– .
1642b	FULHAM POTTERY ENGLAND	Impressed marks, c. 1948– .

FURNIVAL   JACOB FURNIVAL & CO., Cobridge. Staffordshire Potteries. c. 1845–70. *Earthenwares.*

1643 J F & CO. Several printed marks occur (in the Victoria and Albert Museum records) with these initials and the name of the pattern, c. 1845–70. Blue printed earthenwares have been reported from America with these initials and such pattern names as "Rhine".

FURNIVAL **JACOB & THOMAS FURNIVAL**, Miles Bank, Shelton, Hanley. Staffordshire Potteries. c. 1843. *Earthenwares*. Subsequently Thomas Furnival & Co., q.v.

1644   Printed mark of the Royal Arms and the initials J & T F, c. 1843.

FURNIVAL **THOMAS FURNIVAL & CO.**, Miles Bank, Hanley. Staffordshire Potteries. c. 1844–6. *Earthenwares*. Formerly Jacob & Thomas Furnival, q.v. Subsequently Furnival & Clark.

1645 T. F. & CO. Distinguishing detail of printed marks of differing design: name of the individual pattern is often included, c. 1844–6.

FURNIVAL **THOMAS FURNIVAL & SONS**, Elder Road, Cobridge. Staffordshire Potteries. 1871–90. *Earthenwares*. Subsequently Furnivals, see next entry.

1646–8a

Printed monogram type marks, c. 1871–90.

1649   Printed Royal Arms mark, c. 1818–90. Variations occur, with the title placed above the arms.

1650 Crest mark, printed or impressed. Registered in 1878.

FURNIVALS

FURNIVALS (LTD.), Elder Road, Cobridge. Staffordshire Potteries. 1890– . *Earthenwares*. Formerly Thomas Furnival & Sons, see previous entry.

1651 FURNIVALS ENGLAND

Distinguishing name found on several marks of differing design, 1890–5.

1652

Anchor and dagger trade-mark used 1890–1910, in several forms.

1653–5

FURNIVALS, LTD. COBRIDGE ENGLAND.

c. 1905–13   c. 1895–1913   c. 1910–13

"LTD" add to style, c. 1895.

1656–8a

Style changed to "FURNIVALS (1913) LTD" in January 1913.

FUTURA

FUTURA ART POTTERY LTD., Bryan St., Hanley. Staffordshire Potteries. 1947–56. *Earthenwares*.

1659

Printed mark, 1947–56.

4217	FW	*See* F. Winkle & Co. (Ltd.).
—	F & W	*See* Appendix, page 717.
4213	F W & CO.	*See* F. Winkle & Co. (Ltd.).

G

—	G	*See* Appendix, page 717.
1719		*See* Louis H. H. Glover.
2846		*See* Neale (James) & Co.
3176		*See* Protean Pottery.
1744	GA (monogram)	*See* Anne Gordon.
—	G. & A.	*See* Appendix, page 717.
1727	G. BROS.	*See* John & Robert Godwin.
1823		*See* Grimwade Bros.
1771	G. & CO.	*See* George Grainger (& Co.).
1661	G. & CO. L	*See* Gallimore & Co. Ltd.
1770	G. & CO. W	*See* George Grainger (& Co.).

GALBRAITH   **MISS MARGARET J. GALBRAITH,** Sydenham, London S.E.26. 1961– . *Studio-type Pottery.*

1660   Impressed seal type mark, 1961– .

GALLIMORE   **GALLIMORE & CO. LTD.,** Melbourne Works, Longton, Staffordshire Potteries. 1906–34. *Earthenwares.*

1661      Impressed or printed mark, 1906–34.

GALLIMORE   **ROBERT GALLIMORE**, St. James Place, Longton. 1831–40. *Earthenwares, Lustre-wares.* Formerly A. & R. Gallimore. Subsequently Gallimore & Shutbotham.

1662   R. G.   The impressed initials R. G. have been noted on lustre wares and this mark could well relate to Robert Gallimore, although there is no definite proof, c. 1831–40.

809   GALLIMORE TURNER   *See* Caughley Works.

GALLINER   **EDITH M. GALLINER**, Hampstead Garden Suburb, London N.W.11. 1949– . *Studio-type Pottery, Wall Panels and Sculpture.*

1663   Incised, painted or impressed seal mark, 1949– .

GANT   **TONY & JANET GANT**, Putney, London S.W.15. 1957– . *Studio-type Pottery, Stonewares.*

1664   TONY GANT 1963   Signature mark, incised or painted, with year, 1957– .

1664a   T GANT   Variation of signature mark, 1957– .

1665   T. G.   Initial mark on small, inexpensive examples, 1957– .

1666   JANET S GANT 1963   Incised signature marks of Mrs. Gant, with year, 1962– .

1667   J. S. G. 1963   Incised or painted initial marks used by Mrs. Gant, 1962– .

242	GARDEN HOUSE POTTERY	*See* Bancroft & Bennett.

GARDINER		**JUDY GARDINER, MISS.,** London S.W.7. 1958– . *Studio-type Pottery, Stonewares.*
1668	J. G. 63	Incised or painted initial mark, with year, 1958– .
1419	P. GARDNER	*See* Dunmore Pottery (Co.).

GARNER		**ROBERT GARNER** (1733–89), Foley, Fenton. Staffordshire Potteries. Late 18th century.* *Earthenwares.*
1669	R. G.	The initials R. G. occur as part of the design on moulded earthenware "Fair Hebe" jugs of c. 1788. Similar jugs bear the initials of R. M. Astbury. See a paper by R. J. Charleston on J. Voyez in the *Transactions of the English Ceramic Circle,* vol. 5, part 1, and *British Pottery and Porcelain: an illustrated Encyclopaedia of Marked Specimens.*

* A son, also Robert Garner, potted at Lane End until c. 1821 and he made various types of earthenware, including Queen's ware.

GARNKIRK		**GARNKIRK FIRE-CLAY CO.** (various owners), Garnkirk Works, Glasgow, Scotland. c. 1830–80. *Terra-cotta wares.*
1670	GARNKIRK	Impressed mark, c. 1850–80.

GATER		**GATER, HALL & CO.,** New Gordon Pottery (c. 1899–1907), Tunstall. Royal Overhouse Pottery (1907+), Burslem. Staffordshire Potteries. 1895–1943. *Earthenwares.* Formerly Thomas Gater & Co. Subsequently "Barratt's of Staffordshire Ltd.", q.v.
1671	G H & CO.	Distinguishing initials found on several marks of differing design, 1895+.

1672–3		Printed marks, 1914+. The "Corona" mark was continued by "Barratt's of Staffordshire Ltd.", q.v.

1673a	CROWN CORONA EST.P:1819 G.H & Co BURSLEM ENGLAND	Printed mark, 1936–43.
731	G. B. (monogram)	*See* Graham Burr.
335	G. B. & Co.	*See* George Bennett & Co.
1744	G. & B.	*See* Goodwin & Bullock.
1739	G. B. H.	*See* Goodwin, Bridgwood (&) Harris.
1739a	G. B. O.	*See* Goodwin, Bridgwood & Orton.
1739b	G. B. & O.	*See* Goodwin, Bridgwood & Orton.
1823	G. Bros.	*See* Grimwade Bros.
—	G. C. & Co.	*See* Appendix.
2538	G. & C. J. M.	*See* G. M. & C. J. Mason.
934	G. C. P. Co.	*See* Clyde Pottery Co.
1859a	G. & D.	*See* Guest & Dewsbury.
1859	G. & D. L.	*See* Guest & Dewsbury.
1859a	G. & D. L.	*See* Guest & Dewsbury.
1740a	G. & E.	*See* Goodwin & Ellis.

GEDDES

1674   JOHN GEDDES, Verreville Pottery

JOHN GEDDES (& SON), Verreville Pottery, Glasgow, Scotland. c. 1806–27. *Pottery and Porcelain.*

Sam Laidacker, in his *Anglo-American China, Part II* and in correspondence, mentions this form of printed mark as occurring on printed earthenware found in America c. 1806–24. Arnold Fleming, in his *Scottish Pottery*, states that Geddes wares were exported to America.

Any marks with the addition of "& Son" would relate to the period 1824–7. Geddes employed skilled hands from Staffordshire and also purchased wares from Wedgwoods.

GELSON		**GELSON BROS.**, Cobden Works, Hanley. Staffordshire Potteries. 1867–76. *Earthenwares*. Subsequently Thomas Gelson & Co.
1675	GELSON BROS. HANLEY	Distinguishing detail of several marks of differing design, 1867–76.
—	G. E. M.	*See* Appendix, page 718.
GEM		**GEM POTTERY LTD.**, Keele Street, Tunstall. Staffordshire Potteries. 1961– . *Earthenwares*. Wholesalers for Alfred Meakin (Tunstall) Ltd.
1676		Printed mark, 1961.
509 or 510	G. F. B. G F B B T	*See* George Frederick Bowers (& Co.).
3579 or 3580	G. F. S. G F S & CO.	*See* George F. Smith (& Co.).
1721 1746 1822	G. G.	*See* G. Godfrey. *See* Gordon's Pottery. *See* Gladys Grimshaw.
1762 or 1762	G. G. & CO. G. G. & CO. S. P.	*See* George Grainger (& Co.).
3852	G. G. G.	*See* Three G's Pottery.
1763	G. G. W.	*See* George Grainger (& Co.).
3094	G. H.	*See* Portishead Studio Pottery.
3423	GHC (monogram)	*See* Rustington Pottery.

278	G. H. & CO.	*See* Barratt's of Staffordshire Ltd.
1671		*See* Gater Hall & Co.
—	G H & G	*See* Appendix, page 718.
1725	G. & H. H.	*See* Godwin & Hewitt.
1752	G. I. (monogram)	*See* Isobel Goudie.

GIBSON

JOHN & SOLOMON GIBSON, Liverpool, Lancs.   Early 19th century.   *Earthenwares.*

| 1677 | JOHN GIBSON
LIVERPOOL
1813 | H. Boswell Lancaster, in his *Liverpool and Her Potters* (1936), cites a plaque in the Liverpool Museum signed as no. 1677; also a figure of Mercury seated, with the incised mark no. |
| 1678 | SOLOMON GIBSON
1816 | 1678. |

GIBSON

GIBSON & SONS (LTD.), Albany Pottery (also Harvey Pottery), Burslem. Staffordshire Potteries. 1885– . *Earthenwares.*   Formerly Gibson, Sudlow & Co.

1679   Printed mark, c. 1904–9.

| 1679a | G. & S. LTD.
B. | Distinguishing initials found on several printed marks of differing design, 1905. |
| 1679b | G. & S. LTD. | |

1680–3

c. 1909+   c. 1912+   c. 1930+   c. 1930+

1684–5

c. 1930+   c. 1930+

1686–9	*Gibsons* ·HAND PAINTED· ·ENGLAND· c. 1940+	*Gibsons* LTD BURSLEM ENGLAND	ENGLAND GIBSON'S c. 1940+ GIBSON'S MADE IN ENGLAND
1690–1	ROYAL HARVEY STAFFORDSHIRE ENGLAND c. 1950–5		GIBSONS STAFFORDSHIRE ENGLAND c. 1950–

GIBSON

WILFRED GIBSON, Falmouth, Cornwall. 1953– . *Earthenwares and Porcelain Figures, Groups, etc.*

1692	W. G.	Written initials or signature on early figures, 1953+.
1693	Wilfred Gibson	
1694	W᳹G	Painted mark, 1960– .

| 1686–9, 1691 | GIBSONS | *See* Gibson & Sons (Ltd.). |
| 340 | GIGS | *See* Agnes Benson. |

GILBODY

SAMUEL GILBODY (GILLBODY), Liverpool. c. 1755–61. *Porcelains.*

Samuel Gilbody was described as "clay potter" in 1756; in 1758 he was advertising china "equal to any produced in Staffordshire". Dr. B. Watney in the *Transactions of The English Ceramic Circle*, vol. 4, part 5, attributes a class of porcelain to Gilbody but apart from the mug mentioned below, no marked examples have been recorded.

| 1695 | GILBODY—MAKER —EVANS SCT. | Very rare "mark" on print of Frederick the Great on a porcelain mug (perhaps of Worcester manufacture) in the Liverpool Museum, c. 1756–61. See *British Pottery and Porcelain: an illustrated Encyclopaedia of Marked Specimens.* |

John Evans' name occurs on other printed patterns on Liverpool porcelain of the 1760 period. See E. S. Price's *John Sadler, a Liverpool Pottery Printer* (1948).

GILDEA

JAMES GILDEA, Dale Hall Works, Burslem. Staffordshire Potteries. 1885–8. *Earthenwares.* Formerly Gildea & Walker, q.v.

1696

Printed mark, 1885–8.   The word "leaf" refers to the name of the pattern.   Similar marks occur.

GILDEA

GILDEA & WALKER, Dale Hall Works, Burslem.   Staffordshire Potteries. 1881–5. *Earthenwares.* Formerly Bates, Gildea & Walker, q.v.   Subsequently James Gildea, q.v.

1697   G. & W.

Distinguishing initials found on several printed marks of differing design, 1881–5.

1698

Trade-mark, incorporated in various marks, 1881–5.

1699   GILDEA & WALKER
$$\frac{2}{84}$$

Impressed name-mark with month and year numbers, c. 1881–5.

GILL

WILLIAM GILL & SON(S), Providence Pottery, Castleford, Yorkshire. 1880–1932. *Earthenwares.* Formerly G. Gill.

1700

Printed mark, 1880+.   "England" added from 1891.

GIMSON

WALLIS GIMSON & CO., Lane Delph Pottery, Fenton. Staffordshire Potteries. 1884–90. *Earthenwares.* Formerly Pratt & Simpson.

1701   WALLIS GIMSON &
CO.

A printed mark comprising a beehive with the title of the firm below and the name of the pattern above was used by this firm, 1884–90.

GINDER		**SAMUEL GINDER & CO.**, Victoria Works, Lane Delph, Fenton. Staffordshire Potteries. 1811–43. *Earthenwares.*

1702  Distinguishing name found on several printed marks of differing design: name of the individual pattern is often included, *1811–43.*

4020   GJ   *See* Christopher D. Warham.
          (monogram)

—   G. J. & S.   *See* Appendix, page 718.

139   G. L. A. & Bros.   *See* G. L. Ashworth & Bros. (Ltd.).

1703–5 GLADSTONE (CHINA) *See* below also.
3173   *See* George Procter & Co. (Ltd.).

GLADSTONE   **GLADSTONE CHINA (LONGTON) LTD.**, High Street, Longton. Staffordshire Potteries. 1939–52. *China.*

1703 Printed mark, 1946–61. *See* below.

Continued as:

GLADSTONE   **GLADSTONE CHINA** (Proprietors—Thos. Poole & Gladstone China Ltd.), Longton. Staffordshire Potteries. 1952– . *China.*

1704–5   Printed marks, c. 1961. The former "Gladstone China (Longton) Ltd." mark, no. 1703, was continued by the new company from 1952 to 1961.

GLASS   **JOHN GLASS,*** Market Street, Hanley. c. 1784–1838 * *Earthenwares, Basaltes, etc.*

1706   GLASS HANLEY   Impressed marks, c. 1787–1838.*
1706a   J. GLASS HANLEY   A basalt covered sugar, in the Godden Collection, with mark, no. 1706a, would seem to be of the 1822–30 period.

            * Three firms could have used this mark:
               John Glass, Market St., Hanley. c. 1784–1812.
               John Glass & Sons, Market St., Hanley. c. 1818–22.
               John Glass, Market St., Hanley. c. 1822–38.

GLASS
JOSEPH GLASS, Hanley. Staffordshire Potteries. Late 17th century–early 18th century. *Slip decorated Earthenwares.*
    Wedgwood, in his list of Hanley potters of c. 1710–15, lists Glass as a manufacturer of "cloudy sort of dishes painted with Diff't color'd slips, and sold at 3s. and 3s. 6d. a doz.".

1707   JOSEPH GLASS
This name occurs written in slip on rare slip decorated earthenwares. A cradle dated 1703 in the Fitzwilliam Museum is illustrated in *British Pottery and Porcelain: an illustrated Encyclopaedia of Marked Specimens.*

1029   GLASTON
See John Coney.

342   G. L. B. & CO.
See G. L. Bentley & Co. (Ltd.).

GLEBE
GLEBE POTTERY (Agnes M. Raper), Chelsea, London S.W.3. 1924–7. *Studio-type Pottery, models of cottages, etc.*

1708   GLEBE CHELSEA
           CIMS
Incised or painted mark, c. 1924–7.

1709   GLEBE CHELSEA
Impressed or incised mark, c. 1927.

2732   G L M
See Grace L. Moody.

GLOBE
GLOBE POTTERY CO. LTD., Waterloo Road, Cobridge. Staffordshire Potteries and at Shelton from c. 1934. 1914– .*
Earthenwares.

1710–11

Printed marks used from 1914 and no. 1711 from 1917.

        * Firm taken over by Ridgways and continued from Messrs. Ridgways addresses.

1712–13			Printed marks, c. 1930–40. N.B. "Cobridge" gives way to "Shelton" from c. 1934.

1714–17

1947–54   1947–54   1954–   1954–

Post-war printed marks.
N.B. No "Co. Ltd." on marks from 1954.

GLOVER

LOUIS H. H. GLOVER, Barnsley, Yorkshire. 1930– .
Studio-type Pottery.

1718 **4HG** Incised or painted initial mark, often with year added, 1930's–46.

1719 **G** Impressed or painted initial mark, 1946– .

GLYNDE

GLYNDE POTTERY, Glynde Place, Glynde, Sussex. 1960– . *Studio-type Pottery.*

1720 GLYNDE POTTERY Painted or incised name, in writing letters, 1960– .

341 **1660** **2555**	GM (also joined)	*See* Agnes Benson. *See* Margaret Galbraith. *See* Geoffrey Maund.
1133	G. M. C.	*See* Creyke & Sons Ltd.
2556	G M P	*See* Geoffrey Maund.

GODFREY		**G. GODFREY**, Richmond, Surrey. 1961– . *Studio-type Pottery*.
1721	G. G.	Incised initial mark, 1961– . Sometimes with year added.

GODWIN

BENJAMIN E. GODWIN, Cobridge. Staffordshire Potteries. 1834–41. *Earthenwares*. Formerly in partnership with Thomas Godwin.

1722
1723   B. G.

Distinguishing initials found on several printed marks of differing design: name of the individual pattern is often included, 1834–41. Mark no. 1723 is a typical example with initials below. Many child's toy services bear "B. G." marks.

N.B. Another Benjamin Godwin was potting at Cobridge from about 1795 to 1811.

GODWIN

B. C. GODWIN, Navigation Road, Burslem. Staffordshire Potteries. c. 1851.* *Earthenwares*.

1724   B. C. G.

Distinguishing initials found on several printed marks of differing design: name of the individual pattern is often included, c. 1851.

 * This name also occurs in the Cobridge records for 1836, but the marked wares would appear to date from 1851 when the above Burslem address occurs.

GODWIN

GODWIN & HEWITT, Victoria Tile Works, Hereford. 1889–1910. *Tiles*, *etc*. Subsequently Godwin & Thynne.

1725

Printed or impressed mark registered in 1889 and continued to 1910.

GODWIN

JOHN & ROBERT GODWIN, Sneyd Green, Cobridge. Staffordshire Potteries. 1834–66. *Earthenwares*.

1726   J. & R. G.

Distinguishing initials found on several printed marks of differing design: name of the individual pattern is often included, 1834–66.

1727	G. BROS.	The pottery prints in the Victoria and Albert Museum contain several bearing marks incorporating "G. Bros". It is possible that this form of mark was used by John & Robert Godwin, c. 1834–66, or possibly by Gelson Bros, c. 1868–75.

GODWIN

GODWIN, ROWLEY & CO., Market Place, Burslem. Staffordshire Potteries. 1828–31. *Earthenwares*.

1728	G. R. & Co.	Distinguishing initials found on several printed marks of differing design: the words "Staffordshire Stone China" on a scroll below a crown are incorporated in several marks, 1828–31. N.B. These initials could also have been used by Godwin, Rathbone & Co. of the same address, c. 1822.

GODWIN

THOMAS GODWIN, Canal Works, Navigation Road, Burslem. Staffordshire Potteries. 1834–54. *Earthenwares*. Formerly T. & B. Godwin, q.v.

1729	T. G.	Distinguishing initials found on several printed marks of differing design: name of the individual pattern is often included, 1834–54.
1730	THOS GODWIN BURSLEM STONE CHINA	Other printed or impressed marks give the name in full, c. 1834–54.
1730a	THOS GODWIN NEW WHARF	
1730b	OPAQUE CHINA T GODWIN WHARF	Printed mark on American view dish illustrated in companion illustrated encyclopaedia, c. 1840–50.
1731		This printed mark has previously been attributed to Thomas Green, Churchyard Works, Burslem, but as it occurs with Thos. Godwin's name, there can be little doubt that it relates to this potter, c. 1834–54. An example with this mark will be found illustrated in the companion illustrated encyclopaedia of marked specimens.

GODWIN

THOMAS & BENJAMIN GODWIN, New Wharf and New Basin Potteries, Burslem. Staffordshire Potteries. c. 1809–34. *Earthenwares, Creamwares, etc.* Subsequently Thomas Godwin, see previous entry.

| 1732 | T & B G. | Distinguishing details of several printed marks of differing design: name of the individual pattern is often included, 1809–34. The name also occurs in full on several printed marks. |
| 1733 | T. B. G. | |

| 1734 | T. & B. GODWIN NEW WHARF | Impressed mark, c. 1809–34. |

| 869 | GOLD ANCHOR (anchor mark in gold) | *See* Chelsea Porcelain Works. |

GOLDSCHEIDER

GOLDSCHEIDER (STAFFORDSHIRE) POTTERY LTD. (formerly Goldscheider Art Pottery), John Street, Hanley. Staffordshire Potteries. 1946–59. *Earthenwares and Bone China Figures, etc.*

| 1735 | *Goldscheider* | Printed mark, 1946–59. The signature of Marcel Goldscheider. |

GOMSHALL

GOMSHALL POTTERY (Mrs. Molly Coryn), Gomshall, Surrey. 1953– . *Studio-type Pottery.*

| 1736 | GOMSHALL | Incised mark in writing letters, 1953– . |

| 1736a |  | Incised initials of Molly Coryn on early, pre-Gomshall pieces, c. 1939–53. |

GOODE

THOMAS GOODE & CO. (LTD.), South Audley Street, London W.1.

| 1737 | | Many 19th and 20th century marks occur which incorporate this famous retailing firm's name. The name does not generally occur before the 1860's. It should be noted that the addition of "Ltd" in the style indicates a date subsequent to September 1918. |
| 1737a | T. GOODE & Cº LONDON MINTONS CHINA | |

GOODFELLOW		**THOMAS GOODFELLOW**, Phoenix Works, Tunstall. Staffordshire Potteries. 1828–59. *Earthenwares.*
1738	T. GOODFELLOW	Distinguishing detail of several printed marks of differing design: name of the individual pattern is often included, 1828–59.

GOODWIN		**GOODWIN, BRIDGWOOD (&) HARRIS**, Lane End. Staffordshire Potteries. 1829–31. *Earthenwares.* Formerly Goodwin, Bridgwood & Orton (see below), subsequently Goodwin (s) & Harris, q.v.
1739	G. B. H.	Distinguishing initials found on printed marks, 1829–31. An earthenware jug in the Brighton Museum (Willett Collection) commemorates the death of George IV in June 1830 and bears a mark of these initials under a lion. See Plate 3. See also companion illustrated encyclopaedia. This partnership is included in rate records from March 1829 to March 1831. Similar wares bear only the lion mark without the initials. These wares may have been made by Goodwin & Harris, q.v.

GOODWIN		**GOODWIN, BRIDGWOOD & ORTON**, High Street, Lane End. Staffordshire Potteries. 1827–9. *Earthenwares.* Formerly Goodwin & Orton and Goodwin & Co., subsequently Goodwin, Bridgwood & Harris, see above.
1739a	G. B. O.	Distinguishing detail of rare printed marks of differing design: name of the individual pattern is included, 1827–9.
1739b	G. B. & O.	

GOODWIN		**GOODWIN & BULLOCK**, Dresden Works, Longton. Staffordshire Potteries. 1852–6 (and 1858 at High St., Longton). *Porcelains.*
1740		Printed mark, 1852–6.

GOODWIN		**GOODWIN & ELLIS**, Flint Street, Lane End. Staffordshire Potteries. c. 1839–40. *Earthenwares.* Formerly Goodwin & Harris, q.v.
1740a	G. & E.	Distinguishing detail of several printed marks of differing design: name of the individual pattern is often included. 1839–40.

GOODWIN

J. GOODWIN STODDARD & CO., King Street, Foley, Longton. Staffordshire Potteries. 1898–1940. *China*.

1741

Printed mark, 1898–1936.

1742

Printed mark, 1936–40.

GOODWINS

GOODWINS* & HARRIS, Crown Works, Lane End. Staffordshire Potteries. c. 1831–8. *Earthenwares*. Formerly Goodwin, Bridgwood & Harris, q.v.

1743   GOODWINS & HARRIS

Impressed name-mark on printed earthenwares, children's plates, etc., c. 1831–8.

1743a   LION CREST

A printed mark of a crown surmounted by a lion occurs on a reform jug of c. 1832 and was probably used by this firm. See crest on G. B. H. mark no. 1739 shown in Plate 3.

     * In some rate records the name "GOODWINS" appears as "GOODWIN".

GORDON

ANNE GORDON, MRS., Quick's Green, Pangbourne, Berkshire. 1958– . *Studio-type Pottery, Figures and Bird Models*.

1744

Incised or painted mark, often with year added, 1958– .

219   GORDON POTTERY

See William Bailey & Sons.

GORDON'S

GORDON'S POTTERY, Prestonpans, Scotland. 18th century–1832. *Earthenwares*.
See J. Arnold Fleming's *Scottish Pottery* (1923).

| 1745 | GORDON | Rare impressed marks, late 18th–early 19th century. |

| 1746 | G. G. | The initials of George Gordon occur (rarely) in printed marks incorporating the name of the pattern.   Early 19th century. |

GOSS

WILLIAM HENRY GOSS (LTD.), Falcon Pottery, Stoke. Staffordshire Potteries. 1858 (or 1862)–1944.* *Porcelains, Parian and Earthenwares.*

1747	W H G	Impressed or printed marks, c. 1862+.
1748	W H GOSS	
1749	W. H. GOSS COPYRIGHT	

| 1750 | | Printed mark, c. 1862. "ENGLAND" added below from 1891. |

* Retitled Goss China Co. Ltd. from c. 1934 when taken over by Cauldon Potteries Ltd.

GOUDIE

ISOBEL GOUDIE, MISS, Edinburgh, Scotland.   c. 1920–30. *Studio-type Pottery.*

| 1751 | ISOBEL GOUDIE | Signature or initial monogram marks, c. 1920–30. |

| 1752 | | |

GOVANCROFT

GOVANCROFT POTTERIES LTD., Tollcross, Glasgow, Scotland.   1913– . *Earthenwares and Stonewares.*

| 1753–4 | | Printed or impressed marks, 1913–49. |

| 1755–6 | | Printed marks, 1949– . |

CHIEFTAIN WARE   This trade-name was introduced in 1962.

GOW		**DOROTHY W. GOW, MRS.**, London S.W.10. c. 1920–30. *Studio-type Pottery and Figures.*
1757	D. W. G.	Incised or painted mark, c. 1920–30.
1819	G. P.	*See* Greta Pottery.
2969a		*See* Gwendolen Parnell.
229	G. P. CO.	*See* Baker, Bevans & Irwin.
3171	G P & CO or	*See* George Proctor & Co. (Ltd.).
3172	C P & CO L	
3247	G. R.	*See* George Richardson.
1158b	G R C	*See* G. R. Curtis.
1728	G R & CO	*See* Godwin, Rowley & Co.
2195– 2202	GRAFTON CHINA	*See* A. B. Jones & Sons (Ltd.).

GRAINGER		**GEORGE GRAINGER (& CO.)**, Worcester. c. 1839–1902. *Porcelains, Parian, Semi-Porcelain.* Formerly Grainger Lee & Co.
1758	GEO GRAINGER CHINA WORKS WORCESTER	Distinguishing details of several painted or printed marks of differing design: c. 1839–60.
1759	*George Grainger Royal China Works Worcester.*	
1760	G. GRAINGER & CO. WORCESTER	"& Co." was added to most marks from about 1850.
1761	SOCIETY OF ARTS AWARD 1847 G. GRAINGER WORCESTER	An ornate, large circular printed mark occurs on wares of the 1847–50 period.

| 1762 | G. G. & CO. S. P. | Impressed or printed initial marks on the special "semi-porcelain" body, introduced in 1848. The name "Semi-Porcelain" occurs in full on some printed marks. |
| 1762a | S. P. G. G. W. | |

| 1763 | G. W. | Distinguishing detail of several printed marks of differing design: name or number of the individual pattern is often included, 1850–60. |

| 1764 | GRAINGER WORCESTER S. P. | The wording "sole manufacturer of the Semi-Porcelain. Prize Ware" also occurs in the 1848–55 period. |
| 1764a | SEMI PORCELAIN | |

| 1765 | | Printed marks, c. 1850–75. |

| 1766 | CHEMICAL PORCELAIN GRAINGER & CO. MANUFACTURERS WORCESTER | Distinguishing detail of several printed marks of differing design, c. 1850–70. |

| 1767 | G & CO. W. | Distinguishing initials on several marks, 1850–89. |

| 1768 | G. GRAINGER 19 FORE GATE WORCESTER | A rare printed mark was employed in the 1850's. This comprises the name and address on three lines of a folded ribbon-like device. |

| 1769 | | Printed mark used on copies of early Worcester porcelains, c. 1860–80. |

| 1770 | | Printed or impressed mark, c. 1870–89. Later version given below. |

In 1889 the Grainger company was taken over by the Worcester Royal Porcelain Co. Ltd., and production was continued until 1902.

1771   Printed mark, c. 1889–1902. "England" added below from 1891. The shield mark nos. were not used before 1870, or from 1889 with the words "Royal China Works". The date 1823, given in several books, is an error.

Year letters occur under this mark, from 1891, see below:

A	1891	E	1895	I	1899
B	1892	F	1896	J	1900
C	1893	G	1897	K	1901
D	1894	H	1898	L	1902

Typical examples of Grainger wares will be found illustrated in *British Pottery and Porcelain; an illustrated Encyclopaedia of Marked Specimens.*

GRAINGER

GRAINGER, LEE & CO., New China Works, Worcester. c. 1812–c. 39. *Porcelains.* Formerly Grainger, Wood & Co., q.v. Subsequently George Grainger, see previous entry.

1772 Grainger Lee & Co. Worcester Early wares bear the written mark—Grainger Lee & Co., Worcester. Printed marks also occur in several forms from c. 1820, c. 1812–39.

1773 New China Works Worcester Painted mark on floral plate in the Victoria and Albert Museum, c. 1820–30, also occurs on other early specimens.

1774 Royal China Works Worcester Painted marks in this form occur c. 1812–30.

GRAINGER

GRAINGER WOOD & CO., New China Works, Worcester. c. 1801–12. *Porcelains.* Subsequently Grainger, Lee & Co., see previous entry.

Most examples of Messrs. Grainger Wood & Co.'s porcelains were unmarked or bore only the name of the London retailer—Mortlock.

1775 Grainger Wood & Co. Worcester, Warranted Several written marks similar to these were used c. 1801–12 but are rare.

1775a GRAINGER, WOOD WORCESTER, WARRANTED A marked teapot will be found illustrated in *British Pottery and Porcelain: an illustrated Encyclopaedia of Marked Specimens.*

2366b GRANITOFTS *See* Leeds Fireclay Co. Ltd.

GRAY

A. E. GRAY & CO. LTD., Glebe Works, Hanley, c. 1912–33; Whieldon Road, 1934–61, Stoke. Staffordshire Potteries. 1912–61.* *Earthenwares.*

A. E. Gray was formerly a china decorator.

1776

Printed mark, 1912–30.

1777–8

Printed marks, 1930–33. Note "Hanley" address.

1779

Printed mark, 1934–61. "England" or "Made in England" were added to this mark.

    * Retitled "Portmeirion Potteries Ltd.", q.v., from December 31st, 1961.

GRAY

W. A. GRAY (& SONS) (LTD.), Midlothian Pottery (and Newbigging Pottery, Musselburgh from 1880), Portobello, Scotland. c. 1857–1931. *Earthenwares and Stonewares.*

1780   W. A. GRAY

Marks may occur incorporating the initials and the name of Dr. Gray. "& Sons" was added to the style c. 1870 and "Ltd." in 1926.

—   DANIEL GREATBATCH

See Appendix.

GREATBATCH

WILLIAM GREATBATCH (b. 1735, d. 1813), Lane Delph, Fenton. Staffordshire Potteries. c. 1760–c. 1780. *Earthenwares.*

William Greatbatch, a modeller and potter, was closely associated with Josiah Wedgwood from c. 1760. Wolf Mankowitz in his *Wedgwood* (1953) quotes contemporary letters and a bill for modelling designs for Wedgwood; this includes—"Leaf Candlestick, oval fruit basket and stand, pr cornucopia, 3 oblong fruit dishes, 1 pineapple teapot, 1 Chinese teapot". Early Greatbatch wares are not normally marked. See a paper by Donald Towner in the *Transactions of the English Ceramic Circle*, vol. 5, part 4, 1963. Later printed creamwares may bear the name on the print.

1781 PUBLISHED AS THE ACT DIRECTS JANY 4.1778 BY W. GREATBATCH, LANE DELF, STAFFORDSHIRE

Printed signature "mark" on printed teapot in the Franks Collection at the British Museum.*

1782 GREATBATCH

The simple name-mark occurs on some prints of the 1770–80 period.

* Donald Towner in his *English Cream-coloured Earthenware* (1957) illustrates (Plate 66B) a similar signed teapot.

3440 GREEN
or
3441 GREEN LIVERPOOL
(on prints)

See John Sadler.

GREEN

GREEN & CLAY, Stafford St., Longton. Staffordshire Potteries. 1888–91. *Earthenwares.* Formerly Green, Clark & Clay.

1783

Printed or impressed mark, 1888–91.
Another compass point mark occurs on tiles made by the Campbell Tile Co. (Ltd.) from 1882.

GREEN

DAVID GREEN, various teaching posts, Carlisle, Cumberland. 1946– . *Studio-type Pottery.*

1784 DAVID GREEN
1785 D. G.

Impressed name or initial marks, 1946– .

GREEN	**GREEN DENE POTTERY** (Denis Moore), East Horsley, Surrey. 1953– . *Studio-type Pottery.*
1786	Impressed seal type mark, 1953– .
1787	Personal monogram seal of Denis Moore, 1953– .
1788	Personal mark of Michael Buckland, 1953– .
— W. GREEN	*See* Ashtead Potters Ltd.
1311 GREEN DON POTTERY	*See* Don Pottery.
GREEN	**J. GREEN & CO.** (or & SONS), 10 & 11 St. Paul's Churchyard, London. 1834–42 (later at other addresses). *Retailers.*
1789	Porcelains occur with this printed mark. The London directories list this firm of retailers from 1834 to 1842. In 1841 and 42 the style is given as "J. Green & *Sons*".
1789a JAMES GREEN UPPER THAMES ST. & 62 CORNHILL LONDON	Printed marks occur with the name and these addresses; the Cornhill address indicates a date from c. 1870 to c. 1874.
GREEN	**M. GREEN & CO.**, Minerva Works, Fenton. Staffordshire Potteries. 1859–76. *China and Earthenwares.* Formerly T. Green, q.v. Subsequently T. A. & S. Green, q.v.
1790	Printed mark, 1859–76. Other marks occur with the name M. Green & Co.

GREEN

STEPHEN GREEN, Imperial Pottery, Lambeth, London S.E. c. 1820–58. *Stonewares*. Works purchased by John Cliff in 1858.

1791	STEPHEN GREEN LAMBETH	Distinguishing detail of several relief, impressed or incised marks of differing design, c. 1820–58.
1792	STEPHEN GREEN IMPERIAL POTTERIES LAMBETH	
1793	S. GREEN LAMBETH	

A rare marked figure/flask and a moulded jug are illustrated in *British Pottery and Porcelain: an illustrated Encyclopaedia of Marked Specimens.*

GREEN

THOMAS GREEN, Minerva Works, Fenton. Staffordshire Potteries. 1847–59. *China and Earthenwares*. Formerly Green & Richards. Subsequently M. Green & Co., q.v.

| 1794 | T. GREEN FENTON POTTERIES | Distinguishing detail of several printed marks of differing design, 1847–59. |

1795   Printed mark, 1847–59.

GREEN

T. A. & S. GREEN, Minerva Works, Fenton. Staffordshire Potteries. 1876–89.* *China*. Formerly M. Green & Co.

1796   Printed mark, 1876–89; other marks occur with the initials "T. A. & S. G."

      * Continued from 1889 as "Crown Staffordshire Porcelain Co.", q.v.

GREEN

T. G. GREEN & CO. (LTD.), Church Gresley, Nr. Burton-on-Trent, Derbyshire. c. 1864– . *Earthenwares and Stonewares*.
Early wares unmarked.

GRESLEY

1797   Printed church mark, first registered in 1888.

1798–9		Printed marks, c. 1892+ with "England".
1800–1		20th century printed marks.
1802–5		Typical printed marks of the 1930's.
1806–10		Post-war printed marks; similar marks used for different patterns or styles.
1811		New basic mark introduced in 1962.

GREENE

JOHN GREENE (d. 1686), Wrotham, Kent. Second half 17th century. *Slip decorated Earthenwares.*

1812	I. G.	Rare examples of Wrotham earthenwares bear these initials. See *E.C.C. Transactions*, vol. 3, part 2, a paper by A. J. B. Kiddell.

933 —	GREENOCK	*See* Clyde Pottery (Co. Ltd.). *See* Greenock Pottery.

GREENOCK		**GREENOCK POTTERY** (retitled Ladyburn Pottery, c. 1849), various owners, Greenock, Scotland. c. 1820–60. *Earthenwares, Creamwares.*
1813	GREENOCK POTTERY	Distinguishing detail of impressed or printed marks of differing design, c. 1820–c. 49.

1814   J. Arnold Fleming in his *Scottish Pottery* (1923) attributes this mark to James Stevenson & Co. of the Greenock Pottery, c. 1820. But this mark is normally attributed to Andrew Stevenson of Cobridge, Staffs. A printed plate with this mark in the British Museum is decorated with a subject dated 1820, but could have been produced later.

GREENWOOD

S. GREENWOOD, Fenton. Staffordshire Potteries. c. 1790. *Basalt wares.*

1815   S. GREENWOOD   A fine basalt vase (in the British Museum) is illustrated in Grant's *The Makers of Black Basaltes* (1910) but this seems to be the only known example bearing this impressed name-mark.

GREENWOOD

R. M. GREENWOOD, MISS., London W.1. 1948– . *Independent Ceramic Decorator.*

1816   Painted monogram mark, 1948– .

GRENVILLE

GRENVILLE POTTERY LTD., Tunstall. Staffordshire Potteries. 1946– . *Earthenwares.*

1817–18   Printed marks, 1946– *.

* At January 1964 this company was looking for new premises, and was not at that time in production.

1797 1801– 1811	GRESLEY or GRESLEY WARE	*See* T. G. Green & Co. (Ltd.).
—	C. GRESLEY	*See* Appendix, page 719.

GRETA		**GRETA POTTERY,** Summer Street, Stoke. Staffordshire Potteries. 1938–41. *Earthenwares.*
1819	G$_P$	Printed or painted mark, 1938–41.
3358–60	GRIFFIN	*See* Rockingham Works.
4183	(device)	*See* H. M. Williamson & Sons.
GRIFFITHS		**ARTHUR J. GRIFFITHS,** Long Whatton, Nr. Loughborough, Leics. 1948– . *Studio-type Pottery.*
		Arthur Griffiths worked at the Crowan and Leach Potteries before taking teaching posts.
1820		Impressed seal mark, 1948– .
GRIFFITHS		**GRIFFITHS, BEARDMORE & BIRKS,** Flint Street, Lane End. 1830. *Earthenwares.* Formerly Thomas Griffiths & Co. Subsequently Beardmore & Birks.
1821	G. B. & B.	A willow pattern dish in the Godden Collection bears a large printed mark incorporating these initials, the pre-Victorian Royal Arms and the words "Staffordshire Ironstone China". These initials only fit this partnership which occurs in the March 1830 rate records.
GRIMSHAW		**GLADYS GRIMSHAW, MRS.,** Noke, Oxford. 1934– . *Studio-type Pottery and Sculpture.*
1822	G. G.	Incised or painted initial mark, 1934–62.
1822a		Impressed seal type mark, being the name Grimshaw in Chinese characters, 1963–
GRIMWADE		**GRIMWADE BROS.,** Winton Pottery, Hanley and Stoke. Staffordshire Potteries. 1886–1900. *Earthenwares, Majolica and China.*
		Subsequently Grimwades Ltd., see below.

1823 Printed mark, 1886–1900.

GRIMWADES

GRIMWADES LTD., Winton, Upper Hanley and Elgin Potteries, Stoke. Staffordshire Potteries. 1900– . *Earthenwares, Majolica, Jet, etc.* Formerly Grimwade Bros., see above.

1824–8

STOKE POTTERY

c. 1900+   c. 1906+   c. 1906+   c. 1906+   c. 1911+

1829–33 GRIMWADES ENGLAND VITRO HOTELWARE   GRIMWADES ROYAL WINTON IVORY ENGLAND   GRIMWADES ENGLAND   STOKE ON TRENT ENGLAND   ROYAL WINTON IVORY

c. 1930+   c. 1930+   c. 1930+   c. 1930+   c. 1930+

1834–6 BONE CHINA ENGLAND   ROYAL WINTON GRIMWADES ENGLAND   RUBIAN ART POTTERY GRIMWADES ENGLAND

c. 1934–9   c. 1934–50   c. 1934–50

1837–9 *Royal Winton* MADE IN ENGLAND   *Royal Winton* GRIMWADES MADE IN ENGLAND   *Royal Winton* MADE IN ENGLAND

c. 1951+   c. 1951+   c. 1951+

Printed marks, c. 1900 onwards.

GRINDLEY

GRINDLEY HOTEL WARE CO. LTD., Globe Pottery, Tunstall. Staffordshire Potteries. 1908– . *Earthenwares.*

1840 GRINDLEY HOTEL WARE ENGLAND VITRIFIED   Printed mark from 1908.

1841   Printed mark, c. 1946– .

GRINDLEY	**W. H. GRINDLEY & CO. (LTD.)**, New Field Pottery (c. 1880–91), Woodland Pottery (1891–), Tunstall. Staffordshire Potteries. 1880– . *Earthenwares, Ironstones, etc.*

Firm acquired by Alfred Clough Ltd. in 1960.

1842 Printed mark, c. 1880–1914. Early, pre-1891 versions have "Tunstall" in place of "England" as the last word.

1843–5

Printed marks, c. 1914–25.
N.B. "Ltd." added to style and marks from 1925.

1846–9

Printed marks used from 1925.

1850 Printed mark, c. 1936–54. Slight variations occur, with the name of patterns, etc.

1851 Printed mark, c. 1954– .

2160, 2168 1852   GROSVENOR (CHINA)   *See* Jackson & Gosling (Ltd.) and Grosvenor China Ltd., below.

GROSVENOR   **GROSVENOR CHINA LTD.**, Chelson St., Longton. Staffordshire Potteries. 1961– . *Bone China.*

1852 Printed mark, also used by Messrs. Jackson & Gosling Ltd. from the 1950's.

GROSVENOR

F. GROSVENOR (& SON), Eagle Pottery (from 1906), Bridgeton, Glasgow, Scotland. c. 1869–1926. *Stonewares, Earthenwares.*

1853

Printed eagle trade-mark registered by Frederick Grosvenor in 1879 and continued by Grosvenor & Son to 1926.

1854   GROSVENOR & SON

Distinguishing detail of impressed or printed marks of differing design.   Note "& Son" dating from c. 1899.

GROUP

GROUP LETTERS
In 1942 due to war-time controls the Board of Trade divided the production of domestic china and earthenwares into various categories, with the initials A. B. C.   These initials were incorporated in the marks and as the relevant orders were cancelled in March 1947 marks bearing the initials can be dated 1942–7.
   Further groups BY, CY and CZ came into being in 1945.

A typical mark incorporating a group letter.

GROVE

GROVE & STARK, Palissy Works, Longton. Staffordshire Potteries. 1871–85. *Earthenwares.* Formerly R. H. Grove.

1855   G. & S.

Distinguishing initials found on several printed marks of differing design: name of the individual pattern is often included, 1871–85.

1855a   GROVE & STARK
LONGTON

The names in full occur on several printed and impressed marks, 1871–85.

1856

A monogram of the initials G S impressed within an oval occurs on plates registered by Grove & Stark in the early 1880's.

GROVES

LAVENDER GROVES, MISS, 163 Kings Road, London S.W.3.   1952– .   *Studio-type Pottery.*

1857	*GROVES*	Incised or painted mark, 1952– .
1858		Rare examples bear a mark of a "Peke's" head.
1856		*See* Grove & Stark.
1855	G & S	*See* Grove & Stark.
3568	G. S. & Co.	*See* George Skinner & Co.
1679b	G & S Ltd.	*See* Gibson & Sons (Ltd.).
	or	
1679a	G & S Ltd. B	
—	GSH (monogram)	*See* Appendix, page 719.
3504	G. S. & S.	*See* George Shaw & Sons (Ltd.).
2796	G. T. M.	*See* George Thomas Mountford.
3894	G. T. & S.	*See* G. W. Turner & Sons.
—	GUEST BROS.	*See* Appendix.

GUEST

GUEST & DEWSBURY, South Wales Pottery, Llanelly, Carmarthenshire, Wales. 1877–1927. *Earthenwares.* Formerly Holland & Guest.

1859	G. & D. L.	Distinguishing details of several printed marks of differing
1859a	G. D.	design: name of the individual pattern is often included,
	L.	1877–1927. The L stands for the town of Llanelly.

—	G. W.	*See* Appendix, page 719.
171		*See* Avoncroft Pottery.
1763		*See* George Grainger.
4021		*See* George Warrilow (& Sons) (Ltd.).
1697	G. & W.	*See* Gildea & Walker.
4022	G. W. & S.	*See* George Warrilow (& Sons) (Ltd.).
	or	
4023	G. W. & SONS	
	or	
4024	G. W. & SONS LTD.	
3892	G. W. T. S.	*See* G. W. Turner & Sons.
	or	
3893	G. W. T. & S.	
	or	
3891	G. W. T. & SONS	

H

820a	H.	*See* Caughley Works.
1861		*See* Hackwood.
1896–7		*See* Frank & Janet Hamer.
1945		Harborne Pottery.
2114		*See* Hughes & Co.
2130		*See* William Hulme.
—	H. & CO.	*See* Appendix.
1864		*See* Hackwood & Co.
1903		*See* Hammersley & Co.
2030		*See* Hill & Co.
2086	H. LTD.	*See* Hoods Ltd.
81	HA	*See* Allanger Pottery.
123	(also joined)	*See* Hester Armstrong.
1875–6		*See* Anna Hagen.
14	H.A. & CO.	*See* Harvey Adams & Co.
64		*See* Henry Alcock & Co. (Ltd.).
179		*See* H. Aynsley & Co. (Ltd.).
1909	H. & A.	*See* Hammersley & Asbury.
2132		*See* Hulse & Adderley.

HACKWOOD

HACKWOOD, Shelton and Hanley.   19th century.   *Earthenwares, Creamwares, etc.*

Several marks, printed or impressed, bear the name Hackwood or the initial H.

Several potters of this name were working at Shelton or
Hanley in the 19th century and it is difficult to attribute
the "Hackwood" or H marks with certainty. The *main*
potters of this name were:

William Hackwood, Eastwood, Hanley, see mark no.
1867. 1827–43.
Josiah Hackwood, Upper High St., Hanley. 1842–3.
William & Thomas Hackwood, New Hall, Shelton. 1844–
50.
Thomas Hackwood. 1850–5.

1860	HACKWOOD	
1861	H	

Distinguishing details of several impressed or printed marks of
differing design: name of the individual pattern is often
included, 1827–55.

1862

This printed mark occurs on wares with the impressed name
"Hackwood", c. 1830–40.

HACKWOOD

HACKWOOD & CO., Eastwood, Hanley. Staffordshire
Potteries. 1807–27. *Earthenwares, Jaspers, etc.* Subsequently
W. Hackwood, q.v.

Contemporary advertisements and some directories list
Hackwood, Dimmock & Co.—a style not included in rate
records. It is very probable that Hackwood & Co. and Hackwood, Dimmock & Co. were one and the same firm. Chaffers'
mark handbook lists the mark "Hackwood Dimmock & Co.".
In some rate lists (1822 and 1825) this firm is listed as William
Hackwood & Co.

1863   HACKWOOD & CO.
1864   H. & CO.

Distinguishing details of impressed marks, 1807–27.

HACKWOOD

HACKWOOD & KEELING, Market St., Hanley. Staffordshire Potteries. 1835–6. *Earthenwares.*

1865

Distinguishing initials H & K found on several printed marks of
differing design: name of the individual pattern is often included, 1835–6. Mark no. 1865 is a typical example.

HACKWOOD

WILLIAM HACKWOOD, Eastwood, Hanley. Staffordshire
Potteries. 1827–43. *Earthenwares.* Formerly Hackwood & Co.,
q.v. Subsequently William & Thomas Hackwood and William
Hackwood & Son.

| 1866 | W. H. HACKWOOD | Distinguishing initials W. H. found on several printed marks of differing design.   A cup and saucer in the Godden Collection has this form of printed initial mark, also the impressed name "HACKWOOD", c. 1827–43. |
| 1867 | | |

| 3199 | R ——— HACKWOOD | *See* William Ratcliffe. |

HACKWOOD

WILLIAM HACKWOOD & SON, New Hall Pottery Shelton.   Staffordshire Potteries.   1846–9.   *Earthenwares.* Formerly William & Thomas Hackwood.   Subsequently Thomas Hackwood.

1868

Distinguishing initials W. H & S found on several printed marks of differing design: name of the individual pattern is often included, 1846–9.   William Hackwood died in 1849.   The son Thomas continued to 1853.

HADLEY

JAMES HADLEY & SONS (LTD.), Worcester.   1896–1905. *Porcelains, Earthenwares, Terra-cotta.*
    For further information on James Hadley and Hadley Ware see *Victorian Porcelain* (1961) and the companion illustrated encyclopaedia to this mark book.

1869

Incised or impressed signature on figures, groups, vases, etc., modelled by James Hadley for the Worcester Royal Porcelain Co., c. 1875–94.

1870

Printed or impressed mark, 1896–February 1897.

1871

Printed mark, February 1897–June 1900.   *A similar mark without the centre ribbon (and without the word "Faience")* was used from June 1900 to August 1902.

| 1872 | FINE ART HADLEY'S TERRA-COTTA | Impressed mark in this form occurs on rare terra-cotta wares, c. 1897–1902. |

1873		Printed mark, August 1902 to June 30th, 1905.
1874	HADLEY WARE	These words occur on some Hadley styled Royal Worcester Porcelains after 1905.

HAGEN   ANNA HAGEN, MISS, London S.W.4. 1956– . *Studio-type Pottery.*

1875		Incised mark on hand-thrown wares, 1956– .
1876		Impressed seal mark on moulded or pressed dishes, etc., 1956– .

HAINES   HAINES, BATCHELOR & CO., Cannon St., London E.C. 1880–90. *Earthenwares and China Retailers.*

1877	PATTERN H. B.	This firm of retailers used their initials on wares made for them. A design registered in 1883 bears this form of printed mark.

HAILE   T. S. HAILE, Shinners Bridge, Darlington, Devon (and other addresses in England and in America). c. 1936–43 and 1945–8. *Studio-type Pottery.*
See Muriel Rose's *Artist Potters in England* (1955).
G. Wingfield Digby's *The Work of the Modern Potter in England* (1952).

1878		Seal type impressed mark, c. 1936–48. Sam Haile died in 1948.
—	HALDEN	*See* High Halden Pottery.

HALES   HALES, HANCOCK & GODWIN LTD., London E.C.1. 1922–60. *Retailers.* Formerly Hales, Hancock & Co. Ltd. Subsequently Hales Bros.

1879	H. H. & G. LTD.	Distinguishing initials found on several printed marks of differing design, c. 1922+.

1880	 H.H & G.LTD ENGLAND	Printed mark, 1930+.

HALL		HALL BROS. (LONGTON) LTD., Radnor Works, Longton. Staffordshire Potteries. 1947– . *China Figures, Vases, etc.*

1881–2		Printed marks, 1947–51.

1883		Printed mark, 1947– .

HALL		CHRISTINE HALL, Henley-on-Thames, Oxfordshire. 1960– . *Figures and Groups in China or Pottery.*

1884		Painted mark, 1960– .

1885	I. HALL (& SONS)	*See* John Hall (& Sons), below.

HALL		JOHN HALL (& SONS), Sytch Pottery, Burslem. Staffordshire Potteries. 1814–32. *Earthenwares.*
1885 1886	I. HALL HALL *	Distinguishing details of several impressed or printed marks of differing design, 1814–22. N.B. A partnership between John & Ralph Hall was in operation at Burslem from 1802–22 and at Tunstall from 1811–22. John Hall seems to have overlapped this period or the mark I. Hall was sometimes employed.
1887	I. HALL & SONS	Impressed or printed mark, c. 1822–32. The impressed version occurs on a relief moulded hunting jug in the Godden Collection.

    * Earthenware figures occur with the impressed mark HALL. These have been attributed to John Hall or Ralph Hall or to the partnership between the two. Directories do not list these potters as "toy" or figure manufacturers but Samuel Hall is listed as such, see mark no 1890.

HALL		**RALPH HALL (& CO.)** or **(& SON)**, Swan Bank, Tunstall. Staffordshire Potteries. 1822–49. *Earthenwares*. Formerly in partnership with John Hall. Subsequently Podmore Walker & Co., q.v.
1888	R. HALL	Distinguishing name found on several printed marks of differing design: name of the individual pattern is often included, 1822–41.
1889	R. HALL & SON	This form of title is recorded on American subject prints, c. 1836.
1890	R. HALL & CO.	Distinguishing detail of several impressed or printed marks of differing design: name of the individual pattern is often included, 1841–9.
1890a	R H & CO.	Distinguishing detail of several printed marks of differing design, 1841–9.

HALL		**SAMUEL HALL**, Marsh Street, Shelton, Hanley. Staffordshire Potteries. c. 1841*–56. *Earthenwares*.
1891	HALL	Impressed mark on rare earthenware figures, c. 1841*–56. These "HALL" marked figures have been attributed to John and Ralph Hall, see note under mark 1886.

* This potter is also included in White's Directory of 1834.

HALL		**HALL & READ**, Wellington Works, Burslem, 1882, Dresden Works, Hanley, 1883. Victoria Square, Hanley, 1883–8. Staffordshire Potteries. 1882–8. *Earthenwares*.
1892	HALL & READ HANLEY	A printed name-mark of horse-shoe form occurs on a design (of Willow pattern type) registered by this firm in January 1883. Other marks occur with the name in full and the name of the pattern, 1882–8.
	H. & R.	These initials may have been used by this firm, see Appendix, "H & R".

HALLAM		**HALLAM & DAY**, Mount Pleasant Works, Longton. Staffordshire Potteries. 1880–5. *Earthenwares*. Formerly Hallam & Johnson.
1893	H. & D.	Distinguishing initials H. & D. found on several printed marks of differing design, 1880–5. The Royal Arms occur on several marks.

HALLEN		**HENRY HALLEN**, Chesterton, Staffordshire. c. 1810–c. 50? *Earthenwares*.
1894	Henry Hallen May 14th, 1831	Incised signature mark of Henry Hallen, recorded on one specimen only. The working period of this potter is subject to doubt.

HAMADA		**SHOJI HAMADA**, Leach Pottery, St. Ives, Cornwall. c. 1920–23 and 1929–30+ (also worked in Japan; examples sent to England). *Studio-type Pottery*. For examples of Shoji Hamada's work see Muriel Rose's *Artist Potters in England* (1955).
1895	庀	Impressed seal mark, c. 1920– .

HAMER		**FRANK & JANET HAMER**, Terracotta, Ponthir, Nr. Newport, Wales. *Studio-type Pottery, mainly Stonewares*. Formerly at Wolverhampton and at Hellaby (Yorkshire) 1952– .
1896–7	·H· ▪▪	Impressed seal marks, 1952–9.
1898	F. H.	Seal mark of initials of Frank Hamer, 1952– .
1899	J. H.	Seal mark of initials of Janet Hamer, 1952–9.
1900	PONTHIR	Impressed mark used by Janet Hamer at Ponthir, 1959– .
3125	HAMILTON	*See* Pountney & Allies, page 507.

HAMILTON		**ROBERT HAMILTON**, Stoke. Staffordshire Potteries. 1811–26. *Earthenwares*.
1901	HAMILTON STOKE	Distinguishing detail of impressed or printed marks of differing design, 1811–26.

HAMMERSLEY		**HAMMERSLEY & CO.**, Alsager Pottery, Longton. Staffordshire Potteries. 1887–1932+.* *China*.

1902	H. & C.	
1903	H. & CO.	
1904–4a		

Distinguishing details of several impressed or printed marks of differing design, usually with a crown. The crown and "china" occurs on small items without the initials, 1887–1912.

1905–6

Printed marks, 1912–39.

1907–8

Printed marks, 1939– .

  * Continued as *Hammersley & Co. (Longton) Ltd.* from 1932 to present day.

HAMMERSLEY

HAMMERSLEY & ASBURY, Prince of Wales Pottery, Longton. Staffordshire Potteries. 1872–5. *Earthenwares.* Formerly Hammersley, Freeman & Co. Subsequently E. Asbury & Co., q.v.

1909 H. & A.
1910

Distinguishing initials on several printed marks of differing design, with or without the Prince of Wales' crest, 1872–5.

  N.B. Other potters could well have used these initials, if they occur without the crest. Such potters include Hulse & Adderley (1869–75) of Longton.

HAMMERSLEY

J. & R. HAMMERSLEY, New St., Hanley. Staffordshire Potteries. 1877–1917. *China and Earthenwares.* Subsequently R. Hammersley (c. 1917–20).

1911 J. R. H.

Distinguishing initials found on several printed marks of differing design: name of the individual pattern is often included, 1877–1917.

HAMMERSLEY

RALPH HAMMERSLEY (& SON), Overhouse Pottery (c. 1880+), Burslem. Staffordshire Potteries. (At Church Bank Pottery, Tunstall, c. 1860–83 and Black Works, Tunstall, c. 1885–1888.) 1860–1905. *Earthenwares.*

| 1912 | R. H. | Distinguishing initials found on several printed marks of differing design: name of the individual pattern is often included, 1860–83. |

| 1913 | | This form of garter mark occurs on a pattern registered in 1868. |

| 1914 | R. H. & S. | Distinguishing initials found on several printed marks of differing design: name of the individual pattern is often included, 1884–1905. "England" added from 1891. |

| 1915 | R. H. & S. LTD. | A garter-shaped mark occurs with these initials but with the addition of "Ltd."; however, records do not confirm that a limited company was formed.

N.B. A Ralph Hammersley is listed at Hanley c. 1822–3 but the above marks are 1860 onwards. |

| — | C. HAMMON | *See* Appendix. |

HAMMOND

HENRY F. HAMMOND, The Oast Pottery (and Farnham School of Art), Farnham, Surrey. 1934–40 and 1946– . *Studio Pottery, Stonewares.*

For illustrations of Henry Hammond's work see Muriel Rose's *Artist Potters in England* (1955) and George Wingfield Digby's *The Work of the Modern Potters in England* (1952).

| 1916 | | Incised mark, 1934– . |

| 1917 | | Impressed seal mark, 1934– . |

HAMMOND

ROSEMARY J. HAMMOND, MISS, Ravenscourt Pottery, London W.12. 1955–61. *Studio-type Pottery.*

| 1918 | R. J. H. | Painted or incised initials, 1955–61. |

3777   HAMPTON   *See* Swinnertons Ltd.

HAMPSON   **HAMPSON & BROADHURST**, Green Dock Works,
                                Longton. Staffordshire Potteries. 1847–53. *Earthenwares.*
1919   H. & B.   Distinguishing initials found on several printed marks of differ-
                                ing design: name of the individual pattern is often included,
                                1847–53.   See Plate 5.

HANAN   **THELMA P. HANAN, MISS**, London, c. 1947–51. Ports-
                                mouth, c. 1951– . 1947 to March 53.* *Studio-type Pottery.*
1920–1   Incised or painted marks, c. 1947 to March 1953.

                                    * From the autumn of 1951 Miss Hanan worked with Henry Clark at
                                the Island Pottery, Portsmouth. In 1953 Miss Hanan married Henry
                                Clark.   See also Island Pottery.

HANCOCK   **BENJAMIN & SAMPSON HANCOCK**, Bridge Works,
                                Stoke. Staffordshire Potteries. 1876–81. *Earthenwares.*
1922   B. & S. H.   Distinguishing initials found on several printed marks of
                                differing design, 1876–81.

HANCOCK   **F. HANCOCK & CO.**, Campbell Place Works, Stoke.
                                Staffordshire Potteries. 1899–1900. *Earthenwares.*

1923   Printed mark, 1899–1900.

HANCOCK   **ROBERT HANCOCK**, Battersea, Bow, Worcester, Caughley.
                                c. 1755–65. *Engraver.*
                                    For further information see Cyril Cook's *The Life and Work
                                of Robert Hancock* (1948).

1924   Fine quality printed patterns occur with versions of these forms
1925   of signature. Robert Hancock is mainly known for his work
1926   on first period Worcester porcelains, c. 1756–65.   Later work
                                is unlikely to be signed.

HANCOCK		SAMPSON HANCOCK (& SONS), Bridge Works, Stoke. Formerly at Tunstall (c. 1858–70). Staffordshire Potteries. 1858–1937.* *Earthenwares.*
1927	S. H.	Distinguishing initials found on several printed marks of differing design: name of the individual pattern is often included, 1858–91.
1928	S. HANCOCK	Printed marks with name in full. 1858 onwards.
1929 1929a	S. H. & S. S. H. & SONS	Distinguishing details of several printed marks of differing design: name of the individual pattern is often included, 1891–1935.

1930–1   Printed marks, 1900–6.

1932–3   Printed marks, 1906–12.

1934   THE "DUCHESS" CHINA   A circular mark incorporating these words was registered in 1911.

1935   Printed mark, 1912–37.

* New title "S. Hancock & Sons (Potters) Ltd., Corona Pottery, Hanley", from 1935 to 1937.

HANCOCK		HANCOCK, WHITTINGHAM & CO., Swan Bank Pottery, Burslem. Staffordshire Potteries. 1863–72. *Earthenwares.* Subsequently Hancock & Whittingham, see next entry.
1936	H. W. & CO.	Distinguishing initials found on several printed marks of differing design: name of the individual pattern is often included, 1863–72.
HANCOCK		HANCOCK & WHITTINGHAM, Bridge Works, Stoke. Staffordshire Potteries. 1873–9. *Earthenwares.* Formerly Hancock, Whittingham & Co., q.v.

1937 1938	H. & W. 	Distinguishing initials found on several printed marks of differing design: name of the individual pattern is often included, 1873–9. Mark no. 1938 is an example.
697 1414	HAND mark	*See* Buckley Heath & Co. *See* Sir James Duke & Nephews.
2370e	HAND MADE WEST OF ENGLAND POTTERY	*See* Jo Lester.

HANLEY

HANLEY CHINA CO., Burton Place, Hanley. Staffordshire Potteries. 1899–1901. *China.* Formerly Hanley Porcelain Co.

1939 Printed mark, 1899–1901.

HANLEY

HANLEY PORCELAIN CO., Burton Place, Hanley. Staffordshire Potteries. 1892–9. *China.* Formerly Thomas Bevington, q.v. Subsequently Hanley China Co., q.v.

1940 Printed mark, 1892–9.

HANOVER

HANOVER POTTERY (LTD.), Hanover St. (renamed Woodbank St.), Burslem. Staffordshire Potteries. 1948–56. *Earthenwares.* Formerly Staffs Teapot Co., q.v.

1941 Printed or impressed mark, 1948–53.

1942 Printed mark, 1953–6.

HANSSEN

GWYNN, Mrs, and LOUIS HANSSEN, London W.11. 1960– . *Studio-type Pottery, Stonewares.*

1943

Impressed seal mark of Gwynn Hanssen, 1960– .

1944

Impressed seal mark of Louis Hanssen, 1960– .

HARBORNE

HARBORNE POTTERY (E. M. & B. Blumer), Harborne, Birmingham 17. 1956– . *Pottery and Tiles, etc.*

1945

Impressed seal mark, September 1956– .

HARDING

HARDING & COCKSON, Globe Pottery, Cobridge. Staffordshire Potteries. 1834–60. *Earthenwares.*

This firm should not be confused with Cockson & Harding of Hanley.

1946   COBRIDGE
H & C

1947

Distinguishing detail of several printed marks of differing design: name of the individual pattern is often included, 1834–60. The town name Cobridge occurs on most marks. On other marks the name of the partners occurs in full.

HARDING

DEBORAH N. HARDING, MISS, Letchworth, Hertfordshire. 1920's–30's. *Studio-type Pottery.*

1948   D. N. H.

Incised or painted initial mark used in the 1920's.

HARDING

JOSEPH HARDING, Navigation Road, Burslem. Staffordshire Potteries. 1850–1. *Earthenwares.*

1949   J. HARDING

Distinguishing detail of several printed marks of differing design: name of the individual pattern is often included, 1850–1.

HARDING

W. & J. HARDING, New Hall Works, Shelton. Staffordshire Potteries. 1862–72. *Earthenwares.* Formerly Cockson & Harding, q.v.

1950	W. & J. H.	Distinguishing initials found on several printed marks of differing design: name of the individual pattern is often included, 1862–72.

HARLEY

THOMAS HARLEY, Lane End. Staffordshire Potteries. 1802–8. *Earthenwares.* Formerly in partnership with J. G. & W. Weston. Subsequently Harley & Seckerson.

1951–2	HARLEY T. HARLEY	Impressed name-marks, 1802–8. Some fine lustre decorated jugs bear this mark.
1952a	T. HARLEY LANE END	Printed or written marks in writing letters, c. 1802–8.
1952b	MANUFACTᴰ BY T. HARLEY LANE END	A good teapot, with swan knob on the cover, is in the Victoria and Albert Museum. Other teawares are in the Godden Collection and will be found illustrated in *British Pottery and Porcelain: an illustrated Encyclopaedia of Marked Specimens.* Many printed wares bear the name T. Harley as part of the printed decoration.

HARPER

JEREMY HARPER, Potters Croft, Leven, Nr. Hull, August 1960–1 and then: 10 Shambles, York. 1961– . *Studio-type Earthenwares and Stonewares.*

1953		Impressed seal mark, August 1960–1.
1954		Impressed monogram mark, 1960– .
1955		Impressed mark of York pottery, 1961– .
536	HARJIAN	*See* E. Brain & Co. Ltd.

HARRIS

MURIEL HARRIS, MRS., Old Hall Smithy, Washington, Co. Durham. 1953–9.* *Studio-type Pottery.*

1956

Shield mark impressed or printed, 1953–9.

1957

Monogram mark, 1961–   .

    * Continued at St. Margarets-at-Cliffe, Dover, Kent.   1961–

HARRISON

      1958   G. Harrison

GEORGE HARRISON, Lane Delph.*   Staffordshire Potteries. c. 1790–5. *Earthenwares.*

Impressed mark, c. 1790–5.

    * Jewitt quotes an invoice dated August 20th 1793, which included: Large and Less Tureens, Sauce Tureens, Root Dishes, Salad Bowls, Tureen Ladles, Ewers—Blue Edged and Cream Coloured. A blue printed plate is in the Godden Collection.   In 1795 George Harrison & Co. is listed at Lower Lane, Fenton.

HARRISON

      1959   H. & P.
             BURSLEM

HARRISON & PHILLIPS,* Chelsea Works, Burslem. Staffordshire Potteries. 1914–15. *Earthenwares.*

Distinguishing detail of several printed marks of differing design, 1914–15.

    * A firm of this title was at Broad St., Hanley, in 1924.

HARROP

FREDERICK HARROP, Finchley, London N.3.   1952–   .
Studio-type Pottery and Stonewares.

1960 **FSH**

Incised or painted initials, often with date of potting, 1952–   .

HARROP

HARROP & BURGESS, Mount Pleasant Works, Hanley. Staffordshire Potteries. 1894–1903. *Earthenwares.* Subsequently Thomas Burgess.

1961

Printed mark, 1894–1903.

HART		HART & SON, Wych St., London. 1826–69. *Retailers.* Subsequently Hart, Son & Peard Co.
1962	H. & S.	A circular printed mark bearing these initials occurs on wares made for this firm of retailers, c. 1840–69.

HARTLEY		HARTLEY, GREENS & CO., Leeds Pottery, Leeds, Yorkshire. c. 1781–1820. *Earthenwares.* Formerly Humble, Hartley, Greens & Co.
		See also Jewitt's *The Ceramic Art of Great Britain* (1883) and D. C. Towner's *English Cream-coloured Earthenware* (1957).
1963	HARTLEY, GREENS & CO. LEEDS POTTERY	Distinguishing detail of several impressed marks of differing form, c. 1781–1820.

HARTLEY'S		HARTLEY'S (CASTLEFORD) LTD., Phillips Pottery, Castleford, Yorkshire. Hartley's from c. 1898–1960. Utilitarian *Stonewares and Earthenwares. Art wares* from 1953.
1964	HARTROX	Trade-name on decorative wares from 1953 to June 1960.

1964	HARTROX	*See* Hartley's (Castleford) Ltd., above.

HARVEY		ARTHUR EDWARD HARVEY (b. 1893), various teaching posts, Birmingham, Warwickshire. 1920's–30's. *Studio-type Pottery.*
1965	Arthur Edward Harvey	Signature mark, c. 1920's–30's.

HARVEY		HARVEY, BAILEY & CO., Lane End. Staffordshire Potteries. 1833–5. *Earthenwares.*
1966	H. B. & CO.*	Distinguishing initials found on several printed marks of differing design: name of the individual pattern is often included, 1833–5.

* Marks bearing these initials also fit Henry Brown & Co., High Street, Lane End. c. 1828–30.

HARVEY		C. & W. K. HARVEY (also Charles Harvey & Sons), Stafford St., Church St., Charles St., Chancery Lane, Longton. Staffordshire Potteries. 1835–53. *Earthenwares, China, etc.* Stafford Street works continued by Holland & Green, q.v.
1967	HARVEY	Impressed mark, 1835–53.
1968	C. & W. K. H.	Distinguishing initials found on several printed marks of differing design: name of the individual pattern is often included, 1835–53. A palm tree is depicted on several marks.
1969		Printed Royal Arms mark, with initials and name, 1835–53.

HARWOOD		J. HARWOOD, Clarence Pottery, Stockton-on-Tees, Durham. 19th century. *Earthenwares.* Subsequently The Clarence Potteries Co.
1970	HARWOOD	Impressed marks, c. 1849–77.
1971	HARWOOD STOCKTON	

HASTINGS		HASTINGS POTTERY (Bernard J. Cotes), Hastings, Sussex. 1956–9. *Studio-type Pottery.*
1972		Incised mark, 1956–9.
1973		Personal mark of B. J. Cotes, 1956–9.*

* Subsequently at Battle Pottery, q.v., and personal mark no. 1973 continued.

HAUBER		BARBARA HAUBER, MISS, Swaffham Bulbeck, Nr. Cambridge. June 1962*– . *Studio-type Pottery (Stonewares).*
1974	Baba	Written or incised name-mark, June 1962*–

* Miss Hauber formerly worked in Paris.

HAUGHTON		JANET MABEL HAUGHTON, MRS., Cranbrook, Kent. c. 1920–30. *Earthenware Figures.*
1975	JANET HAUGHTON	Incised or painted signature mark, c. 1920–30's.

HAVERFORDWEST

HAVERFORDWEST POTTERY, T. & A. Whalley, Haverfordwest, Pembrokeshire. December 1962– . *Studio-type Earthenwares and Stonewares.*

1976   **HP**   Impressed Haverfordwest Pottery seal mark, 1962– .

1976a   **W**   Impressed mark of Mrs. Ann Whalley, on special pieces, 1962– .

1976b   **W**   Impressed mark of Theodore Whalley, on special pieces, 1962– .

HAWKINS

BETTY HAWKINS, MISS, Ravenscourt Pottery, London W.12. c. 1955. *Studio-type Pottery.*

1977   BETTY HAWKINS   Incised or painted signature, in writing letters, c. 1955.

—   HAWLEY   *See* Appendix, page 720.

HAWLEY

HAWLEY, BROS. (LTD.), Northfield Pottery, Rotherham, Yorkshire. 1868–1903. *Earthenwares.* Formerly W. & G. Hawley, q.v. Subsequently Northfield Hawley Pottery Co. Ltd., q.v.

1978   H. B.   A printed mark comprising the initials H. B. (intertwined) within a shield, with the date 1790 below, was used by Hawley Brothers from 1868 to c. 1898.

1978a   HAWLEY BROS.   The name in full may also occur. "Ltd." may occur on marks from 1897.

1979      The trade-mark of a Lion and Globe was registered in 1898 and occurs printed on wares. This mark was continued by the Northfield Hawley Pottery Co. Ltd. to c. 1919.

HAWLEY		HAWLEY (JOHN) & CO., Foley Pottery, Foley. Staffordshire Potteries. 1842–87. *Earthenwares.*
1980	HAWLEY*	Impressed marks, 1842–87.
1981	HAWLEY & CO.	

* See also Appendix, page 720.

—	Tho HAWLEY	*See* Appendix, page 720.

HAWLEY		**WILLIAM & GEORGE HAWLEY**, Northfield Pottery, Rotherham, Yorkshire. 1863–8. *Earthenwares.* Formerly George Hawley. Subsequently Hawley Bros. (Ltd.), q.v.
1982	W. & G. HAWLEY	Distinguishing detail of several impressed or printed marks of differing design: name of the individual pattern is often included, 1863–8.

HAWLEY		HAWLEY, WEBBERLEY & CO., Garfield Works, Longton. Staffordshire Potteries. 1895–1902. *Earthenwares, Majolica, etc.*
1983		Printed mark, 1895–1902.

HAYNES		**JOYCE HAYNES, MISS**, Tuxford, Nr. Newark-on-Trent, Nottinghamshire. c. 1940– . *Studio-type Pottery, Stonewares and Ash-glaze effects.*
1984	Joyce Haynes	Incised signature mark, with address (Leicester, c. 1940–60; Scarborough, c. 1947–55; Tuxford, c. 1960–) with year of production.
1985		Impressed seal monogram mark, also used c. 1947– .

—	C. HAYTON	*See* Appendix, page 721.

393–4	H. B.	*See* Howard Bissell.
710		*See* Henry Burgess.
1877		*See* Haines Batchelor & Co.
1881–3		*See* Hall Bros. (Longton) Ltd.
1978		*See* Hawley Bros.
2037		*See* Hines Bros.
2925		*See* Oldswinford Pottery.
4447	H. & B.	*See* Appendix, page 721.
726		*See* Thomas Burgess.
1919		*See* Hampson & Broadhurst.
1961		*See* Harrop & Burgess.
1997		*See* Heath & Blackhurst.
2018		*See* Hibbert & Boughey.
1966	H. B. & CO.	*See* Harvey Bailey & Co.
1998		*See* Heath, Blackhurst & Co.
782	HC	*See* Hilary Carruthers.
1096	(also joined)	*See* Hans Coper.
1902	H. & C.	*See* Hammersley & Co.
1946		*See* Harding & Cockson.
2088		*See* Hope & Carter.
2127		*See* Hulme & Christie.
1939	H. C. & CO.	*See* Hanley China Co.
—	H. & D.	*See* Appendix (Hall & Davenport).
1893		*See* Hallam & Day.
1401	H. D. & CO.	*See* H. Dreydel & Co.
1226	H·DUBLIN	*See* Henry Delamain.

HEATH   **J. E. HEATH LTD.**, Albert Potteries, Burslem. Staffordshire Potteries. 1951– . *Earthenwares (Hotel wares, etc.).*

1986–7   Printed marks, 1951– .

HEATH   **JOB HEATH**, Stoke. Staffordshire Potteries. Early 18th century. *Slip-decorated Earthenwares.*

1988	JOB HEATH	This name occurs on a slip decorated Posset-pot with the date 1702 (Ashmolean Museum, Oxford). Stoke parish registers record the marriage in April 1701 of Job Heath, potter.

HEATH

		JOHN HEATH, Sytch Pottery, Burslem. Staffordshire Potteries. 1809–23. *Earthenwares (and China)*, *Figures, etc.*
1989	HEATH	Impressed mark, 1809–23.

HEATH

		JOSHUA HEATH, Shelton, Hanley. Staffordshire Potteries. First half 18th century.* *Earthenwares.*
1990	JOSHUA HEATH	This name occurs on a combed pattern Posset-pot in the Victoria and Albert Museum. A deed of 1745 mentions Joshua Heath, Earthen Potter of Shelton.

* A potter of this name was working at a later period. See next entry.

HEATH

		J. HEATH, Hanley. Staffordshire Potteries. c. 1770–c. 1800. *Earthenwares, Creamwares, etc.*
		Several J. Heaths are recorded in the 18th and early 19th century. One signed the price agreement of 1770. This entry relates to Joshua Heath.
1991	I. H.	Impressed marks of initials I. H. or the name Heath,* c. 1780–
1992	HEATH	1800.

* Similar marks have previously been attributed to John Heath of Derby.

HEATH

		JOSEPH HEATH, High St., Tunstall. Staffordshire Potteries. 1845–53. *Earthenwares.*
1993	J. HEATH	Distinguishing detail of several printed marks of differing design: name of the individual pattern is often included, 1845–53.
		It should be noted that other J (John or Joseph) Heaths were working in Staffordshire in the first half of the 19th century.

HEATH

		JOSEPH HEATH & CO., Newfield Pottery, Tunstall. Staffordshire Potteries. 1828–41. *Earthenwares.*
1994	J. HEATH & CO.	Distinguishing detail of several printed marks of differing design, 1828–41.

| 1994a | J. H. & CO. | Distinguishing initials found on several printed marks of differing design: name of the individual pattern is often included, 1828–41. |
| 1994b | I. H. & CO. | The J is often printed as an I. |

N.B. Some books attribute the initials J. H. & Co. to J. Hall & Co., but I have been unable to trace such a firm in rate records or directories.

HEATH

THOMAS HEATH, Hadderidge, Burslem. Staffordshire Potteries. 1812–35. *Earthenwares.*

| 1995 | T. HEATH | Distinguishing details of several impressed or printed marks of |
| 1996 | T. HEATH BURSLEM | differing design, 1812–35. |

HEATH

HEATH & BLACKHURST and **HEATH, BLACKHURST & CO.**, Hadderidge Pottery, Burslem. Staffordshire Potteries. 1859–77. *Earthenwares.* Formerly W. & G. Harding. Subsequently Blackhurst & Bourne, q.v.

1997	H. & B.	Distinguishing initials found on several printed marks of
1998	H. B. & CO.	differing design: name of the individual pattern is often
1999		included, 1859–77. A garter-shaped mark, as no. 1999, was favoured.

N.B. This firm is also listed in rate records and in other contemporary accounts as Heath Blackhurst & Co.; many printed marks incorporate the initials H. B. & Co. and these probably relate to this firm during the 1860's. At an earlier period these initials fit Harvey Bailey & Co. of Lane End, c. 1833–5.

HEATH

HEATH & GREATBATCH, Union Pottery, Burslem. Staffordshire Potteries. 1891–3. *Earthenwares.* Formerly Buckley & Heath.

| 2000 | | Printed or impressed mark, 1891–3. |

HEATH

HEATH & SON, Burslem. Staffordshire Potteries. Late 18th century, early 19th century. *Earthenwares.*

2001   HEATH & SON*   Impressed mark.   Late 18th century, early 19th century.

> * G. Bemrose in *Nineteenth Century English Pottery and Porcelain* (1952) illustrates a "Castleford" type teapot with the impressed mark Heath & Son. This teapot will also be found illustrated in *British Pottery and Porcelain: an illustrated Encyclopaedia of Marked Specimens*. This specimen is given the period "about 1820", and the firm is given as working at Tunstall; this information is not backed by Mr. Alfred Meigh's records of the Staffordshire potters, which only list Heath & Son about 1797 at Burslem. This entry is taken from Chester & Mort's Directory of c. 1797.

HEATHCOTE   CHARLES HEATHCOTE & CO., Lane End. Staffordshire Potteries. 1818–24. *Earthenwares.*

2002   C. HEATHCOTE & CO.   Distinguishing detail of several printed marks of differing design: name of the individual pattern is often included, 1818–24.   The Prince of Wales' three-feather crest occurs on several marks.

4184–6 HEATHCOTE CHINA   *See* H. M. Williamson & Sons.

HEATHERLEY   HEATHERLEY FINE CHINA (& GLASS CO.) LTD., Worcester and Chessington, Surrey. 1961– . *Decorators and Gilders of Bone China.*

2003   Printed mark, 1961– .

1471   HEATMASTER   *See* Ellgreave Pottery Co. Ltd.

HENDERSON   EILA HENDERSON, MISS, Eastbourne, Sussex. (At London prior to 1954.) 1945– . *Studio-type Pottery.*
Miss Henderson was in partnership with Mrs. D. Tickle, q.v., at the Theda Pottery from c. 1948 to c. 1954, see also Theda Pottery.

2004–4a   Painted or incised marks, 1945– .

HENSHALL

HENSHALL & CO., Longport. Staffordshire Potteries.*
c. 1795. *Earthenwares.*

2005   HENSHALL & CO.   Impressed mark reported by William Chaffers as occurring on a plate in the Sheldon Collection.

> * This title was used c. 1795, but the mark may also have been used by the related firms of Henshall, Williamson & Clowes (c. 1790–5) or by Henshall, Williamson & Co. (c. 1802).

HENSON

DAPHNE HENSON, MRS., Whitton, Middlesex. 1951– .
Studio-type Pottery.

2006

Incised mark, often with date, 1951– .

HERCULANEUM

HERCULANEUM POTTERY (Messrs. Worthington, Humble & Holland, and other owners), Liverpool, Lancashire. c. 1793–1841. *Earthenwares and Porcelains.*

For further information see Chaffers' *Marks and Monograms...* 15th edition, and Jewitt's *Ceramic Art of Great Britain.*

2007–10   HERCULANEUM

Impressed or printed marks, c. 1796–1833.

2007a   HERCULANEUM POTTERY

The full impressed name-mark HERCULANEUM POTTERY is said to date from 1822 and is subsequent to those reproduced above.

2011–12

Printed or impressed Liver bird marks, in many forms, c. 1833–6.

2013

Rare initial mark attributed to Mort Herculaneum Pottery Co., c. 1833–41.

1626   HEREFORDSHIRE   *See* Fownhope Pottery.

HERON		**ROBERT HERON (& SON)**, Fife or Gallatown Pottery, Sinclairtown, Kirkcaldy, Scotland. About 1850–1929. (Pottery established by the Grey brothers, c. 1820.) *Earthen-wares, "Rockingham" wares, etc.*
2014	R H & S	Distinguishing initials found on several printed marks of differing design, 1850–1929.
1015		Printed mark, 1920–9. Other marks include the name of the firm.
HEWITT		**HEWITT & LEADBEATER**, Willow Pottery, Longton. Staffordshire Potteries. 1907–19. *China and Parian.*
1016		Printed mark, 1907–26.* * This mark was continued by the successors—Hewitt Brothers—to c. 1926.
4448	HEWSON	*See* Appendix, page 721.
2115	H. F.	*See* E. Hughes & Co.
4069	H F W & CO. LTD.	*See* H. F. Wedgwood & Co. Ltd.
2064 2070	H & G	*See* Holland & Green. *See* Hollinshead & Griffiths.
2000	H & G B	*See* Heath & Greatbatch.
4449–9a	H. H.	*See* Appendix, page 721.
1879	H H & G LTD	*See* Hales, Hancock & Godwin Ltd.
2049	H H & M	*See* Holdcroft, Hill & Mellor.
2134	H. I.	*See* Henry Ifield.
621	HIAWATHA	*See* Britannia Pottery Co. Ltd., page 105.
HIBBERD		**MARY HIBBERD, MISS**, Forest Hill, London S.E. c. 1920–30. *Earthenware figures.*
2017	MARY HIBBERD	Incised or painted name-mark.

HIBBERT

HIBBERT & BOUGHEY, Market St., Longton. Staffordshire Potteries. 1889. *Earthenwares and China.*

2018

Printed mark on a pattern registered in October 1889.

HICKS

HICKS & MEIGH, High St. (2 works), Shelton. Staffordshire Potteries. 1806–22. *Earthenwares, Ironstones.* Formerly Baddeleys. Subsequently Hicks, Meigh & Johnson, q.v.

This firm made high-grade ironstone or stone china in the style of Mason's Ironstone. Many fine dinner services were produced. They used the name "Stone China".

2019   HICKS & MEIGH

Rare impressed or printed marks with the name in full, c. 1806–22.

2020

Printed Royal Arms mark, c. 1806–22.

N.B. Early version of Royal Arms (see page 552). Various numbers occur with this mark. This mark occurs in several sizes according to the size of the article; large dishes bear marks over three inches in length.

HICKS

HICKS, MEIGH & JOHNSON, High Street, Shelton. Staffordshire Potteries. 1822–35. *Earthenwares and Ironstone.* Formerly Hicks & Meigh, q.v.

2021   II M J
2021a   H M & J

Distinguishing details of several printed marks of differing design, 1822–35.

2022

Royal Arms mark, similar but not so detailed as that version used by Hicks & Meigh (no. 2020). Variations occur with the name of the pattern below or with numbers, 1822–35.

2023

Printed mark, 1822–35. This mark may have been used earlier by Hicks & Meigh. Wares on which it appears seem to pre-date 1830.

2024 · Printed mark, 1822–30.   This device occurs on the named and dated mark following, no. 2025.

2025 · This mark may not have been used.   The copper plate from which this was taken was found by the late Alfred Meigh on the premises.   It is interesting as it includes the Crown and Laurel Wreath device which occurs on wares without any wording—mark no. 2024.

Messrs. Hicks, Meigh & Johnson produced a fine range of "Stone China" (Ironstone) in the Mason's tradition.   This is normally unattributed as the marks have not previously been published.

1755 · HIGHLAND WARE · *See* Govancroft Potteries Ltd.

HIGH HALDEN · **HIGH HALDEN POTTERY,** High Halden, Kent.
A pottery was established here in the 18th century (and by tradition in the 16th century).
During the 19th century there were two potteries, worked by the Farrence and the Kingsnorth families.   These potteries closed c. 1902.
Most wares from these country potteries were unmarked but G. Bemrose in his *19th Century English Pottery and Porcelain* (1952) illustrates a money box marked:

2026 · HALDEN POTTERY

730 · HILBRE · *See* Hilda Burn.

HILDITCH · **HILDITCH & SON,** Church St., Lane End.   Staffordshire Potteries.   1822–30.   *China and Earthenwares.*   Formerly Hilditch & Martin.   Subsequently Hilditch & Hopwood.

2027–9 ·   · Printed marks, 1822–30.

HILL		HILL & CO., St. James Works (c. 1898–1907), Windsor China Works (1907–20), Longton. Staffordshire Potteries. 1898–1920. *China.* Formerly Coggins & Hill, q.v.
2030	H. & CO.	Distinguishing initials found on several impressed or printed marks of differing design, 1898–1920.
HILL		HILL POTTERY CO. (LTD.), Hill Pottery, Burslem. Staffordshire Potteries. c. 1861–7. *China and Earthenwares.*
2031	J. S. H.	Distinguishing initials or monogram (no. 2032) found on several printed marks of differing design: name of the individual pattern is often included, c. 1861–7. See note below.

2032

The monogram mark as reproduced occurs on a pattern registered in the name of the Hill Pottery Company in May 1861 *but* the same mark occurs on a design registered by Samuel Alcock & Co. in 1854. It would seem that different firms working the Hill Pottery, Burslem, used this mark, unless the 1854 Alcock design was re-issued by the Hill Pottery Co., and their monogram added. Examples will be illustrated in the companion picture book of marked specimens.

2033	HILL POTTERY BURSLEM	Several printed marks incorporate this name, and could relate to S. Alcock & Co. or subsequent firms at this pottery.
—	HILLCOCK & WALTON	*See* Appendix, page 721.
2726	HILLSTONIA	*See* Moira Pottery Co. Ltd.
HILTON		DAVID HILTON, The Ham Lane Pottery, Compton Dundon, Somerton, Somerset. 1956– . *Studio-type Pottery, Earthenwares to 1962, then Stonewares.* Formerly at Street, Somerset.
2034		Impressed star mark, 1956– .
2035	D. H.	Incised initials on some individual pieces.
HINE		MARGARET HINE, MISS, Prestwood, Bucks. 1950– . *Studio-type Pottery, Sculpture and Ceramic Murals.*
2036	Margaret Hine	Signature mark in writing letters, 1950– .

HINES

HINES BROTHERS, Heron Cross Pottery, Fenton. Staffordshire Potteries. 1886–1907. *Earthenwares.* Taken over by Grimwades Ltd. in 1907.

2037   H. B.   Impressed initials mark, 1886–1907.

2038   Printed mark, 1886–1907.

1985   HJ   *See* Joyce Haynes.
2046–46a   (also monograms)   *See* Joseph Holdcroft.
2206   *See* A. G. H. Jones.

987   H. J. C.   *See* H. J. Colclough.
989   or
985–6   H. J. C.
                      L.

4266   H. J. W.   *See* H. J. Wood (Ltd.).

2071   H. K.   *See* Hollinshead & Kirkham (Ltd.).

1865   H. & K.   *See* Hackwood & Keeling.
2074   or   *See* Hollinshead & Kirkham (Ltd.).
                    H. & K.
                      T.

—   H. L.   *See* Appendix, page 721.
            (with other initials under)

—   H. L. & Co.   *See* Appendix, page 722.

2110b   H. M.   *See* Hudson & Middleton.
2549   *See* Heber Mathews.
3196   *See* Rainforth & Co.

—   H. M. & Co.   *See* Appendix, page 722.

2021   H. M. J.   *See* Hicks, Meigh & Johnson.
                      or
2021a   H. M. & J.

3611   H. M. S.   *See* Hilda Mary Snowden.
4393   *See* Ymagynatyf Pottery.

| 4185 | H. M. W. & SONS | *See* H. M. Williamson & Sons. |

| —
3662 | H. N. | *See* Appendix, page 722.
See St. Agnes Pottery. |

| 3122 | H. N. & A. | *See* Hulse, Nixon & Adderley. |

| 2042 | HOBSON
B. | *See* George Hobson. |

HOBSON

CHARLES HOBSON (& SON), Albert Street Pottery, Burslem. Staffordshire Potteries. 1865–80. *Earthenwares.* Subsequently G. & J. Hobson.

2039   C. H.
2040   C. H. & S.

Distinguishing details of several impressed or printed marks of differing design: name of the individual pattern is often included, 1865–80.

    N.B. "& S." added c. 1873–5.

2041

The name in full occurs on a garter-shaped mark on a design registered in July 1883.

HOBSON

GEORGE HOBSON, Sneyd Pottery, Albert St., Burslem. Staffordshire Potteries. 1901–23. *Earthenwares.* Formerly G. & J. Hobson, q.v.

2042

TRADE MARK
HOBSON
B

Printed or impressed mark, 1901–23.

HOBSON

G. & J. HOBSON, Albert St. Pottery, Burslem. Staffordshire Potteries. 1883–1901. *Earthenwares.* Formerly C. Hobson, q.v.

2043

This printed mark occurs on the firm's advertisements in 1884. Other forms of mark may occur with the name Hobson's.

| 2043 | HOBSON'S | *See* G. & J. Hobson, above. |

HODGE

JOHN HODGE, Brixton Hill, London S.W.2. c. 1920–35.
Studio-type Pottery.

2044   HODGE
2045   Monogram of J. H.

Incised or painted name or monogram marks, c. 1920–35.

HOLDCROFT

JOSEPH HOLDCROFT,* Sutherland Pottery (from c. 1872),
Longton. Staffordshire Potteries. 1865–1939.† *Earthenwares,
Majolica, Parian, etc.*

2046–46a

Printed or impressed monogram (J H) marks, 1865–1906.

2047

Printed mark, 1890–1939. This mark was continued by
Holdcrofts Ltd. and by Cartwright & Edwards.

* Restyled Holdcrofts Ltd. c. 1906.
† Subsequently taken over by Messrs. Cartwright & Edwards Ltd. who
continued the name and works to 1940.

HOLDCROFT

PETER HOLDCROFT & CO., Lower Works, Fountain
Place, Burslem. Staffordshire Potteries. 1846–52. *Earthenwares.*

2048   P. H. & CO.

Distinguishing initials found on several printed marks of
differing design: name of the individual pattern is often
included, 1846–52.

HOLDCROFT

HOLDCROFT, HILL & MELLOR, High St. Pottery
(c. 1860–5), Queen St. (c. 1866–70), Burslem. Staffordshire
Potteries. 1860–70. *Earthenwares.*

2049   H H & M
2049a   FLAXMAN
             H H & M

Distinguishing initials found on several printed marks of
differing design: name of the individual pattern is often
included, 1860–70. Mark no. 2049a is a typical example.

—   HOLDCROFTS LTD. *See* Joseph Holdcroft.

HOLDEN

    2049b   HOLDEN

JOHN HOLDEN, Knowl Works, Burslem. Staffordshire Potteries. c. 1846. *Earthenwares.*

Impressed mark reported (from America) as occurring on imported English earthenware. The only potter of this name is John Holden of Burslem; his name appears only in Williams Directory of 1846.

HOLDEN

    2050   R. H.

ROZELLE HOLDEN, MRS., East Kilbride, Scotland. 1956– . *Studio-type Pottery.*

Painted or incised initial mark, 1956– .

HOLDEN-JONES

    2051   M. T. H.

MARGARET T. HOLDEN-JONES, MRS., London S.W.16. c. 1940–8. *Studio-type Pottery.*

Incised or painted initial mark, often with year added below, c. 1940–8.

HOLDSWORTH

    2052–4

PETER HOLDSWORTH, Holdsworth Potteries, Ramsbury, Wiltshire. 1945– . *Earthenwares, Stonewares, etc.*

Impressed or printed marks, 1945– .

HOLKHAM

    2055

HOLKHAM POTTERY LTD., Holkham Hall, Holkham, Norfolk. 1961– . *Earthenwares.* Formerly Holkham Studio Pottery, see below.

Printed or impressed mark, April 1961– . Note revised version of mark no. 2056.

HOLKHAM

HOLKHAM STUDIO POTTERY, Holkham Hall, Holkham, Norfolk. 1951–61. *Earthenwares.* Subsequently Holkham Pottery Ltd., see above.

2056 Printed or impressed mark May 1951 to April 1961.   New title and mark introduced in April 1961, see no. 2055.

2074   HOLKIRK WARE   *See* Hollinshead & Kirkham (Ltd.).

HOLLAND   GEORGE FISHLEY HOLLAND, The Pottery, Clevedon, Somerset (1955–9), Dunster Pottery, Dunster, Somerset (1959–). 1955– . *Earthenwares.*

2057   Printed, painted or impressed mark, 1955– . This signature should not be confused with that of W. F. Holland.

2058   DUNSTER   "Dunster" added to signature mark from 1959– .

HOLLAND   ISABEL FISHLEY HOLLAND, MISS, The Pottery, Clevedon, Somerset. 1929–42. *Pottery figures, Tiles, etc.*

2059   I. HOLLAND   The signature mark, in writing letters, of Miss Isabel Fishley Holland is found on "Beatrice Potter" animal figures and other work carried out at her father's (William Fishley Holland) Clevedon pottery, c. 1929–42.

HOLLAND   JOHN HOLLAND, Clay Hills Pottery, Tunstall. Staffordshire Potteries. 1852–4. *Earthenwares.*

2060   J. HOLLAND   This name-mark occurs with the name of the pattern "Carrara" on a blue printed tureen in the Godden Collection. This example also bears the Patent Office registration mark for November 1852.

HOLLAND   WILLIAM FISHLEY HOLLAND, The Pottery, Clevedon, Somerset. c. 1921– . *Earthenwares.* Formerly at Fremington.

W. F. Holland's *Fifty Years a Potter* (1958) is a most interesting account of a country potter's life and work.

2061-3

W J Holland   WJH   FH

Incised initial or signature marks, c. 1921— .
William Fishley Holland, junr., continues
with his father at Clevedon.

HOLLAND	HOLLAND & GREEN, Stafford Street Works, Longton. Staffordshire Potteries. 1853–82. *Earthenwares, Ironstones, etc.* Formerly C. & W. K. Harvey. Subsequently Green, Clarke & Clay.
2064 H. & G. LATE HARVEY	Distinguishing detail of several impressed or printed marks of differing design: name of the individual pattern is often included,
2065 HOLLAND & GREEN	1853–82. The Royal Arms occur in several marks. The name occurs in full on some marks.

HOLLINS	SAMUEL HOLLINS, Vale Pleasant, Shelton. Staffordshire Potteries. c. 1784–1813. *Basalt and other Wedgwood-type wares (often with silvered decoration).*
2066 S. HOLLINS	Impressed name-marks, c. 1784–1813.
2067 HOLLINS	On his death in 1820 Samuel Hollins still had an interest in the New Hall China Works, of which he was a partner.

Typical specimens will be found illustrated in *British Pottery and Porcelain: an illustrated Encyclopaedia of Marked Specimens.*

HOLLINS	T. & J. HOLLINS, Far Green (?), Shelton, Hanley. Staffordshire Potteries. c. 1795–1820. *Earthenwares, Wedgwood-type wares.*
2068 T. & J. HOLLINS	Impressed mark, c. 1795–c. 1820.

HOLLINS	THOMAS, JOHN & RICHARD HOLLINS, Far Green, Hanley. Staffordshire Potteries. c. 1818–22. *Earthenwares, Wedgwood-type wares.*
	In the rate of August 1822, J. & R. Hollins only is listed. The date of this partnership is open to slight doubt.
2069 T. J. & R. HOLLINS	Impressed mark, c. 1818–22.

HOLLINSHEAD

HOLLINSHEAD & GRIFFITHS, Chelsea Works, Burslem. Staffordshire Potteries. 1890–1909. *Earthenwares.*

2070

Printed mark, 1890–1909.

HOLLINSHEAD

HOLLINSHEAD & KIRKHAM (LTD.), Unicorn Pottery, Tunstall. Staffordshire Potteries. (Est. c. 1870 at Burslem, Tunstall from c. 1876.) 1870–1956. *Earthenwares.*
Factory purchased by Johnson Bros. (Hanley) Ltd. in 1956.

2071   H. & K.   Distinguishing details of several impressed or printed marks of
2072   H. & K.   differing design, c. 1870–c. 1900.
        TUNSTALL

2072a   H. & K.   Impressed mark dating from c. 1890 when Wedgwood & Co.'s
        LATE WEDGWOOD   Unicorn Pottery was taken over.

2073

Printed mark, 1900–24.

2074

Printed mark, 1924–56.

2075

Printed mark, 1933–42.

2076

Printed mark, 1954–6.

G. HOLMES   *See* Appendix, page 722.

HOLMES   **HOLMES, PLANT & MAYDEW,** Sylvester Pottery, Burslem.
                          Staffordshire Potteries.   1876–85. *Earthenwares.* Formerly
                          Holmes, Plant & Whitehurst.   Subsequently Holmes & Plant.
2077   H. P. & M. Distinguishing initials found on several printed marks of
                          differing design: name of the individual pattern is often in-
                          cluded, 1876–85.

HOLMES   **HOLMES & SON,** Clayton Pottery, Longton.   Staffordshire
                          Potteries.   1898–1903.   *Earthenwares.*
2078   H. & S.   Impressed or printed mark, 1898–1903.
              LONGTON

2079   Printed mark, 1898–1903.

2770   HOMELEIGH   *See* Morley Fox & Co. Ltd.
              WARE

HONITON   **HONITON ART POTTERIES LTD.,** High St., Honiton,
                          Devon. Est. 1881 (various titles and changes in ownership).
                          Earthenwares.
                          Early wares usually unmarked.
2080   THE HONITON   A printed or impressed mark in circular form was registered in
           LACE ART POTTERY 1915, and includes this wording.
              CO.

2081   COLLARD HONITON   Printed or impressed marks including the name Collard date
              ENGLAND   from 1918 to 1947.

2082   N. T. S. HULL Mark employed by Norman T. S. Hull from 1947 to 1955.
                          Norman Hull also managed the Norman Hull Pottery, see page
                          340.

2083   HONITON POTTERY   Printed, moulded or impressed marks, 1947+.
              DEVON
               or
       HONITON ENGLAND

2084 Printed or impressed mark, 1956– .

HOODS

HOODS LTD., International Works, Fenton. Staffordshire Potteries. 1919–42.* *Earthenwares.*

2085  Trade-mark with various wording or "H. Ltd.", c. 1919–42.*

    * This firm is still in existence but wares sold by them do not now bear this mark.

2086   H LTD.

HOOK

HOOK POTTERY (Miss Deirdre Malone), Hook, Wiltshire. 1957– . *Studio-type Pottery.*

2087   HOOK D. M. 3164   Incised or painted name Hook, with initials D. M. and progressive reference number (the number reached by July 1963 was 3164), 1957– .

HOPE

HOPE & CARTER, Fountain Place, Burslem. Staffordshire Potteries. 1862–80. *Earthenwares.*

    John Hope was formerly in partnership with Pinder and Bourne, as Pinder, Bourne & Hope. A letter in the Victoria and Albert Museum is dated January 13th, 1862, and reads "— Business will be carried on by Thomas Pinder and Joseph Harvey Bourne, under the firm of Pinder, Bourne & Co. at the manufactory at Nile Street, *and by John Hope and John Carter under the firm of Hope & Carter at the manufactory—*" (the letter is here torn).

    Works taken over by G. L. Ashworth & Bros, c. 1880.

2088   H. & C.   Distinguishing initials found on several printed marks of differing design: name of the individual pattern is often included. Several printed marks are of garter form and occur on patterns registered in the firm's name in the 1860's, c. 1862–80.

HOPKINS

ALFRED G. HOPKINS, Lambeth, London. c. 1920's–30's. *Studio-type Pottery, Stonewares.*

2089   A. G. HOPKINS   Impressed or incised name-marks occur. The incised marks
       LAMBETH   sometimes have the year added, c. 1920's–30's.

HORNSEA   **HORNSEA POTTERY CO. LTD.,** Edenfield Works, Hornsea, Yorkshire. c. 1951– . *Earthenwares.*

2090–4

              1951–   1954–   1960–   1962–   Trade-mark
                                                                                   1962+

                             Printed or impressed marks.

3015   Horse's head mark   *See* John Phillips & Co.

HORSLEY   **AGNES HORSLEY,** Canterbury, Kent. c. 1923. *Earthenwares.*

2095   JUBBE   This mark or trade-name was registered under the above name in 1923.

HOWARD   **TOM W. HOWARD,** Loughton, Essex. 1956– . *Studiotype Pottery. Earthenwares, c. 1956–60, "Semi Stoneware", c. 1960– .*

2096   Incised mark, 1956– . "62" relates to the year of production.

HOWARD   **HOWARD POTTERY CO. (LTD.),** Norfolk St., Shelton. Staffordshire Potteries. 1925– . *Earthenwares.*

2097   BRENTLEIGH WARE   Trade-name incorporated in marks, 1925– .

2098   Printed mark, 1925+ .

2099   Printed mark, 1950– .

HOWELL		**HOWELL & JAMES (& CO.),** 5–9 Regent St., London W.1. c. 1820–1922. *Retailers.*
2100	HOWELL & JAMES	Marks or inscriptions occur, incorporating the name of this firm of retailers, from c. 1860 onwards. During the 1870's and 80's this firm held many exhibitions of amateur painting on china and examples can be found still bearing the original labels.
HOY		**AGNETE HOY, MISS,** London W.3. Formerly employed by Bullers Ltd. and by Doultons (Lambeth), 1952–7. 1957– . *Studio-type Pottery, Stonewares and Porcelains.*
2101	AH	Incised monogram mark, 1952– .
2102	Agnete Hoy	Incised, impressed or painted signature mark, 1952– . N.B. Doulton (Lambeth) marks also occur on wares made or designed by Miss Hoy between 1952 and 1957.
1976	HP	*See* Haverfordwest Pottery.
2951	(also joined)	*See* Humphrey Palmer.
3001		*See* Seth Pennington.
3037		*See* Helen Pincombe.
1959	H. & P.	*See* Harrison & Phillips.
1679	H P CO.	*See* Gibson & Sons Ltd.
1940	(also joined)	*See* Hanley Porcelain Co.
2077	H. P. & M.	*See* Holmes Plant & Maydew.
—	H. & R.	*See* Appendix.
2181	H. & R. J.	*See* H. & R. Johnson.
2728	HS (joined)	*See* C. & U. Mommens.
1962	H. & S.	*See* Hart & Son.
2027–9		*See* Hilditch & Sons.
2078		*See* Holmes & Son.
3611a	H S M (monogram)	*See* H. M. Snowden.

| 2379–80 | H T | *See* Linthorpe Pottery. |
| 3871 | (also joined) | *See* Tooth & Co. |

HUBBLE

NICHOLAS HUBBLE, Wrotham, Kent. 17th century. *Slip-decorated Earthenwares.*

2103   N. H.

These initials occur on Wrotham earthenwares and are attributed to two potters of this name (father, d. 1689, and son). Dated examples range between 1649 and 1687.

    An interesting paper (by A. J. B. Kiddell) on Wrotham earthenwares is contained in the *Transactions of the English Ceramic Circle*, vol. 3, part 2. An example will be found illustrated in *British Pottery and Porcelain: an illustrated Encyclopaedia of Marked Specimens.*

HUDDEN

JOHN THOMAS HUDDEN, Stafford St. (British Anchor Works, c. 1874–85), Longton. Staffordshire Potteries. 1859–85. *Earthenwares.*

2104   J. T. H.
2105   J. T. HUDDEN

Distinguishing details of several printed marks of differing design: name of the individual pattern is often included, 1859–85. Several garter-shaped marks occur on patterns registered in the 1860's.

HUDSON

WILLIAM HUDSON,* Alma Works (c. 1889–92), Sutherland Pottery (c. 1892–1941), Longton. Staffordshire Potteries. 1889–1941. *China.* Formerly Middleton & Hudson. Subsequently Hudson & Middleton Ltd., q.v.

2106   W. H.

Distinguishing initials found on several printed marks of differing design, 1889–92.

2107

Printed mark, 1892–1912.

2108

Printed mark, 1912–41.

2109

Printed mark, introduced 1936 and continued by successors, Messrs. Hudson & Middleton Ltd.

    * This firm should not be confused with William Hudson *& Son* of Longton, c. 1875–94.

HUDSON

HUDSON & MIDDLETON LTD., Sutherland Pottery, Longton. Staffordshire Potteries. 1941– . *China*. Formerly W. Hudson, see previous entry.

2110   Former mark of W. Hudson continued (first used c. 1936).

2110a   Former mark of J. H. Middleton & Co. continued (first used c. 1930).

2110b   Printed mark, 1947– .

HUDSON

YVONNE HUDSON, Earnley, Nr. Chichester, Sussex. 1947–8, 1957– . *Studio-type Pottery, Stoneware Sculpture, etc.*

2111   Y. HUDSON   Incised or painted name or initial marks, 1947–8 and 1957– .
2111a   Y. H.

2112      Impressed seal type mark, taken from a Greco-Roman intaglio, with initials Y. H. and last two numerals of the year added, 1963– .

HUGHES

ELIJAH HUGHES & CO., Bleakhill Works, Cobridge. Staffordshire Potteries. 1853–67. *Earthenwares*.

2113   E. HUGHES & CO.   Impressed mark, 1853–67.

HUGHES

E. HUGHES & CO., Opal China Works, Fenton. Staffordshire Potteries. 1889–1953.* *China*.

2114   H.   Impressed mark, 1889–98.

2115   Impressed or printed mark, 1898–1905.

* Retitled Hughes (Fenton) Ltd., 1940. Works closed 1941 and relicensed 1946 and continued to 1953. The new title may occur on marks similar to Nos. 2119–20.

2116–17   Printed marks, 1905–12 and c. 1908–12.

2118–20

1912–41   1914–41   1930–41

Printed marks, 1912–41.

— **HUGHES (FENTON) LTD.**	*See* E. Hughes & Co., above.

HUGHES

THOMAS HUGHES, Waterloo Road, Burslem (c. 1860–76), Top Bridge Works, Longport, Burslem. Staffordshire Potteries (c. 1872–94). 1860–94. *Earthenwares.* Subsequently Thomas Hughes & Son (Ltd.), q.v.

2121   THOMAS HUGHES IRONSTONE CHINA   Impressed mark, 1860–94.

HUGHES

THOMAS HUGHES & SON (LTD.), Unicorn Pottery, Longport, Burslem. Staffordshire Potteries. 1895–1957. *Earthenwares and China.* Formerly Thomas Hughes.

Works taken over by Arthur Wood & Sons. (Unicorn Pottery Ltd. took part of the works, 1961.)

2122   THOS. HUGHES & SON ENGLAND   Distinguishing detail of several impressed or printed marks of differing design, c. 1895 onwards. "Ltd." added to firm's style and marks, c. 1910.

2123      Printed mark, 1910–30. An earlier version occurs from 1895 *without* "Ltd." and "Made in England".

2124		Printed mark, 1930-5.
2125		Printed mark, 1935-57.

HULL

NORMAN HULL POTTERY, Honiton, Devon. 1947-55. *Earthenwares.*

2126   NORMAN HULL POTTERY

Printed or impressed mark, 1947-55.

   N.B. Norman T. S. Hull was also Managing Director, Art Director, etc., of the Honiton Art Potteries Ltd., see page 333.

2082   N. T. S. HULL

See Honiton Art Potteries Ltd.

HULME

HULME & CHRISTIE, Sutherland Pottery, Fenton. Staffordshire Potteries. 1893-1902. *Earthenwares.* Formerly Forester & Hulme, q.v. Subsequently Christie & Beardmore, q.v.

2127

Printed mark, 1893-1902.

HULME

HULME & SONS, Waterloo Works, Lane End. Staffordshire Potteries. c. 1828-30. *Earthenwares.*

2128   HULME & SONS

Distinguishing detail of several printed marks of differing design, c. 1828-30. The full title of this firm is John Hulme & Sons.

HULME

HENRY HULME & SONS, Garfield Pottery, Burslem. Staffordshire Potteries. 1906-32. *Earthenwares.* Formerly Wood & Hulme.

| 2129 | W. & H.
B. | Impressed or printed initials of Wood & Hulme continued by Henry Hulme & Sons, 1906–32. (Mark introduced in 1882.) |

HULME   WILLIAM HULME, Wedgwood Works, Burslem. Staffordshire Potteries. 1891–1941.* *Earthenwares.*

2130 Printed mark, 1891–1936.

2130a Printed or impressed mark, 1936–41.

         * Firm retitled "William Hulme (Burslem) Ltd." c. 1925.

HULME   WILLIAM HULME (Proprietors: Leighton Pottery Ltd.), Argyle Works, Cobridge. Staffordshire Potteries. 1948–54. *Earthenwares.*

2131 Printed mark, 1948–54. This mark also occurs without the words "Imperial Porcelain".

HULSE   HULSE & ADDERLEY, Daisy Bank Works, Longton. Staffordshire Potteries. 1869–75. *China and Earthenwares.* Formerly Hulse, Nixon & Adderley, q.v. Subsequently W. A. Adderley & Co., q.v.

2132 Printed mark, 1869–75.

HULSE   HULSE, NIXON & ADDERLEY, Daisy Bank Works, Longton. Staffordshire Potteries. 1853–68. *Earthenwares.* Subsequently Hulse & Adderley, q.v.

2133   H. N. & A.   Distinguishing initials found on several printed marks of differing design: name of the individual pattern is often included, 1853–68.

2938	H. W.	*See* Oxshott Pottery.
3999–	(or monogram)	*See* Helen Walters.
4000		
1936	H. W. & CO.	*See* Hancock, Whittingham & Co.
1983		*See* Hawley, Webberley & Co.
1937	H. & W.	*See* Hancock & Whittingham.
2484a	HYLTON POT	*See* Maling.
2484a	WORKS	*See* John Phillips (& Co.).

I

158–9	I. A.	*See* Ian Auld.
241	I. B.	*See* Isaac Ball.
1121	ICENI WARE	*See* William Harrison Cowlishaw.
300	I. D. B.	*See* John Denton Baxter.

IDEN

IDEN POTTERY, D. Townsend and J. H. Wood, Rye,* Sussex. October 1961– . *Studio-type Earthenwares and Stonewares.*

2133a

Printed mark, 1961– . D. Townsend's early work (on Rye Pottery wares) from c. 1947 sometimes bear his personal T. D. triangle sign—the central device in his Iden Pottery mark.

* Iden Pottery was established at Iden, near Rye. In 1963 the pottery moved to Rye but retained its original name.

—	I. E.	*See* Appendix, page 722.
197	I. E. B. or	*See* John & Edward Baddeley.
198	I. E. B. W	

IFIELD

HENRY IFIELD, Wrotham, Kent. c. 1656–69. *Slip decorated Earthenwares.*

2134   H. I.   Rare examples of early Wrotham earthenware bear these

initials. Dated examples range between 1656 and 1669.
See *E.C.C. Transactions*, vol. 3, part 2: a paper by A. J. B.
Kiddell. Six initialled specimens will be found illustrated in
*British Pottery and Porcelain: an illustrated Encyclopaedia of
Marked Specimens.*

IFIELD

2135   I. I.

JOHN IFIELD, Wrotham, Kent. c. 1674+. *Slip-decorated
Earthenwares.*
These initials occur on rare examples of Wrotham earthenware.
Dated examples of 1674 and 1676 are recorded.
   See *E.C.C. Transactions*, vol. 3, part 2: a paper by A. J. B.
Kiddell.

IFIELD

2136   T. I.

THOMAS IFIELD, Wrotham, Kent. c. 1620+. *Slip-deco-
rated Earthenwares.*
Rare examples of Wrotham earthenware bear these initials.
Dated examples include 1621, 1632 and 1654. These (or the
first two) are tentatively attributed to Thomas Ifield.
   See *E.C.C. Transactions*, vol. 3, part 2: a paper by A. J. B.
Kiddell. Two examples will be found illustrated in *British
Pottery and Porcelain: an illustrated Encyclopaedia of Marked
Specimens.*

1812	I. G.	*See* J. Greene.
1991	I. H.	*See* J. Heath.
1994b	I. H. & CO.	*See* Joseph Heath & Co.
2135	I. I.	*See* John Ifield.
2295	I. K.	*See* Joseph Kishere.
2384	I. L.	*See* John Livermore.

ILLINGWORTH

D. **ILLINGWORTH**, Scotforth, Lancaster. 1959– .
Studio-type Pottery and Stonewares.

2137	**di**	Impressed mark, 1959–61.
2137a	**DD**	Impressed seal mark, with name Lancaster, 1961– .
	LANCASTER	
1138	IM (monogram)	*See* Cricklade Pottery.
2632	I. M.	*See* John Meir.
2897	I. M. & CO.	*See* North British Pottery Co.
3087	IMP CHINA	*See* Thomas Poole.
4066	IMPERIAL	*See* Wedgwood & Co. Ltd.
—	IMPERIAL	*See* Appendix, page 722.
374	IRONSTONE CHINA	*See* Birks Bros. & Seddon.
980		*See* Cockson & Seddon.
2920	IMPERIAL PARISIAN GRANITE	*See* Old Hall Earthenware Co. Ltd.
4059	IMPERIAL PORCELAIN	*See* Wedgwood & Co. Ltd.
2634	I. M. & S.	*See* John Meir & Son.

INDEO

INDEO POTTERY, Bovey Tracey, Devon. c. 1772–1841. *Earthenwares (Creamwares).*

2138   INDEO   Rare impressed mark, c. 1772–1841.
N.B. The "I" can look like a "J".

2619 (note)   INDIAN STONE-CHINA   *See* Charles Meigh.
2921   *See* Old Hall Earthenware Co. Ltd.

INDUSTRIAL		**INDUSTRIAL CO-OPERATIVE POTTERY SOCIETY LTD.**, Grange Pans, Bo'ness, Scotland. 1892–4. *Earthenwares*. Formerly Bo'ness Industrial Pottery & Manufacturing Society.
2139	INDUSTRIAL POTTERY BO'NESS	Printed mark in oval form, on earthenware mug in the Godden Collection. Printed and coloured over design—"DRILL", of children playing soldiers, c. 1892–4.

The only local reference to this pottery occurs in Slater's Directory of 1893. It occurs in only one *Pottery Gazette Diary*, that of 1894, the entries being gathered in the preceding year, 1893. The winding-up order for this company was made in February 1894.

INGLEBY		**THOMAS INGLEBY & CO.**, High Street, Tunstall. Staffordshire Potteries. c. 1834–5. *Earthenwares*.
2140	T. I. & CO.	Distinguishing detail of printed marks of differing design: name of the individual pattern is often included, 1834–5.
2370d	I. O. W.	*See* Jo Lester.
952	I. R. & CO.	*See* Coalport Porcelain Works.

IRESON		**NATHANIEL IRESON**, d. 1769. Wincanton, Somerset. c. 1730–67. *Delft-type wares*.
2141	IRESON WINCANTON	Rare painted marks, c. 1730+.
2141a	NATHANIEL IRESON	Several specimens are recorded with the place name—Wincanton and a date, 1738, 1739, 1748,* etc. It is not clear if Nathaniel Ireson potted up to the time of his death in 1769. He had varied interests. In his will dated 1765 he is described as a "Mason". *See also* Wincanton Pottery, page 677.

* See Professor F. H. Garner's *English Delftware* (1948). Documentary specimens will be found illustrated in *British Pottery and Porcelain: an illustrated Encyclopaedia of Marked Specimens*.

3966–8	IRISH PORCELAIN	*See* Wade (Ulster) Ltd.
3465	I. S.	*See* Isobel Saul.
3546		*See* John Simpson.
2658	I. S. LONDON	*See* Middlesbrough Pottery Co.

ISIS

2142
ISIS

ISIS POTTERY, Oxford. c. 1947–53.* *Studio-type Pottery.*
Printed or incised mark, c. 1947–53.

    * The dates are approximate only.

ISLAND

2143   ISLAND POTTERY
        SHANKLIN

ISLAND POTTERY (Harry Clark and Thelma P. Clark),
Shanklin, Isle of Wight, 1949–50. Portsmouth, Hampshire,
1950– . 1949– . *Studio-type Pottery and Stonewares.*
Incised or painted name-mark, arranged around base, 1949–50.

2144   ISLAND POTTERY
        PORTSMOUTH

Incised or painted name-mark, arranged around base. Note
address "Portsmouth", 1950– .

2145

Incised or painted initial mark of Harry Clark, arranged in
centre of base. On special individual examples only the
initial mark occurs, not the "Island Pottery" mark, 1949– .

2146

Incised or painted initial mark of Mrs. Thelma Clark. (*née*
Hanan, see page 307), 1951– .

ISLAND

2147   J. O.
        I. O. W.
        SEAVIEW

ISLAND POTTERY STUDIO (SEAVIEW) LTD. (J.
Lester), Seaview, Isle of Wight. May 1956 to October 1958.
Earthenwares. Subsequently D. Buckley, q.v.
Printed or impressed marks comprising the outline of the Isle
of Wight enclosing the initials J. O., I. O. W. with "Seaview"
under, or "Handmade at Seaview", May 1956 to October 1958.

ISLE OF WIGHT

ISLE OF WIGHT POTTERY (S. E. Saunders), Whipping-
ham, Isle of Wight. c. 1930–40. *Earthenwares.*

2148

Printed or impressed mark, c. 1930–40. The central monogram
was used previously by S. E. Saunders. (See mark no. 773.)

ISLEWORTH

ISLEWORTH POTTERY (J. Shore, Shore & Co. and Shore & Goulding), Middlesex. c. 1760–1825. *Earthenwares (and Porcelains?)*

2149	SHORE & CO.	These marks have been attributed to the Isleworth Pottery. Little is known of its history or products.
2150	S. & CO.	
2151	S. & G.	A class of moulded terra-cotta has previously been classed as Isleworth and these sometimes bear similar impressed initial marks. Such wares are German and were made by Schiller & Gerbing in the 19th century.
2151a	S. & G.	
	ISLEWORTH	

4070	ISLINGTON	*See* H. F. Wedgwood & Co. Ltd.
4318	I T	*See* Worcester Porcelains, page 693.
	IVORY	Impressed mark found on late 19th century earthenwares, the name refers to the type of body.
—	I W	*See* Appendix, page 723.
4193	I. W. & CO.	*See* Isaac Wilson & Co.

J

— 2911	J.	*See* Appendix, page 723. *See* Odney Pottery.
2154	J. & CO.	*See* J. Jackson & Co.
1125	JACKFIELD	*See* Craven, Dunnill & Co. Ltd.

JACKSON

CHRISTOPHER P. JACKSON, Harpenden, Herts. 1957– .
Earthenware models of Veteran Cars.

2152   CHRISTOPHER PAUL   Signature mark in writing letters, 1957– .

JACKSON

J. JACKSON & CO., Holmes Pottery, Rotherham, Yorkshire. 1870–87. *Earthenwares.* Formerly Jackson, Dickinson, Greaves & Shaw. Subsequently George Shaw & Sons, q.v.

2153   J. J. & CO.
2154   J. & CO.

Distinguishing initials found on several printed marks of differing design: name of the individual pattern is often included, 1870–87. Several marks incorporate "J. & Co." and these may refer to this firm.

JACKSON

JOB & JOHN JACKSON, Church Yard Works, Burslem. Staffordshire Potteries. 1831–5. *Earthenwares.*

2155   J. & J. JACKSON
2156   JACKSON'S
      WARRANTED

Distinguishing details of several impressed or printed marks of differing design, 1831–5. Other marks incorporate initials J. & Co. and these cannot be attributed with certainty, see note on mark no. 2154.

JACKSON		**JACKSON & GOSLING (LTD.)**, Grosvenor Works, Longton. Staffordshire Potteries. Established c. 1866 at King Street, Fenton. Longton address from c. 1909. Various changes in ownership. 1866– . *China.*
2157 2158	J. & G. J. & G. L.	Distinguishing details of several impressed or printed marks of differing design: name of the individual pattern is often included, c. 1880 onwards. Early wares were not usually marked.

2159–62

c. 1912+   c. 1912+   c. 1914+   c. 1919+

2163–6

c. 1919+   c. 1924+   c. 1930+   c. 1934+

Note addition of "Ltd."

2167–8

c. 1930's+   c. 1950's+

This mark is also
used by Grosvenor
China Ltd.

Printed or impressed marks, c. 1912+.

JACKSON		**JACKSON & PATTERSON**, Sheriff Hill Pottery, Newcastle upon Tyne, Northumberland. 1830–45. *Earthenwares.* Formerly J. Fordy & Co. Subsequently T. Patterson and then George Patterson.
2169	J. & P.	Distinguishing initials found on several printed marks of differing design: name of the individual pattern is often included, 1830–45.
JAMES		**JOHN LEWIS JAMES** (b. 1877), Decorative Earthenware Works, Millwall, London E.14. c. 1920–30. *Earthenwares.*

| 2170 | J. L. James | Signature mark on "reproductions of moorish and Delft wall tiles and thrown pots", c. 1920–30. |
| 2171 | JAMIERE | *See* Robert Jamieson, below. |

JAMIESON

ROBERT JAMIESON, Kings Road, Newcastle under Lyme, Staffordshire.   c. 1896.

2171	JAMIERE	This trade-name was registered in 1896. Robert Jamieson was described as a china and earthenware manufacturer.
3583	JASMI	*See* James Smith.
—	J. B.	*See* Appendix, page 723.
206	(also joined)	*See* Jacob Baggaley.
314		*See* James Beech.
317		*See* J. & M. P. Bell & Co.
344		*See* John Berry.
352		*See* John Bevington.
359		*See* Joan Biggs.
639		*See* James Broadhurst & Sons.
2912		*See* Odney Pottery (Ltd.).
—	J. B. & CO.	*See* Appendix, page 723.
336		*See* J. Bennett & Co.
354		*See* John Bevington & Co.
—	J. B. D.	*See* Appendix, page 723.
640	J. B. & S.	*See* James Broadhurst & Sons.
315	J. B. & S.	*See* James Beech & Sons.
	or	*See* James Broadhurst & Sons.
315a	J. B. & SON	
641	J. B. & S. LTD.	*See* James Broadhurst & Sons.
4032	J. B. W.	*See* James B. Wathen.
	or	
4033	J. B. W. F.	

—	J. C.	*See* Appendix, page 723.
910		*See* Joseph Clementson.
1126		*See* Joan Crawford.
1031		*See* Joanna Connell.
1642c	℄	*See* Fulham Pottery & Cheavin Filter Co. Ltd.
1453	J. C. E.	*See* J. C. Edwards.
882	J. C. L.	*See* John Chew.
4156	J. & C. W.	*See* J. & C. Wileman.
—	J. D.	*See* Appendix, page 724.
1167		*See* John Dan.
301	J. D. B.	*See* John D. Baxter.
—	J. D. & CO.	*See* Appendix, page 724.
1289–90]	(and monogram)	*See* J. Dimmock & Co.
—	J. L.	*See* Jeremy Leach.
1449	J. E.	*See* John Edwards (& Co.).
1450	J. E. & CO.	
2221	J. E. J.	*See* Josiah E. Jones.
872 (note)	Jem	*See* Chelsea Pottery.
—	JEREMY	*See* Jeremy Leach.

JERSEY

JERSEY POTTERIES LTD. or Jersey Potteries (Home Decorations Ltd.), Gorey, Jersey, Channel Islands. 1946– . *Hand-made Earthenwares.*

2172	JERSEY POTTERY C. I.	Painted mark, 1946– .
2173		Impressed or printed mark, 1946– .

2174		Impressed or printed mark, 1951– .

1446	J. E. & S.	*See* James Edwards & Son.
1127 1578	J. F.	*See* Joan Crawford. *See* Joseph Flower.
1127 1563	JF (joined)	*See* Joan Crawford. *See* John Fisher.
45	J. F. A.	*See* J. F. Adderley.
1643	J. F. & CO.	*See* Jacob Furnival & Co.
1481–2	J. F. E. or J. F. E. & Co. Ltd.	*See* J. F. Elton & Co. Ltd.
4157	J. F. & C. W.	*See* James Charles Wileman.
4160	J. F. W.	*See* James F. Wileman.
— 1668 1696 2217 4020	JG (also joined)	*See* Appendix. *See* J. Gardiner. *See* James Gildea. *See* George Jones. *See* Christopher D. Warham.
2157	J. & G.	*See* Jackson & Gosling (Ltd.).
69a	J. & G. A.	*See* J. & G. Alcock.
2158	J. & G. L.	*See* Jackson & Gosling.
1741–2	J. G. S. & Co.	*See* Goodwin, Stoddard & Co.
— 1899 2045 2046–46a 2206	JH (also joined)	*See* Appendix, J.H. *See* Frank & Janet Hamer. *See* John Hodge. *See* Joseph Holdcroft. *See* A. G. H. Jones.

1994a	J. H. & Co.	*See* Joseph Heath & Co.
1065	J. H. C. & Co.	*See* J. H. Cope & Co.
2500a	J. H. M.	*See* J. H. Manning.
3325	JHR & Co. (joined)	*See* Ridgways (Bedford Works) Ltd.
1870–1	J H & S (joined)	*See* James Hadley & Sons.
4003	J. H. W.	*See* J. H. Walton.
4043	J. H. W. & Sons or	*See* J. H. Weatherby & Sons.
4047	J. H. W. & Sons Ltd.	
3442	Jill S.	*See* Jill Salaman.
2153	J. J. & Co.	*See* J. Jackson & Co.
2266	J. K. or	*See* James Kent (Ltd.).
2265	J. K. L.	
— 2351a	J. L.	*See* Appendix, page 724. *See* Jeremy Leach.
2351	J L (within a triangle)	*See* Janet Leach.
877	J. L. C.	*See* Jonathan Lowe Chetham.
2351b	J. L. C. P.	*See* Jeremy Leach.
2351	J. L. D. S.	*See* Jeremy Leach.
2631	J. M.	*See* John Meir.
— 2820 2557 2896	J. M. & Co.	*See* Appendix. *See* James Macintyre & Co. (Ltd.). *See* J. Maudesley & Co. *See* North British Pottery.

2564	J. M.	See John Mayer.
	F	

318	J. & M. P. B. & Co.	See J. & M. P. Bell & Co. (Ltd.).
	or	
320	J. & M. P. B. & Co. (Ld)	

—	J. M. & S.	See Appendix, page 724.
2627	or	See Job Meigh (& Sons).
2633	J. M. & Son	See John Meir & Son.
2635		

2139	JNDEO	See Indeo Pottery.

2147	J. O.	See Island Pottery Studio.
2370	or	See Jo Lester.
	J. O.	
	I. O. W.	

JOHNSON

RHEUBEN JOHNSON AND/OR PHOEBE JOHNSON, Miles Bank, Hanley. Staffordshire Potteries. c. 1817–38.* *Earthenwares.*

2175   JOHNSON HANLEY STONE CHINA

Distinguishing detail of printed marks. The wares would seem to date from c. 1825 onwards to 1838.

> * It is not certain which potter employed this mark. Reuben Johnson was working from c. 1817 to 1823. Phoebe Johnson (widow) continued (as Phoebe Johnson & Son) to c. 1838; she was "leaving the neighbourhood" late in 1840.

JOHNSON

JOHNSON BROS. (HANLEY) LTD., Hanley Pottery (and other Hanley Potteries), Hanley (and at Tunstall, c. 1899–1913). 1883– . Staffordshire Potteries. *Earthenwares (Ironstone, etc.).* Formerly J. W. Pankhurst & Co.

2176

Distinguishing name "Johnson Bros." found on several impressed or printed marks of differing design: name of the individual pattern is often included, 1883–1913.

2177

Printed mark, c. 1900+.

2178-9

Printed marks, c. 1913 onwards.

2180   Printed mark, c. 1955– .

JOHNSON

H. & R. JOHNSON (LTD.), Crystal Tile Works, Cobridge to 1920. Highgate Tile Works (c. 1916+), Tunstall. Staffordshire Potteries. 1902– . *Tiles, etc.*

2181   H. & R. J. ENGLAND   Impressed or printed mark, 1902– .

2182   [CRISTAL shield mark]   Impressed or printed mark, 1916+ .

JOHNSON

JOSEPH JOHNSON, Liverpool. Late 18th century to early 19th century. *Engraver.*

2183   I. JOHNSON LIVERPOOL   This signature mark occurs on a printed earthenware drinking cup in the Schreiber Collection at the Victoria and Albert Museum.

2184   JOSEPH JOHNSON LIVERPOOL   H. Boswell Lancaster in *Liverpool and her Potters* (1936) records a jug dated 1789 with this signature mark on the prints.

JOHNSON

LESLIE JOHNSON. Staffordshire Potteries. c. 1900 20. *Decorator.*

2185   LESLIE JOHNSON HAND PAINTED   Printed or painted name-marks occur on porcelains decorated by this former Doulton artist, c. 1900–20.

JOHNSON

SAMUEL JOHNSON LTD., Hill Pottery,* Burslem. Staffordshire Potteries. 1887–1931. *Earthenwares.*

     * Britannia Pottery from 1916.

2186	S. J.	Distinguishing details of several printed marks of differing design: name of the individual pattern is often included, 1887–1931. "Ltd." should occur from 1912 onwards.
2187	S. J. B.	
2188	S. J. LTD.	

2189   Printed mark, c. 1916–31.

JONES   A. B. JONES & SONS (LTD.), Grafton Works (and other addresses), Longton. Staffordshire Potteries. 1900– . *China and Earthenwares.* Formerly A. B. Jones.

2190	A. B. J. & S.	Distinguishing details of several marks of differing design, 1900– .
2190a	A. B. J. & SONS	
2191	A. B. JONES & SONS	

2192–4   Printed marks, 1900–13.

2195–8

c. 1913+

c. 1920+

c. 1930+

c. 1935+

2199–2202

c. 1949+

c. 1950+

c. 1957+

c. 1961+

Printed marks used from 1913 onwards.

JONES   ALBERT E. JONES (LONGTON) LTD., from c. 1930, Palissy Pottery (formerly Garfield Pottery), Longton. Staffordshire Potteries. 1905–46. *Earthenwares.* Formerly A. E. Jones and A. E. Jones & Co. to c. 1929. Subsequently Palissy Pottery Ltd., q.v.

2203		Printed or impressed mark, c. 1908–36.
2204		Printed mark, 1936–41.
2205		Printed mark, 1937–46, and continued by successors, see page 480.

JONES

A. G. HARLEY JONES, Royal Vienna Art Pottery (and other addresses), Fenton. Staffordshire Potteries. 1907–34. *Earthenwares and China.*

2206	H. J.	Distinguishing details of several marks of differing design:
2207	A. G. H. J.	name of the individual pattern is often included, 1907–34.

2208–12

c. 1907+   c. 1920+   c. 1920+   c. 1921+   c. 1923–34
Many variations occur of this mark.

Printed marks used from 1907 to 1934.

JONES

ELIJAH JONES, Villa Pottery, Cobridge. Staffordshire Potteries. 1831–9. *Earthenwares.*

2213	PUBLISHED BY E. JONES COBRIDGE SEPTEMBER 1, 1838	Impressed "Published by" marks in this form occur on moulded jugs, etc., with the date of introduction of the design.
2214	E. J.	Printed marks occur with these initials and were probably used by this firm, c. 1831–9, but other potters with the same name include: Elijah Jones, Hall Lane, Hanley, 1828–31. Elijah Jones, Phoenix Works, Shelton, 1831–2. Elijah Jones, Mill Street, Shelton, 1847–8.

JONES

FREDERICK JONES (& CO.), Stafford St. (c. 1865–73) and Chadwick St. (c. 1868–86), Longton. Staffordshire Potteries. 1865–86. *Earthenwares.*

2215   F. JONES LONGTON

Distinguishing detail of several impressed or printed marks of differing design: name of the individual pattern is often included, 1865–86.

N.B. This firm is also listed in contemporary records as Frederick Jones *& Co.*

JONES

GEORGE JONES, Barnfield House, Burslem. Staffordshire Potteries. c. 1854. *Earthenwares.*

2216   GEORGE JONES

Impressed mark on earthenware, child's "A.B.C." and motto plate, in the Godden Collection, c. 1854.

JONES

GEORGE JONES (& SONS LTD.), Trent Pottery (c. 1864–1907), Crescent Pottery (c. 1907–57), Stoke. Staffordshire Potteries. 1861–1951. *China (from 1872)*, *Earthenwares*, *Majolica, etc.*

See L. Jewitt's *The Ceramic Art of Great Britain* (1883).

2217

Distinguishing monogram found on several relief, impressed or printed marks, c. 1861 to late 1873 when "& Sons" added to marks. Some marks incorporate the term "Stone China" and "Stoke on Trent".

2218

Printed or impressed mark, c. 1874–1924. "England" was added from 1891. "Crescent China" may occur under mark from c. 1893.

2219

Printed or impressed mark, c. 1924–51.

JONES

JOSIAH ELLIS JONES, Portland Works, Longton. Staffordshire Potteries. 1868–72. *Earthenwares.* Formerly Jones, Shepherd & Co., q.v.

2220		Printed mark with title in full. Other marks may occur with the initials J. E. J., 1868–72.
2221	J. E. J.	

JONES

G. OWEN JONES, London N.W.2. 1954– . *Studio-type Pottery.*

2222	G. Owen Jones	Incised or painted mark in writing letters, 1954– .

JONES

JONES SHEPHERD & CO., Portland Works, Church St., Longton. Staffordshire Potteries. 1867–8. *Earthenwares.* Subsequently J. E. Jones, q.v.

2223	J. S. & Co.	Distinguishing initials found on several printed marks of differing design: name of the individual pattern is often included, 1867–8.

2223a	JONES & SON	*See* page 364.

JONES

JONES & WALLEY, Villa Pottery, Cobridge. Staffordshire Potteries. 1841–3. *Earthenwares, etc.* Subsequently Edward Walley, q.v.

2224	PUBLISHED JULY 1st, 1842 BY JONES & WALLEY COBRIDGE	Impressed or relief "Published by" marks in this form occur on moulded jugs, etc., with the date of introduction of the design, 1841–3.

2224a	J. & W.	Distinguishing initials found on printed marks of differing design: name of the individual pattern is often included, 1841–3.

3325	JONROTH	*See* Ridgways (Bedford Works) Ltd.

JORDAN

J. F. JORDAN, Clapham Common Brick & Tile Company, Clapham, Nr. Worthing, Sussex. c. 1918–39. *Earthenwares.*

2225	JORDAN WARE CLAPHAM	Distinguishing name and place name "Clapham" occurring on several incised marks, 1918–39.
2226	J. JORDAN	Some specimens bear only the name-marks, 1918–39. Many jugs and vases have the appearance of being 18th century wares but all were made between 1918 and 1939.

| 2225 | JORDAN WARE | *See* J. F. Jordan. |

| **JOYNSON** | | **CECILE JOYNSON**, Yatton Court, Beaford, Nr. Winkleigh, Devon. c. 1951. |
| 2227 | CECILE | This trade-name was registered in 1951, under the above name and address for porcelain and earthenware decorated wares. |

—	JP	*See* Appendix (J. Parkshurst), page 727.
2173	(also joined)	*See* Jersey Potteries Ltd.
2973		*See* Judith Partridge.
3178		*See* James Pulham.

| 2169 | J. & P. | *See* Jackson & Patterson. |

| 3154 | J. P. & Co. (L) | *See* John Pratt & Co. Ltd. |

| 3174 | J. P. L. | *See* John Procter. |

| 2991 | J. P. Ltd. | *See* James Pearson Ltd. |

3218	J. R.	*See* James Reeves.
3251		*See* Job Ridgway.
3253		*See* John Ridgway & Co.
3368		*See* John & George Rogers.
3370		*See* John Rogers & Son.

| 3337 | J. R. B. | *See* Joseph Robinson. |

| 3268 | J. R. B. & Co. | *See* John Ridgway, Bates & Co. |

| 952 | J. R. & Co. | *See* Coalport. |
| 3257 | | *See* John Ridgway & Co. |

| 3218 | J R F | *See* James Reeves. |

| 878 | J. R. & F. C. | *See* J. R. & F. Chetham. |

| 1726 | J. & R. G. | *See* John & Robert Godwin. |

| 1911 | J. R. H. | *See* J. & R. Hammersley. |

3368	J. R.	*See* John & George Rogers.
3370	L.	*See* John Rogers & Son.
951	J. ROSE	*See* Coalport.
	or	
947–50	J. ROSE & CO.	
3371	J. R. S.	*See* John Rogers & Son.
3336	J. R. & S.	*See* John Robinson & Son.
3931	J. R. VENTNOR	*See* Ventnor Pottery.
3463	JS	*See* June Sarene.
3513, 3515	(also joined)	*See* John Shelly.
3581		*See* James Smith.
3624		*See* John Solly.
2223	J. S. & CO.	*See* Jones, Shepherd & Co.
3532		*See* J. Shore & Co.
1667	J. S. G.	*See* Tony & Janet Gant.
2031–2	JSH	*See* Hill Pottery Co.
	(monogram)	
3435	J. S. S. B.	*See* James Sadler & Sons (Ltd.).
3505	JSS Ltd.	*See* John Shaw & Sons (Longton) Ltd.
	(joined)	
4138	J. S. W.	*See* Wild Bros.
3791	J. T.	*See* John Tams (& Son) (Ltd.).
3844		*See* John Thomson.
3907		*See* John Twemlow.
3908		*See* J. Twigg.
355	J. & T. B.	*See* James & Thomas Bevington.
1454	J. & T. E.	*See* James & Thomas Edwards.
1559	J. T. F.	*See* John Thomas Firth.
	K. L.	
1644	J. & T. F.	*See* Jacob & Thomas Furnival.

2104	J. T. H.	*See* John Thomas Hudden.
3794 3846	J. T. & S. or J. T. & SONS	*See* John Tams & Son. *See* John Thomson & Sons.
3095	JUBBE	*See* Agnes Horsey.

JUDE

MERVYN AND MRS. NERYS JUDE, Oxshott, Surrey, 1948–54. Cranleigh, Surrey, 1954–63. Glyn Ceiriog, Denbighshire. November 1963– . 1948– . *Studio-type Pottery.*

2228–9   **MJ   M**   Initial and seal type mark of Mervyn Jude arranged in circle, c. 1948– .

2230–1   **NJ   N**   Initial and seal type mark, the latter within double lined circle, of Mrs. Nerys Jude, c. 1948– .

3566a	Jug mark	*See* John Singleman.

JUPP

2231a   MOJ

MAURICE JUPP. *Studio-type Pottery.*
Impressed seal mark.   Other wares may be signed Jupp.
   This modern potter had an exhibition of his work in London in November 1963.   My letter seeking further information has not been answered at the time of going to press.

3934 3934b 3934a	J. V. J. V. JUNR. J. V. & S.	*See* James Vernon (& Sons).
3978 — 4306 4159	JW (also monogram) J. W. & CO.	*See* J. F. Walford. *See* Josiah Wedgwood. *See* James Woodward. *See* James & Charles Wileman.
133	J. W. D.	*See* Ashby Potters Guild.

2952	J. W. P. or	*See* J. W. Pankhurst & Co.
2954	J. W. P. & CO.	
3260	J. W. R. or	*See* John & William Ridgway.
3261	J. & W. R.	
4195	J. W. & S.	*See* J. Wilson & Sons.
4383	J. Y.	*See* John Yates.

POSTSCRIPT

JONES		**JONES & SON**, Hanley. Staffordshire Potteries. c. 1826–8, *Earthenwares*.
2223a	JONES & SON	Distinguishing detail of ornate blue printed mark of a fine platter bearing " British History " subject, c. 1826–8.

K

3180	K.	*See* Kenneth Quick.
2241	K. & CO.	*See* Keeling & Co. (Ltd.).
2282		*See* William Kirkby & Co.
2288		*See* Kirkland & Co.
2242	K. & CO. B.	*See* Keeling & Co. (Ltd.).
2289	K. & CO.	*See* Kirkland & Co.
2291	E.	

KALAN

ANTON & MRS. STEPHANIE KALAN, Mitcham, Surrey. Newport, Essex (from December 1962). 1953–   *Studio-type Pottery and Porcelains.*

2232	A. KALAN	Painted or incised marks in signature form, 1953– .
2233	S. KALAN	

1298	KAOLIN WARE	*See* Thomas Dimmock (Junior) & Co.

KAPOSVARY

KAPOSVARY CONTEMPORARY ART POTTERY (John A. Kaposvary), Porthill, Newcastle, Staffordshire. 1954–   . *Earthenwares.*

2234		Printed mark, 1954– .

KAY		**NORA KAY, MISS,** Gerrards Cross, Buckinghamshire. 1951– . *Studio-type Pottery.*
2235	**NK**	Impressed seal mark, 1951– .
3067–8	KB (monogram)	*See* Katharine Pleydell-Bouverie.
699	K. B. or	*See* Kirsti Buhler.
700	K. B. F.	
2277	K. & B.	*See* King & Barratt (Ltd.).
2298		*See* Knapper & Blackhurst.
4346–7		*See* Worcester, Kerr & Binns.
891a	K. C.	*See* Kenneth Clark.
2234	K C A P	*See* Kaposvary Contemporary Art Pottery.
2301	K. E. & CO. or	*See* Knight Elkin & Co.
2303	K. & E.	
2304a	K. E. B.	*See* Knight Elkin & Bridgwood.
2278	K. E. & B.	*See* King, Edge & Barratt.
2304		*See* Knight Elkin & Bridgwood.

KEELE		**KEELE STREET POTTERY CO. (LTD.),** Keele Street, Tunstall (c. 1913–58), Meir Airport, Longton (1958–). Staffordshire Potteries. 1915– . *Earthenwares.* This firm is one of several pottery firms in the Keele Street Pottery Group. Early wares usually unmarked.
2236	K. S. P.	The initials K. S. P. occur on post-war products.
2237	KEELE ST. POTTERY CO. LTD. GOLDEN PYRAMID ENGLAND	Basic printed mark introduced in 1962. The name of various patterns or styles is added to the centre of this mark.

KEELING		ANTHONY & ENOCH KEELING (Two Works), Tunstall. Staffordshire Potteries. c. 1795–1811. *China and Earthenwares.*
2238	A. & E. KEELING	Distinguishing details of painted marks of differing design, c. 1795–1811.
2239	A. E. KEELING	

KEELING		CHARLES KEELING, Broad St., Shelton. Staffordshire Potteries. 1822–5. *Earthenwares.*
2240	C. K.	Distinguishing initials found on several printed marks of differing design: name of the individual pattern is often included, 1822–5.

KEELING		KEELING & CO. (LTD.), Dale Hall Works (from 1887), Burslem. Staffordshire Potteries. 1886–1936. *Earthenwares.* Formerly J. Gildea & Co.
2241	K. & CO.	Distinguishing details of several printed marks of differing design: name of the individual pattern is often included, 1886–1936.
2242	K. & CO. B.	
2242a	& K. CO.	

2243   Trade-mark, printed, 1886–1936. "England" may be added after 1891. "Ltd." may be added after 1909.

2244   LOSOL   Trade-name, c. 1912 onwards.

2245   Printed mark, c. 1912–36.

KEELING		JOSEPH KEELING, Keelings Lane, Hanley. Staffordshire Potteries. c. 1802–8. *Earthenwares, Basaltes, etc.*
2246	JOSEPH KEELING	Rare impressed mark, c. 1802–8.

KEELING   SAMUEL KEELING & CO., Market St., Hanley. Staffordshire Potteries. 1840–50. *Earthenwares.*

2247   S. K. & CO.   Distinguishing details of several printed marks of differing
2248   S. KEELING & CO.   design: name of the individual pattern is often included,
2249   1840–50. Mark no. 2249 is a typical example of an initial
                               mark.

KEELING   **KEELING, TOFT & CO.**, also **KEELING & TOFT**,
                              Hanley. Staffordshire Potteries. 1805–26. *Wedgwood-type
                              Basalt wares*, *etc*. Subsequently Toft & May.

                                 This firm used two different forms of impressed marks, and
                              worked several different potteries.   The basic marks are:
2250–1   KEELING TOFT & CO.   KEELING & TOFT.
                              With the exception of the fourth rate, of November 1812, all
                              records list Keeling Toft & Co. rather than Keeling & Toft.

                                 Two typical pieces of basalt are illustrated in *British Pottery
                              and Porcelain : an illustrated Encyclopaedia of Marked Specimens.*

KEEN   **LAWRENCE KEEN**, Moat House, Stanmore, Middlesex.
                              1953– . *Studio-type Pottery.*
2252   L·K   Impressed seal mark of the initials L·K or painted initials on
2253   special pieces, 1953– .

2305   K. E. & K.   *See* Knight, Elkin & Knight.

2415–16   KELSBORO ware   *See* Longton New Art Pottery Co. Ltd.

KEMP   **DOROTHY KEMP**, Felixstowe, Suffolk. 1939– .   *Studio
                              Pottery, Slipwares and Stonewares.*
                                 Dorothy Kemp is one of the many talented modern potters
                              who studied under Bernard Leach.

2254   Incised or impressed monogram mark, 1939– .

2255   Incised or impressed marks used by Dorothy Kemp, c. 1939– .

KENN   KENN POTTERY (Miss P. Shillinglow), Kenn, Nr. Exeter,
                                           1945–59. Ringmore, Shaldon, Devon, 1959– . 1945– .
                                           Hand-made Pottery.

2256   Incised mark, 1945– .

KENNEDY   HENRY KENNEDY & SONS (LTD.), Barrowfield Potteries,
                                           Glasgow, Scotland. 1866–1929. *Stonewares.*

2257      Trade-mark, 1866+ .

2257a   THE DELAWARE   A trade-mark incorporating this name and a head crest was
                                           registered in 1923.

KENNEDY   JAMES KENNEDY, Commercial Street, Burslem. Stafford-
                                           shire Potteries. c. 1818–34. *Engraver.*
2258   KENNEDY   Signature mark on printed designs by this independent en-
2258a   J. KENNEDY   graver. A coronation mug of 1831 in the Hanley Museum and
                                           a Reform mug of 1832 in the Godden Collection bear Kennedy's
                                           signature as part of the design.

KENNEDY   WILLIAM SADDLER KENNEDY (& CO.), Washington
                                           Works, Burslem. Staffordshire Potteries. 1843–54. *Earthen-
                                           wares.* Subsequently Kennedy & Macintyre, see following
                                           entry.
2259   W. S. KENNEDY   Distinguishing name found on impressed or printed marks of
                                           differing design, 1843–53.

KENNEDY

2260   W. S. KENNEDY
& J. MACINTYRE

KENNEDY & MACINTYRE, Washington Works, Burslem. Staffordshire Potteries. 1854–60. *Earthenwares.* Formerly W. S. Kennedy, see previous entry. Subsequently J. Macintyre & Co., q.v.

Distinguishing names found on impressed or printed marks of differing design, 1854–60.

KENSINGTON

KENSINGTON FINE ART POTTERY CO., Kensington Works, Hanley. Staffordshire Potteries. 1892–9. *Earthenwares.*

2261

Printed or impressed mark, 1892–9.

KENSINGTON

KENSINGTON POTTERY LTD., Kensington Works, Hanley, c. 1922–37. Trubsham Cross, Burslem, c. 1937– . Staffordshire Potteries. 1922– . *Earthenwares.*

A new company, Price & Kensington Potteries Ltd., was formed in 1961 but the Kensington Pottery and mark continues.

2262

Printed mark, c. 1922– .

KENT

JAMES KENT (LTD.), Old Foley Pottery, Longton. Staffordshire Potteries. 1897– . *China and Earthenwares.*

2263

Printed mark, 1897–1915.

2264–7

c. 1897–1901   c. 1901+   c. 1910+   c. 1913+

N.B. "Ltd." added to title and marks from 1913.

2268–71

c. 1936–9   c. 1945+   c. 1950+   c. 1955+
                                          with mark number 2270.

Printed marks used from 1897 onwards.

KENT

WILLIAM KENT (PORCELAINS) LTD., Auckland St., Burslem. Staffordshire Potteries. 1944–62.* *Earthenwares.* Formerly William Kent.

2272

Printed mark, 1944–62.

2273   w B к

Moulded initial mark on modern earthenware figures, etc., made from 19th century master moulds previous to 1963.

> * Production of ornamental earthenwares ceased on December 31st, 1962. The firm continues to produce electrical porcelains.

—   KERR
            or
—   KERR & BINNS
            or
— W. H. KERR & CO.

See Worcester, Kerr & Binns, page 696.

4394   K. E. S.

See Ymagynatyf Pottery.

KEYES

PHYLLIS KEYES, London. c. 1930–40. *Studio-type Pottery.*

2274

Incised or painted mark, c. 1930–40. Painted decoration on a tinglaze was carried out by Jane Bussy, Simone Bussy, Angelica Garnett, Duncan Grant and Vanessa Bell; their initials may occur.

KEYS		**KEYS & MOUNTFORD**, John St., Stoke. Staffordshire Potteries. 1850–7. *Parian.*
		John Mountford is reputed to have invented the popular parian body while employed by Copeland & Garrett in the early 1840's. See *Victorian Porcelain* (1961). Subsequently J. Mountford, q.v.
2275	K. & M.	Impressed marks on parian wares, 1850–7.
2276	S. KEYS & MOUNTFORD	
2261	K. F. A. P. Co.	*See* Kensington Fine Art Pottery Co.
KING		**KING & BARRATT (LTD.)**, Bournes Bank Pottery, Burslem. Staffordshire Potteries. 1898–1940. *Earthenwares, Jet, etc.*
2277	K. & B.	Distinguishing initials found on impressed or printed marks of differing design, 1898–1940.
1564	Kingfisher mark	*See* John Fisher.
KING		**KING, EDGE & BARRATT**, Bournes Bank Pottery, Burslem. Staffordshire Potteries. 1896–7. *Earthenwares.*
2278	K. E. & B.	Distinguishing initials found on several printed marks of differing design, 1896–7.
		N.B. These initials were used earlier by Knight Elkin & Bridgwood, q.v.
KINGWOOD		**KINGWOOD POTTERIES** (L. D. Wilkinson), Wormley, Nr. Godalming, Surrey. 1947–56. *Earthenwares.* Subsequently West Surrey Ceramic Co. Ltd. Established on same site, mid-1956.
2279	KINGWOOD WILKINSON BROOK SURREY	A circular, printed or impressed mark incorporating this wording was employed 1947–50.

| 2280 | KINGWOOD WORMLEY SURREY ENGLAND | Printed or impressed mark in this form, 1950–6. |

2291   KIRALPO ware   *See* Kirkland & Co.

KIRKBY

2281   W. K. & CO.   **WILLIAM KIRKBY & CO.**, Sutherland Pottery, Fenton.
2282   K. & CO.

Staffordshire Potteries. 1879–85. *China and Earthenwares.* Distinguishing details of several impressed or printed marks of differing design: name of the individual pattern is often included, 1879–85.

2283

2285–6   KIRKHAM   *See* Kirkhams Ltd.

KIRKHAM

WILLIAM KIRKHAM, London Road, Stoke. Staffordshire Potteries. 1862–92. *Earthenwares, Terra-cotta, etc.* Subsequently retitled Kirkhams, then Kirkhams Ltd., q.v.

2284   W. KIRKHAM   Impressed mark, 1862–92.

KIRKHAMS

KIRKHAMS LTD., Kirkham St., London Road, Stoke. Staffordshire Potteries. 1946–61. *Earthenwares.* Formerly Kirkhams.

On December 31st 1961 Messrs. Kirkhams Ltd. and A. E. Gray & Co. Ltd. were combined, under the style of Portmeirion Potteries Ltd., q.v.

2285–6   Printed marks, c. 1946–61.

2287	**Kirkhams Ltd.** STOKE ON TRENT ENGLAND	Printed marks, c. 1952–61.

KIRKLAND

KIRKLAND & CO. (Kirkland & Piddock, c. 1897–8), Albion Pottery, Etruria. Staffordshire Potteries. 1892– .* *Earthenwares.* Formerly Kirkland & Dean.

2288–9	K & Co. K & Co. E	Distinguishing details of several marks of differing design, 1892+.

2290

Printed mark, 1892+.

2291

Printed mark, 1928+.

2292

Printed mark, c. 1938– .

* Retitled "Kirklands (Etruria) Ltd." c. 1938. Retitled "Kirklands (Staffordshire) Ltd." 1947.

KISHERE

JOSEPH KISHERE, Mortlake Pottery, London. c. 1800–43. *Salt-glazed Stonewares, etc.* Formerly Benjamin Kishere.

2293–3a–4	KISHERE	KISHERE MORTLAKE	KISHERE POTTERY
2295		I. K.	MORTLAKE SURREY

Impressed marks occur in any of the above forms, c. 1800–43.

For further information see J. F. Blacker's *The A.B.C. of English Salt-Glaze Stone-Ware* (1922). Examples will be found illustrated in *British Pottery and Porcelain: an illustrated Encyclopaedia of Marked Specimens.*

KITCHING		**KATE KITCHING**, Kay Pottery, Chelsea, London. c. 1920. *Bird Models, etc., in Pottery.*

2296   Incised mark, c. 1920.

2296 Ƙ K *See* Kate Kitching, above.

1559–61 K. L. *See* John Thomas Firth.

1137 K. M. *See* Cricklade Pottery.

2275 K. & M. *See* Keys & Mountford.

4393 K. M. S. *See* Ymagynatyf Pottery.

KNAPPER

KNAPPER & BLACKHURST, Boston Works, Sandyford, Tunstall (1867–71) and Dale Hall, Burslem (1883–8). Staffordshire Potteries. 1867–71 and 1883–8. *Earthenwares.* Distinguishing details (name and initials) of several impressed or printed marks of differing design., c. 1867–71 and 1883–8. The initials K & B may have been used also by Messrs. Knight & Bridgwood of Longton, c. 1884–6.

2297 KNAPPER AND BLACKHURST

2298

KNELLER

FRANK KNELLER, Chelsea Pottery, London S.W.3. 1949– . *Earthenware character figures.*

2299   Incised or painted initial mark on figures, 1949– .

1522 K NICK NACK *See* Fancies Fayre Pottery.

KNIGHT

PHILIP KNIGHT, Lancing, Sussex. 1950– . *Studio-type Pottery, Animals and Portrait busts.*

2300

Impressed seal-type mark, initials in relief, 1962.– .

KNIGHT

KNIGHT ELKIN & CO. (also listed in rates as Elkin & Knight), Foley Potteries, Fenton. Staffordshire Potteries. 1826–46. *Earthenwares.* Subsequently J. K. Knight, q.v.

| 2301 | K. E. & CO. | Distinguishing details of several printed marks of differing design: name of the individual pattern is often included, 1826–46. See Plate 4. |
| 2302 | KNIGHT ELKIN & CO. | |

2303   K. & E.

The initials K. & E. may also relate to this partnership under the style Knight & Elkin.

KNIGHT

KNIGHT ELKIN & BRIDGWOOD, The Foley Potteries, Fenton. Staffordshire Potteries. c. 1829–40.

2304   K. E. & B.

Many printed marks occur in the Victoria and Albert Museum records with these initials.*

N.B. At a later period the initials K. E. & B. would relate to Messrs. King Edge & Barratt, c. 1897.

2304a   K. E. B.

The initial mark K. E. B. has been recorded on blue printed earthenwares of the 1830's; this probably relates to the above partnership.

* These could refer to the above firm which seems to be an alternative title to Knight Elkin & Co. (Bridgwood being the "& Co."). John Ward lists the style Knight Elkin & Bridgwood in 1843 as does also a directory of 1834. At other times the firm is listed as Elkin Knight & Bridgwood. See page 234.

A bill-head in the Gentle Collection is headed *KNIGHT, ELKIN & BRIDGWOOD, MANUFACTURERS OF EARTHENWARE, EGYPTIAN BLACK &c.*

KNIGHT

KNIGHT ELKIN & KNIGHT (also listed as Knight, Elkin & Co.), King St., Fenton. Staffordshire Potteries. 1841–4. *Earthenwares.*

2305   K. E. & K.

Distinguishing initials found on several printed marks of differing design: name of the individual pattern is often included, 1841–4. This firm seems to represent one of the changes in style of Knight Elkin & Co.

KNIGHT

2306	J. K. KNIGHT	
2307	I. K. KNIGHT	

JOHN, KING, KNIGHT, The Foley Potteries, Fenton. Staffordshire Potteries. 1846–53. *Earthenwares.* Formerly Knight, Elkin & Co. Subsequently Knight & Wileman. Distinguishing details of several printed marks of differing design: name of the individual pattern is often included, 1846–53. The name FOLEY sometimes occurs with these marks.

KNOWLES

2308   KNOWLES

MATTHEW KNOWLES & SON, Welshpool & Payne Potteries, Brampton, Derbyshire. c. 1835–1911. *Earthenwares and Stonewares.*
This name-mark has been recorded but has not been seen by the present writer.

Jewitt gives a good account of the Knowles' wares in his *Ceramic Art of Great Britain* (1878 and 1883).

2262	K. P. H.	*See* Kensington Pottery Ltd.
—	K. P. M.	*See* Appendix, page 725.
3180	KQ (monogram)	*See* Kenneth Quick.
2988	KRUSTA	*See* Pearson & Co. Ltd.
2236	K. S. P.	*See* Keele Street Pottery Co. Ltd.
2421	KW	*See* Looe Pottery.
4040	(also monogram)	*See* Kate Watts.
4049		*See* Kate Weaver.
4196		*See* Katherine Wilson.

L

2318 **2320**	L. & SONS LTD.	*See* Lancaster & Sons (Ltd.).
8	L. A.	*See* Leonard Acton.
2401	L. & A.	*See* Lockhart & Arthur.

LAKE

W. H. LAKE & SON (LTD.), Chapel Hill Pottery, Truro, Cornwall. 1872– . *Earthenwares.*

2309–10 LAKE'S CORNISH POTTERY TRURO

LAKE'S HANDMADE
CORNISH POTTERY
TRURO ENGLAND

Printed or impressed marks occur based on the above wording. Although the pottery was established in 1872, the marks indicate a 20th century date.

LAKIN

THOMAS LAKIN, Stoke.* Staffordshire Potteries. 1812–17.* *Earthenwares, Creamwares, etc.* Formerly T. Lakin & Son, c. 1810–12.

2311 LAKIN

Impressed mark on creamwares, 1812–17.*

* This mark has formerly been attributed to a potter of the same name working in Burslem in the 1790's, but from the style of examples it would seem probable that the above details are correct. This mark could have been used by T. Lakin & Son, c. 1810–12.

LAKIN

LAKIN & POOLE, Hadderidge, Burslem. Staffordshire Potteries. c. 1791–5. *Wedgwood-type Wares, Creamwares, etc., and Figures.* Subsequently Lakin, Poole & Shrigley or Poole, Lakin & Shrigley.

| 2312 | LAKIN & POOLE | Impressed marks, c. 1791–5. |

2313   L. & P.
             BURSLEM

2314   POOLE, LAKIN & CO.   Some basaltes bear this mark, which probably relates to the partnership of Poole, Lakin & Shrigley, c. 1795.

An interesting dated (1793) historical group with the impressed "Lakin & Poole" mark is illustrated in G. Godden's *English Pottery and Porcelain*, 1780–1850. Other marked examples will be found in *British Pottery and Porcelain: an illustrated Encyclopaedia of Marked Specimens*.

LAMB   M. LAMB, Kensington, London W.8. c. 1951. *Studio-type Pottery.*

2315   A circular-shaped mark based on this wording and monogram was registered in 1951.

LAMORNA   LAMORNA POTTERY, Lamorna, Nr. Penzance, Cornwall. 1947– . *Earthenwares.*

2316   LAMORNA   Incised or painted mark, 1947– .

2139a   LANCASTER   *See* D. Illingworth.

LANCASTER   LANCASTER & SONS (LTD.), Dresden Works, Hanley. Staffordshire Potteries. 1900–44. *Earthenwares.* Formerly W. Harrop & Co. Subsequently Lancaster & Sandland Ltd., see next entry.

2317   L. S.   Distinguishing initials found on several printed marks of differing design, 1900–6. "& Sons" or "& S." added after 1906. "Ltd" added to most marks from 1906.

2318–21

1906+   1920+   1920+   1930+

2322-4

c. 1935—   c. 1935—

c. 1938-44

These two marks, nos 2322-3, were continued by Lancaster & Sandland Ltd. after 1944.

Printed marks, 1906 onwards.

LANCASTER

LANCASTER & SANDLAND LTD., Dresden Works, Hanley. Staffordshire Potteries. 1944– . *Earthenwares.* Formerly Lancaster & Sons, see previous entry.

2322-3

Former marks used by Lancaster & Sons from 1935, continued.

2325-7

ENGLISH
WARE
LANCASTER
SANDLAND
LTD.
HANLEY
ENGLAND

1944+

ENGLISH WARE
MADE IN ENGLAND
LANCASTER
& SANDLAND
HANLEY
ENGLAND

1944+

LANCASTER
SANDLAND
HAND PAINTED
IN ENGLAND

1949+

2328-30

SANDLAND WARE

LANCASTER &
SANDLAND LTD
HANLEY
STAFFORDSHIRE
ENGLAND.
REGᵈ TRADE MARK

1949+

CHARACTER
LANCASTER
SANDLAND
HAND PAINTED
HANLEY.
ENGLAND
SANDLAND   WARE.

1949+

SANDLAND

MADE IN ENGLAND

1952+

2331-3

**SANDLAND
WARE**
L, & S, LTD.
**STAFFORDSHIRE
ENGLAND**

1955+

SANDLAND
BONE CHINA
STAFFORDSHIRE
ENGLAND

1961+

**SANDLAND
STAFFORDSHIRE
ENGLAND**

1961+

Printed marks, 1944 onwards.

2324   LANCASTER LTD   *See* Lancaster & Sons (Ltd.).

LANE		**PETER LANE,** The Pottery, Andover, Hampshire. 1961– . *Studio-type Pottery.*

2334   Impressed seal mark, 1961– .

2335   Painted or incised mark, 1961– .

2336   Signature mark on important examples, 1961.

LANGDALE   **LANGDALE POTTERY CO. LTD.,** Belgrave Works, Hanley. Staffordshire Potteries. 1947–58. *Earthenwares.*

2337   Printed mark, 1947–58. Other marks were used with the name Langdale.

LANGTON   **LANGTON POTTERY LTD.** (Gordon Plahn), Langton Green, Tunbridge Wells, Kent. 1961– . *Studio-type Pottery.*

     N.B. This potter formerly worked at Sevenoaks, see page 568.

2338   Impressed seal comprising Gordon Plahn's monogram.

     Decorated wares may also bear the incised name Langton in writing letters, 1961– .

2425–7
2430–1   LANGLEY (WARE)   *See* Lovatt & Lovatt.

LAUDER   **ALEXANDER LAUDER** (Lauder & Smith), Barnstaple (and Pottington), Devon. 1876–1914. *Earthenwares.*

2339   LAUDER BARUM   Incised or painted mark, in writing letters, 1876–1914.

LAWLEYS

LAWLEYS LIMITED, Ash Hall, Stoke. Staffordshire Potteries and many Retail Shops. 1921– . *Retailers.*

2340	LAWLEYS	Several printed marks were employed on wares made for this
2341	LAWLEYS LTD.	firm of retailers from c. 1925 to c. 1940. Subsequent wares

Several printed marks were employed on wares made for this firm of retailers from c. 1925 to c. 1940. Subsequent wares bear only the marks of the producing firms. Firms in the Lawley Group comprise Ridgway Potteries Ltd., Swinnertons Ltd. and Alcock, Lindley & Bloore.

LAWRENCE

THOMAS LAWRENCE (LONGTON) LTD., Falcon Works (1897–1957), Sylvan Works (1957–), Longton. Staffordshire Potteries. 1892– . *Earthenwares.*

Established by Thomas Lawrence at Trent Bridge Pottery, Stoke. Title changed to "Thomas Lawrence (Longton) Ltd.", c. 1938. Early wares unmarked.

2342–4

1936+

1944+

1947+

Printed or impressed marks.

685a	L. B.	*See* L. Bruckner.
434	LB	*See* Leo Bonassera.
685	(joined)	*See* L. Bruckner.
2869	LD (joined)	*See* Newlyn Harbour Pottery.
2349b	L^D	*See* David Leach.
2395–5a	L. E.	*See* Lockett & Hulme.
1472	L. E. & S.	*See* Elliot, Liddell & Son.

LEACH

BERNARD HOWELL LEACH, C.B.E., St. Ives, Cornwall.
1921– . *Studio-type Pottery.*

Bernard Leach, the most famous modern English Studio Potter, trained many talented potters at his St. Ives Pottery. Examples of his ware are illustrated in most books on modern pottery. Bernard Leach's *A Potter's Book* (1940) is a most interesting book on pottery technique.

2345

Impressed seal mark.   A circular version also occurs, c. 1921+ .

2346–7a

Personal marks of Bernard Leach, 1921– .

2348

This is the impressed seal mark of the Canadian potter Glenn Lewis, who has worked at the Leach Pottery since 1961.   He may establish his own pottery in England.

LEACH

DAVID LEACH, Lowerdown Pottery,* Bovey Tracey, Devon.
1956– . *Studio-type Pottery, Stonewares and Porcelains.*

2349–9a   D. D. A. L.   Incised or seal marks on St. Ives pottery, c. 1932–56.

2349b

Impressed seal type marks based on this form of initials, 1956– .

* David Leach was formerly at St. Ives with his father, Bernard Leach. The Lowerdown Pottery dates from 1956.

LEACH

JANET LEACH, Leach Pottery, St. Ives, Cornwall.   1956– .
Studio-type Pottery.

Mrs. Janet Leach (*née* Darnell) is the wife of Bernard Leach.

2350

Impressed seal mark, normally occurring with the standard Leach Pottery mark no. 2345.   This seal is made up of the initials J. L., within a triangle, 1956– .

LEACH

JEREMY LEACH, Craft Pottery, London S.E.1.   c. 1959*– . *Studio-type Pottery*.

2351   J. L.
          D. S.
                 Impressed seal used on pottery made at school, c. 1959.

2351a   J L
                 Incised mark (rarely used) on wares made at the St. Ives Pottery, or at the Central School of Arts and Crafts prior to May 1962. Early wares made at Mr. Leach's Craft Pottery were also marked in this manner, c. 1960–2 and June 1963– .

2351b   J. L.
           C. P.
                 Impressed seal introduced at Christmas 1962 and broken in June 1963, from which date the initials J. L. have been incised.

* It is difficult to fix the earliest date for Jeremy Leach's ceramic career for since the age of five he has made pottery under his father's direction at the St. Ives Pottery; such wares were signed "Je" or "Jeremy".

LEACH

JOHNNY LEACH, Leach Pottery, St. Ives, Cornwall.   1950–* *Studio-type Pottery*.

2352
                 Impressed initial seal mark, used prior to 1958.*

* Johnny Leach was at his grandfather's famous pottery at St. Ives until mid-1963 and there his work bore only the Leach Pottery mark (see page 383). He is now teaching in America. The initial mark was used prior to 1958 and will probably be reintroduced later.

LEACH

MARGARET LEACH, MISS (Mrs. Heron), Brockweir, Monmouth (1946–51), Taena Community, Aylburton and Upton St. Leonards, Gloucestershire.   1946*–56. *Studio-type Pottery*.

Miss Margaret Leach worked at the Leach Pottery at St. Ives from January 1943 to November 1945 (she is not related to Bernard Leach).

2353   Impressed seal type "Taena" mark used by Margaret Leach from October 1951 to January 1956. A similar mark is used by L. A. Groves at the Taena Pottery, mark no. 3788.

* In 1946 Margaret Leach started on her own account at the Barnhouse Pottery at Brockweir, Monmouth (see Barnhouse Pottery). In October 1951 Margaret Leach joined the Taena Community at Aylburton, Gloucestershire, where the circular mark number 2353 (below) was first employed and was continued at Upton St. Leonards. In January 1956 she ceased potting on the occasion of her marriage. Her partner, L. A. Groves, continued and still uses the circular Taena mark.

LEACH

MICHAEL LEACH, Yelland Manor Pottery, Fremington, Devon. 1956– . *Studio-type Pottery.*

Michael Leach was trained under his father, Bernard Leach, at the St. Ives Pottery.

2355   **Y**   Circular impressed seal mark, 1956– .

2356   **LM**   Personal initial seal mark of Michael Leach, 1956–

LEADBEATER

EDWIN LEADBEATER, Drury Place, Longton. Staffordshire Potteries. 1920–4. *China.*

2357   *LEADBEATER ART CHINA LONGTON*   Printed or impressed mark, 1920–4.

LEAPER

E. T. LEAPER, Newlyn, Nr. Penzance, Cornwall. 1954– . *Hand-made Pottery.*

2358   LEAPER NEWLYN   Incised marks, 1954– .

2359   *See* also Appendix, page 732

LEAR

SAMUEL LEAR, Mayer St. and High St., Hanley. Staffordshire Potteries. 1877–86. *Jasper Ware, Majolica, China, etc.*

2360   LEAR   Impressed mark on Jasper type wares and earthenwares 1877–86.

LEDGAR

THOMAS P. LEDGAR, Heathcote Road, Longton. Staffordshire Potteries. 1900–5. *China and Earthenwares.* Formerly Wildblood & Ledgar, q.v. Subsequently Ledgar & Smith.

2361   T. P. L.   Distinguishing initials found on several impressed or printed marks of differing design, 1900–5.

LEEDS

LEEDS POTTERY (various proprietors),* Jack Lane, Hunslet, Leeds, Yorkshire. Est. c. 1758. *Earthenwares, Creamwares, Basalt, etc.*

N.B. Only a small proportion of Leeds wares bear factory marks.

2362	LEEDS POTTERY†	Impressed mark, c. 1775–1800+.
2363	Leeds Pottery	Mark on transfer printed creamwares, c. 1790+.
2364	L. P.	Rare impressed or painted initial mark, c. 1780+.
2365	HARTLEY GREENS & CO. LEEDS POTTERY	Impressed mark, c. 1781–1820.

For further information see Jewitt's *The Ceramic Art of Great Britain*, O. Grabham's *Yorkshire Potteries, Pots and Potters*, D. C. Towner's *English Cream-Coloured Earthenware* and *The Leeds Pottery*. Typical examples will be found illustrated in *British Pottery and Porcelain: an illustrated Encyclopaedia of Marked Specimens*.

* After the bankruptcy of 1820, the following potters or firms worked the Leeds Pottery:

Samuel Wainwright, 1825–37.
Leeds Pottery Company, 1837–41.
S. & J. Chappell, 1841–9.
R. Britton & Co., 1850–3.
Warburton & Britton, 1853–61.
Richard Britton, 1861–72.
R. Britton & Sons, 1872–8, see page 106.

† Later copies of pierced creamwares also bear this impressed mark.

LEEDS

LEEDS FIRECLAY CO. LTD., Burmantofts Works, Leeds, Yorkshire. c. 1904–c. 14.* *Earthenwares, Terra-cotta.* Formerly Burmantofts, q.v.

2366	L. F. C.	Distinguishing initials found on several marks of differing design, c. 1904–14.
2366a	LEFICO	Trade-names registered in 1905 and 1906.
2366b	GRANITOFTS	

* This firm continues to the present day for the manufacture of utilitarian wares. Decorative wares were mainly confined to the period c. 1904–14.

W. LEES & SONS   *See* Appendix, page 725.

| 2366a | LEFICO | *See* Leeds Fireclay Co. Ltd., above. |
| 487–8 | LEIGHTON POTTERY | *See* Bourne & Leigh (Ltd.), page 90 and next entry. |

LEIGHTON

LEIGHTON POTTERY LTD., Orme St., Burslem. Staffordshire Potteries. 1940–54. *Earthenwares.*

| 2367 | PRODUCED AT THE LEIGHTON POTTERIES BURSLEM, ENGLAND | Printed mark, c. 1946–54. |

2367a

Printed mark, c. 1946–54.

4089	E. LEFSORE	*See* Josiah Wedgwood & Sons Ltd.
1472	L. E. & S.	*See* Liddle Elliot & Son.
4089	E. LESSORE	*See* Josiah Wedgwood & Sons Ltd.

LESTER

BARBARA LESTER, MRS., London N.10. 1961– . *Studio Pottery.*

| 2368 | LESTER | Painted or incised name-mark, 1961– . |

LESTER

JO LESTER, London, c. 1951–2, Freshwater, Isle of Wight. 1953– . *Studio-type Earthenwares.*

| 2369 | WIGHTCRAFT | Incised trade-name used in London, c. 1951–2. |
| 2370 | | Basic printed* Isle of Wight outline mark with initials JO, IOW, 1953– . |

* On early specimens this mark or the initials were incised through a black patch on the base of the article.

2370a	FRESHWATER	The place name FRESHWATER occurs below this basic mark from 1953 to 1961.
2370b	SEAVIEW	The place name SEAVIEW below the basic mark occurs on wares made at Seaview, 1956–8.
2370c	COWES	The place name COWES below the basic mark occurs on wares made by Joe Lester junior at Cowes, 1959–60.
	TOTLAND M	For the basic Isle of Wight mark with the name Totland or with the initial M see Totland Pottery and J. H. Manning.
2370d	I. O. W.	Incised mark on small pieces that will not take the basic mark, no. 2370.
2370e	HAND MADE WEST OF ENGLAND POTTERY	Several printed marks incorporating this wording (with or without the initials JO) have been used by Jo Lester from 1960 onwards.
2370f	WEST OF ENGLAND HAND MADE POTTERY	

LEWENSTEIN

EILEEN LEWENSTEIN, London N.W.3. 1959*– . *Studio-type Pottery.*

2371

Seal type mark, or painted initials, 1959– .

* Eileen Lewenstein was formerly in partnership with Donald Mills, and at the Briglin Pottery from c. 1948 to 1959.

2973 LEWES

See Judith Partridge.

LEWIS-EVANS

A. LEWIS-EVANS, Stoney Down Pottery,* Lytchett Matravers, Dorset. 1952*– . *Studio-type Stonewares and Porcelains.*

2372

Impressed monogram mark of initials ALE, 1952*– .

* Mr. Lewis-Evans started potting at Welling, Kent, in 1952. He moved to the Stoney Down Pottery in 1957.

LEWIS

REGINALD A. LEWIS, Glympton Studio, Water Orton, Nr. Birmingham. 1948– . *Studio-type Pottery.*

2373

Printed mark, 1948– .

2366 L
    F C

See Leeds Fire Clay Co.

2553 L. F. M.

See Leo F. Matthews.

1198 L. G. D.

See Leslie G. Davie.

2395 L. & H.
    or
    L. & H.
    L. E.

See Lockett & Hulme.

1718 LHHG
    (monogram)

See Louis H. H. Glover.

    LIMITED

See page 11.

2789 LINDLEY WARE

See J. Morton & Son.

LING

LING POTTERY (Dennis Lucas and Eunice Gordon), St. Albans, Hertfordshire. 1954–6. *Studio-type Pottery and Figures.*
    Dennis Lucas subsequently worked at Hastings, see D. Lucas.

2374

Impressed or incised mark, c. 1954–6.

LINGARD

LINGARD WEBSTER & CO. (LTD.), Swan Pottery, Tunstall. Staffordshire Potteries. 1900– . *Earthenwares.*

2375

Impressed or printed mark, 1946– .

LINTHORPE

LINTHORPE POTTERY (John Harrison), Middlesbrough, Yorkshire. 1879–89. *Earthenwares, Glaze effects, etc.*

For further information see O. Grabham's *Yorkshire Potteries, Pots and Potters.* Examples are illustrated in H. Wakefield's *Victorian Pottery* (1962).

2377	LINTHORPE	Impressed mark, often with outline of vase, c. 1879–89.
2378	Chr. Dresser	Incised, impressed or painted signature of Christopher Dresser,* the designer, c. 1879–89.
2379–80	Ⱶ HT	Monogram or initial mark of Henry Tooth, the manager, prior to 1883.

* An interesting article on Dr. Christopher Dresser (by Shirley Bury) is contained in the *Apollo*, December 1962.

LINTON

MURIEL LINTON, MISS, Oxford. 1920–30. *Studio-type Pottery.*

2381	MURIEL LINTON	Signature type mark, c. 1920–30.
1979 2904	LION & GLOBE	*See* Hawley Bros. Ltd. *See* Northfield Hawley Ltd.
2802	LION (rampant)	*See* Murray & Co.
900b	LISA	*See* Clavering Pottery.

LITTLEHAMPTON

LITTLEHAMPTON POTTERY (William Marriner), Littlehampton, Sussex. 1945– . *Earthenwares, Glaze effects, etc.*

2382	LITTLEHAMPTON POTTERY, SUSSEX	Impressed mark in circular form, with anchor in centre, c. 1945– .

2383	W. M. 1953	Incised initial mark of William Marriner, with date.

William Marriner, now in his eighties, worked for the greater part of his life at the Fulham Pottery.

1158c	LITTLETHORPE	*See* G. R. Curtis.

LIVERMORE

JOHN LIVERMORE, Wrotham, Kent. c. 1610–58. *Slip-decorated Earthenwares.*

2384	I. L.	Examples of early Wrotham earthenware bear these initials. Dated examples range between 1612 and 1649. John Livermore died in 1658. See *E. C. C. Transactions*, vol. 3, part 2., a paper by A. J. B. Kiddell.

	LIVERPOOL	*See* Herculaneum Pottery, page 321.

LIVERPOOL

LIVERPOOL.

Many potters made varied wares in Liverpool during the 18th century. Most tin glazed, delft-type earthenwares are unmarked. Typical specimens attributed to Liverpool potters are illustrated in F. H. Garner's *English Delftware* (1948). Most 18th century Liverpool creamware and porcelains are also unmarked, but some printed wares bear the name of the engraver in the design. Some Liverpool potters and engravers are listed under:

Thomas Billinge	page	73.
Francey & Spence		260.
John & Solomon Gibson		271.
Samuel Gilbody		272.
Herculaneum Pottery		321.
Joseph Johnson		356.
Seth Pennington		489.
John Sadler		560.

Standard reference books include:

History of the Art of Pottery in Liverpool, J. Mayer (1882).
Liverpool and her Potters, H. Boswell Lancaster (1936).
Liverpool Porcelain, 18th century, Dr. Knowles Boney (1957).
English Blue and White Porcelain, Dr. B. Watney (1963).

LIVESLEY

LIVESLEY POWELL & CO., Old Hall Lane and Miles Bank, Hanley. Staffordshire Potteries. 1851–66. *Earthenwares (Ironstone, etc.) and China.* Subsequently Powell & Bishop, q.v.

2385   LIVESLEY POWELL & CO.

Distinguishing details of several impressed or printed marks of differing design, 1851–66.

2386   L. P. & CO.

2387   BEST L. P. & CO.

2352   L   *See* Johnny Leach.

2252–3   L. K. (or monogram)   *See* Lawrence Keen.

2428   L. & L.   *See* Lovatt & Lovatt.

LLANGOLLEN

LLANGOLLEN POTTERY, Regent St., Llangollen, North Wales. 1951– . *Hand-made Earthenwares.*

2388   *Llangollen*   Incised mark, c. 1952– .

LLOYD

JOHN (& REBECCA) LLOYD, Shelton, Hanley. Staffordshire Potteries. c. 1834–52.* *Earthenware and China figures, etc.*

2389   LLOYD SHELTON

Rare impressed mark, c. 1834–52.* An initial may occur before the name on some specimens.

* From 1850 to 1852 Rebecca Lloyd continued. A marked figure will be found illustrated in *British Pottery and Porcelain: an illustrated Encyclopaedia of Marked Specimens.*

2356   L^M   *See* Michael Leach.

2408   [monogram]   *See* Mildred Lockyer.

4397   L. & M.   *See* Ynysmedw Pottery.

LOCHHEAD

THOMAS LOCHHEAD, Kirkcudbright, Scotland. 1948– .
Studio-type Pottery.

| 2390 | LOCHHEAD 1949 | Incised name and year mark, 1948–50. |

| 2391 | LOCHHEAD KIRKCUDBRIGHT | Incised name and town mark, 1950–. |

LOCKE

LOCKE & CO. (LTD.), Shrub Hill Works, Worcester.
1895–1904. *Porcelain.*
    Taken over by the "Worcester Royal Porcelain Co. Ltd."

| 2392 | LOCKE & CO. WORCESTER | Written mark, c. 1895–1903. |

2393   Printed mark, c. 1895–1900.

2393a   Printed mark, c. 1900–4. Note addition of "Ltd." above the word "Hill"

| 1264 | LOCKER & CO. | *See* Derby Porcelain Works. |

LOCKETT

LOCKETT BAGULEY & COOPER, Victoria Works, Shelton, Hanley. Staffordshire Potteries. 1855–60. *Porcelains.* Mark on very rare Crimean war memorial ornament in the collection of Mr. and Mrs. E. M. H. Joyce.

2394   PUBLISHED BY LOCKETT BAGULEY & COOPER SHELTON, STAFFS. June 25th, 1856

LOCKETT

LOCKETT & HULME, King St., Lane End. Staffordshire Potteries. 1822–6. *Earthenwares.*

2395   L & H
         L E   Distinguishing detail of several printed marks of differing design, 1822–6.

LOCKETT		**JOHN LOCKETT**, Chancery Lane, Lane End. Staffordshire Potteries. c. 1821–58. *Earthenwares (Jasper Wares, etc.)*. Formerly George Lockett.
2396	J. LOCKETT	Impressed mark, 1821–58. This mark occurs on jasper-type wares, 1821–30.
LOCKETT		**J. & G. LOCKETT**, Lane End. Staffordshire Potteries. c. 1802–5. *Earthenwares*. Subsequently George Lockett & Co.
2397	J. & G. LOCKETT	Impressed mark, c. 1802–5.
LOCKETT		**J. LOCKETT & CO.**, King St., Lane End. Staffordshire Potteries. c. 1812–89 and 1882–1960 at Longton; 1960– at Burslem. *Earthenwares*.
2398	J. LOCKETT & CO.	Impressed or printed marks occur with the name in full. It is difficult to date such marks without evidence of style, etc.
LOCKETT		**JOHN LOCKETT & SONS**, King St., Longton. Staffordshire Potteries. 1828–35. *Earthenwares*. Subsequently John & Thomas Lockett.
2399	J. LOCKETT & SONS	Impressed mark, 1828–35.
LOCKETT		**WILLIAM LOCKETT**, St. Ann's Street, Nottingham. c. 1740–80+.
2400	Wm. Lockett	Incised signature mark in writing letters, c. 1740–80+. Jewitt cites a Nottingham stoneware mug dated 1762, which bears this signature mark on the base. William Lockett is included in freeholders lists of 1740 and 1780.
LOCKHART		**LOCKHART & ARTHUR**, Victoria Pottery, Pollokshaws, Glasgow, Scotland. 1855 to December 1864. *Earthenwares*. Subsequently David Lockhart & Co., q.v. For further information see J. A. Fleming's *Scottish Pottery* (1923).

2401 2402	L. & A. LOCKHART & ARTHUR	Distinguishing details of several impressed or printed marks of differing design, 1855–64.

LOCKHART

DAVID LOCKHART & CO., Victoria Pottery, Pollokshaws, Glasgow, Scotland. 1865–98. *Earthenwares*. Formerly Lockhart & Arthur, above. Subsequently D. Lockhart & *Sons*, below.

2403	D. L. & CO.	Distinguishing detail of several printed marks of differing design, 1865–98.

LOCKHART

DAVID LOCKHART & SONS (LTD.), Victoria Pottery, Pollokshaws, Glasgow, Scotland. 1898–1953. *Earthenwares*. Formerly D. Lockhart & *Co.*, above.

2404    Distinguishing initials D. L. & S. found on impressed or printed marks of differing design, 1898–1953. On other marks "& Sons" is given in full, as no. 2405.

2405   D. L. & SONS

LOCKITT

WILLIAM H. LOCKITT, Wellington Pottery, Hanley. Staffordshire Potteries. 1901–19. *Earthenwares*. Formerly Wellington Pottery Co., q.v.

2406    Printed mark, 1901–13.

2407    Printed mark, 1913–19.

LOCKYER

MILDRED LOCKYER, MISS, various teaching posts. 1928–39. *Studio-type Pottery.*

2408

Incised or painted mark, 1928–39.

LOGAN

TREVOR LOGAN, Alwoodley, Leeds 17, Yorkshire. 1957– . *Studio-type Pottery, Stonewares.*

2409

Impressed mark, 1957– . Trevor Logan started potting in 1943; his impressed triangle mark has been used since 1957.

2497   LONDON
2658   (& anchor mark)

See Malkin, Walker & Hulse, page 411.
See Middlesbrough Pottery Co., page 435.

LONGBOTTOM

SAMUEL LONGBOTTOM, Nafferton Pottery, Nr. Hull, Yorkshire. Late 19th century. *Earthenwares.* Formerly C. Longbottom.

2410   S. L.

Impressed initial mark, late 19th century. Pottery closed April 1899.

LONGPARK

LONGPARK POTTERY CO. (LTD.), Longpark, Torquay, Devon. 1905–40. *Earthenwares.*

2411   LONGPARK
          TORQUAY

Printed or painted mark, 1905–40.

LONGTON

LONGTON HALL WORKS (William Littler & Co.), Longton Hall. Staffordshire Potteries. c. 1749–60. *Porcelains.*

2412–14  Marks painted in underglaze blue, c. 1749–55. This type of mark is only found on early specimens. Workmen's numbers and letters also occur on blue and white examples.

Most specimens of Longton Hall porcelain are unmarked. For further information see Dr. B. Watney's *Longton Hall Porcelain* (1957). Some marked pieces will be found illustrated in *British Pottery and Porcelain: an illustrated Encyclopaedia of Marked Specimens*.

LONGTON

LONGTON NEW ART POTTERY CO. LTD., Gordon Pottery, Longton. Staffordshire Potteries. 1932– . *Earthenwares*.

2415  Printed mark, 1932– . Variations occur but all include the trade-name "Kelsboro".

2416 Printed mark, 1962– .

LONGTON

LONGTON PORCELAIN CO. (LTD.), Victoria Works, Longton. Staffordshire Potteries. 1892–1908. *Porcelains*.

2417 Printed mark, 1892–1908.

LONGTON

LONGTON POTTERY CO. LTD., Bluebell Works, Longton. Staffordshire Potteries. 1946–55. *Earthenwares*.

2418 L. P. CO. LTD.
2419

Distinguishing detail of several printed marks of differing design, 1946–55. The title also occurs in full, as no. 2419.

LOOE

LOOE POTTERY (K. G. and M. Webb), Barbican, Looe, Cornwall. Est. 1932 as the Barbican Pottery. Closed 1962. *Stonewares.*

2420   LOOE   Impressed, printed or incised mark, 1932–62.

2421–2  Initial marks of K. Webb and M. Webb, 1946–62.

Mr. Webb hopes to establish a Studio Pottery at Stenalees, St. Austell, Cornwall, but at the time of writing (early 1963) this has not come to fruition.

2244   LOSOL   *See* Keeling & Co. Ltd.

1470   LOTTIE RHEAD   *See* Ellgreave Pottery Co. Ltd.
           WARE

LOTUS

LOTUS POTTERY (M. C. Skipwith), Stoke Gabriel, South Devon. 1957– . *Earthenwares.*

2423   Printed **mark,** 1957– .

2424   Impressed seal mark, 1957– .

2096   LOUGHTON   *See* Tom W. Howard.

LOVATT

LOVATT & LOVATT, Langley Mill, Nr. Nottingham. 1895– . *Stonewares and Earthenwares.* Formerly Calvert & Lovatt.

Firm retitled *Lovatt's Potteries Ltd.* in 1931 and acquired by J. Bourne & Son Ltd. in 1959 but continued as Lovatt's Potteries Ltd.

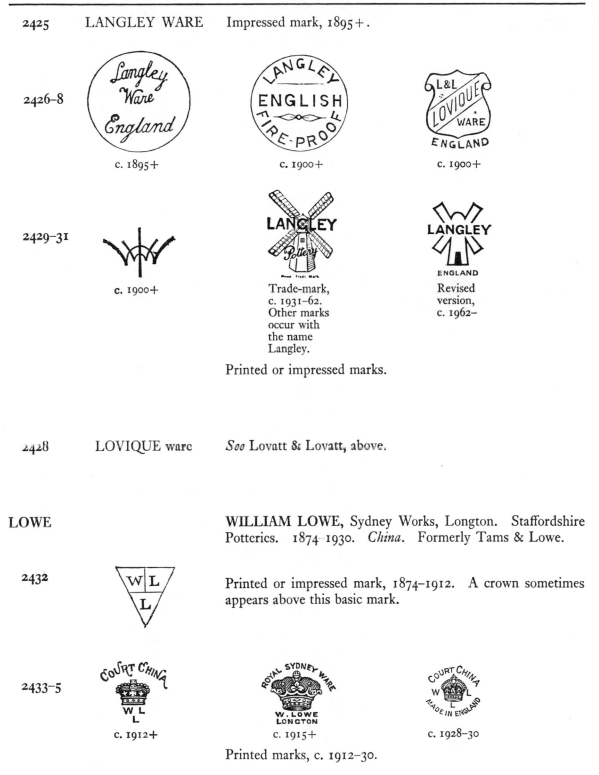

2425   LANGLEY WARE   Impressed mark, 1895+.

2426–8

c. 1895+   c. 1900+   c. 1900+

2429–31

c. 1900+   Trade-mark,   Revised
                 c. 1931–62.   version,
                 Other marks   c. 1962–
                 occur with
                 the name
                 Langley.

Printed or impressed marks.

2428   LOVIQUE ware   *See* Lovatt & Lovatt, above.

LOWE   **WILLIAM LOWE,** Sydney Works, Longton.   Staffordshire
              Potteries. 1874–1930. *China.* Formerly Tams & Lowe.

2432   Printed or impressed mark, 1874–1912.   A crown sometimes
          appears above this basic mark.

2433–5

c. 1912+   c. 1915+   c. 1928–30

Printed marks, c. 1912–30.

LOWE

LOWE, RATCLIFFE & CO., Gold Street Works, Longton. Staffordshire Potteries.   1882–92.   *Earthenwares.*

2436

Printed or impressed mark, 1882–92.

LOWESBY

LOWESBY POTTERY (Sir F. Fowke), Leicestershire. c. 1835–40.   *Earthenwares (Terra-cotta).*

2437   LOWESBY

Impressed marks, c. 1835–40.

2438

LOWESTOFT

LOWESTOFT PORCELAIN FACTORY, Lowestoft, Suffolk.   c. 1757–1802.   *Porcelain (soft paste, bone-ash body).*

Workmen's marks—numbers or letters—occur painted in underglaze blue (often on the inside edge of the foot-rim) on early specimens, c. 1760–75.   The numbers 3 and 5 are relatively common.   Letters of the alphabet were also painted on the inside of the foot-rim but these are rarer than the numerals. It should be noted that workmen's marks on the inside of the foot-rim have been noted on Liverpool, Bow and Worcester porcelains, so that this cannot be taken as a sure sign of Lowestoft manufacture.

2439–45

From c. 1775 to 1790 copies of Dresden and Worcester marks, nos. 2446–8, occur but the above workmen's marks were not continued.

2446–8

2449

Allen
Lowestoft

This unique signature mark occurs on a Chinese porcelain teapot in the Victoria and Albert Museum. Robert Allen decorated and sold china after the factory's closure. This is not a factory mark.

A TRIFLE FROM
LOWESTOFT

All marks occur on blue painted (or printed) examples. Enamelled specimens made from c. 1774 onwards were not generally marked—only one example is recorded. The inscription "A Trifle from Lowestoft" occurs on some rare mugs, inkwells, etc. See *British Pottery and Porcelain: an illustrated Encyclopaedia of Marked Specimens.*

For further information see Chaffers' *Marks and Monograms . . .*, 15th edition, and B. Watney's *English Blue and White Porcelain of the 18th Century* (1963).

Forgeries of Lowestoft porcelain have been made.

2364	L. P.	*See* Leeds Pottery.
2424	LP	*See* Lotus Pottery.
3060	(joined)	*See* R. H. & S. L. Plant.
2417	L P CO. (monogram)	*See* Longton Porcelain Co.
2386	L. P. & CO.	*See* Livesley Powell & Co.
2418	L. P. CO. LTD.	*See* Longton Pottery Co. Ltd.
2313	L. & P.	*See* Lakin & Poole.
2373	L. R.	*See* Reginald A. Lewis.
3326	LR (joined)	*See* Lucie Rie.
2436	L R & CO. (monogram)	*See* Lowe Ratcliffe & Co.
2317	L. S.	*See* Lancaster & Sons.
3404	L. S. & G.	*See* Rubian Art Pottery.
—	L. S. & S.	*See* Appendix, page 725.

2331	L. & S. LTD.	*See* Lancaster & Sandland Ltd.
2318, 2320	L. & SONS LTD.	*See* Lancaster & Sons.
—	LTD.	Any English mark incorporating "Ltd." after the firm's title or initials must be subsequent to 1855. The Old Hall Earthenware Company Ltd. of Hanley was the first *Staffordshire* pottery company to become a limited liability company in March 1861.

LUCAS

DENNIS EDWARD LUCAS, Hastings Pottery,* Cobourg Place, Hastings, Sussex. 1956– . *Studio-type Pottery.* Formerly at Ling Pottery, q.v.

2450

HASTINGS
POTTERY

Incised mark, 1956– .
The words "Hastings Pottery" may be added to the basic mark from 1963 onwards.

* The name "Hastings Pottery" was not used before February 1962.

LUCK

JOHN LUCK, Tunbridge Wells, Kent. Mid-19th century. *Retailer.*

2451   JOHN LUCK
TUNBRIDGE WELLS

Printed mark on local view porcelains sold by this retailer, mid-19th century.

LUNN

DORA LUNN, Shepherd's Bush, London W.12. 1943–55. *Studio-type Pottery.*
Miss Dora Lunn (Mrs. Hedges) had earlier worked the Ravenscourt Pottery, q.v.

2452   DORA LUNN
2453   DORA LUNN
POTTERY

Painted marks, 1943–55.

LUNN

RICHARD LUNN, Cockpit Hill China Works, Derby. c. 1889. *China.*
This was a short lived venture of Richard Lunn's, formerly Art Director at the Derby Crown Porcelain Works. Lunn's advertisements list: "Tea, Breakfast, and Dessert Ware, Japan and Original Patterns. Works of Art in Porcelain and Bisque. Reproductions from the Public Museums."

2454	LUNN-DERBY	A printed mark of a branch above the words LUNN-DERBY was registered in 1889.
2455		This printed mark occurs on advertisements in 1889.
149	LUSTROSA	*See* G. L. Ashworth & Bros. Ltd.
4468	L. W.	*See* Appendix, page 726.
4468a	L. W. & S. or L. W. & SONS	*See* Appendix, page 726.

M

740	M	*See* Cadborough Pottery.
805		*See* Michael Casson.
2460		*See* John Maddock.
2485		*See* Maling.
2827		*See* Patrick McCloskey.
2684–91		*See* Mintons.
2727		*See* C. & N. Mommens.
2804		*See* William S. Murray.
2808		*See* Diana Myer.
2929		*See* Peter O'Malley.
3394		*See* Royal Albion China Co.
2694–6	M. & CO.	*See* Mintons.
2748		*See* Moore & Co. Fenton.
2749		*See* (M) Moore & Co., (Hanley).
2754	M. & A.	*See* Morley & Ashworth.
	MAC, Mc	*See* separate section at end of M, pages 457–9.

MACHIN

MACHIN & POTTS, Waterloo Pottery, Burslem. Staffordshire Potteries. 1833–7. *China, Earthenwares, etc.* Formerly Machin & Baggaley.

2456	MACHIN & POTTS
2456a	MACHIN & POTTS PATENT

Several different, often ornate, marks occur with the name of the partners in full, on wares printed by Potts patent process.

W. W. Potts' first patent, for single-colour printing, was taken out in 1831. Multi-coloured prints date from the patent of 1835. Advertisements in the early 1830's mention "Royal Steam Cylindrical Printing Apparatus. Producing an unequalled variety of novel and elegant patterns".

2457	PUBLISHED AS THE ACT DIRECTS JUNE 20th, 1834 BY MACHIN & POTTS BURSLEM, STAFFORDSHIRE	This firm is mainly known for their patent printing process but a stoneware jug in the British Museum proves they were also orthodox potters. This jug bears the mark, and will be found illustrated in *British Pottery and Porcelain: an illustrated Encyclopaedia of Marked Specimens*.

MACHIN

2458	CONSTITUTION M. & T.	**MACHIN & THOMAS**, Burslem. Staffordshire Potteries. c. 1831–2. *Earthenwares.* A printed earthenware jug, commemorating the "Royal Assent to the Reform Bill, 7 June 1832", is in the Fitzwilliam Museum and bears this mark, within a laurel wreath. See *British Pottery and Porcelain: an illustrated Encyclopaedia of Marked Specimens*.

MACHIN

2459	PUBLISHED AS THE ACT DIRECTS OCTOBER 13, 1832 BY WILLIAM MACHIN BURSLEM STAFFORDSHIRE POTTERIES	**WILLIAM MACHIN**, Burslem. Staffordshire Potteries. c. 1832. *Earthenwares.* Impressed mark on white parian-like bust of A. Clarke in the possession of Messrs. W. W. Warner. Contemporary written records do not list a William Machin at this period. He was very probably the partner in Messrs. Machin & Baggaley of the Waterloo Pottery, Burslem (1809–33), and subsequently Machin & Potts (1833–7), see similar mark, no. 2457.

2460a 2461 & 2469	MADDOCK	*See* John Maddock & Sons.
2466	MADDOCK & CO.	

MADDOCK

JOHN MADDOCK, Newcastle Street, Burslem. Staffordshire Potteries. 1842–55. *Earthenwares.* Formerly Maddock & Seddon, q.v. Subsequently J. Maddock & Son(s), see next entry.

2460  Printed mark with initial M at left-hand side. c. 1842–55. The same mark with the initials M. & S. was used by Maddock & Seddon, c. 1839–42.

2460a **MADDOCK** Distinguishing detail of printed marks of differing design, 1842–55.

MADDOCK **JOHN MADDOCK & SONS (LTD.),** Newcastle St. and Dale Hall, Burslem. Staffordshire Potteries. 1855– . *Earthenwares, Ironstone, etc.* Formerly J. Maddock, see previous entry.

2461 Printed mark used by John Maddock before 1855. Other marks may occur with the name J. Maddock. "& Son" added to style in 1855.

2462–3  Printed marks, c. 1880–96. "Ltd." added to marks after 1896.

2464–7

c. 1896+
See also nos. 2463 and 2470.

c. 1896+
Later variations occur.

c. 1906+

c. 1906+

2468–71

c. 1927+

c. 1935+

c. 1945+

c. 1945+
"Made in England" in place of "England".

2472-5   

c. 1945+ "Ivory Ware" replaces earlier "Royal Ivory".   c. 1955+   c. 1960+   c. 1961+ Slight variations occur.

Printed marks.

MADDOCK

2476   M. & S.

MADDOCK & SEDDON, Newcastle Street, Burslem. Staffordshire Potteries. c. 1839–42. *Earthenwares.* Formerly Maddock & Edwards. Subsequently J. Maddock, q.v. Distinguishing initials found on several printed marks of differing design: name of the individual pattern is often included, as may be the name of the type of body, "Stone China" etc., c. 1839–42.

MADDOX

2477   MADDOX

REGINALD MADDOX, Bingley and Otley, Yorkshire. c. 1925–60.* *Studio-type Pottery.* Signature mark, sometimes with year, c. 1925–60.*

    * Approximate dates only.

MADE IN ENGLAND A term usually found on 20th century English marks. The period that these words were added is usually given with each mark in this book. E. Hughes & Co. added these words to their mark in 1905.

MADELEY

2478   T M R Madeley

MADELEY WORKS (Thomas M. Randall), Madeley, Shropshire. c. 1825–40. *Porcelains and redecorated wares.*

Very rare painted mark, c. 1825–40. Most examples are unmarked.
  See *Country Life*, December 6th 1956, an article by S. W. Fisher, or *British Pottery and Porcelain: an illustrated Encyclopaedia of Marked Specimens.*

MAGARSHACK

CHRISTOPHER MAGARSHACK, Well Walk Pottery, Hampstead, London N.W.3. 1959– . *Studio-type Pottery.*

2479   C. M.   Impressed seal marks incorporating the initials C. M., c. 1959– .

2480   W   Impressed seal or painted mark on enamelled pieces and jewellery, 1959– .

2481   Incised or painted mark on slip decorated wares, 1959– .

MAKIN

GERALD MAKIN, Bilston, Staffordshire. 1958– . *Studio-type Pottery.*

2482   Impressed, incised or painted monogram mark, 1958– .

MAK' MERRY

MAK' MERRY STUDIO (Catherine Blair), Macmerry, E. Lothian, Scotland. c. 1932. *Earthenwares and China.*

2483   MAK' MERRY   This name trade-mark was registered in 1932 for hand-painted porcelain and earthenwares.

MALING

MALING (various Christian names), North Hylton Pottery or Hylton Pottery, Sunderland, Durham. 1762–1815.* *Earthenwares.*

William Maling established this pottery in 1762 for his sons Christopher and John Maling. John's son Robert joined the pottery about 1797, and it was continued by the Malings to July 1815. They then established a new factory at Ouseburn, Newcastle. The early Maling earthenwares were unmarked but the impressed name-mark occurs rarely on early 19th century wares. Colourful patterns, termed in America Gauldy Dutch or Gauldy Welsh, very rarely bear a Maling mark.

2484   MALING   Impressed mark, c. 1800–15.* Also used by Robert Maling at the Ouseburn pottery, see next entry.

* This pottery was continued after 1815 by John Phillips. It was closed about 1867. For further information see *The Potteries of Sunderland and District* by J. T. Shaw.

2484a HYLTON POT WORKS Rare printed or impressed mark, c. 1800–15 or later. Also used by John Phillips, see page 492.

MALING'S

MALING'S OUSEBURN POTTERY, NEWCASTLE. Established 1817 by Robert Maling, general earthenwares were produced including printed and lustred wares.

2484   MALING   Impressed mark, c. 1817–59.*

2485   M.   The impressed initial M. occurs on some Maling type, Newcastle earthenwares, c. 1817–30. From 1859 C. T. Maling succeeded and built the Ford Potteries., see next entry.

* Formerly used at the North Hylton pottery, c. 1800–15, see above.

MALING

C. T. MALING, A. & B Ford Potteries,* Newcastle upon Tyne, Northumberland. c. 1859*–90. *Earthenwares.* Subsequently C. T. Maling & Sons.

2486   MALING   Simple impressed mark, c. 1859–90. A similar mark was used by William Maling at the North Hylton Pottery, Sunderland, before c. 1815, and by Robert Maling from 1817. See previous entry.

2486a   C. T. MALING   Impressed mark on moulded plate with lustre rim and ship print in the centre, in the Godden Collection, c. 1859+.

2486b   C. T. M.   Several marks occur with the initials C. T. M., c. 1859–90.

2487   Impressed or printed mark occurs on advertisement in 1875 and continued by C. T. Maling & Sons to c. 1908.

* In 1853 Christopher T. Maling succeeded his father at the Ouseburn Bridge Pottery; in 1859 he built the Ford Pottery.

MALING

C. T. MALING & SONS (LTD.), A & B Ford Potteries, Newcastle upon Tyne, Northumberland. 1890–July 1963. *Earthenwares.* Formerly C. T. Maling, q.v.

2488-2491

1890+   c. 1908+   c. 1924+   c. 1949-63

Printed marks, 1890-July 1963.

MALKIN   **FREDERICK MALKIN,** Belle Works, Burslem. Staffordshire Potteries. 1891-1905. *Earthenwares.*

2492    Printed mark, c. 1900-5.

MALKIN   **RALPH MALKIN,** Park Works, Fenton. Staffordshire Potteries. 1863-81. *Earthenwares.* Subsequently R. Malkin & Sons, q.v.

2493   Distinguishing initials R. M. found on several printed marks of differing design: name of the individual pattern is often included, 1863-81.

MALKIN   **RALPH MALKIN & SONS,** Park Works, Fenton. Staffordshire Potteries. 1882-92. *Earthenwares.* Formerly R. Malkin, q.v.

2494    Distinguishing initials R. M. & S. found on several printed marks of differing design: name of the individual pattern is often included, 1882-92.

MALKIN   **SAMUEL MALKIN,** Knowle Works, Burslem. Staffordshire Potteries. Early 18th century. *Slip-decorated Earthenwares.*

2495   S. M.   A series of circular moulded and slip decorated dishes bear the initials conspicuously worked into the design. One example is signed in full. Dated examples of 1712(?), 1726, 1727 and 1734 are recorded. See illustrated articles by Hugh Tait, in *Apollo* magazine, January and February 1957. An example will be found illustrated in *British Pottery and Porcelain: an illustrated Encyclopaedia of Marked Specimens.*

MALKIN   **MALKIN, WALKER & HULSE**, British Anchor Pottery, Longton. Staffordshire Potteries. 1858–64. *Earthenwares.* Subsequently Walker, Bateman & Co.

2496      Distinguishing initials M. W. & H. found on several printed marks of differing design: name of the individual pattern is often included, 1858–64.

2497   This impressed mark has been attributed to the Middlesbrough Pottery (page 435) but it occurs on a plate decorated with an *underglaze* blue printed pattern, which was registered in the name of Malkin, Walker & Hulse in January 1864. Just before going to press I have purchased a Sunderland type bowl with splash lustre borders and printed shipping scenes; this example bears a clear impression of this mark. It would therefore seem that mark no. 2497 was used at two, or more, factories. On close comparison between the Malkin, Walker & Hulse mark and the Sunderland type bowl it is seen that the Sunderland-Middlesbrough example has a border made up of dots and the mark is deeper from top to bottom than the above-mentioned plate. Also there is no number above the main mark.

461   MALVERN CHINA-   *See* Booths & Colcloughs Ltd.
3287   WARE   *See* Ridgway Potteries Ltd.

MANN   **MANN & CO.** (Arthur and Edward Mann), Cannon St., Hanley. Staffordshire Potteries. 1858–60. *China and Earthenwares.* Subsequently Mann Evans & Co.
2498   MANN & CO.   Distinguishing detail of several printed marks of differing
            HANLEY   design: name of the individual pattern is often included, 1858–60.

MANNERS

2499   Erna Manners
2499a

ERNA MANNERS, MISS, Ealing, London W.5. c. 1920–35. *Studio-type Pottery.*
Incised or painted signature or initial marks, c. 1920–35.

MANNING

2500

J. H. MANNING, Cowes, Isle of Wight. c. 1956– . *Studio-type Pottery.*

Stamped Isle of Wight mark (as used by Jo Lester, mark no. 2370), with initial M added, c. 1956–61.

2500a   HANDMADE
           J. H. M.
           COWES

Stamped mark, in circular form, c. 1961– .

MANSFIELD

MANSFIELD WORKS (William Billingsley), Mansfield, Nottingham. c. 1799–1802. *Small porcelain works or decorating establishments.*

The researches of the late C. L. Exley indicate that Billingsley left Mansfield for Brampton-in-Torksey in or about June 1802. As he had come from Pinxton in 1799, wares bearing this form of name and address mark can be dated to a three-year period. It is probable that Pinxton and other wares were decorated at Mansfield and that no porcelain was made there.

2501   WILLIAM
          BILLINGSLEY
          MANSFIELD

Signature mark in writing letters, c. 1799–1802. Several slight variations occur in the form of signature mark. Rare signed examples will be found illustrated in *British Pottery and Porcelain : an illustrated Encyclopaedia of Marked Specimens.*

MANSFIELD

2502   M. B.

MANSFIELD BROS. (LTD.), Art Pottery Works, Woodville and Church Gresley, Nr. Burton-on-Trent. c. 1890– .* *Earthenwares and Tiles.*
Impressed mark, c. 1890 onwards.*

* The Woodville works were closed in 1957 but the firm continued at Paisley, Scotland. The products were mainly utilitarian.

MANZONI

CARLO MANZONI, Granville Pottery, Hanley. Staffordshire Potteries. c. 1895–8. *Studio-type individual Pottery.*

2503   Incised mark with year of production, c. 1895–8. Early in 1898 the business of Manzoni & Co. was transferred to the Coleorton Pottery, Ashby-de-la-Zouch, Leicestershire.

A vase is illustrated by H. Wakefield in *Victorian Pottery* (1962). A contemporary photograph showing a selection of wares will be found in *British Pottery and Porcelain: an illustrated Encyclopaedia of Marked Specimens.*

MAPPLEBECK   *See* Appendix.

MARE

JOHN (?) MARE, Shelton, Hanley. Staffordshire Potteries. c. 1800–25. *Earthenwares.*

2504   MARE   Impressed mark on blue printed earthenwares, c. 1800–25.*

    * It is not clear which potter of this name the simple MARE mark refers to. John Mares are recorded at Hanley from c. 1790 to 1827, but several other potters named Mare are also recorded at the same period in the rate books. A blue printed earthenware footbath with the impressed Mare mark will be found illustrated in *British Pottery and Porcelain: an illustrated Encyclopaedia of Marked Specimens.*

—   S. MARE   *See* Appendix.

MARGRIE

VICTOR MARGRIE, Southgate, London, W.14. 1952– . *Studio-type Pottery (Stonewares).*

2505   Impressed seal mark, 1952– .

MARKS

MARGARETE MARKS, MRS., London S.E.19. c. 1952– . *Studio-type Pottery.*
    Mrs. Marks formerly worked the Greta Pottery, q.v.

2506   M   Incised mark, c. 1952– .
        M

MARLOW

REGINALD MARLOW, various addresses and teaching posts. c. 1930– . *Studio-type Pottery.*

2507   Impressed or relief mark, c. 1930– .

MARSHALL

2508   MARSHALL & CO.

MARSHALL & CO., Tunstall (?). Early 19th century. *Earthenwares.*

Impressed mark recorded by L. Jewitt as being on a "shell piece" in the Mayer Museum. This firm is not recorded in the surviving rate records and the address and period is not known. Jewitt in 1878 stated, "early 19th century".

MARSHALL

2509   JOHN MARSHALL & CO.

JOHN MARSHALL (& CO.) (LTD.), Bo'ness Pottery, Bo'ness, Scotland. 1854–99. *Earthenwares.*

A printed mark with the title in full occurs on a plate in the Wenger Collection. This example bears the pattern registration number for 1884. This title was used from 1867 to 1897 ("Ltd." was added from 1897 to 1899). Formerly John Marshall, c. 1854–66.

MARSHALL

RAY MARSHALL, Bridgefoot Cottages, Stedham (from c. 1957), Nr. Midhurst, Sussex. 1945– . *Studio-type Pottery (Stonewares).*

Ray Marshall worked at the Milland Pottery until 1957.

2510

Impressed seal type mark, 1945–7.

2511   B

Incised or impressed B (Bridgefoot) mark, 1957– .

2511a   Ray Marshall
              1963

Most wares signed in full, in writing letters, with year of production.

MARSHALL

WILLIAM MARSHALL, The Leach Pottery, St. Ives, Cornwall. 1954– . *Leach Pottery.*

2512

Incised mark, 1954–6.

2512a

Impressed seal marks, 2512a and 2513, 1956– .

2513		Examples with the personal mark of William Marshall should also have the Leach Pottery mark, see page 383.

MARTIN

MARTIN BROTHERS (Robert Wallace; Walter; Edwin & Charles), Fulham and Southall, London. 1873-1914.* *Individual Studio-type Stonewares.*

All marks incised or impressed.

2514	R. W. Martin fecit.	Early examples, 1873-5, may be signed in this form.
2515	Pomona House, Fulham	This very rare address mark has been noted with the date 1873.
2516		Incised name and address mark, "Fulham" occurs only in the 1873-4 period. "B.4" refers to the object.
2517		"London" occurs from end of 1874 to 1878 (but may occur on very small objects of later date). N.B. Letter prefix to object number discontinued from end of 1874.
2518-18a		Marks 2518 and 18a, 2519 and 19a, with place name "Southall", c. 1878-9.

2519-19a	SOUTHALL MARTIN POTTERY	MARTIN SOUTHALL POTTERY	

Oval impressed mark, c. 1878-9.

2520		"London and Southall" used c. 1879-82. N.B. Object number discontinued c. 1881.
2521 2521a	R. W. M. E. B. M.	Initial marks of R. W. Martin and Edwin B. Martin are very rarely found.
2522		"Bros." or "Brothers" added in 1882. Mark continued in this form to May 1914 when "London" deleted. N.B. The month and year of production appears incised, with the mark on most specimens. For further information see *A Catalogue of the Martinware in the Collection of F. J. Nettlefold* by C. R. Beard (1936), Chaffers' *Marks and Monograms* . . . (1963) and *Victorian Pottery* by H.

Wakefield (1962). Examples will also be found illustrated in *British Pottery and Porcelain: an illustrated Encyclopaedia of Marked Specimens.*

    * The last firing was carried out in 1914 but Robert Wallace Martin continued to model up to 1923. Captain Butterfield later endeavoured to re-establish the pottery.

MARTIN	**DOROTHY B. MARTIN, MISS,** Brighton, Sussex. c. 1920–35. *Studio-type Pottery.*

2523

    Incised or painted monogram mark, c. 1920–35.

MARTIN	**MARTIN, SHAW & COPE,** Lane End, Longton. Staffordshire Potteries. c. 1815–24. *Earthenwares, Ironstone and China.* Subsequently Martin & Cope.

2524   MARTIN SHAW   Distinguishing detail of printed marks of differing design,
            & COPE   1815–24.
    IMPROVED CHINA

2723   MASHA   *See* Mary Mitchell-Smith.

MASK

2525   MASK ST. IVES   **MASK POTTERY** (D. and J. Val Baker*), St. Ives, Cornwall. 1953– . *Studio-type Pottery.*
An impressed or printed mark comprising this wording within a shield outline, 1953– .

    * Denys Val Baker is the author of an interesting book, *Pottery Today* (1961).

2542   MASON & CO.   *See* Charles James Mason & Co.

MASON	**CHARLES JAMES MASON,** Fenton Works, Lane Delph. Staffordshire Potteries. c. 1845–8. (Also 1851–4 at Daisy Bank, Longton.) *Ironstone, Earthenwares.* Formerly Charles James Mason & Co., see next entry.

2526–8

Printed variations of basic Mason's Ironstone mark (no. 2530) c. 1845+.

2529

Note angular crown or ribbon version, and the difference between these later versions and the earlier (used with early impressed mark) seen below for comparison. This form of mark with the registration mark of 1849 is reproduced in Plate 3.

2530

Earlier version of standard mark, used by G. M. and C. J. Mason from 1813 to 1829.

N.B. Mark continued by Francis Morley, page 449, and G. L. Ashworth & Bros., see page 38.

MASON

CHARLES JAMES MASON & CO., Patent Ironstone China Manufactory, Lane Delph. Staffordshire Potteries. 1829–45. *Ironstone wares.* Formerly G. M. and C. J. Mason, q.v. Subsequently C. J. Mason, q.v.

Several printed marks occur with initials C. J. M. & Co. or title C. J. Mason & Co., 1829–45.

2531–3   FENTON
STONE WORKS
C. J. M. & CO.
GRANITE CHINA

The staple patent Ironstone mark, no. 2530, was also continued.

2534

A variation with "Improved" Ironstone china occurs c. 1840+.

2535	MASON'S CAMBRIAN ARGIL	Impressed or printed marks on special bodies, c. 1825–40.
2536	MASON'S BANDANA WARE	

MASON

G. M. & C. J. MASON (also listed in rates, etc., as G. & C. Mason), Patent Ironstone China Manufactory, Lane Delph. Staffordshire Potteries. 1813–29. *Ironstones.* Subsequently C. J. Mason & Co., q.v.

2537	G. M. & C. J. MASON	Marks incorporating the initials of George Miles and Charles
2538	G. & C. J. M.	James Mason occur before 1829.

The earliest marks of "Mason's Ironstone China" (patented in July 1813) were *impressed.*

2539	MASON'S PATENT IRONSTONE CHINA	These early marks (c. 1813–25) occur in different forms— impressed in one line, in two or more or in circular form, and
2540	PATENT IRONSTONE CHINA	may be placed in unexpected places.

2530  The staple form of printed Patent Ironstone China mark occurs from c. 1820 onwards. Later versions occur, see mark no. 2529 and Ashworth's, page 38. Early versions occur without the word "Mason's" over the crown.

2541  Printed mark, c. 1825+. Slight variations occur with different borders. "No. 306" refers to the pattern.

2542 CHINA CHIMNEY PIECE. MASON & CO. PATENTEES STAFFORDSHIRE POTTERIES (Pre-Victorian Royal Arms) PATENT IRON STONE CHINA

A special large ornate printed mark occurs on rare Ironstone China fireplaces. The pre-Victorian Royal Arms occurs in the centre, see Plate 6. Note unusual title—"Mason & Co.", which may refer to C. J. Mason & Co., c. 1825–37.

For further information on Mason wares see R. G. Haggar's *The Masons of Lane Delph* (1952) and G. Godden's *British Pottery and Porcelain 1780–1850* (1963). Typical examples will be found illustrated in *British Pottery and Porcelain: an illustrated Encyclopaedia of Marked Specimens.*

MASON		MILES MASON (Islington Pottery, Liverpool (c. 1792–1800)), then Victoria Pottery (c. 1800–6) and Minerva Works, Lane Delph (c. 1806–16). Staffordshire Potteries. c. 1792–1816. *Porcelain.*
2543	M. MASON	Impressed marks, c. 1800–16.
2544	MILES MASON	

2545   Printed mark on Willow (and other Chinese) type patterns. The name MILES MASON may occur with this mark, c. 1800–16.

Typical specimens will be found illustrated in *British Pottery and Porcelain: an illustrated Encyclopaedia of Marked Specimens.*

MASON

WILLIAM MASON, Lane Delph. Staffordshire Potteries. c. 1811–24. *Earthenwares.*

2546   W. MASON   A fine 20-inch blue printed scenic platter bears this rare printed mark, 1811–24.

MASON'S
or
MASON'S IRONSTONE

See (listed in chronological order):
    G. M. & C. J. Mason, c. 1813–29.
    Charles James Mason & Co., c. 1829–45.
    Charles James Mason, c. 1845–8 and c. 1851–4.
    Francis Morley (& Co.), c. 1848–62.
    G. L. Ashworth & Bros., c. 1862– .
For a full account of the Masons and illustrations of typical wares see R. G. Haggar's *The Masons of Lane Delph* (1952) and *British Pottery and Porcelain: an illustrated Encyclopaedia of Marked Specimens.*

MASON

MASON HOLT & CO., Dresden Works, Longton. Staffordshire Potteries. 1857–84. *China.*

2547   M. H. & CO.   Distinguishing initials found on several impressed or printed marks of differing design, 1857–84.

MASSEY

MASSEY WILDBLOOD & CO., Peel Works, Longton. Staffordshire Potteries. 1887–9. *China.* Formerly Hulme & Massey. Subsequently Wildblood & Heath, q.v.

2548	M. W. & CO.	Distinguishing initials found on several printed marks of differing design, 1887–9. N.B. Some directories also list R. V. Wildblood at this period.

MATHEWS

HEBER MATHEWS, various teaching posts and at Lee, Nr. Woolwich, Kent. 1931–58. *Studio-type Pottery (Stonewares and Porcelains)*.

2549

HM

Incised mark, 1931–58.
    Heber Mathews died January 31st, 1959.

For illustrations of Heber Mathews' work see *Apollo*, August 1947.

MATTHEWS

BASIL MATTHEWS, The Studio, Wolverhampton, Staffordshire. 1946– . *Earthenware figures, Animals, etc.*

2550

Basil Matthews

Printed or painted mark, 1946– .

MATTHEWS

MATTHEWS & CLARK, Melbourne Works, Longton. Staffordshire Potteries. c. 1902–6. *China and Earthenwares*.

2551

Printed mark registered in 1902 and continued to 1906.

MATTHEWS

JOHN MATTHEWS, Royal Pottery, Weston-super-Mare, Somerset. 1870–88. *Terra-cotta, etc.* Formerly C. Phillips. Subsequently C. G. Warne.

2552

JOHN MATTHEWS
LATE PHILLIPS
·ROYAL POTTERY·
WESTON-SUPER-MARE

Impressed mark, 1870–88.

MATTHEWS

LEO. F. MATTHEWS, Walford Heath, Shropshire. 1954– . *Studio-type Pottery.*

2553 Painted or incised initial mark, 1954– .

3163 Mattona Ware *See* Price Bros. (Burslem) Ltd.

MAUND

GEOFFREY MAUND (Geoffrey Maund Pottery Ltd.), Croydon, Surrey. 1952– . *Hand-made Earthenwares.*

2554–5   Impressed marks, c. 1953– .

2556 Printed or impressed mark, c. 1961– .

MAUDESLEY

J. MAUDESLEY & CO., Well St. and Cross St., Tunstall. Staffordshire Potteries. 1862–4. *Earthenwares.*

2557 STONE WARE J. M. & CO.

A printed mark incorporating the initials J. M. & Co. is believed to relate to this firm, 1862–4. Other, earlier, firms also used these initials, see the Appendix.

MAW

MAW & CO. (LTD.), Benthall Works, Broseley, Nr. Jackfield, Shropshire (formerly at Worcester). Est. c. 1850– . *Tiles (Art Pottery from c. 1875).*

2558 MAW
2558a MAW & CO.
2559 MAW & CO. BROSELEY

Distinguishing details of impressed, moulded or printed marks of differing design, c. 1850– . "Broseley" occurs from c. 1857.

2560 FLOREAT MAW SALOPIA

A circular mark incorporating this wording was introduced c. 1880. "England" was added to basic marks from c. 1891.
See Jewitt's *The Ceramic Art of Great Britain.* A vase

decorated by Walter Crane is illustrated in H. Wakefield's *Victorian Pottery* (1962) and in *British Pottery and Porcelain: an illustrated Encyclopaedia of Marked Specimens.*

2572	MAYER BROS.	*See* Thomas, John & Joseph Mayer.
2565a	MAYER & CO.	*See* Joseph Mayer & Co.

MAYER

2561 E. MAYER

ELIJAH MAYER, Cobden Works, Hanley. Staffordshire Potteries. c. 1790–1804. *Wedgwood-type Wares, Creamwares and Basaltes.* Subsequently E. Mayer & Son, see next entry. Impressed mark, c. 1790–1804.

Typical examples will be found illustrated in *British Pottery and Porcelain: an illustrated Encyclopaedia of Marked Specimens.*

MAYER

2562 E. MAYER & SON

ELIJAH MAYER & SON,* Cobden Works, Hanley. Staffordshire Potteries. 1805–34. *Wedgwood-type Earthenwares, also China.* Formerly E. Mayer, above.
Impressed or printed name-mark, 1805–34.

* In most rate records the name of Joseph Mayer is given, but in directories the trading name "E. Mayer & Son" is given.

MAYER

2563

2563a

MAYER & ELLIOTT, Fountain Place and Dale Hall, Longport. Staffordshire Potteries. 1858–61. *Earthenwares.* Formerly Mayer Bros. & Elliott. Subsequently Liddle *Elliott & Son,* q.v.
Distinguishing initials M & E found on several printed marks of differing design, 1858–61. Impressed month and year numbers occur: $\frac{11}{60}$ for November 1860.

MAYER		JOHN MAYER, Foley. Staffordshire Potteries. 1833–41. *Earthenwares.*
2564	J M F	Distinguishing detail of several printed marks of differing design, 1833–41.

MAYER

JOSEPH MAYER & CO., High St., Church Works from 1831, Hanley. Staffordshire Potteries. c. 1822–33. *Earthenwares.*

Joseph Mayer was the son of Elijah. Joseph continued his father's works probably under various styles—E. Mayer & Co., J. Mayer & Co., or Mayer & Co. The rate records, etc., are

2565   JOSEPH MAYER & CO.   complicated. The following marks have been recorded.
          HANLEY   The exact period is open to question, c. 1822–33.

2565a   MAYER & CO.

MAYER

THOMAS MAYER (ELTON POTTERY) LTD., Elton Pottery, Stoke. Staffordshire Potteries. 1956– . *Earthenwares.*

2566   MADE IN ENGLAND

Monogram mark, 1956–60.

2567   ELTON POTTERY
          MADE IN
          ENGLAND

Printed or impressed mark, 1960– .

MAYER

THOMAS MAYER, Cliff Bank Works, Stoke (c. 1826–35), and Brook St., Longport (c. 1836–8). Staffordshire Potteries. c. 1826–38. *Earthenwares.*

2568   T. MAYER   Distinguishing details of several printed marks of differing
2569   T. MAYER, STOKE   design: name of the individual pattern is often included, c. 1826–38. The addition of "Stoke" signifies a date before 1836.

Thomas Mayer's blue printed wares were extensively exported to the United States of America and American devices occur in the marks.

MAYER		THOMAS, JOHN & JOSEPH MAYER, Furlong Works and Dale Hall Pottery, Burslem. Staffordshire Potteries. 1843–55. *Earthenwares, China, Parian, etc.*

Messrs. T. J. & J. Mayer exhibited in the Exhibitions of 1851, 1853 and 1855. Their products were varied and highly regarded. Interesting moulded parian wares were a feature. Subsequently Mayer Bros. & Elliot.

2570 T. J. & J. MAYER Distinguishing detail of several printed marks of differing design: name of the individual pattern is often included, 1843–55. Mark no. 2571 is a typical example.

2571

2572 MAYER BROS. The title "Mayer Bros." also occurs.

MAYER

MAYER & MAUDESLEY, Tunstall. Staffordshire Potteries. 1837–8. *Earthenwares.*

2573 M. & M. Printed marks are recorded with these initials and are attributed to this firm, 1837–8.

In Ward's *Stoke-on-Trent* (1843) this firm is listed as producing "China toys, also Black Egyptian" (basaltes). Several firms listed in this 1843 book ceased before publication.

MAYER

MAYER & NEWBOLD, "Staffordshire Porcelain Manufactory", Market Place, Lane End. Staffordshire Potteries. c. 1817–33. *Porcelains and Earthenwares.* Formerly T. & J. Johnson. Subsequently Richard Newbold.

2574 M. & N. Distinguishing details of several painted or printed marks of
2575 MAYᴿ & NEWBᴰ differing design, c. 1817–33. Examples will be found illustrated
2576 Mayer & Newbold in the companion picture book of marked specimens.
2577

MAYER

MAYER & SHERRATT, Clifton Works, Longton. Staffordshire Potteries. 1906–41. *China.*

2578–80

M&S
L

c. 1906

MELBA CHINA
ENGLAND

c. 1921+

GUARANTEED
MADE IN
ENGLAND

c. 1925–41

Various printed marks from 1906.

2575	MAY^R & NEWB^D	*See* Mayer & Newbold.
2502	M. B.	*See* Mansfield Bros. (Ltd.).
3693	M. & B.	*See* Minton.
1737a —	M. C.	*See* Gomshall Pottery. *See* Nottingham Stonewares.
2551	M. & C. L	*See* Matthews & Clark.
1787	MD (joined)	*See* Green Dene Pottery.
2654	M. E. & CO.	*See* Middlesbrough Earthenware Co.
2563	M. & E.	*See* Mayer & Elliott.

MEAKIN

ALFRED MEAKIN (LTD.), Royal Albert, Victoria and Highgate Potteries, Tunstall. Staffordshire Potteries. 1875– .*
Earthenwares.

2581 ALFRED MEAKIN
2582 ALFRED MEAKIN
LTD.

Distinguishing details of several impressed or printed marks of differing design, 1875– . Note the addition of "Ltd." after 1897.

2583–5

c. 1875–97

ALFRED MEAKIN.LTD

c. 1897+

c. 1891+

Earlier versions occur without "Ltd."

* Firm retitled "Alfred Meakin (Tunstall) Ltd." from c. 1913. Newfield Pottery taken over c. 1930.

2586-9

c. 1891+   c. 1907+   c. 1914+   c. 1914+

Typical printed marks ("England" added from 1891).

A. MEAKIN (TUNSTALL) LTD.

2590-3

ç. 1930+   c. 1937+   c. 1937+   c. 1937+

Note "Ltd." does not appear in the marks from c. 1930 onwards.

2594-5

Post-war marks, several slight variations occur.

MEAKIN

CHARLES MEAKIN, Eastwood Pottery, Hanley. Staffordshire Potteries. 1883–9. *Earthenwares.* Formerly at Burslem.

2596

Printed mark, 1883–9. Similar marks without "Hanley" relate to earlier potters at Burslem (1870–82).

MEAKIN

HENRY MEAKIN, Abbey Pottery, Cobridge. Staffordshire Potteries. 1873–6. *Earthenwares.*

2597

Printed mark incorporating the name H. Meakin, 1873–6. Other "H. Meakins" of the period include Harry Meakin, Lichfield St., Hanley, c. 1870. Henry Meakin, Grove St., Cobridge, c. 1882.

MEAKIN

J. & G. MEAKIN (LTD.), Eagle Pottery and Eastwood Works, Hanley. Staffordshire Potteries. 1851– . *Earthenwares, Ironstones, etc.*

2598   J. & G. MEAKIN

Distinguishing detail of several impressed or printed marks of differing design: name of the individual pattern is often included, 1851– . The Royal Arms occur in many marks.

Later printed marks include:

2599–2602

c. 1890+   c. 1890+   c. 1890+   c. 1907+

Earlier versions without "England".

2603–5

c. 1912+   c. 1912+   1912

"SOL" and sun face trade-marks registered in 1912. Many variations occur with different trade-names, etc.

2606–11

J & G MEAKIN ENGLAND

c. 1939+

Post-war variation of no. 2605.

c. 1953+   c. 1955+   c. 1958+   c. 1962

2612   "ROMANTIC ENGLAND"

A series of printed, Romantic England, scenic patterns was started in 1947. Various ornate marks are used and incorporate this wording.

Eastwood Pottery sold 1958; Eagle Pottery then enlarged and modernised.

MEEDS

WILLIAM MEEDS & SON (LTD.), Burgess Hill, Sussex. Late 19th century to 1939. *Terra-cotta and Pottery Wares.*

This pottery was established in or before 1714. Its products were mainly bricks and utilitarian wares. From 1855 to 1866 directories list James Meeds. From 1870 to 1887 the style is William & Frederick Meeds. In 1890 the style is William Meeds & Son; in 1907 "Ltd." is added.

2613   W. MEEDS & SON, Manufacturers, Burgess Hill, Sussex

Impressed mark on ancient looking earthenware pot of different coloured clays, in the Worthing Museum, c. 1890–1907.

MEIGH

CHARLES MEIGH, Old Hall Works, Hanley. Staffordshire Potteries. 1835–49. *Earthenwares, Stonewares, etc.* Formerly J. Meigh & Sons, q.v. Subsequently C. Meigh, Son & Pankhurst, q.v.

2614   CHARLES MEIGH
2614a   C. M.

2615

Many impressed marks bear the name in full, with date of introduction of the design or other information, 1835–49. The Royal Arms were incorporated in many marks. *Most* printed marks incorporate the initials C. M. with the name of the pattern and type of body: "Porcelain Opaque", etc.; no. 2615 is an example.

2616   NOV. 12, 1846 REGISTERED No. 88068 CHARLES MEIGH. YORK MINSTER

Many marks incorporate the diamond shaped pattern registration mark, or the date of registration. These marks occur on ornate moulded wares of the 1840's.

Although most of Charles Meigh's varied products bear his name in full, often with a date, some marks occur on services, etc., with printed or impressed marks similar to these basic examples:

2617–19

These marks were also used by J. Meigh & Sons, page 429, and by Charles Meigh & Son, page 429. Other wording was used in mark no. 2618, "Indian Stone China" or "French China".

MEIGH		CHARLES MEIGH & SON, Old Hall Pottery, Hanley. Staffordshire Potteries. 1851–March 61. *Earthenwares.* Formerly C. Meigh, Son & Pankhurst, q.v. Subsequently Old Hall Earthenware Co. Ltd., q.v.

2620

Distinguishing initials C. M. & S. or M. & S. found on several printed marks of differing design: name of the individual pattern is often included, 1851–61.

2620a M. & S.
2621 C. MEIGH & SON
        MEIGH'S

Several marks, including Royal Arms marks, occur with the name Meigh, Meigh's or C. Meigh & Son.

2622
        CHINA

2623 OPAQUE
        PORCELAIN

This mark printed or impressed occurs on wares, alone or with other marks, 1851–61. The words are slightly curved.

Mark numbers 2617–19 also occur on Charles Meigh & Son's wares.

MEIGH

CHARLES MEIGH, SON & PANKHURST, Old Hall Pottery, Hanley. Staffordshire Potteries. 1850–1. *Earthenwares.* Formerly Charles Meigh, q.v. Subsequently Charles Meigh & Son, q.v.

2624 C. M. S. & P.

Distinguishing initials found on several printed marks of differing design: name of the individual pattern is often included, 1850–1.

MEIGH

JOB MEIGH (& SON), Old Hall Pottery, Hanley. Staffordshire Potteries. c. 1805–34 (& Son from c. 1812). *Earthenwares.* Subsequently Charles Meigh, q.v.

2625 MEIGH

Impressed mark, 1805–34.

2626 OLD HALL

Impressed or printed mark, 1805+.

2627 J. M. & S.

The initials J. M. & S. may have been used from c. 1812 to 1834, but these initials usually relate to J. Meir & Son, depending on the period, see page 430.

2628

Printed mark on good quality printed plate in the Godden Collection, c. 1815–25.

MEIGH

W. & R. MEIGH, Bridge Bank Works, Stoke. Staffordshire Potteries. 1894–9. *Earthenwares.* Subsequently F. Hancock & Co.

2629

Printed mark, 1894–9.

250–1   MEIR CHINA
252   MEIR WARE
249   MEIR WORKS

See Barker Bros. (Ltd.), page 54.

MEIR

2630   JOHN MEIR

JOHN MEIR, Staffordshire Potteries. Late 17th century to early 18th century. *Slip-decorated Earthenwares.*
A slip-decorated earthenware cradle is inscribed: "John Meir 1708 made thi——".

MEIR

2631   J. M.
2632   I. M.

JOHN MEIR, Greengates Pottery, Tunstall. Staffordshire Potteries. c. 1812–36. *Earthenwares.* Subsequently J. Meir & Son, see next entry.
Distinguishing details of several printed marks of differing design: name of the individual pattern is often included, 1812–36.

MEIR

2633   J. M. & S.
2634   I. M. & S.
2635   J. M. & SON

JOHN MEIR & SON, Greengates Pottery, Tunstall. Staffordshire Potteries. 1837–97. *Earthenwares.* Formerly John Meir, above.
Distinguishing details of several impressed or printed marks of differing design: name of the individual pattern is often included, 1837–97. See Plate 5. Impressed month and year

| 2636 | J. MEIR & SON | numbers occur on some specimens: $\frac{11}{76}$ for November 1876. |
| 2637 | MEIR & SON | "England" occurs on marks from c. 1890. |

Typical marks include:

2639–41

The attribution of the initials I. M. & S. is confirmed by two similar plates in the Godden Collection, one of which is marked with these initials, one with the name in full.

MEIR

RICHARD MEIR, Shelton.* Staffordshire Potteries. Late 17th century to early 18th century. *Slip-decorated Earthenwares.*

2642 RICHARD MEIR

This name occurs on slip-decorated earthenwares. Some examples bear dates between 1682 and 1708.

* A "Richard Meire earth potter" was at Shelton in 1689 (Deed). The name Richard Meer occurs on a Posset-pot dated 1682. It is not unusual to find 17th century names spelt in different ways.

2579–80	MELBA	*See* Mayer & Sherratt.
2643		*See* Melba China Co. Ltd.
3288		*See* Ridgways Potteries Ltd.
2372–3		*See* H. A. Wain & Sons Ltd.

MELBA

MELBA CHINA CO. LTD., Stafford St., Longton. Staffordshire Potteries. 1948–51. *China.*

2643

Printed mark, 1948–51.

273-4   MELBAR WARE   *See* Barlows (Longton) Ltd.

1616   MELBOURNE WORKS   *See* Thomas Forester & Co.

MELLON   ERIC JAMES MELLON, Gallery 65, Bognor Regis, Sussex.
                          1942-4 and 1951- . *Studio-type Pottery, Stonewares, Tiles
                          and Sculpture.*

2644   ERIC JAMES   Incised or painted signature mark in writing letters, 1951- .
          MELLON

2644a   MELLON   Incised or painted marks in writing letters, often with last two
                          numerals of year added, i.e. 63 for 1963.

MELLOR   MELLOR, VENABLES & CO., Hole House Pottery, Bur-
                          slem. Staffordshire Potteries. 1834-51. *Earthenwares and China.*
2645   M. V. & CO.   Distinguishing details of several impressed or printed marks of
2646   MELLOR, VENABLES   differing design: name of the individual pattern is often
          & CO.   included, 1834-51.
                              Messrs. Mellor, Venables & Co. produced a range of printed
                          earthenwares for the American market.

MELLOR   MELLOR, TAYLOR & CO., Top Bridge Works (c. 1882-3),
                          Cleveland Works (c. 1884-1904), Burslem. Staffordshire
                          Potteries. 1880-1904. *Earthenwares.*

2647-8      Printed or impressed marks, 1880-1904.

MENDEL   RENEE MENDEL, MISS, London N.10. 1942- . *Terra-
                          cotta figures and studio-type Pottery.*

2649   Incised or painted initial (R. M.) mark, 1942- .

1028   MENDIP   *See* John Coney.

MENZIES

LLEWELYN, FREDERICK, MENZIES-JONES, Eton College, Windsor, Berkshire. 1938–58 (approximate dates). *Studio-type Pottery.*

2650   Circular impressed seal of initials M. I., c. 1938–58.

4405   MERLIN POTTERY   *See* postscript, page 745.

2663   MERZAYSIDE WARE   *See* Midland Pottery Co.

3719   M. E. S.   *See* Erick & Meira Stockl.

METHVEN

DAVID METHVEN & SONS, Kirkcaldy Pottery, Kirkcaldy, Fifeshire, Scotland. First half 19th century to c. 1930. *Earthenwares.*

2651   D. M. & S.   Early wares were generally unmarked. Marks from c. 1875
2652   METHVEN   onwards include the initials or name, as nos. 2651–3.
2653   D. METHVEN & SONS   David Methven died in 1861 but the various successors (the Young family) continued the old title.

3642   MEXBRO   *See* Sowter & Co.

1621   M. F.   *See* Moira Forsyth.
2999   *See* Pendley Pottery.

—   M. & F.   *See* Appendix, page 726.

2767   M. F. & Co.   *See* Morley Fox & Co. Ltd.
2769   or
      M. F. & Co. Ltd.

2776c   F   *See* Marion Morris.
         M M

695   M. G. H.   *See* Buckfast Abbey Pottery.

1957   MH   *See* Muriel Harris.
     (joined)

2840   Mh·   *See* F. Barrie Naylor.
     (joined)

| 2547 | M. H. & CO. | *See* Mason Holt & Co. |
| 2718 | | *See* Minton, Hollins (& Co.) (Ltd.). |

| 2697–8 | M. & H. | *See* Minton. |

| 2682 | MHP (joined) | *See* Milton Head Pottery. |

| 2650 | MI (joined) | *See* L. F. Menzies-Jones. |

| 42a | MICRATEX | *See* William Adams & Sons (Potters) Ltd. |

| 2656a | MIDDLESBRO | *See* Middlesbrough Pottery Co. |
| 2657 | | *See* Middlesbrough Earthenware Co. |

| 4193 | MIDDLESBROUGH | *See* Isaac Wilson & Co. |

MIDDLESBROUGH

MIDDLESBROUGH EARTHENWARE CO., Middlesbrough-on-Tees, Yorkshire. 1844–52. *Earthenwares.* Formerly Middlesbrough *Pottery* Co., see below. Subsequently Isaac Wilson & Co., q.v.

| 2654 | M. E. & CO. | Distinguishing initials found on several impressed or printed marks of differing design, 1844–52. Several marks include an anchor. |

| 2657 | MIDDLESBRO POTTERY (with anchor device) | This standard, impressed, Middlesbrough mark is normally attributed to 1834–44 but it was almost certainly also used by this company to 1852. |

| 4194 | MIDDLESBROUGH POTTERY | *See* Isaac Wilson & Co. |

MIDDLESBROUGH

MIDDLESBROUGH POTTERY CO., Middlesbrough-on-Tees, Yorkshire. 1834–44. *Earthenwares, Creamwares, etc.* Subsequently Middlesbrough *Earthenware* Co., see previous entry.

| 2655 | M. P. Co. | Distinguishing details of impressed or printed marks of differing design, c. 1834–44. |
| 2656 | MIDDLESBRO' POTTERY CO. | |

2656a	MIDDLESBRO' POTTERY	Mark no. 2656a occurs on examples in the Godden Collection; the mark also shows a view of the pottery with seven kilns, c. 1834–44.

2657   MIDDLESBRO' POTTERY* (with anchor device)

An anchor occurs with several marks: one form has the name MIDDLESBRO' POTTERY arranged round the anchor,* another form has the initials M. P. Co., c. 1834–44.

2657a

2658

Another mark is recorded by Chaffers and other writers and comprises the anchor with the word "London"; numbers may also occur above this mark.

Just before going to press I purchased a Sunderland-type bowl with printed and splash lustre decoration. This example has a clear impression of mark no. 2658 but the period would seem to be subsequent to that of the Middlesbrough Pottery Co. as the bowl bears a print of the "Great Eastern Leviathan" launched in 1858 (her first Atlantic crossing was June 1860). See also note relating to mark no. 2497, Malkin Walker & Hulse.

2658a   Impressed crown

An impressed crown mark on earthenwares is attributed by some authorities to the Middlesbrough Pottery. Such a mark occurs on a lustre and floral painted plate in the Godden Collection, c. 1830–40.

* This mark of the anchor, with the words "Middlesbro Pottery" arranged in a curve above the anchor, was most probably also used by the Middlesbrough Earthenware Co. to 1852, judging by the style of some pieces bearing this mark.

MIDDLETON

B. MIDDLETON, Looe, Cornwall. c. 1950's–60's.* *Earthenwares.*

2659   BERT MIDDLETON LOOE

Impressed mark on blue decorated vases, jugs, etc.

* The writer purchased a marked example of B. Middleton's ware, as new, in 1962, but letters seeking further information have not been answered.

MIDDLETON

J. H. MIDDLETON (& CO.), Delphine Pottery, Longton. Staffordshire Potteries. 1889–1941. Formerly Middleton & Hudson. Subsequently Hudson & Middleton Ltd., q.v.

2660–2

c. 1891+   c. 1930–41   c. 1930–41

Various printed marks with trade-name DELPHINE.

MIDLAND   MIDLAND POTTERY CO. (J. J. Bate & Son Ltd.), Raven-head, St. Helens, Lancs. 1932–40. *Earthenwares (teapots).*

2663   Printed or impressed mark, 1932–40.

MIDWINTER   W. R. MIDWINTER (LTD.), Albion and Hadderidge Potteries, Burslem. Staffordshire Potteries. Est. c. 1910– . *Earthenwares.*

Early wares were generally unmarked. Pre-war marks include:

2664–5   c. 1932–41

Post-war marks include:

2666–9

New versions of mark no. 2664 above, note **Group** letter, see page 295.   c. 1946+   c. 1950+

2670–2

"STYLECRAFT" c. 1953+   c. 1961+

Note month and year numbers, 4–61 for April 1961.   c. 1962+

MILES		MICHAEL MILES, West Sussex College of Arts & Crafts, Worthing, Sussex. 1954– . *Studio-type Pottery, also Stonewares and Tiles.*
2673	M. Miles	Incised or painted initial mark, 1954–60.
2674	M. M. 63	Painted or incised initial mark, with year, 1958– .

MILLAND		MILLAND POTTERY, Mr. & Mrs. Hawkins, Milland, Liphook, Hampshire. 1948– . *Earthenwares.*
2675		Printed or impressed mark, 1948– .

MILLAR		JOHN MILLAR, South Saint Andrew Street, Edinburgh. 1840–82. *Retailer.*
2676	JOHN MILLAR	Printed marks incorporating the above name and address occur on Victorian pottery and porcelain sold by this firm. From 1840 to 1843 the address was 11 South St. Andrew Street, and then at number 2.

MILLS		DONALD MILLS (Donald Mills Pottery Ltd.), London S.E.1. 1946–55. *Studio-type Pottery, Stonewares.*
2677	*Donald Mills*	Signature registered as a trade-mark in 1948 and continued to c. 1955, often with year added.
2678	D. M.	Printed initial mark, c. 1946–55.

MILLS		HENRY MILLS, Bryan St., Hanley. Staffordshire Potteries. c. 1892. *Earthenwares.*
2679		Printed mark, c. 1892. Another Henry Mills was potting at Shelton, 1841–50.

MILNE

2680   MILNE CORNWALL
          & CO.

MILNE CORNWALL & CO., Portobello, Scotland. c. 1830–40. *Stonewares.* Subsequently John Tough
Rare impressed mark, c. 1830–40.

MILNER

2681   RENLYM

G. E. MILNER, Dalehall, Burslem. Staffordshire Potteries. 1957– . *China.*
Printed marks incorporating the trade-name RENLYM, 1957– .

MILTON

MILTON HEAD POTTERY CO. LTD., Brixham, Devon. 1951– . *Earthenwares.*

2682

Monogram mark incised or painted, 1951– .

2683

Printed mark, c. 1951– .

3893   MINORIES

See William Walker.

MINTON

MINTON (various titles), Stoke. Staffordshire Potteries. Est. 1793– . *Porcelains, Earthenwares, Parian, Majolica, etc.*
   Early wares generally unmarked or bear the pattern number only.

2684

Painted mark on early porcelains, c. 1800–30. The mark occurs with or without pattern numbers under. It is difficult to date the early patterns with certainty. The Minton firm possess the original pattern books and they date pattern 184 to 1799; 539 to 1810; 909 to 1812.

2684a   CROSSED SWORDS
          MARK

Some Minton porcelain of the 1820 period bears a very rare painted mark of the crossed swords (of Dresden) with the pattern number below.

Very many printed marks occur with the initials of the various partnerships M = c. 1822–36, M & B = c. 1836–41, M & Co. = 1841–73, M & H = 1845–68.   Other examples have the name in full.   Typical examples include:

2685–7

2688–91

Note "M" at bottom.

Mark no. 2690 occurs on moulded earthenwares of the 1830's and 1840's, often with the pattern registration mark (page 527).   For information on Minton pattern numbers see *Victorian Porcelain* (1961).

2692   M   Impressed mark found on rare earthenwares of the 1830–45
         STONE   period.

2693–93a

Minton & Boyle printed marks, c. 1836–41.   Many other examples occur with the initials M & B.

2694–6

Minton & Co. printed marks, c. 1841–73.   Several other marks occur with the initials M. & Co.

2697–8

Minton & Hollins printed marks, c. 1845–68.   Other variations occur with the initials M. & H.

From 1842 onwards small year cyphers have been impressed into the body.   Such marks occur in sets of three: month letter, potter's mark and the year cypher.   The key to the year cyphers is reproduced below.

2699

Key to Month Letters

J   January
F   February
M   March
A   April
E   May
I   June
H   July
Y   August
S   September
O   October
N   November
D   December

1842	1843	1844	1845	1846	1847	1848	1849
1850	1851	1852	1853	1854	1855	1856	1857
1858	1859	1860	1861	1862	1863	1864	1865
1866	1867	1868	1869	1870	1871	1872	1873
1874	1875	1876	1877	1878	1879	1880	1881
1882	1883	1884	1885	1886	1887	1888	1889
1890	1891	1892	1893	1894	1895	1896	1897
1898	1899	1900	1901	1902	1903	1904	1905
1906	1907	1908	1909	1910	1911	1912	1913
1914	1915	1916	1917	1918	1919	1920	1921
1922	1923	1924	1925	1926	1927	1928	1929
1930	1931	1932	1933	1934	1935	1936	1937
1938	1939	1940	1941	1942

2700   Incised or impressed into early Parian figures, c. 1845–50. Often in conjunction with year cypher, see page 440.

2701      Mark in relief on Parian figures produced c. 1847–8 for the "Summerly's Art Manufactures". See *Victorian Porcelain*. See also Plate 8.

2702   Rare printed mark on porcelains, c. 1851.

2703   Painted "Ermine" mark, c. 1850 onwards, indicating a special soft glaze. The "Ermine" mark with or without the addition of the letter "M" was occasionally used as the factory mark in the 1850's. Its earliest recorded use is on a dish, dated May 21st, 1850, in the Godden Collection.

2704–4a      Printed marks of the 1860's.

2705   B. B.   The impressed initials B. B. occur on mid-19th century earthenwares, and refer to Best Body.

2706   MINTON   Impressed mark used from c. 1862 to 1871 when S was added. This mark occurs with the impressed year cyphers.

2707   Standard printed Globe trade-mark, c. 1863–72. Later versions are crowned or have S added to Minton.

2708   Printed mark on wares decorated at Minton's short-lived "London Art Pottery Studio", c. 1871–5. See *Victorian Porcelain*.

| 2709 | | Impressed mark used on Sevres styled porcelains, and incorporating the year of manufacture, c. 1868–80. |

| 2710 | TOFT or C. TOFT | Signature mark on intricate copies of "Henri Deux" wares, c. 1870–7. |

| 2711 | MINTONS | Impressed mark from 1873. Note "S" added to earlier version, no. 2706. |

| 2712 | | Several printed marks commemorate special events and these usually include the date. Other marks incorporate the name of the retailer, Messrs. T. Goode & Co., etc. |

| 2713 | | Revised version of standard printed mark no. 2707, c. 1873 onwards. Note crown added, also "S" added to earlier Minton. "England" added below from 1891. "Made in England" occurs c. 1902–11. The crown was deleted on some earthenwares from c. 1901. |

| 2714 | MINTONS ENGLAND | Impressed or moulded mark, c. 1890–1910. |

| 2715 | | Printed mark on earthenwares, c. 1900–8. |

| 2716 | | New version of standard Globe mark, c. 1912–50. |

| 2717 | | Revised standard mark, introduced early in 1951. BONE CHINA, MADE IN ENGLAND may occur under this mark. For further information on Mintons see: Jewitt's *Ceramic Art of Great Britain* (1878 and 1883). *Victorian Porcelain*, G. Godden (1961). *Victorian Pottery*, H. Wakefield (1962). Typical examples will be found illustrated in *British Pottery and Porcelain: an illustrated Encyclopaedia of Marked Specimens*. |

MINTON

MINTON HOLLINS (& CO.) (LTD.), Patent Tile Works, Stoke. Staffordshire Potteries. 1868– .* *Tiles.* Formerly Minton.

| 2718 | M. H. & CO. | Distinguishing details of impressed, moulded or printed marks |
| 2719 | MINTON HOLLINS & CO. | of differing design, 1868– . |

* The present style is Minton Hollins Ltd. "Ltd." was added c. 1928. N.B. This firm of tile manufacturers should not be confused with the main Minton firm.

MIST

JAMES MIST, 82 Fleet St., London. c. 1810–15. *Earthenwares, Basaltes, Porcelains, etc.* Formerly Abbott & Mist, q.v.

Mist is believed to have been only the London agent for Staffordshire manufacturers. Previous writers have given earlier dates for these marks but the first directory entry is in 1810. "James Mist, no. 82 Fleet Street, City of London, Glass and Chinaman" was declared bankrupt early in 1815.

| 2720 | MIST | The name Mist occurs impressed on a white stoneware type jug in the British Museum and on other similar wares, c. 1810–15. |

| 2721 | J. MIST
82 FLEET STREET
LONDON | The name and address mark occurs impressed on rare examples of Turner type stonewares with relief figure motifs on coloured grounds. See the companion illustrated encyclopaedia of |
| 2721a | JAS MIST
No. 82, FLEET ST. | marked specimens. This form of mark also occurs painted on porcelains, c. 1810–15. |

| 739 | MITCHELL | *See* Cadborough Pottery. |

MITCHELL

MARY MITCHELL-SMITH, MISS, London N.W.8. 1940– . *Earthenware figures and groups.*

| 2722 | M. M. S. | Early incised or painted marks, 1940–5. |
| 2723 | Masha | |

| 2724 | Mary Mitchell-Smith | Standard incised signature mark, c. 1940– . |

| 2228–9 | MJ
(also joined) | *See* Mervyn and Mrs. Nerys Jude. |

| 2820 | M J & Co | *See* J. Macintyre & Co. (Ltd.). |
| 2822 | (joined) | |

2510	M K (in diamond)	*See* Ray Marshall.
2408	ML (joined)	*See* Mildred Lockyer.
2750	M. L. & Co.	*See* Moore, Leason & Co.
2315	MLJ (joined)	*See* M. Lamb.
2506 2674 2776b	M. M.	*See* Margarete Marks. *See* Michael Miles. *See* Marion Morris.
2573 3158 3162	M. & M.	*See* Mayer & Maudesley. *See* Price Brothers. *See* Price Bros. (Burslem) Ltd.
2722	M. M. S.	*See* Mary Mitchell-Smith.
2574	M. & N.	*See* Mayer & Newbold.
2832	MN&Co. (joined)	*See* McNeal & Co. (Ltd.).

MOGRIDGE

MOGRIDGE & UNDERHAY LTD., London E.C.4. c. 1912+. *Retailers and agents.*

2725 TRADE MARK M&M "EMUNDU"

Printed trade-mark and name registered in 1912, and continued for many years.

MOIRA

MOIRA POTTERY CO. LTD., Moira, Nr. Burton-on-Trent, Leicestershire. c. 1922– . *Stonewares.*

2726 HILLSTONIA

Trade-names of wholesalers, impressed or stencilled on Moira stonewares, c. 1922– .

2231a	MO J. I. MOLE	*See* Maurice Jupp. *See* Appendix.

MOMMENS

C. & U. MOMMENS, South Heighton, Nr. Newhaven, Sussex. 1951– . *Studio-type Pottery and moulded Animal models.*

2727   M
   SOUTH HEIGHTON
     1951

Incised mark, with year of production, 1951– .

2728

Incised or painted mark on Mr. C. H. N. Mommens' animal models made at South Heighton, 1951– .

2728a

Incised or painted mark used by Mrs. Ursula Mommens (see Darwin) on her tin glazed and other earthenwares, from c. 1935 onwards. Mrs. Mommens started to produce stonewares in 1963.

MONKTON

MONKTON COMBE POTTERY (Mrs. Rachel Warner), Nr. Bath, Somerset. 1946–53. *Studio-type Pottery.* Subsequently P. Wright, q.v.

2729 MONKTON COMBE

Impressed mark, "Monkton Combe" in border of double line circle. Incised monogram RW (no. 2730) in centre, c. 1946–53.
  N.B. A similar monogram has been used by W. Rawsthorne since 1958, see page 523.

2730

MOODY

ESME MOODY, East Grinstead, Sussex. 1955–61. *Studio-type Pottery.*

2731 E. L. M.
2731a E. M.

Incised or painted initial marks, 1955–61.

MOODY

GRACE L. MOODY, MISS, Winterslow, Wiltshire and Bridestow, Nr. Okehampton, Devon. Early 1960– . *Studio-type Earthenwares.*
  At the time of writing (late 1963), Miss Moody was moving her studio from Winterslow to Bridestow.
  Before establishing her own studio Miss Moody designed for the industry and held various teaching posts.

2732 G. L. M.

Impressed seal-type mark incorporating these initials. A similar initial mark is sometimes incised, 1960– .

MOORCROFT

	W. MOORCROFT (LTD.), Washington Works, Burslem. Staffordshire Potteries. 1913– . *Earthenwares.*
2733 MOORCROFT BURSLEM	Printed or impressed mark, 1913+.

2734

William Moorcroft's signature mark. Registered as a trademark in 1919 but previously used on articles decorated by Moorcroft while at Macintyres.

2734a

William Moorcroft died in 1945 and his son, Walter, continues the pottery on traditional lines. A similar signature mark is used or the painted initials W. M.

2735   MOORCROFT
MADE IN ENGLAND

Modern wares also have the printed mark—Moorcroft and "Made in England".

MOORE

BERNARD MOORE, Wolfe St., Stoke. Staffordshire Potteries. 1905–15. *Earthenwares and Porcelain (glaze effects).* Formerly Moore Bros., next entry.

2736

Painted initial mark in several forms, 1905–15.

2737   ᛒᴇʀɴᴀʀᴅ
ʙᴍᴏᴏʀᴇ

Painted or printed mark, 1905–15; the year may be added to these marks.

The talented decorators of Bernard Moore's wares included John Adams, Hilda Beardmore, Dora Billington, George Buttle, Gertrude Jackson, Hilda Lindop, Annie Ollier and Reginald R. Tomlinson. These artists signed their work with monograms of their initials.

MOORE

MOORE (BROS.), St. Mary's Works, Longton. Staffordshire Potteries. 1872–1905. *Porcelains.* Formerly Samuel Moore (& Son).

The Moore Bros. moulds, designs, etc., were sold in September 1905. The St. Mary's Works were sold to Wild & Co. and Bernard Moore continued at Stoke, see Bernard Moore.

| 2738 | MOORE | Impressed or printed mark, c. 1868–75. |

| 2739 | MOORE BROS. | Impressed mark late 1872–1905. |

| 2740 | | Printed mark, c. 1880+. "England" added from c. 1891. |

| 2741 | MOORE BROTHERS ENGLAND | Late impressed mark, 1891–1905. |

| 2742 | | Printed mark, 1902–5. |

MOORE

(SAMUEL) MOORE & CO. (R. T. Wilkinson, using old style, from 1861), Wear Pottery, Southwick, Sunderland, Durham. 1803–74. *Earthenwares*. Formerly John Brunton. Subsequently Messrs. Glaholm, Lisle & Robson.

2743	MOORE & CO. SUNDERLAND	Many impressed or printed marks were used from c. 1803 to
2744	MOORE & CO.	c. 1874, incorporating any of the listed forms of initials or
2745	S. MOORE & CO.	names. The name of the pattern "The Bottle", etc., occur on
2746	S. M. & CO.	printed earthenwares. Examples will be found illustrated in
2747	SAMUEL MOORE & CO.	*British Pottery and Porcelain: an illustrated Encyclopaedia of Marked Specimens*.

MOORE

MOORE & CO., Old Foley Pottery, Fenton. Staffordshire Potteries. 1872–92. *Earthenwares*. Subsequently Moore, Leason & Co., q.v.

| 2748 | M. & CO.* | Distinguishing initials found on impressed or printed marks of differing design, 1872–92. |

* A similarly styled firm was at Hanley, c. 1898–1903, and used a mark with the same initials, see below. Mintons also used these initials, see mark nos. 2694–6.

MOORE

(M) MOORE & CO., Victoria Works, Hanley. Staffordshire Potteries. 1898–1903. *Earthenwares*.

2749		Printed mark, c. 1898–1903. "England" may occur with this mark.

MOORE

MOORE, LEASON & CO., Old Foley Pottery, Fenton. Staffordshire Potteries. 1892–6. *Earthenwares*. Formerly Moore & Co., q.v.

2750	M. L. & CO.	Distinguishing detail of several impressed or printed marks of differing design, 1892–6.
2751		Printed mark, 1892–6.

MORAY

BARBARA MORAY, THE COUNTESS OF, London S.W.1. 1948–55. *Studio-type Pottery*.

2752	B. M.	Impressed mark of the intertwined initials B. M. *with a coronet above*, 1948–55.

MORGAN

MORGAN WOOD & CO., Hill Works, Burslem. Staffordshire Potteries. 1860–70. *Earthenwares*. Formerly Barker & Co.

2753	M. W. & CO.	Distinguishing detail of several printed marks of differing design, 1860–70. One mark incorporates a bee.

MORLEY

MORLEY & ASHWORTH, Broad St., Hanley. Staffordshire Potteries. 1859–62. *Earthenwares, Ironstones, etc.* Formerly F. Morley, q.v. Subsequently G. L. Ashworth & Bros., q.v.

2754	M. & A.	Distinguishing details of several impressed or printed marks of differing design: name of the individual pattern is often included, 1859–62.
2755	MORLEY & ASHWORTH HANLEY	

2756–8

Samples of different printed marks.

— MORLEY CLAY *See* Appendix, page 726.

MORLEY **FRANCIS MORLEY (& CO.)**, Broad St., Shelton, Hanley. Staffordshire Potteries. 1845–58. *Earthenwares, Ironstones, etc.* Formerly Ridgway & Morley, q.v. Subsequently Morley & Ashworth, q.v.

2759 F. M. Distinguishing details of several impressed or printed marks of
2760 F. M. & CO. differing design: name of the individual pattern is often
2761 F. MORLEY & CO. included, 1845–58. See Plates 3 and 5.

Typical examples include:

2762–4

2765–6

N.B. Masons' printed Ironstone mark no. 2529 continued by Francis Morley from c. 1845 also used by successors.

MORLEY **MORLEY FOX & CO. LTD.**, Salopian Works, Fenton. Staffordshire Potteries. 1906–44. *Earthenwares.* Formerly William Morley. Subsequently William Morley & Co. Ltd., see next page.

Various marks were used incorporating the initials M. F. & Co., etc.   Other marks include:

2767–70   MORLEY, FOX MADE IN ENGLAND. & COMPANY, LTᴰ   MADE IN M.F.& Co.LTD. ENGLAND   HOMELEIGH WARE

c. 1906   c. 1920+   c. 1920+   c. 1929+

2771–2   Crown Manor WARE   MORLEY WARE MADE IN ENGLAND   Mark numbers 2771 and 2772 were subsequently used by William Morley & Co. Ltd.

c. 1938+   c. 1938+

2772   MORLEY WARE   *See* Morley Fox & Co. Ltd.
2773–6   or William Morley & Co. Ltd., below.

MORLEY

WILLIAM MORLEY & CO. LTD., Salopian Works, Fenton. Staffordshire Potteries. 1944–57. *Earthenwares.* Formerly Morley Fox & Co., Ltd., see above.

2773–6   MORLEY WARE MADE IN ENGLAND

Several printed marks, including nos. 2771 and 2772 formerly used by Morley Fox & Co. Ltd. were continued c. 1944–57. Month and year marks occur, i.e. II/IV for February 1944.

MORRIS

MARION MORRIS, MRS., Sheering, Hertfordshire. c. 1950– . *Pottery figures.*

2776a   MARION MORRIS   Painted or incised signature mark on individual pottery figures, etc., c. 1950– .

2776b   M M   Incised or painted initial marks sometimes placed on early
2776c   F   figures, c. 1950–5.
             M M

MORRIS		**ROWLAND JAMES MORRIS**, born 1847, died 1909. *Ceramic Modeller, etc.*
2777	R. J. MORRIS	Incised signature on ceramics. R. J. Morris designed for various late 19th century manufacturers.

MORRIS		**THOMAS MORRIS**, Anchor Works, Longton. Staffordshire Potteries. 1897–1901. *China.*
2778		An impressed or printed anchor was used as a trade-mark, c. 1897–1901. The initials T. M. may also occur with the anchor.
2779	T. M.	N.B. There were two potters of this name, see also entry below.

MORRIS

THOMAS MORRIS, Regent Works, Longton. Staffordshire Potteries. 1892–1941. *China.*

2780–2

c. 1892+   c. 1912+   c. 1928+

Printed marks, c. 1892+.

MORTLOCK		**J. MORTLOCK** or **MORTLOCKS LTD.**, Oxford St. and other addresses, London. Established 1746, ceased c. 1930. *Retailer.*
		John Mortlock was one of the leading 19th century retailers and was associated with several factories in the 1810–30 period.
2783	MORTLOCKS	On some early wares the name Mortlock appears, in writing letters.
2783a	MORTLOCK	Very rare impressed name-mark on earthenware plate in the Godden Collection, c. 1820–5.
2784	MORTLOCK'S STUDIO LONDON	Mark on wares decorated at Mortlock's Studio in Orchard St., London, c. 1880.

2785   Many printed marks occur in the 1870's and 80's. The example cited occurs on pieces with registration marks for 1875.

2786   Several marks include the name of the manufacturer as well as Mortlock's name.

2787   Printed trade-mark first registered in 1877.

2788   **MORTLOCK'S OXFORD STREET**   Printed name-mark within an oval floral ribbon border, c. 1885–1930.

MORTON   **J. MORTON & SONS,** Lindley Moor Pottery, Nr. Huddersfield, Yorkshire. "Established 450 years", closed 1945. *Earthenwares.*

2789   LINDLEY WARE   Impressed mark, c. 1900–45.

MORTON   **J. T. MORTON,** Filey, Yorkshire. c. 1920–48.* *Leeds-type Creamwares.*

2790   J. T. MORTON FILEY   Incised signature mark, in writing letters, c. 1920–48.

* Subsequently potted for a few years at Scarborough.

MOSELEY   **JOHN MOSELEY,** Cobridge and Burslem. Staffordshire Potteries. c. 1802–22.* *Earthenwares (Wedgwood-type Wares).* Formerly Moseley & Dale.

2791   MOSELEY   Impressed mark, often on Wedgwood-type wares, basalts, etc., c. 1802–22.*

* Contemporary records list two separate manufacturers under John Moseley. One at Cobridge c. 1802–18 and one at Burslem, c. 1809–22.

MOTLEY

JOAN MOTLEY, MISS, London S.W.3, c. 1946–57 and Much Wenlock, Shropshire, c. 1957– . 1946– . *Studio-Pottery, Figures, Dishes, etc.*

2792   MOTLEY

Painted or incised name-mark, 1946–57.

2793

Painted or incised mark, 1946– .

MOUNT

MOUNT SAINT BERNARD ABBEY, Charnwood Forest, Nr. Coalville, Leicestershire. 1949– . *Earthenwares.*

2794

Trade-mark registered in 1951– .

Illustrations and an interesting account of Mount Saint Bernard Abbey pottery is contained in Vincent Eley's *A Monk at the Potters Wheel* (N.D.).

MOUNTFORD

ARTHUR J. MOUNTFORD, Salisbury Works, Burslem. Staffordshire Potteries. 1897–1901. *Earthenwares.*

2795

Printed mark, 1897–1901.

MOUNTFORD

GEORGE THOMAS MOUNTFORD, Alexander Pottery, Stoke. Staffordshire Potteries. 1888–98. *Earthenwares.* Subsequently Myott, Son & Co., q.v.

2796

Printed mark, c. 1888–98.

MOUNTFORD

JOHN MOUNTFORD, John St., Stoke. Staffordshire Potteries. 1857–9.* *Parian figures, etc.* Formerly Keys & Mountford, q.v.

2797   J. MOUNTFORD
              STOKE

Incised signature mark, in writing letters, c. 1857–9.*

* John Mountford is listed as at the Dresden Pottery, Stoke, in James's Directory of 1864, but this is the only reference after 1859.

MOUSEHOLE

MOUSEHOLE POTTERY (Mr. & Mrs. B. Picard), Mousehole, Cornwall. 1953– . *Studio-type Pottery.*

2798		Impressed seal or painted mousehole mark, 1953– .
2799	MOUSEHOLE POTTERY	Incised name of pottery or potters, in writing letters, 1953– .
2800	BILL PICARD	
2801	BIDDY PICARD	
—	M. & P.	*See* Appendix, page 727.
2655 2657a	M. P. Co.	*See* Middlesbrough Pottery Co.
4366	MPW (joined)	*See* Muriel Wright.
2507 2510	M. R.	*See* Reginald Marlow. *See* Ray Marshall.
2809 2810	M. S. & CO.	*See* Myott, Sons & Co. (Ltd.).
2476 2578 2620 (note)	M. & S.	*See* Maddock & Seddon. *See* Mayer & Sherratt. *See* Charles Meigh & Son.
3479	MSP (monogram)	*See* Marjorie Scott-Pitcher.
2458	M. & T.	*See* Machin & Thomas.
2051	M. T. H.	*See* Margaret T. Holden-Jones.
2725	M. & U.	*See* Mogridge & Underhay.
1126	MULL	*See* Joan Crawford.

MURRAY

W. F. MURRAY & CO. (LTD.), Caledonian Pottery, Ruther-glen, Glasgow, Scotland. 1870–98. *Earthenwares, Basaltes, Stonewares, etc.* Subsequently Caledonian Pottery Co. Ltd.

For an account of the various firms working the Caledonian Pottery, see J. A. Fleming's *Scottish Pottery* (1923).

2802

Impressed or printed mark of a lion rampant used by W. F. Murray & Co. late in the 19th century.

MURRAY

WILLIAM S. MURRAY, various addresses in England. Southern Rhodesia from 1940. c. 1919–40+. *Studio-type Pottery.*

2803

W. S. MURRAY
1924
LONDON

Incised or painted signature mark in writing letters, with year added, 1919+.

2804

Impressed seal mark, 1919–40, in England.

William Staite Murray died in February 1962.

For illustrations of William Staite Murray's work and for further information on his career see M. Rose's *Artist Potters in England* (1955) and G. Wingfield Digby's *The Work of the Modern Potter in England* (1952).

MUSSELBURGH

2805

MUSSELBURGH POTTERY, Edinburgh, Scotland. Early 19th century. *Earthenwares.*

The raised crown is a rare mark attributed to the Musselburgh Pottery, c. 1835. A marked Toby jug, in the Royal Scottish Museum, is illustrated in an interesting article by H. J. S. Banks in *Apollo*, December 1957.

2645   M. V. & Co.   *See* Mellor, Venables & Co.

2422   MW   *See* Looe Pottery.
2828   (and joined)   *See* Warren McKenzie.

—	M. W. & Co.	*See* Appendix, page 727.
2548		*See* Massey, Wildblood & Co.
2753		*See* Morgan Wood & Co.
2496	M. W. H.	*See* Malkin, Walker & Hulse.

MYATT

MYATT POTTERY CO., Bilston, Staffordshire. 19th century. *Earthenwares.*

2806

MYATT

Impressed trade-mark registered in 1880, with a note that this mark had been used by applicants and predecessors for 30 years before 1875. Continued to c. 1894.

N.B. A similar mark was used by a Staffordshire potter of this name early in the 19th century, see below.

Advertisements of this firm list "Rockingham, green and yellow ware, Bristol Stoneware, Flower Vases, Plaques in Terra-cotta, Ornamented glazed wares".

JOSEPH (?) MYATT, Lane Delph and Fenton. Staffordshire Potteries. Late 18th to early 19th century. *Earthenwares, Wedgwood-type Wares.*

2807   MYATT

Impressed mark, late 18th to early 19th century.

Many potters of this name were working in the Potteries from c. 1790 into the 19th century. It is difficult to state with certainty which used this mark, or to fix the period to narrow limits. An 18th century red earthenware teapot with the impressed Myatt mark is in the Victoria and Albert Museum. See *British Pottery and Porcelain: an illustrated Encyclopaedia of Marked Specimens.*

N.B. A similar mark was used by the Myatt Pottery Co. to c. 1894, see entry one above.

MYER

DIANA MYER, London N.W.3. 1958– . *Studio-type Pottery.*

2808

Painted mark, 1958– .

MYOTT

MYOTT, SON & CO. (LTD.), Alexander Pottery, Stoke (1898–1902), Cobridge (1902–46) and Hanley (c. 1947–). Staffordshire Potteries. 1898– . *Earthenwares*. Formerly G. T. Mountford, q.v.

2809–12

c. 1898–1902

c. 1900+

c. 1907+

c. 1930+

2813–16

c. 1930+

c. 1936+

China-Lyke (c. 1959+)

c. 1961+

2817

c. 1961+

Various printed marks. A "Stoke" address indicates a date prior to 1903.
Other marks include the name Myott. Cups and small mass-produced objects bear a moulded mark—MYOTT ENGLAND.

2812   MYOTT'S   *See* Myott, Son & Co. (Ltd.), above.

MACINTYRE

JAMES MACINTYRE & CO. (LTD.), Washington Works, Burslem. Staffordshire Potteries. c. 1860– .* *Earthenwares*. Formerly Kennedy & Macintyre.

2818   MACINTYRE   Early printed or impressed marks without "& Co.", c. 1860–7.
2819   J. MACINTYRE

2820   J. M. & CO.   From 1867 several marks occur with the initials J. M. & Co. or a
2821 J. MACINTYRE & CO. monogram or the name in full with "& Co." added, c. 1867–94.

* From c. 1928 only electrical wares have been produced by this firm.

2822–3

An illustrated advertisement of 1888 will be reproduced in the companion illustrated encyclopaedia.

2824–5

Impressed or printed marks with "Ltd." added to title, c.1894–1928.*

* From c. 1928 only electrical wares have been produced by this firm.

MACKEE

2826   A. M.
        L.

ANDREW MACKEE, Foley Works, Longton. Staffordshire Potteries. 1892–1906. *China and Earthenwares.*
Distinguishing initials found on impressed or printed marks of differing design, 1892–1906.

McCLOSKEY

PATRICK McCLOSKEY, Hove, Sussex. 1948– . *Studio-type Pottery, slip-decorated wares and Figures.*

2827

Impressed seal type mark, 1948– .

McKENZIE

2828   M
        W

WARREN McKENZIE, Leach Pottery, Cornwall, 1950–2, Dartington, Devon, 1963– . 1950– .* *Studio-type Pottery.*
Incised or seal mark of initials, 1950–2.*

2828a

Impressed seal mark on Dartington wares, 1963– .*

* Warren McKenzie is an American potter who came to and worked at the Leach Pottery for two years from 1950. He then returned to America but at the time of writing (mid-1963) he has rented T. S. Haile's former pottery at Dartington, Devon, where he proposes to stay for at least one year.

McKNIGHT   **WILLIAM K. McKNIGHT & CO.**, Belfast, Ireland.   1960–.
Wholesalers.

2829   Printed mark on ceramics sold by this firm, 1960–   .

3827   John McLellan   *See* Tewkesbury Pottery.

McNAY   **CHARLES W. McNAY & SONS**, Bridgeness Pottery,
Bo'ness, Scotland.   Est. 1887–1958.   *Earthenwares.*

2830–1   Post-war label type marks incorporating the
trade-name DALMENY, c. 1946–58.

McNEAL   **McNEAL & CO. (LTD.)**, Stanley Pottery, Longton. Staffordshire Potteries.   1894–1906.   *Earthenwares.*

2832   Printed mark, 1894–1906.

N

1249	N	*See* Derby Porcelain Works.
2841		*See* James Neale (& Co.).
2873		*See* New Hall Porcelain Works.
3796	NANKIN WARE	*See* John Tams (& Sons) Ltd.

NANTGARW

NANTGARW CHINA WORKS, Nantgarw, Glamorgan, Wales. c. 1813–14 and 1817–22.* *Porcelain (a fine translucent body)*.

2833	NANT GARW	Impressed marks, 1813–22.*
2834	NANTGARW	

2835   NANT GARW   C. W.

The initials C. W. (sometimes given as G. W.) stand for China Works. A unique plate in the H. Sherman Collection has the words "China Works" in full. Some reproductions bear mark no. 2835, the letters are larger than the originals.

2836   NANTGARW

Painted or stencilled mark.

N.B. This mark was also used on later copies of Nantgarw porcelains.

For further information on the history of the Nantgarw works and for illustrations of typical objects the reader is referred to *The Pottery and Porcelain of Swansea and Nantgarw* by E. M. Nance (1942) and *Nantgarw Porcelain* by W. D. John (1948).

* The exact date of the factory's closure is open to some doubt. Billingsley and Walker left in 1820, There was a sale of stock in May 1821 and a final sale as late as October 1822. See articles by P. J. Williams in *The Antique Collector*, April and August issues, 1963.

NAPER

ELLA NAPER, MRS., St. Buryan, Cornwall. c. 1920–35. *Studio-type Pottery.*

2837   ELLA NAPER   Signature type mark, c. 1920–30.

NAUTILUS

NAUTILUS PORCELAIN CO., Glasgow, Scotland. 1896–1913.* *China, Parian-type Wares, etc.*

2838–9   Printed marks, 1896–1913.*

* From 1898 to 1901 the firm was restyled the POSSIL POTTERY CO. and a revised version of mark no. 2838 above was used, see page 505.

NAYLOR

F. BARRIE NAYLOR, Mees-yr-haf Educational Settlement, Treallaw, Rhondda, Wales. 1954– . *Studio-type Pottery.*

2840   Incised mark, monogram of the initials M. Y. H., 1954– . See Plate I.

—   N. B.   *See* Appendix, page 727.

527–9   NB
          (joined)   *See* Norah Braden.

NEALE

(JAMES) NEALE & CO., Church Works, Hanley. Staffordshire Potteries. c. 1776–c. 86. *Earthenwares, Wedgwood-type Creamwares, Basaltes, etc.* Formerly in partnership with H. Palmer.

2841   N   Impressed initial or name-marks, nos. 2841–4, c. 1776–8.
2842   NEALE   No. 2844 occurs in circular form.
2843   I. NEALE   N.B. All these marks are without the later addition of "&
2844   I. NEALE. HANLEY   Co."

2845   NEALE & CO.   Impressed name-mark with the addition of "& Co.", c. 1778–86.*

* It is probable that this form of mark was continued to c. 1795 by Messrs. Neale & Wilson. The many changes in the title of this firm and its London shop are very complicated. Different styles would seem to have been used at the same period. A Neale & Wilson bill-head is dated 1784.

2846 Crown and C (or G) impressed marks occur on Neale & Co.'s wares, sometimes in conjunction with mark nos. 2842 or 2845, c. 1776–86. A fine part dessert bearing these marks will be found illustrated in the companion illustrated encyclopaedia of marked specimens. This mark has also been seen on wares of the 1820 period.

An interesting article in *The Connoisseur*, December 1947, illustrated a wide range of wares; other examples will be found in *British Pottery and Porcelain: an Illustrated Encyclopaedia of Marked Specimens*.

NEALE

NEALE & BAILEY (or NEALE & CO.), Church Works,* Hanley. Staffordshire Potteries and London. c. 1790–1814. *Earthenwares*. Formerly Neale, Maidment & Bailey.

Although Neale & Bailey are listed by Alfred Meigh as at Church Works, Hanley, it would appear that they were agents for several firms of potters and had premises at 8 St. Paul's Churchyard, London.

There is an overlap of periods with the partnership of Neale & Wilson, see page 463.

The Neale & Bailey firm placed a large order for Derby porcelain in 1793.

2847   NEALE & BAILEY   Impressed or printed name-mark, c. 1790–1814. Rarely found.

NEALE

NEALE, HARRISON & CO., Shaw Works (Providence Works, c. 1885), Hanley. Staffordshire Potteries. 1875–85. *Earthenwares and China*.

2848   N. H. & CO.   Distinguishing detail of several printed marks of differing design: name of the individual pattern is often included, c. 1875–85.

NEALE

NEALE & PALMER, Church Works, Hanley. Staffordshire Potteries. c. 1769–76.* *Earthenwares, Wedgwood-type Wares*. Subsequently J. Neale (& Co.).

2849   NEALE & PALMER   Impressed marks, c. 1769–76.*

* It is not known at what period in the association between James Neale and Humphrey Palmer this mark was used. It is probable that during most of this period the mark of Palmer was used, see page 480.

NEALE

NEALE & WILSON, Church Works, Hanley. Staffordshire Potteries. c. 1784–95. *Earthenwares, Wedgwood-type Wares, Creamwares, etc.* Subsequently R. Wilson, q.v.

2850   NEALE & WILSON   Impressed marks, c. 1784*–95.

2851   NEALE & CO.   It is probable that the mark Neale & Co. was also used at this period.

       * A bill dated April 1784 bears Neale & Wilson's name, and is made out for leaf-edged dishes and plates supplied to Josiah Wedgwood.

—   NEALE & WILTON   *See* Appendix, page 727.

—   NEEID   *See* Appendix, page 727.
           or
—   NEELD

1117   NELSON WARE   *See* Elijah Cotton, Ltd., page 176.
1119

755–6   N
       W   E   *See* Campbell Tile Co. (Ltd.), page 124.
         S

NEWBOLD

C. NEWBOLD, Arncliffe, Skipton, Yorks. 1961– . *Studio-type Pottery (Stonewares).*

2852   Incised or painted marks, 1961– .

2853

426   NEW BRIDGE POTTERY   *See* Edward F. Bodley & Son.

NEWCASTLE

NEWCASTLE POTTERY, various owners, Newcastle upon Tyne, Northumberland. Early 19th century. *Earthenwares.*

    There were several potteries at, or near, Newcastle upon Tyne.

Most Newcastle wares, when marked, bear marks incorporating the name of the manufacturer (see Fell and Sewell, pages 245 and 591) but a mug printed with a Nelson subject of 1805 or shortly after bears mark no. 2854.

2854   NEWCASTLE POTTERY

See the companion illustrated encyclopaedia of marked specimens.

1773   NEW CHINA WORKS   *See* Grainger, Lee & Co.

NEW CHELSEA

NEW CHELSEA CHINA CO. LTD., Chelson St., Longton. Staffordshire Potteries. 1951–61. *China.* Formerly New Chelsea *Porcelain* Co. Ltd., see below. Subsequently Grosvenor China Ltd., q.v.

2855

Printed mark, 1951–61.

NEW CHELSEA

NEW CHELSEA PORCELAIN CO. (LTD.), Bagnall St. (renamed Chelson St.), Longton. Staffordshire Potteries. c. 1912–51.* *China.*
* Firm retitled "NEW CHELSEA CHINA CO. LTD." from September 1951, see entry one above.

2856–9

c. 1912+   c. 1913+   c. 1919+   c. 1936+

2860–1

        Various printed marks.

c. 1936+   c. 1943+

NEWCOMB

2862   NEWCOMB NEEDHAM HARLESTON, NORFOLK

GODFREY (and MARY) NEWCOMB, Needham Pottery, Harleston, Norfolk. April 1958– . *Studio-type Pottery.*
Printed mark, in oval form, 1958– .

| 2863 | MARY NEWCOMB | Incised signature marks, on large examples, in writing letters, |
| 2864 | GODFREY NEWCOMB | 1958– . |

2863   MARY NEWCOMB   *See* Godfrey (& Mary) Newcomb, above.

1245   NEW D.   *See* Derby Porcelain Works.

NEW DEVON

NEW DEVON POTTERY LTD., Newton Abbot, Devon. 1957– . *Earthenwares.*

2865

Printed mark, 1957– .

NEWLAND

WILLIAM NEWLAND, Prestwood, Buckinghamshire. 1948– . *Studio-type Pottery, Ceramic Sculpture and Architectural Wares.*

2866

WN 53

Painted or incised initial mark with year numbers.

2867   William Newland 58

Signature mark, in writing letters, with year.

2868

W N 6 3

Painted mark incorporating initials and year numbers.

NEWLYN

NEWLYN HARBOUR POTTERY (Dennis Lane), Newlyn, Cornwall. 1956– . *Studio-type Pottery.*

2869

D

Incised or impressed initial mark of Dennis Lane, 1956– .

2870   NEWLYN HARBOUR POTTERY

Standard, impressed mark, 1956– .

NEW HALL

NEW HALL POTTERY CO. LTD., New Hall Works, Hanley. Staffordshire Potteries. August 1899 to 1956. *Earthenwares.* Formerly Plant & Gilmore.

2871

Printed mark, c. 1930–51.

2872

Restyled mark, 1951–6. This mark is reversed in this reproduction; it occurs printed in black on a white ground.

NEW HALL

NEW HALL PORCELAIN WORKS (various partnerships), Shelton, Hanley. Staffordshire Potteries. 1781–1835. *Porcelain* (*very rarely Earthenwares*).

    For further information and illustrations of typical wares see *New Hall Porcelain* by G. E. Stringer (1949). R. J. Charleston, in an interesting article in *The Connoisseur* magazine of April 1956, gives interesting information on the closure of the Bristol factory and on the subsequent establishment of the New Hall factory.

2873   N 76
2874   No 76

Painted pattern numbers, usually in red enamel, c. 1781–1812. See Plate 7. See also Postscript page, 745, mark 4403.

    N.B. These pattern numbers occur on the larger pieces only, on teapots, sugar bowls, creamers, etc., not on tea-bowls and saucers. The numbers occur on early hard paste wares.

2875

Printed mark, c. 1812–35. Found on Bone China only.

    Specimens will be found illustrated in the author's *British Pottery and Porcelain 1780–1850* and in *British Pottery and Porcelain: an illustrated Encyclopaedia of Marked Specimens.*

NEWPORT

NEWPORT POTTERY CO. LTD., Newport Lane, Burslem. Staffordshire Potteries. 1920– . *Earthenwares.*

2876–8

c. 1920+   c. 1938+   c. 1945+

Printed marks.

NEW PARK		**NEW PARK POTTERIES LTD.**, Park Works, Longton. Staffordshire Potteries. 1935–57. *Earthenwares.*
2879	N. P. P. LTD.	Distinguishing details of several printed marks of differing design: name of the individual pattern is often included, 1935–57.
2880	NEW PARK POTTERIES LONGTON	
2881	NEW PARK	

NEW PEARL

NEW PEARL POTTERY CO. LTD., Brook Street Potteries, Hanley. Staffordshire Potteries. 1936–41.* Formerly Pearl Pottery Co. Ltd.

2882

Printed mark, 1936–41.*

   * This firm was closed during the war and the factory was sold in 1947.

NEW WHARF

NEW WHARF POTTERY CO., New St., Burslem. Staffordshire Potteries. 1878–94. *Earthenwares.* Subsequently Wood & Son, q.v.

2883	N. W. P. CO.	Distinguishing details used in several printed marks of differing design: name of the individual pattern is often included, 1878–94.
2884	N. W. P. CO. B.	
2885	N. W. P. CO. BURSLEM	

2886

Printed mark, c. 1890–4.

2103   N. H.   *See* N. Hubble.

3662

See St. Agnes Pottery.

2848   N. H. & CO.   *See* Neale Harrison & Co.

NICHOLSON   **THOMAS NICHOLSON & CO.**, Castleford, Yorkshire. c. 1854–71. *Earthenwares.* Formerly Wood & Nicholson. Subsequently Clokie & Masterman.

2887
2888   T. N. & CO.   Distinguishing detail of several printed marks of differing design: name of the individual pattern is often included, as mark no. 2888, c. 1854–71.

NIGLETT   **JOHN NIGLETT**, Bristol, Gloucestershire. c. 1714–54+.* *Painter and Potter.*

In 1714 John Niglett was apprenticed to Thomas Dixon of the Brislington Pottery. He was later a painter and potter on his own account. A Poll Book of 1754 lists Niglett as a potter at Redcliff, Bristol.

2889   N
J E
1733   Initial mark on unique blue painted delft type earthenware dish in the Bristol Museum. See *British Pottery and Porcelain: an illustrated Encyclopaedia of Marked Specimens.*

* His date of retirement or death is not recorded.

2230–1   NJ
(also joined)   *See* Mervyn & Nerys Jude.

2889   N
J E   *See* John Niglett.

2235   NK
(joined)   *See* Nora Kay.

2874   No.
(with number after)   *See* New Hall Porcelain Works.

3151   No. 123
(printed)   *See* F. & R. Pratt Co. (Ltd.).

NORFOLK   **NORFOLK POTTERY CO. LTD.**, Norfolk St., Shelton. Staffordshire Potteries. 1958– . *Earthenwares.*

2890–1    Printed marks, 1958– .

NORMAN		**RICHARD NORMAN**, Chailey, Sussex. Early 19th century. *Earthenwares.*
2892	RICHARD NORMAN	Impressed or incised mark, early 19th century.

NORNESFORD		**NORNESFORD LTD.**, Commerce St., Longton. Staffordshire Potteries. 1920+. *China.*
2893	NORNESFORD MADE IN ENGLAND CHINA	A circular mark incorporating this wording was registered by this firm in 1920. It does not seem to relate to a manufacturer.

NORRIS		**CONINGSBY NORRIS**, 55 Tything, Worcester. c. 1835–1879. *Decorator and Gilder.*
		Norris is included in Bentley's Guide of 1840–1 under the heading: China Gilding and Enamellers. (In Pigot's Directory of 1835 he is listed as a dealer.) In 1851 he is listed as "Manufacturer of Burnished gold china Tea and Breakfast Sets, Desserts, Ornaments &c.". Many of his blanks were obtained from G. F. Bowers of Staffordshire.
2894	C. NORRIS WORCESTER	Rare painted marks in script, c. 1840–60.
2895	WORCESTER	On a porcelain tea-set some few pieces bear the name-mark, no. 2894; most specimens bear only the place name Worcester.

NORTH BRITISH		**NORTH BRITISH POTTERY**, James Miller & Co., Dobbies Loan, Glasgow, Scotland. 1869–75. *Earthenwares.* Subsequently A. Balfour & Co.
2896	J. M. & CO.	Distinguishing initials found on several printed marks of differing design: name of the individual pattern is often included. A garter-shaped mark in the Victoria and Albert Museum collection bears the initials J. M. & Co. with the address "North British Pottery, Glasgow". A lion rampant is in the centre of the garter. This mark is with a letter dated 1872, c. 1869–75.
2897	I. M. & CO.	
2898	J. M. CO.	

NORTH STAFFORDSHIRE		**NORTH STAFFORDSHIRE POTTERY CO. LTD.**, Globe Pottery, Cobridge, then Cobridge Road, Hanley. Staffordshire Potteries. 1940–52.* *Earthenwares.*

    * Pottery taken over by Ridgway Potteries Ltd. and trade-name continued.

2899   Basic trade-mark registered in 1944.

2900   Printed mark, c. 1945–52.

2901   Revised mark, c. 1952+,* without word "Cobridge".
     * Pottery taken over by Ridgway Potteries Ltd. and trade-name continued.

NORTHEN   **W. NORTHEN (& CO.)**, Union Potteries, London S.E. 1847–92. *Stonewares.*

2902   W. NORTHEN POTTER VAUXHALL LAMBETH   Impressed marks occur with name in full, c. 1847–87. "& Co." may occur from 1887 to 1892.

2903   W. NORTHEN POTTER   A fully marked stoneware bottle in the form of a fish will be found included in the companion illustrated encyclopaedia of marked specimens.

NORTHFIELD   **NORTHFIELD HAWLEY POTTERY CO. LTD.**, Northfield Pottery, Rotherham, Yorkshire. 1903–19. *Earthenwares.* Formerly Hawley Bros. (Ltd.), q.v.

2904   Impressed or printed mark, c. 1903*–19.
     * This mark may also have been used by Hawley Bros. before this date.

NORTON   **WILFRED NORTON**, London N.W.3. 1920–56. *Studio-type Pottery.*

2905   Incised or painted mark, 1920–56.

NORWAY		**CARLO NORWAY**, London S.W. c. 1920–35. *Studio-type Pottery and Figures.*

2906   Incised or painted device mark.

Carlo Norway   Incised or painted signature mark, c. 1920–35.

NOTTINGHAM

NOTTINGHAM STONEWARES, c. 1700 into 19th century.

A class of hard, salt glazed stoneware normally of a russet brown colour was produced at, or near, Nottingham in the 18th century. Most examples are unmarked but the following name "marks" or inscriptions have been recorded:

"John Asquith maker, 1756".

"M. C. (Moses Colclough?) maker at Nottm., 1771".

"——Wm. Lockett——", c. 1739–c. 80. See also mark no. 2400.

"Nottingham". Several specimens are recorded with the place name "Nottingham", with various names, inscriptions and dates.

For further information and illustrations see an interesting article by E. N. Stretton, Esq., in *Apollo*, May 1956. Also *British Pottery and Porcelain: an illustrated Encyclopaedia of Marked Specimens.*

NOWELL

C. D. NOWELL, Dane Bank, Disley (c. 1946–51), Prestbury, Nr. Macclesfield (c. 1951–9), Cheshire. 1946–59. *Studio-type Pottery.*

2907   Signature type mark with "DISLEY", c. 1946–51. This occurs with or without the house outline.

2908   Signature type mark with "PRESTBURY", c. 1951–9.

PRESTBURY

2879   N. P. P. Ltd.   *See* New Park Potteries Ltd.

1089	N. S.	*See* Copeland & Garrett.
3653		*See* Josiah Spode.
2900–1	N. S. POTTERY CO. LTD.	*See* North Staffordshire Pottery Co. Ltd.

| | NUMBERS | Number marks occur on several 18th century porcelains. These are painters' marks. Number marks in underglaze blue occur on Bow porcelain, Longton Hall porcelain and Lowestoft porcelain; at this latter factory the painters' marks were normally painted on the inside of the foot-rim, if the article has a foot-rim. |

Numbers painted on New Hall and other porcelains normally relate to the pattern, not the painter. Some pattern numbers on Pinxton porcelains have the letter prefix P.

3931	NV (joined)	*See* Nicholas Vergette.
4100a	N W	*See* Josiah Wedgwood (& Sons Ltd.).
2883	N. W. P. CO.	*See* New Wharf Pottery Co.
	or	
2884	N. W. P. CO. B.	

O

ODNEY

2909	ODNEY
2910	ODNEY HAND MADE ENGLAND

ODNEY POTTERY (LTD.), Grove Farm, Cookham, Berks.
1937–56. *Earthenwares.*
Impressed marks, 1937–56.

2911
2912

J

ĴB

Painted initial marks used by John Bew (1897–1954) at Odney Pottery, c. 1950–4.

2917	O. H. E. C.
	or
2918	O. H. E. C. (L)

See Old Hall Earthenware Co. Ltd.

1638   OLDCOURT WARE   *See* J. Fryer & Son.

OLDFIELD

| 2913 | J. OLDFIELD |
| 2914 | OLDFIELD & CO. |

OLDFIELD & CO., Brampton, Nr. Chesterfield, Derbyshire.
c. 1838–88. *Earthenwares.* Formerly Oldfield, Nadin, Wright, Hewitt Co.
Distinguishing details of several impressed marks of differing design, c. 1838–88.

OLD FORGE

OLD FORGE POTTERY (H. J. C. Sturton), Puttenham, Nr. Guildford, Surrey. 1955– . *Studio-type Pottery, Stonewares.*

2915	THE OLD FORGE POTTERY ENGLAND PUTTENHAM, SURREY	Printed or impressed marks comprising the title and/or the outline of an anvil 1955– .

2916

2626	OLD HALL	*See* Job Meigh (& Sons), page 429.
2922		*See* Old Hall Earthenware Co. Ltd., below.
2922a		*See* Old Hall Porcelain Works Ltd.
3246		*See* A. G. Richardson & Co. Ltd., page 532.

OLD HALL

OLD HALL EARTHENWARE CO. LTD.*, Old Hall Pottery, Hanley.   Staffordshire Potteries.   1861–July 1886. *Earthenwares.*   Formerly Charles Meigh & Son, q.v. Subsequently Old Hall Porcelain Works Ltd., see below.

2917	O. H. E. C.	Distinguishing initials found on several printed marks of differ-
2918	O. H. E. C. (L)	ing design: name of the individual pattern is often included, March 1861–86.

2919
Printed or impressed mark, 1861–86.

2920	IMPERIAL PARISIAN GRANITE (EAGLE CREST) OLD HALL E'WARE CO. (LIMᴰ)	Ornate printed mark, one of several with the title in full, 1861–86.

2921,
2623

INDIAN STONE CHINA   OPAQUE PORCELAIN

Impressed marks formerly used by Charles Meigh and continued by Old Hall Earthenware Co. Ltd.

2922

OLD HALL 1790

Printed trade-mark registered in 1884 and continued by successors, see mark no. 2922a.

* This Company was the first limited liability company in the Staffordshire Potteries and was incorporated in March 1861.

OLD HALL

2922a

OLD HALL PORCELAIN WORKS LTD., Old Hall Pottery, Hanley. Staffordshire Potteries. 1886–1902. *Porcelains and Earthenwares.* Formerly Old Hall *Earthenware* Co. Ltd., see page 474.

Former mark of Old Hall Earthenware Co. Ltd. continued by new company. Used from 1884. "England" added from c. 1891 and continued to c. 1902.

    N.B. The trade-name "Old Hall" was also used by A. G. Richardson & Co. Ltd., see page 532.

OLD HAMPSTEAD

2923   OLD HAMPSTEAD POTTERY CO.

OLD HAMPSTEAD POTTERY CO., London N.W.3. 1948–51. *Earthenwares.* Subsequently retitled "Seviers Pottery Ltd.", q.v.

Printed or impressed mark, 1948–51.

2588
2590   OLD ROYAL CHINA   *See* Sampson Smith Ltd.

738   OLD SUSSEX WARE   *See* Cadborough Pottery.

OLDSWINFORD

2924   OLDSWINFORD

2925

OLDSWINFORD POTTERY,* Hagley Road, Oldswinford, Stourbridge, Worc. 1955–60.* *Studio-type Pottery.*

Basic mark, used with the name of the individual potter, c. 1955–60.

Monogram mark of Howard Bissell, c. 1955– .
    * Title changed to Swincraft Productions, c. 1960. See Howard Bissell.

OLLIVANT

2926   O. P.
2926a   O. P. L.
2927   OLLIVANT

2928

OLLIVANT POTTERIES LTD., Etruscan Works, Stoke. Staffordshire Potteries. 1948–54. *Earthenwares.* Formerly H. J. Ollivant.

Distinguishing initials found on several printed marks of differing design: name of the individual pattern is often included, 1948–54.

A similar mark occurs with the initials O. P. only, c. 1948–54.

O'MALLEY
                    PETER O'MALLEY, Chelsea, London S.W.3.   1953– .
                    Studio-type Pottery.

2929   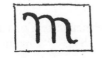   Impressed mark, 1953– .

4218   ONE SHILLING   *See* Winkle & Wood.

ONIONS
                    I. ONIONS, Broseley, Shropshire.   Mid-19th century.
                    Terra-cotta tiles, etc.

2930   I. ONIONS   Stamped mark on terra-cotta reliefs.   An example from
                    Holland House is dated 1847.   See *Country Life*, April 21st,
                    1960, Correspondence.

2926   O. P.   *See* Ollivant Potteries Ltd.
           or
2926a   O. P. L.

2623 OPAQUE PORCELAIN *See* Charles Meigh & Son.
                    See Old Hall Earthenware Co. Ltd.

OPERATIVE
                    OPERATIVE UNION POTTERY, High Street, Burslem.
                    Staffordshire Potteries.   Mid-19th century.   *Earthenwares.*

2931 OPERATIVE UNION Impressed mark on printed and moulded earthenware plates
        POTTERY   in the Victoria and Albert Museum (no. c. 317–1931) and in the
                    British Museum, 1840–50.

                       This "pottery" does not occur in local records.   The
                    address "Society of Operative Potters, High Street, Burslem"
                    is printed on the front of these plates.   Jewitt records "High
                    Street Pottery (Burslem).   This manufactory, usually known
                    as 'Union Bank' through its having been for some time worked
                    by the Potters' Trade Union,——".   Whittingham, Ford &
                    Co. were working this pottery from 1868.

ORANGE
                    ORANGE TREE POTTERY (Mrs. Alethea Short), Rainton
                    Gate, Co. Durham.   1952– .   *Studio-type Pottery.*

2932   Impressed or printed mark.   1952– .

ORCHARD

2933   ORCHARD POTTERY

2933a

OSBORNE

2934

4042   OVENWA

OVERSTONE

2935

Overstone

2936   OVERSTONE
        POTTERY

OXSHOTT

2937   OXSHOTT

2938   HW

2939   hw

ORCHARD POTTERY (B. J. Cotes), Addiscombe, Surrey. 1954–6. *Studio-type Pottery and Stonewares.* B. J. Cotes subsequently worked the Hastings Pottery, q.v. Impressed marks, 1954–6.

OSBORNE CHINA CO. LTD., Mount Pleasant, Longton. Staffordshire Potteries. 1909–40. *China.*

Printed mark, 1909–40.

See Wearside Pottery Co.

OVERSTONE POTTERY, Mrs. Sheila Willison, Moulton, Northants. 1950– . *Studio-type Pottery.*

Painted or incised mark. W. W. used during the Wright & Willison partnership, c. 1950–4.

Impressed or painted mark, c. 1954– .

OXSHOTT POTTERY, Oxshott, Surrey. 1919– . *Studio-type Pottery.*
Standard name-mark, 1919– .

Incised initials of Henry Wren, with or without the name Oxshott, c. 1919–47.

2940   Initials of Mrs. Denise K. Wren, with or without the name Oxshott, c. 1919– .

2941   Impressed Wren seal mark of Miss Rosemary Wren, introduced in 1945. The name "Oxshott" occurs under the bird from 1950.

OXSHOTT

P

275a	P	*See* William Barnes.
2274		*See* Phyllis Keyes.
3000		*See* Seth Pennington.
3022		*See* Pilkingtons.
3048		*See* Pinxton.
3120		*See* Pountney & Allies.
3175		*See* J. & H. Procter (& Co.).
3566a		*See* John Singleman.
4087		*See* Josiah Wedgwood.
4232		*See* Charles Wollaston.
1618	P 66	*See* Audrey H. Forse.
2985	P. & Co.	*See* Pearson & Co.
	or	
3109	P. & Co. Ltd.	*See* Pountney & Co. (Ltd.).
59–60	PA	*See* Peter Ainslie.
873	(also joined)	*See* Peggy Cherniavsky.
3121	P. & A.	*See* Pountney & Allies.
	or	
3122	P. A. B. P.	
863	PAD (OR PATCH)	*See* Chelsea-Derby.
	MARK	*See* Derby Porcelain Works.
		See also Plate 8.
4363	PADMORE	*See* Worcester Porcelains.
—	PALIN & CO.	*See* Appendix.
	or	
	J. PALIN	

2203–5 2943–43a	PALISSY	*See* A. E. Jones (Longton) Ltd. *See* Palissy Pottery Ltd.

PALGRAVE

PALGRAVE POTTERY, Mr. and Mrs. J. Colliers, Tuns, Broome, Nr. Bungay, Suffolk. 1953– . *Studio-type Pottery.*

2942

Impressed, incised or painted P. P. initial mark, 1953– .

PALISSY

PALISSY POTTERY LTD., Chancery Lane, Longton. Staffordshire Potteries. 1946– . *Earthenwares.* Formerly A. E. Jones (Longton) Ltd., q.v.

2943–43a

Former marks of A. E. Jones (Longton) Ltd. continued.

2944–7

2948

Printed marks used in addition to nos. 2943–3a from 1948– .

N.B. Several marks based on the design of no. 2948 occur with the names of different patterns, c. 1946+. "Eastern Scenes" introduced c. 1962.

PALMER

HUMPHREY PALMER, Church Works, Hanley. Staffordshire Potteries. c. 1760–78. *Earthenwares (Wedgwood-type Basaltes, etc.).* Subsequently J. Neale (& Co.), q.v.

2949
2950

PALMER

Impressed marks, c. 1760–78.

N.B. The mark of the partnership Neale & Palmer was also used during some of this period, see mark no. 2849.

2951	H. P.	These initials are listed as an impressed mark of Humphrey Palmer, by T. H. Ormsbee in his *English China and its marks*. The present writer has not seen this mark.

PANKHURST

J. W. PANKHURST & CO., Charles St. and Old Hall St., Hanley. Staffordshire Potteries. 1850–82. *Earthenwares* (*Ironstone, etc.*). Formerly W. Ridgway, q.v.

2952	J. W. P.	Distinguishing details of several printed marks of differing
2953	J. W. PANKHURST	design: name of the individual pattern is often included,
2954	J. W. P. & CO.	c. 1850–82.
2955	J. W. PANKHURST & CO.	N.B. "& Co." added from c. 1852.
2956	J. PANKHURST & CO.	

PARAGON

PARAGON CHINA (CO.) LTD., Atlas Works, Longton. Staffordshire Potteries. 1920– .* *Porcelain.* Formerly Star China Company, q.v.

    N.B. The trade-name "Paragon" was used on marks by the Star China Co. from c. 1900.

2957–60

 c. 1932+   c. 1939–49   c. 1949–52   c. 1952+

2961–3

 c. 1952+    c. 1956+   c. 1957+

Printed marks used from c. 1932 onwards.

   * Taken over by T. C. Wild & Sons Ltd. in 1960 but continued under the same title.

3684–7	PARAGON CHINA	*See* Star China Co.
2211	PARAMOUNT	*See* A. G. H. Jones.

PARAMOUNT

PARAMOUNT POTTERY CO. LTD., Meir Airport (formerly at Ranelagh St., Hanley), Longton. Staffordshire Potteries. 1946– . *Earthenwares.*

2964–5

PARAMOUNT
POTTERY
STAFFORDSHIRE
ENGLAND

Printed marks:
    No. 2964, 1946– .
    No. 2965, 1958– .

PARDOE

THOMAS PARDOE, Bristol, etc.   Early 19th century. *Decorator.*

    Thomas Pardoe was a talented flower painter. He was employed at the Derby Porcelain factory from the mid-1780's, and later at Worcester. He was employed at the Cambrian Pottery at Swansea from about 1795 to c. 1809. In about 1809 Thomas Pardoe went to Bristol where he *decorated* porcelain and earthenware purchased in the white from Coalport and other sources. It is only this independent work that is signed; his earlier painting on Derby, Worcester and Swansea wares are not signed. Thomas Pardoe died in 1823. His son W. H. Pardoe also decorated wares. For further information see E. Morton Nance's *The Pottery and Porcelain of Swansea and Nantgarw* (1942).

2966	Pardoe 28 Bath Street, Bristol Warranted	Painted, in colours or gold, signature marks on wares decorated by Thomas Pardoe. The Bath Street address indicates a date between about 1812 and 1816. Other specimens are dated in full, c. 1809–20. From about 1821 Thomas Pardoe was at Nantgarw.
2966a	Pardoe, Bristol	
2966b	Pardoe, 1814	

PARDOE

WILLIAM HENRY PARDOE, Nantgarw, Neath and Cardiff. c. 1820+. *Decorator.*

2966c   PARDOE. CARDIFF   Rare printed mark on a vase decorated by W. H. Pardoe at Cardiff, c. 1826–35. This artist had earlier painted at Nantgarw and at Neath. He was the son of Thomas Pardoe, see previous entry.

PARK

IRENE PARK, MRS., Padiham, Lancashire. 1952– . *Studio-type Pottery.*

2967      Lancashire witch, painted mark, 1952– .

PARKINSON   **RICHARD PARKINSON LTD.**, Brabourne Lees, Nr.
                                 Ashford, Kent. 1952– . *Porcelain Figures, Animals, etc.
                                 and useful Wares.*

2967a   RICHARD   Name impressed in full often with trade-mark no. 2967b,
          PARKINSON   1952– .
          LTD.

2967b

PARNELL   **GWENDOLEN PARNELL, MISS**, Glebe Place (c. 1916–17),
                                 Upper Cheyne Row (c. 1918–21), Paradise Walk (c. 1921–36),
                                 Chelsea, London S.W.3. 1916–36. *Pottery figures, etc.*

2968   CHELSEA CHEYNE   Incised mark used from July 1918. This occurs with slight
          1923   variations, and often has the year of manufacture added.

2969   G. P.   The initials G. P. with a drawing of a rabbit was used by Miss
                                 Parnell as a personal mark, c. 1916–36.
                                    For illustrations of typical Parnell "Chelsea Cheyne"
                                 figures see *The Cheyne Book of Chelsea China and Pottery*
                                 (1924), Plates 36–7.

PARR   **HARRY PARR**, 14a Cheyne Row, Chelsea, London S.W.3.
                                 c. 1919–40 and 1945+.* *Studio-type Pottery figures.*

2970   HY PARR   Incised or impressed signature mark—in writing letters usually
          CHELSEA 1922   with year of production added, c. 1919–40.
                                    The Cheyne Book of Chelsea China and Pottery (1924) illus-
                                 trates four typical Parr figures.

                                    * Harry Parr produced some ceramic sculpture for a few years from
                                 1945.

PARROTT

PARROTT & CO. (LTD.), Albert Street Pottery, Burslem. Staffordshire Potteries. c. 1921– .* *Earthenwares.*

2971

Printed trade-mark registered in 1921.

2972

Slightly redrawn mark, c. 1935– . The trade-name "Coronet Ware" may occur with this mark.

* The *manufacture* of pottery has been discontinued.

PARTRIDGE

JUDITH PARTRIDGE, MISS, Lewes, Sussex. 1954–61 and 1962– . *Studio-type Pottery, Majolica.*

2973

Painted mark, 1954–61. An impressed seal of the joined initials J.P. also occurs without the word "Lewes".

2973a   RODMELL
     SUSSEX. ENGLAND.

The painted monogram no. 2973 has been used with the wording "Rodmell, Sussex, England" since September 1962. Rodmell is near Lewes.

2974

Incised or painted monogram on wares made at Alan Caiger-Smith's Aldermaston Pottery, 1961 to March 1962.

2540   PATENT IRONSTONE   *See* G. M. & C. J. Mason, page 418.
          CHINA

PATIENCE

THOMAS PATIENCE, Temple St., Bristol. Pre-1785. *Stonewares.*

2975   PATIENCE

The impressed mark "Patience" has been recorded on 18th century stonewares and probably relates to the above Thomas Patience, mentioned by Jewitt.

PATTERSON

PATTERSON & CO. (George Patterson), Sheriff Hill Pottery, Newcastle upon Tyne, Northumberland. 1830*–1904. *Earthenwares.*

2976 PATTERSON & CO. Several printed or impressed marks incorporating this name are believed to relate to the above firm, 1830–1904.

2977 PATTERSON & CO. TYNE POTTERY†
N.B. It should be noted that other potters or firms named Patterson worked the near-by Carr's Hill Pottery, also the St. Anthony's Pottery:

Carr's Hill Pottery
    T. Patterson, c. 1887–8.
    Patterson & Parkinson, c. 1889–90.
    Patterson & Scott, c. 1891–2.
St. Anthony's Pottery
    Patterson & Parkinson, c. 1891–2.
    T. Patterson, c. 1893–1908.

* The name Patterson & Co. occurs in an 1837 directory but some wares appear to pre-date this.
† Examples with mark no 2977 appear to be of the 1820-30 period.

PATTISON

ALFRED PATTISON, 18th or early 19th century.

2978 ALFRED PATTISON This signature mark, in writing letters, occurs on a stoneware figure of a greyhound in the Glaisher Collection at the Fitzwilliam Museum, Cambridge. It is of a type of stoneware made in the Nottingham district.

PATTISON

J. PATTISON, High St., Lane End., Longton. Staffordshire Potteries. c. 1818-30. *Earthenware figures.*

2979 JOHN PATTISON 1825
This very rare signature mark, in writing letters, occurs on an earthenware figure of Venus* in Captain E. Bruce George's collection.
N.B. The rate records, etc., list James not John Pattison.

* This figure is illustrated by R. G. Haggar in his *Staffordshire Chimney Ornaments* (1955), Plate 70.

PAYNE

PAYNE, Salisbury, Wiltshire. c. 1834–41. *Retailer.*

2980 PAYNE SARUM This printed mark occurs on wares decorated with local views, etc., and sold by this retailer, c. 1834–41.

658 p b *See* Yvette (& Paul) Brown.

650	P. B.	*See* Percy Brown.
3104	or	*See* Poulson Bros. (Ltd.).
3105	P. BROS.	

| 651 | PB
(joined) | *See* Percy Brown. |

| 3132 | P. & B. | *See* Powell & Bishop. |

| 3038 | P. B. & CO. | *See* Pinder Bourne & Co. |

| — | P. B. F. B. | *See* Appendix. |

| 3043 | P. B. & H. | *See* Pinder Bourne & Hope. |

| 3054 | P. B. L. | *See* Plant Bros. |

| 3137 | P. B. & S. | *See* Powell, Bishop & Stonier. |

| 3017 | P. & C. | *See* Physick & Cooper. |

| 539 | PEACOCK POTTERY | *See* E. Brain & Co. Ltd., page 97. |

| 2988 | PEANCO | *See* Pearson & Co. (Chesterfield) Ltd. |

PEARCE

ALFRED B. PEARCE, Ludgate Hill, London E.C.4. 1866–1940. *Retailers.*

| 2981 | ALFRED B. PEARCE
39 LUDGATE HILL
LONDON | Printed marks occur with the name and address of this firm of retailers, 1866–1940. |

| 4086 | PEARL | *See* Josiah Wedgwood (& Sons Ltd.). |

| 4260– | PEARL CHINA | *See* Enoch Wood & Sons. |

PEARL

PEARL POTTERY CO. (LTD.), Brook Street Potteries, Hanley. Staffordshire Potteries. 1894–1936. *Earthenwares.* Subsequently New Pearl Pottery Co. Ltd., q.v.

2982 Printed or impressed mark, 1894–1912.

2983 Printed mark, 1912+.

2984  Printed mark, 1914–36.
 N.B. From c. 1930–42 a similarly named firm, "Pearl Pottery (Burslem) Ltd.", was working at the Sytch Pottery, Burslem.

PEARL WARE
or
PEARL STONE WARE

Name for special earthenware body, used by many 19th century firms. Impressed or incorporated in printed marks. See also Chetham & Woolley, page 144. The impressed mark PEARL or WEDGWOOD PEARL occurs on Wedgwood wares of the 1840–68 period, mark no. 4086.

PEARSON

PEARSON & CO., Whittington Moor Potteries, Chesterfield, Derbyshire. Est. c. 1805– . *Earthenwares and Stonewares.*

2985   P. & CO.
2986   PEARSON & CO.
          WHITTINGTON
          MOOR

Early impressed mark, prior to 1880.

2987  Impressed or printed mark, c. 1880+.

PEARSON & CO.
(CHESTERFIELD) LTD.

Re-named "PEARSON & CO. (CHESTERFIELD) LTD.". c. 1925.

2988  Trade-name, c. 1928+. The trade-name "PEANCO" was also used.

2989   Post-war standard trade-mark, to present day.

PEARSON   COLIN PEARSON, The Quay Pottery, Aylesford, Kent. 1962– . *Studio-type Pottery.*

2990   Impressed seal mark, 1962– .
    Colin Pearson was formerly at the Aylesford Priory Pottery and used initial marks, C.P. See page 43.

PEARSON   JAMES PEARSON (LTD.), Oldfield and London Potteries, Brampton, Nr. Chesterfield, Derbyshire. 19th century to 1939.* *Stonewares, etc.*
    Early wares unmarked.

2991   J. P. LTD.   Impressed or printed initial mark, 1907+.

2992   Trade-name, 1920+.

2993   Printed mark on cooking wares, etc., 1930+.
    * This firm was merged with "Pearson & Co. (Chesterfield) Ltd." in 1939.

—   R. PEARSON   *See* Appendix.

PELLATT   APSLEY PELLATT (& CO. LTD.), various addresses, London. c. 1789– . *Retailers.*

2994   APSLEY PELLATT & CO.   The name of this old established firm of china and glass retailers occurs on some marks, mainly during the second half of the 19th century or during the present century.

PELLATT		**PELLATT & GREEN**, St. Paul's Church Yard, London. c. 1805–30. *Retailers.*
2995	PELLATT & GREEN LONDON	Marks sometimes occur with the name of this firm of retailers. Swansea porcelain has been recorded with the name of this firm, c. 1805–30.

PELLATT		**PELLATT & WOOD**, Baker Street, London. c. 1870–90. *Retailers.*
2996	PELLATT & WOOD	Printed marks incorporate the name of this firm, c. 1870–90.

—	PENCOYD	*See* Appendix, page 728.

PENDLEY

PENDLEY POTTERY (Murray Fieldhouse), Pendley Manor, Tring, Hertfordshire. 1949– . *Studio-type Pottery, Stonewares.*

2997-9

Incised or printed marks, c. 1949– . P. P. mark stands for Pendley Pottery. The initials M. F. for Murray Fieldhouse; other initials occur on wares by other potters working at Pendley.

PENNINGTON

SETH (or **JAMES**) **PENNINGTON**, Liverpool. c. 1760–80+. *China and Earthenwares.*

3000   P

Rare painted mark in gold or colour, c. 1760–80 (approximate dates). *James* Pennington worked c. 1761–74 but it is not certain which Liverpool potter of this name employed the P mark.

    Most Liverpool wares are unmarked.

3000a   PENNINGTON

This name-mark is given by some authorities. It is unlikely that S. or J. Pennington used their name as a mark. Other potters of this name were working in Staffordshire in the 19th century.

3001   **HP**   The joined initials HP occur on Liverpool type porcelains of the 1780 period, and probably relate to the Pennington's, rather than the Herculaneum Pottery (which specimens appear to pre-date). Two examples with this mark are illustrated in the *Connoisseur*, October 1940. It should be noted that the P marked child's teaset illustrated in this same article as made by Pennington is of mid-19th century date and cannot relate to any Liverpool potters of this name.

3470–1   PENRITH   *See* A. Schofield.

PEOVER   **FREDERICK** (or **MRS. ANN**) **PEOVER**, High Street, Hanley. Staffordshire Potteries. 1818–22. *Porcelain.*

3002   PEOVER   Impressed name-mark, very rarely found, 1818–22.

PERRETT   **BETTY PERRETT, MRS.**, Storrington, Sussex. 1950– . *Studio-type Pottery, Tin-glazed Earthenwares.*

3003   PERRETT   Incised or painted name-mark, 1950– .

PERRIN   **IDA PERRIN, MRS.**, Bushey Heath, London. 1921–33. *Decorator of Earthenwares.*

3004      This mark (without the words Bushey Heath) was registered by I. S. Perrin in 1924.

3004a   F. P.   Fred Passenger (formerly with William De Morgan) painted pottery and tiles for Mrs. Perrin in the De Morgan style to about 1933. His initials may occur on some specimens.

PEYMAN   **JOSEPHINE PEYMAN, MISS**, Kensington, London S.W.7. 1949–59. *Studio-type Pottery and Animal models.*

3005   JOSEPHINE PEYMAN
1958   Incised or painted signature mark, with year, 1949–59.

4007	P. & F. W.	*See* Peter & Francis Warburton.
596	P. G.	*See* Sampson Bridgwood & Son (Ltd.).
2052 2054	PH (also joined)	*See* P. Holdsworth.
1940	P. H. CO.	*See* Hanley Porcelain Co.
2048	P. H. & CO.	*See* P. Holdcroft & Co.
3155 3156	P. H. G. or P. H. & G.	*See* Pratt, Hassall & Gerrard.

PHILLIPS

3006

PHILLIPS (various initials and styles), various addresses, London. c. 1799–1929. *Retailers*.

Many printed marks were used on wares sold by this firm. The following changes in style and address give an approximate guide to dating:

W. P. & G. Phillips, 358–9 Oxford Street, c. 1858–97.
W. P. & G. Phillips, 155 New Bond Street, c. 1859–89.
Phillips & Co., 15–21 Mount Street, c. 1897–1906.
Phillips Ltd., 43–4 Bond Street, c. 1908–29.

PHILLIPS

3007   EDWARD PHILLIPS
SHELTON
STAFFORDSHIRE

EDWARD PHILLIPS, Cannon Street, Shelton. Staffordshire Potteries. 1855–62. *Earthenwares*.

Printed marks incorporating the name in full, 1855–62.

PHILLIPS

3008   PHILLIPS
LONGPORT
3008a   E. & G. P.
3009   E. & G. PHILLIPS
LONGPORT

EDWARD & GEORGE PHILLIPS, Longport. Staffordshire Potteries. 1822–34. *Earthenwares (blue printed, etc.)*. Subsequently G. Phillips, see below.

Distinguishing details of several printed marks of differing design: name of the individual pattern is often included, 1822–34.

PHILLIPS

GEORGE PHILLIPS, Longport. Staffordshire Potteries. 1834–48. *Earthenwares.*

3010   PHILLIPS

3011

Different impressed or printed marks with the name Phillips or G. Phillips occur, often with the name of the pattern, c. 1834–48. The Staffordshire knot device (3011) occurs with the words "Phillips" and "Longport".

3012

PHILLIPS

JOHN PHILLIPS (& CO.), North Hylton Pottery, Sunderland, Durham. c. 1815–67. *Earthenwares.* Formerly Maling, q.v.

3013   JOHN PHILLIPS
        HYLTON POT
             WORKS

3013a   J. PHILLIPS
        HYLTON POTTERY

2484a   HYLTON POT
             WORKS

Distinguishing details of several printed marks of differing design. Some of these name-marks occur as part of the printed design, c. 1815–67.

N.B. John Phillips also owned and worked the Garrison Pottery at Sunderland and John Phillips marks without the Hylton address may relate to the Garrison works. See "Sunderland", page 603.

3014   FROM THE MANU-
        FACTORY OF
        J. PHILLIPS,
        SUNDERLAND

PHILLIPS

JOHN PHILLIPS & CO., Aller Pottery, Newton Abbot, Devon. 1868–87. *Earthenwares, mainly architectural.* Subsequently "Aller Vale Art Pottery", q.v.

3015   ΦΙΛΕΩ ΙΠΠΟΝ.

Printed or impressed mark *with horse's head*, 1868–87.

PHILLIPS

PHILLIPS & MALING, North Hylton Pottery, Sunderland, Durham. 1780–1815. *Earthenwares.* Formerly Maling, q.v. Subsequently J. Phillips, q.v.

3016   PHILLIPS & MALING   This mark is said to occur, although the Director of the local museum has not seen a marked specimen, 1780–1815.   See also Maling, page 408.

PHILLIPS   **THOMAS PHILLIPS & SON**, Furlong Pottery, Burslem. Staffordshire Potteries.   c. 1845-6.   *Earthenwares.*

3016a   T. PHILLIPS & SON   Printed or impressed name-mark, c. 1845-6.
        BURSLEM

1615   PHOENIX CHINA   *See* Thomas Forester & Sons (Ltd.).
           or
1615a   PHOENIX WARE

PHYSICK   **PHYSICK & COOPER**, Anchor Works, Hanley.   Staffordshire Potteries.   1899–1900.   *Earthenwares.*   Formerly Physick & Brassington.   Subsequently Art Pottery Co., q.v.

P & C

3017   Printed mark, c. 1899–1900.

        ENGLAND

2800-1   Bill or Biddy   *See* Mousehole Pottery.
            PICARD

PICKARD   **BAAJIE PICKARD**, Glasgow. Scotland.   1953–   .   *Studio-type Pottery—Stonewares.*

3018–20   *Baajie Pickard.*   BP

          Painted marks, 1953–

PIERCE   **W. PIERCE & CO.**, Benthall, Shropshire.   c. 1800–18. *Earthenwares.*

3021   W. PIERCE &CO.   Chaffers records this name-mark, and states that it pre-dates the year 1818, when Bathurst succeeded W. Pierce.

PILKINGTON'S

3022   P

3023

3024-5

PILKINGTON'S TILE & POTTERY CO. LTD., Clifton Junction, Nr. Manchester, Lancashire. *Earthenwares, Lustre and glaze effects.* Ornamental wares from c. 1897 to March 1938 and 1948–57.

Early wares, c. 1897–1904, were unmarked or bear an incised "P".

Trade-mark registered in 1904. Printed c. 1904–5, subsequently impressed to 1914.

N.B. Roman numerals occur under this mark and denote the year of potting, vi = 1906.

Impressed marks, the basic mark without the words occurs on small items. Some wares bear only the words "ROYAL LANCASTRIAN", c. 1914–38. "England" was added to c. 1920. "Made in England", c. 1920–38.

The initials or monogram of the designer or artist occur on most items:

3026-30

3031-5

These initials are those of: Lewis F. Day; R. Joyce; Jessie Jones; Gordon M. Forsyth; Gwladys Rodgers; Walter Crane; C. E. Cundall; Annie Burton; William S. Mycock; and Dorothy Dacre.

For further information see A. Lomax's *Royal Lancastrian Pottery* (1957) or *Apollo*, October 1961.

3036

Messrs. Pilkington's re-opened their pottery department (as opposed to their main concern, the production of tiles) in August 1948 and continued this to August 1957. The initial P with the outline of the Lancastrian Rose was used as a mark.

PINCOMBE

HELEN PINCOMBE, The Forge, Oxshott, Surrey.   1950– .
Studio-type Pottery.

3037      Impressed seal mark, c. 1950– .

PINDER

PINDER, BOURNE & CO., Nile St., Burslem.   Staffordshire Potteries.   January 1862–82* *Earthenwares.*   Formerly
Pinder, Bourne & Hope, see below.

3038   P. B. & CO.   Distinguishing details of several printed marks of differing
3039   PINDER, BOURNE   design: name of the individual pattern is often included,
            & CO.   1862–82.

3040–2

Several variations of the above marks occur.   Impressed month
and year number may be found on some specimens, 7.81 for
July 1881.

   * The firm and works were purchased by Doultons in 1878 for £12,000
but the title was retained until early in 1882 when it became "Doulton &
Co. Ltd." see page 213.

PINDER

PINDER, BOURNE & HOPE, Fountain Place (c.1851–60),
Nile Street (c. 1860–2), Burslem.   Staffordshire Potteries.
1851 to January 1862. *Earthenwares.*   Formerly Thomas Pinder,
see below.   Subsequently Pinder, Bourne & Co., see above.

3043   P. B. & H.   Distinguishing details of several printed marks of differing
3044   PINDER BOURNE   design: name of the individual pattern is often included, 1851
            & HOPE   to January 1862.

3045

PINDER		**THOMAS PINDER**, Swan Bank Works, Burslem. Staffordshire Potteries. 1849–51. *Earthenwares.* Subsequently Pinder, Bourne & Hope, see previous entry.
3046	PINDER BURSLEM	Printed or impressed mark, c. 1849–51.

PINXTON WORKS

PINXTON WORKS (John Coke, William Billingsley, John Cutts, etc.) Pinxton, Derbyshire. c. 1796–1813. *Porcelains.*

Most Pinxton porcelains are unmarked. Various impressed letters occur and an interesting entry in the factory records for Feb. 25th, 1797, reads "Twenty letters to mark ware at 1½d." Some puce marked Derby porcelains of the 1790's also have impressed letters, which are workmen's marks.

Other marks included the written name Pinxton; this is rare but occurred on a fine fluted teaset sold by Messrs. Godden of Worthing Ltd. Other examples are recorded. Sometimes the pattern number is prefixed by the cursive letter P, or this letter may occur without a number.

3047–51

After William Billingsley left c. 1799 John Coke continued and rarely used a mark of a crescent and a star (from his family arms) and arrow-like marks. c. 1799–1806. The factory was subsequently worked by John Cutts. During the closing years the Pinxton works may have been only a decorating establishment. Cutts left for Wedgwoods in 1813 and the Pinxton works closed.

The reader is referred to two very interesting articles (based on factory records) by I. M. Booth in the *Connoisseur*, January and February 1963 and a recent book, *The Pinxton China Factory*, C. L. Exley (1963). Basic information is contained in the present writer's *British Pottery and Porcelain, 1780–1850* and typical specimens will be found illustrated in *British Pottery and Porcelain: an illustrated Encyclopaedia of Marked Specimens.*

PITCAIRNS

PITCAIRNS LTD., Pinnox Pottery, Tunstall. Staffordshire Potteries. 1895–1901. *Earthenwares.*

3052		Printed mark, 1895–1901.

2053	P. J. H.	*See* P. Holdsworth.
2300	Pk	*See* Philip Knight.
3060	P. L.	*See* R. H. & S. L. Plant (Ltd.).
2336–7 3129	PL (joined)	*See* Peter Lane. *See* Alfred & Louise Powell.

PLANT

BENJAMIN PLANT, Lane End, Longton. Staffordshire Potteries. c. 1780–1820. *Earthenwares*.

3053

Rare incised signature marks, c. 1780–1820. These dates are approximate only. A rare signed and dated (1814) example will be found illustrated in *British Pottery and Porcelain: an illustrated Encyclopaedia of Marked Specimens*.

PLANT

PLANT BROS., Crown Pottery, Burslem (c. 1889–98), then Stanley Works, Longton. Staffordshire Potteries. 1889–1906. *China*. Subsequently combined with R. H. & S. L. Plant, q.v.

3054

Printed mark, 1898–1906. Note the initial L for Longton. A similar mark without L or with B may occur before 1898.

PLANT

ENOCH PLANT, Crown Pottery, Burslem. Staffordshire Potteries. 1898–1905. *Earthenwares*.

3055

Printed or impressed crown mark, 1898–1905.
    N.B. Other manufacturers used this mark, see pages 757–8.

PLANT

J. PLANT & CO., Stoke Pottery, Stoke. Staffordshire Potteries. 1893–1900. *Earthenwares.* Formerly J. & R. Plant. Stoke Pottery taken over by Grimwade Bros., c. 1900.

3056

Printed mark, 1893–1900. This mark may also have been used by predecessors, c. 1889–93.

PLANT

R. H. PLANT & CO., Carlisle Works, Longton. Staffordshire Potteries. 1881–98. *China.* Subsequently R. H. & S. L. Plant, q.v.

3057

Printed mark, 1881–98.

PLANT

R. PLANT & SONS, Warwick Works, Longton. Staffordshire Potteries. 1895–1901. *Earthenwares.* Formerly Plant & Baggaley.

3058

Printed mark, 1895–1901. An illustrated advertisement of 1895, showing typical forms and patterns, will be reproduced in the companion illustrated encyclopaedia.

PLANT

R. H. & S. L. PLANT (LTD.), Tuscan Works, Longton. Staffordshire Potteries. c. 1898– . *China.* Formerly R. H. Plant, q.v.

    Several printed marks occur incorporating the initials R. H. & S. L. P, or the trade-name "Tuscan", c. 1898 onwards. Examples are reproduced below:

3059–62

c. 1898+

c. 1902+

c. 1907+

c. 1936+

3063–5   TUSCAN CHINA
          METALLISED
          MADE IN ENGLAND
          c. 1936+

c. 1947+

c. 1961+

N.B. Year numerals occur in or below the later marks, i.e. 62 indicates 1962.

PLANT

THOMAS PLANT, Lane End.   Staffordshire Potteries. 1825–50.   *Earthenware figures, etc.*
    Son of Benjamin Plant, page 497.

3066   T P

Rare painted mark on earthenware figures, etc., c. 1825–50. A rare earthenware lion with these initials is illustrated in *British Pottery and Porcelain: an illustrated Encyclopaedia of Marked Specimens.*

PLEYDELL

KATHARINE PLEYDELL-BOUVERIE, various addresses; from 1946 at Kilmington Manor, Nr. Warminster, Wiltshire. 1925– .   *Studio-type Pottery, Stonewares.*
    Katharine Pleydell-Bouverie was one of Bernard Leach's first pupils at St. Ives in 1924.

3067–8

Various incised initial or seal marks, 1925– .
    For illustrations of Katharine Pleydell-Bouverie's work see Muriel Rose's *Artist Potters in England* (1955) and G. Wingfield Digby's *The Work of the Modern Potter in England* (1952).

PLOWMAN

THOMAS PLOWMAN, Clay Brook Pottery, Hammersmith, 1958–63.   Marchmont Street, London W.C.1.   1963– . *Studio-type Pottery.*

3069

Impressed seal type mark, used on individual items, 1958– . See Plate 2.

3070   C. B. P.

Impressed initials on standard, repeatable items.   The initials stand for Clay Brook Pottery.   This form of mark was only used from c. 1960 to 1962.

3070a   T. P.

The initials T. P. (sometimes joined) are painted on some wares which do not bear the standard impressed mark no. 3069, c. 1960– .

PLYMOUTH		**PLYMOUTH PORCELAIN WORKS** (William Cookworthy) Plymouth, Devon. 1768–70.* *Porcelain (hard paste).*
3071	2	Painted (sign for tin) mark in underglaze blue, or in overglaze enamel, c. 1768–70. Workmen's marks may occur but are not factory marks.
508	T°	The impressed T° mark was also used at Plymouth but also occurs on Bristol as well as Bow and Worcester porcelains.

For full details of the history of Plymouth Porcelain, and illustrations, see F. Severne Mackenna's *Cookworthy's Plymouth and Bristol Porcelain* (1946) and B. Watney's *English Blue and White Porcelain of the 18th Century* (1963). Some specimens will be found illustrated in *British Pottery and Porcelain: an illustrated Encyclopaedia of Marked Specimens.*

* In 1770 the works were moved to Bristol and joined with the Bristol factory (page 103). If the above tin mark occurs with the Bristol cross the date is subsequent to 1770.

PLYMOUTH		**PLYMOUTH POTTERY CO. LTD.**, Coxside, Plymouth, Devon. 1856–63. *Earthenwares.*
3072	 P. P. COY. L. STONE CHINA	Jewitt records this mark in his *Ceramic Art of Great Britain* but the initials could also relate to other firms at a later date: Pearl Pottery Co. Ltd., c. 1894–1936. Primrose Pottery Co. Ltd., c. 1912–13. Paramount Pottery Co. Ltd., c. 1947.
3842–3	PMT (joined)	*See* Pauline Thompson.
1016	P. N.	*See* Ernest Collyer.

POCOCK		**ALFRED POCOCK**, Slinfold, Sussex. c. 1920–35. *Studio-type Pottery.*
3073	19 ⌐AP 27.	Incised or painted monogram mark, with year. A. L. Pocock was formerly gem sculptor to the Russian Court Jewellers.

PODMORE

PODMORE CHINA CO., Sylvan Works, Hanley. Staffordshire Potteries. 1921–41. *China.* Closed 1941–6, subsequently Sylvan Pottery Ltd., q.v.

3074

Printed mark, 1921–41.

PODMORE

PODMORE, WALKER & CO. (PODMORE, WALKER & WEDGWOOD), Well Street (c. 1834–53), Amicable Street (c. 1850–9), Swan Bank (c. 1853–9), Tunstall. Staffordshire Potteries. 1834–59. *Earthenwares.* Subsequently Wedgwood & Co. (Amicable Street Works) and Beech & Hancock (Swan Bank Works), q.v.

3075
3076

P. W. & CO.

Distinguishing detail of several printed marks of differing design: name of the individual pattern is often included, 1834–59. Mark no. 3076 is a typical example.

3077

P. W. & W.

The initials P. W. & W. for Podmore Walker & Wedgwood may occur, c. 1856–9.

3078
3079

WEDGWOOD
WEDGWOOD & CO.

It should be noted that the above firm also used the name (and mark) "Wedgwood" or "Wedgwood & Co.".

3080

The printed mark here reproduced is taken from official files and occurs on a pattern registered by Podmore Walker & Co. in 1849. The "& Co." was Enoch Wedgwood but it was found advantageous to use the name Wedgwood alone. From c. 1860 the firm was retitled "Wedgwood & Co.", see page 655. Marks nos. 3078–80 are often taken for those of the main Wedgwood firm.

POINTON

POINTON & CO. LTD., Norfolk St. Works, Hanley. Staffordshire Potteries. 1883–1916. *China.* Formerly R. G. Scrivener & Co., q.v.

3081

Printed mark, 1883–1916. "England" added below from 1891.

3081a

POINTON

Impressed mark, 1883–1916.

POLESWORTH		**POLESWORTH POTTERY**, Polesworth, Warwickshire. c. 1800. *Earthenwares, slip decorated.*
3082	POLESWORTH POTTRY	Inscription on slip-decorated earthenware jug, dated 1801, in the Fitzwilliam Museum, Cambridge. This should not be regarded as a mark and it is probable that all Polesworth wares are unmarked.

POLLARD

WILLIAM POLLARD, Swansea and Carmarthen, Wales. c. 1829–32. *China painter.*

William Pollard (1803–54) was a talented painter of flowers employed at the Swansea works. His factory work is unsigned but rare pieces decorated on his own account are recorded with the place name Carmarthen and these belong to the 1829–32 period. His career and work are discussed at length in E. Morton Nance's *The Pottery and Porcelain of Swansea and Nantgarw* (1942).

3083	Pollard, Carmarthen	Painted mark on porcelains decorated by William Pollard at Carmarthen, Wales, c. 1829–32.
2515	POMONA HOUSE	*See* Martin Bros.
1900	PONTHIR	*See* Frank Hamer.
—	R. POOL	*See* Appendix, page 728.
—	POOLE or POOLE POTTERY or POOLE POTTERY LTD.	*See* Carter, Stabler & Adams Ltd.

POOLE

J. E. POOLE, Hadderidge, Burslem. Staffordshire Potteries. c. 1796–7+ ? *Earthenwares.*

3084	POOLE	The impressed mark POOLE occurs on late 18th or early 19th century wares. Haggar in *The Concise Encyclopaedia of English Pottery and Porcelain* attributes this mark to John Ellison Poole, who had formerly been in partnership as:

Lakin & Poole, c. 1791–5; Poole Lakin & Shrigley, c. 1795; Poole & Shrigley, c. 1795–7.

John Poole was adjudged bankrupt in 1797 but may have re-established himself as a potter after this.

2314	POOLE, LAKIN & CO. *See* Lakin & Poole.

POOLE

POOLE POTTERY LTD., Poole, Dorset. February 1963– .
Earthenwares. Formerly Carter, Stabler & Adams Ltd., q.v.

Former marks (nos. 790, 792–a) of Carter, Stabler & Adams
Ltd. continued by retitled company. See Carter, Stabler &
Adams Ltd.

POOLE

RICHARD POOLE, Shelton, Hanley. Staffordshire Potteries.
1790–5. *Earthenwares.*

3085   R. POOLE   Impressed mark, 1790–5.

792a   POOLE STUDIO   *See* Carter, Stabler & Adams (Ltd.).

POOLE

THOMAS POOLE, Cobden Works, Longton. Staffordshire
Potteries. 1880–1952.* *China and Earthenwares.* Formerly
in partnership as Johnson & Poole.

3086   Impressed or printed crown mark (also used by other manufacturers, see pages 757–8, 1880–1912).

3087–8       Printed marks, 1912+.

3089   Printed mark, c. 1929–40.

3090   Printed mark, c. 1940–52.*

* Firm retitled "*Thomas Poole (Longton) Ltd.*" c. 1925. This firm was
merged with Gladstone China Ltd. in 1948 and after 1952 continued under
"Royal Stafford China", see page 553.

POOLE		**POOLE & UNWIN**, Cornhill Works, Longton. Staffordshire Potteries. 1871–6. *Earthenwares, Figures, Stonewares, etc.* Formerly Poole, Sutherland & Hallam. Subsequently Joseph Unwin (& Co.), q.v.
3091	P. & U.	Printed or impressed initial mark, often in a diamond shaped outline, c. 1871–6. A very rare Staffordshire earthenware figure with this mark is illustrated in the companion encyclopaedia of marked specimens.
	Porcelain Opaque	Term for a special earthenware body, used by several 19th century firms including Sampson, Bridgwood & Son and Charles Meigh.

PORT DUNDAS		**PORT DUNDAS POTTERY CO. LTD.**, Bishop St., Port Dundas, Glasgow, Scotland. Mid-19th century to 1932. *Stonewares.* Formerly James Miller & Co.
3092	PORT DUNDAS GLASGOW POTTERY	Impressed or painted marks including the name "Port Dundas", mid-19th century to 1932.
3093	PORT DUNDAS GLASGOW POTTERY COY	A patented process of printing was employed on some utilitarian stonewares. An interesting account is given in Jewitt's *The Ceramic Art of Great Britain* (1878 and 1883). An example will be found included in *British Pottery and Porcelain: an illustrated Encyclopaedia of Marked Specimens.*

PORTISHEAD		**PORTISHEAD STUDIO POTTERIES** (Miss Gwen Horlick), Woodhill, Portishead, Bristol. 1950 to March 1961. *Studio-type Pottery.*
3094		Incised or painted mark, 1950 to March 1961. Miss Horlick died March 8th, 1961.

PORTLAND		**PORTLAND POTTERY LTD.**, Regal Works, Cobridge. Staffordshire Potteries. 1946–53.** *Earthenwares.*

* This firm was taken over by Ridgways in 1953 and mark no. 3098 continued.

3095 — Trade-mark registered in 1946, including the initials P P with C for Cobridge.

3096 PORTLAND POTTERY
3097 PORTLAND POTTERY
      LTD.

Distinguishing details of several printed marks of differing design: name of the individual pattern is often included, 1946–53.

3098 — Printed mark, continued by Ridgway Potteries Ltd.* Note month and year number under mark.

    * This firm was taken over by Ridgways in 1953 and mark no. 3098 continued.

PORTMEIRION

PORTMEIRION POTTERIES LTD., Grays Pottery, Stoke. Staffordshire Potteries. January 1962– . *Earthenwares.* Formerly A. E. Gray & Co. Ltd., q.v., and Kirkhams Ltd., q.v.

3099
PORTMEIRION
POTTERY
STOKE-ON-TRENT
MADE IN ENGLAND

Printed mark in oval form as no. 3100, basic version, January 1962– .

3100

Several variations occur with the name of the designer, etc., January 1962– .

690 PORTOVASE *See* A. W. Buchan & Co.

POSSIL

POSSIL POTTERY CO., Denmark St., Possil Park, Glasgow, Scotland. 1898–1901. *Earthenwares and China.*

3101  Printed trade-mark, c. 1898–1901.

3102 NAUTILUS
      PORCELAIN

The Nautilus mark no. 2839, given on page 461, was also used. See also Nautilus Porcelain Co.

ANNE POTTS   *See* Fulham Pottery & Cheavin Filter Co. Ltd.

POTTS   **WILLIAM WAINWRIGHT POTTS,** St. George's Works, New Mills Works, Nr. Derby, Derbyshire. c. 1831+. *Printed Earthenwares.* Subsequently at Burslem.*

3103      This rare mark occurs on earthenwares *decorated* by Potts' patent process. The first patent is dated September 17th, 1831, and relates to an improved method of printing earthenware, porcelain, etc., by means of engraved cylinder rollers "as is generally used by calico printers". A second Potts patent of December 3rd, 1835, relates to coloured printing, the pattern being obtained from "raised or elevated surfaces and not from the engraved cut, indented or depressed parts of the roller, block or implement employed".

Potts exhibited at the 1851 Exhibition (his address being Waterloo House, Burslem); his machine was "calculated to produce as much work for transferring as 40 men can do in the same time by hand-printing".

* The address on the 1831 patent is New Mills, as on mark no. 3103. On the 1835 patent the name and address is given as "William Wainwright Potts, of Burslem . . . China and Earthenware Manufacturer".

POULSON   **POULSON BROS. (LTD.),** West Riding Pottery, Ferrybridge, Yorkshire. 1884–1927. *Earthenwares.*
N.B. Messrs. T. & E. L. Poulson worked the "Ferrybridge Pottery" (before 1897) which should not be confused with the "West Riding Pottery".

3104   P. B.   Distinguishing details of several printed or impressed marks of
3105   P. BROS.   differing design, 1884–1927.

POUNTNEY   **POUNTNEY & CO. (LTD.),** Bristol Victoria Pottery, Temple Backs, Bristol, Gloucestershire. 1849– . *Earthenwares.* Formerly Pountney & Goldney, q.v.

3106   P. & CO.   The early wares of Pountney & Co. were generally unmarked.
3107   POUNTNEY & CO.   Marks incorporating the initial P. & Co. or Pountney & Co. may occur from 1849 to 1889.

3108   BRISTOL   This mark occurs on some special glaze effects produced in
              +   1884. Other wares may also bear this form of mark, 3/84
            3/84   denotes the date of manufacture: = March 1884.

| 3109 | P. & CO. LTD. | Distinguishing details of several printed marks of differing |
| 3110 | POUNTNEY & CO. LTD. | design from 1889: name of the individual pattern is often included. Note addition of "Ltd.". |

3111–14

c. 1889+   c. 1900+   c. 1900+   c. 1930+

3115–19

c. 1939+   c. 1954+   c. 1954+   c. 1958+   c. 1958–

Printed marks, c. 1889– .

POUNTNEY

POUNTNEY & ALLIES, Bristol Pottery, Temple Backs, Bristol, Gloucestershire. c. 1816–35. *Earthenwares.* Formerly Carter & Pountney. The partnership was dissolved on March 28th, 1835. Subsequently Pountney & Goldney, see below.

3120	P	Distinguishing details of several printed, impressed or painted
3121	P. & A.	marks of differing design, c. 1816–35.
3122	P. A.	
	B. P.	
3123	P. A.	
	BRISTOL POTTERY	

3124 — Impressed mark with title in full, c. 1816–35.

3125 HAMILTON — The written name Hamilton occurs on some wares decorated in the classical style, c. 1820–30.

POUNTNEY

POUNTNEY & GOLDNEY, Bristol Pottery, Temple Backs, Bristol. 1836–49. *Earthenwares.* Formerly Pountney & Allies, see above. Subsequently Pountney & Co., q.v.

3126 BRISTOL POTTERY — Impressed marks, 1836–49.

| 3127 | POUNTNEY & GOLDNEY | The Pountney & Goldney mark occurs in the horse-shoe form of no. 3124. |

POWELL

ALFRED AND LOUISE POWELL, Decorators for Wedgwoods in Staffordshire, and independently in London at Red Lion Square. c. 1904–39. *Hand-painted Earthenwares.*

Earthenwares painted by Alfred and Louise Powell normally bear Wedgwood impressed marks, as that firm supplied the blanks. Apart from wares painted in London, the Powells helped to re-establish Wedgwood's hand painting department in the 1920's and they also designed for Wedgwoods.

| 3128 | | Personal painted mark of Alfred Powell (d. 1960), c. 1904–39. |
| 3129 | | Personal painted mark of Louise Powell, c. 1906–39. Mrs. Powell was the grand-daughter of the celebrated 19th century Wedgwood artist Emile Lessore. |

POWELL

JOHN POWELL, 91 Wimpole Street, London W.1. c. 1810–30. *China painter and seller.*

A John Powell was employed at the Chamberlain Works at Worcester in 1808. John Powell exhibited paintings on porcelain at the Royal Academy (from various London addresses) between 1811 and 1830. These were mainly floral and figure subjects. He is not listed at Wimpole Street in directories after 1822.

| 3130 | Powell, 91 Wimpole St. | Painted mark on a Swansea porcelain cup in the Allen Collection at the Victoria and Albert Museum. Similar marks in colour or gold have been reported on other Swansea and Nantgarw porcelains, c. 1810–20. |
| 3130a | J. Powell, China enameller to their R. & I. Highnesses the Princess Charlotte, Prince Leopold and Princess Sophia of Gloucester 19 Wimpole Street | Very rare painted mark on a pair of vases in the possession of Messrs. Godden of Worthing Ltd. and illustrated in *British Pottery and Porcelain, an illustrated Encyclopaedia of Marked Specimens,* c. 1816–17.* |

* Mention of Princess Charlotte and Prince Leopold would seem to indicate the period 1816–17, as they were married in 1816 and Princess Charlotte died in November 1817. In a directory of 1818 he is listed as "China painter to his S. H. Prince Leopold & the Princess Sophia of Gloucester", Princess Charlotte is no longer mentioned.

POWELL

WILLIAM POWELL (& SONS), Temple Gate Pottery, Bristol. c. 1830–1906. *Stonewares.*

William Powell is famous for the glaze he invented for his stonewares in 1835. This was taken up by most manufacturers of the period. See W. J. Pountney's *Old Bristol Potteries* (1920).

Business sold to Price, Sons & Co. in 1906, this firm then traded as "Price, Powell & Co.".

3131

Impressed mark, c. 1830+.

3131a   BRISTOL TEMPLE GATE POTTERY

Impressed mark, c. 1830+.

POWELL

POWELL & BISHOP, Stafford St. Works and other addresses, Hanley. Staffordshire Potteries. 1876–8. *China and Earthenwares.* Formerly Livesley Powell & Co. Subsequently Powell, Bishop & Stonier, see next entry.

3132   P. & B.
3132a   BEST
       P. & B.
3133   POWELL & BISHOP

Distinguishing details of several printed or impressed marks of differing design, 1876–8.

3134

This triangle mark is given by Jewitt.

3135

This Caduceus mark was registered as a trade-mark in 1876 and occurs with the initials P. & B. or with the initials or names of succeeding partnerships.

3136

One of several printed marks with the title in full, 1876–8.

POWELL

POWELL, BISHOP & STONIER, Stafford Street Works and other addresses, Hanley. Staffordshire Potteries. 1878–91. *China and Earthenwares.* Formerly Powell & Bishop, see above. Subsequently Bishop & Stonier, q.v.

3137   P. B. & S.   Distinguishing detail of several printed or impressed marks of differing design: name of the individual pattern is often included, 1878–91.

3138   This basic form of trade-mark was registered in 1880 and was continued by Bishop and Stonier after 1891. The Caduceus mark (no. 3135,) was also used, with the initials P. S. & S., 1878–91.

For further information see Jewitt's *The Ceramic Art of Great Britain.*

POWELL

POWELL & WELLS STUDIO POTTERY, Darnley Terrace, London W.11., from October 1958, formerly at Redhill, Surrey. May 1954– . *Studio-type Pottery.*

3139   P. W.   Painted or incised mark, 1954– .

3140   POWELL & WELLS   Printed mark, c. 1958– .
            STUDIO POTTERY

3141   D/PW   Painted or incised mark of Daphne Samson, at Powell & Wells Pottery.

3142   E/PW   Painted or incised mark of Elizabeth Yarner.
                        The above marks often include the date of production.

358   P P   *See* Joan A. Biggs.
2982   *See* Pearl Pottery Co. Ltd.
2997–8   *See* Pendley Pottery.

3095   P. P. C.   *See* Portland Pottery Ltd.

2983–4   P. P. CO. LTD.   *See* Pearl Pottery Co. Ltd.

3072   P. P. COY L.   *See* Plymouth Pottery Co. Ltd.

2997 $\frac{PP}{MF}$ *See* Pendley Pottery.

3094	P. P. S.	*See* Portishead Studio Potteries.

332 3346	PR (joined)	*See* Bembridge Pottery. *See* Bryan Rockford.

—	P. R.	*See* Appendix, page 728.

3145 3149 3157	PRATT	*See* F. & R. Pratt & Co. (Ltd.), below. *See* William Pratt.

PRATT

F. & R. PRATT & CO. (LTD.), High St., Fenton. Staffordshire Potteries. Est. c. 1818– .* *Earthenwares (printed decoration), Terra-cotta, etc.* Formerly Felix Pratt.

3143 3144 3145	F. & R. P. F. & R. P. & CO. PRATT	Distinguishing details of several printed marks of differing design: name of the individual pattern is often included, c. 1818–60. Note "& Co." added from c. 1840.

3146		Sample of early initial mark, without "& Co." and therefore pre-1840.

3147		Printed mark with initials and "& Co.", 1840+.

3148		Rare printed mark, c. 1847–60. Found on fine quality Etruscan pattern vases, and fine printed wares. See companion illustrated encyclopaedia of marked specimens. Vases of this type are mentioned in the Art Union magazine, August 1847.

* Messrs. F. & R. Pratt & Co. was taken over in the 1920's by Cauldon Potteries Ltd.; the original title and name is continued on marks.

3149–50	PRATT FENTON . F.&R.PRATT.&Cº 349 FENTON	Printed mark, on multi-coloured printed wares, of pot lid type (a speciality of this firm). Most examples are un-marked, c. 1850+. These marks with "England" added are subsequent to 1891 and usually of 20th century date.
3151	No. 123	Some specimens bear only the relevant pattern number, printed.
3152	F.&R.PRATT.&Cº ORIGINAL ENGRAVED PRINTINGS MADE IN ENGLAND AT THE [crown] Royal Cauldon Factory Est 1774	Pre-war printed mark of the 1930's.
3153	F.&R.PRATT & CO ORIGINAL ENGRAVED PRINTINGS Made by Royal Cauldon Est [crown] 1774	Post-war printed mark used by Cauldon Potteries Ltd. on re-issued Pratt printed designs.

Typical examples of Victorian Pratt wares will be found illustrated in *British Pottery and Porcelain: an illustrated Encyclopaedia of Marked Specimens.*

PRATT   **JOHN PRATT & CO. LTD.**, Lane Delph Pottery, Fenton. Staffordshire Potteries. 1872–8. *Earthenwares.* Formerly J. Pratt & Co.

3154	WATER-LILY J.P.&Cº (L)	Printed mark with the name of the pattern and the initials J. P. & Co. (L), 1872–8. N.B. Similar marks without "(L)" could relate to J. Pratt & Co., c. 1851–72, or to Joseph Peake & Co., c. 1835, or to James Pope & Co., c. 1849–50.

PRATT   **PRATT HASSALL & GERRARD**, High Street, Lane Delph, Fenton. Staffordshire Potteries. 1822–34. *Porcelain and Earthenwares.*

3155 3155a	P. H. G. P. H. & G.	Distinguishing details of several printed marks of differing design, 1822–34.

PRATT

PRATT & SIMPSON, Lane Delph Pottery, Fenton. Staffordshire Potteries. 1878–83. *Earthenwares.*

3156   P. & S.

A simple circular printed mark occurs with the name of the pattern and the initials P. & S., 1878–83.

PRATT

WILLIAM PRATT, Lane Delph. Staffordshire Potteries. c. 1780–99. *Earthenwares.*

3157   PRATT

Rare mark on coloured and moulded figures, jugs, etc. William Pratt (d. 1799) was succeeded by his wife Ellen who may have used the same mark to c. 1808.

It is difficult to state with certainty which potter of this name employed the above mark.

A large range of moulded jugs etc. are termed "Pratt" but similar wares were made by many other potters. A marked "Pratt" example is illustrated in *British Pottery and Porcelain: an illustrated Encyclopaedia of Marked Specimens.*

2908   PRESTBURY

See C. D. Nowell.

PRICE

PRICE BROTHERS, Crown Works, Burslem. Staffordshire Potteries. 1896–1903. *Earthenwares.*

3158

Printed mark, 1896–1910.*

* Continued by successors Price Brothers (Burslem) Ltd., see below.

PRICE

PRICE BROS. (BURSLEM) LTD., Top Bridge Works and Albion Works, Burslem. Staffordshire Potteries. 1903 to end of 1961.* *Earthenwares.* Formerly Price Brothers, see above. Subsequently, from January 1st, 1962, "Price & Kensington Potteries Ltd.", see next entry.

Former mark of Price Bros. continued, see no. 3158, above. Subsequent printed marks include:

3159–61

**PRICE
ENGLAND**

c. 1925+

c. 1925+

PALM ATHLO
PRICE BROS.,
ENGLAND

c. 1925+
with various pattern names above

3162–4

c. 1928

c. 1930+

c. 1934–61*

* Continued to 1963, see next entry.

PRICE

PRICE & KENSINGTON POTTERIES LTD., Longport. Staffordshire Potteries.   January 1962– .   *Earthenwares.* Formerly Price Bros. (Burslem) Ltd. and Kensington Pottery Ltd., q.v.

3165

Former mark of Price Bros. (Burslem) Ltd. continued by new company to 1963.

3166

Printed mark, 1963– .

PRIMAVESI

F. PRIMAVESI (& SON), Cardiff and Swansea, Wales. c. 1850–1915.   *Earthenwares, etc., Retailers.*

3167

F. PRIMAVESI & SON
CARDIFF

These printed marks occur on earthenwares sold by this firm of retailers, c. 1850–1915.   "& Son" would appear to date from c. 1860.

3168

128   Prince of Wales's crest   *See* E. Asbury & Co.

3898   *See* John Turner.

3530   Princess Anne   *See* Shore & Coggins.

PRINKNASH   **PRINKNASH BENEDICTINES**, Prinknash Abbey, Glou-
                                       cester. 1945– . *Earthenwares.*

3169   Printed or impressed mark, 1945– . Variations occur, all
                                       with the word "Prinknash".

PRIORY   **PRIORY CERAMICS LTD.***, Heckmondwike, Yorkshire.
                                       1961– . *Earthenwares.*

3170   PRIORY   Trade-mark name registered in January 1961 for use on
                                       earthenware figures, etc.

                                         * A firm of this title operates at Youghal, Co. Cork, Ireland. Hand-
                                       made vases, jugs, dishes, etc., have been produced from 1960 and bear this
                                       name.

PROCTER   **GEORGE PROCTER & CO. (LTD.)**, Gladstone Pottery,
                                       Longton. Staffordshire Potteries. 1891–1940. *China.* For-
                                       merly Procter, Mayer & Woolley.

3171   G. P. & CO.   Distinguishing detail of several printed marks of differing
3172   G. P. & CO.   design: name of the individual pattern is often included,
             L.   1891–1940.

3173   Printed mark, 1924–40.

PROCTER

3174   J. P.
                    L.

JOHN PROCTER, Dresden Works, etc., Longton. Staffordshire Potteries. 1843–6. *Earthenwares.*
Impressed or printed initial marks, c. 1843–6.

    N.B. These initials also fit John Procter of Longton, c. 1880–2.

PROCTER

J. & H. PROCTER (& CO.), Heathcote Pottery (c. 1857–9), New Town Pottery (c. 1859–75) and Heathcote Road Pottery (c. 1876–84), Longton. Staffordshire Potteries. 1857–84. *Earthenwares.*

3175

WARRANTED
P.

Printed or impressed mark, c. 1857–84.

PROTEAN

PROTEAN POTTERY (H. J. Gee), Dunster Steep, Dunster Somerset. July 1959– . *Studio-type Pottery and Jewellery.*

3176   PROTEAN DUNSTER   Impressed mark, 1959– .
                 G

3468   P
                    S
                (joined)

See Paula Schneider.

3156   P. & S.

See Pratt & Simpson.

3058   P. & S.
                    L.

See R. Plant & Sons.

3094   P. S. P.

See Portishead Studio Potteries.

3969   P. S. W.

See Philip S. Wadsworth.

3177   PUBLISHED BY——

Many impressed, moulded or applied pad marks will be found with the words "Published by" followed by the firm's name (or modeller's name) and the date that the design was *first* published. Objects bearing this mark are always sculptured or modelled as the wording relates to the Sculpture Copyright Act of 1797 (amended, 1814). Many modelled jugs of the 1830's and 1840's bear "Published by——" marks. A selection of jugs bearing this type of mark is illustrated in Godden's *British Pottery and Porcelain, 1780–1850.*

| 3091 | P. & U. | *See* Poole & Unwin. |

PULHAM

JAMES PULHAM, Broxbourne, Herts.   c. 1843–1918. *Terracotta.*

3178	J. P.	Impressed mark on terra-cotta vases, etc., c. 1843–1918.
—	P. V.	*See* Appendix, page 728.
3139	P. W.	*See* Powell & Wells Studio Pottery.
4367	PW (joined)	*See* Peter Wright.
3075	P. W. & CO. or	*See* Podmore, Walker & Co.
3077	P. W. & W.	

Q

3180	QK (joined)	*See* Kenneth Quick.
3305	QUARTZ CHINA	*See* William Ridgway (& Co.).
3527–9	QUEEN ANNE	*See* Shore & Coggins.
4024	QUEENS CHINA	*See* George Warrilow (& Sons).
1154 3179	QUEENSBERRY	*See* Crown Staffordshire Porcelain Co. Ltd. *See* Queensbury China Ltd., below.

QUEENSBURY

QUEENSBURY CHINA LTD., Belgrave Works, Longton. Staffordshire Potteries. 1954–5. *China.*

3179   QUEENSBURY   Distinguishing detail of printed marks of differing design, 1954–5.

QUICK

KENNETH QUICK, Leach Pottery, St. Ives, Cornwall. 1945–63*. *Studio-type Pottery.*

3180

Incised initial mark, 1945– .

3181
3182   TREGENNA HILL   Impressed or incised marks on wares made at the Tregenna Hill Pottery, c. 1955–60.

    * Kenneth Quick was apprenticed to the Leach Pottery in 1945. He worked on his own at the Tregenna Hill Pottery c. 1955–60 but then returned to the Leach Pottery and in 1963 went to Japan, where he was drowned in July 1963.

R

—	R	*See* Appendix.
501		*See* Bow China Works.
3199–200		*See* William Ratcliffe.
3250		*See* Job Ridgway.
3362		*See* Roeginga Pottery.
3233	R. & CO.	*See* Reid & Co.

RADFORD
(signature on printed wares)

The signature "Radford" occurs on some 18th century earthenwares and relates to the engraver Thomas Radford. He was employed at the Cockpit Hill Works at Derby, c. 1760–80 (see Derby Pot Works, page 204), and subsequently in Staffordshire where he engraved designs for Greatbach of Fenton, and other potters to c. 1802.

4268	E. RADFORD	*See* H. J. Wood (Ltd.), page 686.
3183	G. RADFORD	*See* Radford Handcraft Pottery, below.

RADFORD HANDCRAFT

RADFORD HANDCRAFT POTTERY, Amicable Street, Burslem. Staffordshire Potteries. 1933–48. *Earthenwares.*

3183	G. RADFORD BURSLEM	Signature mark (printed), 1933–48.

RADFORD

SAMUEL RADFORD (LTD.), High St., Fenton (formerly at Longton). Staffordshire Potteries. 1879–1957. *China.*

3184–8

c. 1880+   c. 1891+   c. 1913+   c. 1913+   c. 1924+

3189–93

c. 1925+   c. 1928+   c. 1928+   c. 1928+   c. 1938–57

Various printed marks from c. 1880 to 1957.

3186–7	RADFORDIAN	*See* Samuel Radford (Ltd.), above.
1881–3	RADNOR	*See* Hall Bros. (Longton) Ltd.

RAINBOW

RAINBOW POTTERY CO., Green St., Fenton. Staffordshire Potteries. 1931–41. *Earthenwares.*

3194

**RAINBOW POTTERY
FENTON
MADE IN ENGLAND**

Printed or impressed mark, 1931–41.

RAINFORTH

RAINFORTH & CO., Petty's Pottery, Holbeck Moor, Leeds, Yorkshire. 1792–1800. *Earthenwares, Creamware.*

3195   RAINFORTH & CO.
3195a   RAINFORTH & C

Printed or impressed marks (rare), 1792–1800.

3196   H. M.

Impressed mark, found inside covers etc., may relate to this pottery at Holbeck Moor or to the Leeds Pottery period, c. 1775. See D. C. Towner's *English Cream-coloured Earthenware* (1957).

RAINHAM

RAINHAM POTTERY LTD., High St., Rainham, Kent. *Earthenwares.* Pottery established in 1938 as Roeginga Pottery, closed 1939. Reopened in 1948 by Alfred Wilson Ltd. Titled "Rainham Pottery Ltd." from November 1956– .

3197	RAINHAM	Impressed or painted mark c. 1948. With or without "Made in England". Painted, decorator's initials also occur with this basic mark.
—	R. A. K. & CO.	*See* Appendix, page 729.
2053	RAMSBURY	*See* P. Holdsworth.
1512	RANLEIGH WARE	*See* Era Art Pottery Co.

RAOH

RAOH SCHORR CREATIONS, Bolton Studios, London S.W.10. c. 1945–c. 50. *Earthenwares and Porcelain.*

3198

This trade-mark was registered, under the above name, in 1946. The Raoh Schorr Studio continues but no pottery has been made after about 1950.

RATCLIFFE

WILLIAM RATCLIFFE, New Hall Works, etc. Hanley. Staffordshire Potteries. c. 1831–40. *Earthenwares.*

3199

R
HACKWOOD

Printed or impressed mark, c. 1831–40.

3200

Printed mark in underglaze blue, c. 1831–40.

RATCLIFFE

RATCLIFFE & CO., Clarence Works (Gold Street Works c. 1891–96), Longton. Staffordshire Potteries. 1891–1914. *Earthenwares*

3201

RATCLIFFE
ENGLAND.

Printed mark, 1891–1914.

RATHBONE

RATHBONE SMITH & CO., Soho Pottery, Tunstall. Staffordshire Potteries. 1883–97. *Earthenwares.* Subsequently Smith & Binnall, q.v.

3202   R. S. & CO.   Distinguishing details found on several printed marks of
                                 differing design: name of the individual pattern is often in-
                                 cluded, 1883–97.   Mark no. 3203 is a typical example.

3203

RATHBONE   T. RATHBONE & CO., Newfield Pottery, Tunstall.
                                 Staffordshire Potteries. 1898–1923. *Earthenwares.*
                                 Several marks incorporating the initials T. R. & Co.* Ex-
                                 amples include:

3204–6

                  c. 1898+   c. 1912+   c. 1919–1923

                            * These initials were also used at an earlier period by Thomas Rathbone
                          & Co. of Portobello, see below.

RATHBONE   THOMAS RATHBONE & CO., Portobello, Nr. Edinburgh,
                                 Scotland. c. 1810–45. *Earthenwares.*
                                    Works reopened in 1856 by Dr. Gray and later traded as
                                 "W. A. Gray & Sons".

3207   T. R. & CO.*   Distinguishing detail of printed or impressed marks of differing
3208   T. RATHBONE   design, c. 1810–45.
                  P

                                    * These initials were used at a later period by T. Rathbone & Co. of
                                 Tunstall, see entry above.

RAVENSCOURT   RAVENSCOURT POTTERY (Miss Dora Lunn), Ravens-
                                 court Park, London W.6.   1916 to December 1928.* *Earthen-
                                 wares.*

3209   RAVENSCOURT   Impressed, printed or incised mark, c.1916–28.*

                                    * The title "Ravenscourt Pottery" was used in the 1940's and 50's for a
                                 pottery at Goldhawk Road, London W.12. Miss Dora Lunn later potted
                                 under her own name, see D. Lunn, page 402.

RAWSTHORNE

WINIFRED RAWSTHORNE, Winthorn Pottery, Bramcote, Nottingham. 1958– . *Studio-type Pottery.*

3210   Incised or painted monogram mark, 1958– . A similar mark was used at the Monkton Combe Pottery, see page 445.

3210a   WINTHORN   Name added to monogram mark from November 1959– .

RAY

GEORGE RAY, Lane End. Staffordshire Potteries. Early 19th century. *Modeller.*

3211   G. Ray   Name mark on bust of William Turner, in the Hanley Museum.
        Lane End   Ray was a modeller, but a potter of this name was working in Longton and Hanley in the 1840's and 50's.

298	R. B.	*See* Richard Batterham.
707		*See* Ruth Burchard.
3334		*See* Robinson Bros.
637	R. B. & S.	*See* Richard Britton & Son.
—	R. C.	*See* Appendix, page 729.
3212	R. & C.	*See* Read & Clementson.
3213	R. C. & A.	*See* Read, Clementson & Anderson.
965	R. C. & CO.	*See* R. Cockran & Co.
3248	R (C) LTD.	*See* Richardsons (Cobridge) Ltd.
1000–1	R. C. R.	*See* S. & E. Collier.
—	R. D.	*See* Appendix, page 729.
—	Rd. No. or Rd	*See* Registration numbers, page 526.
—	R. & D.	*See* Appendix, page 729.
3214–15		*See* Redfern & Drakeford (Ltd.).
1520	RE (joined)	*See* Raymond R. Everett.

READ

READ & CLEMENTSON, High Street, Shelton, Hanley. Staffordshire Potteries. 1833–5. *Earthenwares* (*Ironstones*). Subsequently Read, Clementson & Anderson, q.v.

3212   R & C

Distinguishing detail of several printed marks of differing design: name of the individual pattern is often included, 1833–5. Mark no. 3212a is a typical example.

3212a

Later in the century, the initials refer to other manufacturers.

READ

READ, CLEMENTSON & ANDERSON, High Street, Shelton, Hanley. Staffordshire Potteries. c. 1836. *Earthenwares*. Formerly Read & Clementson, see previous entry.

3213   R. C. & A.

A good quality printed plate in the Godden Collection bears a printed mark, incorporating the initials R. C. & A. and the name of the pattern, c. 1836. See *British Pottery and Porcelain: an illustrated Encyclopaedia of Marked Specimens.*

—   REAL STONE CHINA *See* Appendix, page 729.

868   RED ANCHOR
        (anchor mark in red)

See Chelsea Porcelain Works.

REDFERN

REDFERN & DRAKEFORD (LTD.), Chatfield Works (c. 1892–1902), Balmoral Works (c. 1902–33), Longton. Staffordshire Potteries. 1892–1933. *China*.
Taken over by Royal Albion China Co., q.v.

3214

BALMORAL CHINA,

Printed or impressed mark, c. 1892–1909.

3215

Printed mark, 1909–33.

REED		J. REED (JAMES to 1849 then continued by son, JOHN), Rock Pottery, renamed Mexbro Pottery (c. 1849), Mexborough, Yorkshire. c. 1839–73. *Earthenwares*. Subsequently Sidney Woolfe & Co., q.v.
3216	REED	Impressed mark. Several printed marks also occur with the name REED, 1839–73. Reed purchased some Rockingham moulds, etc., in 1842.

REED & TAYLOR		REED & TAYLOR, Ferrybridge Pottery (c. 1840–56, subsequently L. Woolf & Sons, see Ferrybridge, page 246) and Rock Pottery (c. 1820–39, subsequently J. Reed, see entry above), Yorkshire. c. 1820–56. *Earthenwares*.
3217	R. & T.	Distinguishing detail of several printed marks of differing design: name of the individual pattern is often included, c. 1820–56. These initials could also relate to the firm of Ray & Tideswell of Lane End, Staffordshire, c. 1830–46.

REEVES		JAMES REEVES, Victoria Works, Fenton. Staffordshire Potteries. 1870–1948. *Earthenwares*.
3218	J. R.	Distinguishing details of several printed or impressed marks of differing design: name of the individual pattern is often included, 1870–1948. "England" or "Made in England" occurs on 20th century wares.
3218a	J. R. F.	
3219	J. REEVES	
3220–1		

REGAL		REGAL POTTERY CO. (LTD.), Elder Road, Cobridge. Staffordshire Potteries. 1925–31. *Earthenwares*.
3222		Printed mark, 1925–31.

3222	REGAL WARE	*See* Regal Pottery Co. (Ltd.).
3242		*See* A. G. Richardson.
3248		*See* Richardsons (Cobridge) Ltd.

REGENCY   REGENCY CHINA LTD., Sutherland Road, Longton.
                                 Staffordshire Potteries.   1953–   .   *China*.

3223   Printed trade-mark registered in 1953–   .

3403   REGINA   *See* Royal Tara.
(note)

REGISTRATION MARKS AND NUMBERS

A diamond-shaped device occurs on Victorian ceramics from 1842 to 1883.   The purpose of this mark was to show that the design or shape had been registered at the Patent Office in London and was thereby protected from piracy by other manufacturers for an initial period of three years.   The various letters and numbers in the corners of the diamond will show (with the aid of the key reproduced on page 527) the *earliest* possible date of manufacture.   Although the majority of registered designs were taken out by English manufacturers, some were registered by foreign manufacturers or their agents and it must not be presumed that all objects bearing this device are of English manufacture.

The diamond device will be found both printed or impressed (or moulded).   As a very general rule printed marks related to the added decoration.   Impressed or moulded marks generally relate to the shape of the object, so that several different *patterns* can be found on a tureen bearing one moulded or impressed mark which refers to the form of the tureen.

The letters and numbers (from which the date of registration can be ascertained) were arranged in two different ways.   From 1842 to 1867 the year *letter* appears in the top panel (below the class number IV, in the case of all porcelain and pottery objects).   From 1868 to the end of 1883 the year letter appears in the right-hand panel.

Many of the marks included in this book have been taken from the official Patent Office files which show each design registered between 1842 and 1883.   Several of the pulls from the original copper plates (from which the printed design was transferred) include the marks in use by the manufacturer at that period.   A selection of early wares bearing this diamond shaped mark will be found illustrated in my *British Pottery and Porcelain, 1780–1850* (1963).

From January 1884 registered designs were numbered consecutively and these numbers appear on wares with the prefix "Rd" or "Rd. No."   A guide to dating patterns on forms registered between 1884 and 1909 is printed on pages 527–8.

TABLE OF REGISTRATION MARKS
1843–1883

3224

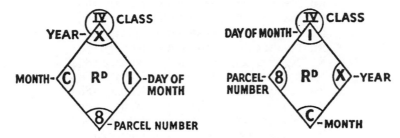

Above are the two patterns of Design Registration Marks that were in current use between the years 1842 and 1883. Keys to "year" and "month" code-letters are given below.

The left-hand diamond was used during the years 1842 to 1867. A change was made in 1868, when the right-hand diamond was adopted.

INDEX TO YEAR AND MONTH LETTERS

YEARS

1842–67		1868–83	
Year Letter at Top		*Year Letter at Right*	
A = 1845	N = 1864	A = 1871	L = 1882
B = 1858	O = 1862	C = 1870	P = 1877
C = 1844	P = 1851	D = 1878	S = 1875
D = 1852	Q = 1866	E = 1881	U = 1874
E = 1855	R = 1861	F = 1873	V = 1876
F = 1847	S = 1849	H = 1869	W = (Mar. 1x6)
G = 1863	T = 1867	I = 1872	1878
H = 1843	U = 1848	J = 1880	X = 1868
I = 1846	V = 1850	K = 1883	Y = 1879
J = 1854	W = 1865		
K = 1857	X = 1842		
L = 1856	Y = 1853		
M = 1859	Z = 1860		

MONTHS (BOTH PERIODS)

A = December	G = February	M = June
B = October	H = April	R = August (and
C or O = January	I = July	September 1st–19th
D = September	K = November (and	1857)
E = May	December 1860)	W = March

TABLE OF DESIGN REGISTRATION NUMBERS, FOUND ON WARES FROM 1884

Rd. No.   1   registered in January 1884
Rd. No.   19754   registered in January 1885
Rd. No.   40480   registered in January 1886

Rd. No. 64520 registered in January 1887
Rd. No. 90483 registered in January 1888
Rd. No. 116648 registered in January 1889
Rd. No. 141273 registered in January 1890
Rd. No. 163767 registered in January 1891
Rd. No. 185713 registered in Jauuary 1892
Rd. No. 205240 registered in January 1893
Rd. No. 224720 registered in January 1894
Rd. No. 246975 registered in January 1895
Rd. No. 268392 registered in January 1896
Rd. No. 291241 registered in January 1897
Rd. No. 311658 registered in January 1898
Rd. No. 331707 registered in January 1899
Rd. No. 351202 registered in January 1900
Rd. No. 368154 registered in January 1901
Rd. No. 385500* registered in January 1902
Rd. No. 402500* registered in January 1903
Rd. No. 420000* registered in January 1904
Rd. No. 447000* registered in January 1905
Rd. No. 471000* registered in January 1906
Rd. No. 494000* registered in January 1907
Rd. No. 519500* registered in January 1908
Rd. No. 550000* registered in January 1909

Approximate numbers only

REICH		**TIBOR REICH,** Alderminster Pottery, Alderminster, Worcestershire. c. 1952–54. *Pottery.*
3226	TIGO	Trade-name for special type of glazed pottery introduced by Tibor Reich, c. 1952+.
3227	Designed by Tibor Reich Alderminster Pottery	Printed or written mark, c. 1952–4.
3228	Designed by Tibor Reich, produced by Denby Pottery.	Printed or written mark on similar wares produced at the Denby Pottery, c. 1954–60.
REICHEL		**CHRISTA REICHEL, MISS,** Canonbury Studio.* London N.1. c. 1950's to September 1962. *Studio-type Pottery.*
3229	CHRIS	Incised or painted marks, c. 1950's–62.

* The studio was taken over by Miss S. Dawson, q.v., in September 1962.

3230	CHRIS CANONBURY STUDIO 1962	The name Canonbury also occurs as Canombury.
—	REID & CO. (18th century)	*See* Appendix, page 729.

REID & CO.

REID & CO., Park Place Works, Longton. Staffordshire Potteries. 1913–46. *China.* Subsequently Roslyn China, q.v.

3231–5

c. 1913+   c. 1922+   c. 1924+   c. 1937+   c. 1937–46

Various printed marks.

2130	RELIABLE	*See* W. Hulme.

RENDELL

JOSEPH RENDELL, Croydon, Surrey. c. 1920–35. *Studio-type Pottery and Figures.*

3236   P. RENDELL — Signature mark, c. 1920–35. Joseph Rendell's father, James, was also a potter.

2681	RENLYM	*See* G. E. Milner.

REYCHAN

STANISLAS REYCHAN, Garden Studio, London N.W.8. c. 1950– . *Pottery Sculpture and Ornaments.*

3237   S. REYCHAN — Impressed, c. 1950– .

3238   **SR** — Impressed seal mark, c. 1950– . See Plate 2.

1623	R. F.	*See* Robert Fournier.
1632		*See* Richard Freeman.
303	rfb (joined)	*See* Richard Franz Bayer.
—	F R L R	*See* Appendix (F. Raymond), page 729.
1580	R. F. & S.	*See* R. Floyd & Sons.
—	R. G.	*See* Appendix, page 729.
1662		*See* Robert Gallimore.
1669		*See* Robert Garner.
1046	R G C (joined)	*See* Ronald G. Cooper.
3480	R. G. S. or	*See* R. G. Scrivener & Co.
3481	R. G. S. & CO.	
1912	R. H.	*See* R. Hammersley (& Son).
2050		*See* R. Holden.
1925	RH (joined) or	*See* R. Hancock.
1926	R. H. f.	*See* Worcester Porcelains.
1890a	R H & CO	*See* Ralph Hall (& Co.).
4267	CHARLOTTE RHEAD	*See* H. J. Wood (Ltd.).
—	R. H. L. P.	*See* Appendix, page 729.

RHODES

RHODES & PROCTOR, Swan Bank Pottery, Burslem. Staffordshire Potteries. 1883–5. *Earthenwares.* Formerly Tundley, Rhodes & Proctor, q.v.

3239	R. & P.	Distinguishing detail occurring on several printed marks of differing design: name of the individual pattern is often included, 1883–5.

3057	R. H. P. & CO.	*See* R. H. Plant & Co.
1914	R. H. & S.	*See* R. Hammersley (& Son).
2014		*See* R. Heron & Son.
—	R. H. & S. Ltd.	*See* Appendix, page 730.
3059	R. H. & S. L. P	*See* R. H. & S. L. Plant (Ltd.).
634	RIALTO CHINA	*See* British Art Pottery Co.

RICHARDS

DONALD RICHARDS, Marton-cum-Grafton, Yorkshire. 1961*– . *Studio-type Pottery, Stoneware.*

3240   D. R. 63

Painted or incised initial mark, with year of production, 1961*– .

    * Some examples may bear dates between 1949 and 1961 but Donald Richards has only been producing pottery on a commercial scale from 1961.

RICHARDS

FRANCES E. RICHARDS, Highgate, London. 1922–31. *Studio-type Pottery.*

3241

Incised mark, with year of production—in 1920's.
    Marked examples of Frances Richards pottery are preserved in the Victoria and Albert Museum.

RICHARDSON

ALBERT G. RICHARDSON, Regal Pottery, Cobridge. Staffordshire Potteries. c. 1920–1. *Earthenwares.* Subsequently Richardsons (Cobridge) Ltd., q.v.

3242

Printed mark, c. 1920–1.
    N.B. The initials A. G. R. were also used by A. G. Richardson *& Co. Ltd.*, see below.

RICHARDSON

A. G. RICHARDSON & CO. LTD., Gordon Pottery, Tunstall. Staffordshire Potteries, then Britannia Pottery, Cobridge, c. 1934– . 1915– . *Earthenwares.*

3243  Printed trade-mark c. 1916+, with or without A. G. R. & Co. Ltd. under.

3244-6

c. 1925+   c. 1930+   c. 1934+

Printed marks, c. 1925– .

RICHARDSON

GEORGE RICHARDSON, Wrotham, Kent. c. 1642–77. *Slip-decorated Earthenware.*

3247   G. R.

Examples of early Wrotham earthenware bear these initials. Dated examples range between 1642 and 1677.

See E. C. C. Transactions, vol. 3, part 2. A Paper by A. J. B. Kiddell. Six initialled specimens will be found illustrated in *British Pottery and Porcelain: an illustrated Encyclopaedia of Marked Specimens.*

RICHARDSONS

RICHARDSONS (COBRIDGE) LTD., Regal Pottery, Cobridge. Staffordshire Potteries. 1921–5. *Earthenwares.* Formerly Albert G. Richardson, q.v.

3248

Printed mark, 1921–5.

RIDDLE

RIDDLE & BRYAN (Riddle & Co.), Longton. Staffordshire Potteries. c.1835–40. *Lustred Earthenwares.*

3248a   RIDDLE & BRYAN, Longton.

Printed mark on copper lustre jug, sold at Sothebys in January 1964. c. 1835–40.

This hitherto unrecorded printed mark occurs on part of the clock face panels on each side of a jug. R. G. Haggar records the fact that George Bryan withdrew from the Riddle & Co. partnership in 1840; the firm continued as Riddle & Lightfoot to 1851.

RIDGWAY

RIDGWAY & ABINGTON, Church Works, Hanley. Staffordshire Potteries. c. 1835–60. *Earthenwares, Moulded jugs, etc.* Formerly W. Ridgway, Son & Co., q.v.

The two partners were Edward James Ridgway and Leonard James Abington. The name Abington occurs with one and also with two "b"s. Subsequently E. J. Ridgway.

3249   PUBLISHED BY E. RIDGWAY & ABINGTON HANLEY JANUARY 4 1838   Impressed marks, several variations occur with different dates, c. 1835–60.

RIDGWAY

JOB RIDGWAY, Cauldon Place, Shelton, Hanley. Staffordshire Potteries. c. 1802–8. *Earthenwares.* Formerly Job & George Ridgway. Subsequently Job Ridgway & Sons, see below.

3250   R   An R within a Chinese-type square seal has been given as a mark of Job Ridgway, c. 1802–8.

3251   J. R.   Many printed marks incorporate the initials J. R. but in most cases these marks relate to John Ridgway (c. 1830+). The wares of Job Ridgway were usually unmarked.

RIDGWAY

JOB RIDGWAY & SONS, Cauldon Place, Shelton, Hanley. Staffordshire Potteries. c. 1808–14. *Earthenwares.* Formerly Job Ridgway, see above. Subsequently J. & W. Ridgway, q.v.

3252   RIDGWAY & SONS   Impressed or printed marks occur incorporating "Ridgway & Sons" c. 1808–14.

N.B. This form of title could also have been used by E. J. Ridgway & Sons (c. 1867–72).

RIDGWAY

JOHN RIDGWAY (& CO.), Cauldon Place, Shelton, Hanley. Staffordshire Potteries. c. 1830–55. *Porcelains and Earthenwares.* Formerly J. & W. Ridgway. Subsequently Ridgway, Bates & Co.

3253   J. R.
3254   JOHN RIDGWAY
3255   JHN RIDGWAY
3256   I. RIDGWAY

Distinguishing details of several printed or impressed marks of differing design: name of the individual pattern is often included, c. 1830–41. Note "& Co." occurs on later marks.

3257–8

Many variations of the Royal Arms mark occur, some are without the initials J. R. or J. R. & Co. under the arms. A mark without the initials occurs on a design registered by John Ridgway in September 1841.

3258a   Crown
         Mark
    See Plate 5

It will be observed that on teasets the saucers and large pieces bear the full Royal Arms mark, but the cups have only a printed crown, see Plate 5.

3259   J. R. & CO.
3259a   J. RIDGWAY & CO.
3259b   JOHN RIDGWAY
           & CO.

Distinguishing details of several printed marks of differing design: name of the individual pattern is often included, c. 1841–55. Note addition of "& Co." Many of these Ridgway marks include the Royal Arms.

RIDGWAY

JOHN & WILLIAM RIDGWAY, Cauldon Place and Bell Works, Shelton, Hanley. Staffordshire Potteries. 1814– c. 1830. *Earthenwares and China.* Formerly Job Ridgway & Sons, see above.

3260   J. W. R.
3261   J. & W. R.
3262   J. & W. RIDGWAY

Distinguishing details of several printed or impressed marks of differing design: name of the individual pattern is often included, c. 1814–30. Typical examples include:

3263–5

3266

This form of vase and anchor mark occurs impressed or in relief, or printed, c. 1814+ and was also used by William Ridgway & Co. after 1830.

3267   RIDGWAY

This impressed name-mark has been seen on a very fine large porcelain vase, with fruit painted panels, green ground and gilt enrichments, and probably relates to this partnership.

RIDGWAY

JOHN RIDGWAY BATES & CO., Cauldon Place, Shelton, Hanley. Staffordshire Potteries. 1856–58. *Porcelain and Earthenwares.* Subsequently Bates, Brown-Westhead-Moore & Co., q.v.

| 3268 | J. R. B. & CO. | Printed marks incorporating initials, 1856–58. |

3269

| 3270 | MESSRS. JOHN RIDGWAY BATES & CO. CAULDON PLACE STAFFORDSHIRE POTTERIES | A plate in the Victoria and Albert Museum (illustrated in *Victorian Porcelain*, Plate 97) has this mark, of the style in full. |

| 3270a | J RIDGWAY BATES & CO. | Impressed mark on parian bust, in the Godden Collection, dated 1858. |

RIDGWAY

RIDGWAY, MORLEY, WEAR & CO., Broad St., Shelton, Hanley. Staffordshire Potteries. 1836–42. *Earthenwares.* Formerly Hicks, Meigh & Johnson. Subsequently Ridgway & Morley, see below.

| 3271 3272 | R. M. W. & CO. RIDGWAY, MORLEY WEAR & CO. | Distinguishing details of several printed marks of differing design: name of the individual pattern is often included, 1836–42. Typical examples include: |

3273-5

FLORAL
R.M.W.&C°.
FLORENCE ROSE

RIDGWAY

RIDGWAY & MORLEY, Broad Street, Shelton, Hanley. Staffordshire Potteries. 1842–44. *Earthenwares.* Formerly Ridgway, Morley Wear & Co.

| 3276 3277 | R. & M. RIDGWAY & MORLEY | Distinguishing details of several printed marks of differing design: name of the individual pattern is often included, 1842–44. Typical examples include: |

3278–80

3281–3

c. 1842–44

RIDGWAY

RIDGWAY POTTERIES LTD., Ash Hall, Stoke. Stafford-shire Potteries. February 1955– . *Earthenwares.* Formerly Ridgway & Adderley Ltd., see page 539.

Ash Hall is the administrative address. Potteries in the Ridgway group include:

Booths, Church Bank Pottery, Tunstall.
Colcloughs, Regent Works, Longton.
Paladin Works, Fenton.
North Staffordshire Pottery, Cobridge.
Portland Pottery, Cobridge.
Bedford Works, Shelton.
Adderley Floral China Works, Longton.
Gainsborough Works, Longton.

Many marks include the name of the pottery concerned.

3284

Basic Ridgway mark (introduced by Ridgways (Bedford Works) Ltd., c. 1950). Several variations occur and the names of different firms or potteries occur in place of Ridgway.

3285–88

3289–90

Other printed marks, also used formerly by Booths & Colcloughs Ltd., etc. before the amalgamation, are reproduced on next page.

3291–4

Recent (1962) marks used by Ridgway's associate Potteries.

3295–7

Recent (1962) marks used by the main "Ridgway Potteries Ltd." Company.

RIDGWAY

RIDGWAY & ROBEY, Hanley. Staffordshire Potteries. c. 1837–9. *Porcelain figures.*
The partners were William Ridgway & Ralph Mayer Robey.

3298   PUBLISHED JUNE 15, 1839 BY RIDGWAY & ROBEY HANLEY STAFFORDSHIRE POTTERIES

Printed mark on very rare porcelain character figures, Kate Nickleby etc., 1839.
See companion illustrated encyclopaedia of marked specimens.

3252   RIDGWAY & SONS   *See* Job Ridgway & Sons.

RIDGWAY

RIDGWAY, SPARKS & RIDGWAY, Bedford Works, Shelton, Hanley. Staffordshire Potteries. 1873–9. *Earthenwares.* Formerly E. J. Ridgway & Son. Subsequently Ridgways, see below.

3299   R. S. R.   Distinguishing details of several printed marks of differing design: name of the individual pattern is often included, 1873–9. Mark no. 3299a is a typical example.

3299a

RIDGWAY

WILLIAM RIDGWAY (& CO.), Bell Works, Shelton, and Church Works, Hanley.   Staffordshire Potteries.   c. 1830–54*.   *Earthenwares.*   Formerly J. & W. Ridgway, q.v.

| 3300 | W. RIDGWAY | Printed and impressed marks, c. 1830–4. |
| 3301 | W. R. | |

3302   W. RIDGWAY & CO.
3303   W. R. & CO.
3303a

Distinguishing details of several printed or impressed marks of differing design: name of the individual pattern is often included, 1834–54.   "& Co." first occurs in Rate records for 1834.   Mark no. 3303a is a typical example of a "W R & Co" printed mark.

3304   PUBLISHED BY
W RIDGWAY & CO
SHELTON
STAFFORDSHIRE

Many "Published by ——" marks occur with the name in full and with the date of publication.

3305   QUARTZ CHINA

This term is included in some W. Ridgway marks of the 1830–50 period.

* William Ridgway Son & Co. were also working at Hanley from c. 1838 to 1848, see next entry.   Some W. Ridgway marks were later reissued by Ridgways, see page 539.

RIDGWAY

WILLIAM RIDGWAY, SON & CO., Church Works (and Cobden Works c. 1841–6), Hanley.   Staffordshire Potteries.   c. 1838–48.   *Earthenwares.*   Subsequently Ridgway & Abington.

3306   PUBLISHED BY
W. RIDGWAY, SON
& CO. HANLEY
SEPTEMBER 1, 1840

Many "Published by" marks occur in this form with various dates.

3307   W. R. S. & CO.

Distinguishing initials found on several printed marks of differing design: name of the individual pattern is often included, 1838–48.   The vase and anchor device occurs on several marks, see mark Nos. 3308.   Mark No. 3309 is a typical initial mark, but similar "Humphrey Clock" marks were used at later periods.

3308–9

RIDGWAYS

RIDGWAYS, Bedford Works, Shelton, Hanley.   Staffordshire Potteries. Late 1879–1920.* *Earthenwares.* Formerly Ridgway Sparks & Ridgway, q.v.   Continued as Ridgways (Bedford Works) Ltd., see below.

3310

Trade-mark registered in 1880.   Early versions do not have "Stoke-on-Trent".

3311–14

c. 1905+

c. 1905+

c. 1912+

c. 1912+

Printed marks, c. 1905–20.

3315–16

Reissued former marks, note addition of "England" after 1891.

RIDGWAYS

RIDGWAYS (BEDFORD WORKS) LTD., Bedford Works, Shelton, Hanley. Staffordshire Potteries. 1920–52.* *Earthenwares.*   Formerly Ridgways, see above.

Former marks of Ridgways continued, new marks include:

3317–20

WILLOW

c. 1927+

c. 1927+

IVORY CHINA
BEDFORD
MADE IN ENGLAND

c. 1934+

c. 1934+

3321–24

RIDGWAYS, BEDFORD WORKS
ENGLAND

c. 1930+

MADE IN ENGLAND

c. 1930+

c. 1930+

Est. 1792
RIDGWAY
Made in England

c. 1950+
Continued by subsequent firms.

* Retitled "Ridgway & Adderley Ltd." from October 21st 1952 (old marks continued) and continued with Booths & Colcloughs Ltd. from January 1st 1955 as Ridgway, Adderley, Booths & Colcloughs Ltd. but renamed **RIDGWAY POTTERIES LTD.** from February 28th 1955, see page 536.

| 3325 | JONROTH | Some printed marks incorporate the name Jonroth and/or a monogram of JHR & Co. Such marked pieces were made for the American firm of John H. Roth & Co. from the 1930's to c. 1956. |

| RIE | | LUCIE RIE, MRS., Albion Mews, London W.2. c. 1938– . *Studio-type Pottery.* |

| 3326 | | Impressed seal mark, c. 1938– . |

| RIGBY | | RIGBY & STEVENSON, Boston Works (1894–1907), Pelham Street Works (1907–1954), Hanley. Staffordshire Potteries. 1894–1954. *Earthenwares.* |

| 3327 | R. & S. | Distinguishing detail of several printed marks of differing design: name of the individual pattern is often included, 1894–1954. |

| RILEY | | JOHN & RICHARD RILEY, Nile Street (c. 1802–1814), Hill Works (c. 1814–1828), Burslem. Staffordshire Potteries. 1802–28. *Earthenwares and China.*
 Riley's Hill works were later taken over by Samuel Alcock. |

| 3328 | | Several different painted, printed or impressed marks occur with the name "Riley", 1802–28. The Rileys exported decorative "Gaudy Dutch" earthenwares to America. |

| 3329 | | |

| 3330 | RILEY 1823 | One of several jugs with this mark moulded in the base will be found illustrated in *British Pottery and Porcelain: an illustrated Encyclopaedia of Marked Specimens.* |

| RING | | RING & CO., Bristol Pottery, Bristol. c. 1789–1813. *Earthenwares.* |

Joseph Ring established a factory for Staffordshire type creamwares in 1785. He was killed by a falling kiln in 1788. The works were continued by his widow with William Taylor as manager and partner from c. 1789. Directories from 1793 to 1812 list the firm as Ring & Carter. Subsequently Carter, Ring & Pountney.

3331	RING & CO.	Very rare impressed mark on a creamware coffee pot in the Bristol Art Gallery (illustrated in the companion illustrated volume). This mark probably relates to the period 1789–1812, see note above. See also W. J. Pountney's *Old Bristol Potteries* (1920).

RIVERS

WILLIAM RIVERS, Bedford Row, Shelton, Hanley. Staffordshire Potteries. c. 1818–22. *Earthenware, Creamware, etc.*

3332	RIVERS	Impressed mark, c. 1818–22.
791	rj	*See* Carter, Stabler & Adams Ltd.
1918	R. J. H.	*See* R. Hammond.
4027	R. J. W.	*See* R. J. Washington.
	or	
4028	R. J. W.	
3338	R. & L.	*See* Robinson & Leadbeater (Ltd.).
—	R. L. & S.	*See* Appendix, page 730.
1143	R. M.	*See* Cromer Pottery.
2493		*See* Ralph Malkin.
2649	RM (joined)	*See* Renee Mendel.
3276	R. & M.	*See* Ridgway & Morley.
3375		*See* Roper & Meredith.
154	R. M. A.	*See* Richard M. Astbury.

1816	RMG (joined)	*See* R. M. Greenwood.
2494	R. M. & S.	*See* Ralph Malkin & Sons.
3815	R M T F T W	*See* Robert Minton Taylor.
3271	R. M. W. & Co.	*See* Ridgway, Morley, Wear & Co.
3391	R. & N.	*See* Rowley & Newton (Ltd.).

ROBERTSON

SEONAID MAIRI ROBERTSON, MISS, Edinburgh and Yorkshire. 1944– .* *Studio-type Pottery.*

3333   S. M. R.   Incised or painted initial mark, 1944– .*

> * Miss Robertson has not been able to pot for some years, due to an accident, but she hopes to start again in a year or two. (G.G. 1963.)

ROBINSON

ROBINSON BROTHERS, Castleford and Allerton Potteries, Castleford, Yorkshire. 1897–1904. *Stonewares.* Subsequently J. Robinson & Son, see below.

3334   R. B.   Distinguishing detail of several printed or impressed marks of differing design: name of the individual pattern is often included, 1897–1904.

ROBINSON

F. S. ROBINSON, Ducketts Wood Pottery, Thundridge, Hertfordshire. 1961– . *Studio-type Pottery.*

From 1959 Mr. Robinson worked with A. G. Shelley at the Ducketts Wood Pottery but from 1961 he has worked the pottery on his own.

3335   Impressed seal type mark of the initials F. R. in a square outline. 1961– .

ROBINSON

JOHN ROBINSON & SON, Castleford and Allerton Potteries, Castleford, Yorkshire. 1905–33. *Stonewares.* Formerly Robinson Bros., see above.

3336   J. R. & S.   Impressed initial mark, c. 1905–33.

ROBINSON

JOSEPH ROBINSON, Knowle Works, Burslem. Staffordshire Potteries. 1876–98. *Earthenwares.*

3337   J. R.
              B.

3337a   J. ROBINSON
          BURSLEM

Distinguishing details of several printed or impressed marks of differing design: name of the individual pattern is often included, 1876–98.

ROBINSON

ROBINSON & LEADBEATER (LTD.), Wolfe Street (and other addresses), Stoke. Staffordshire Potteries. 1864–1924. *Parian figures, etc.* Taken over by J. A. Robinson & Sons Ltd. and subsequently Cauldon Potteries Ltd., q.v.

Early parian wares unmarked. An illustrated advertisement of 1896 will be reproduced in the companion illustrated encyclopaedia.

3338

Impressed mark, usually on the *back* of the base of parian figures or groups, c. 1885+.

3339

Printed mark, c. 1905–24. Note addition of "Ltd.", after 1905.

ROBINSON

ROBINSON & SON, Foley China Works, Longton. Staffordshire Potteries. 1881–1903. *China.* Subsequently E. Brain & Co., q.v.

3340   R. & S.
           L.

3341   ESTABLISHED

Distinguishing detail of several printed or impressed marks of differing design: name of the individual pattern is often included, 1881–1903.

Printed trade-mark, several variations occur. The words Foley China* often occur with these marks, c. 1881–1903.

3342   FOLEY CHINA*

    N.B. A firm of this title was also working at Longton c. 1864–9.

   * The name "Foley" was used by other manufacturers: E. Brain & Co., Wileman & Co.

ROBINSON

W. H. ROBINSON, Baltimore Works, Longton. Staffordshire Potteries. 1901–4. *China.* Subsequently Robinson & Beresford.

3343   Printed mark, 1901–4.

ROBINSON   **ROBINSON & WOOD,** Broad Street, Shelton, Hanley. Staffordshire Potteries. 1832–6. *Earthenwares.* Subsequently Robinson, Wood & Brownfield, see below.

3344   R. & W.   Distinguishing detail of several printed marks of differing design: name of the individual pattern is often included, 1832–6.

ROBINSON   **ROBINSON, WOOD & BROWNFIELD,** Brownfield's Works, Cobridge. Staffordshire Potteries. 1838–41. *Earthenwares.* Formerly Robinson & Wood, see above.

3345   R. W. & B.   Distinguishing detail of several printed marks of differing design: name of the individual pattern is often included, 1838–41. See Plate 6.

1562   ROCK   *See* John Fisher.

ROCHFORD   **BRYAN ROCHFORD,** Willowdene, Cheshunt, Herts. July 1960– . *Studio-type Pottery.*

3346   Rochford Pottery monogram, July 1960– .

3347   Personal seal mark used by Bryan Rochford, 1960– .

ROCK   **HELEN, FRAZER, ROCK,** London N.W. c. 1920–32. *Studio-type Pottery.*

3348   HELEN FRAZER ROCK   Signature or monogram mark, c. 1920–32.

3349

ROCKINGHAM

ROCKINGHAM WORKS (various owners), Nr. Swinton, Yorkshire. c. 1745–1842. *Earthenwares (and Porcelain from c. 1826).*

Early wares were unmarked.

3350	BINGLEY	Rare impressed mark, c. 1778–87.

3351	BRAMELD	Many impressed "Brameld" earthenware marks occur from 1806 to 1842. Various crosses or stars or numbers were added after the name "Brameld". Marks nos. 3351–5. Porcelains were not made before 1825. Marks nos. 3353–4 rarely occur on porcelains c. 1826–30. Mark no. 3352 c. 1830–42. The name also occurs on a raised oval pad of coloured clay.
3352	ROYAL ROCKINGHAM WORKS BRAMELD	
3353	ROCKINGHAM WORKS, BRAMELD	
3354	ROCKINGHAM BRAMELD	
3355	BRAMELD & CO.	

3356

Rose Jar

Several printed marks occur but these mainly give only the name of the pattern. The example reproduced, no. 3356, occurs on an earthenware plate with the impressed mark "Brameld," c. 1815–42.

It has formerly been believed that the Brameld marked earthenwares were produced before 1830 but recent research on factory documents by Messrs. A. Eaglestone and T. A. Lockett shows that earthenware was made up to the closure in 1842.

3357	B	A rare example in the Godden Collection has a printed mark incorporating the name of the pattern, "Parroquet", and "B". It also has the impressed Brameld mark.

N.B. The impressed mark "ROCKINGHAM" occurs on some green glazed Wedgwood earthenwares but with the Wedgwood mark.

3358

Rockingham Works Brameld

The "griffin" mark printed, at first in red, c. 1826–30. On some rare examples the griffin crest occurs without any wording. This "griffin" mark also occurs impressed on rare biscuit figures, etc.

3358a	ROCKINGHAM CHINA WORKS SWINTON, 1826	Painted mark on rare early porcelain cup, dated 1826.

3359

Later versions of the griffin mark, printed in puce after 1830. Note later wording "Royal Rock(ingham) Works" and/or "China Manufacturers to the King ——", c. 1830–42. The use of the wording " . . . to the King" should have ceased in 1837.

3360

Rare examples of the "griffin" mark with the wording "Manufacturers to the Queen" were probably decorated by Alfred Baguley after the closure of the Rockingham works in 1842—see page 48. This form of wording was not used before 1837.

N.B. Not all Rockingham wares are marked, in early teasets the saucers only are marked, and the cups etc. are not.

For an interesting account, and illustrations, of Rockingham wares see *The Connoisseur Year Book 1962*, pages 140–6, also Jewitt's *The Ceramic Art of Great Britain* (1883) and *British Pottery and Porcelain: an illustrated Encyclopaedia of Marked Specimens*.

The Rotherham Museum and Libraries Committee will be publishing in 1964 a book by A. A. Eaglestone and T. A. Lockett entitled *The Rockingham Pottery*. This will include much fresh information on Rockingham wares.

211   ROCKINGHAM WORKS, MEXBRO   *See* A. Baguley.

RODDY   **E. RODDY (& CO.)**, Newcastle St., Burslem. Staffordshire Potteries. 1925–8.* *Earthenwares.*

3361   STAFFORDSHIRE RODDY WARE ENGLAND   A circular printed mark occurs with this wording, c. 1925–8.

* Other firms of this title manufactured tiles or sanitary wares.

2973a   RODMELL   *See* Judith Partridge.

ROEGINGA   **ROEGINGA POTTERY** (O. C. Davies), Rainham, Kent. 1938–9. *Earthenwares.*
Reopened in 1948, by Alfred Wilson Ltd., see also Rainham Pottery Ltd., page 520.

| 3362 | $\mathcal{R}$ | Incised mark, c. 1938–9. |

| 3363 | GBD monogram | Monogram GBD mark on wares decorated by Mrs. Davies, c. 1938–9. |

ROGERS

ERIC ROGERS, Handsworth, Birmingham, Warwickshire. 1920–35. *Studio-type Pottery.*

| 3364 | ERIC ROGERS | Incised or painted signature mark, c. 1920–35. |

ROGERS

JAMES ROGERS, Donyatt, Nr Ilminster, Somerset. c. 1800–1900. *Earthenwares.*

The Rogers, James, his son James and then Abraham made typical West Country sgraffito decorated earthenwares during the 19th century. Most examples are unmarked.

| 3365 | Jas Rogers Maker Octr 10th 1848 | A puzzle jug sold at Sotheby's in 1960 bears this incised signature. |

| 3366 | ROGERS & SONS CROCK STRETT POTTERY | Impressed mark on puzzle jug in the Glaisher Collection at the Fitzwilliam Museum, Cambridge. This example is dated 1864. See *British Pottery and Porcelain: an illustrated Encyclopaedia of Marked Specimens.* |

ROGERS

JOHN & GEORGE ROGERS, Dale Hall, Longport. Staffordshire Potteries. c. 1784–1814. *Earthenwares.* Subsequently J. Rogers & Son, see below.

| 3367 | ROGERS | Impressed mark, c. 1784–1814+. This form of mark may also have been used by John Rogers & Son after 1814.

Ward in his *Borough of Stoke-upon-Trent* (1843) noted that John & George Rogers "were noted for the excellence of their table-ware". |

| 3368 | J. R. L. | This initial mark *may* relate to these potters, but see next entry. |

ROGERS		**JOHN ROGERS & SON (SPENCER ROGERS)**, Dale Hall, Longport. Staffordshire Potteries. c. 1814–36. *Earthenwares.* Formerly J. & G. Rogers, see above.
3369	ROGERS	Impressed mark, formerly used by J. & G. Rogers and continued, c. 1784–1836. Many well potted blue printed objects occur with this impressed name-mark, most specimens seem to be of the 1800–20 period.
3370	J. R. L.	This initial mark is given by Chaffers and other authorities as that of this firm but it seems unlikely that it relates to Messrs. J. & G. Rogers or to J. Rogers & Son.
3371 3372	J. R. S. ROGERS & SON	These two impressed marks are given by T. H. Ormsbee in his *English China and its marks* (1959), c. 1814–36.
3366	ROGERS & SONS	*See* James Rogers.

ROMAINE		**WINEFRIDE ROMAINE-WALKER, MISS**, London W. 1920's. *Pottery figures, etc.*
3373	WINEFRIDE ROMAINE-WALKER	Signature mark on figures and animal models, 1920's.

ROOKE		**BERNARD ROOKE**, Alan Gallery, Forest Gate, London S.E.23. 1961– . *Studio-type Pottery.*
3374	BERNARD ROOKE	Signature mark, 1961– . Many examples are unmarked.

238	ROPE LANE POTTERY	*See* W. Balaam.

ROPER		**ROPER & MEREDITH**, Garfield Pottery, Longton. Staffordshire Potteries. 1913–24. *Earthenwares.*
3375–6		Printed marks, 1913–24.

	ROSE or J. ROSE or I. ROSE & CO. or J. ROSE & CO. or JOHN ROSE & CO.	*See* Coalport Porcelain Works.
3356	"ROSE JAR"	*See* Rockingham Works.

ROSE

MURIEL ROSE, MISS, Temple Sheen, London S.W.14. 1959– . *Studio-type Pottery.*

3377   MURIEL ROSE   Incised, or painted signature, in writing letters, 1959– .

ROSINA

ROSINA CHINA CO. LTD., Queen's Pottery, Longton. Staffordshire Potteries. 1941– . *China.* Formerly G. Warrilow & Son Ltd.

From c. 1941 to 1946 the marks previously used by G. Warrilow & Son Ltd. were continued.

Rosina marks from 1946 include:

3378–81

c. 1946+

c. 1948+   c. 1952+   1952+

ROSLYN

ROSLYN CHINA, Park Place Works, Longton. Staffordshire Potteries. 1946 to July 1963. *Bone China.* Formerly Reid & Co., q.v.

3382

Former mark of Reid & Co., continued to c. 1950.

3383-5

c. 1950+   c. 1955+   c. 1958—63

Printed marks, c. 1950 to July 1963. The trade-name Roslyn was also used by Reid & Co., see page 529.

ROSS

ROGER, ROSS TURNER, Chesilborne (1949–57), then Abbotsbury, Dorset (c. 1957–). 1949– . *Earthenwares, Slip-wares, Lustres, etc.*

3386

Incised or painted initial mark with last two numbers of year, 1949– .

3387   ROSS TURNER

Incised signature mark in writing letters, with "Abbotsbury" from 1957– .

3388

Incised or painted initial mark of Mrs. Hilda Ross Turner, c. 1957– .

3389–9a

Joint marks of Roger and Hilda Ross Turner, c. 1957– .

4226   ROUTH

See Wold Pottery Ltd.

ROUTH

ROUTH LANE POTTERY, Miss Ann Wrightson, Tilehurst, Nr. Reading, Berkshire. 1958– . *Majolica and Slip decorated Earthenware.*

3390   ROUTH LANE POTTERY TILEHURST

Stamped mark, 1959–61.

3390a   ROUTH LANE POTTERY, TILEHURST, BERKS.

Stamped mark, 1961– . Note addition of word "Berks".

ROWLEY

ROWLEY & NEWTON (LTD.), Park Place Works, Longton. Staffordshire Potteries. 1896–1901. *Earthenwares and China.* Formerly Rowley & Jervis. Subsequently Rowley & Son.

3391   R. & N.   Distinguishing detail of several printed or impressed marks of
3391a   differing design: name of the individual pattern is often in-
                   cluded, 1896–1901. The lion crest, as mark no. 3391a, is often
                   included in marks.

3293   ROYAL ADDERLEY   *See* Ridgway Potteries Ltd.

4146–8   ROYAL ALBERT   *See* Thomas C. Wild (& Sons Ltd.).
          or
4144–5   ROYAL ALBERT
          CROWN CHINA

ROYAL

ROYAL ALBION CHINA CO., Albion Street, Longton. Staffordshire Potteries. 1921–48. *China.*

3392–4

Printed marks c. 1921+. Variations occur.

ROYAL

ROYAL ALLER VALE & WATCOMBE POTTERY CO., St. Mary Church, Torquay, Devon. c. 1901–62. *Earthenwares.* Formerly Aller Vale Art Pottery, q.v. Production ceased on September 30th, 1962.

3395   ROYAL ALLER VALE   Impressed or printed name-marks, c. 1901+.
3396   DEVON MOTTO
        WARE
3397   ROYAL
        TORQUAY
        POTTERY

3398   Printed or impressed mark, c. 1958–62.

| 1026–7 | ROYAL ALMA | *See* Thomas Cone Ltd. |

ROYAL ARMS

The British Royal Arms, and many close copies, occur in the printed or impressed marks of many 19th and 20th century British manufacturers. It should be noted that foreign firms also copied these arms.

The basic form of mark can be a guide to dating, for all arms engraved after 1837 will have the simple quartered shield but the pre-1837 arms have an inescutcheon or extra shield in the centre. See example below. The inescutcheon had a cap over the top during the 1801–14 period and this was replaced by a crown from 1814 to 1837.

Example of pre-1837 Royal Arms mark with inescutcheon.

Example of post-1837 Royal Arms mark with simple quartered shield.

929	ROYAL ART POTTERY	*See* Clough's Royal Art Pottery, Ltd.
574	ROYAL BARUM	*See* C. H. Brannam.
2882	ROYAL BOURBON	*See* New Pearl Pottery Co. Ltd.
4236 4238	ROYAL BRADWELL	*See* Arthur Wood & Son (Longton) Ltd.
824–5	ROYAL CAULDON	*See* Cauldon Potteries Ltd.
2855 2861	ROYAL CHELSEA	*See* New Chelsea China Co. Ltd. *See* New Chelsea Porcelain Co. Ltd.
2118	ROYAL CHINA	*See* E. Hughes & Co.
3880–1	ROYAL CROWN POTTERY	*See* Trentham Bone China Ltd.
1333	ROYAL DOULTON	*See* Doulton & Co. Ltd., Burslem and Lambeth.

369a	ROYAL ESSEX ART POTTERY	*See* Edward Bingham.
2199–2202	ROYAL GRAFTON	*See* A. B. Jones & Sons Ltd.
1690	ROYAL HARVEY	*See* Gibson & Sons (Ltd).
3225	ROYAL LANCASTRIAN	*See* Pilkingtons.
2367a	ROYAL LEIGHTON	*See* Leighton Pottery Ltd.
855	ROYAL MAYFAIR	*See* Chapmans Longton Ltd.
2890–1	ROYAL NORFOLK	*See* Norfolk Pottery Co. Ltd.
	ROYAL PRINCE	*See* Hall Bros. (Longton) Ltd.
896	ROYAL SEMI-PORCELAIN	*See* Edward Clarke (& Co.)

ROYAL

ROYAL STAFFORD CHINA (Thomas Poole and Gladstone China Ltd.), Longton. Staffordshire Potteries. 1952– . *Porcelain.* Formerly Thomas Poole and Gladstone China Ltd., see pages 503 and 274.

3399–3402   ROYAL STAFFORD BONE CHINA MADE IN ENGLAND

Printed marks 1952. The name "Royal Stafford China" and marks no. 3399 and 3400 were formerly used by Messrs. Thomas Poole, see page 503.

2118	ROYAL STAFFORDSHIRE CHINA	*See* E. Hughes & Co.
4170–1 4176	ROYAL STAFFORDSHIRE POTTERY	*See* Arthur J. Wilkinson (Ltd.).
854 856	ROYAL STANDARD	*See* Chapmans Longton Ltd.

983–4 3675–6	ROYAL STANLEY	*See* Colclough & Co. *See* Stanley Pottery Ltd.
3710	ROYAL STUART	*See* Stevenson, Spencer & Co. Ltd.

ROYAL

ROYAL TARA, Tara Hall, Galway, Ireland. 1942– . *China.*

3403 — Printed mark, 1942– . Other marks occur with the name "Royal Tara" or "Regina".

3397	ROYAL TORQUAY POTTERY	*See* Royal Aller Vale & Watcombe Pottery Co.
255&a	ROYAL TUDOR WARE	*See* Barker Bros. Ltd.
4068	ROYAL TUNSTALL	*See* Wedgwood & Co. Ltd.
3291	ROYAL VALE	*See* Ridgway Potteries Ltd.
3311	ROYAL VITRIFIED	*See* Ridgways.
3398	ROYAL WATCOMBE	*See* Royal Aller Vale & Watcombe Pottery Co.
114a	ROYAL WESTMINSTER	*See* Anchor Porcelain Co.
1837–9	ROYAL WINTON	*See* Grimwades Ltd.
—	ROYAL WORCESTER	*See* Worcester Porcelains.
3445 3447	ROYAL YORK	*See* Salisbury (Crown) China Co.
2321	ROYALL & LANSAN	*See* Lancaster & Sons (Ltd.)
3346	RP (joined)	*See* Bryan Rochford.
3239	R. & P.	*See* Rhodes & Proctor.
—	R. R. S. & Co.	*See* Appendix, page 730.

3184–92	RS	*See* Samuel Radford (Ltd.).
3542	(joined)	*See* Raymond Silverman.
3705		*See* Ralph Stevenson.
3327	R. & S.	*See* Rigby & Stevenson.
	or	*See* Robinson & Son.
3340	R. & S. L	
3202	R. S. & CO.	*See* Rathbone Smith & Co.
3299	R. S. R.	*See* Ridgway, Sparks & Ridgway.
3706	R. S. & S.	*See* Ralph Stevenson & Son.
3713	R. S. W.	*See* Stevenson & Williams.
3426	R. S. W. RYE	*See* Rye Pottery.
3217	R. & T.	*See* Reed & Taylor.
3405	RUBAY ART WARE	*See* Rubian Art Pottery Ltd.

RUBIAN

RUBIAN ART POTTERY LTD., Park Works, Fenton. Staffordshire Potteries. 1906–33.* *Earthenwares.* Formerly H. K. Barker & Co. Ltd.

3404	L. S. & G.	Impressed or printed mark, 1906–30.
3405	RUBAY ART WARE	Trade-name, c. 1926–33.

* This firm was a branch of Grimwades from c. 1913. See also Grimwades Ltd., page 293

RUNNAFORD

RUNNAFORD POTTERY (William Young), Runnaford Combe, Buckfastleigh, Devon. 1951– . *Pottery Figures, Groups, etc.*

3406	RUNNAFORD POTTERY DEVON	Printed or written marks. The signature in writing letters, 1951– .
3407	WILL YOUNG	

RUSCOE		WILLIAM RUSCOE, Stoke-on-Trent prior to 1944, Exeter from 1944. c. 1920– . *Pottery Figures, etc.*

3408 Incised or painted mark, 1920+.

3409 Incised or painted monogram, with year. c. 1925+.

3410 WM RUSCOE Signature mark in writing letters, c. 1925–50.

3411 WILLIAM RUSCOE Signature mark in writing letters. "William" in full from c. 1950.

RUSKIN — RUSKIN POTTERY (W. Howson Taylor), Smethwick, Nr. Birmingham. 1898 to July 1935. *Earthenwares.*

The Ruskin Pottery closed in July 1935 and W. Howson Taylor (b. 1876) died on September 22nd, 1935.

For further information see L. B. Powell's *Howson Taylor, Master Potter* (c. 1936).

3412 TAYLOR Early impressed mark, c. 1898+.

3413-14 Painted or incised marks, c. 1898+.

3415 Impressed mark, within oval, c. 1904–15. The year of production usually occurs in full with this mark.

3416 RUSKIN Several impressed marks occur with the name "Ruskin"
ENGLAND c. 1904+. "Made in England" dates from about 1920
3417 RUSKIN POTTERY onwards.
3418 RUSKIN
3419 RUSKIN
MADE IN ENGLAND

3420 W. HOWSON TAYLOR Printed or incised mark, "W. Howson Taylor" is in writing
RUSKIN letters, c. 1920+.
ENGLAND

RUSSELL		**EVADNE RUSSELL, MISS,** Burgess Hill, Sussex. 1950– . *Studio-type Pottery, of an individual nature.*
3421		Painted mark, of the initials ER joined, 1950– .

RUSTINGTON

RUSTINGTON POTTERY, Worthing Road, Rustington, Sussex. 1947– . *Studio-type Pottery.*

3422   Impressed or printed trade-mark, 1947– .

3423   Initial mark of G. H. Champion on Rustington pottery, 1947– , but now seldom used as Mrs. E. E. Champion now does most of the throwing.

4155	R. V. W.	*See* Richard Vernon Wildblood.
3344	R. & W.	*See* Robinson & Wood.
3345	R. W. & B.	*See* Robinson, Wood & Brownfield.
1402	R W D	*See* Ruth Duckworth.
4114	R. W. F.	*See* Reginald F. Wells.
3521	R. W. M.	*See* Martin Bros.

RYDER		**FRANCES E. RYDER, MRS.,** Blackheath, London S.E.3. 1920–35. *Studio-type Pottery.*
3424	Frances E. Ryder	Incised or painted signature mark, c. 1920–35.
738 & a	Rye	*See* Cadborough.
1199	or	*See* Leslie G. Davie.
3429–32	Rye Pottery	*See* Rye Pottery.

RYE

RYE POTTERY (various owners), Bellevue Pottery, Rye, Sussex. 1869– . *Pottery.*

Early Rye pottery was often unmarked. "Old Sussex Ware, Rye" and "Rye Pottery" marks were used by W. Mitchell (& Sons) at the nearby Cadborough Pottery, see page 122.

3425	SUSSEX WARE	Incised mark, in writing letters with date. Late 19th century–early 20th century. The place name Rye and the year are sometimes added to this basic mark.

3426

Impressed or incised S. R. W. (Sussex Rustic Ware) mark, c. 1869–c. 1920.

3427

Impressed or incised S. A. W. (Sussex Art Ware) mark, c. 1920–39.

The factory was closed during the war years, 1939–45, and was reopened by John C. Cole and Walter V. Cole in 1947. The following impressed or printed marks have been used by the Coles.

3428–32

1947–53

RYE
1947–54

c. 1955–6

1955–6

MADE IN
RYE
POTTERY
ENGLAND
1957–

3433

Painted or incised initial mark of Walter V. Cole found on some individual pieces, some examples may have the year and the word Rye added, c. 1957– .

S

—	S	*See* Appendix, page 730.
813–17		*See* Caughley Works.
2967b		*See* Richard Parkinson Ltd.
3538		*See* John Shorthose.
3566		*See* John Singleman.
3648a		*See* Josiah Spode.
3660b		*See* Sheila Sprague.
3750		*See* C. P. Sutcliffe & Co. Ltd., page 604.
4117		*See* Reginald F. Wells.
3727	S. BROS.	*See* Stubbs Bros.
805b	S	*See* Michael & Sheila Casson.
	(with crescent or C above)	
2150	S. & CO.	*See* Isleworth.
3643		*See* Sowter & Co.
3778	S. LTD.	*See* Swinnertons Ltd.
3633	S. & SONS	*See* Southwick Pottery.
3678	SA	*See* Ann Stannard.
	(joined)	
76	S. A. & CO.	*See* Samuel Alcock & Co.

SADLER		E. SADLER, Fremington, Nr. Barnstaple, North Devon. Late 19th century. *Earthenwares.*
3434	E. SADLER FREMINGTON N. DEVON	Incised mark in writing letters on motto jug in the Worthing Museum, late 19th century.

SADLER		JAMES SADLER & SONS (LTD.), Wellington and Central Potteries, Burslem. Staffordshire Potteries. c. 1899– . *Earthenwares, mainly Teapots.* Formerly Sadler & Co.
3435	ENGLAND J. S. S. B.	Impressed mark, 1899–c. 1937.
3436	SADLER BURSLEM ENGLAND	Impressed or printed mark, 1937+.
3437		Printed mark, c. 1947– .

SADLER		JOHN SADLER, Messrs. Sadler & Green, Liverpool, Lancs. c. 1756–99. *Printers—not manufacturers.*
3438	J. SADLER— LIVERPOOL	John Sadler invented a process of ceramic printing, c. 1756. Wedgwood and other potters sent their wares to be printed by
3439	SADLER LIVERPOOL	the Sadler & Green partnership. Tiles were also decorated, in red and/or black (underglaze blue was not employed). Speci-
3440	GREEN	mens are sometimes marked. Sadler retired c. 1770 and Guy
3441	GREEN LIVERPOOL	Green continued to 1799, the "GREEN" marks are of the later period. Signed tiles are illustrated in the companion illustrated encyclopaedia.

SALAMAN		JILL SALAMAN, MISS (Mrs. Hamer), Selsey, Sussex. 1929–50. *Studio-type Pottery and Tiles.*
3442		Signature mark, 1929–50.

SALISBURY		SALISBURY CROWN* CHINA CO., Salisbury Works, Longton. Staffordshire Potteries. c. 1927–61.† *Bone China.*

* "CROWN" deleted from firm's title in 1949.
† Firm taken over by Thomas Poole and moved to Chadwick Street, Longton, from November 1961.

3443-5

SALISBURY CHINA
Bradley's
ENGLAND
c. 1927-37

SALISBURY
FINE BONE
CHINA
MADE IN
ENGLAND
c. 1937+

ROYAL YORK
BONE CHINA
MADE IN
ENGLAND
c. 1940

3446-8

SALISBURY
CHINA
MADE IN ENGLAND
FINE BONE
c. 1946+

ROYAL YORK
BONE CHINA
ENGLAND
c. 1952+

SALISBURY
BONE
CHINA
c. 1959-61

Printed marks, 1927-61.

3454-5	SALON CHINA	*See* Salt & Nixon.
810	SALOPIAN	*See* Caughley Works.
3449		*See* Salopian Art Pottery Co.

SALOPIAN

SALOPIAN ART POTTERY CO., Benthall, Nr. Broseley, Shropshire. 1882–c. 1912. *Earthenwares.*

3449   SALOPIAN

Impressed mark on *earthenwares*, 1882–1912. Wares with this mark should not be confused with CAUGHLEY PORCELAIN marked in the same manner. A diamond-shaped mark with the word "Salopian" was registered in 1882.

SALT

RALPH SALT, Marsh Street, Hanley. Staffordshire Potteries. c. 1820–46. *Earthenware Figures, Animals, etc.*
     Ralph Salt was succeeded, on his death in 1846, by his son Charles, who died c. 1864.

3450   SALT

Impressed name-mark usually on relief scroll on back of figure bases, c. 1820–46. Examples are included in the companion illustrated encyclopaedia of marked specimens. Porcelain was also manufactured but no marked examples have been recorded.

SALT		**SALT BROS.,** Brownhills Pottery, Tunstall. Staffordshire Potteries. 1897–1904. *Earthenwares.* Formerly Brownhills Pottery Co., q.v. Taken over by T. Till & Sons.

3451
SALT BROS.
TUNSTALL
ENGLAND

Impressed or printed mark.

3452

Printed mark, c. 1897–1904.

SALT

SALT & NIXON (LTD.), Gordon Pottery (Jubilee Works from 1910), Longton. Staffordshire Potteries. 1901–34. *China.*

3453–55

c. 1901–21   c. 1914–21   c. 1921–34

Printed marks.

1605   SAMFORD WARE   *See* Samuel Ford & Co.

SAMPSON
BRIDGWOOD

See Sampson *Bridgwood* & Son (Ltd.).

SAMUEL

AUDREY SAMUEL, MISS, Kensington, London W.8. 1949– . *Studio-type Pottery.*

3456

Incised or painted mark, 1949– .

SANCTUARY

MAISIE SANCTUARY, MRS., Laleham-on-Thames, Middlesex. 1949– . *Pottery Figures and Animals.*

3457
SANCTUARY 1963

Painted or incised signature mark, 1949– .

2328–33 SANDLAND (WARE)   *See* Lancaster & Sandland Ltd.

SANDLANDS

SANDLANDS & COLLEY, LTD., Lichfield Pottery, Hanley. Staffordshire Potteries. 1907–10.* *China and Earthenwares.* Formerly Sandlands Ltd.

3458

Printed mark, 1907–10.*

* Continued by W. Sandland to c. 1913, old mark probably continued.

SANDYGATE

SANDYGATE POTTERY LTD., Sandygate, Kingsteignton, Devon. 1950– . *Earthenwares.*

3459–60

Impressed or printed marks.

—   WILLIAM SANS   *See* Appendix, page 730.

SANT

SANT & VODREY, Abbey Pottery, Cobridge. Staffordshire Potteries. 1887–93. *Earthenwares.* Formerly Wood & Hawthorne, q.v.

3461

Printed or impressed mark, 1887–93.

SARACEN

SARACEN POTTERY (CO.), Possil Park, Glasgow, Scotland. 1875–1900. *Earthenwares, various.*

3462   B. M. & CO.
SARACEN POTTERY

Impressed or printed mark used by Bailey Murray & Co., 1875–84. From c. 1884 to c. 1900 the style was SARACEN POTTERY CO.

SARENE		JUNE SARENE, MRS., Pinner, Middlesex. 1954– . *Studio-type Pottery*.
3463 3464	J. S.	Incised or painted initial or monogram marks, 1954– .

SAUL		ISOBEL SAUL, MISS, Southbourne-on-Sea, Hampshire. c. 1920's. *Pottery*.
3465 3466	I. S. ISABEL SAUL	Initial or signature marks, c. 1920's.

SAUNDERS		SAMUEL E. SAUNDERS, East Cowes, Isle of Wight. 1927–30. *Pottery*.
773		Initial trade-mark registered in 1927. After 1930 S. E. Saunders was at the Isle of Wight Pottery and at the Carisbrooke Pottery (see pages 347 and 127).

SAVIAC		SAVIAC WORKSHOPS (David S. Ballantyne), Highcliffe, Hants. c. 1935– . *Studio-type Pottery*.
3467	S. W.	Incised or painted initial mark rarely used, most wares unmarked, more widely used after 1961.

382	SAVOY CHINA	*See* Birks, Rawlins & Co.
772 (note)	SAXON STONE	*See* Thomas & John Carey.
3493 3637	S. B. & CO.	*See* Thomas Sharpe. *See* Southwick Pottery.
3482	S. & B. or	*See* Sefton & Brown.
3483	S. & B. F. B.	

3577	S. & B. T.	*See* Smith & Binnall.
263 593 595 597	S. B. & S. or S. B. & SON	*See* Samuel Barker & Son. *See* Sampson Bridgwood & Son (Ltd.).
921	S. C.	*See* Stephen Clive.
3524 3526	S. & C.	*See* Shore & Coggins.
—	SCAMMELLS	*See* Appendix, page 731.
3683–5 922	S. C. CO.	*See* Star China Co. *See* Stephen Clive.
3531	S. C. H. L.	*See* Shore, Coggins & Holt.

SCHNEIDER

PAULA SCHNEIDER, MRS., London N.16. 1956– .
Studio-type Pottery.

3468   Incised or painted mark, 1956– .

SCHOFIELD

A. SCHOFIELD (Proprietor, H. Thorburn), Wetheriggs Pottery, Nr. Penrith, Cumberland. Est. 1913 but earlier potteries were on this site. *Earthenwares.*

3469	SCHOFIELD	Incised signature, in writing letters, c. 1920–53.
3470	SCHOFIELD PENRITH	Impressed mark, c. 1920– .
3471	CUMBERLAND POTTERY PENRITH	Incised mark, in writing letters, with monogram H. T. (mark no. 3472). One would expect this rare form of mark to relate to this pottery but Mr. Thorburn states that he has not used such a monogram.
3472		This pottery was closed from 1940 to 1946.

422	SCOTIA POTTERY	*See* Edward F. Bodley & Co.

3638	SCOTT	*See* Southwick Pottery.
3629	or	
3639	A. SCOTT (& CO.)	
3630a		
3640	or	
	A. SCOTT (& SON(S))	

SCOTT

SCOTT BROTHERS, Portobello, Nr. Edinburgh, Scotland. c. 1786–96.* *Earthenwares.* Works subsequently continued by Cookson & Jardine, Thomas Yoole and then Thomas Rathbone & Co., q.v.

3473	SCOTT BROS.	Impressed marks, c. 1786–96.
3474	SCOTT BROTHERS*	
3475	SCOTT	
	P. B.	

* The mark SCOTT BROTHERS was also used at the Southwick Pottery. An interesting class of brown earthenware decorated with yellow transfer printed motifs has been for many years attributed to the Portobello Pottery. A good range is illustrated by G. Carroll Lindsay in *Antiques* magazine (U.S.A.), May 1962. However, if the dates given by Fleming and other authorities for the Scott Brothers' working period are correct, some at least of these wares must have been made by Scott Brothers of the Southwick Pottery, Sunderland (see page 587). It seems very likely that dishes bearing the impressed mark SCOTT BROTHERS were made at the Southwick Pottery, not at Portobello. A flower pot with the "SCOTT P. B." mark will be found illustrated in *British Pottery and Porcelain: an illustrated Encyclopaedia of Marked Specimens*. The initials P.B. may in this case be read as referring to Portobello.

SCOTT

GERALD SCOTT, Redland, Bristol. c. 1942– . *Studio-type Pottery, Stonewares, Terra-cotta and Sculpture.*

3476	GERALD SCOTT	Signature mark on important work, c. 1942– , often with year of production.
3477		Incised or painted initial mark, c. 1947–51.
3478		Incised or painted mark, c. 1951– , with year of production.

3631   SCOTT & SON(S)   *See* Southwick Pottery.

SCOTT-PITCHER   MARJORIE SCOTT-PITCHER, MRS., Mermaid Street, Rye, Sussex. 1954– . *Studio-type Pottery and Figures.*

3479   Painted or incised mark, 1954– .

Scratch cross mark   A scratched or incised saltire cross mark occurs on some early English porcelains, mainly in the 1750's. This cross mark may well be nothing more than a workman's mark, or it may indicate a special body, etc. The scratched cross has been noted on early Worcester and Liverpool porcelains, also on Bow and Bristol examples. A mug with the date 1754 and a scratched cross is illustrated in the *Transactions* (no. III) *of the English Porcelain Circle*, p. 82. It should not be regarded as a factory mark.

SCRIVENER   **R. G. SCRIVENER & CO.**, Norfolk Street Works, Hanley. Staffordshire Potteries. 1870–83. *China and Earthenwares.* Subsequently Pointon & Co. Ltd., q.v.

3480   R. G. S.   Distinguishing details of several printed or impressed marks of
3481   R. G. S.   differing design: name of the individual pattern is often
       & CO.   included, 1870–83.

1468   S. E.   *See* Samuel Elkin.

—   T. SEABORN   *See* Appendix, page 731.

82   SEAHAM POTTERY   *See* John Allason.

2147   SEAVIEW   *See* Island Pottery Studio.
2370b   *See* Jo Lester.

308   SEAVIEW POTTERY   *See* D. Beckley.

3773   S. & E.   *See* Swift & Elkin.

3926   SEEBY   *See* Upchurch Pottery.

SEFTON		**SEFTON & BROWN**, Ferrybridge Pottery, Ferrybridge, Yorkshire. 1897–1919. *Earthenwares.* Formerly T. & E. L. Poulson. Subsequently T. Brown & Sons Ltd., q.v.
3482	S. & B.	Distinguishing details of several printed or impressed marks of differing design, 1897–1919.
3483	S. & B.	
	F. B.	
SELMAN		**J. & W. SELMAN**, Gritten Street, Tunstall. Staffordshire Potteries. c. 1864–5. *Earthenwares Figures, etc.*
3484	SELMAN	Rare impressed mark, 1864–5.
SELOUS		**DOROTHEA SELOUS, MISS** (Mrs. D. Jamieson), London N.W.6. c. 1920–35. *Studio-type Pottery.*
3485	SELOUS	Signature-type mark, 1920–35.
3702	SEMI NANKIN CHINA	*See* Andrew Stevenson.
1764a	SEMI PORCELAIN	*See* George Grainger (& Co.).
SENESHALL		**"SENESHALL CATS"**, Kensington Church St., London W.8. 1960– . *Earthenware Models of Cats.*
3486	SENESHAL CATS	Painted or incised name-mark on pottery cats, 1960– .
691	SENOLITH	*See* A. W. Buchan & Co.
3720	mS^e	*See* Eric & Meira Stockl.
773	SES (joined)	*See* Samuel E. Saunders.
SEVENOAKS		**SEVENOAKS POTTERY LTD.** (Gordon Plahn), Sevenoaks, Kent. 1958*–61. *Studio-type Pottery.*

* An earlier "Sevenoaks Pottery", c. 1955–7, is not connected with the Sevenoaks Pottery Ltd., or with Gordon Plahn.

3487
3488

Impressed seal-type marks, 1958–61. Gordon Plahn then moved to Langton Green, see page 381.

SEVIERS

SEVIERS POTTERY LTD., Hampstead, London N.W.3. c. 1951– . *Earthenwares.* Formerly Old Hampstead Pottery Co.

3489   SEVIERS   Written or incised mark, 1951– .

3665   SEWELL   *See* St. Anthony's Pottery.
                 or
3667   SEWELL & CO.
                 or
3666   SEWELL & DONKIN

1560   S. F.   *See* John Thomas Firth.
                 K. L.

1622   S. F.   *See* Robert & Sheila Fournier.
3739   (also joined)   *See* Felix Summerly.

3578   S. & F.   *See* Smith & Ford.

1543   S. F. & CO.   *See* S. Fielding & Co.

1628   SFS   *See* Sylvia Fox-Strangways.
                (joined)

2151   S. & G.   *See* Isleworth.

—   SH   *See* Appendix, page 731.
1267   (also joined)   *See* Derby Porcelain Works, page 203.
1927   *See* S. Hancock (& Sons), page 308.
1267   *See* Stevenson & Hancock.

4494a	S. H. & CO.	*See* Appendix.
1929	S. H. & S.	*See* S. Hancock (& Sons).
	or	
1929a	S. H. & SONS	

SHARPE

THOMAS SHARPE (SHARPE, BROTHERS & CO.), Swadlincote, Burton-on-Trent, Derbyshire. c. 1821– . *Earthenwares and Stonewares.*

    After 1838 retitled Sharpe Brothers & Co.

3490	SHARPE MANUFACTURER SWADLINCOTE	Impressed marks, c. 1821–38.
3491	T. SHARPE	
3492	THOMAS SHARPE	
3493	S. B. & CO.	Initial marks, in various forms, c. 1838–95. "Ltd." added from 1895. This firm produced mainly sanitary wares.

SHARPE

SHARPE (WILLIAM) & CO., Brampton China Manufactory, Brampton-in-Torksey, Lincolnshire. c. 1803–7*. *China* (?).

3494	BRAMPTON MANUFACTORY	These two marks are listed on the authority of G. B. Hughes and are included in his "Victorian Pottery and Porcelain" (1959).
3495	S. W. W. B. B.	N.B. The present writer has not seen the initial mark. It would seem unlikely to have been used. The trading name "Sharpe & Co." is given in *The London Gazette*. The initials are those of the partners William Sharpe (Plumber and Glazier), Samuel Walker, James Walker (Farmer), Benjamin Booth (Printer) and William Billingsley. It seems unlikely that their initials would have been used as a mark, as their names were not generally known.

    * The notice concerning the dissolution of partnership is dated November 1807 and relates to July 15th, 1807, but it is stated that "the business of a china manufacturer from that time has been and is now carried on in the name of Samuel Walker".

SHARPUS

Several printed marks occur with the name of the china retailers, SHARPUS of London. The various changes in the firm's title help to date such marks.   These changes, obtained from London directories, are:

Sharpus & Co., 1801–2.
R. (& E.) Sharpus, 1803.
E. Sharpus, 1803–34.
F. Sharpus, 1835.
Thos. & F. Sharpus, 1836–7.
Thomas Sharpus & Co., 1838–43.
Sharpus & Cullum, 1844–71.
This was followed by Cullum & Sharpus, 1872–93.

—	SHAW	*See* Appendix, page 731.

SHAW

ANTHONY SHAW (& CO.) (& SON), Tunstall (c. 1851–6) and Burslem (c. 1860–c. 1900). Staffordshire Potteries. 1851–c. 1900.   *Earthenwares.*

3496	ANTHONY SHAW	Distinguishing details of several printed or impressed marks of differing design: name of the individual pattern is often included, 1851–82. The Royal Arms often form the main part of Anthony Shaw's marks.
3497	A. SHAW	
3498	A. SHAW BURSLEM	
3499	SHAWS	
3500	SHAW BURSLEM	

—	& SON	Added to style and marks from c. 1882 to c. 1898.
—	& CO.	Substituted for "& Son" from c. 1898 until the firm was taken over by A. J. Wilkinson Ltd., c. 1900.
—	C. & J. SHAW junr.	*See* Appendix, page 731.

SHAW

SHAW & COPESTAKE, Drury and Sylvan Works, Longton. Staffordshire Potteries.   1901– .   *Earthenwares.*

New factory open at Barford Street, Longton, 1957.   Early wares probably unmarked.

3501–3

c. 1925–36   c. 1936–40   c. 1946–

Printed or impressed marks.

SHAW		**GEORGE SHAW & SONS (LTD.),** Holmes Pottery, Rotherham, Yorkshire. 1887–1948. *Earthenwares.* Formerly J. Jackson & Co., q.v.
3504	G. S. & S.	Distinguishing detail of several printed marks of differing design: name of the individual pattern is often included, 1887–1948.
	JOHN SHAW (18th century)	*See* Appendix, page 732.

SHAW	**JOHN SHAW & SONS (LONGTON) LTD.,** Willow Pottery (and other addresses), Longton. Staffordshire Potteries. 1931–63. *China and Earthenwares.* Formerly J. Shaw & Sons.

3505–7

c. 1931+   c. 1949+   c. 1959–63

Printed marks.

SHAW		**RALPH SHAW,** Cobridge. Staffordshire Potteries. Early 18th century. *Earthenwares.*
3508	Made by Ralph Shaw, October 31, Cobridge gate	Unique inscription in slip on earthenware cradle in the Hanley Museum. This is dated 1740 or 1746.

SHAW		**SHAW & SONS,** Sandyford Pottery, Tunstall. Staffordshire Potteries. 1892–1910. *Earthenwares.*
3509	S. & S. S.	Impressed or printed initial mark, 1892–1910.
—	R. SHAWE or	*See* Appendix, page 732.
—	R. SHAW'S	

—	William Sheldon	*See* Appendix, page 732.
3510–12 4164–5	SHELLEY	*See* Shelley Potteries Ltd., below. *See* Wileman & Co., page 672.

SHELLEY

SHELLEY POTTERIES LTD. (Shelley, c. 1925–9), The Foley, Longton. Staffordshire Potteries. 1925– . *China.* Formerly Wileman & Co., q.v.

N.B. Name "Shelley" formerly used by Wileman & Co.

3510–12

c. 1925–40   c. 1945–

Printed marks.

SHELLY

JOHN SHELLY, Bath Pottery, Bath, Somerset, c. 1949–56, and Dorset, c. 1957–60, and The Old Manor, Littlehempston, Totnes, Devon. c. 1961– . *Studio-type Pottery.*

3513

Initial mark, impressed, 1949–56.

3514   BATH POTTERY   The name Bath Pottery may also occur, 1949–56.

3515

Later version of impressed initial mark, used in Dorset from 1957 and subsequently at Littlehempston, 1957– . Note that the top of the J is raised above the cross piece from 1957.

1493   SHELTON IVORY   *See* Empire Porcelain Co.

SHEPHERD

ALFRED SHEPHERD & CO., Eagle Works, Longton. Staffordshire Potteries. 1864–70. *Earthenwares.*

3516   A. SHEPHERD & CO.   Distinguishing detail of several printed marks of differing design: name of the individual pattern is often included, 1864–70.

SHERWIN   **SHERWIN & COTTON**, Vine St. (and other addresses), Hanley. Staffordshire Potteries. 1877–1930. *Tile manufacturers.*

3517   Impressed mark, 1877–1930.

3518   SHERWIN & COTTON Name impressed or incised on back of tiles and plaques, 1877–1930.

SHERWOOD   **PHYLLIS SHERWOOD, MRS.,** Epsom, Surrey. 1960– . *Studio-type Pottery.*

3519   PHYLLIS SHERWOOD, Incised or painted signature mark in writing letters, 1960– .
       EPSOM

SHIRLEY   **RALPH SHIRLEY,** Foston, Derby. 1959– . *Studio-type Pottery.*

3520   SHIRLEY. FOSTON   Printed mark, words in double line circle, 1959– .

SHIRLEY   **THOMAS SHIRLEY & CO.,** Clyde Pottery, Greenock, Scotland. c. 1840–57. *Earthenwares.* Formerly Clyde Pottery Co. (Andrew Muir & Co.). Subsequently Clyde Pottery Co., q.v.

3521   T. S. & COY   Impressed initial marks, c. 1840–57.
3522   T. S. & C.

2149   SHORE & CO.   *See* Isleworth, page 348.

SHORE   **SHORE & COGGINS,** High Street and Edensor Works, Longton. Staffordshire Potteries. 1911– . *China.* Formerly Shore, Coggins & Holt, q.v.

3523–6      Bell China

     c. 1911+   c. 1922+   c. 1930+   c. 1936+

3527-30

c. 1949+   c. 1950+   c. 1959+   c. 1959+

Printed marks.

SHORE

SHORE, COGGINS & HOLT, Edensor Works, Longton. Staffordshire Potteries. 1905–10. *China and Earthenwares.* Formerly J. Shore & Co., q.v.   Subsequently Shore & Coggins, q.v.

3531   Printed mark, c. 1905–10.

SHORE

J. SHORE & CO., Edensor Works, Longton.   Staffordshire Potteries. 1887–1905. *China.* Subsequently Shore, Coggins & Holt, q.v.

3532   J. S. & CO.   Distinguishing detail of several printed marks of differing design: name of the individual pattern is often included, 1887 1905.

SHORTER

SHORTER & SON (LTD.), Copeland Street, Stoke. Staffordshire Potteries. 1905– . *Earthenwares.* Formerly Shorter & Boulton.

3533-5

c. 1914–36   c. 1936–40   c. 1940+

Printed marks.

SHORTHOSE

SHORTHOSE & CO., Shelton, Hanley. Staffordshire Potteries. c. 1817 and 1822. *Earthenwares.* See also Shorthose & Heath and John Shorthose.

3536	SHORTHOSE & CO.	Impressed, printed or written mark. This form of title only occurs in the Rate Books in 1817 (marked Void in 1819), and 1822, but was probably also used by Shorthose & Heath, see below. Examples will be found illustrated in *British Pottery and Porcelain : an illustrated Encyclopaedia of Marked Specimens*.

SHORTHOSE

SHORTHOSE & HEATH, Shelton, Hanley. Staffordshire Potteries. c. 1795–1815. *Earthenwares.* See also John Shorthose.

3537	SHORTHOSE & HEATH	Impressed or printed name-marks, c. 1795–1815. The style Shorthose & Co. may also have been used at this period. See previous entry.

SHORTHOSE

JOHN SHORTHOSE, Hanley. Staffordshire Potteries. c. 1807*–23. *Earthenwares.*

3538	S	Impressed initial and name-marks, c. 1807–23, the S mark may relate to another potter. Arrow marks are attributed to this potter but also occur on other wares. John Shorthose made good quality lustre wares, often with white relief patterns; examples are rarely marked.
3539	SHORTHOSE	

* The name John Shorthose also occurs c. 1783. There is an overlap of dates with Shorthose & Heath, c. 1795–1815, and with Shorthose & Co., c. 1815–7. John Shorthose was probably connected with these firms. See previous two entries.

SIBLEY

SIBLEY POTTERY (LTD.), Wareham, Dorset. 1922–62. *Earthenwares and Stonewares.*

3540	*Sibley*	Incised mark, rarely used, 1922–38.
3540a		Impressed mark, 1946–53.
3540b		Impressed or printed mark, 1953–62.

SIGGERY

JOHN SIGGERY, Herstmonceux, Wiston, etc., Sussex. Early 19th century. *Pottery.*

3541   MADE BY JOHN SIGGERY, POTTER WISTON, SUSSEX.

Inlaid inscriptions on pottery flasks, dated 1812 and 1835, in the Fitzwilliam Museum, Cambridge. Other examples are recorded, including one dated 1794. It is possible that two potters of this name, father and son, worked in Sussex.

3541a   MADE BY JOHN SIGGERY HERSTMON^x SUSSEX.

1003   SILCHESTER WARE

See S. & E. Collier.

4356   SILLAX

See Worcester Porcelains, page 699.

SILVERMAN

RAYMOND SILVERMAN, Dulwich, London S.E.22. 1962– . *Studio-type Pottery.*

3542   **RS**

Impressed seal-type mark, 1962– .

—   SIMPSON

See Appendix, page 732.

SIMPSON

J. SIMPSON, 28 Theobald's Road, London. Mid-19th century. *Parian Figures and Earthenwares.*

3543   J. SIMPSON

This name-mark has been recorded as found on parian figures. J. Simpson exhibited parian statuettes and earthenware table, tea and dessert services at the 1851 Exhibition.

SIMPSON

RALPH SIMPSON (1651–1724?). Staffordshire Potteries. Late 17th century to early 18th century. *Slip-decorated Earthenware.*

3544   RALPH SIMPSON

Slip-decorated dishes in the Victoria and Albert; the British and the Fitzwilliam Museums bear the name Ralph Simpson on the front and are similar to the Toft dishes. See *British Pottery and Porcelain: an illustrated Encyclopaedia of Marked Specimens.*
William Simpson and John Simpson made similar wares.

| SIMPSON | | **JOHN SIMPSON**, Burslem. Staffordshire Potteries. Early 18th century. *Slip-decorated Earthenwares.* |

3545
3546   JOHN SIMPSON
I. S.

This name occurs on slip decorated earthenwares. A two-handled posset-pot is dated 1735. Some examples bear the initials I. S. and have been attributed to John Simpson. Wedgwood in his list of Burslem potters, c. 1710–15, mentions three of this name. Ralph and William Simpson made similar wares.

SIMPSON

T. A. SIMPSON (& CO. LTD.), Furlong Tile Works, Burslem. Staffordshire Potteries. From 1902 (formerly at other addresses) to present day. *Tiles.*

3547   Lion and shield mark   Printed or impressed, 1908–39, not now used.

SIMPSON

WILLIAM SIMPSON, Burslem and/or Hanley and/or Tunstall. Staffordshire Potteries. Late 17th century to early 18th century. *Slip-decorated Earthenwares.*

3548   WILLIAM SIMPSON   This name occurs on a slip-decorated posset-pot, dated 1685. A William Simpson is mentioned in Tunstall Court Rolls of 1671, also by Wedgwood in his list of Burslem potters, c. 1710–15. A potter of this name was also working at Hanley and died in 1748.

SIMPSON

W. B. SIMPSON & SON (LTD.), St. Martins Lane, London W.C.2. c. 1873– . *Decorators, mainly of Tiles.*

3559   W   B
S
&   S

Distinguishing detail of printed or impressed marks of differing design, c. 1873– .

SIMPSONS

SIMPSONS (POTTERS) LTD., Elder Works, Cobridge. Staffordshire Potteries. 1944– . *Earthenwares.* Formerly Soho Pottery Ltd., q.v.

3560–2

c. 1944+

Solian ware
SIMPSONS (POTTERS) LTD.
COBRIDGE
ENGLAND.

c. 1944+

六月玫瑰
LIOH YÜEH
MEI XUEI
SIMPSONS (POTTERS) LTD
COBRIDGE
ENGLAND

c. 1951+

3563-5

c. 1954+   c. 1957+   c. 1959+

Other printed marks occur including the name of the pattern, etc., with the name of the firm in full. Other marks include the trade-name "Ambassador Ware".

—   A. SINGER   *See* Appendix, page 709.

SINGLEMAN   **JOHN SINGLEMAN,** Sheffield Paul, Penzance, Cornwall. 1948-61. *Studio-type Pottery, Terra-cotta and Stonewares.*

3566   S   Impressed seal mark of initial S in circle, 1950-61. See Plate 2.

3566a   JUG MARK   Some rare early wares bear an impressed mark comprising the
         P   outline of a jug, with the letter P inside the outline, c. 1948-9.

2186   S. J.   *See* Samuel Johnson (Ltd.), page 357.
2188   S. J. LTD.
2187   S. J. B.

734   S. & J. B.   *See* Samuel & John Burton.

2247   S. K. & CO.   *See* Samuel Keeling & Co.

SKEY   **GEORGE SKEY,** Wilnecote Works, Nr. Tamworth, Staffordshire. Ornamental wares 1862-1900, later sanitary wares. *Earthenwares, Terra-cotta and Stonewares.*

3567   GEORGE SKEY   Impressed mark, 1862-c. 1900. An earthenware lion with
        WILNECOTE WORKS   this mark will be found illustrated in *British Pottery and Porce-*
        NR. TAMWORTH   *lain: an illustrated Encyclopaedia of Marked Specimens.*

SKINNER

GEORGE SKINNER & CO., Stafford Pottery, Stockton-on-Tees, Yorkshire. c. 1855–70. *Earthenwares.* Formerly William Smith & Co., q.v.   Subsequently Skinner & Walker, q.v.

3568   G. S. & Co.

Distinguishing detail of several printed marks of differing design; name of the individual pattern is often included, c. 1855–70.   Some wares bearing a "G. S. & Co." printed mark also have the impressed mark of William Smith & Co. (no. 3599) showing that they were potted by this firm and decorated by their successors, George Skinner & Co.   Several special patterns were made for foreign markets.

SKINNER

SKINNER & WALKER, Stafford Pottery, Stockton-on-Tees, Yorkshire.   1870–c. 80.   *Earthenwares.*   Formerly G. Skinner & Co. (see also W. Smith & Co.).   Subsequently Ambrose Walker & Co.

3569   S. & W.
        QUEEN'S WARE
        STOCKTON

3569a   S. & W's
        PEARL WARE

3570   QUEEN'S WARE
        STOCKTON

Distinguishing details of several printed or impressed marks of differing design, c. 1870–80.

2410   S. L.

See Samuel Longbottom.

3673   S. & L.

See Stanley & Lambert.

SLACK

SLACK & BROWNLOW, Tonbridge, Kent.   Ornamental wares, c. 1928–34.   *Earthenwares.*

3571

CASTLE WARE.

3572   TONBRIDGE WARE

Printed or impressed mark, c. 1928–34.   The name "Tonbridge Ware" also occurs.

SLATTER		**MILDRED SLATTER, MRS.**, High Wycombe, Buckinghamshire. 1956– . *Studio-type Pottery.*

3573 Impressed seal mark, also incised or painted, 1956– . See Plate 2.

2495   S. M.   *See* Samuel Malkin.

2746   S. M. & CO.   *See* (Samuel) Moore & Co.

SMALL   **ISOBELLA R. SMALL, MISS**, Bangor, Northern Ireland. c. 1920's. *Studio-type Pottery.*

3574   ISOBELLA R. SMALL   Signature type mark, c. 1920's.

SMITH   **AMBROSE SMITH & CO.**, Burslem. Staffordshire Potteries. c. 1784–6. *Earthenwares.*

3575   A. S. & CO.   Impressed or printed initial mark, c. 1784–6.

SMITH   **SMITH & BARNETT LTD.**, Longton. Staffordshire Potteries. c. 1926– . *Wholesalers, etc.*

3576   SMITH & BARNETT LTD.   Distinguishing detail of several printed marks of differing design, c. 1926 .

SMITH   **SMITH & BINNALL**, Soho Pottery, Tunstall. Staffordshire Potteries. 1897–1900. *Earthenwares.* Formerly Rathbone, Smith & Co., q.v. Subsequently Soho Pottery, q.v.

3577   Printed mark, 1897–1900.

SMITH   **SMITH & FORD**, Lincoln Pottery, Burslem. Staffordshire Potteries. 1895–8. *Earthenwares and Tiles.* Formerly Smith, Ford & Jones. Subsequently Samuel Ford & Co., q.v.

3578   Printed mark, 1895–8.

SMITH		**GEORGE F. SMITH**, North Shore Pottery, Stockton-on-Tees, Durham. c.1855–60. *Earthenwares.* Formerly W. Smith junr. & Co., q.v. Subsequently G. & W. Smith.
3579 3580	G. F. S. G. F. S. & CO.	Distinguishing details of several printed or impressed marks of differing design: name of the individual pattern is often included, c. 1855–60.

SMITH		**JAMES SMITH**, Glebe Pottery, Stoke. Staffordshire Potteries. 1898–1924.* *China and Earthenwares.*

3581 Printed mark, c. 1898–1922.

3582   JAMES SMITH   The name also occurs in full on some marks.

3583 Printed or impressed mark, c. 1922–4.

       * Restyled James Smith & Partners Ltd., c. 1922.

SMITH		**SAMPSON SMITH (LTD.)**, various addresses, Longton. Staffordshire Potteries. c. 1846–1963. *Earthenwares, Figures, etc. China in 20th century.*
		  Most 19th century wares unmarked.
		  Various owners have carried on the old Sampson Smith title. "Ltd." was added to the style, c. 1918. From 1954 Sampson Smith Ltd. was one of the Alfred Clough group.

3584	SAMPSON SMITH 1851 LONGTON	Very rare relief mark on earthenware dogs, jugs or figures, c. 1851–90, and on some re-issues.
3585	S. S.	The impressed initials S. S. were very rarely used as a mark in the 19th century.

3586–90

       c. 1923–30   c. 1925–30   c. 1930–41   c. 1930–41   c. 1945–63

20th century printed marks.

SMITH

3591   T. SMITH & CO.
OLD KENT RD.
LONDON

THOMAS SMITH & CO., Canal Potteries, Old Kent Road, London S.E. 1879–93. *Stonewares.*

Distinguishing detail of several impressed or incised marks of differing design, c. 1879–93.

SMITH

3592   T. SMITH

THEOPHILUS SMITH, Smithfield Works,* Tunstall. Staffordshire Potteries. 1790–c. 97. *Earthenwares, Figures, etc.*

Impressed mark, 1790–c. 97.

      * Works taken by John Breeze, and renamed Greenfield.

SMITH

3593   W. S. JUNR. & CO.
3594   W. S. Jr. & CO.

3595   W. S.
STOCKTON

WILLIAM SMITH (JUNR.) & CO., North Shore Pottery (closed 1884, new works built at West Hartlepool), Stockton-on-Tees, Durham. c. 1845–84. *Earthenwares.* Formerly J. Smith.

Distinguishing details of several printed or impressed marks of differing design: name of the individual pattern is often included, 1845–55.

      Subsequently G. F. Smith (& Co.), see page 582, and G. & W. Smith. William Smith from c. 1870.

Impressed or printed initials, with or without "Stockton", c. 1870–84.

      N.B. Similar marks were used by William Smith of the Stafford Pottery, Stockton-on-Tees, see next entry.

SMITH

3596   W. S. & CO.
3597   W. S. & CO.
STAFFORD
POTTERY

3598   W. S. & CO'S
WEDGEWOOD

3599   W. S. & CO'S
QUEEN'S WARE
STOCKTON

WILLIAM SMITH (& CO.), Stafford Pottery, Stockton-on-Tees, Yorkshire. c. 1825–55. *Earthenwares.* Subsequently G. Skinner & Co., then Skinner & Walker, q.v.

Distinguishing details (marks 3596–601) of several printed or impressed marks of differing design, c. 1825–55.

The name "Wedgwood" not used after 1848, but after this date the middle E may have been introduced.

3600	W. S. & CO. WEDGWOOD WARE	William Smith & Co. catered for export markets, a marked plate in the Godden Collection has a printed subject with a German inscription. See *British Pottery and Porcelain: an illustrated Encyclopaedia of Marked Specimens.*
3601	W. SMITH & CO.	

4508	VEDGWOOD	*See* Appendix.

SMITH — W. T. H. SMITH (LTD.), Cable Pottery, Longport. Staffshire Potteries. 1898–1905. *Earthenwares and Tiles.*

3608		Printed marks, 1898–1905.

3333	S. M. R.	*See* Seonaid Mairi Robertson.

SNEYD — THOMAS SNEYD, Miles Bank, Shelton, Hanley. Staffordshire Potteries. 1846–7. *Earthenwares.* Formerly Sneyd & Hill, see below.

3609	T. SNEYD HANLEY	Impressed mark, c. 1846–7. Other authorities have attributed this mark to an earlier period. This is not borne out by records or by the style of marked examples. A marked vase will be found illustrated in the companion picture book of marked specimens.

SNEYD — SNEYD & HILL, Miles Bank, Hanley. Staffordshire Potteries. c. 1845. *Earthenwares.* Subsequently T. Sneyd, see above.

3610	SNEYD & HILL HANLEY STAFFORDSHIRE POTTERIES	Printed mark, c. 1845.

3453–5	S. & N. L.	*See* Salt & Nixon.
—	SNIZER	*See* Appendix, page 732.

SNOWDEN

HILDA M. SNOWDEN, MISS, Thackley, Bradford, Yorkshire. 1950– . *Studio-type Pottery.*
Some wares were not marked.

3611	H. M. S.	Impressed or incised initial marks, 1950– .

3611a

816	So	*See* Caughley Works.
3644	S. & O. C.	*See* Sowter & Co.

SOHO

SOHO POTTERY (LTD.), Soho Pottery, Tunstall. Staffordshire Potteries. 1901–6.* *Earthenwares.* Formerly Smith & Binnall, q.v. Subsequently Simpsons (Potters) Ltd., q.v.

3612

Printed mark, c. 1901–6. Note "Tunstall" address.

3613–16

c. 1906–22   c. 1913–30   c. 1930+   c. 1930+

3617–19

c. 1930+   c. 1930+   c. 1930

* Elder Works, Cobridge, from 1906 to 1944. Note Cobridge in later marks and trade-name "Solian' introduced c. 1913.

SOIL | SOIL HILL POTTERY, also known as Swill Hill Pottery, or Swilling End Pottery, Nr. Halifax, Yorkshire. *Earthenwares.*

This pottery was established by John Catherall about 1770 and was continued by his son Samuel. Most wares are unmarked but some inscriptions occur such as:

3620 | A. Kiton, Soil Hill Pottery, 1828.

3621 | S. C., born March 19th, 1807, and made this pot April 29th, 1868, at Swilling End.

3622 | SOIL HILL POTTERY | In about 1897 the Soil Hill Pottery was taken over by Isaac Button; his sons have continued to the present day under the name Isaac Button. The name Isaac Button may be added on some specimens. Mark no. 3622 is of 20th century date.

2604+ | SOL | *See* J. & G. Meakin Ltd.

3614
3616
3618 | SOLIAN | *See* Soho Pottery (Ltd.).

SOLLY | JOHN SOLLY, Maidstone, Kent. Established September 1953– ; some experimental work before this. *Studio-type Pottery.*

3623 | W. J. S. | Impressed or incised initial mark on early wares, 1950–5.

3624 | J. S. | Impressed J. S. seal mark, 1953– .

3625 | MAIDSTONE JOHN SOLLY KENT | Standard impressed mark, 1953– .

4116 | SOON | *See* Reginald F. Wells.

2519 | SOUTHALL | *See* Martin Bros.

833 | SOUTH CHAILEY | *See* Chailey Pottery.

1129–30 | SOUTHCLIFFE | *See* Creigian Pottery.

2727 | SOUTH HEIGHTON | *See* C. & N. Mommens.

SOUTH WALES

SOUTH WALES POTTERY, Chambers & Co., c. 1839–54, Coombs & Holland, c. 1854–58, Llanelly, Wales. c. 1839–58. *Earthenwares*.

This pottery was continued by Messrs. Holland & Guest and then Guest & Dewsberry to c. 1927.

3626	CHAMBERS, LLANELLY
3627	SOUTH WALES POTTERY W. CHAMBERS
3627a	SOUTH WALES POTTERY
3628	S. W. P.

Distinguishing detail of several printed or impressed marks of differing design, c. 1839–58. The Chambers marks, nos. 3626–7, are prior to 1855.

SOUTHWICK POTTERY

SOUTHWICK POTTERY (Anthony Scott & Co., Scott & Sons, etc.), Sunderland, Durham. c. 1800–97. *Earthenwares*. Formerly Atkinson & Co., q.v.

Many impressed and printed marks were used and these by their changing styles help to date the objects. Many printed marks are incorporated in the printed design.

The main changes in style were:

3629	A. SCOTT & CO.	} c. 1800–29.
3629a	SCOTT, SOUTHWICK	

3630	ANTHONY SCOTT & SONS	
3630a	A. SCOTT & SONS	
3631	SCOTT & SONS	} c. 1829–38.
3632	SCOTT & SONS, SOUTHWICK	
3633	S. & SONS	

3634	SCOTT BROTHERS & CO.	
3635	SCOTT BROTHERS	
3636	SCOTT BROS.	} c. 1838–54.
3637	S. B. & CO.	
3638	SCOTT	

3639	A. SCOTT	} c. 1854–72 and c. 1882–97.
3638	SCOTT	

3640	A. SCOTT & SON	
3641	S. & S.	} c. 1872–82.
3638	SCOTT	

3639	A. SCOTT	} c. 1882–97 (and 1854–72).
3638	SCOTT	

N.B. These Scott marks should not be confused with Scott Bros. of Portobello, see page 566.
See *The Potteries of Sunderland and District*. Specimens will be found illustrated in *British Pottery and Porcelain: an illustrated Encyclopaedia of Marked Specimens*.

SOWTER

SOWTER & CO., Mexborough Old Pottery, Mexborough, Yorkshire. c. 1795–1804. *Earthenwares*. Subsequently P. Barker and then Samuel Barker, q.v.

3642	SOWTER & CO. MEXBRO.	Impressed mark, c. 1795–1804.

3643	S. & CO.	This impressed mark, no. 3644, occurs on moulded "Castle-
3644	S. & O. C.	ford" type teapots, and probably relates to this firm. See *British Pottery and Porcelain: an illustrated Encyclopaedia of Marked Specimens*.

3723	SP (joined)	*See* Peter Stoodley.

1762a	S. P. G. G. W.	*See* George Grainger & Co.

3784	S. P. LTD.	*See* Sylvan Pottery Ltd.
3788		

SPARKS

GEORGE SPARKS, Worcester. c. 1836–54. *Decorator of Worcester and Coalport Porcelains*.

3645	Sparks Worcester	Written mark, c. 1836–54. See Plate 7.

3646	SPARKS BY APPOINTMENT TO HER MAJESTIE QUEEN ADELAIDE & H.R.H. THE DUCHESS OF KENT WORCESTER	Many printed marks occur, with long inscriptions. Some include the words Coalport Porcelain, all include the name SPARKS, c. 1836–54. A marked scenic tray is illustrated in G. Godden's *Victorian Porcelain* (1961).

3659a   SPODE & COPELAND   *See* Josiah Spode.

SPODE

JOSIAH SPODE, Stoke-on-Trent.   Staffordshire Potteries. c. 1784 to April 1833.   *Earthenwares, Porcelains. Stone-china, etc.*   Subsequently Copeland & Garrett, q.v.

3647

Gilt workman's mark painted very small on some early porcelains, c. 1790–1805.   A similar workman's mark also occurs on Coalport porcelains, c. 1810–20.

3648

Spode
or
SPODE

Impressed or blue printed marks on *earthenwares*, c. 1784+. Early wares rarely marked.   Some rare early wares have a very large upper case mark.

3648a

SPODE
S.

This *impressed* name-mark or the letter "S" occurs *very* rarely on *early* porcelain, c. 1784–1805.   See companion illustrated encyclopaedia.

3648b

Spode 967
Spode 1166

Written mark with pattern number on earthenwares and porcelain, c. 1790–1820.   See Plate 7 for typical examples.   The pattern number changes with each different pattern.

3649

Impressed mark on early porcelains, c. 1790–1820.

3650

SPODE

Printed mark on printed earthenwares and porcelains, c. 1805+.

3651

Printed mark in black on stone-china, c. 1805–15.   Printed in blue, c. 1815–30.   The bottom half also occurs alone.   The painted mark "Spode Stone China" also occurs.

3652

3653

SPODE'S
NEW STONE
N. S.

Impressed marks, c. 1805–20, on "New Stone" earthenware body.   See G. Godden's *British Pottery and Porcelain, 1780–1850*.

3654-6

Printed marks, on special earthenware bodies, c. 1805–33.

3657   Printed mark, usually in puce, on felspar porcelains, c. 1815–27. Many fine specimens bear this basic mark.

3658   Several slight variations occur of mark no. 3657, this example with the Stoke and London address is very rare. An example in the Copeland works museum has the date 1821 added.

3659	SPODE, SON & COPELAND
3659a	SPODE & COPELAND

Rare painted, impressed or printed marks with the style under which the London shop traded from c. 1797 to 1816.

3659b   SPODE ICH DIEN

A very rare printed mark on a porcelain plate with blue border and rose painted centre has been reported. It comprises the Prince of Wales' feather crest with the word "Spode" below and the motto "Ich Dien"; this may be a special mark for a Royal service, c. 1806–10. Messrs. Spodes were appointed Potters to the Prince of Wales in 1806.

N.B. Many modern COPELAND marks include the name SPODE.

A good selection of Spode wares is illustrated in A. Hayden's *Spode and his Successors* (1925). See also *British Pottery and Porcelain: an illustrated Encyclopaedia of Marked Specimens.*

3659a   SPODE & COPELAND   *See* Josiah Spode, above.
or
3659   SPODE, SON & COPELAND

SPRAGUE   **SHEILA SPRAGUE, MRS.,** East Peckham, Kent. 1956– . *Studio-type Pottery—Mainly useful wares.*

3660   SPRAGUE   Painted or incised name-mark, 1956–61.

3660a   S. S.   Painted, incised or impressed initial mark, 1961 to early 1963.

3660b   S.   Impressed seal mark in oval form, early 1963– .

| 371 | SPRINGBURN | *See* Campbellfield Pottery Co. |

| 984 | SR | *See* Colclough & Co. |
| 3238 | (joined) | *See* Stanislas Reychan. |

| 3585 | S. S. | *See* Sampson Smith Ltd. |
| 3660a | | *See* Sheila Sprague. |

| 3641 | S. & S. | *See* Southwick Pottery. |
| 3751 | | *See* Daniel Sutherland & Sons. |

| 3509 | S. & S. S. | *See* Shaw & Sons. |

| 4211 | S. T. | *See* Winchcombe Pottery. |

ST. AGNES   ST. AGNES POTTERY, A. and N. Homer, St. Agnes, Cornwall. 1953–7. *Earthenwares.*

3661–2   Impressed seal marks, c. 1953–7.

| 245 | ST. ALBAN WARE | *See* Barina Potteries Ltd. |

ST. ANTHONY'S

ST. ANTHONY'S POTTERY, Sewell, Sewell & Donkin, Sewell & Co., etc., Newcastle upon Tyne, Northumberland. c. 1780–1878. *Earthenwares, Creamwares, etc.*

3663	ST. ANTHONY'S	Impressed mark, 1780–1820.
3664	SEWELL ST. ANTHONY'S	Impressed or printed marks with name "Sewell", 1804–c. 28.
3664a	SEWELL	Some very fine lustre-decorated pottery was made at this period.
3665	SEWELL & DONKIN	Impressed or printed name-marks (nos. 3665–6), 1828–52.
3666	SEWELLS & DONKIN	
3667	SEWELL & CO.	Subsequently Sewell & Co., 1852–78.

STABLER **HAROLD & PHOEBE STABLER,** Poole, Dorset and London. Early 20th century. *Earthenwares.*

Harold Stabler (1872–1945) was a partner in the Poole Pottery (Messrs. Carter, Stabler & Adams) from 1920. He was also a Designer, Potter and Silversmith. Phoebe Stabler (his wife), a talented artist and designer, died in December 1955.

3668 Phoebe Stabler 1910 Incised or painted signature marks on early earthenware figures with year of production. Examples in the Victoria and

3669 Stabler 1911 Albert Museum bear these marks.

1148 STAFFS (with crown above) *See* Crown Staffordshire Porcelain Co. Ltd.

STAFFS TEAPOT **STAFFS TEAPOT CO. LTD., THE,** Crown Pottery (and other addresses), Burslem. Staffordshire Potteries. 1929–48. *Teapots.* Subsequently Hanover Pottery (Ltd.), q.v.

3670 THE STAFFS TEAPOT Co.Ltd. CROWN POTTERY. BURSLEM. ENGLAND. Printed mark, 1929–48.

1147 STAFFORDSHIRE (with crown above) *See* Crown Staffordshire Porcelain Co. Ltd.

110 STAFFORDSHIRE FLORAL BONE CHINA *See* Charles Amison (& Co.) (Ltd.).

301a STAFFORDSHIRE KNOT IMPRESSED *See* John Denton Baxter.

STAFFORDSHIRE **STAFFORDSHIRE TEA SET CO. LTD.,** Plex Street Pottery, Tunstall. Staffordshire Potteries. 1947– . *Earthenwares.*

3671 STAFFS TEASET Co.Lᵗᵒ PLEX ST. POTTERY TUNSTALL MADE IN ENGLAND Printed mark, 1947– .

3672

Printed mark, 1950– .

852,
854

STANDARD CHINA

See Chapmans Longton Ltd.

107–9,
111

STANLEY
STANLEY
BONE CHINA
STANLEY CHINA, etc.

See Charles Amison (& Co. Ltd.).

STANLEY

STANLEY & LAMBERT, Newtown Pottery, Longton. Staffordshire Potteries. c. 1850–4. *Earthenwares.*

3673

S. & L.

3674

Distinguishing detail of several printed marks of differing design: name of the individual pattern is often included, 1850–4. Mark no. 3674 is a typical example.

STANLEY

STANLEY POTTERY LTD., Edensor Road, Longton. Staffordshire Potteries. 1928–31. *Earthenwares and China.* Formerly Colclough & Co., q.v.

3675–6

Printed marks, formerly used by Colclough & Co., continued to 1931.

STANNARD

ANN STANNARD (and Marigold Austin), Potbridge, Odiham, Hampshire. 1959– . *Studio-type Pottery.*

3677

Basic painted mark, 1959– .

3678–9

Monogram potters marks, 1959– .

STANTON

HARRY E. STANTON, Burslem. Staffordshire Potteries. and other addresses. 1910–40.* *Studio-type Pottery.*

3680   STANTON   Name-mark, incised or painted, 1910–40.*

* These dates are only approximate.

STANYER

A. STANYER, New Street Pottery, Burslem. Staffordshire Potteries. c. 1916–41. *Earthenware Teapots, Jugs, etc.*

3681–2   A. S.   A. S.   Impressed marks, c. 1916–41.
        B.   ENG.
        ENG.   B.

779   STAG'S HEAD   *See* John Carr & Sons, page 128.

689   STAR MARK   *See* A. W. Buchan & Co. (Ltd.).
2034   *See* D. Hilton.
3688   *See* Star Pottery.

STAR

STAR CHINA CO., Atlas Works (and other addresses), Longton. Staffordshire Potteries. 1900–19. *China.* Subsequently Paragon China (Co.) Ltd., q.v.

3683–7

    c. 1900+   c. 1904+   c. 1912+   c. 1913+   c. 1915+

Printed marks, c. 1900–19.

STAR

STAR POTTERY (Johnstone Wardlaw), Possil Park, Glasgow, Scotland. 1880–1907. *Earthenwares and Stonewares.*

3688   Impressed or printed mark, 1880–1907.

STEEL

DANIEL STEEL, St. James St. (c. 1790–1818), Scotia Works (c. 1802), Nile Street (c. 1821–4), Burslem. Staffordshire Potteries. 1790–1824. *Earthenwares, Wedgwood-type Jasper wares, etc.*

3689   STEEL

3690   STEEL BURSLEM

Impressed marks, 1790–1824.

Examples are illustrated in *British Pottery and Porcelain: an illustrated Encyclopaedia of Marked Specimens.*

Jasper examples with mark no. 3689, the name without the place name Burslem, may have been made by Henry Steel of Marsh Street, Shelton. His trade card lists *only* "—— all kinds of Jasper ornaments of a superior quality".

STEELE

STEELE & WOOD, London Road, Stoke. Staffordshire Potteries. 1875–92. *Tiles, etc.*

3691

Printed or impressed mark, 1875–92.

4035   STELLA

See Constance Stella Watson.

STEPHAN

PETER STEPHAN, Jackfield, Shropshire. First half 19th century? *Blue-printed Earthenwares and Tiles.*

3692–92a

Impressed and printed marks. Local directories of 1856 and 1871 list a Peter Stephan as an artist but it is not clear if this is the potter referred to by Jewitt (in the past tense) in 1878.

STERLING

STERLING POTTERY LTD., Fenton. Staffordshire Potteries. 1947–53. *Earthenwares.* Formerly Sterling Pottery Co.

3693–4

c. 1947+

c. 1949–53   c. 1950–3

Printed marks, c. 1947–53.

STEVENS

EILEEN STEVENS, MRS., Ifield, Crawley, Sussex. 1952– .
Studio-type Pottery.

3695   E.S   Incised or painted mark, 1952–5.

3696   Revised version, 1955–60.

3697   New initial mark, 1960– .

STEVENSON

ANDREW STEVENSON, Cobridge. Staffordshire Potteries.
c. 1816–30. *Earthenwares.* Formerly Bucknall & Stevenson.

3698	Andrew Stevenson July 8th, 1807	Incised mark on wall vase sold in Sothebys at 1962. The name does not occur in written records at this early date, except for a directory entry in 1811.

3699 3699a	STEVENSON A. STEVENSON	Impressed marks, c. 1816–30.

3700
also
(1814)

Impressed mark, formerly attributed to Ralph Stevenson but now thought to have been used by Andrew. See also Greenock Pottery, page 291. A marked plate in the British Museum bears a printed subject bearing the date 1820.

3701

Impressed mark, including the name A. Stevenson. A slight variation of this circular mark occurs in the Godden Collection, c. 1816–30. See Plate 2.

3702

Printed mark on blue printed earthenwares, attributed to Andrew Stevenson, c. 1816–30.

STEVENSON

RALPH STEVENSON, Lower Manufactory, Cobridge.
Staffordshire Potteries. c. 1810–32.* *Earthenwares.*
For an interesting account of the Stevenson family see *Antiques* magazine, June 1955, an article by N. Emery.

  * Many Stevenson marks may have been used by either Andrew or Ralph Stevenson.

3703	STEVENSON / STAFFORDSHIRE. (crown mark)	Impressed marks, nos. 3703–4, c. 1810–32.
3704	R. STEVENSON	
3705	R. S.	The initials R. S. occur on several different printed marks, c. 1810–32.
3706	R. S. & S.	**RALPH STEVENSON & SON**, from c. 1832 to 1835.
3707	R. STEVENSON & SON	Distinguishing details of several printed marks of differing design: name of the individual pattern is often included, 1832–5.

STEVENSON

3708   STEVENSON, ALCOCK & WILLIAMS

STEVENSON, ALCOCK & WILLIAMS, Cobridge. Staffordshire Potteries. c. 1825. *Earthenwares.*

Printed name-marks, c. 1825.

STEVENSON

1267

STEVENSON & HANCOCK, and subsequent owners, King Street, Derby. c. 1859–1935. *Porcelains (and Bisque).* Formerly Stevenson, Sharpe & Co., q.v. See also under Derby Porcelain Works.

Painted mark, 1861–1935. From 1859 to 1861 the basic mark without the initials S. H. was used.

Subsequent owners of the King Street works continued to use the S. H. mark until the concern was purchased by the Royal Crown Derby Company in 1935. See *Victorian Porcelain* (1961).

STEVENSON

1266

STEVENSON, SHARP & CO., King Street, Derby. c. 1859. *Porcelains.* Formerly Locker & Co. Subsequently Stevenson & Hancock, see previous entry.

Printed mark, c. 1859, rare.

STEVENSON

STEVENSON, SPENCER & CO. LTD., Enson or Dresden Works, Longton. Staffordshire Potteries. 1948–60.* *China.*

3709–11

c. 1948+   c. 1951+   c. 1952+

Printed marks.

    * Distributors only from 1960.

STEVENSON

WILLIAM STEVENSON, Hanley. Staffordshire Potteries. c. 1802. *Earthenwares.*

3712

```
W. STEVENSON
   HANLEY
   MAY 2
    1802
```

This rare mark occurs on a jasper-type pedestal in the Victoria and Albert Museum (no. 2581–1901), 1802.

STEVENSON

STEVENSON & WILLIAMS, Lower Manufactory, Cobridge. Staffordshire Potteries. c. 1825.* *Earthenwares.*

3713   R. S. W.

Distinguishing detail of several printed or impressed marks of differing design, c. 1825, name of individual pattern is often included.

3714

Printed mark, c. 1825.

    * This would appear to be a short-lived partnership between Ralph Stevenson and Aldborough Lloyd Williams. The partnership is not listed in directories but it is mentioned in a mortgage deed of 1825.

STEVENTON

JOHN STEVENTON & SONS LTD., Royal Pottery, Burslem. Staffordshire Potteries. 1923– .* *Earthenwares.* Formerly Brown & Steventon Ltd., q.v.

3715

Printed mark with title in full, c. 1923–36.*

    * This firm still continues but is now mainly concerned with the production of tiles and sanitary wares.

STEWART		**ROBERT STEWART** (Robert Stewart Ceramics Ltd.), Paisley, Renfrewshire, Scotland. 1960– .

3716 — Printed mark on decorated earthenware covered jars, etc., 1960– .

STIFF

JAMES STIFF (& SONS), London Pottery, Lambeth, London S.E. c. 1840–1913.* *Stonewares.*
    Continued as JAMES STIFF & SONS, from c. 1863.

3717   J. STIFF   Distinguishing detail of several impressed marks of differing design, c. 1840–63.

3718   J. STIFF & SONS   Distinguishing detail of several impressed marks of differing design, c. 1863–1913.

    * Works taken over by Doultons.

STOCKL

ERIC & MEIRA STOCKL, Stroud Green, London N.4. 1956– . *Studio-type Pottery, Stoneware.*

3719   M. E. S.   Painted or incised, joint initial mark, 1956–61.

3720   Painted, incised or impressed mark, 1961– .

3568   STOCKTON   *See* Skinner & Walker.
3570   *See* William Smith (junr.) & Co.
3595

—   J. W. STOCKWELL   *See* Appendix, page 733.

2423   STOKE GABRIEL   *See* Lotus Pottery.

1824   STOKE POTTERY   *See* Grimwades Ltd.
3056   *See* J. Plant & Co.

STONE

STONE & CO., Nonsuch Pottery, Ewell, London. c. 1867 to early 20th century. *Pottery, Stonewares and Tiles.* Formerly Stone & Swallow.

3721   STONE & CO.   Impressed mark, c. 1867 to early 20th century.

	STONE CHINA STONE WARE	Names for Ironstone-type earthenwares, used by many 19th century manufacturers. See Hicks & Meigh and Hicks, Meigh & Johnson.

STONER

FRANK STONER, London. c. 1930.

3722   FRANK STONER

Incised mark on very rare earthenware Toby-type jugs made in a similar style to 18th century examples, c. 1930.

STOODLEY

PETER STOODLEY, Bournemouth, Hampshire. 1951– .
Studio-type Pottery and Stonewares.

3723

Impressed seal mark, 1951– .

STRITCH

JOHN STRITCH, Limerick, Ireland. 1761+. *Tin-glazed (Delft type) Earthenware.*

In 1762 the Dublin Society awarded a premium to John Stritch and Christopher Bridson of Limerick "for erecting a manufactory of earthenware in imitation of delft or white ware".

3724   Made by John Stritch
       Limerick, 1761

Inscription in blue (in writing letters) on rare armorial plates dated 1761. Two of these plates are illustrated by W. B. Honey in the *Transactions of the English Ceramic Circle*, vol. 2, no. 8, p. 156. One example, with signature, is illustrated in *British Pottery and Porcelain: an illustrated Encyclopaedia of Marked Specimens.* Another example is in the British Museum.

STRINGER

HARRY H. STRINGER, London S.W.13. 1953– . *Studio-type Pottery.*

3725

Impressed seal mark, 1953– .

3726

Impressed mark used 1957 at Fulham Pottery.

| 2899–2901 | STRONG AS THE ROCK | *See* North Staffordshire Pottery Co. Ltd. |

STUBBS

STUBBS BROS., Argyle Works, Fenton. Staffordshire Potteries. 1899–1904. *China.*

3727

Printed mark, c. 1899–1904. This mark may have been continued by successors Messrs. Stubbs Bros. and John Chew Ltd. to c. 1907.

STUBBS

JOSEPH STUBBS, Dale Hall, Longport, Burslem. Staffordshire Potteries. c. 1822 35. *Earthenwares, blue printed, etc.*
There is an overlap of directory entries for Joseph Stubbs and Messrs. Stubbs & Kent, see next entry.

3728   STUBBS

Impressed mark, c. 1822–35.

3729   JOSEPH STUBBS
             LONGPORT

Impressed or printed mark in circular form, c. 1822–35.

STUBBS

STUBBS & KENT, Dale Hall, Longport, Burslem. Staffordshire Potteries. c. 1828–30. *Earthenwares, blue printed, etc.*

3730

Impressed or printed mark, c. 1828–30. A similar mark was used by Joseph Stubbs, see previous entry.

STUDIO

STUDIO SZEILER (LTD.), Hanley, c. 1951–5. Burslem, c. 1955– . Staffordshire Potteries. c. 1951– . *Earthenwares (Figures, etc.).*

3731–4

c. 1951+   c. 1954+   c. 1956–   c. 1962–

Printed or impressed marks.

| — | S. U. | *See* Appendix, page 733. |
| — | W. SUCKERS | *See* Appendix, page 733. |

SUDLOW

R. SUDLOW & SONS LTD., Adelaide Pottery, Burslem. Staffordshire Potteries. 1893– . *Earthenwares.* Formerly R. Sudlow.

3735-6   Printed or impressed marks, c. 1920 onwards.

| — | SULTANA | *See* Appendix, Fife Pottery. |

SUMMERBANK

SUMMERBANK POTTERY LTD., Tunstall. Staffordshire Potteries. 1952– . *Earthenwares.*

3737   SUMMERBANK   Distinguishing detail of several printed marks of differing design, 1952– .

3738

SUMMERBANK POTTERY
STAFFORDSHIRE
ENGLAND

Printed mark on bird models, 1954+ .

SUMMERLY

FELIX SUMMERLY (HENRY COLE), Summerly's Art Manufactures, c. 1846–50.

"Felix Summerly" (Henry Cole) caused ceramics, silver, etc., to be designed by leading Victorian designers and manufacturers. Examples were sold under the name "Summerly's Art Manufactures". See *Victorian Porcelain* (1961).

3739   Distinguishing detail of several printed or applied marks of differing design, c. 1846–50.

SUNDERLAND

SUNDERLAND OR "GARRISON" POTTERY, Sunderland, Durham. c. 1807–65. *Earthenwares (printed and lustre wares).*

Most Sunderland marks incorporate the name of the various partnerships which are listed in date order. Most of these marks are impressed.

| 3740 | J. PHILLIPS | } c. 1807–12. |
| 3741 | J. PHILLIPS SUNDERLAND POTTERY | |

| 3742 | PHILLIPS & CO. | } c. 1813–19. |
| 3743 | DIXON & CO.* | |

| 3744 | DIXON, AUSTIN & CO. | } c. 1820–26. |

| 3745 | DIXON, AUSTIN, PHILLIPS & CO. | } c. 1827–40. |
| 3746 | DIXON, AUSTIN & CO. | |

| 3747 | DIXON PHILLIPS & CO. | } c. 1840–65. |

3748   SUNDREX   A later firm the SUNDERLAND POTTERY CO. (LTD.) was established c. 1913, and continued to c. 1927; the trade-name was "SUNDREX".

Other potteries at Sunderland are listed under the name of the potter, firm or works. Examples will be found illustrated in *British Pottery and Porcelain: an illustrated Encyclopaedia of Marked Specimens.*

* The mark Dixon & Co. was sometimes used at later periods.

SUNFIELD   **SUNFIELD POTTERY** (J. R. S. Dugdale-Bradley), Clent Grove, Nr. Stourbridge, Worcestershire. 1937– . *Earthenwares and Stonewares.*

3749
HAND MADE IN ENGLAND   Impressed or printed mark, 1937– . The production of stonewares dates from 1952. Earthenwares have been produced from 1937 to the present day.

3748   SUNDREX   *See* Sunderland.

3534–5   SUNRAY POTTERY   *See* Shorter & Son (Ltd.).

4120	SURREY CERAMICS	*See* West Surrey Ceramics Co. Ltd.

SUTCLIFFE   **C. P. SUTCLIFFE & CO. LTD.,** Higher Broughton, Manchester, Lancashire. c. 1885–1901. *Tiles.*

3750   Printed or impressed mark, c. 1885–1901.

307	SUTHERLAND ART WARE	*See* Frank Beardmore & Co.
2107–9	SUTHERLAND CHINA	*See* W. Hudson.
2110 & 2110b		*See* Hudson & Middleton Ltd.

SUTHERLAND   **DANIEL SUTHERLAND & SONS,** Park Hall Street, Longton. Staffordshire Potteries. 1865–75. *Parian, Majolica and Stonewares.* Formerly Daniel Sutherland. Subsequently Hugh Sutherland.

3751	S. & S.	Impressed or printed initial marks, c. 1865–75.
3461	S. & V.	*See* Sant & Vodrey.
3467	S. W.	*See* Saviac Workshops.
3568	S. & W.	*See* Skinner & Walker.

SWANSEA   **SWANSEA PORCELAIN,** Swansea, Wales. 1814–22. *Porcelains.*

3752	SWANSEA	Impressed mark, with or without trident, 1814–22.
3753	SWANSEA	Printed or written mark, 1814–22.
3754 3755	DILLWYN & CO. DILLWYN & CO. SWANSEA	Impressed marks, rare, c. 1814–17.

| 3756 | BEVINGTON & CO. | Impressed mark, rare, c. 1820. |

For illustrations of typical Swansea porcelain see *The Pottery and Porcelain of Swansea and Nantgarw*, E. Morton Nance (1942) and *Swansea Porcelain*, W. D. John (1957).

SWANSEA POTTERY

SWANSEA POTTERY, Cambrian Pottery, Swansea, Wales. c. 1783 (earlier wares unmarked) to 1870. *Pottery.*

| 3757 | SWANSEA | Impressed mark, c. 1783+. |

3758	CAMBRIA	Impressed or printed marks in several forms, c. 1783–c. 1810.
3759	CAMBRIAN	
3760	CAMBRIAN POTTERY	

3761–3

Impressed workmen's marks found on Swansea plates, dishes, etc., c. 1800–10. The spade-like mark was also used at the Leeds Pottery.

3764	DILLWYN & CO.	Impressed or printed marks, in various forms, c. 1811–17.
3765	DILLWYN & CO. SWANSEA	
3766	D. & CO.	

| 3767 | BEVINGTON & CO. | Impressed mark, c. 1817–24. |

3768	DILLWYN	Impressed marks, nos. 3768–70, c. 1824–50.
3769	DILLWYN SWANSEA	
3770	D	

| 3771 | CYMRO STONE CHINA | Impressed mark on special body, c. 1847–50. |

| 3772 | DILLWYN'S ETRUSCAN WARE | Printed mark, in ornate frame, c. 1847–50. |

| 1519a | EVANS & GLASSON SWANSEA | Impressed or printed name-marks, c. 1850–62. |

1514	D. J. EVANS & CO.	Distinguishing details of several printed marks of differing
1518	D. I. EVANS & CO.	design: name of the individual pattern is often included,
1517	EVANS & CO.	c. 1862–70.

N.B. Many printed marks occur on Swansea earthenwares which do not include the name of the firm—only the pattern or type of body.

For detailed information on Swansea earthenwares, see E. Morton Nance's *The Pottery and Porcelain of Swansea and Nantgarw* (1942).

SWIFT

SWIFT & ELKIN, Stafford and Flint Streets, Longton. Staffordshire Potteries. 1840–3. *Earthenware.* Subsequently J. Swift.

3773   S. & E.   Distinguishing detail of several printed marks of differing design: name of the individual pattern is often included, 1840–3. These initials are often in flowing writing letters.

SWINNERTONS

SWINNERTONS LTD., various addresses, Hanley. Staffordshire Potteries. 1906– . *Earthenwares.*

3774–6

SWINNERTONS HANLEY.
c. 1906–17

SWINNERTONS LTD. SEMI PORCELAIN ENGLAND
c. 1917–30

Swinnertons England
c. 1930+

3777–9

HAMPTON IVORY ENGLAND
c. 1930+

MADE IN ENGLAND S LTD
c. 1930+

SWINNERTONS STAFFORDSHIRE ENGLAND
c. 1946+

3780–2

VITRION SWINNERTONS STAFFORDSHIRE ENGLAND
c. 1946+

SWINNERTONS STAFFORDSHIRE ENGLAND
c. 1946+

ROYAL WESSEX WHITE IRONSTONE MADE IN ENGLAND BY SWINNERTONS
c. 1962+

Printed marks, 1906– .

1460   S. W. P.   *See* David Eeles.
3628   *See* South Wales Pottery.

3495   S. W. W. B. B.   *See* (William) Sharpe & Co.

814   Sx   *See* Caughley Works.
       or
815   S^x

SYKES		**STEVEN SYKES**, Richmond, Surrey. 1948–55.* *Studio-type Pottery.*
* Steven Sykes subsequently concentrated on architectural ceramics.
3783	Steven Sykes	Signature mark, 1948–55.
3502–3	SYLVAC	*See* Shaw & Copestake Ltd.
1426	SYLVAN CHINA	*See* Dura Porcelain Co. Ltd.

SYLVAN

SYLVAN POTTERY LTD., Hanley. Staffordshire Potteries. 1946– . *Earthenwares.* Formerly Podmore China Co., q.v.

3784–6

3787–7a

Printed marks, 1946– .
    N.B. The addition of the letter B in the marks dates wares as being used prior to 1948.

T

841	T	*See* Chamberlain (& Co.).
507		*See* Tebo.
3863		*See* Jacob Tittensor.

TAENA TAENA POTTERY, L. A. Groves, Upton St. Leonards, Gloucester. 1948– . *Earthenwares.*

3788 Impressed or incised mark, 1948– . A similar mark was used by Miss Margaret Leach at Aylburton.

TALOR WILLIAM TALOR (or **TALLOR**), Burslem. Staffordshire
(or TALLOR) Potteries. c. 1700. *Slip-decorated Earthenwares.*

3789   WILLIAM TALOR   This name occurs on rare slip-decorated dishes. One example
3789a   WILLIAM TALLOR   is dated 1700. An example in the Brighton Museum is inscribed William Tallor. See the companion illustrated encyclopaedia of marked specimens.

TAMS, ANDERSON   Marks incorporating these names have been recorded on
   & TAMS   earthenwares of the 1820–40 period. However the firms are not listed in Staffordshire directories or rate records.

TAMS DENIS V. TAMS, Stoke-on-Trent, Staffordshire. 1950– .
Studio-type Pottery, Stonewares.

3790   D. V. Tams   Incised signature mark, with date, 1950– .
      June 1963

TAMS

JOHN TAMS (& SON) (LTD.), Crown Pottery, Longton. Staffordshire Potteries. c. 1875– . *Earthenwares.*

3791 J. T.
3792 J. Tams

Distinguishing details of several printed marks of differing design: name of the individual pattern is often included, 1875–90.

3793

Printed trade-mark, on some versions the initials J. T. replace the monogram, c. 1875+.

From 1903 to 1912 the firm's title was changed to JOHN TAMS & SON.

3794 J. T. & S.

Distinguishing detail of several printed marks of differing design, c. 1903–12.

3795

Variation of earlier mark with addition of "& S.", c. 1903–12.

Firm retitled JOHN TAMS LTD. from 1912. The following printed marks were used. Mark number 3795 was continued.

3796–7

c. 1913+

c. 1930

3798–801

VITRIFIED HOTELWARE

c. 1952+

PRODUCTS

c. 1955+

MADE IN ENGLAND

c. 1958+

TAMS
ENGLAND

c. 1960

Various other marks both impressed and printed incorporate the words TAMS ENGLAND.

TAMS

See John Tams (& Sons) (Ltd.).

TAMS		**TAMS & LOWE**, St. Gregory's Pottery, Longton. Staffordshire Potteries. 1865–74. *Earthenwares.* Subsequently W. Lowe, q.v.
3802	T. & L.	Distinguishing detail of several printed marks of differing design: name of the individual pattern is often included, 1865–74.
—	S. TAMS & CO.	*See* Appendix, page 733.
1796	T. A. & S. G.	*See* T. A. & S. Green.
3412	TAYLOR	*See* Ruskin Pottery.
TAYLOR		**TAYLOR & CO.** (or **TYLER & CO.**), Tyne Pottery, Newcastle upon Tyne, Northumberland. c. 1820–5.* *Earthenwares.*
3803 3804	TAYLOR & CO. TYLER & CO. TYNE POTTERY NEWCASTLE	Rare printed mark, occurring as part of the printed decoration. The spelling Tyler & Co. has been reported, c. 1820–5.*

     * This firm is listed in local directories for 1821–3. In 1827 the firm is listed as Taylor & Son.

TAYLOR		**GEORGE TAYLOR**, Hanley. Staffordshire Potteries. c. 1784–1811. *Earthenwares, Basaltes, etc.* George Taylor, junior, continued potting to c. 1813.
3805 3806	G. TAYLOR GEO. TAYLOR	Impressed or incised marks, c. 1784–1811. N.B. A slip-decorated dish of Toft type, in the Fitzwilliam Museum, Cambridge, bears this name but it is not certain that it refers to a potter of this name, c. 1670. This dish will be found illustrated in *British Pottery and Porcelain: an illustrated Encyclopaedia of Marked Specimens.*
TAYLOR		**TAYLOR & KENT (LTD.)**, Florence Works, Longton. Staffordshire Potteries. 1867– . *Porcelains.*
3807	T. & K. L.	Distinguishing detail of several printed or impressed marks of differing design: name of the individual pattern is often included, 1867– .

The principal printed marks have been:

3808–10	c. 1880+	c. 1906+ c. 1912+

c. 1939+   c. 1950+   c. 1961+

3811–13

TAYLOR

NICHOLAS TAYLOR, Denholme Pottery, Denholme, Yorkshire. 1893–1909. *Earthenwares.*

3814   N. Tayler
        Denholme

Incised signature type mark, 1893–1909.

TAYLOR

ROBERT MINTON TAYLOR, Tile Works, Fenton. Staffordshire Potteries. 1869–75. *Tiles.*

3815   R. M. T.
        F. T. W.
3816   ROBERT MINTON
        TAYLOR
        TILE WORKS,
        FENTON, NEAR
        STOKE-ON-TRENT

Impressed or relief moulded marks, 1869–75.

TAYLOR, TUNNICLIFFE

TAYLOR, TUNNICLIFFE & CO. (LTD.), various addresses, Hanley. Staffordshire Potteries. 1868– . *Earthenwares and China.*

From about 1898 only utilitarian objects have been produced.

3817   T. T.
3818   T. T. & CO.

Distinguishing details of several printed marks of differing design: name of the individual pattern is often included, c. 1868–80.

3819–22

Printed marks, c. 1875–98.

| 3420 | W. HOWSON TAYLOR | *See* Ruskin Pottery. |

356   T. B.   *See* Thomas Bevington.

3868   T. & B.   *See* Tomkinson & Billington.

447   T. B. & CO.   *See* Thomas Booth & Co.

1733   T. B. G.   *See* Thomas & Benjamin Godwin.
or
1732   T. & B. G.

438   T. B. & S.   *See* T. & R. Boote Ltd.
448   *See* Thomas Booth & Son.
655   *See* T. Brown & Sons Ltd.

1023–4   T. C.   *See* Thomas Cone Ltd.
1022   or
           T. C.
           L.

1609   T. & C. F.   *See* T. & C. Ford.

4142   T. C. W.   *See* Thomas C. Wild.

3834   T.D.   *See* Theda Pottery.
(joined)

TEBO   "TEBO" (THIBAUD?), Ceramic modeller or "repairer".*
c. 1750–75.

508   Impressed marks, found chiefly on Bow porcelains, c. 1750–60, and rarely on Worcester porcelains, c. 1760–9, also on Plymouth, c. 1769–70, and Bristol porcelains, c. 1770–4. In 1775 this modeller was employed by Wedgwood.

T°

* A "repairer" assembled the finished figure, group, etc., from separate moulded parts.

507

T

3131a	TEMPLE GATE POTTERY	*See* William Powell.

TENBY

TENBY POTTERY (Anthony Markes), Tenby, Pembroke-shire. 1959– . *Studio-type Pottery.*

3823	TENBY POTTERY	Incised mark, in writing letters, 1959– .

3824 — **AM** — Initial marks on pieces potted and decorated by Anthony Markes, 1959– .

3824a — **am**

TERRINGTON

TERRINGTON POTTERY (Mrs. Brenda Dennis), Terring-ton, St. Clements, Norfolk. 1959– . *Slip-decorated wares, Animal Models and Tiles.*

3825	BD. TERRINGTON NORFOLK	Painted mark, 1959– .

TEWKESBURY

TEWKESBURY POTTERY (John and Una McLellan), Tewkesbury, Gloucester. 1959– . *Studio-type Pottery.*

3826	TEWKESBURY POTTERY	Incised or painted mark, in writing letters, 1959– .
3827	John McLellan	Signature mark, incised or painted, 1959– .

3828 — **UNA** — Initial mark of Una McLellan, 1959 .

—	T. F.	*See* Appendix, page 733.
1606		*See* Thomas Ford.
1534	T. F. & CO.	*See* Thomas Fell (& Co.).
1612		*See* Thomas Forester & Co.
1645		*See* Thomas Furnival & Co.

1614	T. F. & S.	*See* Thomas Forester & Sons (Ltd.).
	or	
1615	T. F. & S. (LTD.)	

| 1645–8 | F. T. & SONS (ornate monograms) | *See* Thomas Furnival & Sons. |

1665	T. G.	*See* Tony & Janet Gant.
1729		*See* Thomas Godwin.
1795		*See* Thomas Green.

| 449 | T. G. B. | *See* Thomas G. Booth. |

| 450 | T. G. & F. B. | *See* T. G. & F. Booth. |

| 1798 | T. G. G. & CO. LTD. | *See* T. G. Green & Co. (Ltd.). |

3182	TH	*See* Kenneth Quick.
3388	(joined)	*See* Roger Ross Turner.
3472		*See* A. Schofield.

| — | T. H. & CO. | *See* Appendix, page 733. |

THALMESSINGER

ANNE H. THALMESSINGER, MISS, Yateley, Camberley, Surrey. 1961– . *Studio-type Pottery.*

3829		Painted or incised initial mark, 1961–2.
3830		Painted initial mark, 1962– .
3831		Impressed seal-type mark, 1962– .

THANET

THANET POTTERY LTD. (David White and M. L. Dening), Westwood, Margate, Kent. 1961– . *Earthenwares.*

| 3832 | THANET POTTERY | Moulded or impressed mark, 1961– . |

THEDA

THEDA POTTERY (E. Henderson and D. Tickle), Hampstead, London N.W.6. 1948–54. *Studio-type Pottery.* Subsequently at Eastbourne, see page 320.

3833   THEDA   Pottery name-mark, rarely used, 1948–54.

3834–5   Personal marks used by Mrs. D. Tickle, 1948–54.

3836–7   Personal marks used by Miss E. Henderson, 1948–54.

THOMAS

URIAH THOMAS & CO., Marlborough Works, Hanley. Staffordshire Potteries. 1888–1905. *Earthenwares, Majolica, etc.*

3838   Printed or impressed mark, 1888–1905. With "England" after 1891.

HANLEY

THOMPSON

JOSEPH THOMPSON, Wooden Box or Hartshorne Pottery, Nr. Ashby de la Zouch, Derbyshire. c. 1818–56. *Earthenwares, Stonewares, Terra-cotta.*

After 1856 the title was changed to THOMPSON BROTHERS and later marks incorporate this style.

3839   J. THOMPSON   Impressed mark, 1818–56.

3840   JOSEPH THOMPSON WOODEN BOX POTTERY DERBYSHIRE   Impressed mark, in circular form, 1818+.

3841   J. THOMPSON HARTSTONE NEAR ASHBY DE LA ZOUCH   Printed mark, on printed jug in the Godden Collection, 1840–56.

THOMPSON

PAULINE THOMPSON, Ginge Brook Pottery, East Hendred, Berkshire. 1950– . *Studio-type Pottery.*

3842 Incised or painted marks, 1950– .

3843

THOMSON

JOHN THOMSON (& SONS), Annfield Pottery, Glasgow, Scotland. c. 1816–84.* *Earthenwares.*

3844   J. T.
3845   J. T.
          ANNFIELD

Distinguishing detail of several printed or impressed marks of differing design, c. 1816–65.

3846   J. T. & SONS
3847   J. T. & SONS
          GLASGOW
3848   J. THOMSON & SONS
          GLASGOW

Distinguishing details of several printed marks of differing design: name of the individual pattern is often included, c. 1866–84. Note the addition of "& Sons" to earlier forms of the mark.

* The date of closure is given by A. Fleming in his *Scottish Pottery* as 1884 but the firm is listed in Glasgow directories to 1896 as "flint millers and earthenware manufacturers of Annfield Pottery".

THORLEY

THORLEY CHINA LTD., Wellington Works, Longton. Staffordshire Potteries. Est. 1940– . *China Jewellery and Fancies.*

3849 Printed mark, c. 1950– .

THORNTON

HAROLD THORNTON, Burnley, Lancashire. c. 1933– . *Studio-type Pottery, Stonewares.*

3850 Impressed seal mark, c. 1933– .

THOROGOOD

STANLEY THOROGOOD, several teaching posts—Burslem Art School, etc., c. 1900–50. *Pottery, Figures, Groups, Plaques, etc.*

3851	STANLEY THOROGOOD	Incised or painted signature mark, c. 1900–50.
3902	T. H. & P.	*See* Turner, Hassall & Peake.
3389–90	THR (joined)	*See* Roger Ross Turner.

THREE G's

THREE G's POTTERY (Mrs. Lloyd), Worthing, Sussex. Established c. 1953 at Rowlands Castle, Hampshire. *Earthenwares.*

3852		Incised mark, c. 1953– .
2136	T. I.	*See* Thomas Ifield.
2140	T. I. & Co.	*See* Thomas Ingleby & Co.
3226	TIGO	*See* Tibor Reich.
1483	T. I. & J. E.	*See* Thomas, Isaac & James Emberton.

TILL

THOMAS TILL & SON(S), Sytch Pottery, Burslem. Staffordshire Potteries. c. 1850–1928. *Earthenwares.* Formerly Barker, Sutton & Till, q.v.

3853	TILL	Distinguishing details of several printed marks of differing
3854	TILL & SON	design: name of the individual pattern is often included,
3855	T. TILL & SON	c. 1850–61.

N.B. "& Son" changed to "& Sons", c. 1861, and various marks subsequently incorporate this style.

3856–60

c. 1861   c. 1867   c. 1880   c. 1919   c. 1922–8

Printed marks, c. 1861–1928.

—	TINTAGEL POTTERY	*See* Appendix.

TITTENSOR		**CHARLES TITTENSOR** (various partnerships), Shelton. Staffordshire Potteries. c. 1815–23. *Earthenware Figures and printed wares.*
3861	TITTENSOR	Impressed mark on figures, etc., and printed on printed wares, very rare, c. 1815–23.

An unusual earthenware figure with this mark is illustrated in *British Pottery and Porcelain: an illustrated Encyclopaedia of Marked Specimens*. Some rare specimens with this mark appear to be earlier than the working period of Charles Tittensor, and other potters of this name may have used this mark. Other marked "Tittensor" figures are illustrated in *Apollo*, May 1943. See also *Apollo*, December 1950.

TITTENSOR		**JACOB TITTENSOR**, Stoke. Staffordshire Potteries. c. 1780–95. *Earthenwares, Figures.*
3862	Jacob Tittensor made this October 2 in the year of our Lord 1789	Signature mark in writing letters, on unique plaque, c. 1780–95.
3863	T	The rare impressed mark T occurs on a figure in the Brighton Museum and may relate to this potter. An incised T mark has also been recorded.

3802	T. & L.	*See* Tams & Lowe.
3808–9	T. L. K. or	*See* Taylor & Kent Ltd.
3807	T. & K. L.	
2566	TM	*See* Thomas Mayer (Elton Pottery) Ltd.
2780	(joined)	*See* Thomas Morris.
2779	T. M.	*See* Thomas Morris.
2478	T. M. R.	*See* Madeley Works.

2887	T. N. & CO.	*See* Thomas Nicholson & Co., page 468.
508	T°	*See* Tebo.
2710	TOFT or C. TOFT	*See* Minton.

TOFT

TOFT, JAMES (b. 1673), **RALPH** (b. 1638), **THOMAS** (d. 1689), Hanley. Staffordshire Potteries. c. 1670–c. 1710. *Earthenwares, slip-decorated.*

3864	James Toft	The name of various members of the Toft family occurs, as
3865	Ralph Toft	part of the decoration, on slip-decorated earthenware dishes,
3866	Thomas Toft	etc. Examples can be seen in the Victoria and Albert Museum,

the Hanley and other museums. Specimens will be found illustrated in *British Pottery and Porcelain: an illustrated Encyclopaedia of Marked Specimens.* Some examples bear dates. Specimens by Thomas Toft are the most often found, over thirty signed examples are recorded.

TOLLOW

VERA TOLLOW, MISS, Wallington, Surrey. 1954– . *Studio-type Pottery.*

3867	Tollow.	Painted mark, 1954– .

TOMKINSON

TOMKINSON & BILLINGTON, High St., Longton. Staffordshire Potteries. 1868–70. *Earthenwares.*

3868	T. & B.	Distinguishing initials found on several printed marks of differing design: name of the individual pattern is often included, 1868–70. See Plate 4.
1538	TOMLINSON & CO.	*See* Ferrybridge Pottery.
3571	TONBRIDGE CASTLE WARE or	*See* Slack & Brownlow, page 580.
3572	TONBRIDGE WARE	

TONI   **TONI RAYMOND POTTERY** (R. A. Smith and G. W. Hiscock), Torquay, Devon. 1961– . *Earthenwares, Table wares, Figures, etc.*

3869   Impressed or printed marks, 1961– .

—   TONQUIN CHINA   *See* Appendix, page 733.

TOOTH & CO.   **TOOTH & CO. (LTD.)**, Bretby Art Pottery, Woodville, Nr. Burton-on-Trent, Derbyshire. Est. 1883 as Tooth & Ault, Continued as Tooth & Co. 1887– . *Earthenwares.*

3870   Trade-mark registered in 1884, printed or impressed. "England" added from 1891. "Made in England" occurs on 20th century examples.

3871   Initial mark used by Henry Tooth, c. 1883–1900.

3872   CLANTA   Name-marks introduced, c. 1914.
3873   CLANTA
        WARE

3799   "TOP-O-THE-WORLD"   *See* John Tams (& Sons) (Ltd.), page 609.

TORQUAY   **TORQUAY TERRA-COTTA CO. LTD.**, Hele Cross, Torquay, Devon. 1875–1909. *Terra-cotta, Figures, Plaques, Vases, etc.*

3874   TORQUAY   Impressed mark, 1875–1909.

3875   TORQUAY   Impressed or printed mark, in various forms, 1875–90.
      TERRA-COTTA CO.
        LIMITED

3875a   Impressed or printed mark, 1875–1909.

3875b   Printed or impressed mark, 1900–9.

TORQUIL   **TORQUIL POTTERY**, R. Moon, Henley-in-Arden, War-
                                           wickshire. 1958– . *Studio-type Pottery.*

3876   REG MOON   Incised or painted signature mark, 1958– .

3876a   TORQUIL   Incised or painted mark, 1958– .

3876b   TORQUIL POTTERY   Stamped mark, in circular form, note place name Cookham,
            COOKHAM   used 1958 to May 1960.
          HAND MADE

3876c   TORQUIL POTTERY   Stamped mark, in circular form, May 1960– .
          HAND MADE

3876d   HENLEY-IN-ARDEN   Stamped mark, in circular form, May 1960– .
         TORQUIL POTTERY
           HAND MADE

TOTLAND   **TOTLAND POTTERY**, Kenneth A. Scotcher, Totland Bay,
                                           Isle of Wight. October 1958– . *Studio-type Pottery.*

3877   Printed mark, 1958– .

                                               Mr. Scotcher was trained under Jo Lester, and uses the basic
                                           Lester, Isle of Wight mark (no. 2370) with the addition of the
                                           place name TOTLAND.

TOWER   **JAMES TOWER**, Corsham, Wiltshire. 1950– . *Studio-
                                           type Pottery.*

3878   James Tower   Incised or painted name marks, in writing letters with year of
                    63   manufacture, 1950– .
3878a   Tower
                    63

104	TOWERS CRAFT WARE	*See* Alton Towers.

TOWNSEND

GEORGE TOWNSEND, St. Gregory's Pottery (and other addresses), Longton. Staffordshire Potteries. c. 1850–64. *Earthenwares.*

3879   G. TOWNSEND   Distinguishing name found on several printed marks of differing design: name of the individual pattern is often included, c. 1850–64. The Royal Arms occur in several of these marks.

—	T. P.	*See* Appendix, page 733.
3066		*See* Thomas Plant.
3070a		*See* Thomas Plowman.

2361	T. P. L.	*See* Thomas P. Ledgar.

3386	TR (joined)	*See* Roger Ross Turner.

436	T. & R. B.	*See* T. & R. Boote.

3204–6	T. R. & CO.	*See* T. Rathbone & Co.
3207		*See* Thomas Rathbone & Co.

3181	TREGENNA HILL	*See* Kenneth Quick.

1279	TRENTHAM	*See* Devonshire Potteries Ltd. and Trentham Bone China Ltd.,
3880–1		below.

TRENTHAM

TRENTHAM BONE CHINA LTD., Royal Crown Pottery, Longton. Staffordshire Potteries. 1952–7. *China.*

3880   Printed mark, 1952–7.

3881   Printed mark, 1955–7.

TREY

TREY, MARIANNE DE (Mrs. Haile), Shinner's Bridge, Dartington, South Devon. 1947– . *Studio-type Pottery.* Marianne de Trey formerly worked in America.

3882   Incised or painted mark, 1945– . This mark also occurs within a triangle outline.

3883   Impressed seal mark within circle or square, 1945– .

    A "mark" of this form has been given in several recent books and attributed to Marianne de Trey. Such a mark has *not* been used by this potter.

TRIBE

BARBARA TRIBE, Sheffield Paul, Penzance, Cornwall. 1962– . *Figures, etc., in Terra-cotta or Stoneware. Also Studio-type Pottery.*

Barbara Tribe was the wife of the late John Singleman, q.v. She is well known for her sculpture (ceramic sculpture from about 1946). On the death of her husband she continued his pottery.

3884   BARBARA TRIBE   Signature-type mark, early 1962– .

2085   TRIOOD   *See* Hoods Ltd.

331   T. R. P.   *See* Bembridge Pottery.
4387   *See* Yellowsands Pottery.

3886   T. R. & P.   *See* Tundley, Rhodes & Proctor.

3522   T. S. & C.   *See* Thomas Shirley & Co.
        or
3521   T. S. & COY.

3817   T. T.   *See* Taylor, Tunnicliffe & Co. (Ltd.).
        or
3818   T. T. & CO.

3904   T. & T.   *See* Turner & Tomkinson.

3914	T. T. H.	*See* Thomas Twyford.
3838	T. U. & CO. (joined)	*See* Uriah Thomas & Co.
754a	M. TUDOR-JONES	*See* Campden Pottery.

TUDOR

WILLIAM TUDOR, High Wycombe, Buckinghamshire. 1947– . *Studio-type Pottery.*

3885   Impressed monogram seal mark, 1947– .

TUNDLEY

TUNDLEY, RHODES & PROCTOR, Swan Bank Pottery, Burslem. Staffordshire Potteries. 1873–83. *Earthenwares.* Subsequently Rhodes & Proctor, q.v.

3886   T. R. & P.   Distinguishing detail of several printed marks of differing design: name of the individual pattern is often included, 1873–83.

TUNNICLIFF

MICHAEL TUNNICLIFF(E), High St., Tunstall. Staffordshire Potteries. 1828–41. *Earthenware Figures, Jugs, etc.*

3887   TUNNICLIFF
TUNSTALL   Name-mark on raised fancy scroll, 1828–41.

1221	TUNSTALL WARE	*See* Thomas Dean & Sons.
808	TURNER	*See* Caughley Works.

TURNER

TURNER & ABBOT(T), Lane End, Longton. Staffordshire Potteries. c. 1783–7. *Wedgwood-type Jasper wares, etc.*
    This was a short-lived partnership between John Turner and Andrew Abbott. Abbott was subsequently in partnership with Mist. It is possible that Abbott was the selling agent rather than a practical potter. A very interesting advertisement of January 1785 is quoted in the *Transactions of the English*

Ceramic Circle, vol. 4, part 5, and in the author's *English Pottery and Porcelain*, 1780–1850. This partnership is also mentioned in the Lygo–Duesbury correspondence during 1787. See *The English Ceramic Circle Transactions*, vol. 3, part 5, p. 204.

3888   TURNER & ABBOTT   Impressed mark, c. 1783–7.

3899   TURNER & CO.   *See* John Turner.

809   TURNER GALLIMORE   *See* Caughley Works.

TURNER

TURNER, GODDARD & CO., Royal Albert Pottery, Tunstall. Staffordshire Potteries. 1867–74. *Earthenwares.*

3889   TURNER, GODDARD & CO.   Distinguishing detail of several printed marks of differing design, 1867–74. See Plate 4, a jug with this mark in the Godden Collection is dated July 1867.

TURNER

G. W. TURNER & SONS, Victoria Works, Tunstall. Staffordshire Potteries. 1873–95. *Earthenwares.* Formerly Turner & Tomkinson, q.v.

3890   TURNERS   Impressed marks, 1873–95.
3891   G. W. T. & SONS
3892   G. W. T. S.   Distinguishing details (marks nos. 3891–4) of several printed
3893   G. W. T. & S.   marks of differing design: name of the individual pattern is
3894   G. T. & S.   often included, 1873–95.

3895   Printed Royal Arms mark, 1891–5.

3897   I. TURNER   *See* John Turner.

TURNER		JOHN TURNER (Turner & Co., etc.), Lane End, Longton. Staffordshire Potteries. c. 1762–1806. *Earthenwares, Cream-wares, Wedgwood-type wares—Jaspers, etc. Rarely Porcelains.*

On John Turner's death in 1787, he was succeeded by his sons—John and William. The firm closed in 1806. Several changes in style were used for brief periods—Turner & Abbott (c. 1784–6), Turner Abbott & Co. (c. 1799)—but for the main period the basic mark was TURNER.

3896	TURNER	Impressed mark, c. 1770+. Some very rare porcelains bear this impressed mark. Some jasper portrait and figure subject plaques of Wedgwood type bear this mark; others of the same set bear only impressed numbers.
3897	I. TURNER	Rare impressed mark, c. 1770–87.
3898	TURNER.	Printed or impressed mark from 1784 when John Turner was appointed potter to the Prince of Wales.
3899	TURNER & CO.	Impressed marks with "& Co." probably used c. 1780–6 and 1803–6.
3900	*Turner's-Patent.*	Painted mark on rare stone-ware type earthenwares, 1800–5. This body was patented in January 1800 and the rights sold to Spode in 1805.

Examples of Turner's wares will be found illustrated in *British Pottery and Porcelain: an illustrated Encyclopaedia of Marked Specimens.*

291	TURNER JASPER WARE	*See* Bates, Elliot & Co.
TURNER		**TURNER, HASSALL & PEAKE,** Copeland Street and Liverpool Road, Stoke. Staffordshire Potteries. 1865–9. *Earthenwares, Parian, etc.* Subsequently Turner, Hassall, Peake & Poole.
3901	TURNER, HASSALL & PEAKE	Distinguishing details of several printed or impressed marks of differing design: name of the individual pattern is often
3902	T. H. & P.	included, 1865–9.

TURNER		**TURNER & TOMKINSON**, Victoria Works, Tunstall. Staffordshire Potteries. 1860–72. *Earthenwares.* Subsequently G. W. Turner & Sons, q.v.
3903	TURNER & TOMKINSON	Distinguishing details of several printed marks of differing design: name of the individual pattern is often included,
3904	T. & T.	1860–72. The initials T. T. are often in a fancy form, as mark no. 3905.

3905   **T & T**

—   WM. TURNER   *See* Appendix, page 734.

TURNER

TURNER & WOOD, Copeland Street Works, Stoke. Staffordshire Potteries. 1880–8. *Parian, Porcelain, Majolica, Earthenwares.* Formerly Poole, Stanway & Wood.

    An advertisement of 1883 lists china dessert, tea, breakfast and five o'clock tea sets. Vases, ornaments, baskets, etc., in china, earthenware, stoneware, majolica, parian, terra-cotta. Over 4,000 various articles and designs—"new models being weekly introduced". Jewitt (*Ceramic Art of Great Britain*, 1883) also lists wares made by this firm; the majority of items were unmarked.

3906   TURNER & WOOD STOKE   Impressed mark on parian bust of Queen Victoria, dated 1887 (Godden Collection).

3890   TURNERS   *See* G. W. Turner & Sons.

3900   TURNER'S PATENT   *See* John Turner.

1223–5   TUSCAN   *See* Decoro Pottery Co.
3060–5   *See* R. H. & S. L. Plant Ltd.

—   T. W.   *See* Appendix, page 734.

3885   TW (joined)   *See* William Tudor.

4140   T. W. & CO.   *See* Thomas C. Wild & Co.
4283   *See* Thomas Wood & Co.

| 4284 | T. W. & S. | *See* Thomas Wood & Sons. |

TWEMLOW

JOHN TWEMLOW, Shelton. Staffordshire Potteries. c. 1795–7. *Earthenwares, Basaltes, etc.*

| 3907 | J. T. | These initials occur under the handle of a basalt teapot, formerly in the Grant Collection, c. 1795–7. Jewitt in his *Ceramic Art of Great Britain* quotes from an invoice of John Twemlow (1797) in which many Egyptian black (basalt) teapots are mentioned. |

| 2096 | TWH
(joined) | *See* T. W. Howard. |

TWIGG

J. TWIGG (& CO.), Newhill Pottery, c. 1822–66, Kilnhurst Old Pottery, c. 1839–81, Nr. Swinton, Yorkshire. c. 1822–81. *Earthenwares.*

For the greater part of the working period the firm's style was Twigg Brothers or J. Twigg & Bros. but marks do not use this form of title.

| 3908 | J. T. | Initial mark impressed or printed with name of pattern, c. 1822. |

| 3909
3910 | TWIGG
TWIGG'S | Impressed mark, c. 1822+.* |

| 3911 | TWIGG
NEWHILL | Impressed mark, c. 1822–66. |

| 3912 | TWIGG
K. P. | Impressed mark, c. 1839–81. K. P. relates to the Kilnhurst Pottery. |

| 3913 | J. TWIGG
& CO. | Rare printed mark recorded on plate, c. 1841–6. In this case the "& Co." is very small and below "J. Twigg".

For further information the reader is referred to O. Grabham's *Yorkshire Potteries, Pots and Potters* (1916). |

* Several books attribute these marks to the middle of the 18th century —this is incorrect.

TWYFORD

THOMAS TWYFORD, Bath Street Works and Cliffe Vale Potteries (c. 1888+), Hanley. Staffordshire Potteries. 1860–98.* *Earthenwares.*

N.B. This firm made mainly sanitary wares.

3914

Printed or impressed mark, 1860–98. Other marks incorporate the name or initials T. T.

* From 1898 the firm has been Twyfords Ltd.

TYDEMAN

ELEANOR TYDEMAN, MISS, East Dulwich, London S.E. 15. c. 1920–35. *Studio-type Pottery.*

3915   E. T.

Incised or painted monogram mark of the initials E. T., c. 1920–35.

3804   TYLER & CO.
                also
        TYNE POTTERY

See Taylor & Co.

U

1285	U. C. & N.	*See* Dicker Potteries.
3927–9	U. H. P. CO. (LTD.).	*See* Upper Hanley Pottery (Co. Ltd.)
3922	U. H. & W.	*See* Unwin, Holmes & Worthington.
2829	ULNIMACK	*See* William K. McKnight & Co.

ULSTER

ULSTER POTTERY, Coalisland, Ireland. Late 19th century. *Porcelain.*

3916   THE ULSTER POTTERY COALISLAND, IRELAND

Stencilled mark on Belleek-type wares, late 19th century.

3921	U. M. & T.	*See* Unwin, Mountford & Taylor.
3828	U. N. A.	*See* Tewkesbury Pottery.

UNION

UNION POTTERY, Southwick, Sunderland, Durham. c. 1802. *Earthenwares.*

Very little is known about this pottery apart from an advertisement for a foreman in 1802.

3917   UNION POTTERY

Very rare mark, occurring as part of the printed decoration on a pottery mug.* It has also been recorded impressed on a lustred watch stand.

* See companion illustrated encyclopaedia of marked specimens.

UNIVERSAL

UNIVERSAL POTTERY (LONGTON) LTD., Sèvres Works, Longton. Staffordshire Potteries. 1949 to December 1962. *China and Earthenwares.*

3918–19a

1949+

1956+

c. 1958–62

Printed marks, 1949–62.

3918–19a UNIVERSAL
WARE

See Universal Pottery (Longton) Ltd.

UNWIN

JOSEPH UNWIN (& CO.), Cornhill Works, Market Lane, Longton. Staffordshire Potteries. 1877–1926. *Earthenwares, Figures, etc.* Formerly Poole & Unwin, q.v.

3920 UNWIN

Moulded name-mark, within a diamond-shaped outline, recorded on a Staffordshire earthenware group of two harvesters, c. 1877–90.

Other potters of this name are recorded but, as a similar figure bears the initial mark of Poole & Unwin, it is probable that the UNWIN mark relates to this Longton potter. His advertisements mention "Earthenware figures for home and export". "& Co." was added to the style in 1891.

UNWIN

UNWIN, MOUNTFORD & TAYLOR, Upper Hanley Pottery, Hanley. Staffordshire Potteries. c. 1864. *Earthenwares.* Subsequently Unwin, Holmes & Worthington, see next entry.

3921 U. M. & T.

Distinguishing initials found on several printed marks of differing design: name of the individual pattern such as "Railway" is included, c. 1864.

UNWIN

UNWIN, HOLMES & WORTHINGTON, Upper Hanley Pottery, Hanley. Staffordshire Potteries. c. 1865–8. *Earthenwares.* Formerly Unwin, Mountford & Taylor, q.v. Subsequently Unwin & Holmes.

| 3922 | U. H. & W. | Distinguishing initials found on several printed marks of differing design: name of the individual pattern is often included, c. 1865–8. The name in full also occurs in some marks, as no. 3923. |
| 3923 | | |

UPCHURCH

UPCHURCH POTTERY (William and James Baker), Rainham, Kent. Established in 1913 by S. Wakeley. *Earthenwares*. Closed January 1961.

3924	UPCHURCH	Standard impressed mark, 1913–61.
3925	UPCHURCH SEEBY	Impressed mark, 1945–61.
3926	SEEBY	The name SEEBY also occurs painted. This relates to the firm of agents at Reading through which wares were sold.

UPPER

UPPER HANLEY POTTERY CO. (LTD.), Hanley (c. 1895–1902) and Brownfield's Works (c. 1902–10), Cobridge. Staffordshire Potteries. 1895–1910. *Earthenwares*.

| 3927 | U. H. P. CO. ENGLAND | Impressed or printed initial mark, in various forms, 1895–1900. |

| 3928 | | Printed mark, 1895–1900. |

| 3929 | U. H. P. Co. Ltd. ENGLAND | "Ltd." added to style and marks from c. 1900. See nos. 3929 and 3929a, c. 1900–10. |

| 3929a | | |

| 1862 | URN MARK | *See* Hackwood. |
| 3838 | U T & Co. (monogram) | *See* Uriah Thomas & Co. |

V

3932a	V	*See* Nicholas Vergette.
994	VALE	*See* Colclough China Ltd.
988		*See* H. J. Colclough.
3285		*See* Ridgway Potteries Ltd.

VAN		**VAN DER STRAETEN**, Linton, Nr. Cambridge. 1948– . *Individual studio-type Earthenwares.*

3930		Printed or impressed mark, 1948– .

4507a	V & B	*See* Appendix.
—	VEDGWOOD	*See* Appendix, page 734.

VENABLES		**VENABLES & BAINES**, Nile Street, Burslem. Staffordshire Potteries. c. 1851–3. *Earthenwares.* Subsequently John Venables & Co., q.v.
3930a	VENABLES & BAINES	Printed or impressed name-mark, 1851–3.

VENABLES		**JOHN VENABLES & CO.*** Nile Street, Burslem. Staffordshire Potteries. c. 1853–5. *Earthenwares.* Formerly Venables & Baines, q.v.

   * This firm also traded as VENABLES MANN & CO.

3930b	J. VENABLES & CO.	Printed or impressed name-mark, c. 1853–5.

VENTNOR — VENTNOR POTTERY, John Reilly, Ventnor, Isle of Wight. 1960– . *Studio-type Pottery and Tiles.*

3931	J R VENTNOR	Painted or incised initial and place-name mark, 1960 .
3931a	HAND PAINTED AT THE VENTNOR POTTERY STUDIOS	Stamped mark on decorative tiles, 1960– .

VERGETTE — NICHOLAS VERGETTE, Camberwell School of Art and other posts. 1946–58.* *Studio-type Pottery, also Tiles, etc.*

3932	N.V	Painted or incised marks, 1946+.
3932a	V.	
3933	VERGETTE	Signature mark in writing letters, c. 1946+.

* Nicholas Vergette moved to America in 1958.

VERNON — JAMES VERNON (& SON), Waterloo Pottery, Burslem. Staffordshire Potteries. 1860–80. *Earthenwares.* Formerly James Vernon & Co. Subsequently J. & G. Vernon.

3934	J. V.	Distinguishing initials found on several printed marks of differing design: name of the individual pattern is often included, 1860–74. "& Son" added to style and marks from c. 1875.
3934a 3934b	J. V. & S. J. V. junr.	Distinguishing details of several printed marks of differing design: name of the individual pattern is often included, c. 1875–1880.
802	VICTORIA	*See* Cartwright & Edwards.

VICTORIA

VICTORIA PORCELAIN (FENTON) LTD., Fenton. Staffordshire Potteries. 1949–57. *Earthenwares.* Subsequently Victoria & Trentham Potteries Ltd.

3935

Printed mark, 1949–57. Other marks also include the firm's name in full.

VICTORIA

VICTORIA & TRENTHAM POTTERIES LTD., Fenton. Staffordshire Potteries. 1957–60. *China and Earthenwares.* Formerly Victoria Porcelain (Fenton) Ltd., see previous entry.

3936

Printed mark, 1957–60.

VIKING

VIKING POTTERY CO., Cobridge. Staffordshire Potteries. 1950– . *China and Earthenwares.* Formerly Viking Tile Co.

3937–8

Printed marks, 1950– .

4068a   VITRILAIN   *See* Wedgwood & Co. (Ltd.).

236
(note)   VITSIL   *See* Bakewell Bros. Ltd.

VODREY'S

VODREY'S POTTERY, Dublin, Ireland. 1872–85.* *Pottery.*

3939   VODREY DUBLIN   Impressed mark, c. 1872–85.*
              POTTERY

* The closing date is open to doubt.

VOYEZ

JEAN (JOHN) VOYEZ, Staffordshire Potteries. c. 1768–1790(?). *Modeller, etc.*

The reader is referred to a most detailed paper by Mr. R. J. Charleston and contained in the *Transactions of the English Ceramic Circle*, vol. 5, part 1. See also the American magazine, *Antiques*, January, March and October 1963.

3940	J. VOYEZ	The signature mark of this modeller rarely occurs on earthenwares. The best-known examples of his work are the "Fair Hebe" jugs which are signed I. VOYEZ and dated 1788. Examples are in the Victoria and Albert Museum and other collections. See *British Pottery and Porcelain: an illustrated Encyclopaedia of Marked Specimens.*
3941	I. VOYEZ	
3942	J. VOYEZ SCULPSIT	
3943	VOYEZ & HALES FECIT	Rare impressed mark on vases in the British Museum, c. 1770–1780.
3943a	VOYEZ	This impressed mark has been reported on an undecorated, moulded creamware ladle, late 18th century. An example apparently marked I. VOYEZ is illustrated in *Antiques*, October 1963.
3943	VOYEZ & HALES	*See* Jean Voyez, entry above.
1463	VULCAN WARE	*See* Elektra Porcelain Co. Ltd.
VYSE		**CHARLES VYSE**, Cheyne Row, Chelsea, London. 1919–63.* *Earthenware figures and groups* (c. 1920–30), *Glaze effect Stonewares, etc.* Formerly worked in Staffordshire Potteries.
3944	C. V.	Impressed or incised initial marks, with year of production added, 1919– .
3945	C. V. CHELSEA	
3946	Charles Vyse	Signature mark in writing letters, with year.
3947	19 V 27 CHELSEA.	Painted marks, with year of production.
3948	VYSE 1935	Incised or painted marks on attractive, simple (Chinese styled) stonewares with glaze effects, with year of production added. On some specimens the V and Y are joined and can be read as a W giving the name or initials WSE.
3948a	C. VYSE 1927	

* A exhibition of Charles Vyse's work held in London during December 1963 was advertised as his last exhibition: "Charles Vyse has been exhibiting his pottery since 1926, and this is his last exhibition. He has to leave his studio, and the large built-in kiln necessary for the very high temperature firing of these pieces is impossible to move. His work, about 4,000 pieces, is in museums and private collections throughout the world, and is recognised by Connoisseurs as among the finest produced since the Chinese of the Sung Dynasty."

3949	C. VYSE CHELSEA	Impressed or incised mark. The year of production has not been added to post-war pieces.
3950	C. ^{V.} P. CHEYNE CHELSEA	A rare painted mark in this form on earthenware figures probably relates to the Charles Vyse Pottery, rather than to Miss Parnell who used the name "Chelsea-Cheyne".

W

47	W. A. A.	*See* William Alsager Adderley (& Co.).
	or	
48	W. A. A. & CO.	
27	W. A. & CO.	*See* William Adams & Sons (Potters) Ltd.
4065–6	WACOL	*See* Wedgwood & Co. (Ltd.).
3954 3962–4	WADE	*See* George Wade & Sons Ltd., below, and Wade, Heath & Co. (Ltd.).

WADE   **WADE & CO.**, Union Pottery, Burslem. Staffordshire Potteries. 1887–1927. *Earthenwares.* Formerly Wade & Colclough. Subsequently Wade, Heath & Co. Ltd., q.v.

3951   WADE'S   Impressed mark, 1887–1927.

3952   W. & CO. B.   Distinguishing initials found on several printed marks of differing design: name of the individual pattern is often included, 1887–1927.

WADE   **GEORGE WADE & SON, LTD.**, Manchester Pottery, Burslem. Staffordshire Potteries. 1922– . *Earthenwares.*

3953–5

c. 1936+   c. 1936+   c. 1947–

Printed marks, c. 1936– .

WADE   **WADE, HEATH & CO. (LTD.)**, High Street Works (1927–1938), Royal Victoria Pottery, from 1938, Burslem. Staffordshire Potteries. 1927– . *Earthenwares.* Formerly Wade & Co., q.v.

3956–8

c. 1927+   c. 1934+   c. 1934+

3959–61

c. 1936+   c. 1936+   c. 1939+
                                                       with or without the
                                                       word FLAXMAN

3962–4

c. 1953–   c. 1953–   c. 1957–

Printed or impressed marks, 1927– .

WADE

WADE (ULSTER) LTD., Ulster Pottery, Portadown, Co. Armagh, Northern Ireland. 1953– . *Earthenwares—"Irish Porcelain"*.

3965

Impressed mark, 1953– .

3966

"Irish Porcelain" mark, impressed or printed, from October 1953. "Made in Ireland" added below from April 1954. "By Wade, Co. Armagh" also added. "E" is the potter's mark, other initials occur.

3967

Printed mark, c. 1954– .

3968   Embossed mark on die-pressed wares, c. 1955– . The letter below is the potter's mark.

WADSWORTH   **PHILIP S. WADSWORTH,** various addresses. 1933– .*
Studio-type Pottery.

3969   P. S. W.   Incised or impressed initial marks, c. 1933– .*

* Since the war Mr. Wadsworth has only potted intermittently.

WAGSTAFF   **WAGSTAFF & BRUNT,** Richmond Pottery (from c. 1898), Longton. Staffordshire Potteries. 1880–1927. *Earthenwares and China.*

This firm supplied many commemorative wares, and marks occur on Jubilee pieces of 1897. Wagstaff & Brunt may have been dealers, although their name occurs in *Pottery Gazette* lists of manufacturers.

3970   WAGSTAFF & BRUNT   Distinguishing details of several printed marks of differing
              LONGTON   design: name of the individual pattern is often included,
3971   W. & B.   1880–1927.
              LONGTON

WAIN   **H. A. WAIN & SONS LTD.,** Melba Works, Longton. Staffordshire Potteries. 1946– . *Earthenwares, Animals, etc.*

3972–3   Printed marks, 1951– .

The name Melba was also used by other firms, see page 431.

WAINE   **CHARLES WAINE (& CO.) (LTD.),** Derby Works, Longton. Staffordshire Potteries. 1891–1920. *China.* Formerly Waine & Bates.

3974   C. W.   Distinguishing initials found on several printed marks, 1891–1913.

3975 Printed mark, 1891–1913.

C. Waine & Co. renamed C. Waine Ltd. from 1913.

3976 Printed mark, c. 1913–20.

1050 WAISTEL *See* Waistel Cooper.

4065–6 WACOL
or
WACOL WARE *See* Wedgwood & Co. Ltd.

WALDRAM **BEATRICE A. WALDRAM, MISS,** Hampstead, London N.W.3. 1920–35. *Studio-type Pottery.*

3977 B. A. WALDRAM Incised or painted signature mark, with or without the word "Hampstead", c. 1920–35.

309 WALES *See* Beddgelert Pottery.
1202 *See* C. Davis.

WALFORD **J. F. WALFORD,** Redhill, Surrey, and Crowborough, Sussex. 1948– . *Studio-type Pottery.*

3978 Impressed seal-type mark, 1948– .

WALKER **WALKER (& SON),** Rotherham, Yorkshire. c. 1772+. *Earthenwares.* Formerly Platt & Walker, c. 1767–72.

3979 WALKER This name-mark on 18th-century earthenwares may relate to the little-known manufacturer Samuel Walker of Rotherham. See a paper by A. J. B. Kiddell in *The Transactions of the English Ceramic Circle*, vol. 5, part 3, 1962.

WALKER

AGATHA WALKER, MISS, Long Crendon, Thame, Oxford-shire. c. 1920–35. *Studio-type Pottery, Figures.*

3980

Incised or painted mark, c. 1920–35.

WALKER

WALKER & CARTER, British Anchor Pottery, Longton. Staffordshire Potteries. 1866–72 and at Stoke, c. 1872–89. *Earthenwares.* Formerly Walker, Bateman & Co.

3981   W. & C.

Distinguishing initials found on several printed marks of differing design: name of the individual pattern is often included and an anchor is depicted on several marks, 1866–89.

WALKER

THOMAS WALKER, Lion Works, Tunstall. Staffordshire Potteries. 1845–51. *Earthenwares.*

3982   T. WALKER
3982a   THOS WALKER

Various blue printed earthenwares bear marks incorporating the name T. or Thos Walker, c. 1845–51. (Rate records for 1853 list the representatives of the *late* T. Walker.)

N.B. Other potters of this name were at Longton, c. 1846–9 and 1856–7. The initial marks T. W. may relate to the above Tunstall potter, see Appendix, p. 734.

WALKER

WILLIAM WALKER, 112 Minories, London. c.1795–1800.* *Retailer.*

3983   WALKER MINORIES

Impressed mark on pair of dolphin formed creamware sauce-boats in the Schreiber Collection at the Victoria and Albert Museum, c. 1795–1800.

* William Walker—China, Glass and Tea man is listed in a directory of 1797. In 1804 the firm was styled Walker & Nash.

WALLACE

(J.) WALLACE & CO., Newcastle or Forth Bank Pottery, Newcastle upon Tyne, Northumberland. 1838–93. *Earthenwares.* Formerly Redhead, Wilson & Co.

3984   WALLACE & CO.

Impressed mark, 1838–93.

The firm is listed in local directories as J. Wallace & Co. from 1838 to 1857 and then as Wallace & Co. to 1893. This firm continued at other addresses, as flower-pot manufacturers to 1904.

WALLACE

WINIFRED WALLACE, MRS., Ravenscourt Pottery, London W.12. 1955–61. *Studio-type Pottery.*

3985   W. W.

Painted or incised initial marks, 1955–61.

WALLER

BARBARA WALLER, Empshott, Liss, Hampshire. 1942–1953. *Studio-type Pottery, Figures and Animal models.*

3986   Barbara Waller
3987   B. Waller

Signature marks, 1942–53.

    Barbara Waller worked with Charles Vyse at his Chelsea pottery, and the above signature marks will be found on several Vyse models.

WALLEY

EDWARD WALLEY, Villa Pottery, Cobridge. Staffordshire Potteries. 1845–56. *Earthenwares, Parian, etc.* Formerly Jones & Walley, q.v.

3988

Printed mark, 1845–56. Other marks occur with the name and address, see Plate 8.

3989   IRONSTONE
            CHINA
          E. WALLEY

Impressed mark, 1845–56.

3990   W

Distinguishing initial found on several printed marks of differing design: name of the individual pattern is often included, 1845–56.

WALLEY

JOHN* WALLEY, High Street, Burslem. Staffordshire Potteries. 1850–67. *Earthenwares.*

3991   J. WALLEY
3992   J. WALLEY'S
              WARE

Printed or impressed marks, c. 1850–67.

3993   JOHN WALLEY
              1854

Incised mark on earthenware "egg".

    * Other Staffordshire potters of this name include:
      John Walley, Shelton, Hanley, c. 1813.
      John Walley, Market Street, Tunstall, c. 1854.
      John Walley, Hope Street, Hanley, c. 1853–64.
    The above marks could also relate to the last two listed.

WALLIS   E. WALLIS MISS, Disley, Cheshire. 1935–58. *Studio-type Pottery.*

3994   E. W.   Impressed initials in seal-type mark, 1935–58.

1701   WALLIS GIMSON   *See* Wallis *Gimson* & Co.
                    & CO.

WALLWORK   ALAN WALLWORK, Alan Gallery, London S.E.23.   1959– .
                                    Studio-type Pottery and Architectural ceramics.

3995   W.   Incised, impressed or painted initial on standard pieces,
                                    1959– .

3996   Initial mark on individual work, 1959– .

                                      N.B. The initials A. W. also used by Bernard Rooke who
                                    works at the Alan Gallery.

WALSH   WALSH & EARDLEY, Liverpool, Lancashire.   Early 19th
                                    century.   *Creamwares and Delft-type Earthenwares.*

3997   WALSH & EARDLEY   Very rare printed name-mark on a creamware jug in the Allman
                                    Collection.*   This jug bears prints of the Farmers' Arms and
                                    Charity.   The firm's name is incorporated in the print.
                                    Early 19th century.

                                       * This example is illustrated in *The Connoisseur*, October 1940.

WALTERS   HELEN WALTERS, MISS, Stroud Green, Hornsey, London
                                    N.4.   1945– .   *Studio-type Pottery.*

3998   Incised mark on Doulton wares, 1945–53.

3999   Painted or incised initial marks with last two numerals of year,
                                    1953– .

4000 Painted or incised initial marks with last two numerals of year, 1953— .

WALTON **WALTON POTTERY CO. LTD.** (William Gordon), Old Whittington, Nr. Chesterfield, Derbyshire. 1946*–56. *Salt-glazed Stonewares.*

4001 Incised or impressed mark, 1946–56.

* William Gordon carried out experiments in 1939. The pottery was re-established after the war.

WALTON **JOHN WALTON**, Navigation Road, Burslem. Staffordshire Potteries. c. 1818*–35. *Earthenware figures and groups.*

4002 Impressed name-mark on raised scroll, usually found at the back of a figure base, c. 1818*–35.

For further information on John Walton and his figures see R. Haggar's *Staffordshire Chimney Ornaments* (1955). Examples will be found illustrated in *British Pottery and Porcelain: an illustrated Encyclopaedia of Marked Specimens.*

N.B. William Walton of Hope Street, Shelton, also made figures, c. 1846, as did James Walton of Hanley, c. 1846–60, and Joshua Walton of Hanley, c. 1834–41.

* The first record of John Walton as a potter occurs in a directory of 1818 but it would seem likely that he had been potting for some years prior to this date.

WALTON **J. H. WALTON**, Baltimore, or Albion China Works, Longton. Staffordshire Potteries. 1912–21. *China.* Formerly Walton & Co.

4003 Distinguishing initials found on several printed or impressed marks of differing design, 1912–21.

1206 WANSTEAD *See* Clare Dawkins.

WARBURTON **JOHN WARBURTON**, Hot Lane, Cobridge. Staffordshire Potteries. c. 1802–25. *Earthenwares, Creamwares, Basaltes, etc.*

4004 WÁRBURTON Impressed mark, c. 1802–25.

WARBURTON

JOHN WARBURTON, Carr's Hill Pottery, Gateshead, Newcastle upon Tyne. c. 1750–c. 95.* *Earthenwares.*

4005	J. WARBURTON N. ON TYNE	This signature mark is recorded by Chaffers as occurring on a transfer printed, yellow ware jug.
4005a	J. WARBURTON N. C. TYNE	A printed creamware teapot in the Brighton Museum bears this very rare mark, as part of the print. See the companion illustrated encyclopaedia of marked specimens.

* This pottery was continued by Isaac Warburton c. 1795–1801 and then by Ellen Warburton. It closed c. 1817.

WARBURTON

PETER WARBURTON, Bleak Hill, Cobridge. Staffordshire Potteries. c. 1802–12. *Earthenware and China.*

Formerly in partnership with Francis Warburton, see next entry. Peter died in January 1813.

4006	WARBURTON'S PATENT	Printed or written mark, with crown above used on wares printed in gold or silver, c. 1810–12.

WARBURTON

PETER & FRANCIS WARBURTON, Bleak Hill, Cobridge. Staffordshire Potteries. c. 1795 to March 1802. *Earthenwares, Figures, etc.*

The partnership was dissolved on March 29th, 1802. Peter continued the works to 1813, Francis established a factory at La Charité-sur-Loire, France.

4007	P. & F. W.	Impressed mark, c. 1795–1802.
4008	P. & F. WARBURTON	Impressed mark, rare, on two figures of Harvesters,* c. 1795–1802.

* See an article by R. G. Haggar, *Apollo*, November 1955.

4006	WARBURTON'S PATENT	*See* Peter Warburton.
4009	WARDELLA	*See* Gertrude J. Wardle, below.

WARDLE

GERTRUDE J. WARDLE, Southport, Lancashire. 1949– . *Studio-type Pottery.*

4009	WARDELLA	Impressed, incised or painted mark, 1949–56.

| 4010 | G. J. WARDLE | Signature marks, in writing letters, 1956– . |
| 4011 | G. JOYCE WARDLE | |

WARDLE

WARDLE & ASH, James Street, Shelton, Hanley. Staffordshire Potteries. 1859–62. *Parian, Majolica, Figures, etc.*

| 4012 | W. & A. | Impressed initial mark, 1859–62. |

WARDLE

WARDLE & CO. (LTD.), Washington Works, Hanley. Staffordshire Potteries. 1871–1935.* *Earthenwares, Parian, Majolica, etc.* Formerly James Wardle.

| 4013 | WARDLE | Impressed mark, c. 1871+. "England" added from 1891. |

| 4014 | | Printed mark, c. 1885–90. |

| 4015 | | Printed mark, c. 1890–1935. |

| 4016 | | Printed mark, c. 1902–9. |

WARDLE ART POTTERY CO. LTD.

* Retitled WARDLE ART POTTERY CO. LTD. in 1910 and continued at Stoke as a branch of A. J. Robinson, c. 1910–24, and to 1935 as a branch of Cauldon Potteries Ltd. at Shelton.

WARDLE

JOHN WARDLE & CO., Denaby Pottery, Nr. Mexborough, Yorkshire. 1866–70. *Earthenwares, printed Creamwares, etc.* Formerly Wilkinson & Wardle, q.v.

JOHN WARDLE & CO.

NEAR ROTHERHAM
DENABY POTTERY

4017   Printed mark, 1866–70.

WARHAM

CHRISTOPHER D. WARHAM, New Malden, Surrey. 1949– . *Studio-type Pottery.*

4018   C. D. W.   Incised initial mark, 1949–56.

4019   Impressed seal-type mark, 1956–9.

4020   Impressed seal-type mark, 1959– .

WARRILOW

GEORGE WARRILOW (& SONS) (LTD.), Queens Pottery, Longton. Staffordshire Potteries. 1887–1940. *China.* Formerly Warrilow & Cope. Subsequently Rosina China Co. Ltd., q.v.

4021   G. W.   Distinguishing initials found on several printed marks of differing design: name of the individual pattern is often included, 1887–92.

4022   G. W. & S.
4023   G. W. & SONS

ROSINA
QUEENS CHINA
GW & S Lᵀᴰ
ENGLAND

4024

Distinguishing initials found on several printed marks of differing design: name of the individual pattern is often included, 1892–1928. Note addition of "& S." or "& SONS". "Ltd." added to marks and style from 1928, and continued to 1940. Several marks include the trade-name "Queens China".

WARRINGTON

WARRINGTON POTTERY & CO. LTD., Registry Street Works, Stoke. Staffordshire Potteries. 1912–30. *Useful Earthenwares and Stonewares.*

4025   Printed mark, 1912–30.

23–4   W. A. & S.   *See* William Adams & Sons (Potters) Ltd.

WASHINGTON   **WASHINGTON POTTERY LTD.**, College Road, Shelton. Staffordshire Potteries. 1946– . *Earthenwares.*

4026   Printed mark, 1946– . Other marks include the name in full.

WASHINGTON   **R. J. WASHINGTON**, various addresses, Derby, Margate, Dewsbury, Chelmsford, c. 1937– .

4027   R. J. W.   Impressed seal-type initial mark, in outline, c. 1937–40.

4028   R. J. W. 63   Incised initial mark with year of production on post-war wares, c. 1946– .

WATCOMBE (WATCOMBE TERRA-COTTA CLAY CO., etc.)   **WATCOMBE POTTERY CO.** (Watcombe Terra-cotta Clay Co., etc.), St. Mary Church, South Devon. 1867–1901. *Earthenwares, Terra-cotta ornamental wares, Busts, Figures, etc.* Subsequently combined with the Royal Aller Vale Pottery. See Royal Aller Vale and Watcombe Pottery Co., page 551.

4029   WATCOMBE TORQUAY   Impressed marks, 1867+.

4030   WATCOMBE POTTERY

4031   Printed mark, 1875–1901.

Jewitt in his *Ceramic Art of Great Britain* (1883) gives an interesting contemporary review of the Watcombe wares.

WATHEN		**JAMES B. WATHEN,** Victoria Works, Fenton, Staffordshire Potteries. 1864–9. *Earthenwares.* Formerly Wathen & Lichfield, see next entry. Subsequently James Reeves, q.v.
4032	J. B. W.	Distinguishing initials found on several printed marks of differing design: name of the individual pattern is often included, 1864–9.
4033	J. B. W. F.	

WATHEN		**WATHEN & LICHFIELD,** Victoria Works, Fenton. Staffordshire Potteries. 1862–4. *Earthenwares.* Formerly S. Ginders & Co., q.v. Subsequently J. B. Wathen, see previous entry.
4034		Distinguishing detail (W. & L. Fenton) found on several printed marks of differing design: name of the individual pattern is often included, 1862–4.

WATSON		**CONSTANCE STELLA WATSON, MISS,** London W.11. 1920–35. *Studio-type Pottery.*
4035	STELLA	Incised or painted name-mark, c. 1920–35.

WATSONS		**HENRY WATSON POTTERIES LTD.,** Wattisfield, Suffolk. *Earthenwares and Stonewares.* The Watson family have been potting at Wattisfield from at least 1808. The early wares were unmarked.
4036	WATTISFIELD WARE	Impressed mark, c. 1947– .
4037		Printed or impressed mark, c. 1948– .

WATSON'S		**WATSON'S POTTERY,** Prestonpans, Scotland. Second half 18th century to 1840. *Earthenwares, Figures, etc.*
4038	WATSON	Impressed mark, late 18th, to early 19th century.
4039	WATSON & CO.	Printed marks incorporating name, c. 1800–40.

WATTS		**KATE WATTS, MISS,** London W.1. 1960– . *Studio-type Pottery, Stonewares.*
4040	K. W.	Impressed seal-type initial mark, in a circle, 1960– .
WAYTE & RIDGE		**WAYTE & RIDGE,** Waterloo Place Works, Longton. Staffordshire Potteries. c. 1864. *Earthenware Figures, China, Parian, etc.*
4041	W. & R. L.	These initials, which often occur in a diamond-shaped outline on earthenware figures, have previously been attributed to the above short-lived firm. Definite evidence has just come to hand proving that these initials were used on wares (usually Continental) sold by Messrs. Wittman & Roth, Importers, of London, c. 1870–96.
275 660–1	W. B.	*See* William Barnes. *See* William Brownfield (& Son).
3970 4078 4239 4241 4242	W. & B.	*See* Wagstaff & Brunt. *See* Josiah Wedgwood. *See* Wood & Baggaley. *See* Wood & Bowers. *See* Wood & Brownfield.
4240	W. & B. LTD.	*See* Wood & Barker Ltd.
	W. B. & C.	*See* Appendix.
337	W B H	*See* William Bennett (Hanley) Ltd.
2273	W B K	*See* William Kent (Porcelains) Ltd.
664 or 665–5a	W. B. & S. W. B. & SON(S)	*See* William Brownfield & (Sons).
3559	W. B. S. & S.	*See* W. B. Simpson & Son (Ltd.).
—	W C	*See* Appendix.
4163	W & C (joined)	*See* Wileman & Co.

3981	W. & C.	*See* Walker & Carter.
4244		*See* Wood & Challinor.
4246		*See* Wood & Clarke.
4245	W. C. & Co.	*See* Wood, Challinor & Co.
	W. C. Jr. L. P.	*See* Appendix, page 735.
1244	W. D. C.	*See* Derby Porcelain Works.
1485	W. E.	*See* William Emberton.

WEARSIDE

WEARSIDE POTTERY CO., Millfield, Sunderland. 1928–1957. *Earthenwares, useful Wares.* Formerly Sunderland Pottery Co. Ltd.

4042

Printed or impressed mark, 1928–57.

WEATHERBY

J. H. WEATHERBY & SONS (LTD.), Falcon Pottery, Hanley. Staffordshire Potteries. 1891– . *Earthenwares.*

4043 J. H. W. & SONS

Distinguishing initials found on several printed marks of differing design: name of the individual pattern is often included, 1891 onwards.

4044

Printed mark, 1892+.

4045 FALCON WARE

Trade-name used from 1925.

4046

Printed mark, 1928+.

4047–8   Printed marks, 1936– .

WEAVER   **KATE WEAVER**, South Croydon, Surrey. 1957– . *Studio-type Pottery.*

4049   Painted mark, 1957– . A rubber stamp mark of the initials K. W. may be introduced during 1964.

WEBB'S   **WEBB'S WORCESTER TILERIES CO. (LTD.),** (Henry C. Webb), Rainbow Hill, Worcester. 1870–c. 1905. *Tiles, etc.*

4050   WEBB'S WORCESTER   Impressed or moulded marks, c. 1870–1905.
              TILES
4051   HENRY C. WEBB,
           WORCESTER

1110   W. E. C.   *See* W. & E. Corn.
1109   W. & E. C.

WEDD   **ANNE WEDD, MISS,** Brixton, London S.W.9. 1955– . *Studio-type Pottery.*

4052   Incised mark, with year numbers, 1955–7.

4053   Impressed seal-type mark, 1958– .
                                 N.B. A similar mark is used by A. Wyllie, see page 703.

4054   Impressed seal-type mark, 1961– .

3598	WEDGEWOOD	*See* William Smith & Co.
4276b	WEDG-WOOD	*See* John Wedge *Wood*.
3078 **4073–5** etc. **4103**	WEDGWOOD	*See* Podmore, Walker & Co. *See* Josiah Wedgwood (& Sons Ltd.). *See* Ralph Wedgwood (& Co.).
4076–7	WEDGWOOD & BENTLEY	*See* Josiah Wedgwood (& Sons Ltd.).
1539 **3079** **4055** **4104**	WEDGWOOD & CO.	*See* Ferrybridge Pottery. *See* Podmore, Walker & Co. *See* Wedgwood & Co. (Ltd.). *See* Ralph Wedgwood (& Co.).

WEDGWOOD

WEDGWOOD & CO. (LTD.), Unicorn and Pinnox Works, Tunstall. Staffordshire Potteries. 1860– . *Earthenwares, Stone-china, etc.* Formerly Podmore, Walker & Co., q.v.

N.B. The marks of this firm are often mistaken for those of Josiah Wedgwood & Sons Ltd. The Tunstall firm includes "& Co." in the style and marks. This "Wedgwood & Co." mark was also used at the Ferrybridge Pottery, see page 246.

4055 WEDGWOOD & CO. Distinguishing name found on several impressed marks, which often include the name of the body "Imperial Iron Stone China" date etc., 1860+.

4056

Printed "trade-mark"; the addition of these words indicate a after the Act of 1862.

4057

Printed mark, c. 1890–1906.
    N.B. "Ltd." added to style and marks from 1900.

4058 WEDGWOOD & CO.
 LTD. Impressed mark, 1900+.

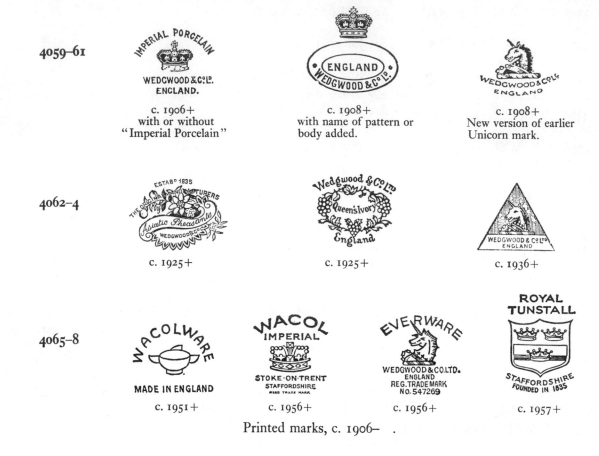

4059–61		
c. 1906+ with or without "Imperial Porcelain"	c. 1908+ with name of pattern or body added.	c. 1908+ New version of earlier Unicorn mark.
4062–4		
c. 1925+	c. 1925+	c. 1936+
4065–8		
c. 1951+	c. 1956+	c. 1956+	c. 1957+

Printed marks, c. 1906–   .

4068a   VITRILAIN   Trade-name for special body introduced in 1962.

WEDGWOOD   **H. F. WEDGWOOD & CO. LTD.**, Islington Works, Longton. Staffordshire Potteries. c. 1954–9. *China and Earthenwares.*

4069   H. F. W. & CO. LTD.   Distinguishing details of several printed marks of differing
4070   ISLINGTON   design, 1954–9. Typical examples are reproduced below.

4071–2

4276a   J. WEDGWOOD   For "J. Wedgwood" marks see John Wedge *Wood* not Josiah Wedgwood (& Sons, Ltd.).

WEDGWOOD

JOSIAH WEDGWOOD (& SONS LTD.), Burslem, c.1759+. Etruria, c. 1769+, Barlaston, 1940– . c. 1759– . *Earthenwares, Basaltes, Jaspers, Porcelains, Parian, Majolica, etc.* Formerly in partnership with Thomas Whieldon.

The very early wares were unmarked. Experimental (?) examples are recorded with an incised signature or the initials J. W. "in Josiah's unmistakable handwriting". See a Paper by Donald Towner, *English Ceramic Circle Transactions*, vol. 5, part 4, 1963.

4073   wedgwood

4074   WEDCWOOD

Impressed marks, in individually stamped lower case letters, or slightly curved as no. 4074, c. 1759–c. 69.

4075   WEDGWOOD

Standard impressed mark. Various sizes, c. 1759 onwards, unless otherwise stated below.

N.B. From 1860 a system of three-letter dating was used, see Table, page 658. From 1891 "ENGLAND" occurs impressed and in the 20th century "MADE IN ENGLAND".

WEDGWOOD & BENTLEY PARTNERSHIP, c. 1768–80.

4076   WEDGWOOD & BENTLEY

4077   WEDGWOOD & BENTLEY ETRURIA

Impressed mark (rarely incised) in various sizes on plaques and ornamental wares. Sometimes in oval form. The addition of "Etruria" is rare.

4078   W. & B.

Impressed initial mark on small ornamental items, intaglios, etc. Seals made by J. Voyez in the mid-1770's bore the initials W. & B. and were sold as true Wedgwood and Bentley examples.

4079

Impressed or raised mark on ornamental vases, etc. The word "Etruria" is sometimes missing, c. 1769–80. Note, "Wedgwood & Bentley" marks were used only on ornamental wares.

4080   Wedgwood.

Impressed mark with lower case letters, c. 1780–98. For this mark on creamware figures see Ralph Wedgwood (& Co.), page 661.

4081   WEDGWOOD & SONS

Impressed mark, very rare, c. 1790.

4082   JOSIAH WEDGWOOD Feb. 2nd 1805

Rare mark found only on tripod incense burners, c. 1805.

4083   WEDGWOOD

Printed mark on *bone china*, c. 1812–22, in red, blue or gold.

4084	WEDGWOOD'S STONE CHINA	Printed mark on rare stone china wares, c. 1827–61.
4085	WEDGWOOD ETRURIA	Impressed mark, in various forms, c. 1840–5.
4086 4087	PEARL P	Impressed name of Pearl body, c. 1840–68; after this date the initial "P" was used.
4088	AAO or other letters impressed in sets of three	Impressed three-letter date marks on earthenwares from 1860 onwards, see Table. It should be noted that the first letter which should denote the month was sometimes misplaced and is the second letter.
	WEDGWOOD	The standard impressed WEDGWOOD mark also occurs on all examples bearing the three letters.

TABLE OF IMPRESSED YEAR LETTERS, OCCURRING IN GROUPS OF THREE LETTERS

4088

The third letter denotes the year of potting as shown in this table.

O = 1860	O = 1885	
P = 1861	P = 1887	
Q = 1862	Q = 1888	
R = 1863	R = 1889	
S = 1864	S = 1890	
T = 1865	T = 1891★	From 1886 to 1897 the earlier (1860–1871) letters are repeated
U = 1866	U = 1892	
V = 1867	V = 1893	
W = 1868	W = 1894	★From 1891 'ENGLAND' should occur on specimens
X = 1869	X = 1895	
Y = 1870	Y = 1896	
Z = 1871	Z = 1897	
A = 1872		
B = 1873		
C = 1874		
D = 1875		
E = 1876		
F = 1877	A = 1898	
G = 1878	B = 1899	
H = 1879	C = 1900	From 1898 to 1906 the letters used from 1872 to 1880 re-occur, but 'ENGLAND' should also appear.
I = 1880	D = 1901	
J = 1881	E = 1902	
K = 1882	F = 1903	
L = 1883	G = 1904	
M = 1884	H = 1905	
N = 1885	I = 1906	

From 1907 the sequence was continued, but a "3" replaces the first letter. From 1924 a "4" replaces the "3". After 1930 the month is numbered in sequence and the last two numbers of the year are given, i.e. 1A 32 = January 1932, "A" being the workman's mark. On some later, post-war examples the last two numbers only are given, i.e. 53 = 1953.

Month letters (the first or second of the three impressed letters) for the period 1860–4 were:

J	January	Y	May	S	September
F	February	T	June	O	October
M	March	V	July	N	November
A	April	W	August	D	December

These were changed and from 1864 to 1907 the months were shown by these letters:

J	January	M	May	S	September
F	February	T	June	O	October
R	March	L	July	N	November
A	April	W	August	D	December

It has been noted that sometimes the month letter varies from those here given. This is probably due to an error on the part of the workman.

4089		Signature of the celebrated figure subject artist—Emile Lessore, c. 1858–76. Examples of his work are illustrated in *British Pottery and Porcelain: an illustrated Encyclopaedia of Marked Specimens.*
4090	ENGLAND	Impressed, or added to printed mark from 1891.
4091	WEDGWOOD	Printed mark on porcelains (and rarely on earthenwares) from c. 1878. "England" added below from 1891. Some porcelains also bear the standard impressed mark "WEDGWOOD".
4092	WEDGWOOD ETRURIA. ENGLAND	Rare impressed mark on earthenwares, c. 1891–1900.
4093	MADE IN ENGLAND	Impressed or printed with standard mark from c. 1898, but mainly found after about 1910.
4094	WEDGWOOD	Printed mark, c. 1900 onwards, on porcelain with ENGLAND or MADE IN ENGLAND under. Note the addition of three stars under the vase, these do not occur on the first version of this mark, c. 1878–1900.

4095	WEDGWOOD BONE CHINA MADE IN ENGLAND	Later version of the Portland vase mark, with the words BONE CHINA added, c. 1920+.
4096	**WEDGWOOD**	Impressed mark (in sans serif type) used from c. 1929 to present day. On some specimens the old type was used but any specimen with sans serif type mark is subsequent to 1929.
4097	WEDGWOOD BONE CHINA MADE IN ENGLAND	Post-war version of Portland Vase mark printed by REJAFIX machine.
4098	WEDGWOOD Bone China MADE IN ENGLAND	New version of above marks, first introduced in December 1962. The name of the pattern or its number may be added below this basic mark.
4099	of ETRURIA WEDGWOOD & MADE IN ENGLAND BARLASTON	Printed mark on creamwares, etc., c. 1940– .
4100	BARLASTON	This name occurs from 1940 onwards and is the address of the firm. The standard name-mark Wedgwood also occurs.
4100a	N W or NORMAN WILSON	Impressed or painted initials or name found on fine glaze effect wares of attractive simple form, produced as individual specimens by Norman Wilson from 1927 to December 1962. The standard Wedgwood mark should occur on these pieces.
4101	ETRURIA	This name should not occur on wares made after 1950 with the exception of some printed marks on old patterns.
4101a	ENGRAVED BY WEDGWOOD STUDIO	Wording used on engraved patterns, from 1952.

4102	WEDGWOOD ETRURIA BARLASTON	Very rare mark on examples laid in the foundations of the Barlaston factory in 1938. Old employees were presented with a replica, and some of these have found their way into the market.

Warning

Several other potters used the name Wedgwood (or close imitations) on their wares. English copyists are listed on page 655. No true Wedgwood marks include "& Co." or a middle "E".

N.B. Many of the above standard marks will occur with slight additions, i.e. the name of the artist, designer, type of body, or pattern.

Several recent books on Wedgwood give helpful aids to dating—by pattern numbers, prefix letters, etc. *Wedgwood Counterpoint* (1962) by Harry M. Buten, of the Buten Museum of Wedgwood, Merion, Pennyslvania, U.S.A., is particularly helpful.

Very many reference books have been written on Wedgwood wares; the most recent include:

Wedgwood Ware, W. B. Honey (1948).
Wedgwood, W. Mankowitz (1953).
Wedgwood Counterpoint, H. Buten (1962).

The *Proceedings of the English Wedgwood Society* (1956+) also contains much interesting material. A selection of wares will be found illustrated in *British Pottery and Porcelain: an illustrated Encyclopaedia of Marked Specimens.*

WEDGWOOD

RALPH WEDGWOOD (& CO.) (1766–1837), Burslem. Staffordshire Potteries, c. 1785–96. Ferrybridge Pottery, Yorkshire, c. 1796–1801 (see page 246). c. 1785–1801 (approximate dates only). *Earthenwares.*

4103	WEDGWOOD	The impressed mark WEDGWOOD occurs on creamware figures of the 1785–95 period. These were probably made by Ralph Wedgwood, as even if Josiah Wedgwood made creamware figures at this period the quality is not up to the standard one would expect of the main Wedgwood firm. It is possible that Wedgwoods farmed out orders for figures to other potters who added the Wedgwood mark. D. Towner in his *English Cream-coloured Earthenwares* suggests that these figures were made by Enoch Wood for Wedgwood. Examples of these marked figures and of other Ralph Wedgwood wares will be found illustrated in *British Pottery and Porcelain: an illustrated Encyclopaedia of Marked Specimens.*

4104   WEDGWOOD & CO.   Good quality creamwares of the 1790–1800 period occur with this impressed mark. These wares were probably made by Ralph Wedgwood & Co. at the Hill Works, Burslem, before 1796 or by Tomlinson, Foster, Wedgwood & Co. of the Ferrybridge Pottery, Yorkshire, after Ralph Wedgwood had joined this firm, having become bankrupt at Burslem. This Yorkshire partnership and their use of the WEDGWOOD & CO. mark ceased about 1801.

4081   WEDGWOOD & SONS   *See* Josiah Wedgwood & Sons Ltd.

WEETMAN   **WEETMAN FIGURES**, Sandyford, Tunstall. Staffordshire Potteries. 1952– . *China and Earthenware Figures and Giftware.*

4105   WEETMAN FIGURES   Printed or impressed marks, 1952 + .
        SANDYFORD

4106   WEETMAN
            SANDYFORD

4107

4107   WEETMAN   *See* Weetman Figures, above.
            GIFTWARE

WELCH   **ROBIN WELCH**, London W.C.1. 1960–2.* *Studio-type Pottery.*

4108   ROBIN WELCH, 62   Painted signature mark. Last two numbers of year added to best specimens, 1960–2.

                           * Robin Welch left for Australia at the end of 1962. After two years he hopes to go to Japan.

WELLBRIDGE   **WELLBRIDGE POTTERY** (Mrs. F. Nash), Wool, Dorset. 1954– . *Studio-type Pottery.*

| 4109 | WELLBRIDGE | Incised or painted name-mark in writing letters, 1954– . |

| 1086–7 | WELLINGTON CHINA | *See* J. H. Cope & Co. (Ltd.). |

| 4187 | WELLINGTON POTTERY | *See* John Williamson. |

WELLINGTON

WELLINGTON POTTERY CO., Hanley.   Staffordshire Potteries.   1899–1901.   *Earthenwares.*   Formerly Bednall & Heath, q.v.   Subsequently W. H. Lockitt, q.v.

| 4110 | | Printed or impressed mark, c. 1899–1901. |

WELLS

WELLS POTTERY (Geoffrey Barfoot), Wells, Somerset. January 1961– .   *Studio-type Pottery.*

| 4111 | WELLS | Incised mark, 1961– . |

WELLS

REGINALD WELLS (1877–1951), Wrotham, Kent, c. 1909; Chelsea, London, c. 1910–24; Storrington, Sussex, c. 1925–51. c. 1909 (or before) to 1951.   *Studio-type Pottery, Stonewares, Figures, etc.*

| 4112 | COLDRUM | Early experimental slip-decorated pottery made at or near |
| 4112a | COLDRUM WROTHAM | Wrotham, Kent, c. 1909. |

| 4113 | COLDRUM CHELSEA | Impressed or incised mark, c. 1910–24. |

| 4114 | | Incised initial mark, c. 1910+. |

| 4115 | R. F. WELLS | Signature mark, incised or painted, often very freely written, c. 1910+. |

| 4116 | SOON | Impressed or incised mark, c. 1918–51. |

4117   S   The letter S occurs on some wares made at Storrington from 1925.

Interesting articles on Reginald Wells and his work are contained in the *Apollo* magazine of May 1925, and *The Studio* of December 1925.

2015   WEMYSS WARE   *See* R. Heron (& Son).

WENFORD   **WENFORD BRIDGE POTTERY**, St. Tudy, Nr. Bodmin, Cornwall. c. 1939–42 and 1949– . *Studio-type Pottery, Stonewares.*

4118   Impressed Wenford Bridge Pottery mark, c. 1939–42 and 1949– .

769   Impressed seal mark of the principal—Michael Cardew. This potter works in Northern Nigeria and returns to England for about two months each year.   See Michael Cardew.

4119   C. K. A.   Incised or painted initials of the Ghanaian potter Clement Kofi Athey, who worked with Michael Cardew in Africa from 1942. This potter worked for a brief period at Wenford Bridge Pottery during 1962 and rare specimens bear his initials *with* the impressed Bridge mark above.   Other wares with these initials were made in Africa.

763   WESCONTREE WARE   *See* Candy & Co. Ltd.

2370f   WEST OF ENGLAND   *See* Jo Lester.
          HAND MADE
          POTTERY

WEST   **WEST SURREY CERAMICS CO. LTD.**, Wormley, Nr. Godalming, Surrey. 1956– . *Earthenwares.*

4120		Printed or impressed mark, 1956– .

WESTMINSTER

WESTMINSTER POTTERY LTD., Hanley. Staffordshire Potteries. 1948–56. *Earthenwares.*

4121–2  **Westminster Hanley, Staffs Made in England**   Printed marks, c. 1948–56. The trade-name "CASTLECLIFFE WARE" was registered in 1952.

—	T. WETHERILL	*See* Appendix, page 735.
3586–8	WETLEY CHINA	*See* Sampson Smith Ltd.
4224	W. E. W.	*See* W. E. Withinshaw.
1553 1553a	W. F. W. F. B.	*See* William Fifield.
4130	W. F. & CO.	*See* Whittingham, Ford & Co.
2062	W.F.H. (joined)	*See* W. F. Holland.
4131	W. F. & R.	*See* Whittingham, Ford & Riley.
1692	W. G.	*See* Wilfred Gibson.
1700	WG & SC (joined)	*See* William Gill & Sons.
1866 2106	W. H.	*See* W. Hackwood. *See* W. Hudson.
2129 4149 4365	W. & H.	*See* Henry Hulme & Sons. *See* Wildblood & Heath. *See* Worthington & Harrop.
2128 4273	W. & H. B.	*See* Henry Hulme & Sons. *See* Wood & Hulme.

4128	W. H. & CO.	*See* Whittaker, Heath & Co.
1747	W. H. G.	*See* William Henry Goss (Ltd.).
4216	WHIELDON WARE	*See* F. Winkle & Co. (Ltd.).

WHITE

WILLIAM J. WHITE, Fulham Pottery, Fulham, London S.W.6. Second half 18th century to first half 19th century. *Stonewares.*

In 1813 the pottery was managed by William White's son. In 1862 the pottery passed to MacIntosh & Clements and in 1864 to C. J. C. Bailey, q.v. This Fulham Pottery was on the site of John Dwight's early stoneware works.

4123	W. W. 1800	Incised initial or signature marks. These dated examples were formerly in the Jewitt Collection.
4124	W. J. WHITE fecit Dec. 8, 1800	
4125	W. WHITE	Figures have been recorded with the mark of W. White.

WHITEHOUSE

ELIZABETH WHITEHOUSE, The Old Bakery, Boscastle, Cornwall. 1957*– . *Studio-type Pottery.*

4126	E. W. B.	Incised initial mark, c. 1957– .

* Elizabeth Whitehouse formerly worked at the Wenford Bridge, Crowan and Leach Potteries.

—	WHITENING	*See* Appendix, page 735.
—	W. H. J.	*See* Appendix, page 735.
2406	W. H. L. H.	*See* William H. Lockitt.

WHITTAKER

WHITTAKER & CO., Hallfield Pottery, Hanley. Staffordshire Potteries. 1886–92. *Earthenwares.* Formerly Whittaker, Edge & Co. Subsequently Whittaker, Heath & Co., see next entry.

4127  Printed mark, c. 1886–92. Other pattern names occur in the central panel.

WHITTAKER

WHITTAKER, HEATH & CO., Hallfield Pottery, Hanley. Staffordshire Potteries. 1892–8. *Earthenwares.* Formerly Whittaker & Co., see previous entry.

4128   W. H. & CO.

Distinguishing initials found on several printed marks of differing design, 1892–8. The words "Hanley" and "England" may also occur.

WHITTALL

ELEANOR WHITTALL, MISS, London N.W.1. 1944– . *Studio-type Pottery—Stonewares and Porcelains.*

4129

Impressed seal, an owl-like device originally made up of the initials E. E. W., c. 1944– . Porcelains from 1958.

WHITTINGHAM

WHITTINGHAM, FORD & CO., Union Bank or High Street Pottery, Burslem. Staffordshire Potteries. 1868–73. *Earthenwares.* Subsequently Buckley, Wood & Co., q.v.

4130   W. F. & CO.

Distinguishing initials found on several printed marks of differing design: name of the individual pattern is often included, 1868–73.

WHITTINGHAM

WHITTINGHAM, FORD & RILEY, Newcastle Street, Burslem. Staffordshire Potteries. 1876–82. *Earthenwares.* Subsequently Ford & Riley, q.v.

4131   W. F. & R.

Distinguishing initials found on several printed marks of differing design: name of the individual pattern is often included, 1876–82.

1868	W. H. & S.	*See* W. Hackwood & Sons.
	or	*See* Wildblood, Heath & Sons (Ltd.).
4150–1	W. H. & S. L	
	or	
4152	W. H. & S. Ltd	

WICKHAM HELEN WICKHAM, MISS, London N.W.2. c. 1920–35. *Earthenware Figures, etc.*

4132 Painted mark on earthenware figure in the Victoria and Albert Museum, made in 1923.

4133 HELEN WICKHAM Incised or painted signature mark, c. 1920–35.

—	WIEGWOOD	*See* Appendix, page 735.
2369	WIGHTCRAFT	*See* Jo Lester.
4311	WIGORNIA	*See* Worcester Porcelains.

WILD WILD & ADAMS (LTD), Longton. Staffordshire Potteries. 1909–27. *Earthenwares.*

4134 W. & A. Printed or impressed marks with initials, 1909–27. N.B. Ltd. added from 1923.

4135

4136 Printed name-mark, c. 1923–7.

WILD		**WILD BROS.**, Edensor Crown China Works and Salisbury Crown China Works, Longton. Staffordshire Potteries. 1904–27. *China*.

4137 — Printed or impressed crown mark, 1904+.

4138 — J. S. W. — Several marks incorporating the initials J. S. W., or W. Bros occur, 1904–27.

4139 — Standard printed mark, c. 1922–7.

WILD — **THOMAS C. WILD & CO.**, Albert Works, Longton. Staffordshire Potteries. 1896–1904. *China*.

4140 — T. W. & CO. — Printed or impressed marks with initials, c. 1896–1904.

4141 — T. C. W.

Continued as:

WILD — **THOMAS C. WILD**, St. Mary's Works, etc. Longton. 1905–17. *China*.

4142 — Printed mark, 1905–7.

4143 — Printed mark, 1907–22.

Continued as:

WILD

THOMAS C. WILD & SONS (LTD.), St. Mary's Works, Longton. 1917– . *China*.

4144–8

c. 1917+   c. 1927+   c. 1935+   c. 1935+   c. 1945+

Printed marks, 1917– .

WILDBLOOD

WILDBLOOD & HEATH, Peel Works, Longton. Staffordshire Potteries. 1889–99. *China*. Formerly R. V. Wildblood, q.v.

4149

Printed mark, c. 1889–99.

Continued as:

WILDBLOOD

WILDBLOOD, HEATH & SONS (LTD.), Peel Works, Longton. 1899–1927. *China*.

4150–2

c. 1899+   c. 1908+   c. 1915–1927
                                note "LTD."

Printed marks, 1899–1927.

WILDBLOOD

JOHN WILDBLOOD, Swillington Bridge Pottery, Nr. Methley, Yorkshire. First half of 19th century. *Pottery*.

4153	JOHN WILDBLOOD SWILLINGTON BRIDGE POTTERY JULY 12, 1831	Rare incised mark on pottery plaque, illustrated by O. Grabham in his *Yorkshire Potteries, Pots and Potters* (1916).

WILDBLOOD

WILDBLOOD & LEDGAR, Bridge Works, Longton. Staffordshire Potteries. 1896–1900. *Earthenwares.* Subsequently T. P. Ledgar, q.v.

4154   W. & L.   Distinguishing initials found on several printed or impressed marks of differing design, 1896–1900.

WILDBLOOD

RICHARD VERNON WILDBLOOD, Peel Works, Longton. Staffordshire Potteries. 1887–8. *China.* Formerly Massey, Wildblood & Co., q.v.   Subsequently Wildblood & Heath, q.v.

4155   Printed mark, 1887–8.

WILEMAN

JAMES & CHARLES WILEMAN, Foley China Works, Fenton, Longton. Staffordshire Potteries. 1864–9. *China and Earthenwares.* Formerly Henry Wileman.

4156   J. & C. W.   Distinguishing initials found on several printed marks of
4157   J. F. & C. W.   differing design, c. 1864–7.

4158   C. J. W.   Rare marks incorporate the initials of Charles J. Wileman, c. 1869.

4159   J. W. & CO.   The firm also traded under the style J. Wileman & Co., c. 1864–9.

Continued by:

WILEMAN   **JAMES F. WILEMAN** 1869–92.
4160   J. F. W.   Distinguishing initials and name found on several printed
4161   J. F. WILEMAN   marks of differing design, 1869–92.

4162

Continued by:

WILEMAN

WILEMAN & CO., Foley Potteries and Foley China Works, Fenton, Longton. 1892–1925. *China and Earthenware*. Subsequently Shelley's, see Shelley Potteries Ltd.

4163–5

c. 1892+   c. 1911+   c. 1923+

Other marks include the name FOLEY CHINA.

WILKES

EDWARD R. WILKES, Staffordshire Potteries. 1900–30. *Decorator*.

4166   E. R. WILKES 1921

4167

Signature mark on rare earthenware vases made by A. G. Richardson of Cobridge, c. 1920–21, and decorated by Edward Wilkes. This decorator had earlier worked for Bernard Moore c. 1905–13 and signed his work with a monogram of the initials E. W. R. (mark no. 4167). Edward also decorated for George Howson & Son of Hanley and for Messrs. Malkin Tile Works Company.

WILKINSON

ARTHUR J. WILKINSON (LTD.), Royal Staffordshire Pottery (and formerly at Central Pottery), Burslem. Staffordshire Potteries. 1885– . *Earthenwares, Ironstones, etc*. Formerly Wilkinson & Hulme.

4168–70

c. 1891+   c. 1896   c. 1907
Earlier versions
without "Ltd."

4171-3

c. 1910

c. 1930+

c. 1930+

4175-6

c. 1930+

c. 1947+

Printed marks, 1891–1947. Many other marks incorporate the name in full, "Ltd" was added c. 1896.

WILKINSON

WILKINSON & WARDLE, Denaby Pottery, Nr. Mexborough, Yorkshire. 1864–6. *Earthenwares.* Subsequently John Wardle & Co., q.v.

4177-8

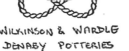

Printed or impressed marks, c. 1864–6.

WILLIAMSON

H. M. WILLIAMSON & SONS, Bridge Pottery, Longton. Staffordshire Potteries. c. 1879–1941. *China.*

4179-81

c. 1879+

c. 1903+

c. 1903+

4182-4

c. 1907–12

c. 1908+

c. 1912+

| 4185–6 | BEST BONE HEATHCOTE CHINA MADE IN ENGLAND c. 1928–41 | MADE IN ENGLAND Heathcote China BEST BONE c. 1928–41 | Printed marks, 1879–1941. |

| 3407 | WILL YOUNG | *See* Runnaford Pottery. |

WILLIAMSON

JOHN WILLIAMSON, Wellington Pottery (Est. c. 1797), Glasgow, Scotland.   1844–94.   *Terra-cotta, etc.*

4187	WELLINGTON POTTERY	Impressed or printed mark, c. 1797–1894.
4188	WILLIAMSON WELLINGTON POTTERY	Impressed or printed marks, c. 1844–94.
4189	WILLIAMSON WELLINGTON POTTERY GLASGOW	

—	WILLOW	*See* Appendix, page 735.
2016	WILLOW ART CHINA	*See* Hewitt & Leadbetter.
4190	WILLS BROS.	*See* W. & T. Wills, below.

WILLS

W. & T. WILLS, Euston Road, London N.W.1.   1858–97. *Terra-cotta, Figures, Busts, Vases (also Metal wares).*

| 4190 | WILLS BROS. | Impressed or incised marks, 1858–97. |
| 4191 | W. & T. WILLS | An ornate marked terra-cotta tankard in the Victoria and Albert Museum was shown at the 1862 Exhibition. See *British Pottery and Porcelain: an illustrated Encyclopaedia of Marked Specimens.* |

4198	C WILSON	*See* Robert Wilson.

WILSON		**DAVID WILSON (& SONS)**, Church Works, Hanley. Staffordshire Potteries. c. 1802–18. *Earthenware and China. Lustred wares.* Formerly Robert Wilson, q.v. From 1815 the style became David Wilson & Sons, or Messrs. Wilsons.
4192	WILSON	Impressed mark c. 1802–18 but formerly used by Robert Wilson from c. 1795. Some very fine lustre wares were made by David Wilson, some specimens have attractive patterns in gold over a lustre or coloured ground. See *British Pottery and Porcelain: an illustrated Encyclopaedia of Marked Specimens*.

WILSON		**ISAAC WILSON & CO.**, Middlesbrough Pottery, Middlesbrough, Yorkshire. 1852–87. *Earthenwares.* Formerly Middlesbrough Earthenware Co., q.v.
4193 4193a	I. W. & CO. I. W. & CO. MIDDLESBROUGH	Distinguishing details of several printed marks of differing design: name of the individual pattern is often included, 1852–87. The initials may also occur impressed.
4194	 MIDDLESBROUGH POTTERY Anchor device	An impressed mark of a crown (on best earthenwares), with the name "Middlesbrough Pottery" over an anchor, is recorded with I. Wilson & Co's printed marks, 1852–87. Mark no. 2658 may have been used by Isaac Wilson & Co.

WILSON		**J. WILSON & SONS**, Park Works, Fenton. Staffordshire Potteries. 1898–1926. *China.* Formerly Wilson & Co.
4195	 J.W.&S.	Printed mark, 1898–1926.

WILSON		**KATHERINE WILSON, MISS**, South Croydon, London. 1949– . *Studio-type Pottery.* Miss Wilson works with Miss Zerkowitz, see page 707.

4196	K W	Impressed, incised or painted initial mark, 1949– .

4100a	NORMAN WILSON	*See* Josiah Wedgwood (& Sons Ltd.).

WILSON

ROBERT WILSON, Church Works, Hanley. Staffordshire Potteries. 1795–1801. *Earthenwares, Creamwares, etc.* Formerly Neale & Wilson, q.v. Subsequently David Wilson, q.v.

Robert Wilson died in 1801. It should be noted that Daniel and then David Wilson continued the Church Works to c. 1815 (and as "& Sons" to 1818). They may have continued to use these marks.

4197	WILSON	Impressed marks, 1795–1801. Continued by David Wilson (& Sons) to c. 1818.

4198		

—	C. G. W.	This impressed mark has for many years been attributed to the Wilsons; this is incorrect.

WILSON

WILSON & PROUDMAN, Coleorton Pottery, Ashby-de-la-Zouch, Leicestershire. 1835–42.* *Earthenwares, Stonewares.* Subsequently J. Wilson.

N.B. Jewitt gives the first partnership as Wilson, Lount and Proudman; this is probably an error, as Lount is a nearby place name.

4199	WILSON & PROUDMAN	Impressed mark, 1835–42.*

* Directory records include John Wilson in 1846. From 1854 or before to 1877 the entries read—Wilson, Thomas, Ironstone, Cane ware manufacturer, Nr. Lount. From c. 1877 to c. 1894 the firm is listed as Wilson Bros.

WILTSHAW

WILTSHAW & ROBINSON (LTD.), Carlton Works, Stoke. Staffordshire Potteries. 1890–1957.* *Earthenwares and China.*

4200–2

c. 1890+

c. 1894 onwards, variations occur.

c. 1906 onwards.

4203–5

c. 1914

c. 1925+

c. 1925–57

* Retitled CARLTON WARE LTD., from January 1958.

WIMBLE

DENNIS WIMBLE, Horsham, Sussex. c. 1958– . *Studio-type Pottery.*

Early wares generally unmarked.

4206

$$19\,\mathcal{W}\,61$$

Impressed mark, with year of production, c. 1958– .

WINCANTON

WINCANTON POTTERY (Nathaniel Ireson.) Somerset. c. 1735–50.* *Delft-type Earthenwares.*

4207	Wincanton
4208	Wincanton 1738
4209	Nathaniel Ireson, 1748

Painted town and name-marks, sometimes with dates in the 1730's and 40's. Marked examples are very rare. See *British Pottery and Porcelain: an illustrated Encyclopaedia of Marked Specimens.*

  * It would appear that Ireson ceased potting c. 1750; in his will of 1765 he is described as Mason. He died in 1769.

WINCHCOMBE

WINCHCOMBE POTTERY (Michael Cardew), c. 1926–39. Raymond Finch, 1939– . Winchcombe, Gloucestershire. c. 1926– . *Studio-type Pottery.*

4210		Standard Winchcombe Pottery mark, normally impressed in circle, c. 1926– .
769		Personal seal mark of Michael Cardew at Winchcombe c. 1926–1939 (and later at Wenford Bridge).
4211	S. T.	Initial seal mark of Sidney Tustin, occurs on wares from the 1950's.
4212	W. S.	Initial mark on test pieces, 1962.
1058–60	WINDSOR	*See* Co-op Wholesale Society.

WINKLE   **F. WINKLE & CO. (LTD.)**, Colonial Pottery, Stoke. Staffordshire Potteries. 1890–1931. *Earthenwares.* Formerly Winkle & Wood, see next entry. Taken over by Ridgways (Bedford Works) Ltd.

4213	F. W. & Co. ENGLAND	Distinguishing detail of several printed or impressed marks of differing design: name of the individual pattern is often included, 1890–1910.
4214	F. WINKLE & CO.	Several marks incorporate the name in full, 1890–1910. N.B. "Ltd." added after 1911.
4215		Printed mark, 1890–1925.
4216		Printed or impressed mark, 1908–25.

4217      Printed mark, 1925–31.

WINKLE

4218      **WINKLE & WOOD**, Pearl Pottery, Hanley. Staffordshire Potteries. September 1885–90. *Earthenwares.* Formerly Wood, Hines & Winkle. Subsequently F. Winkle & Co., see previous entry (Wood retained the Pearl Pottery). Printed mark, 1885–90.

585   WINSCOMBE   *See* Bridge Products Co.

WINTERBURN

                                 MOLLY WINTERBURN, MISS, London S.W.15. 1958– *Studio-type Pottery.*

4219      Impressed seal type or painted mark, 1958– .

WINTERTON

                                 WINTERTON POTTERY (LONGTON) LTD., Longton. Staffordshire Potteries. 1927–54. *Earthenwares.*

4220–23

          c. 1927–41   c. 1939–41   c. 1947–54   c. 1949–54

          Printed marks, 1927–54.

3210a   WINTHORN   *See* Winifred Rawsthorne.

1825   WINTON   *See* Grimwades Ltd.

2967   WITCH MARK   *See* Irene Park.

WITHINSHAW		W. E. WITHINSHAW, Churchyard and Crown Works, Burslem. Staffordshire Potteries. 1873–8. *Earthenwares and China*. Formerly Wood & Clarke, q.v. Subsequently F. J. Emery.
4224	W. E. W.	Distinguishing initials found on several printed or impressed
4224a	W. E. WITHINSHAW	marks of differing design, 1873–8. Other marks include the name in full.
3978	W. J. (joined)	*See* J. F. Walford.
736	W. & J. B.	*See* William & James Butterfield.
1950	W. & J. H.	*See* W. & J. Harding.
3623	W. J. S.	*See* John Solly.
2281	W. K. & CO.	*See* William Kirkby & Co.
4347	K. B. W.	*See* Worcester Porcelains (Kerr & Binns, period).
2432–3	W. L. or	*See* William Lowe.
2435	W. L. L.	
4034	W. & L.	*See* Wathen & Lichfield.
4154		*See* Wildblood & Ledgar.
2383	W. M.	*See* Littlehampton Pottery.
2866	W. N.	*See* William Newland.
1783	W. N. E.	*See* Green & Clay.
755–6	W. N. E. S.	*See* Campbell Tile Co. (Ltd.).
2905	W N L	*See* Wilfrid Norton.

WOLD		**WOLD POTTERY LTD.**, Mr. and Mrs. Dixon, Routh, Nr. Beverley, Yorkshire. June 1954– . *Hand-thrown pottery.*
4225	WOLD	Incised or painted name-mark in writing letters, 1954– .
4226	HAND-THROWN ROUTH BEVERLEY YORKSHIRE	Impressed mark, 1954– .
4230	WOLFE & CO.	*See* Thomas Wolfe.

WOLFE

WOLFE & HAMILTON, Church Street, Stoke. Staffordshire Potteries. c. 1800–11. *Earthenwares, Creamwares and China.*

A directory of 1809 lists this firm as "manufacturers of china and earthenware, Stoke Pottery, and 42 Old Dock, Liverpool". Continued by Thomas Wolfe, junr., from mid-1811, see next entry.

4227	WOLFE & HAMILTON	Impressed or painted name-marks found on creamwares, c. 1800–11.
4227a	WOLFE & HAMILTON STOKE	

WOLFE

THOMAS WOLFE, Church Street, Stoke. Staffordshire Potteries. c. 1784–1800 and c. 1811–18. *Earthenwares, Creamwares, Basaltes, etc.*

Thomas Wolfe was an interesting, little-known potter, his wares were exported in quantity and he was reputedly the first potter to employ steam power at his works, c. 1793. He also had a porcelain factory at Liverpool. Thomas Wolfe died in 1818.

4228	WOLFE	Impressed mark, rare, c. 1784–97 and 1811–18.
4229	W	The impressed letter W. has also been attributed to Thomas Wolfe or his son. This initial mark was also used by Enoch Wood.

4230	WOLFE & CO.	From about 1800 to 1811 Thomas Wolfe was in partnership with Robert Hamilton, see previous entry. A mark "Wolfe & Co." has been noted and may relate to this partnership, or to a partnership for making porcelain at Liverpool, c. 1796–1800.

WOLLASTON

CHARLES WOLLASTON, Bognor Regis, Sussex and Canterbury, Kent. 1951– . *Studio-type Pottery*.

Charles Wollaston

Signature mark, 1951– .

4231

Impressed seal mark, used at Bognor Regis and at Canterbury, 1951– .

4232

Impressed seal mark on "Canterbury Pottery" wares, 1962– . The above signature and W seal also occur on individual pieces made at Canterbury.

— 4247	WOOD	*See* Appendix, page 736. *See* Enoch Wood.
—	AARON WOOD	*See* Appendix, page 736.

WOOD

ARTHUR WOOD, Bradwell Works, Longport. Staffordshire Potteries. 1904–28. *Earthenwares, mainly Teapots*. Formerly Capper & Wood, q.v.

4233

A. W.
L.
ENGLAND

Impressed or printed mark. With or without "England", 1904–28.

Continued as:

WOOD

ARTHUR WOOD & SON (LONGPORT) LTD., Bradwell Works, Longport. Staffordshire Potteries. 1928– . *Earthenwares*.

4234-6

c. 1928+   c. 1934+   c. 1945+

4237-8

c. 1954+   c. 1954+

Printed marks, 1928– . On some modern moulded wares, such as Staffordshire dogs, the moulded name WOOD only appears.

WOOD

WOOD & BAGGALEY, Hill Works, Burslem. Staffordshire Potteries. 1870–80. *Earthenwares*. Subsequently J. Baggaley, q.v.

4239   W. & B.

Distinguishing initials found on several printed marks of differing design: name of the individual pattern is often included, 1870–80. A bee-hive device occurs on several marks.

WOOD

WOOD & BARKER LTD., Queen Street Pottery, Burslem. Staffordshire Potteries. 1897–1903. *Earthenwares*. Formerly Thomas Wood & Sons, q.v.

4240

Printed mark, 1897–1903.

WOOD

WOOD & BOWERS, Waterloo Road, Burslem. Staffordshire Potteries. 1839. *Earthenwares*.

4241   W. & B.

Printed mark with initials and name of pattern, 1839.
    N.B. These initials were also used by Wood & Brownfield, c. 1841–50, see next entry, and later by Wood & Baggaley, (1870–80).

WOOD		**WOOD & BROWNFIELD**, Cobridge Works, Cobridge. Staffordshire Potteries. c. 1838–50. *Earthenwares*. Formerly Robinson, Wood & Brownfield, q.v. Subsequently W. Brownfield, q.v.
4242	W. & B.	Distinguishing initials found on *many* impressed and printed marks, often with the name of the pattern, c. 1838–50.
4243	W. & B. PEARL WHITE COBRIDGE	Impressed mark within borders, c. 1838–50. See also mark nos. 4239 and 4241.

4256   WOOD & CALDWELL   *See* Enoch Wood.

WOOD		**WOOD & CHALLINOR**, Brownhills Pottery, 1828–41. Woodland Pottery 1834–43. Tunstall. Staffordshire Potteries. 1828–43. *Earthenwares*.
4244	W. & C.	Distinguishing initials found on several printed marks of differing design: name of the individual pattern is often included, 1828–43.

WOOD		**WOOD, CHALLINOR & CO.**, Well Street Pottery, Tunstall. Staffordshire Potteries, c. 1860–64. *Earthenwares*.
4245	W. C. & CO.	Distinguishing initials found on several printed marks of differing design: name of the individual pattern is often included, c. 1860–4.

WOOD		**WOOD & CLARKE**, Church Works, Burslem. Staffordshire Potteries. c. 1871–2. *Earthenwares*. Formerly E. Clarke. Subsequently W. E. Withinshaw, q.v.
4246	 W. & C.	Printed mark with lion rampant, the name of the pattern and the initials W. & C., c. 1871–2.

WOOD

ENOCH WOOD, Fountain Place, Burslem. Staffordshire Potteries. c. 1784–90 (or 1792). *Earthenwares, Basaltes, Creamwares, Porcelains.*

Enoch Wood was a talented modeller and potter. His trade card lists—"Table-services, enamel'd with arms, crests, or other ornaments; Egyptian black teapots, vases, Busts, Figures, Seals, &c. Colour'd ware in all its Branches". Enoch Wood died in 1840. See G. Godden's *British Pottery and Porcelain 1780–1850* (1963).

4247	WOOD
4248	E. WOOD
4249	E. W.
4250	W
4251	W (***)

Impressed name or initial marks, c. 1784+. "E WOOD" and "W" occurs on a creamware dinner service dated 1792. See companion illustrated encyclopaedia of marked specimens. Mark no. 4251 occurs on earthenwares and on porcelain.

4252	ENOCH WOOD SCULPSIT
4253	E. WOOD SCULPSIT
4254	ENOCH WOOD

Impressed, moulded or incised signature marks on figures, busts, plaques, etc., modelled by Enoch Wood. Some of these bear dates prior to 1784 when Enoch Wood set up his own works. Mark no. 4255 occurs impressed on fine busts of John Wesley. Similar marks with different names and dates occur.

4255

THE REVᴰ JOHN WESLEY M.A. died Mar 2. 1791 ENOCH WOOD SCULP BURSLEM

Continued as:

WOOD

WOOD & CALDWELL, Fountain Place, Burslem. c. 1790 (or 1792) to July 1818. *Earthenwares, etc.*

4256 WOOD & CALDWELL Impressed mark on creamwares, figures, groups and busts, c. 1790–1818.

Continued as:

WOOD

ENOCH WOOD & SONS, Fountain Place (and other addresses), Burslem. July 1818–46. *Earthenwares, etc.*

4257

4258   ENOCH WOOD
       & SONS
       BURSLEM
   STAFFORDSHIRE

Impressed marks, 1818–46. Many similar marks occur on finely printed blue wares made for the American market.

4259

4260   E. W. & S.
4261   E. WOOD & SONS
4262   E. & E. WOOD
4263   E. & E. WOOD
        BURSLEM
4264   E. & E. W.

Many printed marks incorporate the name or initials E. W. & S. in various forms as nos 4260–4, c. 1818–46. The initials E. & E. W. were used c. 1840. An impressed mark "PEARL CHINA" occurs on a E & E W marked plate in the Godden Collection. The initials E & E relate to Enoch and Edward Wood.

     This firm exported vast amounts of pottery to North America. Documents relating to a single shipment sent to a Philadelphia china broker total 262,000 pieces.

WOOD

H. J. WOOD (LTD.), Alexandra Pottery, Burslem. Staffordshire Potteries. 1884– . *Earthenwares.*

4266–8

c. 1884+

c. 1930+

c. 1935+

4269–71

c. 1948+

c. 1960+

c. 1962+

This form of mark may occur with different pattern names.

Printed marks 1884– .

WOOD		
		WOOD & HAWTHORNE, Abbey Pottery, Cobridge. Staffordshire Potteries. 1882–7. *Earthenwares*. Subsequently Sant & Vodrey, q.v.
4272	WOOD & HAWTHORNE. ENGLAND	Printed name-mark with Royal Arms above, and name of pattern or body, "Ironstone China", etc., 1882–7.

WOOD		
		WOOD & HULME, Garfield Pottery, Burslem. Staffordshire Potteries. 1882–1905. *Earthenwares*. Subsequently H. Hulme & Sons.
4273	W. & H. B.	Printed or impressed initial mark, 1882–1905.

WOOD		
		ISAIAH WOOD, "Back of George",* Burslem. Staffordshire Potteries. 1710–15. *Earthenwares*.
4274	ISA WOOD 1712	Incised signature mark (unique) on pottery lantern in the British Museum and illustrated by Hugh Tait in *Apollo* magazine, November 1957.

> * This address is given by Josiah Wedgwood in his list of "Pot-works in Burslem about the year 1710 to 1715". Isaiah Wood was born in 1682 and died in 1715.

WOOD		
		J. B. WOOD & CO, Heathcote Works, Longton. Staffordshire Potteries. 1897–1926. *Earthenwares*.
4275		Printed or impressed mark, 1910–26.

WOOD		
		JOHN WEDGE *WOOD*, Burslem (1841–4), Tunstall (1845–60). Staffordshire Potteries. 1841–60. *Earthenwares*.
4276	W. W.	Impressed mark on printed plate in Godden Collection, also with printed name-mark, no. 4276b.
4276a		Several different printed marks occur with the name J. WEDGWOOD, c. 1841–60. This has often been mistaken for a mark of the Josiah Wedgwood firm. This latter firm did not use marks with the initial J.

4276b

The marks of John Wedge Wood often have a slight gap or dot between "WEDG" and "WOOD".

WOOD

WOOD & PIGOTT, Well Street, Tunstall. Staffordshire Potteries. 1869–71. *Earthenwares.*

4277 W. & P.

Distinguishing initials found on several printed marks of differing design: name of the individual pattern is often included, 1869–71. The name "Pigott" occurs with one and with two "g"s.

WOOD

RALPH WOOD, Hill Top Pottery, Burslem. Staffordshire Potteries. *Earthenwares, Figures, etc.*
   N.B. There were three generations of potters named Ralph Wood:
       Ralph Wood, 1715–72.
       Ralph Wood, 1748–95.
       Ralph Wood, 1781–1801.

4278	R. WOOD	
4278a	Ra WOOD	
4279	Ra WOOD BURSLEM	
4280	Ralph Wood	

Impressed or incised marks (often with model number of figure or group), c. 1770–1801. The earlier Wood figures and groups are decorated with semi translucent coloured glazes. Later wares have opaque overglaze colours. Some examples bear only the model number impressed or incised.

4281

Rebus mark of trees (wood), c. 1770–90. Very rare.

For illustrations of typical Wood figures the reader is referred to F. Falkner's *The Wood Family of Burslem* (1912) and R. K. Price's *Astbury, Whieldon and Ralph Wood figures, and Toby Jugs* (1922). Some examples will also be found illustrated in *British Pottery and Porcelain: an illustrated Encyclopaedia of Marked Specimens.*

WOOD

THOMAS WOOD, Staffordshire Potteries. c. 1775. *Earthenwares.*

4282	THOMAS WOOD MAKER 1775.	This incised inscription occurs on a unique creamware tea-caddy,* with bust portraits of George III and Queen Charlotte. No potter of this name is recorded and it may be that this inscription was added by a workman of this name. * Sold by Sotheby & Co. in January 1963.

WOOD

4283   T. W. & CO.

THOMAS WOOD & CO., Wedgwood and Queen Street Potteries, Burslem. Staffordshire Potteries. 1885–96. *Earthenwares.*

Printed or impressed marks 1885–96.

Continued as:

WOOD

THOMAS WOOD & SONS, Queen Street Pottery, Burslem. 1896–7. *Earthenwares.* Subsequently Wood & Barker Ltd., q.v.

4284

Distinguishing initials T. W. & S. found on several printed marks of differing design: name of the individual pattern is often included, 1896–7.

WOOD

WOOD & SON(S) (LTD.), Trent and New Wharf Potteries, Burslem. Staffordshire Potteries. 1865– .* *Earthenwares, Ironstones, etc.*

Early wares unmarked.

4285

Printed mark, 1891–1907. Note "& SON", changed to "& SONS" from c. 1907. "Ltd." from c. 1910.

4286–8

c. 1910+

c. 1910+

c. 1917+

* Trading as Wood & Sons (Holdings) Ltd. from 1954.

4289–92

c. 1930+   c. 1930+   c. 1931+   c. 1936

4293–7

c. 1940+
and similar marks
with different
names.

c. 1952+   c. 1957+   c. 1958+   c. 1960–

Printed marks c. 1907 onwards—other marks occur, all with the name in full.

WOOD

WOOD, SON & CO., Villa Pottery, Cobridge. Staffordshire Potteries. 1869–79. *Earthenwares, Ironstones.* Subsequently W. E. Cartlidge.

4298

Printed mark, 1869–79.

WOOD

W. WOOD & CO., Albert Street Works, Burslem. Staffordshire Potteries. 1873–1932. *Earthenwares, Door-furniture, etc.* Formerly Wiltshaw & Wood (who probably used same initials).

4299   W. W. & CO.   Distinguishing initials found on several printed or impressed marks of differing design, 1873+.

4300

Printed mark, 1880–1915.

4301

Printed mark, 1915–32.

3840	WOODEN BOX POTTERY	*See* Joseph Thompson.
1435	WOODLAND	*See* Eastgate Potteries Ltd.
—	WOODNORTH & CO.	*See* Appendix.
4288, 4290–3	WOODS	*See* Wood & Son(s) (Ltd.).

WOODS

RICHARD WOODS, Malvern, Worcestershire. Second half 19th century. *Retailer.*

4305   R. WOODS   Printed marks on local view and other items sold by this retailer, c. 1850+.

771   WOODWARD & CO.   *See* Cardigan Potteries.

WOODWARD

JAMES WOODWARD (LTD.), Swadlincote Pottery, Burton-on-Trent. 1859–88. *Terra-cotta, Majolica, etc. mainly Sanitary wares from c. 1880.*

4306   Printed or impressed mark, 1859–88.

WOOLDRIDGE

WOOLDRIDGE & WALLEY, Knowle Works, Burslem. Staffordshire Potteries. 1898–1901. *Earthenwares.* Subsequently Wooldridge & Hickman.

4307   W. & W.   Distinguishing initials found on several printed marks of
       B.   differing design: name of the individual pattern is often included, 1898–1901.

WOOLISCROFT

GEORGE WOOLISCROFT,* Well Street (c. 1851), High Street (c. 1853), Sandyford Potteries (c. 1860–4), Tunstall. Staffordshire Potteries. 1851–3 and 1860–4. *Earthenwares.*

4308   G. WOOLISCROFT*   Printed or impressed mark, with type of ware, "Ironstone" etc., name of pattern and G. Wooliscroft,* 1851–3 and 1860–4.

              * This name occurs with one and with two "l"s.

WOOLLEY

RICHARD WOOLLEY (1765–1825), Turner's Pottery, Longton. Staffordshire Potteries. 1809–14. *Earthenwares.* Formerly Chetham & Woolley, q.v.

4309   WOOLLEY   Impressed mark on a set of fine earthenware vases with figure relief motifs, in the Fitzwilliam Museum, Cambridge, 1809–14. See companion illustrated encyclopaedia of marked specimens.

WOOLLISCROFT

G. WOOLLISCROFT & SON (LTD.), Patent Tile Works, Hanley. Staffordshire Potteries. 1880– . *Tiles, etc.*

4310      Printed or impressed mark, 1880+ .

WORCESTER   *See* Worcester Porcelains, below, also:
Chamberlain(s) (& Co.).
George Grainger (& Co.).
Grainger, Lee & Co.
Grainger, Wood & Co.
James Hadley & Sons (Ltd.).
Locke & Co. (Ltd.).
Coningsby *Norris.*

WORCESTER

WORCESTER PORCELAINS, produced at the main factory at Worcester, c. 1751– . *Porcelains (and in 19th century Earthenware, Parian, etc.).*
FIRST, OR "DR. WALL", PERIOD

4311   WIGORNIA   *Very* rare embossed moulded mark, c. 1751.

4312a, b, c, d

Many different painters' marks occur on early specimens painted in underglaze blue, 1751–65. Similar marks will be found on other early porcelains.

4313–14a

Crescent marks, c. 1755–90, painted in underglaze blue usually on blue decorated examples. The filled-in crescent (no. 4314) is printed and occurs on blue printed porcelains. A painted or gilt crescent occurs on some pieces probably decorated outside the factory. (The gold crescent also occurs on French hard paste reproductions.) Variations of the crescent mark occur. The Lowestoft factory copied this mark.

4315

The square or fret mark, hand painted in underglaze blue, c. 1755–75. Very many variations occur. This mark also occurs on reproductions, most of which are of hard paste porcelain, or of earthenware. It should be noted that *early* Worcester porcelain with overglaze enamel decoration is seldom marked.

4316

4317

1924

1926

Several signature marks occur *in the design* of some of the fine Worcester printed wares. The initials R. H. relate to the engraver—designer Robert Hancock (also worked at Bow, etc.). The anchor is the rebus of Richard Holdship. Several variations of the four basic marks here reproduced were used but most printed porcelains were unmarked.

The standard work on Robert Hancock's printed designs is C. Cook's *The Life and Work of Robert Hancock* (1948) with supplement issued in 1955. See also page 307.

508

The impressed or moulded mark "Tᵒ" rarely occurs on Worcester baskets and vases, c. 1760–9. See also page 612.

4318

This impressed mark has been reported to me as occurring on a very rare pair of Worcester figures of a Turk and his companion, c. 1765–70.

4319–20

W marks painted or printed in underglaze blue, c. 1755–70. Several variations occur.

4321

Mock Oriental marks, painted in underglaze blue, c. 1753–65. Variations abound. Similar marks also used at the Bow factory.

4322–3		Crossed swords mark (of Dresden) painted in underglaze blue. Occurs, with or without numerals, on printed and enamelled specimens, c. 1760–70.
4324		The Chelsea anchor mark occurs painted or gilt on rare specimens of Worcester porcelain painted by independent decorators such as Giles, c. 1760.
4325–6		Copies of other factory marks—Sevres and Chantilly—were occasionally used, c. 1760–70.

A very fine selection of early Worcester porcelain can be seen at the Victoria and Albert Museum, London.

Standard reference books include:

Worcester Porcelain, R. L. Hobson (1910).

Worcester Porcelain, F. Severne Mackenna (1950).

Worcester Porcelain, F. A. Barrett (1953).

Coloured Worcester Porcelain of the First Period, H. Rissik Marshall (1954).

B. Watney's *English Blue and White Porcelain of the 18th Century* (1963).

FLIGHT PERIOD—1783–92

4327		Blue painted crescent mark continued from earlier period, but generally smaller in size. 1783–92.
4328		Blue painted Flight mark with crescent, c. 1783–8.
4329		Crowned version c. 1788–92 found on the celebrated "Hope" Service (see companion illustrated encyclopaedia) made for the Duke of Clarence. The crown was added after the King's visit to the works in 1788.
4330		
4331	FLIGHT	Painted Flight mark, in various forms. The name also, rarely, occurs impressed as no. 4331, c. 1783–92.
4331a	WORCESTER Manufactory FLIGHT	Very rare printed mark, the words enclosed in an oval with crown above, c. 1788–92.

	BARR AND FLIGHT & BARR PERIOD, c. 1792–1807

4332 BARR WORCESTER
PORCELAIN
MANUFACTURERS
TO THE KING

Very rare painted mark, on a special presentation vase, sold at Sotheby's in 1963. c. 1800.

4333–4 **B B**ₓ

Incised "B" mark in various forms, often found on tea wares, c. 1792–1807. The period 1792–1803 is usually given for the incised B marks but an example dated 1806 has this mark.

4335 *F & B*

Incised initial mark, c. 1792–1807. Rarely used.

4336

"Barr" printed mark, used by the Royal Worcester Company on an experimental body, c. 1896.

4337 *Flight&Barr*

Written marks in various forms, c. 1792–1807. All Flight & Barr marks are rare.

4338 FLIGHT & BARR
WORCESTER
MANUFACTURERS
TO THEIR MAJESTIES

BARR, FLIGHT & BARR PERIOD, c. 1807–1813
(The earlier title Flight & Barr was retained for the London shop.)

4339 BFB

Standard impressed mark found on all wares, with or without written or printed marks, c. 1807–13.

4340 Barr, Flight & Barr
Worcester

Flight & Barr
Coventry Street,
London.
Manufacturers to their
Majesties and
Royal Family

Many written marks occur under a crown. The example cited is one of the fullest versions; all include the style Barr, Flight & Barr and can be dated c. 1807–13. Written marks normally occur on the best specimens.

4341	BARR FLIGHT & BARR ROYAL PORCELAIN WORKS WORCESTER ——— LONDON HOUSE NO. 1 COVENTRY STREET	Several different printed marks occur. All include the style Barr, Flight & Barr, c. 1807–13. Most have a crown and/or the Prince of Wales' crest above the wording.

FLIGHT, BARR & BARR PERIOD, c. 1813–40

4343		Standard impressed mark with or without crown, c. 1813–40.
4344	Flight Barr & Barr Worcester	Various written marks with style—Flight, Barr & Barr, c. 1813–40. Many variations of these written marks occur. Printed marks also occur and are similar to those used in the previous period but with the new title.

Works continued by Chamberlains, c. 1840–52 see page 138. Rare examples of the 1840 period bear both Flight, Barr & Barr and Chamberlain marks, such examples represent stock taken over by Chamberlains. Typical examples of Worcester porcelains of the period c. 1750–1900 will be found illustrated in *British Pottery and Porcelain: an illustrated Encyclopaedia of Marked Specimens.*

KERR & BINNS (W. H. KERR & CO.) PERIOD, 1852–62

4345		Standard mark, printed or impressed, c. 1852–62. Note that this does not have a crown above. A crown was added in 1862. Some examples have this impressed mark with a printed crown added when decorated after 1862.
4346		Printed shield mark used on the finest specimens from c. 1854 to 1862. The last two numbers of the year are placed in the central bar. The artist's initials or signature occurs on the bottom left-hand corner. The TB monogram is that of Thomas Bott, see *Victorian Porcelain* (1961).
4347		Very rare painted mark incorporating the year numerals.

4348

Rare printed mark, c. 1856–62. Some other marks give the style W. H. Kerr & Co. instead of Kerr & Binns.

4348a See Plate 4

A service made for Queen Victoria has a special ornate mark, reproduced in Plate 4, no. 4348a.

Continued by the

"WORCESTER ROYAL PORCELAIN COMPANY LTD." (ROYAL WORCESTER), 1862 to present day.

For an account of the Worcester wares from c. 1852 to 1900 the reader is referred to R. W. Binns' *Worcester China—1852–1897* (1897) and to the present writer's *Victorian Porcelain* (1961).

4349

Standard Royal Worcester printed mark, c. 1862 to 1875.
  Note (a) Crown added to earlier Kerr & Binns mark.
      (b) C in centre, not a crescent.
      (c) Open crown perched on main mark.
  When two numbers occur below this mark they denote the year, i.e. 73 = 1873, also from 1867 a system of dating by year letters was used. The letters were placed below this and subsequent marks, the key is:

A	1867	K	1875	U	1883
B	1868	L	1876	V	1884
C	1869	M	1877	W	1885
D	1870	N	1878	X	1886
E	1871	P	1879	Y	1887
G	1872	R	1880	Z	1888
H	1873	S	1881	O	1889
I	1874	T	1882	a	1890

4350

Standard printed* mark, c. 1876–91.
  Note (a) Crescent in centre, formerly a C.
      (b) Crown filled in and settled down to fit circle.
      Compare with previous mark, no. 4349.
  Year letters occur below printed versions of this mark, see above Table.

* Various impressed versions of this standard mark were employed but these do not show changes in detail or year marks.

4351 Rare printed or impressed mark, c. 1862–75.

4352 Various impressed marks were used, c. 1865–80. Some are in an oval outline. Another has a crown over the word Worcester.

4353 Rare painted mark, c. 1870–85.

4354 Standard printed mark from 1891 when the words "Royal Worcester England" were added round former mark. Recent variations are given, nos. 4357–60. From 1892, dots were added, one for each year, see Table below. "Made in England" added in 20th century.

TABLE, SHOWING DATING MARKS FROM 1892, WITH MARK NO. 4354.

1892 · One dot added above "Royal".
1893 ·· Two dots, one either side of "Royal Worcester England".
1894 Three dots.
1895 Four dots.
1896 Five dots,
and so on progressively until by 1915 there were 24 dots—some placed below the main mark.
1916 Dots replaced by a star, below the mark.
1917 One dot added to star.
1918 Two dots added to star,
and so on until by 1927 there were eleven dots with the star.
1928 Dots and star, replaced by a small square.
1929 Small diamond.
1930 Changed to ÷
1931 Changed to two inter-linked circles.
1932 Changed to three inter-linked circles.
1933 One dot added to three circles.
1934 Two dots added to three circles,
and so on until 1941 when there were nine dots. From 1941 to 1948 no changes were made in year marks.
1949 "V" placed under mark.
1950 "W" placed under mark.
1951 One dot added to "W", and so on to

1955	Five dots with "W".
1956	R replaced former "W". Dots continued progressively, so that in
1963	there are thirteen dots with the circled R device.

N.B. *New* patterns introduced in 1963 and subsequently will have the year of registration added in full.

4355   W   A script capital W in gold occurs on some of the finest examples of modern Royal Worcester.

4356   Printed mark on Royal Worcester Laboratory Porcelain, 1931– .

4357   Standard printed mark, c. 1938–43. Note large "BONE CHINA" each side of crown.

4358   New version, with the words "Bone China" reduced in size, c. 1944–55.

4359   Version, with words "Bone China" *below* "Royal Worcester", c. 1956– .

4360   Revised version, c. 1959– . Year marks occur with these marks, see Table. At the time of writing (1963) both this mark and the one above are in use.

4361   FIREPROOF   Special marks occur on Royal Worcester Fireproof wares made from c. 1940.

4362	*Orange Blossom and Butterfly*	Special marks were used on the famous Dorothy Doughty bird models. This is an example of c. 1946. Others can be dated by reference to changes in the standard mark and year marks, as given above. The standard book on Miss Doughty's bird models is *The American Birds of Dorothy Doughty* by G. Savage (1963).
4363	PADMORE— WORCESTER	Some marks occur with the name PADMORE and with place name Worcester, these occur on wares decorated by Padmore in Worcester. He was not a manufacturer.

WORTHINGTON

4364	WORTHINGTON & GREEN	**WORTHINGTON & GREEN**, Brook Street Works, Shelton, Hanley. Staffordshire Potteries. 1844–64. *Earthenwares, Parian, etc.* Subsequently Worthington & Son. Impressed name-mark on applied pad on parian jugs, etc., 1844–64.

WORTHINGTON

4365	W. & H.	**WORTHINGTON & HARROP**, Dresden Works, Hanley. Staffordshire Potteries. 1856–73. *Earthenwares.* Subsequently William Harrop. Distinguishing initials found on several printed marks of differing design: name of the individual pattern is often included, 1856–73.

2730 4210	WP (joined)	*See* Monkton Combe Pottery. *See* Winchcombe Pottery.
4277	W. & P.	*See* Wood & Pigott.
4110	W. P. & CO.	*See* Wellington Pottery Co.
2730 3210 3408–9	WR (joined)	*See* Monkton Combe Pottery *See* Winifred Rawsthorne. *See* William Ruscoe.
3301	W. R.	*See* William Ridgway (& Co.).
— 774 4200–2	W. & R.	*See* Appendix. *See* Carlton Ware Ltd. *See* Wiltshaw & Robinson (Ltd.).

4041	W. &. R L.	*See* Wayte & Ridge.
3303	W. R. & CO.	*See* William Ridgway (& Co.).
4114	W. R. F.	*See* Reginald F. Wells.
4368	WRIGHT	*See* Peter Wright.

WRIGHT · **MURIEL WRIGHT**, Kettering, Northants. 1951– . *Studio-type Pottery, Stonewares from 1961.*

4366		Painted mark, c. 1951.

WRIGHT · **PETER WRIGHT**, Monkton Combe Pottery, Nr. Bath, Somerset. 1953– . *Studio-type Pottery.*

4367		Painted or incised marks on individual examples, c. 1953– .
4368		Signature marks, often in writing letters, c. 1953– .
4369	Peter Wright	
4370		Standard incised or painted mark on repeat items, c. 1953– .

3307	W. R. S. & CO.	*See* William Ridgway Son & Co.
3595 4212	W. S.	*See* William Smith (junr.) & Co. *See* Winchcombe Pottery.
805a	W	*See* Michael and Sheila Casson.
3596– 3600	W. S. & CO.	*See* William Smith (& Co.).
3948	WSE	*See* Charles Vyse.

1436	W. & S. E.	*See* William & Samuel Edge.
3593	W. S. JUNR. & CO.	*See* William Smith (Junr.) & Co.
	or	
3594	W. S. JR. & CO.	
4179–80	W. & SONS	*See* H. M. Williamson & Sons.
—	W. S. & S.	*See* Appendix, page 736.
—	W. T. & CO.	*See* Appendix, page 737.

WULSTAN

WULSTAN POTTERY CO. LTD., Sefton Works, Hanley. Staffordshire Potteries. c. 1940–58. *Earthenwares.*

4371   Printed mark, slight variations occur, c. 1940–58 (closed c. 1941–6).

3433   *See* Rye Pottery.

2480	W. W.	*See* Christopher Magarshack
2935		*See* Overstone Pottery.
3985		*See* Winifred Wallace.
4123		*See* William J. White.
4178		*See* Wilkinson & Wardle.
4276		*See* John Wedge *Wood*.
4307	W. & W. B.	*See* Wooldridge & Walley.
4299	W. W. & CO.	*See* W. Wood & Co.
	or	
4300–1	W. & W. CO.	

WYE

WYE POTTERY (Adam Dworski), Clyro, Radnorshire, Wales. June 1956– . *Earthenwares.*

| 4373 | WYE POTTERY | Incised or painted factory marks, 1956– . |
| 4374 | WYE
CLYRO
WALES | |

4375   Incised personal mark of Adam Dworski on large vases, etc., 1956– .

WYLLIE

ARTHUR & AILEEN WYLLIE, Fulham, London S.W.6., c. 1954–9, and at Morningside, Edinburgh 10, Scotland, c. 1959– . 1954– . *Terra-cotta figures, Groups, Animals, etc.*

| 4376 | AILEEN & ARTHUR WYLLIE | Signature marks, 1954– . |
| 4377 | ARTHUR WYLLIE | |

4378   Monogram mark of Arthur Wyllie, 1954– .
         N.B. A similar mark is used by A. Wedd, see page 654.

4379   Monogram mark of Aileen Wyllie on animals etc., 1954– .

WYSE

HENRY T. WYSE (b. 1870), Edinburgh, Scotland. c. 1920–35. *Studio-type Pottery.*

4380   WYSE   Incised or painted signature mark, c. 1920–35.

4400   W. Z.   *See* W. Zillwood.

Y

5	Y	*See* William Absolon.
2355		*See* Michael Leach.

YALE

YALE & BARKER, various addresses, Longton. Staffordshire Potteries. c. 1841–5 and c. 1850–3.* *Earthenwares.*

4381	Y. & B.	Distinguishing initials Y. & B. found on several printed marks
4382	SEMI CHINA	of differing design: name of the individual pattern is often
	WARRANTED	included, 1841–53.
	Y. & B.	

* From 1845 to c. 1853 the partnership would seem to have been styled Yale Barker & Hall, who may have used marks with the initials Y.B. & H.

YATES

JOHN YATES, Broad Street, Shelton, Hanley. Staffordshire Potteries. c. 1784–1835. *Earthenwares, Basaltes, etc.*

| 4383 | J. Y. | Distinguishing initials found on several printed or impressed marks of differing design, c. 1784–1835. |

| 4384 | YATES | Impressed mark on basalt teapot in the Victoria and Albert Museum may relate to John Yates. Other potters of this name include William Yates, c. 1790–5. From 1795 John and William were in partnership to c. 1813. An interesting trade card in the British Museum refers to a firm Yates & Co, which had a retail establishment at 31 St. Pauls, London. "Yates & Co., manufacturers of Staffordshire earthenware in all its branches. Both useful and ornamental." The Victoria and Albert Museum teapot will be found illustrated in *British Pottery and Porcelain: an illustrated Encyclopaedia of Marked Specimens.* |

YATES   **WILLIAM YATES**, Leeds, Yorkshire. Mid-19th century.
                                   Retailer.

4385   YATES   Printed or painted marks on wares sold, not manufactured by
                LEEDS   Yates, c. 1840–76.

4381–2   Y. & B.   *See* Yale & Barker.

—   Y B & H   *See* Yale & Barker (note).

YELLOWSANDS   **YELLOWSANDS POTTERY** (T. R. Parsons and S.
                                   Finnemore), Bembridge, Isle of Wight. 1927–32. *Studio-
                                   type Pottery.*

4386   Impressed or painted mark, 1927–32.

4387   T. R. P.   Painted initial mark of T. R. Parsons, with year of production.*

4388   Initial or name-marks used by Sybil Finnemore (Mrs. Parsons).*

4389   FINNEMORE   An early example in the Victoria and Albert Museum is signed
4390   S. FINNEMORE   and dated 1928.

                                        * These marks were continued at the Bembridge Pottery, q.v., from 1949.

2111a   YH   *See* Yvonne Hudson.

YMAGYNATYF   **YMAGYNATYF POTTERY**, Chelsea, London. c. 1922–39.
                                   Studio-type Pottery.

4391   YMAGYNATYF   Incised or impressed mark, with initials of potter:
4392   K. M. S., in circle   K. M. Shuffrey.
4393   H. M. S., in oval   Helen Shuffrey.
4394   K. E. S., in diamond   K. E. Shuffrey.

                                   A selection of Ymagynatyf Pottery is illustrated in *The
                                   Cheyne Book of Chelsea China and Pottery* (1924), Plate 44.

4395	Y. M. P.	*See* Ynysmedw Pottery.

YNYSMEDW   **YNYSMEDW POTTERY** (W. Williams, c. 1854–60., G. Lewis & Morgan, c. 1860–70, W. T. Holland, c. 1870+), Nr. Swansea, Wales. c. 1840*–70+. *Earthenwares, Stonewares, Terra-cotta.*

4395	Y. M. P.	Impressed initial mark, c. 1850+
4396	Y. P.	Impressed initial mark with numbers under, c. 1850.
4397	L. & M.	The initials L. & M. may have been used c. 1860–70.

  * At first bricks and terra-cotta was produced. The manufacture of finer earthenware dates from c. 1850. Blue printed wares were made c. 1850–9.

803–4	YORK	*See* Barbara Cass.
1955		*See* J. Harper.
3407	WILL YOUNG	*See* Runnaford Pottery.
4396	Y. P.	*See* Ynysmedw Pottery.
4386	Y. P. I. W.	*See* Yellowsands Pottery.

Z

ZADEZ		**DOUGLAS ZADEZ**, Cobham, Surrey. 1947– . *Studio-type Pottery.* Prior to 1956 D. Zadez traded as "Cobham (Surrey) Pottery Ltd.", q.v.
4398	D. Z. Cobham	Incised initial mark, with or without "Cobham", 1947– .
1462	ZANOBIA WARE	*See* Elektra Porcelain Co. Ltd.
522	Z. B. or	*See* Zachariah Boyle (& Sons).
523	Z. B. & S.	
ZERKOWITZ		**ELSA ZERKOWITZ, MISS,** South Croydon, Surrey. 1949– . *Studio-type Pottery.*
4399		Incised or painted mark, 1949– .
ZILLWOOD		**W. ZILLWOOD,** Amesbury, Nr. Salisbury, Wiltshire. Late 18th to early 19th centuries. *Pottery.*
4400	W. Z.	Incised mark, c. 1800. Examples in the Salisbury Museum bear dates that are spurious, i.e. 1603, 1604.

N.B. Numbers after 4400 are included in the Appendix, page 708 onwards.

Appendix

Here are listed in alphabetical sequence a number of unidentified marks. These have been separated from the main section in order that this should contain only definitely identifiable and datable marks.

Some foreign marks that are sometimes mistaken for English are included here as are a number of "marks" found in other works but which the writer does not believe exist. Several obvious errors are also listed with relevant notes on their sources.

Reference numbers have only been added to those marks that are known to occur.

	A	A—painted in underglaze blue. This mark occurs on a small porcelain teapot and cover, with a matching cream jug and saucer in the Victoria and Albert Museum (c. 50, 51 and 52—1961). They are described as "Probably English—about 1755". These attractive specimens have a decided Continental appearance.
4401	A. M. S.	These initials occur in a bow knot type outline, on a dinner service made by Wedgwood & Co. of Tunstall. This service bears the registration mark for June 1880. The initials probably relate to the retailer.

ANCHOR MARKS

4402	An impressed anchor mark occurs on fine quality porcelain services of Davenport type and of the period c. 1810–25.
4402a	At a later period, c. 1850, the anchor occurs within a leaf border on porcelains.
4402b	An impressed anchor occurs on a silver lustred earthenware teapot (c. 1825) in the Victoria and Albert Museum. This is illustrated in *British Pottery and Porcelain: an illustrated Encyclopaedia of Marked Specimens*.

N.B. Not all anchor marks should be attributed to the Davenport factory.

AS (monogram)	The initials AS in monogram are attributed to Alfred Singer of the Vauxhall Potteries, London, and are said to occur on parian figures decorated with lace effects. Jewitt does not mention this type of ware when writing of Singer. This attribution is open to some doubt.
A. S. & CO.	These initials occur, impressed, on English porcelain dessert services, etc., c. 1870. The initials fit the following Staffordshire firms. Alfred Shepherd & Co., c. 1864–70. Eagle Works, Stafford Street, Longton. Adams, Scrivener & Co., c. 1862–9. Dresden Works, Stafford Street, Longton. A. Shaw & Co., c. 1898–1900. Mersey Pottery, Burslem.

4403   B   Various printed marks of the period c. 1820–40 incorporate the initial B, with the name of the pattern, etc. This initial could fit many Staffordshire potters and until a specimen is found with an impressed name-mark as well as the printed B initial it would be dangerous to attribute these marks. An impressed marked BRAMELD plate in the Godden Collection also bears a printed mark incorporating the initial B. See Rockingham, page 545.

4403a   B   This initial also occurs impressed under the handle on some basalt teapots. An example in the Castle Museum, Norwich, bears moulded decoration relating to Nelson's death and the battle of Trafalgar, and can therefore be dated approximately 1805. The initial B may relate to the Barkers of the Mexborough Old Pottery, Yorkshire (c. 1804+), or to several Staffordshire manufacturers.

            This printed mark has been given by some writers as that of Robert Bloor of Derby, c. 1811–48. I have not seen this mark and doubt its attribution. I would be pleased to hear of any porcelains bearing this mark.

—	B & Co	This impressed mark has been reported on Sunderland type, lustre-bordered, wall plaques. It has been suggested that these were made by Ball Brothers but they do not seem to have used the style Ball & Co.
	E. BARKER	This name appears as part of the print on late 18th or early 19th century Sunderland earthenwares; the name relates to the engraver, not the manufacturer.
4404	CHARLES BARLOW SMITHFIELD WORKS HANLEY	A jug of c. 1885 has been seen with an indistinct mark which appears to be as here printed but the name and address do not occur in directories. A Patent taken out in October 1882 by C. Barlow refers to a method of ornamenting pottery with bright and dead gold effects.
	BAYLON	This impressed mark is included in the British Museum Catalogue of British Pottery and Porcelain. It is an example of a foreign name-mark that can be thought to relate to an English potter. This mark was used by Abraham Baylon on his earthenwares made at Carouge, near Geneva, Switzerland.
4405	B. B.	The initials B. B. occur on a printed mark incorporating the pre-Victorian Royal Arms. The initials do not fit any pre-1837 Staffordshire firm but the arms are so like those on Messrs. Griffiths, Beardmore & Birks wares that it would seem likely that the BB mark was used by their successors, Messrs. Beardmore & Birks of Lane End, c. 1831–43.
4405a	B. & B.	Several earthenware mugs, etc., occur with printed railway scenes and with these initials under a scroll on the base. The same initials occur under the Royal Arms on other wares. Possible manufacturers include: Beardmore & Birks, Longton, c. 1831–43. Bailey & Ball, Longton, c. 1843–50. Bridgwood & Burgess, Longton, c. 1846–7. N.B. Earlier firms, such as Baggaley & Ball, also used these initials.
BEECH		H. BEECH, Burslem. Staffordshire Potteries. First half 18th century. *Salt-glaze wares*.

4406	BEECH	Impressed mark, first half 18th century.

N.B. This reported mark and its attribution is open to doubt.   H. Beech is included in a list of Burslem potters of the 1710–15 period, as a maker of Butter Pots. Various other potters of this name may well have used this mark at a *later* date.   It is doubtful if H. Beech marked wares during the first half of the 18th century.

4407 B. H. & CO.

Many printed marks incorporate the name of the pattern and the initials B. H. & CO.   The initials fit the following 19th century Staffordshire firms:
> Beech, Hancock & Co., Burslem, c. 1851–5.
> Bennett, Hurd & Co., Burslem, c. 1865–6.
> Buckley, Heath & Co., Burslem, c. 1885–90.
> Bailey, Hackney & Co., Hanley, c. 1889.

4408 B. & L.

These initials occur on earthenware mugs, etc., printed with railway scenes.   The initials fit the following Staffordshire firms:
> Bill & Lawrence, Lane End, c. 1832.
> Bowers & Lloyd, Burslem, c. 1846.
> Bryan & Lawton, Longton, c. 1854.
> Burgess & Leigh, Burslem, from 1862.

4408a B & M LATE ELIJAH MAYER

This mark occurs impressed on both the front and back of a figure subject basalt plaque in the Godden Collection.   I have been unable to fit the initials to any firm connected with Elijah Mayer, or with Hanley.   It is difficult to date this mark, as Elijah Mayer died in January 1813 but the firm, trading as Elijah Mayer & Son, continued to c. 1834.

4409 IRONSTONE B. & M.

This mark is given by Chaffers and other writers as having been used by Bagshaw & Meir of Burslem (c. 1802–8).   However, this firm is of too early a date for the word IRONSTONE.   The mark was probably used by:
> Booth & Meigh, Lane End, c. 1828–37.
> or Brougham & Mayer, Tunstall, c. 1853–5.

JOSEPH BOON

A creamware mug sold at Sothebys in June 1963 is inscribed "Joseph Boon, 1776". This should not be regarded as a true factory mark. A Joseph Boon is recorded as potting between 1784 and 1814.

4410 ENOCH BOOTH — The signature mark, Enoch Booth, has been quoted as a mark of this Tunstall manufacturer of salt glaze and cream-coloured earthenware.   The initials E. B. with the date 1743 occur on a bowl in the British Museum but this is probably an inscription rather than a true mark.   A blue decorated salt glaze mug in the Fitzwilliam Museum, Cambridge, is inscribed "17 Enoch Booth 42". See *British Pottery and Porcelain: an illustrated Encyclopaedia of Marked Specimens.*

BOTHWELL GOODFELLOW — Chaffers lists this firm and mark.   His entry has been copied by most writers without checking.   Contemporary records list BATHWELL, see Bathwell & Goodfellow, page 60.

4411 BRITANNICUS DRESDEN CHINA — This wording occurs on blue printed marks on good quality well potted ironstone wares of Hicks & Meigh type, c. 1820.

A. BROOM — Geoffrey Bemrose, in his *Nineteenth Century English Pottery and Porcelain* (1952), wrote: "In recent years, excellent figures bearing the names of potters as yet unknown have passed through the London sale rooms. Specimens marked A. BROOM ———." This was taken up by R. G. Haggar in his *The Concise Encyclopaedia of English Pottery and Porcelain* under the heading "BROOM, A. Figure maker: mark A. BROOM recorded". These figures are in fact inscribed "BY A BROOM" or "BUY A BROOM"; this is the *title* of the model and does not relate to the manufacturer's name!

4412 (crown) B. & S. — Printed marks with the initials B. & S. under a crown occur on early 19th century wares.   Staffordshire firms of the period with these initials include:
Bucknall & Stevenson,* Cobridge, c. 1808.
Barton & Swift, Burslem, c. 1811.
Booth & Son, Lane End, c. 1830–5.
Broadhurst & Sons, Longton, c. 1855–62.

* This is open to doubt as in some records the firm is listed as Stevenson & Bucknall.

4413 B. & T. — Several earthenware mugs, etc., occur printed with railway scenes and with these initial markings.   Staffordshire firms with these initials include:
Bettany & Tomlinson, Lane End, 1843–4.
Barker & Till, Burslem, 1846–50.
Barrow & Taylor, Hanley, 1859.

4414	B. T. & S.	Initial mark on earthenwares of the 1840 period. No pottery firms seem to fit these initials. One is tempted to rearrange the partnership of Messrs. Barker Sutton & Till of Burslem, c. 1834–43.
4415	W. BULLOCK PUBLISHED JULY 1st 1805	This mark occurs impressed on a fine pair of basalt vases illustrated in Grant's *The Makers of Black Basaltes*. The maker is not recorded and the name W. Bullock may relate to the modeller, not the manufacturer.
	C	Several 19th century printed marks include the manufacturers initial C. Without other evidence it is unwise to attribute these marks to any one of the many potters with this initial.
	C. A. & SONS	A mark incorporating these initials with the word "England" is reproduced in an American book as being that of the Bellevue Pottery Company, Hull, "Est. 1802". The mark is late 19th century and probably relates to Charles Allerton & Sons of Longton, c. 1860 into 20th century. See mark No. 85.
4416	C. C.	The initials C. C. occur on printed marks on scenic centred printed earthenwares of the 1840's. The name Catskill Moss (referring to the border motifs) also occurs on these C. C. marks. One mark of this class occurs with the design registration mark of December 16th, 1844; this was taken out in the name of William Ridgway, Son & Co. of Hanley.
—	C. & C. P. (Art-Union)	These initials occur on several types and makes of English ceramics from 1865. The words "Art Union" may follow the initials. The initials relate to the Ceramic and Crystal Palace Art-Union and wares bearing the initials were awarded to subscribers. The name Crystal Palace Art-Union may occur on wares issued between 1858 and 1865.
	RICHARD CHAFFERS	This "mark" was given in previous editions of Chaffers' mark book and has been copied by other writers. However, this is an inscription on one special piece and cannot be regarded as a factory mark; in fact no mark is known on porcelains made by Richard Chaffers at Liverpool in the 18th century.

CHRISTIAN

The name CHRISTIAN was printed by Chaffers as a sub-heading. Subsequent writers have turned this into a mark and a recent book states that the name occurs "impressed or painted overglaze". Philip Christian of Liverpool did not use such a name-mark on his 18th century porcelain.

This mark of a monogram of the initials C.K. with the word Patent within a hexagonal border occurs, often moulded in relief, on earthenwares and porcelains which have an English appearance in the Moore manner. The word Patent serves to confirm the English attribution but the mark is that of the Bohemian potter Carl Knoll. This mark was used by him from about 1870.

4417   COOPER & CO.

A Staffordshire earthenware jug by Cooper & Co. was sold at Sotheby's in 1954. This was moulded with a bust of Josiah Wedgwood, and enamelled in bright colours. This example was not seen by the writer and the form of mark is not recorded. Several Staffordshire firms of this title are recorded:

William Cooper & Co., Longton, c. 1851.
Thomas Cooper & Co., Longton, c. 1855–60.
J. Cooper & Co., Audeley, c. 1860.
Cooper & Co., Burslem, c. 1870.
Cooper & Co., Longton, c. 1879.

There were also several firms of this name during the first part of the 20th century.

4418   CROSSED SWORDS
MARK

Four pieces of English teaware of the 1820 period in the Victoria and Albert Museum bear a painted mark of the cross swords (taken from the Dresden factory) with the pattern number 186 below. These pieces were painted with landscapes and the waste bowl bears the date 1820.* Several English manufacturers used the crossed swords, many examples of floral encrusted Coalbrookdale porcelain of the 1820's are marked in this manner.* Fine quality Derby porcelains and figures also bear a blue crossed swords mark.

* See *British Pottery and Porcelain, 1780–1850.* G. Godden, 1963.

CROWN
(impressed)

An impressed crown occurs on English creamwares of the 1820–40 period. A marked plate in the Godden Collection has a bold lustre and enamelled pattern and would seem to have been made at a North Country factory.

4419	C. R. & S. or C. R. & SON(S)	Several printed marks incorporating these initials occur on earthenwares of the 1820–40 period. I have been unable to fit the initials to any firm.
	JOSEPH DAY	This name occurs incised on the back of an earthenware plaque in the Allman Collection. No potter of this name is recorded.
4420	D. & B.	Several printed marks incorporate the initials D. & B. Wares with this mark seem to be of the 1830–40 period and firms with these initials include: Deakin & Bailey, Lane End, c. 1828–30. Dalton & Burn, Newcastle upon Tyne, c. 1833+. Deaville & Badderley, Hanley, c. 1854.
4421	D. & K. R.	These initials occur on marks incorporating the Royal Arms. The initials relate to the foreign firm for whom the wares were made. Wares made by Edge, Malkin & Co. in the 1870's bear these initials.
4422	DRAB PORCELAIN	This impressed mark occurs on a printed earthenware plate in the British Museum. A fine dish seen in the stock of David Newbon of London bears this mark. The earthenware dish is of a moulded pattern found in salt glaze wares; the pattern in this case is picked out in pink lustre. c. 1810–20.
4423	D. & S.	Many simple printed marks occur with the initials D. & S. and the name of the pattern. These marks probably relate to Dimmock & Smith of Hanley, c. 1842–59, but these initial marks could also have been used by Deakin & Son of Lane End, c. 1833–41, or at a later period by Dean & Stokes of Burslem, c. 1867–8.
4424	D. W.	Several printed Royal Arms marks occur with the initials D. W. The initials relate to the retailer (probably foreign). Wares made by Ashworth Brothers and Cork, Edge & Malkin bear these marks and the patterns were registered in the 1860's.

4425	E WARRANTED STAFFORDSHIRE	This form of printed mark occurs. It is difficult to attribute single initial marks. This E mark could have been used by *many* potters named Edge, Edwards, Ellis, etc., period c. 1830–50.
—	E C & C	This mark is recorded in S. Laidacker's *Anglo-American China*, part II (1951). I have been unable to trace any firm with these initials. It could be the misread mark E C & Co of Edward Challinor & Co. of Fenton, c. 1853–60, also recorded at Tunstall in 1851 and 1853–4.
4426	E. G.	The initials within this mark have been read as E. C. and attributed to Edward Challinor, c. 1862–7, or Edward Clarke, c. 1865–76. However they appear to read E. G. The discovery of a very clear mark will settle the question.
—	E. H.	This initial mark is recorded on printed earthenwares. It could relate to the following Staffordshire potters. E. Hallen, Burslem, c. 1851 and 1854. Elijah Hughes, Cobridge, c. 1853–67. Elijah Hodgkinson, Hanley, c. 1867–72.
4427	E. I.	*See* I.E., page 722.
4428	J. ELLIS & CO.	This mark presents difficulties. *The Concise Encyclopaedia of English Pottery and Porcelain* (1957) attributes this mark to "James Ellis—Modeller 1818, and earthenware toy manufacturer, Shelton 1830". The same author, in *Staffordshire Chimney Ornaments*, states that the mark is impressed in parian and relates to J. Ellis & Company. The mention of parian does not fit in with the 1818–30 dates cited above. No firms styled J. Ellis & Co. are listed in the Potteries rate records.
4429	WM. FAIRBAIRNS	A printed garter type mark with crown above occurs with the name "WM. FAIRBAIRNS". The only potter named Fairbairns that I can trace is Robert of the Newbottle Potteries, Sunderland.
4430	F. E. N. HAND MADE ENGLAND	This mark has been seen on pottery of the 1930–50 period. Further information would be welcomed.

FIFE

FIFE POTTERY, Kirkcaldy, Scotland. First half 19th century. *Earthenwares.*

4431

SULTANA.

This "mark" occurs on a print in the Victoria and Albert Museum, together with a note to the Staffordshire engravers. The note is dated 5th April 1844 and gives the address "Fife Pottery by Kirkcaldy". Similar "marks" with different names of patterns were no doubt used.

J. Arnold Fleming in his *Scottish Pottery* gives an interesting account of the Fife or Kirkcaldy Pottery, which for most of the 19th century was worked by David Methven (& Sons), see page 433.

—

FOSTERS STUDIO POTTERY CO.

This wording occurs on modern pottery with the wording "Made in the West Country". These wares were probably made at Plain An Gwarry, Redruth, Cornwall, but my letters have not been answered.

4432

T. FRADLEY

This impressed mark occurs on specimens of slip-decorated earthenwares in the Wenger (and other) Collections. This name does not occur in the rate records. *John* Fradley occurs in Shelton Church rate records of 1830.

4433

FREELING & CO.

Chaffers records this name-mark as occurring on cream-coloured earthenware with raised oak-leaves. No details are known.

4434

F. S. C.

These initials occur impressed within a diamond shaped outline, on the base of earthenware pot of Pratt type, c. 1850–60. The significance of this mark is not known.

4435

F. & W.

These initials occur with the name of the pattern on printed marks on mid-19th century earthenwares. The initials do not fit any Staffordshire firms and may relate to a foreign retailer.

G.

Several printed marks on earthenwares of the 1820–40 period include the manufacturers initial G. This could relate to many potters.

4436

G. & A.

Two printed earthenware plates in the Godden Collection bear a circular impressed mark of the initials G. & A. and the name ALBION POTTERY. This mark was probably used at the

Albion Pottery, Newcastle upon Tyne.   Jewitt wrote in 1883: "The (the old Ouseburn Bridge Pottery) were reopened under the name of the Albion Pottery by Bell Brothers about 1863, next by Atkinson & Galloway, and lastly by Mr. W. Morris, and were finally closed in 1872." It should be noted that Jewitt lists the firm as Atkinson & Galloway; to fit this mark the names would have to be reversed.

—	G C & CO	These impressed initials occur on creamwares of the 1810–20 period. Examples appear to be of the Sunderland type, sometimes with splash lustre rims, etc., and printed—shipping subjects. The only firm I can trace with these initials is Greens, Clarke & Co. of the Don Pottery, Yorkshire, c. 1807–34.
4438	G. E. M.	These initials occur on prints in the Victoria and Albert Museum Collection but the initials do not fit any Staffordshire firm.
4439	G. H. & G.	Chaffers reproduced a printed mark with these initials which do not fit any known firm. The subject of the earthenware dish bearing this mark was taken from Byron and would seem to be of the 1830–40 period.
4440	G. J. & S.	These initials occur on earthenware mugs, etc., printed with railway subjects. The initials do not fit any Staffordshire manufacturers before 1867 (George Jones & Sons) and this date is very late for this type of subject.
	DANIEL GREATBATCH	A Whieldon type earthenware tea caddy, decorated with relief pattern and translucent coloured glazes has the incised name and date, "Daniel Great-Batch 1755". See an interesting paper by Donald Towner in the *Transactions of the English Ceramic Circle*, vol. 5, part 4, where it is indicated that Daniel Greatbatch made this specimen while working for Whieldon or while working on his own account.

I have been unable to trace any record to show that Daniel Greatbatch was a potter.   He was certainly known to Whieldon, for in 1749 Thomas Whieldon noted "Hired Daniel Great-batch's son".   This fact can be explained by information given by Simeon Shaw in 1829 (*History of the Staffordshire Potteries*): "The father of William Greatbatch (Daniel Great-batch) was a farmer at Berryhill, and supplied coals to the manufacturers at Fenton ... and among others, to Mr. Whieldon ... on the back of horses...." It is probable that the above-mentioned inscribed tea caddy was made at the Whieldon works as a gift, or that it was a special piece made by

Daniel's son, William, to show the proficiency he had acquired while apprenticed to Whieldon. Many names and dates occur on old pottery—it should not be taken for granted that these always refer to the manufacturer; most are special presentation examples.

There were many potters named Greatbatch in the 18th century and much research still remains to be carried out to prove, one way or the other, that Daniel Greatbatch was a potter. It may be that Shaw's information quoted above is incorrect.

4441   C. GRESLEY   The impressed mark C. GRESLEY has been reported on a creamware tureen painted with flowers. The mark may relate to the place name CHURCH GRESLEY, where several potteries were situated.

4442   G. S. H. (?)   This mark (sometimes with different wording) is usually attributed to Edward Steele of the Cannon Street Works, Hanley, c. 1875–1900. However, the initials in the centre do not seem to comprise the initials E. S. and Jewitt writing in 1883 stated that "Mr. Steele uses no mark". This, or a *very* similar mark, was used by Griffin, Smith & Hill of Phoenixville, U.S.A., and occurs in their catalogue of majolica type wares.

    GUEST BROS.   Acid engraved marks occur incorporating the words GUEST BROS. 1877 PATENT. This mark relates to a patent taken out in November 1877 by Edward and Thomas Guest of Kingswinford, Staffordshire, for "Improvements in Ornamenting surfaces of China, Majolica and Earthenware and other vitreous or semi-vitreous surfaces". This refers to acid engraved motifs. The Guest Brothers were glass decorators and the wares bearing the above mark would not have been made by them, only decorated by their patent process. These wares were still being advertised in the 1880's.

4443   G. W.   Several simple printed marks occur on mid-19th century wares with the initials G. W. These marks could have been used by the following Staffordshire potters:

       George Wood, Hanley, c. 1850–4 and 1864.
       George Woolliscroft, Tunstall, c. 1851–4 and 1860–4.
       George Wrigley, Burslem, c. 1860.
       or by Grainger of Worcester (on porcelains).*

* Since writing this note and just before going to press I saw a porcelain service of the 1850 period bearing two printed marks, one incorporating the initials GW, the other reading Geo Grainger, China Works, Worcester. The initials therefore relate to Grainger, Worcester, when they occur on porcelains.

Other Staffordshire potters of an earlier and later period had the initials G.W.

4444 H & CO

Many printed marks incorporate the initials H. & Co. Several early varieties were used by Hackwood & Co. of Hanley, c. 1807–27. Later marks could have been used by the following Staffordshire firms:

Hopkins & Co., Burslem, c. 1841–3.
Hallam & Co., Longton, c. 1845–8.
Hobson & Co., Longton, c. 1876–8 and 1889–93.
Hett & Co., Hanley, c. 1864.
Hampson & Co., Longton, c. 1865.
Holdcroft & Co., Burslem, c. 1870–1.

HALL & DAVENPORT
H. & D.

Jewitt in his *Ceramic Art of Great Britain* (1878 and 1883) records Messrs. Hall & Davenport at Woodville Pottery, Nr. Burton-on-Trent, c. 1833–58. Therle Hughes in *More Small Decorative Antiques* (1962) writes that examples "might be marked H. & D". I have not seen such a mark.

4445 CLEMENT HAMMON
JERSEY STONE

A transfer-printed stone china cup in the Victoria and Albert Museum bears this mark. The name Clement Hammon does not occur in records of Staffordshire potters.

HAWLEY

O. Grabham in *Yorkshire Potteries, Pots and Potters* (1916) illustrates (fig. 90) an earthenware teapot, which would appear to be of the period 1810–20 with the impressed mark "Hawley". This is included in the section on the Northfield Pottery, Rotherham, which George Hawley did not take over until c. 1855. Mr. Grabham also states that he had seen a Toby jug with a similar mark. It would seem that a potter named Hawley was working in the early part of the 19th century, either in Yorkshire or in Staffordshire but the place or Christian name is not known for certain. See also (J) Hawley & Co., page 316. The impressed mark HARLEY may also be misread as HAWLEY when the piece is not clearly stamped.

4446 THO HAWLEY

R. G. Haggar in *The Concise Encyclopaedia of English Pottery and Porcelain* (1957) records this impressed mark as occurring on an earthenware bust of John Wesley but it cannot be definitely stated which potter this refers to. Several potters named Hawley were working in Yorkshire and in Staffordshire but the Christian name Thomas is not recorded.

	C. HAYTON	The name C. Hayton occurs on Worcester or Coalport plates and other articles painted by this *artist*. He was not a manufacturer. Recorded examples are painted with flowers and landscapes; date specimens of 1821, 1822, 1823 and 1825 are recorded.
4447	H. & B.	Several examples of earthenware mugs, etc., printed with railway subjects are recorded with the initial mark H. & B. Staffordshire firms with these initials include:
		Hampson & Broadhurst, Longton, c. 1847–53.
		Hulme & Booth, Burslem, c. 1851–4.
		Heath & Blackhurst, Burslem, c. 1859–77.
4448	HEWSON	Chaffers reproduces this name-mark (impressed?) as appearing on a transfer printed earthenware bowl, no other information is given.
4449	H. H. 2528	Mr. Stanley Fisher, in an article in the *Apollo* magazine of April 1953, illustrated a creamware figure candlestick bearing this impressed mark. This authority attributed the mark to Harrison & Hyatt of Fenton (c. 1797–1808). This information is open to doubt, the figure has a continental appearance and the name Hyatt may be an error for "Myatt", in which case the initials do not fit this English firm.
4449a	H H	A porcelain saucer in the Godden Collection bears a circular printed mark with the initials H H and the pattern number. It is of mid-19th century date and the probable makers are:
		Hilditch & Hopwood of Lane End, 1832–58.
		Hall & Holland of Tunstall, 1838–43.
		Harris & Hulme of Longton, 1840–1.
		(also listed as Hulme & Harris).
4450	HILLCOCK & WALTON	Printed mark on earthenware oval dish in the British Museum decorated with underglaze blue print of willow pattern type, c.1830–40. I have been unable to trace manufacturers of this name.
4451	H. L. or H. L. L. or with other initials under	These impressed initials occur on porcelains which seem to be of early 20th century date, and may well refer to Hobsons (Longton) Ltd., c. 1907–24. This attribution was based on the initial letter L. (for Longton) under some marks but I have subsequently seen a fine dessert service of the same make with impressed initial marks H. L. on the plates and H. L. on the G. F.

dishes.   I have also seen a dessert service with the impressed mark H. L.   It would therefore seem that the initial under the B.

H. L. does not necessarily refer to Longton.

  These porcelains are always of good quality and colourful and would appear to be of earlier date than they are.

4452   H. L. & CO.   These initials occur on printed earthenwares of the 1850–6 period and may relate to Hancock, Leigh & Co. of Tunstall, c. 1860–2.

4453   This mark has been seen on porcelains of the 1910–30 period. This initial mark may relate to J. H. Middleton & Co. of Longton, c. 1889–1941.

            H. N.   G. Bernard Hughes in his *Victorian Pottery and Porcelain* (1959) states that combed traditional oval earthenware dishes made at Hounslow after 1810 were impressed with the initials H. N.

      GEORGE HOLMES   This name occurs incised on a Derby porcelain figure formerly in the Leverhulme Collection.   It is not a factory mark but an inscription added by the workman ("repairer") who assembled the figure.

            H. & R.   The initials H. & R. occur as a printed mark on earthenwares of the 1880's.   The initials fit the following two Staffordshire firms:
  Hall & Read, Wellington Works, Burslem, c. 1882;
    Victoria Sq. and George St., Hanley, c. 1883–8.
  Hughes & Robinson, Globe Pottery, Cobridge, c. 1888–94.

4427   I. E.   Rare examples of Wrotham slip-decorated earthenware bear the initials I. E. and dates ranging between 1687 and 1721. These initials are tentatively attributed to John Eaglestone of Wrotham, Kent.   See *E.C.C. Transactions*, vol. 3, part 2, a paper by A. J. B. Kiddell.

4454      This ornate Royal Arms mark occurs on good quality Ironstone wares of the 1815–25 period.   Note the central inescutcheon or inner shield which occurs on pre-Victorian Royal Arms.

4455   I. W.   Printed marks with the name of the pattern and the initials
I. W. occur on earthenwares of the 1835–65 period. The
initial J. is often printed as I and Staffordshire firms with the
initials J. W. include:
  James Warren, Longton, c. 1841–53.
  John Walley, Burslem, c. 1850–67.
Many other firms also used these initials at an earlier and
later period. The name Isaac Wilson of Middlesbrough
should also be mentioned in connection with these I. W. marks.

                 J.   Many printed marks occur with the manufacturer's initial J.
This fits many potters.

4456   J. B.   These initials occur on English earthenwares printed for the
American market, with "Texas Campaign" subjects and other
patterns. The initials and period fit:
  James Beech of Tunstall, c. 1834–89.
  Joseph Birch of Hanley, c. 1847–51.
Many other potters both before and after the 1830–50 period
had the initials J. B.

4457   J. B. & CO.   These initials occur on printed marks on earthenwares during
              H.   the 1830–60 period.   The initials fit the following Hanley firms:
  James Barlow & Co., c. 1822–39.
  John Brindley & Co., c. 1824–30.
  John Buckley & Co., c. 1856.

              J. B. D.   The initials have been recorded on a printed mark comprising
the Prince of Wales' crest and the Staffordshire knot, c. 1820–30.
I cannot trace a manufacturer with these initials* but the mark
is indistinct and the initials may have been misread.

  * Since writing this I have discovered an earthenware plate bearing a very
clear impression of this mark, the initials are in fact J.D.B. not JBD as
recorded in an early mark book. See John Denton BAXTER.

4458   J. C.   These initials have been seen on good quality English porcelains
of the 1840–50 period.   Joseph Clementson of Hanley, c. 1841–
64, used these initials in printed marks on earthenwares.

| | J. D. with anchor | The initials J. D. with an anchor have been attributed to the Davenport factory. Such a mark, if it exists, is unlikely to have been used at the Davenport Works. A mark of this type occurs on glass made by John Derbyshire of Manchester in the second half of the 19th century. |

4459   J. D. & Co.

These initials occur in printed marks on earthenwares of the 1830–60 period. These marks could have been used by:
James Dimmock & Co., Hanley, c. 1840–50.
James Deakin & Co., Lane End, c. 1846–58.
or J. Dawson & Co. of the Ford Pottery, Sunderland, c. 1800–48.

J. G.

This initial mark has been reported on blue printed earthenwares. Many 19th century manufacturers fit these initials. The most likely include:
John Gerrard of Hanley, c. 1824–36.
John Gibson of Tunstall, 1841–6.
John Goodwin of Longton, c. 1841–51.
James Godwin of Cobridge, c. 1846–50.
John Gerrard of Hanley, c. 1846–53.

J.H.

A child's earthenware plate in the Godden Collection has an impressed mark of the initials J H under a Staffordshire knot. This plate has a moulded border and a printed scene—"Prayer Meeting in Uncle Tom's Cabin". Staffordshire potters of the period with these initials include:
John Hawthorn of Burslem, 1853–4 and 1860–7.
John Holland of Tunstall, 1852–4.
John Hebb of Fenton, 1856–7.
John Hughes of Cobridge, 1864.
John Holloway of Hanley, 1862–7.

4460   J. L.

These initials occur on printed marks of the period c. 1830–50. These marks probably refer to John Lockett of Lane End, c. 1821–58, but many short-lived firms or potters also used these initials.

J M & CO.

4461

or with initials

4462   J M & S

This form of printed mark occurs on blue printed earthenwares of the 1830–45 period. It occurs with the initials J. M. & CO., also with J. M. & S. I have been unable to trace any firms who used both sets of initials. The separate initials could have been used by:
Joseph Machin & Co., Burslem, c. 1828–30.
Joseph Mayer & Co., Burslem, c. 1841.
and by the Scottish firms of

James Miller & Co., Glasgow.
John Miller & Co., Bo'ness.
J. M. & S. marks were used by:
    Job Meigh & Son, Hanley, c. 1812–34.
    John Meir & Son, Tunstall, c. 1841–97.
    John Maddock & Son, Burslem, c. 1855–69.

K. P. M.   These initials have been attributed to the "Kennedy Porcelain
Manufactory, Burslem" but no such firm is listed in rate lists
or directories.   The initials normally relate to the KOENIG-
LICHE PORZELLAN MANUFACTUR of Berlin.   Many
Lithophanes bear this initial mark and are German, not English.

4465   WILLIAM LEES & SONS.   I have been unable to trace an
English *manufacturer* using this title.

4466   LION CREST.   A crest mark of a lion rampant, with crown
over, all printed in underglaze blue rarely occurs on a class of
English porcelain of the 1790 period.   At first examples with
this mark were attributed to the Caughley factory, and subsequently to Zachariah Barnes of Liverpool (see *Apollo*
magazine, July 1947).   The porcelain appears very hard and
similar to that produced at the New Hall factory in Staffordshire.
The attribution of this mark must be regarded as open.

Only two patterns have been noted with this mark—both
printed in underglaze blue, of Willow pattern type.   A typical
cup and saucer will be found illustrated in my *British Pottery
and Porcelain: an illustrated Encyclopaedia of Marked Specimens*.
"See also B. Watney's *English Blue and White Porcelain* (1963),
where this mark is attributed to New Hall.

4467   L. S. & S.   These initials occur on printed garter type marks of the period
c. 1870–80.   I have been unable to match the initials to a
manufacturer.   However, these initials are given in *Pottery
Gazette Diaries* under the heading of W. Gimson & Co. of
Fenton, c. 1884–90.

4468	L. W.	Several printed marks have been seen with these initials on mid-19th century English earthenwares, and these may relate to Lewis Woolf of the Ferrybridge Pottery, Pontefract, Yorkshire, c. 1856–70.
4468a	L. W. & S. or L. W. & SONS	The initials L. W. & S. also occur as part of several printed marks and these probably relate to Lewis Woolf & Sons of the Ferrybridge Pottery, c. 1870–83.
	MAPPLEBECK	This name occurs below the Royal Arms on an attractive earthenware candlestick in the Godden Collection; the date of registration is also given—December 5th, 1846. This name does not refer to the manufacturer.
	S. MARE NEWCASTLE 1816	This "mark" is incised in the back of an oval plaque in the Victoria and Albert Museum. The plaque is moulded and coloured and shows two portraits facing inwards. This piece is attributed to "S. Mare's factory", which I have been unable to trace. In a 1838 directory Sarah Marr is listed at the North Quay at near-by Sunderland. It is probable that this "mark" is the signature of a workman or potter, rather than a true factory mark. The City Librarian at Newcastle upon Tyne has been unable to trace a local potter of this name and suggests that the inscription could relate to Newcastle under Lyme in Staffordshire.
4469	M. & F.	Printed marks occur with these initials which could have been used by the following Staffordshire firms: Mills & Fradley, Shelton, c. 1827–35. Meakin & Farrall, Shelton, c. 1850–5.
	I MOLE	A pair of earthenware cow creamers (of a type made by many English potters) were sold at Sotheby's in July 1963 and bore this impressed mark. I have been unable to trace an English potter of this name.
4470	MORLEY CLAY	The impressed mark MORLEY CLAY occurs on a biscuit (unglazed) china group of two greyhounds in the Victoria and Albert Museum. Period c. 1840–45, maker unknown.

4471   M. & P.   These initials occur on printed earthenwares of the 1830–50 period.   Staffordshire firms with these initials include:
Machin & Potts, Burslem, c. 1834–39.
Meakin & Proctor, Lane End, c. 1845.

4472   M. W. & CO.   Chaffers attributes a mark bearing these initials to M. WORONZOU & CO. of Llanelly, Wales. This firm were agents, not potters. Staffordshire firms using these initials include:
Malkin, Walker & Co., Longton, c. 1850–60.
Morgan, Wood & Co., Burslem, c. 1860–70.
Massey, Wildblood & Co., Longton, c. 1887–9.

4473   N. B.   These initials have been noted impressed on a green glazed earthenware leaf dish. This could have been made by Noah Bentley of Hanley, c. 1865–7.

NEALE & WILTON   An American mark book lists Neale & Wilton, also Neeld and
NEELD   Neeid.   These entries are probably errors for Neale & Wilson,
NEEID   and Neale. See pages 463 and 461.

4474   PALIN & CO.   This title occurs on Staffordshire type blue printed earthenwares but the name is not recorded in the rate records or directories.

4475   J. PALIN   R. G. Haggar in *The Concise Encyclopaedia of English Pottery and Porcelain* (1957) states that this name occurs painted in yellow underneath the base of a figure of Venus in a private collection.

PARKSHURST   J. PARKSHURST, Brighton. c. 1960. *Pottery.*

4476   J. P.   Impressed initials of pottery bowl purchased at a Brighton College of Art Exhibition in 1960. I have been unable to ascertain if this potter continued as a commercial potter after this period.

P. B. F. B.

A printed mark incorporating these initials has been seen on mid-19th century blue printed wares. The initials do not fit any Staffordshire firm and they may relate to Poulson Brothers of the Ferrybridge Pottery, Yorkshire.

R PEARSON

The impressed mark R Pearson has been noted on blue printed earthenwares but I am unable to trace a Pearson with this initial. Other potters of this name were:
    John Pearson of Burslem, c. 1830–6.
    Edward Pearson of Burslem, c. 1850–4.
    Edward Pearson of Cobridge, c. 1853–73.
The reported mark may have been misread regarding the initial.

4477   PENCOYD

There is a slip-decorated earthenware puzzle jug in the British Museum, inscribed "September the 4th in the year of our 1822 —this was made a pencoyd in the parish of coychurch, near Bridgend county of Glamorganshire". This is a documentary example but the inscription cannot be regarded as a factory mark.

4478   R. POOL

A 17th or early 18th century, slip-decorated drinking vessel in the Victoria and Albert Museum (c. 24–1949) bears the following inscription in slip: "Robert Pool mad this cup and with a gud poset fil".* It is not clear if Robert Pool was a potter, or a workman who decorated this unique example.

  * This piece will be found in the companion illustrated encyclopaedia of marked specimens.

P. R. This seemingly English mark (and others with the initials P. R.) is believed to have been used by Petrus Regout of Maastricht, Holland, in the middle of the 19th century.

P. V.

The initials P. V. or the wording "made for P. V." occur on reissues of railway subject earthenwares intended for the American market, although many examples were sold in England. The initials stand for Peasant Village, and production of these wares continued into the 1950's.

R

Some silver lustred teawares of the 1815–30 period bear an embossed "R" mark. One example in the Art Institute of Chicago is illustrated in John & Warren's *Old English Lustre Pottery*, no. 27b. It is attributed to J & W Ridgway but none of their other wares are marked in this manner.

4479	R. A. K. & CO.	A blue printed jug of the 1840 period bears a mark incorporating these initials which I have been unable to relate to any firm.
4480	1 F 9 R L 1 R 2	This incised mark occurs on an example of Studio-type pottery by F. Raymond, in the Victoria and Albert Museum (no. c. 506–1934). The date should be read as 1921 not 1912. I have been unable to trace records of this potter.
4481	R. C.	These initials have been seen impressed on parian figures, etc., together with the model number. The initials were probably used as a mark by R. Cooke of Hanley, c. 1871–9.
4482	R. D.	Printed marks incorporating these initials have been noted on earthenwares of the 1840–50 period. The initials may therefore relate to Richard Dudson of Hanley, c. 1838–44, or to Richard Daniel of Stoke, c. 1841–54.
	R. & D.	Marks with these initials occur on Victoria and Albert Museum prints. I have been unable to fit the initials to a 19th century English firm but they may relate to a foreign firm.

4483   Printed marks incorporating the words Real Stone China (or Real Ironstone China) were used by many manufacturers from about 1820. Some occur on Ashworth's wares and some on those of Hicks, Meigh & Johnson (1822–35).

	REID & CO.	This name was given by Chaffers as a mark used by William Reid of Liverpool in the middle of the 18th century. This information has been copied by other writers but is incorrect. William Reid did not use a mark. A firm of this name was at Longton from 1914 to 1946.
4484	R. G.	Printed marks with these initials occur on earthenwares of the 1840 period. These initials may relate to Robert Gallimore of Fenton, c. 1840–50.
4485	R. H. L. P.	Printed marks with these initials have been attributed to Reuben Hall of Longport, Staffordshire, c. 1854. This attribution is open to some doubt as Reuben Hall is believed to have been a decorator or gilder not a manufacturer.

4486   A printed crowned garter type mark very similar to that used by Ralph Hammersley & Sons. In this case the abbreviation "Ltd." occurs below the initials R. H. & S. I have been unable to fit these initials to a Limited Company.

4487   R. L. & S.   These initials occur on earthenware mugs, etc., printed with railway subjects; I have been unable to trace a manufacturer to fit the initials. Period mid-19th century.

4488   R. R. S. & CO.   These initials occur with the Ridgway Urn and anchor devices. Possible firms include:
    Ridgway Smith & Ridgway, Shelton, c. 1793–1800.
    Ridgway, Sparks & Ridgway, Shelton, c. 1873–9,
but the first is too early and the second too late. The mark may relate to a short-lived unrecorded partnership c. 1820–40.

4489   S   Several printed marks occur on earthenwares of the 1820–50 period. The initial fits many manufacturers.

       SAMSON & CO. of Paris specialised in reproductions of collectable wares of most countries and periods. It has been claimed that all Samson's reproductions bear one of several "trade-marks". If this is true many other firms must have produced the wares attributed to this firm, for most French fakes bear forged marks of the originals.

Many Samson copies of English porcelains bear a painted mark similar to two crossed "s's". Their reproductions of Battersea type enamels also bear this mark, and are of 19th century manufacture. A fine marked Samson (hard paste) porcelain copy of a Chelsea rabbit tureen is illustrated in *British Pottery and Porcelain: an illustrated Encyclopaedia of Marked Specimens*.

4490   WILLIAM SANS   The name William Sans occurs on some examples of Toft type slip-decorated earthenware. Little is known of William Sans, the approximate period is late 17th century to early 18th century.

4491   "SCAMMELLS STAFFORDSHIRE WAREHOUSE"   A large pottery jug sold at Sotheby's in 1953 bore this inscription under the lip. The name probably refers to a retailer rather than a manufacturer. This specimen was dated August 1824 and was probably painted by the Bristol painter, W. Fifield, see page 248.

4492   T. SEABORN   The printed name T. SEABORN has been seen on Ironstone wares of the 1825–45 period. The name is probably that of a retailer.

4493   This impressed Chinese type *seal* mark occurs on a large circular 18th century salt glaze dish in the possession of Messrs. Tilley & Co. This dish is probably the only marked example of English white salt glazed earthenware. This mark also occurs on unglazed red earthenwares, as does other similar Chinese type devices.

4494   S. H.   These initials occur on mid-19th century earthenwares (porcelains with these initials were probably made by Stevenson & Hancock, and successors, at Derby, see page 597). Staffordshire firms with these initials include:
     Samuel Hall, Hanley, c. 1834 and 1841–56.
     Samuel Hallen, Burslem, c. 1851–4.
     Stephen Hughes, Burslem, c. 1853–4.

4494a   S H & CO   This initial mark has been reported on printed earthenwares of the 1830–40 period. These marks could relate to:
     Samuel Heath & Co. of Lane End, c. 1831.
     Stephen Hughes & Co. of Cobridge, c. 1835–55.
     Samuel Hamilton & Co. of Lane End, c. 1840.

   SHAW   The mark Shaw has been attributed to the Liverpool potter, Thomas Shaw, c. 1740–70. This potter almost certainly did not use such a mark. There have been over twenty Staffordshire potters of this name.

4495   C. & J. SHAW, JUNR.   This name-mark occurs on a mid-19th century printed earthenware dish in the Godden Collection. I have been unable to trace these potters.

JOHN SHAW 1742 — A very rare salt glaze earthenware mug of brown body, decorated with incised motifs and with this signature and date under the handle, was sold at Sotheby's in May 1953. The description indicates that John Shaw was the maker but I have not traced an 18th century Staffordshire potter of this name.

R. SHAWE
or
R. SHAWS — Chaffers printed the name R. Shawe as a sub-heading; other writers have copied this believing that it was intended to be a mark. Ralph Shaw(e) was potting in Burslem in the 1730's; he did not use a mark.

WILLIAM SHELDON — Two fine quality and attractive circular portrait plaques in the possession of Messrs. Winifred Williams (Antiques) of Eastbourne have this signature incised in the back; they are also dated November 1796. This name is not that of a manufacturer.

William Sheldon was employed by Josiah Wedgwood and one plaque depicts this master potter (the other shows Edward Bourne). It is probable that these signed and dated plaques are unique specimens.

4496   SIMPSON — A splash silver lustre decorated earthenware open-work basket in the Victoria and Albert Museum bears an indistinct impressed mark which has been read as SIMPSON, the period would seem to be c. 1810–30. This mark, if Simpson, could relate to Nicholas Simpson of Brook Street, Shelton, Staffordshire Potteries, c. 1821–4. This potter is recorded as an earthenware manufacturer. The mark, however, is so indistinct that different interpretations are possible.

4497   SNIZER — Chaffers records a green glazed honey pot "signed" Snizer, Lambeth. He states that Snizer is believed to have been the last maker of delft type earthenwares in England. The Chief Librarian at Lambeth has been unable to find any local references to this potter.

4498   — ST. LEDGER. An example of Studio-type pottery in the Circulation department of the Victoria and Albert Museum bears this incised cross mark. Museum records show that the specimen was made by Miss St. Ledger and was purchased in 1950. I have been unable to trace further details concerning this potter. A similar mark was used by E. T. Leaper, see page 385.

4499	J. W. STOCKWELL	An earthenware cow creamer in the stock of Messrs D. M. & P. Manheim of London has this incised name-mark under the base. I have been unable to trace a potter of this name. The period would appear to be c. 1830–50.
4500	S. U.	These initials have been noted on mid-19th century earthenwares. I have been unable to trace the manufacturer.
4501	W. SUCKERS	Messrs. Burton & Hobson record an impressed mark of the name W. SUCKERS above an anchor (c. 1820). This manufacturer does not seem to be recorded.
4502	S. TAMS & CO.	This name-mark is given by several writers as a Longton potter, c. 1830–50, but I cannot trace such a potter or firm in contemporary records of this period. There may be a link with the also unlisted partnership of Tams & Anderson and Tams, Anderson & Tams, q.v.
4503	T.F. (joined)	Several books give a mark of the initials T.F. as a Bow porcelain mark, the initials are given as those of Thomas Frye. The so-called initial mark certainly occurs on mid-18th century Worcester and Bow porcelain but is not connected with Thomas Frye, the one-time proprietor of the Bow factory.
4504	T. H. & CO.	These initials occur impressed and printed on earthenwares of the 1820–50 period. The initials could relate to the Castleford firm of Taylor, Harrison & Co., c. 1821–5, or to the following Staffordshire firms: Thomas Hanson & Co., Hanley, c. 1841. Thomas Hobson & Co., Longton, c. 1864–6.
—	TINTAGEL POTTERY	I have seen various printed and painted marks incorporating the word TINTAGEL. These marks occur on post-war Studio-type pottery. The marks were probably used by Kathleen Everard and P Cunningham Quam of the Tintagel Pottery, Tintagel, Cornwall, but my letters seeking confirmation and further details have not been answered.
4505	TONQUIN CHINA	This wording occurs in ornate printed marks on Ironstone-type earthenwares of the 1820 period.
	T. P.	The initials T. P. occur on English earthenwares made for the Russian firm of TRACHTENBERG & PANTHES. This mark is taken from a pattern registered in 1869. The initials

T. P. also occur on other printed English earthenwares and these may relate to one of the following potters:

Thomas Poulson of Hanley, c. 1825–6.
Thomas Pinder of Burslem, c. 1848–51.

Other potters with these initials worked at a later period.

TRIANGLE. This impressed or incised mark is given in several books as a Bristol mark. It is in fact an 18th century Dresden mark and occurs on biscuit figures and groups.

4506   WM. TURNER

An earthenware candlestick in the Allman Collection bears the inscription—WM. TURNER. There were two Staffordshire potters of this name, one at Lane End, c. 1809–30, and one at Fenton, c. 1807–12, but this inscription may relate to a workman rather than a potter as the period of this piece would seem to be c. 1790.

4507   T. W.

Several printed marks incorporating the initials T. W. occur on earthenwares of the 1830–50 period. Staffordshire potters with these initials include:

Thomas Wright, Hanley, c. 1822–5.
Thomas Williams, Stoke, c. 1827.
Thomas White, Hanley, c. 1840–1.
Thomas Worthington, Hanley, c. 1842.
Thomas Walker, Tunstall, c. 1845–57.
Thomas Wynne, Longton, c. 1850–1.

4507a   V & B

Printed and impressed "V & B" marks occur on 19th century earthenwares. These initials could relate to Venables & Baines of Burslem, c. 1851–3, but it is probable that they were used by Villeroy & Boch of Germany and Luxemburg.

4508   VEDGWOOD

This impressed mark occurs on an English earthenware plate in the Godden Collection, c. 1840–50. This has a printed centre pattern and a moulded floral patterned border. It was probably made at one of the many Yorkshire potteries, the mark being intended to look like that of Wedgwood but different enough to escape legal action.*

* Since writing the above note, and just prior to sending the M.S. to the publishers, I have discovered two plates with this mark in the Victoria and Albert Museum. One of these is similar, both in style of decoration and in form, to a plate in my own collection which bears the impressed mark W. S. & CO's. WEDGEWOOD This mark was used by William Smith & Co. of the Stafford Pottery, Stockton-on-Tees, Yorkshire, and it would therefore seem that this VEDGWOOD mark was used by this firm, who sought to pass their wares off as true Wedgwood. In this case they were successful, for the two plates in the Victoria and Albert Museum were officially described as made by the Staffordshire firm!

	W. B. & C. STAFFORDSHIRE	This printed mark occurs on an earthenware platter with underglaze blue Willow pattern in the Godden Collection. The initials do not fit any Staffordshire firm but probably relate to W. Bourne & Co. of the Bell Works, Burslem, c. 1812–18.
—	W C HANLEY	This form of printed mark has been reported. I cannot fit the initials and place name Hanley to any potter before 1872. William Cartledge, Sun Street, Hanley, c. 1872. William Clews, William Street Pottery, Hanley, c. 1882–8.
4509	W. C. Jr· L. P.	Printed marks incorporating these initials occur on wares of the 1830–50 period. The initials probably relate to William Copestake, junior, of Lane End (Longton), c. 1834–60. The initials L.P. could stand for Longton Potteries.
4510	T. WETHERILL	Name-mark recorded by R. M. Kovel (*Dictionary of Marks— Pottery and Porcelain* (1953). Local Lambeth (London) records do not list a T. Wetherill. It is probable he was a modeller not a potter.
	WHITENING	The impressed mark WHITENING occurs on two earthenware plates in the British Pottery section at the Victoria and Albert Museum. I have been unable to trace the name among English records and it may well be that these plates are of Continental manufacture. One is decorated for the Dutch(?) market with a figure-painted religious subject "De Communie".
4511	W. H. J.	These initials occur on a coloured stoneware bust, of Castleford type, in the Victoria and Albert Museum (c. 5–1921). I have been unable to fit the initials to any manufacturer.
	WILLIAM WEDGWOOD	*See* page 737.
4512	WIEGWOOD	This impressed mark occurs on a basalt teapot and cover (Grant Collection) and on a creamware wicker-work basket. The basalt teapot is very similar to a covered sugar bowl marked WEDGWOOD & CO., and it may be that this WIEGWOOD mark was also used at the Ferrybridge Pottery, perhaps after their WEDGWOOD & CO. mark of the 1796–1801 period.
4513	WILLOW	The impressed mark WILLOW occurs on some English earthenwares bearing blue printed patterns other than the well-known Willow pattern. The period of these WILLOW marked pieces is c. 1820–40. The Willow Pottery Company was a short-lived company at Longton, c. 1903–5.

4514	WOOD	The impressed mark WOOD occurs on earthenware figures of the 1820–30 period. It is possible that these were made by Ephraim Wood of Burslem who is recorded as a figure maker from about 1818 to c. 1830. The examples are too late in period for the better-known potter, Ralph Wood. The impressed mark "Wood" usually relates to Enoch Wood of Burslem but there were several other potters of this name who could have used this form of mark.
	AARON WOOD	The signature mark Aaron Wood has been given by many writers. It certainly occurs on moulds made by this member of the Wood family in the middle of the 18th century but does *not* occur as a mark on wares.
WOOD		**ROBERT WOOD**, Burslem (?). Staffordshire Potteries. Late 17th century to early 18th century. *Earthenwares.*
	The best is not too good for you. Robbort Wood.	A unique posset-pot in the Hanley Museum has this inscription in slip. It is open to question if this name refers to the potter.
4515	WOODNORTH & CO.	The impressed mark WOODNORTH & CO. occurs on a printed earthenware plate in the Bethnal Green Museum. The plate is engraved with a "Free Trade" subject by James Brindley and bears the date 1819. James Brindley was at Burslem at this period but the name Woodnorth & Co. does not occur in records. A similar marked plate was sold at Sotheby's in 1955.
	W. & R.	Some decorative flower bowls, etc., in the form of flowers, etc., bear the painted initials W. & R. sometimes with a registered number below. These objects were sold by the importers and wholesalers Wittman & Roth in the 1880's. Examples will be found illustrated in the companion illustrated encyclopaedia of marked specimens.
	W. S. & S.	These initials are found on soft earthenwares of the 1820–60 period. Some American writers have attributed these initials to a non-existent Staffordshire firm of Walley, Smith & Skinner. The initials were used by the Bohemian firm of W. Schiller & Son of Bodenbach and by Wilhelm Sattler & Son of Aschach, North Bavaria. Such wares are normally of a terra-cotta coloured body; the descriptive name "Lava" is also used in their advertisements.

4516   W. T. & Co.

These initials occur on a moulded earthenware mug in the British Museum. The mark has previously been attributed to a period in the middle of the 18th century but it would appear to be much later. The initials would fit William Tomlinson & Co. of the Knottingley or Ferrybridge Pottery, near Pontefract, Yorkshire, c. 1792–6. An earthenware jug in the Victoria and Albert Museum also has the impressed initials W. T. & Co., and bears on the front a Royal portrait with the initials "G.R." placed each side. See *British Pottery and Porcelain : an illustrated Encyclopaedia of Marked Specimens*.

The initials W. T. & Co. also occur on mid-Victorian earthenwares, and they could relate to the Staffordshire firms of:

William Taylor & Co. of Cobridge, c. 1834–45 and 1867–89, or   William Turner & Co. of Burslem, c. 1869–80.

**WILLIAM
WEDGEWOOD**

A rare small creamware jug painted with flowers and with mask lip spout and rope twisted handle was sold at Sothebys in February 1964. The name "William Wedgewood" was incised on the base. This example was attributed to Rothwell or Leeds and the jug would certainly seem to be of Yorkshire origin, rather than Staffordshire.

Glossary

TERMS USED IN THE MAIN SECTION

Basalt. A black unglazed body introduced by Josiah Wedgwood and copied (and adapted) by many manufacturers late in the 18th and early in the 19th century. A contemporary term for the basalt type body was "Egyptian Black". Typical examples will be found illustrated in *British Pottery and Porcelain: an illustrated Encyclopaedia of Marked Specimens*. See also *British Pottery and Porcelain 1780–1850* and M. H. Grant's *The Makers of Black Basaltes* (1910), the standard reference book on this subject.

Body. Ceramic term for the type of ware of which an example is made, "porcelain body", "ironstone body", etc.

Cane Ware or Cane Body. A dry looking unglazed, cane coloured earthenware body used on a small scale from c. 1780 onwards by Wedgwoods and other manufacturers.

Ceramic or Ceramics. A general term used for fired clays of various types, it covers Porcelain, Earthenwares, Ironstones, etc.

Creamware. A refined cream-coloured earthenware body introduced in the second half of the 18th century to replace the earlier salt glazed stonewares and delft type earthenwares. Most English manufacturers from about 1770 produced creamwares. The standard reference book is D. Towner's *English Cream-Coloured Earthenware* (1957).

Delft-wares. Tin-glazed earthenwares, the opaque white tin glaze giving a surface coating to the clay coloured earthen warebody. Named after the Dutch delft-wares but produced at several English potteries: Bristol, Lambeth, Liverpool, etc.

Egyptian Black. See Basalt.

Hard Paste. A true porcelain made in England at the Bristol, Plymouth and New Hall factories. It has a hard, cold appearance and a fracture will appear conchoidal or glass-like. The enamel colours tend to rest on the top of the glaze and do not merge with it as they do on soft paste porcelain.

Inescutcheon. See Royal Arms, page 552.

Ironstone. A hard, heavy earthenware body introduced by C. J. Mason in 1813. Other manufacturers produced similar durable earthenwares early in the 19th century under various names, Stone China, etc. The name Ironstone is today used to cover all bodies of this type. The body was very suitable for dinner services and other articles which have to withstand heat and rough usage, and was made by most manufacturers during the 19th century. Typical examples will be found illustrated in *British Pottery and Porcelain: an illustrated Encyclopaedia of Marked Specimens*.

Jasper. A fine coloured (usually blue) unglazed stoneware body introduced by Josiah Wedgwood c. 1774. Similar Jasper wares were produced by other firms in the 18th and 19th century. Messrs. Josiah Wedgwood & Sons Ltd. have continued to produce their Jasper to this day, with their traditional white relief motifs. Specimens will be found illustrated in the companion illustrated book of marked specimens.

Lustre (Decoration). A shiny surface in imitation of silver, copper, etc., produced by metallic films. Several different effects—"Splash Lustre", "Moonlight Lustre", etc., occur and different methods of decoration were employed from early in the 19th century. Lustre decoration was normally applied to earthenware rather than porcelain. See *British Pottery and Porcelain 1780–1850*, and articles in the *Connoisseur*, October 1951, and in *Antiques* magazine, April 1951, and *Old English Lustre Pottery* by W. D. John and Dr. Warren Baker, 1951 and 1962.

Majolica. Originally a tin-glazed earthenware (in imitation of the Italian Maiolica wares) introduced by Mintons in 1850. The name has since been applied to a wide range of Victorian earthenwares decorated with coloured glazes.

Parian. A white (normally unglazed) body introduced in the 1840's for the reproduction of marble statues, etc., on a small scale at low cost. This versatile body was capable of being moulded into intricate shapes and was used for many types of articles: jugs, vases, figures, groups, centrepieces, etc., etc. See *Victorian Porcelain* (1961).

Pâte-sur-Pâte. An expensive and painstaking form of ceramic decoration in which the white design on a coloured ground is slowly built up and tooled to give a cameo-like effect. See *Victorian Porcelain* (1961).

Porcelain. A refined ceramic body of many varieties. The chief characteristic is that porcelains are translucent (in varying degrees) as opposed to earthenwares, which are opaque.

Queen's Ware. A fine cream-coloured earthenware perfected by Wedgwood and named after Queen Charlotte. Visually the same as creamware.

Rockingham Type Wares. A name given to earthenwares decorated with a rich purple-brown glaze. Originated at the Swinton (Rockingham) works and copied by many other manufacturers. Several late 19th century advertisements list "Rockingham" wares.

Royal Arms. See page 552.

Sgraffito. A traditional form of decoration in which the design is incised through a contrasting coating of clay or glaze, exposing another colour. Much used by West Country potters in the 17th, 18th and 19th centuries and by Studio Potters in the present century.

Slip Wares. Earthenwares decorated by means of slip (clay, often tinted, diluted to the consistency of cream) applied in a manner similar to that used to decorate an iced cake. Much used by 17th and 18th century Staffordshire Potters (noticeably the Toft family) and by modern Studio Potters.

Soft Paste. An artificial type of porcelain chiefly made in England and not fired to as high a temperature as Continental and other true or hard paste porcelains. The wares feel comparatively warm and friendly. The added enamel decoration tends to sink slightly into the glaze. A chip or fracture will appear granular, not glass-like as will hard paste porcelains. Apart from Bristol, Plymouth and New Hall, all English porcelains mentioned in this book are of soft paste; reproductions made on the Continent are hard paste.

Stoneware. A hard, highly fired variety of earthenware, normally holding water without the need for glazing. Much used by modern Studio Potters.

Studio Pottery or Studio Potters. Hand made pottery (as opposed to machine made factory products) produced by one potter or by a small team. Most true Studio Pottery is of an individual nature. The first English Studio Potters were probably the Martin Brothers of Lambeth, c. 1873–1914.

As can be seen from entries in this book, the number of present-day Studio potters is very great and they are to be found in most parts of the country. Their wares express modern taste and creative talents better than mass produced factory wares. Reference books include George Wingfield Digby's *The Work of the Modern Potter in England* (1952) and Muriel Rose's *Artist Potters in England* (1955).

Terra-cotta. Red unglazed earthenwares. Many figures, vases, etc., were produced in this type of body which, being porous, is not very suited to useful wares.

Bibliography

Reference books mentioned in the main section are here listed in date order.

For E. C. C., see English Ceramic Circle, 1931–   .

Rate Records of the Staffordshire Potteries, 1807–59.

History of the Staffordshire Potteries.   S. Shaw.   1829.

The Borough of Stoke-upon-Trent.   J. Ward.   1843.

A Century of Potting in the City of Worcester.   1751–1851.   R. W. Binns.   1865 and 1877.

The Old Derby China Factory. J. Haslem.   1876.

The Ceramic Art of Great Britain.   L. Jewitt.   1878.   Revised 1883.

History of the Art of Pottery in Liverpool.   J. Mayer.   1882.

Worcester China, 1852–1897.   R. W. Binns.   1897.

William Adams, an old English Potter.   W. Turner.   1904.

Staffordshire Pots and Potters.   G. W. & F. A. Rhead.   1906.

Worcester Porcelain.   H. L. Hobson.   1910.

The Makers of Black Basaltes.   M. H. Grant.   1910.

The A.B.C. of XIX Century English Ceramic Art.   J. F. Blacker.   c. 1911.

Trapnell Catalogue of Bristol and Plymouth Porcelain.   1912.

The Wood Family of Burslem.   F. Falkner.   1912.

The Adams Family.   P. W. L. Adams.   1914.

Yorkshire Potteries, Pots and Potters.   O. Grabham.   1916.

Old Bristol Potteries.   W. J. Pountney.   1920.

Catalogue of Works by William De Morgan.   Victoria and Albert Museum.   1921.

The A.B.C. of English Salt Glaze Stoneware.   J. F. Blacker.   1922.

Astbury, Whieldon and Ralph Wood Figures and Toby Jugs.   R. K. Price.   1922.

Scottish Pottery.   J. A. Fleming.   1923.

The Cheyne Book of Chelsea China and Pottery.   R. Blunt.   1924.

Spode and his Successors.   A. Hayden.   1925.

English Porcelain Circle's Transactions.   1928–1931.
   (Continued as The English Ceramic Circle's Transactions, q.v.).

Bristol Porcelain.   F. Hurlbutt.   1928.

English Ceramic Circle's Transactions.   1931–   .

A Catalogue of Martinware in the Collection of F. J. Nettlefold.   C. R. Beard.   1936.

Liverpool and her Potters.   H. Boswell Lancaster.   1936.

A Potter's Book.   B. Leach.   1940.

The Pottery and Porcelain of Swansea and Nantgarw.   E. M. Nance.   1942.

Cookworthy's Plymouth and Bristol Porcelain.   F. Severne Mackenna.   1946.

Champion's Bristol Porcelain.   F. Severne Mackenna.   1947.

English Delftware.   F. H. Garner.   1948.

John Sadler, A Liverpool Pottery Printer.   E. S. Price.   1948.

Wedgwood Ware.   W. B. Honey.   1948.

Nantgarw Porcelain.   W. D. John.   1948.

Chelsea Porcelain, The Triangle and Raised Anchor Wares.   F. Severne Mackenna.   1948.

New Hall Porcelain.   G. E. Stringer.   1949.

Worcester Porcelain.   F. Severne Mackenna.   1950.

Caughley and Coalport Porcelain.   F. A. Barrett.   1951.

Old English Lustre Pottery.   W. D. John & W. Baker.   1951 and 1962.

Chelsea Porcelain, The Red Anchor Wares.   F. Severne Mackenna.   1951.

Anglo-American China.   Part II.   S. Laidacker.   1951.

Chelsea Porcelain, The Gold Anchor Period.   F. Severne Mackenna.   1952.

The Work of the Modern Potter in England.   G. Wingfield Digby.   1952.

19th Century English Pottery and Porcelain.   G. Bemrose.   1952.

The Masons of Lane Delph.   R. G. Haggar.   1952.

Worcester Porcelain.   F. A. Barrett.   1953.

A Dictionary of Marks.   Pottery and Porcelain.   R. M. & T. H. Kovel.   1953.

Wedgwood.   W. Mankowitz.   1953.

Crown Derby Porcelain.   F. Brayshaw Gilhespy.   1954.

Coloured Worcester Porcelain of the First Period.   H. R. Marshall.   1954.

Artist Potters in England.   M. Rose.   1955.

Staffordshire Chimney Ornaments.   R. G. Haggar.   1955.

Proceedings of the English Wedgwood Society.   1956.

British Potters and Pottery Today.   C. G. E. Bunt.   1956.

The Concise Encyclopaedia of English Pottery and Porcelain.   W. Mankowitz and R. G. Haggar.
    1957.

Swansea Porcelain.   W. D. John.   1957.

English Cream-Coloured Earthenware.   D. Towner.   1957.

Royal Lancastrian Pottery, 1900–38.   A. Lomax.   1957.

Longton Hall Porcelain.   Dr. B. Watney.   1957.

Liverpool Porcelain, 18th century.   Dr. Knowles Boney.   1957.

Fifty Years a Potter.   W. F. Holland.   1958.

Victorian Pottery and Porcelain.   G. B. Hughes.   1959.

English China and its marks.   T. H. Ormslee.   1959.

A Pride of Potters (The Adams family).   D. Peel.   1959.

Bow Porcelain Exhibition.   British Museum Catalogue.   H. Tait.   1959.

English Porcelain Figures of the 18th Century.   E. A. Lane.   1961.

The Potteries of Sunderland and District.   J. T. Shaw, Sunderland Library.   1961.

Derby Porcelain.   F. Brayshaw Gilhespy.   1961.

Pottery Today.   D. Val. Baker.   1961.

Victorian Porcelain.   G. Godden.   1961.

Victorian Pottery.   H. Wakefield.   1962.

Wedgwood Counterpoint.   H. Buten.   1962.

More Small Decorative Antiques.   T. Hughes.   1962.

English Blue and White Porcelain.   Dr. B. Watney.   1963.

The American Birds of Dorothy Doughty.   G. Savage.   1963.

The Pinxton China Factory.   C. L. Exley.   1963.

The Leeds Pottery.   D. Towner.   1963.

English Pottery and Porcelain, 1780–1850.   G. Godden.   1963.

Marks & Monograms . . . W. Chaffers.   New revised 15th edition, 1964.

British Pottery and Porcelain: an illustrated encyclopaedia of marked specimens.   G. Godden.   In preparation.

Postscript

Recent marks not included in main section.

4401 HAND PAINTED
by
BOULTON
Made in England

Mark used by William Boulton of Newton Abbott, Devon, on earthenwares from 1963.
William Boulton was formerly designer and decorating manager to Messrs. Shaw & Copestake Ltd.

4402

Recent mark introduced by J. E. Heath Ltd. (see page 317). First used in February 1963 for wares designed for the Australian market.

4403

Painted mark observed on many specimens of New Hall porcelain (see page 466) of the 1790–1810 period. This device occurs in several slightly different forms, as it is hand painted. It is not clear whether it is a workman's mark or a factory sign.

4404

Printed mark used by Wood & Sons Ltd. (see page 689) from 1963. Other marks occur with the new trade-name "Alpine ware", 1963.

4405 MERLIN POTTERY
HAILSHAM, SUSSEX

Impressed mark on Sussex traditional earthenwares made by Norman Benjamin Bridges (a former Dicker potter) at the Merlin Pottery, from February 1963.

ON THE FOLLOWING PAGES OCCUR

AN INDEX OF MONOGRAMS
A pictorial list of potters' initial marks, alphabetically presented

AND

AN INDEX OF SIGNS AND DEVICES
A pictorial list of marks arranged under the predominant subject feature of the mark

Index of Monograms

Here are listed the complicated initial marks that are difficult to interpret.
Simple joined initial marks that are easily decipherable are included in the main section under the first or most prominent initial.

647		Alan Brough	177		Aylesford Priory Pottery
3679		Ann Stannard	173		Aylesford Priory Pottery
741		Alan Caiger-Smith	3661		St. Agnes Pottery
116		D. Annan	163		Ault & Tunnicliffe Ltd.
1618		A. Forse	892		Kenneth Clark
3830		Anne Thalmessinger	125b		Peter G. Arnold
2372		A. Lewis-Evans	452		Booths (Ltd.)
62		Albert Potteries Ltd.	657		Y. Brown
1063		A. Coote	729		Burmantofts

528		Norah Braden	1133a		G. M. Creyke & Sons
685		L. Bruckner	1045		M. Cooper
215		C. J. C. Bailey	2338 3487		Langton Pottery Ltd. Sevenoaks Pottery Ltd.
3068		Katharine Pleydell-Bouverie	1001		S. & E. Collier
714		Burgess & Leigh (Ltd.)	786		Carter, Stabler & Adams
463		Boscean Pottery	3684–5 Part		Star China Co.
668		Brownfield's Guild Pottery	956		Coalport Porcelain Works
3347		Bryan Rochford	1024		Thomas Cone Ltd.
674		Brownhills Pottery Co.	1251		Derby Porcelain Works
954		Coalport Porcelain Works	3975		Charles Waine (& Co.) (Ltd.)
362		Dora Billington (really D but first initial looks like C)	2137a		D. Illingworth
1103		D. Corke	1217		Deacon Pottery
1593		Charles Ford	1300		J. Dimmock (junr.) & Co.
996a		Coldstone Kiln	1268		Derby Porcelain Works
2695		Mintons	954		Coalport Porcelain Works

No.	Monogram	Name	No.	Monogram	Name
3363		Roeginga Pottery	1647		T. Furnival & Sons
1215		G. Day	1648		T. Furnival & Sons
2255		Dorothy Kemp	1648a		T. Furnival & Sons
1787		Green Dene Pottery	2299		Frank Kneller
2523		Dorothy B. Martin	3335		F. S. Robinson
2728a		C & U Mommens	1820		A. J. Griffiths
705		M. E. Bulmer	1672		Gater, Hall & Co.
1481a		J. F. Elton & Co. Ltd.	3423		Rustington Pottery
3836		Theda Pottery	1752		I. Goudie
2499a		Erna Manners	2482		G. Makin
410		E. M. Blensdorf	1856		Grove & Stark
4167		E. R. Wilkes	1920		T. Hanan
4399		Elsa Zerkowitz	3850		Harold Thornton
1572		W. J. Fletcher	1876		A. Hagen
1646		T. Furnival & Sons	2925		Oldswinford Pottery

1954	J. Harper	3180	K. Quick
2145	Island Pottery	2256	Kenn Pottery
2211	A. J. H. Jones	2296	K. Kitching
2046–7	J. Holdcroft	3696 3697	E. Stevens
694	Buckfast Abbey Pottery	3020	B. Pickard
1878	T. S. Haile	1353	Doultons (Lambeth).
3349	H. F. Rock	805	M. Casson
2728	C. & U. Mommens	2523	D. B. Martin
3871	Tooth & Co. (Ltd.)	2499a	E. Manners
1983	Hawley, Webberley & Co.	2482	G. Makin
1290	J. Dimmock & Co.	2767	Morley, Fox & Co., Ltd.
2217	G. Jones & Sons Ltd.	2999	Pendley Pottery
1870	J. Hadley & Sons	1138	Cricklade Pottery
2973	Judith Partridge	2793	J. Motley
		2823	J. Macintyre & Co. (Ltd.)

2315		M. Lamb	3128 3129			A. & L. Powell
2832		McNeal & Co. (Ltd.)	1482			P. Elwood
1307		R. Dodd	1505			Empire Porcelain Co.
2013		Herculaneum Pottery	4232			C. Wollaston
4366		M. Wright	3842–3			P. Thompson
2510		R. Marshall	2942			Palgrave Pottery
3479		M. Scott-Pitcher	3095			Portland Pottery Ltd.
2725		Mogridge & Underhay	332			Bembridge Pottery
2840		F. B. Naylor	3468			Paula Schneider
2832		McNeal & Co. (Ltd.)	3347			B. Rockford
2856		New Chelsea Porcelain Co.	1520			R. R. Everett
2933a		Orchard Pottery	1046			R. G. Cooper
3073		A. L. Pocock	4114			R. Wells
651		P. Brown	1623			R. Fournier
2338 3487		Langton Pottery Ltd. Sevenoaks Pottery Ltd.	4316 part			Worcester Porcelains

2436		Lowe, Ratcliffe & Co.
3281		(R. & M.) Ridgway & Morley
3346		Bryan Rochford
3185 3189		S. Radford (Ltd.)
3678		A. Stannard
3727		Stubbs Bros.
786		Carter, Stabler & Adams
3720		E. & M. Stockl
1628		S. Fox-Strangways
3581		J. Smith
3477		G. Scott
3573		M. Slatter
3723		P. Stoodley
3238		S. Reychan
773		Carisbrooke Pottery and S. E. Saunders

3586		S. Smith (Ltd.)
3829		A. H. Thalmessinger
3875a		Torquay Terra-Cotta Co. Ltd.
3820		Taylor, Tunnicliff & Co. (Ltd.)
3834		Theda Pottery
1227		T. De Leliva
3793, 3795 part part		J. Tams (& Son) (Ltd.)
3389, 3389a		R. Ross Turner
3414		Ruskin Pottery
3829		A. II. Thalmessinger
2780 part		Thomas Morris
2566		J. Mayer (Elton Pottery) Ltd.
3838		U. Thomas & Co.
3885		William Tudor
2096		T. W. Howard

3828		Tewkesbury Pottery
3835		Theda Pottery
3932		N. Vergette
3980		A. Walker
4053 4378		A. Wedd A. Wyllie
1166		W. B. Dalton
4163		Wileman & Co.
4231		C. Wollaston
4215		F. Winkle & Co.
1700		William Gill & Sons
4132		H. Wickham
4182		H. M. Williamson & Sons
2096		T. W. Howard

221 part		W. & J. A. Bailey
2730		Monkton Combe Pottery
3210		W. Rawsthorne
3409		W. Ruscoe
4114		R. Wells
4139		Wild Bros
4143		T. C. Wild
4353		Worcester Porcelains
276		Barnhouse Pottery
3433		Rye Pottery
2429		Lovatt & Lovatt
3732		Studio Szeiler (Ltd.)

Index of Signs and Devices

Here are listed signs and devices that are difficult to index in the main section.

For purposes of easy reference the signs and devices appearing on the following pages have been grouped together under the main subjects listed below. Thus all marks featuring animals—except in the case of crests and coats-of-arms—have been brought together under the same head. *Other devices are listed in alphabetical order.* Marks which are difficult to designate are grouped together, at the end, under Miscellaneous.

To avoid unnecessary duplication, where two of the listed subjects occur together in the same device, the mark has been included under the heading of the more prominent of the two features. If the full title or initials are given with the device mark it will not be included in this index section.

Anchor Marks

61		W. H. & J. H. Ainsworth	505		Bow Porcelain Works
4402		Appendix, page 708	622+		British Anchor Pottery Co. Ltd.
114 114a		Anchor Porcelain Co.	772	ANCHOR DEVICE	T. & J. Carey

860–2		Chelsea-Derby
867–9		Chelsea Porcelain
953		Coalport Porcelain Works
1184		Davenport
1246		Derby Porcelain Works
860		Derby Porcelain Works
1531	F	Thomas Fell (& Co.)
2778		Thomas Morris
3266		J. & W. Ridgway
3692		P. Stephen
4306		J. Woodward
4324		Worcester Porcelains
1650		T. Furnival & Sons (Furnivals (Ltd.))

N.B. Many foreign firms also used anchor marks

Animal Devices

3339		Robinson & Leadbeater (Ltd.)
3954		G. Wade & Son Ltd.
1858		L. Groves
2798		Mousehole Pottery
3015	Horse's Head	J. Phillips & Co.
2042		G. Hobson
440		T. & R. Boote
604		Donald Brindley Pottery Ltd.
779	STAG'S HEAD	J. Carr & Sons
2112		Yvonne Hudson

Lion Marks

46		J. F. Adderley.
4466	LION CREST	Appendix, page 725
1294		J. Dimmock & Co.
1739	See Plate 3	Goodwin, Bridgwood (&) Harris
1979		Hawley Bros. (Ltd.)

2780	Thomas Morris
2802	W. F. Murray & Co. (Ltd.)
2904	Northfield Hawley Pottery Co. Ltd.
3087	Thomas Poole
3391a	Rowley & Newton (Ltd.)
3547	LION & SHIELD DEVICE T. A. Simpson (& Co. Ltd.)

Fish Marks

1168	J. Dan
2450	D. E. Lucas
4370	P. Wright

Bell Device

| 319 | J. & M. P. Bell & Co. (Ltd.) |
| 323 | Belle Vue Pottery |

Bird Marks

| 2012 | Herculaneum Pottery |
| 2941 | Oxshott Pottery |

1544	COCK BIRD MARK S. Fielding & Co. (Ltd.)
07a 86 1156	F. Beardmore & Co. Christie & Beardmore Crystal Porcelain Pottery Co. Ltd.
2127	Hulme & Christie
3930	Van der Straeten
1750	W. H. Goss (Ltd.)
262	S. Barker & Son
1274	Derlwyn Pottery
1853	F. Grosvenor (& Son)
2196	A. B. Jones & Sons (Ltd.)
1564	J. Fisher
4129	E. Whittall
3955	G. Wade & Son Ltd.
1594	C. Ford

Bottle Device

| 2257 | H. Kennedy & Sons (Ltd.) |

Bridge Marks

9   L. Acton

584   Bridge Pottery

4118   Wenford Bridge Pottery

604 BULL MARK D. Brindley

Castle Marks

572   C. H. Brannam

593   S. Bridgwood & Son

925   Clokie & Co. (Ltd.)

2488   C. T. Maling & Sons (Ltd.)

2489
2490   C. T. Maling & Sons (Ltd.)

2491

61   W. H. & J. H. Ainsworth

2922
& a   Old Hall Earthenware Co. Ltd.
    Old Hall Porcelain Works Ltd.

3571   Slack & Brownlow

Church Marks

1202   C. Davis

1797
1799
1800   T. Green & Co., Ltd.

Crests and Coats of Arms

128   Prince of   E. Asbury & Co.
      Wales' crest

301a   J. D. Baxter
1910   Hammersley & Asbury.

78   Royal Arms   S. Alcock & Co.
   etc.   G. L. Ashworth & Bros. (Ltd.)

N.B. Very many other firms used the Royal Arms but they normally added their initials or name. Where these occur the reader should refer to the main section under the relevant initial or name.

For the difference between pre- and post-1837 Royal Arms see page 552.

2020   Hicks & Meigh

Shield Marks

494   Bovey Pottery Co., Ltd.

1956   M. Harris

680   Brown-Westhead, Moore & Co.

673
3452   Brownhills Pottery Co.
    Salt Bros.

1725		Godwin & Hewitt
3198		Raoh Schorr Creations
3453		Salt & Nixon
486		Bourne & Leigh Ltd.
1494		Empire Porcelain Co.

Compass Points

1783		Green & Clay
755		Campbell Tile Co. (Ltd.)

Crab Mark

1143a		Cromer Pottery

Crescent Marks

452		Booths (Ltd.)

506	Bow Porcelain Works
811–12	Caughley Works
2447–8	Lowestoft Porcelain Factory
3049	Pinxton Works
4313 4	Worcester Porcelains

Cross Marks

608–10		Bristol Porcelain Scratch Cross mark, page 567
—		Appendix, (Samson & Co.)
2359 4498		E. T. Leaper Appendix, St. Ledger
3998		H. Walters

Crown Marks

1250		Derby Porcelain Works
1253		Derby Porcelain Works
1254		Derby Porcelain Works
1261		Derby Porcelain Works
1268		Derby Porcelain Works
1322		Doric China Co.
1673		Gater Hall & Co.
1753		Govancroft Potteries Ltd.
1756		Govancroft Potteries Ltd.

1824		Grimwades Ltd.
1904a		Hammersley & Co.
2024		Hicks, Meigh & Johnson
2208		A. G. Harley *Jones*
2658a	CROWN IMPRESSED	Middlesbrough Pottery Co.
2805	CROWN DEVICE	Musselburgh
2846		J. Neale & Co.
3055		E. Plant
3086		T. Poole
3175	CROWN DEVICE	J. & H. Procter (& Co.)
3258a (note)		J. Ridgway (& Co.)
3376		Roper & Meredith
3394		Royal Albion China Co.
4137		Wild Bros.
862		Chelsea-Derby

866		Chelsea Porcelain
1149		Crown Staffordshire Porcelain Co., Ltd.
1150		Crown Staffordshire Porcelain Co., Ltd.
1268		Derby (Derby Crown Porcelain Co., Ltd.)
1251		Derby Porcelain Works
2023		Hicks, Meigh & Johnson

Geometrical Shapes—Circle Marks

4345 4349 4350 4354 4357– 60		Worcester Porcelains

With or without crown above.

638		R. Britton (& Sons)
1786		Green Dene Pottery
2505		V. Margrie
1943		G. & L. Hanssen
2353		Margaret Leach

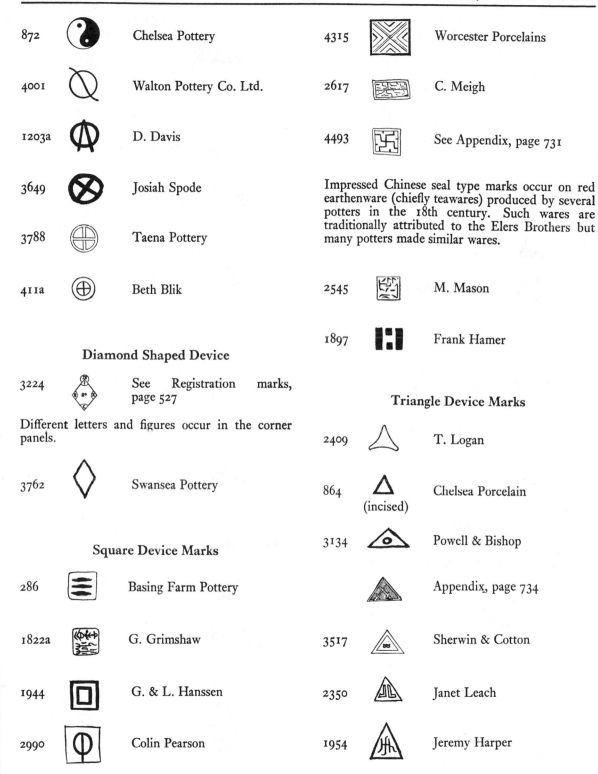

872   Chelsea Pottery

4001   Walton Pottery Co. Ltd.

1203a   D. Davis

3649   Josiah Spode

3788   Taena Pottery

411a   Beth Blik

Diamond Shaped Device

3224   See Registration marks, page 527

Different letters and figures occur in the corner panels.

3762   Swansea Pottery

Square Device Marks

286   Basing Farm Pottery

1822a   G. Grimshaw

1944   G. & L. Hanssen

2990   Colin Pearson

4315   Worcester Porcelains

2617   C. Meigh

4493   See Appendix, page 731

Impressed Chinese seal type marks occur on red earthenware (chiefly teawares) produced by several potters in the 18th century. Such wares are traditionally attributed to the Elers Brothers but many potters made similar wares.

2545   M. Mason

1897   Frank Hamer

Triangle Device Marks

2409   T. Logan

864 (incised)   Chelsea Porcelain

3134   Powell & Bishop

   Appendix, page 734

3517   Sherwin & Cotton

2350   Janet Leach

1954   Jeremy Harper

Key Device

1144		Crosskeys Pottery
2274		P. Keyes

Kiln Device

2130		W. Hulme

LETTERS IMPRESSED   Pinxton Porcelain Works

M mark

2684		Mintons

Numbers and Chinese Type Characters

818–20   Caughley Works

Numbers of small size painted in underglaze blue occur on several types of 18th century porcelains, notably on Bow and Lowestoft.

944	(impressed)	Coalport Porcelain Works
3071		Plymouth Porcelain Works

'S' Device

2345		Bernard Leach
2967b		R. Parkinson Ltd.

Shell Device

3883		M. de *Trey*

Ship Marks

49 50 2132		W. A. Adderley (& Co.) Adderleys Ltd. Hulse & Adderley
1076		W. T. Copeland (& Sons Ltd.)
1228a		Della Robbia Co., Ltd.
1776 & 9		A. E. Gray & Co. Ltd.
1814		Greenock Pottery
1850–1		W. H. Grindley & Co. (Ltd.)
3677		A. Stannard
3700		A. Stevenson
3937		Viking Pottery Co.

Signature Marks

Very many modern Studio potters use signature marks; these are listed under their name. Those that may be difficult to interpret or trace are here listed.

4362		Worcester Porcelains
1735		Goldscheider (Staffordshire) Pottery Ltd.

2057	G. F. Holland
2061 2062	W. F. Holland
4089	Josiah Wedgwood (& Sons Ltd.)
2677	D. Mills
2734 2734a	W. Moorcroft (Ltd.)
2908	C. D. Nowell

Sphinx Marks

| 219 | W. Bailey & Sons |

689	STAR	A. W. Buchan & Co.
2034	DEVICE	D. Hilton
3688		Star Pottery

Swords (crossed) Marks

611–12	Bristol Porcelain
943	Coalport Works
1255	Derby Porcelain Works
2446	Lowestoft Porcelain Factory
2684a	Minton
4322–3	Worcester Porcelains
	These are copies of the Dresden factory marks

| 3413 | Ruskin Pottery |
| 352 | J. Bevington |

Teapot Device

| 2663 | Midland Pottery Co. |

Tree Device Marks

3488	Sevenoaks Pottery Ltd.
4281	Ralph Wood
309	Beddgelert Pottery
4345 4349	Worcester Porcelains, Royal Worcester

Wheel Device

4310	Woolliscroft & Son (Ltd.)
2905	Wilfrid Norton
5	W. Absolon

Miscellaneous

1663	E. M. Galliner
2793	J. Motley
3069	T. Plowman
98	Alpha Potteries

1788		Green Dene Pottery	299a 1973		Battle Pottery Hastings Pottery
2481		C. Magarshack	3850		H. Thornton
2257		H. Kennedy & Sons (Ltd.)	2512a		W. Marshall
1461		A. W. G. Ehlers	2513		W. Marshall
2916		Old Forge Pottery	499		Bow Porcelain Works
386 3135		Bishop & Stonier Powell & Bishop Powell, Bishop & Stonier	500		Bow Porcelain Works
656		Y. (& P.) Brown	1248		Derby Porcelain Works
1635		R. Fry	2906		Carlo Norway
2004a		E. Henderson	3980		A. Walker
3837		Theda Pottery	3478		G. Scott
3835		Theda Pottery	1640		T. Fuchs
2700		Mintons	2650		L. F. Menzie-Jones
2703		Mintons	1820		A. J. Griffiths
3725		H. Stringer	1895		Shoji Hamada
2374		Ling Pottery	1916		H. F. Hammond

No.	Mark	Description	No.	Mark	Description
1917		H. F. Hammond	2649		R. Mendel
2412		Longton Hall Porcelain	1920		T. P. Hanan
2413		Longton Hall Porcelain	1921		T. P. Hanan
2414		Longton Hall Porcelain	2146		Island Pottery
2905		Wilfrid Norton	2145		Island Pottery
2990		Colin Pearson	3050 3051		Pinxton Works
3071		Plymouth Porcelain Works			Appendix (Samson & Co.)
3501		Shaw & Copestake	2348		Leach Pottery (Glenn Lewis)
3761		Swansea Pottery	3238		Stanislas Reychan
3763		Swansea Pottery	1199		L. G. Davie
584		Bridge Pottery	3015	ΦΙΛΕΩ ΙΠΠΟΝ.	J. Phillips & Co.
4312a 4312b 4312c 4321d		Worcester Porcelains	3875a		Torquay Terra-Cotta Co. Ltd.
			1002	Thumb print	S. & E. Collier
4321		Worcester Porcelains	3932		N. Vergette
1262		Sèvres factory (French) mark copied on some English Porcelains including Coalport, Derby, Worcester	2094		Hornsea Pottery Co. Ltd.

638		Richard Britton & Sons	1353		Doulton & Co. Ltd. (Lambeth)
1976a		Haverfordwest Pottery	1132		J. W. Cresswell
1976b		Haverfordwest Pottery	3647		Josiah Spode
1897		Frank Hamer	2828a		Warren McKenzie
4403		Postscript, page 745			